Guides to
Library Collection
Development

Guides to Library Collection Development

JOHN T. GILLESPIE

RALPH J. FOLCARELLI

1994
LIBRARIES UNLIMITED, INC.
Englewood, Colorado

To Carol

LIBRARIES UNLIMITED, INC.
P.O. Box 6633
Englewood, CO 80155-6633
1-800-237-6124

Library of Congress Cataloging-in-Publication Data

Gillespie, John Thomas, 1928-
    Guides to library collection development / John T. Gillespie,
Ralph J. Folcarelli.
    xii, 441 p. 19x26 cm.
    Includes bibliographical references and index.
    ISBN 1-56308-173-3
    1. Bibliography--Bibliography. 2. Collection development
(Libraries)--United States--Handbooks, manuals, etc.
I. Folcarelli, Ralph J. II. Title.
Z1002.G55   1994
025.2'1'0973--dc20   94-13621
                                  CIP

Contents

Adult Sources

13 SOCIAL SCIENCES (*continued*)

14 HUMANITIES 235

INTRODUCTION

In the past decade the term *library collection development* has taken on a new meaning because of several factors, including the expansion of interlibrary loan systems, the development of massive library networks that share materials, and the increased use of electronic technology such as databases and fax transmission of documents. As a result of these developments, even the smallest of libraries is now able to give its patrons access to a tremendous amount of resources hitherto unavailable. In order to identify and make accessible these resources, bibliographies have become an increasingly important component in the collections of today's libraries.

The purpose of this book is to supply information on these bibliographic sources, not only to help in the process of selecting and acquiring materials for the library collection, but also to locate additional items for readers' advisory and interlibrary loan purposes. Additionally these bibliographies can be used for collection evaluation. It is hoped that this volume will fulfill these aims for school, public, and academic libraries, though public libraries serving large metropolitan areas, universities with extensive graduate programs, and other research-oriented libraries may have to find additional, more specialized bibliographies.

The bibliographies included in this work were published and reviewed from 1986 through late 1993. In some cases, exceptions have been made to accommodate still useful publications from 1985. Although most of the works included are completely bibliographic in nature, others were found with sufficiently valuable and extensive bibliographic content to warrant their inclusion, even though part of their contents was nonbibliographical. This will account for the inclusion of titles that would not normally be classified as bibliographies, for example, some handbooks, subject encyclopedias, directories, and biographical dictionaries.

The bibliographies were identified by consulting a number of selection and reviewing sources. The most important of these were the periodicals *Booklist, Choice, Horn Book, Library Journal, School Library Journal, Voice of Youth Advocates (VOYA)*, and *Wilson Library Bulletin*. Among the many retrospective sources consulted were volumes in the H. W. Wilson Standard Catalog series, *Recommended Reference Books for Small and Medium-sized Public Libraries*, and *American Reference Books Annual*. Both of the latter are annual publications of Libraries Unlimited. Only recommended titles from these sources were considered for inclusion.

The annotations were prepared by consulting and adapting reviews, other secondary sources like publisher's catalogs, or in some cases by personal examination. Bibliographic material was verified in publisher's catalogs and *Books in Print, 1992-1993* (Bowker). Only titles currently in print were included, with the exception of a few important works that are still readily accessible in library collections.

The annotations were intended to give the reader an indication of the scope of the work, its size (often the actual number of entries), kinds of material included, its purpose, arrangement, nature of entries, indexes, special features, and a recommendation statement. In the interest of brevity, sometimes only the most salient aspects of a work were cited, particularly in very specialized sources.

Preceding each entry, there is an indication of audience and type of library level:

C = materials for children or for adults working with children (preschool through grade six)

Y = material for young adults or adults working with young adults (junior and senior high school)

A = material for adults from college age on

Readers should be aware that materials are listed only once in the text. Books that contain material suitable for more than one age group (i.e., Children, Young Adult, and Adult) have been placed in the area most appropriate to the books' contents. It is essential, therefore, that all sections of this directory, including the subject index, be consulted to obtain complete coverage of materials suitable for a specific age group. The use of the indicators C, Y, and A aids identification of materials in each section.

The length of the annotation is not an indication of the importance of the work. However, an asterisk (*) after an audience code signifies a work that is highly recommended. This recommendation refers only to its use in collection development and not its general importance.

The book is divided into three major parts. Part I, "Periodicals and Serials," is an annotated list of periodicals useful in collection development, arranged first by intended audience, then by print or nonprint media, and then alphabetically by title. Parts II and III list retrospective sources arranged first by subjects and then alphabetically by title. Part II, "Children and Young Adult Sources," lists sources specifically useful in working with children and young adults. In addition, adult titles in the remainder of the book that would also be valuable in developing young adult collections are identified by the symbol Y. Part III, "Adult Sources," lists comprehensive bibliographies of general adult-level reference materials, and adult-level materials in the social sciences, humanities, and science and technology.

Works cited within annotations are of two types. Those without bibliographic information are given individual entries, while those with bibliographic information are cited only for informational purposes. Major series are given separate descriptive entries, but individual titles in these series might have separate entries if they are considered of great importance. To facilitate access to the citation, there are two indexes: by title and author or editor of main entry, and by subject. This guide was intended to be comprehensive; however, to make it a practical one, extremely esoteric and specialized works have been excluded.

The authors would like to express thanks to the personnel of the libraries who cooperated in the preparation of this book, particularly those of the graduate library schools at the C. W. Post Center of Long Island University and the State University of New York at Albany, and those of the Huntington and Great Neck public libraries on Long Island, New York.

Periodicals
and
Serials

1 General Audience

General

A

1. American Book Publishing Record Monthly. 1960. 12/yr. $129.95 ($159.95 annual cum.). R. R. Bowker, 121 Chanlon Road, New Providence, NJ 07974.

This publication lists the books published within a given month by Dewey sequence for nonfiction and alphabetically by author for fiction. There are also sections for juvenile fiction and mass market paperbacks plus author and title indexes and a subject guide. Entry information includes full bibliographic information, LC classifications, LC card numbers, and subject headings. Annual cumulations are available. Though not a selection aid, this will help to verify the availability of recent publications.

Bibliographies, General

C*; Y*; A*

2. Booklist. 1905. 22/yr. $56 ($70 Canada). American Library Association, 50 E. Huron St., Chicago, IL 60611.

One of the oldest and best reviewing journals in America, *Booklist* has received an editorial face-lift in recent years that has improved both its appearance and content and made it an even more valuable selection aid for all level of public and school libraries. After a section, "Upfront: Advance Reviews," which gives pre-publication reviews of important new adult fiction and nonfiction that are anticipated will be in demand in libraries, there is a section of reviews of adults books, many of which are also recommended for young adults (these are indicated by 'Y'). In a section, "Adult Books for Young Adults," these books are again cited with specific recommendations for YA audiences. There follows sections on books for older readers (grade 7 and up), books for middle readers (grades 4 through 6), and books for the young (preschool through grade three). Each book included has passed a preliminary review for quality before consideration for inclusion; those of exceptional value are starred. Reviews are staff written and are noted for perceptive, incisive comments. The frequent retrospective bibliographies on specific topics are an added bonus. There is a nonprint review section that evaluates videos, filmstrips, audiobooks, etc. at all levels and a closing section, "Reference Books Bulletin," that gives thorough, perceptive reviews of reference books and materials. A semi-annual and annual index is included in the February 15 and August issues respectively. A must for all libraries. *Children's Literature; Young Adult Literature; Adult Books and Reading*

Y; A

3. Environmental Index. 1992. 4/yr. $99. UMI/Data Courier, P.O. Box 1307, Ann Arbor, MI 48106.

This bibliography contains citations culled from about 1,000 sources on such topics as ecology, energy, endangered species, chemicals, pollution, and waste management. All entries, whether for subjects, personal names, institutions, or place names, are found in a single alphabet without indexes. Full bibliographic information is given for each citation. This index is aimed at the general reader and high school student, rather than the serious researcher, and therefore will be appropriate for general collections.

Environment; Ecology

A

4. Forthcoming Books. 1966. 6/yr. $199 ($225. Canada). R. R. Bowker, 121 Chanlon Road, New Providence, NJ 07974.

This periodical supplements *Books in Print*. Each volume begins with books published in a given summer of a year and also lists the books that are scheduled for publication in the next five months. Thus an individual issue updates and expands the previous one and grow larger until a volume has been completed. Materials are arranged by Library of Congress subject headings. Bibliographic information includes ISBNs and LC numbers. Materials listed include adult trade books, technical and science books, young adult and juvenile titles, college texts, paperbacks, imports, revised editions, and reprints. There are separate author, title, and subject indexes. Although this is not a selection tool, it can be very helpful in identifying books to be considered for future purchase. Useful in academic and large public libraries.

Adult Books and Reading

C; Y; A

5. **Freebies.** 1978. 6/yr. $6.97. Freebies Publishing Co., P.O. Box 20283, Santa Barbara, CA 93120.

This bibliography lists approved free and inexpensive material for both children and adults. Included are newsletters, pamphlets, pictures, maps, catalogs, and some nonprint material. All are arranged by subject. Each item is annotated and includes ordering directions. A useful tool for building vertical file material. *Vertical File Materials; Free Material*

Y; A

6. **Government Periodicals and Subscription Services.** 4/yr. free. Superintendent of Documents, U.S. Government Printing Office, Washington, DC 20402.

This is an extremely valuable one of the *Subject Bibliographies* available free from the Superintendent of Documents. This work lists with annotations and ordering information, key periodicals published by various government agencies. The items are arranged by title and there is an agency index with a list under each entry of the periodicals currently available. This is a very useful buying guide for secondary school and public libraries. *Periodicals; United States—Government Publications*

C; Y; A*

7. **Kirkus Reviews.** 1933. 24/yr. $255. Kirkus Service, Inc., 200 Park Ave., S., New York, NY 10013.

Noted for their realistic, straightforward reviews, this publication evaluates books months before their actual publishing date, which allows libraries time to anticipate demand and order in advance accordingly. A loose-leaf format is used for easy filing in binders. Each issue is divided into two parts, one dealing with adult books (there are sections for fiction and nonfiction, each arranged alphabetically by author), and one arranged the same way for children's and young adult books. Books of unusual merit are given a "pointer." These books are highlighted at the beginning of each section. The price will probably restrict this useful selection tool to purchase in medium-sized public libraries and up.

Adult Books and Reading; Children's Literature; Young Adult Literature

Y*; A*

8. **Library Journal.** 1876. 20/yr. $69. R. R. Bowker, P.O. Box 1977, Marion, OH 43302.

This is one of the most read and consulted journals in the library world, both for its articles and special columns, as well as its reviews. In the former area, each issue (semimonthly except for January, July, August, and December) has articles on current library conditions and concerns at the public, college, and special library levels. The February 15 and September 15 issues respectively are on Spring and Fall book announcements, and the January issue highlights the best books of the year. There is also an annual roundup of the best in science and technology and a buying guide issue. In the regular review section, books are arranged by broad subjects (e.g., arts and humanities) with many subdivisions (e.g., poetry). Reviews are written and signed by practitioners or subject specialists. There are also departments that review magazines, videos, audio cassettes, reference materials, and professional reading. This is a must for all libraries serving an adult population. As well, all but the smallest of senior high schools will find it extremely valuable.

Adult Books and Reading

C; Y; A

9. **MultiCultural Review.** 1992. 4/yr. $59. MultiCultural Review, Greenwood Publishing, 88 Post Road West, Box 5007, Westport, CT 06881-5007.

This acquisition journal evaluates multicultural print and nonprint materials suitable for both children, young adults, and adults. In addition to penetrating reviews of material associated with American ethnic, racial, and religious experiences, there are several articles per issue that give overviews on various facets of these subjects. The reviews, which are organized by subject areas, cover new books, magazines, and audio/video materials. An effort is made to include material from both mainstream and alternative publishers. In school, public and academic libraries where this coverage is needed, this is an excellent selection aid. *Children's Literature; Young Adult Literature; Adult Books and Reading; Multiculturalism*

C; Y; A*

10. **The New York Times Book Review**. 1890. 52/yr. $22. The New York Times, 229 W. 43 St., New York, NY 10036.

This standard book reviewing source can be purchased as part of the Sunday edition of the *New York Times* or separately by subscription. The latter method assures the purchaser of receiving it at least a week before it is released generally. This 50- to 60-page publication reviews the fiction and nonfiction of general appeal to the American reader. The reviews vary in length from two pages to about 15 to 20 lines in the "In Short" section. The reviewers are identified by name. There are special sections on mystery and detective fiction and on new paperbacks. The best seller lists (for both hard cover and paperback books) are determined by nation-wide surveys of bookstores. About five of six children's books are reviewed per issue, although there are two supplements per year on children's books. Other annual supplements include ones on business books, science and technology, and university press books. This is an essential purchase for libraries from the senior high school and up. Other noteworthy weekly newspaper book reviewing supplements are *The Los Angeles Times Book Review* and *The Washington Post Book World*.

Adult Books and Reading; Children's Literature; Young Adult Literature

C*; Y*; A*

11. **Science Books and Films**. 1965. 5/yr. $20. American Association for the Advancement of Science, 1333 H St., NW, Washington, DC 20005.

This excellent reviewing source for science materials gives coverage to books, films, and filmstrips on the life sciences, physical sciences, social sciences, and mathematics suitable for students from the elementary grades through college. College texts are included but not those for grades K through 12. The reviews are arranged by Dewey Decimal Class numbers with author, title, and subject indexes. The reviews are astute, practical, and from the scientist's point of view. Levels of difficulty are noted and each book is given one of four possible overall ratings from 'not recommended' to 'highly recommended.' This is an excellent reviewing source for work with all levels of students. The latest compilation of reviews excerpted from this publication is *Science Books and Films' Best Books for Children, 1988-91* (300p., $40. 0-87168-505-1) available from the above address. *Science*

Y*; A*

12. **Vertical File Index**. 1932. 11/yr. $45 ($50 Canada). H. W. Wilson Co., 950 University Ave., Bronx, NY 10452.

Through the years, this publication has become a mainstay for building vertical files. It is a subject index to inexpensive pamphlets and paperbacks, government publications, charts, posters and maps, art exhibition catalogs, and selected university publications. Examples of the topics covered are energy, taxes, hobbies, consumer issues, and nutrition. Entries give prices and ordering information. Each issue contains a title index and there is a semiannual cumulated subject index.

Vertical File Materials; Free Material

C; Y; A*

13. **Wilson Library Bulletin**. 1914. 11/yr. $46 ($52 Canada). H. W. Wilson Co., 950 University Ave., Bronx, NY 10452

This is one of the oldest and widely read general periodicals about libraries and librarianship. Despite its age, it is thoroughly modern in content and approach. Each issue has a number of feature articles on subjects of current interest in the library world. There are also extensive reviewing sections beginning with the audiovisual reviews (usually on recordings and videos), followed by a technology section (software reviews and reference materials on discs). In the section called "Books and Periodicals," there are separate brief sections on picture books for children, books for middle grades, a young adult column, mystery stories, science fiction, art, university press books, periodicals, and current reference books (the largest of these reviewing sections). Though none of these is exhaustive, each gives critical introductions to the best and most important in each category. The *Bulletin* is a very stimulating, energetic publication that is a must purchase particularly in public libraries.

Reference Books; Children's Literature; Young Adult Literature; Adult Books and Reading

Y; A

14. **Worldwide Brochures: The Official Travel Brochure Directory**. 1991. 4/yr. $156. Worldwide Brochures, 1227 Kenneth St., Detroit Lakes, MN 56501.

A typical issue of this quarterly lists more than 7,000 full-color travel brochures from all over the globe in about 800 pages including full ordering information for the 3,000 companies and agencies from which these materials are available free. This will be a boon to building vertical file collections and can also be used by patrons to obtain their own travel information. It is also available as a software product for IBM or compatible PCs. Unfortunately the price may discourage some libraries from purchasing it; however, larger public libraries will find a valuable tool for keeping travel collections current.

Travel; Vertical File Materials

Nonprint Media

Y; A

15. **Compute! The Leading Magazine of Home, Educational, and Recreational Computing**. 1979. 12/yr. $9.97. Compute! Publications, Inc., 324 W. Wendover Ave., Ste. 200, P.O. Box 5406, Greensboro, NC 27408.

This popular, general computing magazine emphasizes the everyday applications of computer technology at home and school. There are many general articles in each issue on such topics as word processing, games, and computer security, plus reviews of programs, announcements, and a discussion of hardware. Similar in scope is *PC Magazine* (1982. 22/yr. $40. Ziff-Davis Publishing Co., Box 2445, Boulder, CO 80322), and, for advanced users, *Byte: The Small Systems Journal* (1975, 12/yr. $23. McGraw-Hill, Inc., One Phoenix Mill Lane, Peterborough, NH 03458). Both contain reviews of both software and hardware. See also *Home Office Computing*. These magazines will be useful for general reading purposes in senior high and public libraries but of limited value in selecting computer products.

Computer Software; Computers

C; Y; A

16. **The Computing Teacher: Journal of the International Council for Computers in Education**. 1979. 9/yr. $29. International Council for Computers in Education, University of Oregon, 1787 Agate St., Eugene, OR 97403-9905.

Though this is not exclusively a reviewing journal, it does include lists of software useful in schools, plus a few reviews. However most of the articles deal with how to teach computer use and how to use computers in teaching. Somewhat similar in scope and number of reviews included are the more scholarly *Computers in Education* (1976. 4/yr. $155. Pergamon Press. Inc., Maxwell House, Fairview Park, Elmford, NY 10523) and *Computers in the Schools* (1984, 4/yr. $48. Haworth Press, Inc. 75 Griswold St., Binghamton, NY 13904). These are important professional journals but of limited value in the selection process. See also *Technology and Learning*. *Computers; Computer Software*

Y; A

17. **Home Office Computing**. 1983. 12/yr. $20. Scholastic, Inc., 730 Broadway, New York, NY 10003.

This periodical was once called *Family and Home Office Computing* and before that *Family Computing*. It is a good general magazine that emphasizes practical uses of computers in nontechnical articles. There are both hardware and software reviews, and a feature "Software Guide" in each issue lists and annotates software related to education, business and entertainment. There is also an annual "Buyer's Guide to Computers." *Computers; Computer Software*

C; Y; A

18. **Video Librarian**. 1986. 11/yr. $35 ($40 Canada). Video Librarian, P.O. Box 2725, Bremerton, WA 98310.

This 10 page magazine opens with introductory material on practical advice about videos, but its heart are the approximately 50 reviews per issue written chiefly by the editor on new video cassettes. The reviews are arranged into four sections; children's, documentaries, how-to, and miscellaneous. The annotations are both descriptive and critical. Each video is rated by a star system from one star (poor) to four (excellent). Especially fine products also receive the Editor's Choice honor. Availability addresses, length, price, and producers are given for each video. Libraries anxious to build quality video collections will find this publication useful. *Videocassettes*

C; Y; A*

19. **Video Rating Guide for Libraries** 1990. 4/yr. $110. ABC-CLIO, 130 Cremona Drive, Box 1911, Santa Barbara, CA 93116-1911.

This quarterly video evaluation guide is an excellent guide to evaluation of videos. It has a library market orientation. Approximately 2,000 are evaluated per year (about 500 per issue). The reviewers are librarians and subject specialists. Vidoes are rated by stars, from one to five. Entries include full title, production information, cataloging data, and audience levels. The reviews are lengthy and thorough. There are indexes by subject, title, price, and audience, and a "Best of Issue" listing. This is a fine selection aid for videos in all types of libraries.   *Videocassettes*

Y; A
   20.   **Wired Librarian's Newsletter**. 1983. $15. Eric Anderson, 393 E. Huron St., Jackson, OH 45640.
     This lively newsletter discusses the use of computer hardware and software in libraries and contains frank and perceptive reviews of both of these types of products. There are also book reviews of professional materials.   *Computers; Computer Software*

2 Children and Young Adult

General

Y*

21. **The ALAN Review**. 1972. 3/yr. $15. Assembly on Literature for Adolescents, National Council of Teachers of English, 1111 Kenyon Road, Urbana, IL 61801.

This periodical is devoted to an examination of literature for young adults. In each issue there are articles that focus on particular topics explored in YA literature (e.g., divorce, historical novels), as well as many profiles of individual authors and/or specific aspects of their work. In the center are four pages of pull-out, signed reviews of both hardcover and paperback books suitable for readers in junior and senior high grades. Features include, "The Library Connection" in which librarian-teacher cooperation is often discussed, "The Publisher Connection," and "The Membership Connection" in which there is current news about ALAN activities. *Young Adult Literature*

C*; Y

22. **Appraisal: Science Books for Young People**. 1967. 4/yr. $39 ($50 Canada). Children's Science Book Review Committee, School of Education, 605 Commonwealth Ave., Boston, MA 02215.

This journal reviews trade books in science and mathematics for children from preschool to high school. There are approximately 90 books reviewed per issue arranged alphabetically by author. For each book there are two reviews of about 15 lines each: one by a librarian and the other by a subject specialist. Each review also contains a rating (E=excellent; VG=very good; G=good; F=fair; U=unsatifactory; *=qualifications) and an age suitability indication. Each issue also contains a section that updates series by indicating and annotating new books that have been added. There are about 40 of these reviews per issue. The index is cumulated for each year by author, title and subject. *Science*

C

23. **Bayviews**. 1990. 10/yr. $25. Association of Children's Librarians of Northern California, P.O. Box 12471, Berkeley, CA 94701.

This association of librarians issues this review journal with a Western perspective ten times a year. Reviews are signed by the participating librarians and the total number of reviews printed per year now averages about 1,200. There is also an annual selection of the best books of the year printed in a separate list, *The ACL Distinguished Book List*. A single copy is available for 75 cents from the above address.

Children's Literature

C*; Y

24. **Book Links: Connecting Books, Libraries and Classrooms**. 1991. 6/yr. $18 (U.S. and Canada). American Library Association, 50 E. Huron St., Chicago, IL 60611.

This new magazine offers ideas for stimulating reading and integrating children's books into the school curriculum. Each issue has annotated lists of books on various subjects, places, events, or people, plus profiles on individual authors. There are also essays that link together books on similar themes. There is a two month calendar at the back that lists occasions to use specific types of books. This most attractive, colorful periodical averages 40 pages per issue and is intended for librarians working with children from preschool through the eighth grade. *Children's Literature; Young Adult Literature*

Y*

25. **The Book Report: The Journal for Junior and Senior High School Librarians**. 1982. 5/yr. $39 ($49 Canada). Linworth Publishing, Inc., 5701 N. High St. (Ste. One), Worthington, OH 43085-3963.

This lively periodical is a combination reviewing journal and a manual on how to bring students and books together. Before the review section, there are many features in each issue that include a section on tips and other "bright ideas" from readers, material on how to motivate readers and how to teach library skills, a section on the use of computers in libraries, and a feature "Books and Other Things," that gives news on professional books, government documents, pamphlets, and bibliographies. The review section is divided into fiction and nonfiction, with many subdivisions by genres and subjects. There are about 120 reviews per issue. Each is about 15 to 20 lines in length and indicates grade levels and if the book is recommended or not. Books specifically for young adults as well as adult books suitable for young adults are included. Reviews are written by practicing librarians. Some software, videos, CD-ROM products, and paperbacks are also included. Black and white reproductions of dustjackets are used extensively in the review section. This is an excellent, highly recommended reviewing journal for all librarians working with young adults. It will be particularly useful in high schools. *Young Adult Literature*

C
26. **Bookbird**. 1962. 4/yr. $30. EBSCO, attention Betty Hand, P. O. Box 1943, Birmingham, AL 35201.

This is a joint publication of the International Board on Books for Young People (IBBY) and the International Institute for Children's Literature and Reading Research. It originates in Denmark and, in addition to giving news about IBBY and its affiliates, there are numerous articles on children's books, for example, the section on "Books of International Interest" highlights important books in a country-by-country arrangement. Each issue contains profiles of a specific author and illustrator and lists international prize winners. This is a fascinating world-wide view of children's literature. *Children's Literature*

C
27. **Books for All Kids**. 1990. 4/yr. Books for All Kids, 3336 Aldrich Ave. South, Minneapolis, MN 55408.

This book reviewing journal evaluates children's literature from the standard criteria with special attention paid to racial and ethnic minorities, disabled characters, male and female roles, characters of various ages, gay and lesbian characters, and families of varies types. Send a stamped self addressed envelope and $1.00 to *Books for All Kids* for more information and sample reviews. *Children's Literature*

C
28. **Canadian Children's Literature**. 1975. 4/yr. $16. C C Press, P.O. Box 335, Guelph, Ont. N1H 6K5.

This journal is devoted "to the literary analysis, criticism, and review of books written for Canadian children." Each of the four quarterly issues has a particular theme or topic covered in a series of bibliographic essays. There follows a book reviewing section. Most of the articles are in English, although some are in French. This periodical will be of primary interest in Canadian libraries.
Children's Literature; Children's Literature, Canadian

C*; Y
29. **Center for Children's Books. Bulletin**. 1947. 11/yr. $32 ($27 for individuals). University of Chicago Press, 5720 S. Woodlawn, Chicago, IL 60637.

This is one of the most respected reviewing sources of books for children and young adults (preschool through junior high). There are approximately 60 reviews per issue usually written by members of the editorial staff although some are contributed by the specialists that make up the advisory committee. Books are arranged in one alphabet by author's last name. Each review is about 10-15 lines in length and contains a rating: *=special distinction; R=recommended; Ad=additional purchase; M=marginal; and NR=not recommended. The reviews are astute and perceptive. At the end of each review there are subjects listed that indicate curricular use and developmental values. The last page is an unannotated bibliography of new books, articles, and pamphlets of interest to the professional. There is a combined author and title annual index in the July/August issue. This is a highly recommended selection aid particularly for elementary schools and children's rooms in public libraries. *Children's Literature; Young Adult Literature*

C
30. **Children's Book News**. 1978. 4/yr. free. Children's Book Centre, 229 College St. West., 5th Floor, Toronto, Ont. M5T 1R4.

Each issue of the quarterly publication contains book announcements of children's books for preschoolers through the ninth grade. Annotations are about 50 words each. Though noncritical in nature, this publication informs librarians about new children's books, particularly those originating in Canada. There is also a news section with material on developments in the field of children's literature in Canada.
Children's Literature, Canadian

C

31. **Children's Book Review Service**. 1972. 14/yr. $40. Children's Book Review Service, 220 Berkeley Place, No. 1D, Brooklyn, NY 11217.

Each of the monthly issues of this reviewing service contains about 60 to 80 reviews that are written by librarians and teachers. An issue is divided into three parts, one for picture books, one for young readers, and another for older readers (ages 10 to 14). Each review is 50 to 100 words in length. This will be of value in elementary schools and children's rooms in public libraries. *Children's Literature*

C

32. **Children's Magazine Guide**. 1948. 9/yr. $45 ($49. Canada). R. R. Bowker, 121 Chanlon Road, New Providence, NJ 07974.

This should more accurately be called *Children's Magazine Index* because it supplies an index to the nonfiction contents of about 40 magazines suitable for children from ages six through 14 such as *Boy's Life* and *Highlights for Children*. Entries are arranged by subject, and there is a separate index to articles in nine professional magazines like *School Library Journal* and *Horn Book*. The August issue contains the annual cumulation. These annual issues covering 1987 on are available for $20 each. Though not intended as a buying guide, this will nevertheless be a helpful guide in choosing magazines for elementary schools and children's rooms in public libraries. *Children's Periodicals*

33. (This entry number not used.)

C*; Y

34. **Curriculum Review**. 1960. 6/yr. $35. Curriculum Advisory Service, 517 S. Jefferson St., Chicago, IL 60607.

This periodical is an invaluable reviewing source of instructional materials for school libraries. The reviews are divided into four main sections: language arts, mathematics, science, and social studies and includes reviews of both print and nonprint materials. Each issue begins with several feature articles on a timely curricular topic. Many of these also contain useful retrospective bibliographies. A separate section deals with computers and computer education. Ordering information is given for the products reviewed and there is index to reviews in each issue. This is an excellent guide for both elementary and high schools for collection building in academic areas.

Children's Literature; Young Adult Literature; Instructional Materials

C*; Y*

35. **Emergency Librarian**. 1973. 5/yr. $40 ($45 if billed). Dyad Services, Dept. 284, Box C34069, Seattle, WA 98124-1069.

This Canadian publication offers practical tips on management and many evaluations of materials for school librarians. Each issue has a section on professional reading which contains about 15 reviews. There are also reviews of new paperbacks and recordings for children and young adults, software reviews, a videofile and a feature called "Footnotes," that often lists pamphlets, bibliographies, and useful books. Other features found in most issues are bestseller lists (one for Canada; one for U.S.), a section called "Outstanding New Books, K-12," (about 20 books are noted with annotations), and a profile of an outstanding Canadian author or illustrator. This periodical contains many useful hints for successful school library management plus many practical suggestions for effective collection development.

Children's Literature; Young Adult Literature

Y

36. **English Journal**. 1912. 8/yr. $40. National Council of Teachers of English, 1111 Kenyon Road, Urbana, IL 61801.

This is essentially a professional journal that discusses issues, trends, and practices in the teaching of English in junior and senior high schools. Although it is not primarily a reviewing journal, there are sections that review professional books, media, and computer software regularly. As well, there are frequently bibliographic articles that survey young adult literature from the perspective of a particular concern, subject, or author. *Young Adult Literature*

C
37. **The Five Owls**. 1986. 6/yr. $18 ($23 Canada). The Five Owls, Dept. L, 2004 Sheridan Ave. S., Minneapolis, MN 55405.

The purpose of this attractive publication is "to encourage reading and literacy among young people by advocating children's books with integrity: those that can be judged intelligent, beautiful, well-made and worthwhile in relation to books and literature in general." Each issue is 16 pages and, in addition to articles about children's literature, contains about 10 to 15 book reviews, tips on collection building, interviews with authors, and ideas on how to use books with young people. A distinguished publication that will be of value in children's rooms and large elementary schools. *Children's Literature*

C; Y
38. **Free Materials for Schools and Libraries**. 1979. 5/yr. $17 ($20 if billed). Free Materials for Schools and Libraries, Dept. 284, Box C34069, Seattle, WA 98124-1069.

This publication, edited in Canada, contains listings of completely free materials available for libraries. Each piece of material has been reviewed professionally for accuracy, suitability, and quality, and each is annotated with descriptive information. Full ordering instructions are given. This is very helpful in developing vertical files in libraries serving children and young adults.

Free Material; Vertical File Materials

C*; Y
39. **The Horn Book Magazine: About Books for Children and Young Adults**. 1924. 6/yr. $36. Horn Book Magazine, Park Square Bldg., 31 James Ave., Boston, MA 02116.

This is one of the oldest and most prestigious reviewing sources in the field of children's literature. Each issue contains articles about individual authors or illustrators and scholarly essays on topics related to children, their reading, and education. The review section is divided by age group. Most of the books are favorably reviewed because they have been screened for quality in advance. *The Horn Book Guide to Children's and Young Adult Books* (2/yr. $45) gives more inclusive reviews. *Horn Book* reviews delve into perceptive details that might escape the reviewers in other journals. In addition to the regular reviews, there is a section on professional news and publications, and others on paperbacks, new editions and reprints, and outstanding paperbacks. This stimulating periodical is extremely important in children's rooms and elementary school libraries for assuring quality book selection. Because of the highly selective nature of the reviews of young adult books, it is of lesser importance in junior high schools.

Children's Literature; Young Adult Literature

C; Y
40. **Interracial Books for Children Bulletin**. 1966. 8/yr. (several double issues) $28 ($33. Canada). Council on Interracial Books for Children, 1841 Broadway, New York, NY 10023.

This interesting periodical contains articles on multicultural coverage in children's and young adult books, past and present, educational services to these minority groups, and pertinent issues such as bilingual education. An important part of each issue is "Bookshelf," which reviews "books that relate to minority themes." They are evaluated by members of the minority group depicted. A stimulating periodical that should be available in elementary schools and children's collections in public libraries.

Children's Literature; Young Adult Literature; Multiculturalism

Y
41. **Journal of Reading**. 1957. 8/yr. membership. International Reading Association, 800 Barksdale Road, Box 8139, Newark, DE 19714-8139.

This companion to *The Reading Teacher* is a journal for professionals working with adolescent and adult learners. In addition to information on concerns in this area and teaching strategies, there are reviews of instructional materials, professional books, books for young adults, tests, and software. There is also a section on current research and one devoted to reading supervisors and their interests.

Young Adult Literature; Reading

C; Y
42. **Journal of Youth Services in Libraries**. 1987. 4/yr. $40 ($50 Canada). American Library Association, 50 E. Huron St., Chicago, IL 60611.

This quarterly is the official publication of two divisions of the American Library Association, the Association for Library Service to Children, and the Young Adult Services Division. It began in 1942 as

Top of the News and in 1987 took its present name. Although it contains information on activities and programs of these division, it also has articles on working with children and YAs, as well as on content analyses of books for these groups and on individual authors and illustrators. Although it does not review juvenile books, these articles are often useful in book selection. There are sections on current research, technology and new professional books. *Children's Literature; Young Adult Literature*

Y*

43.   **KLIATT Young Adult Paperback Book Guide: An Annotated List of Current Paperback Books for Young Adults**. 1966. 8/yr. $33. KLIATT Paperback Book Guide, 425 Watertown St., Newton, MA 02158.

This periodical is issued eight times a year, three times as large magazine-sized booklets, and five times in shortened newsletter formats. The booklets contain about 300 to 400 reviews each, and the newsletters average about 75 books. All types of paperbacks are reviewed: both trade and mass market, as well as young adult titles and adult titles suitable for young adults. Some of the subject divisions are: fiction, literature, biography, education and guidance, social studies, history and geography, science, arts, and recreation. Symbols used in the reviews indicate the suitability of the work from advanced to low reading ability; M means mature contents, and a * signifies a publication of exceptional merit. The reviews are short but give a good indication of both content and quality. This selection aid is highly recommended for both junior and senior high schools and young adult collections in public libraries. *Young Adult Literature*

C

44.   **Language Arts**. 1924. 8/yr. $40. National Council of Teachers of English, 1111 Kenyon Rd., Urbana, IL 61801.

This authoritative periodical deals with the teaching of English primarily in the elementary grades (although some of the articles are also pertinent for junior high teachers). The articles deal with composition skills, language, and literature. In the latter area there are sometimes articles on themes and authors in children's literature. As well there are selective reviews of children's books and other professional materials. This is a basic title for elementary schools that will also be of some help in collection building. *Children's Literature; Reading*

C*

45.   **Library Talk: The Magazine for Elementary School Librarians**. 1988. 5/yr. $35. Linworth Publishing, Inc., 5701 N. High St., Ste. 1, Worthington, OH 43085.

This companion to *The Book Report* is aimed at librarians in elementary schools. Each issue contains articles on how to bring children and books together, as well news items and reports on new bibliographies, media, and professional publications. The reviews are grouped under headings like poetry, arts and crafts, nonfiction, reference books and general series books, mysteries (including science fiction and fantasy), general fiction (divided by grade level), easy readers, and folk tales, etc. The reviews in each section are by a single individual. There is a separate annotated section on paperbacks. This attractive magazine is illustrated with many black and white dust jacket reproductions. It is of great value in selecting materials in both elementary schools and children's rooms in public libraries. *Children's Literature*

C

46.   **Perspectives: Choosing and Using Books for the Classroom**. 1990. 5/yr. $24.95 Christopher Gorden Publishers, Inc., 480 Washington St., Norwood, MA 02062.

This is a relatively new addition to the growing number of reviewing sources for children's literature. Written from the standpoint of the classroom teacher, this periodical stresses literary values in books for children and how these books can be used creatively in the classroom. Included are fiction, nonfiction, and general works of literature including books of poetry. *Children's Literature*

C

47.   **The Reading Teacher**. 1947. 9/yr. $30. International Reading Association, 800 Barksdale Road, Box 8137, Newark, DE 19714.

This periodical deals with various aspects of reading instruction at the elementary school level. Many of the articles deal with trends and issues affecting the teaching of reading, and others focus on a particular theme or genre in children's literature. The latter often contain good bibliographies for collection development. A regular feature is also "Children's Books," a bibliographic essay on a special theme that will cite as many as 50 to 60 individual titles. There are also reviews of professional books. This is a useful tool for elementary school teachers that can also be used by librarians for background information on children's literature. *Children's Literature; Reading*

C*; Y*
48. **School Library Journal**. 1954. 12/yr. $76. School Library Journal, P.O. Box 1978, Marion, OH 43305.

This is an excellent all-purpose magazine for school librarians and public librarians that work with children and young adults. The first sections are devoted to features and articles that deal with various aspects of school and public services to young people. There are also departments on recent news, a calendar of events, and similar updates. The sections devoted to reviews represent about ⅔ of the text. First, there are audiovisual reviews that cover such media as films and videos, filmstrips, and recordings, with a separate section on computer software. The book reviews are divided into four areas: preschool and primary, grades 3-6, junior high and up, and adult books for young adults. These reviews total about 4,200 items per year (3,200 are books) and are written chiefly by practitioners. Both recommended and not recommended titles are included. Reviews are signed and indicate grade level suitability. Books of unusual merit are starred, and twice per year in a separate publication, *Star Track,* that is included in the subscription, all of the starred reviews for the past six months are reproduced. Each December there is a list of the best books of the year as chosen by the editors. This issue also contains the annual index by author and title. There is also an annual list of the best reference books of the year. This publication is a must for all library collections involved with children and young adults. *Children's Literature; Young Adult Literature*

C
49. **Science and Children.** 1963. 8/yr. $42. National Science Teachers Association, 1742 Connecticut Ave. NW, Washington, DC 20009.

This is a magazine about the teaching of science in elementary school with some material also for the junior high grades. Articles are on concerns and problems involved in instruction in science classrooms with many ideas for new approaches and improvements. For collection building, there are some reviews of books, curriculum materials, and software, although this is not primarily a selection tool. *Science*

Y
50. **Science Teacher.** 1934. 9/yr. $43. National Science Teachers Association, 1742 Connecticut Ave. NW, Washington, DC 20009.

Like its companion periodical, *Science and Children*, this is an official publication of the National Science Teachers Association, and, therefore, includes association news. The emphasis in the articles in this magazine is teaching science at the secondary school level. Although it is not intended as a major selection aid, there are some reviews of books, professional materials, and software. *Science*

C; Y
51. **Social Education**. 1937. 7/yr. $55. National Council for the Social Studies, 3501 Newark St. NW, Washington, DC 20016.

This is the official publication of the National Council for the Social Studies and concentrates on articles about teaching various topics in social studies. Many of these contain bibliographies for both students and teachers. Of particular importance is a feature of the May/June issue, the annual list of "Notable Children's Trade Books in the Field of Social Studies" (see entry 348). The section called "Resources" also includes articles, many of which are bibliographies of educational materials on specific subjects. Most of the material in this periodical is directed to elementary and junior high schools. *Social Studies*

C; Y*
52. **VOYA: Voice of Youth Advocates**. 1978. 6/yr. $32.50 ($37.50 Canada). Scarecrow Press, 52 Liberty St., Metuchen, NJ 08840.

There is no other publication for teachers and librarians that so accurately conveys the needs, concerns, and attitudes of young adults as *VOYA*. Each issue has about four or five interesting, sometimes controversial, articles on young adult reading and recreational interests, important authors, techniques of bringing adolescents and books together, or bibliographies on specific topics. The reviews section (over ⅔ of each issue) is divided into various sections: audiovisual (mostly films and video cassettes); fiction; science fiction, fantasy, and horror (a particularly strong area); nonfiction; professional; reference; and reprints. Book reviews are written and signed by practicing librarians and are uniquely coded for the book's quality (one to five Qs) and potential popularity (one to five Ps). Although the emphasis is on material for junior and senior high schools, there also reviews of books aimed at a middle school audience. Each issue has a title index. This lively, provocative publication deserves a place in all junior and senior high schools and young adult departments in public libraries where it will be an excellent aid for collection building.

Young Adult Literature; Instructional Materials

Nonprint Media

Y; A

53. **AFVA Evaluations**. 1946. 2/yr. membership. American Film and Video Association, Inc., 920 Barnsdale Road, Ste. 152, LaGrange Park, IL 60525.

For many years, this periodical was known as *EFLA Evaluations* because it was the official journal of the Educational Film Library Association. It changed its name in 1987 to reflect a change in emphasis and the media covered. It now reviews on a selective basis educational films and videos that are suitable for school and public libraries. Also from this organization is *Sightlines* (1967. 4/yr. $20) which contains articles on film and video production and a few reviews. *Films; Videocassettes*

C

54. **Children's Video Report**. 1985. 6/yr. $35. Great Mountain Productions, 145 W. 96 St., New York, NY 10025.

This is a comprehensive guide to videos for children. An average issue is about eight pages in length and contains several short reviews and five or six major reviews of about 250 words each. The reviewers are professionals in child development and media evaluation. Issues also contain ideas for video programming and related activities for young people. This would be of value both for parents and librarians in medium to large public libraries and school district professional collections.

Videocassettes; Children's Videocassettes

C; Y

55. **The Digest of Software Reviews: Education**. 1983. 12/yr. $42.95. School and Home Courseware, 3999 N. Chestnut Diag., Ste. 333, Fresno, CA 93726-4797.

This periodical is a digest of published reviews of educational software for grades K through 12. About 60 journals and newsletters are scanned, their reviews tabulated, and the most frequently reviewed items listed with excerpts from the reviews. In addition to the software evaluations, each issue contains guest editorials by educators, news items, and software announcements. This magazine gives the most complete review coverage of software for this age group. Unfortunately, it takes some time before the reviews can be collected and published. Nevertheless, this is a valuable tool in district-wide curriculum collections.

Computer Software

C; Y

56. **EPIEGRAM: Equipment and Materials**. 1972. 9/yr. $65 ($75 Canada). Epie Institute, P.O. Box 839, Water Mill, NY 11976.

This newsletter was formerly issued in two parts, one on materials and the other on equipment. This combined journal contains information related to curriculum and instruction but primarily it evaluates educational products and equipment. It is a valuable asset to district-wide school collections that need guidance in buying expensive curriculum related items.

Instructional Materials; Education Equipment and Supplies

Y

57. **INFOWORLD: The PC News Weekly**. 1979. 52/yr. $100. C W Communications, 1060 Marsh Road, Menlo Park, CA 94025.

This weekly tabloid covers microcomputers and news about them. In addition to articles on trends, new products, and various applications of existing software, there are reviews of new hardware and software. Another popular magazine that covers similar territory is *PC World* (12/yr. $29.90 PCW Communications, 501 Second St., Ste. 600, San Francisco, CA 94107). *Computers; Computer Software*

C; Y

58. **Landers Film Review: The Information Guide to 16mm Films**. 1956. 4/yr. $45. Landers Associates, P.O. Box 27309, Escondido, CA 92027.

This highly respected guide to 16mm films reviews about 125 per issue. The reviews are thorough and describe content as well as technical aspects. Suitability and usage possibilities are also stressed. There is a directory of sources in each issue and title and subject indexes. Although the use of films in schools has largely been replaced by video cassettes, this is a valuable reference tool at the elementary and secondary school level and in public libraries with large film collections. *Films*

C*; Y*

59. **Media and Methods: Educational Products, Technologies and Programs for Schools and Universities**. 1964. 5/yr. $29. American Society of Education, 1429 Walnut St., Philadelphia, PA 19102.

This periodical covers various forms of nonprint media and their use in education. Each issue has about five or six articles on media projects and products and their management in the classroom and library. As well there is a department on new products and a review section that includes material on video cassettes, filmstrips, books, databases, software, and videodiscs. There are also lists of catalogs to send for and directories of equipment manufacturers. This has proven to be a great asset in libraries from elementary school through junior college levels. *Audiovisual Materials; Instructional Materials*

C

60. **Oppenheim Toy Portfolio**. 1991. 4/yr. $15. Oppenheim Toy Portfolio, 40 E. 9th St., New York, NY 10003.

The scope of this selection aid is somewhat broader than the title would suggest because the author reviews books and videos as well as toys. Issues are arranged by age group from infants, toddlers, and preschoolers, to five- to eight-year-olds. In a typical issue there are reviews of about 30 books, 30 toys, and about 10 videos. *Toys; Children's Literature; Videocassettes*

C*

61. **Parents Choice: A Review of Children's Media**. 1978. 4/yr. $18. Parent's Choice Foundation, Box 185, Waban, MA 02168.

This tabloid-sized newspaper reviews books, television, movies, home videos, recordings, toys, games, computer programs, and rock 'n roll for children up to about age 12. The articles are both informative and entertaining. As well they try to represent a child's point of view and interests. Of particular value is the once-per-year Awards Issue which lists with annotations the best in toys, picture books, movies, story books, rock 'n roll, audio recordings, videos, television, magazines, computer programs, paperbacks, and video games. This is an excellent selection aid for both librarians as well as parents.

Instructional Materials; Children's Literature

C*; Y*

62. **Technology and Learning**. 1980. 8/yr. $24. Pitman Learning, 2451 E. River Road, Dayton, OH 45439.

This periodically was formerly known as *Classroom Computer Learning* and before that as *Classroom Computer News*. As its old names would suggest, the emphasis in this periodical is on using computers in education although other media like videodiscs are given coverage. There are many practical articles plus news items about new products, software developments, conferences, meetings, and other educational activities. There are about four very thorough reviews of software products per issue plus other material on texts, catalogs, and periodicals. Of great importance in schools are the annual software awards in which the best educational software is highlighted. The top five are featured, plus others arranged by subject areas like science and social studies. A total of about 50 are so honored each year. This periodical is valuable in both elementary and high schools. *Computer Software; Instructional Materials*

3 Adult

General

A
63. **Bestsellers**. 1989. 4/yr. $45. Gale Research Inc., P.O. Box 33477, Detroit, MI 48232-5477.

Each issue of this quarterly highlights about 25 to 30 books that are currently popular or for various reasons are currently in the news. Each entry is about four pages in length and contains biographical information about the author, a brief summary of the book, an excerpt, quotations from reviews, and other pertinent background information. This will be valuable for both reader's guidance and selection in public libraries. *Bestsellers; Adult Books and Reading*

A
64. **Books in Canada**. 1971. 9/yr. $20. Canadian Review of Books, Ltd., 366 Adelaide St., Ste. 432, Toronto, Ont. M5A 3X9.

This book reviewing journal reviews English language books currently being made available in Canada. Although reviews of Canadian material predominate, other important books are included regardless of country of origin. There are usually some interesting features articles and in the section "Books Received," new Canadian books are listed. *Canadian Literature*

A
65. **Books: 100 Reviews; The West Coast Review of Books**. 1974. 6/yr. 8 issues: $11.97 ($16.97 Canada). Rapport Publishing Co., Inc., 5265 Fountain Ave., Upper Terrace, Los Angeles, CA 90029.

Once known as simply *The West Coast Review of Books*, this reviewing journal is popular in both tone and scope and contains reviews of general fiction and nonfiction titles. Individual reviews are initialed and rated from one star (poor) to five stars (excellent). This is an interesting publication that is interesting to skim. *Adult Books and Reading*

A*
66. **Choice: Current Reviews for Academic Libraries**. 1964. 11/yr. $148 ($165 Canada). $225. on cards ($245. Canada). Choice, 100 Riverview Center, Middletown, CT 06457.

In its almost 30 years of existence, this has become the premier current book selection aid for college libraries. In its pages there are about 6,600 reviews per year arranged into four main sections: reference, the humanities, science and technology, and the social and behavioral sciences. Each contains many subdivisions by subject. Reviews are signed and are usually by academic subject specialists. Each review is numbered by volume and a consecutive digit within each volume. Some nonprint items are included. Each review is about 15 to 20 lines or about 150 words in length. There is an index in each issue and an annual cumulative index for each volume that is by author, title, and nonprint item. This is an essential purchase for all academic libraries and large public libraries. *Adult Books and Reading*

A
67. **Collection Building**. 1978. 4/yr. $55. Neal-Schuman, 23 Leonard St., New York, NY 10013.

This interesting periodical gives many tips on collection building for both academic and public libraries. Issues contain case studies in collection building, usage studies, and many bibliographic essays on how to collect information on special subjects. Others list libraries with strong collections in particular subjects. There is a section on government documents that often lists important publications on a particular subject. Many articles give tips on selection, and some are actually core bibliograpies on specific subjects. This is an extremely useful selection aid for both academic and medium to large public libraries.

Libraries—Collection Development

A

68. Consumer Health and Nutrition Index. ed. by Alan M. Rees. Oryx, quarterly. $89.50 per year. ISSN 0883-1963.

This quarterly index covers the literature of nutrition and health care as found in general interest magazines, health newsletters, and special publications. Such topics as AIDS, drug abuse, parenting, cancer, and pregnancy are covered. Each fourth issue cumulates the previous three plus adding new entries. This then become the single annual volume. This will be useful in large public and academic libraries.

Health; Nutrition

A

69. Current Index to Journals in Education, CIJE. Gale, monthly, $225. per year ISSN 0011-3565.

This monthly index provides access to the contents of articles appearing in over 700 periodicals. Available separately are the semiannual cumulations also priced at $225 per year. There is a special combination subscription price of $430. This index is a valuable extension of the basic material found in Wilson's *Education Index*; however, its price will restrict its purchase to large libraries or district-wide curriculum centers. *Education; Periodicals—Education*

A

70. Garden Literature: An Index to Periodical Articles and Book Reviews. 1992. 4/yr. (individuals $50) Garden Literature Press, Sally Williams, 398 Columbus Ave., Ste. 181, Boston, MA 02116.

This relatively new index appears four times per year and indexes garden related articles, using a subject approach, from over 100 periodicals. There is also a separate section per issue (usually about 30 pages) which is an author and title index to book reviews. The last issue per year is a cumulative index. In addition to the standard areas involved in gardening, this work covers such topics as conservation, important people in the field, acid rain, and wetlands. Individual plants are found under scientific names with references from common names. This gives comprehensive coverage for both laypeople and professionals and, therefore, depending on the locality, will be of value in medium sized and larger public libraries as well as specialized collections. *Gardening*

A

71. The Informed Librarian: Professional Reading for the Information Professional. 1992. 12/yr. $129. Infosources Publishing, 140 Norma Rd., Teaneck, NJ 07666.

This is a relatively new periodical which averages 16 to 32 pages per issue and functions as a kind of *Current Contents* for librarians in that it reprints the table of contents of over 100 library and information science-related journals and new books on these subjects. An article delivery service is also available. Write to the above address for further information. For large libraries and those specializing in library and information science. *Library Science; Information Science*

A

72. Lector. 1982. 6/yr. $40. Hispanic Information Exchange, P.O. Box 4273, Berkeley, CA 94704.

Using a general subject approach, this reviewing journal covers Spanish-language and bilingual Hispanic literature. Preceding the reviews, there are usually several articles that explore publishing in the area and its output. Both adult and juvenile publications are covered, and there are recommendation codes at the end of each review which give rating and audience suitability. This is a useful selection tool for libraries that serve a large Hispanic population. *Spanish Literature*

A

73. Locus: The Newspaper of the Science Fiction Field. 1968. 12/yr. $35 ($40. Canada). Locus Publications, 34 Ridgewood Lane, Oakland, CA 94611.

This hugely entertaining magazine for science fiction buffs begins with news items about the world of science fiction publishing, its authors, awards, groups, conventions, and meetings. There is also a series of reviewing columns (usually about six) each by a different reviewer and containing chatty reviews of about six books each. Other sections include one for short reviews, an article on science fiction around the world, lists of forthcoming books in the U.S. and Britain, an annotated catalog of books and magazines received, and a chart on the month's best sellers. Children's and young adult books are included for review. This is a fine guide to fantasy and science fiction for both acquisition librarians and patrons.

Science Fiction; Fantasy

A

74. **Monthly Catalog**. 1895. 12/yr. $166. U.S. Government Printing Office, Superintendent of Documents, Washington, DC 20402.

Each issue of this massive bibliography of materials, published by the various branches of the federal government, is arranged by the Superintendent of Documents classification numbering system which roughly is by such issuing agencies as departments, the House of Representatives and Library of Congress. Each entry gives full bibliographic information, content notes, price, subject headings, Library of Congress classification number, Dewey and OCLC numbers, and LC card number. There are several indexes: by author, title, subject, series/reports, stock number, and title keyword. There are also annual cumulations of the indexes. The *Monthly Catalog* will be of value only in very large public and depository libraries. On various microform format there are many commercially available indexes that cumulate the *Monthly Catalog* beyond this annual level. They are generally very expensive and intended only for libraries having large collections of government documents. Some are: *Government Publications Index* (Information Access Co., $1,650 per year), *Federal Government Publications Catalog* (Brodart, $1,500 per year), *Government Documents Catalog Subscription* (Auto-Graphics, $1,400 per year). The U.S. Government Printing Office also publishes a more modest *Publications Reference File* ($142 per year) on microfiche that includes only those in-print items that are for sale by the Government Printing Office.

United States—Government Publications

A

75. **Monthly Checklist of State Publications**. 1910. 12/yr. $26. U.S. Government Printing Office, Superintendent of Documents, Washington, DC 20402.

This monthly bibliography is compiled by the Library of Congress staff and is arranged by state. For each state there is a listing of the most important documents that are considered to be of general interest throughout the country. This is a valuable selection aid for larger public libraries.

United States—Government Publications

A

76. **New Technical Books: A Selective List with Descriptive Annotations**. 1915. 6/yr. $15. New York Public Library, Science and Technology Division, Room 120, Fifth Ave. and 42nd Street, New York, NY 10018.

This is a highly respected guide to important new books in science and technology. The arrangement is by Dewey Decimal Classification numbers, although Library of Congress numbers are also included. Each entry is briefly annotated in four to eight sentences that are mainly descriptive, although inclusion in the list is an indication of recommendation. This is an extremely useful bibliography for academic and large public libraries. *Science; Technology*

A

77. **New York Review of Books**. 1963. 22/yr. $34. New York Review, Inc., 250 W. 57 St., New York, NY 10107.

This is more a literary journal than a book selection aid. Each issue contains about nine essays that begin as a lengthy book review but often become forums on current concerns and social problems. The books reviewed, however, are usually of significance and therefore should be considered for purchase in academic and medium to large public libraries. *Adult Books and Reading*

A

78. **Preview: Professional and Reference Literature Review**. 1988. 12/yr. $25. Mountainside Publishing, Inc., 321 S. Main St. #300, Ann Arbor, MI 48104.

The purpose of this periodical is twofold, first to help acquisition librarians choose among new reference materials and professional publications, and second to keep librarians up-to-date on new publications in the library science and related fields. Each issue gives review summaries from about 100 periodicals covering about 300 books. Each issue is divided about equally between coverage of professional literature and that on reference resources. Special sections highlight software for library applications, new editions, and children's reference sources. The coverage of reviews of new reference materials emphasizes works not commonly covered in the review media, such as small press books. This is an excellent selection aid for larger public and academic libraries. *Reference Books; Library Science*

A*

79. **Publishers Weekly**. 1872. 52/yr. $89. Publishers Weekly, P.O. Box 1979, Marion, OH 43305.

This is an essential periodical for publishers, booksellers, and others involved with books and the book trade. Through a number of regular features and specialized departments, it supplies information about trends, current book news, bookselling practices, and technology. There are many statistics reports, interviews with leaders in the field, and reports on best sellers and sales of rights. Of particular value for book selectors is the "Forecast" section which reviews fiction, nonfiction, paperbacks, and children's books prior to publication and makes prediction concerning possible popularity. There are several special issues each year including two on children's books (Fall and Spring announcements) and one preceding the American Booksellers Association conference. This is fascinating reading and will be of value particularly in academic and larger public libraries. *Adult Books and Reading*

A

80. **Rave Reviews**. 1986. 6/yr. $24. Rave Reviews, 55 Bergen St., Brooklyn, NY 11201.

This is a popularly written magazine on newsprint that is a guide to books intended for the average reader. Under such headings as contemporary fiction, thrillers, horror, science fiction, mystery, and historical romance, there are staff reviews that describe and predict popularity of books for recreational readers. Each books is also rated by a star system: one star =forget it, to five stars=don't miss it. At the end of each issue, there are lists of the best in recreational reading in both hard cover and paperback books, each with a three or four line annotations. This publication might be of interest to public library patrons and of some use in alerting librarians to the newest in popular readings. *Adult Books and Reading*

A

81. **Reference Services Review**. 1972. 4/yr. $45. Pierian Press, P.O. Box 1808, Ann Arbor, MI 48106.

The stated purpose of this periodical is to "review and evaluate a wide variety of publications having reference value within academic, public, school, and special library settings" and "to provide subject bibliographers and reference librarians with information useful to the functions of collection development and assessment." Each issue begins with seven or eight articles on reference service and materials, usually two of which are special bibliographies on a particular subject. At the end is a section, "Reviews and Recommendations," which contains annotated lists of new reference books, series additions, and material on automated data banks. This publication has been found to be helpful in developing both reference collections and their use in college libraries and medium public libraries. See also entries for *RQ* and *Reference and Research Book News*. *Reference Books*

A

82. **Romantic Times: For Readers of Romantic and Contemporary Fiction**. 1981. 6/yr. $24. Romantic Times Publishing Group, 163 Joralemon St., Brooklyn, NY 11201.

This companion to *Rave Reviews* is a popularly written guide to romantic fiction. In addition to profiles of authors and other news items, there are about 170 new books (mostly paperbacks) reviewed in each issue and rated from three to five hearts: three hearts=fair, and five hearts=classic. Also, the steaminess of the contents are also indicated: sensual (somewhat explicit); spicy (very explicit), and sexy (erotic). This guide might be of value to both patrons and librarians where there is a demand for this genre.

Romances—Fiction; Adult Books and Reading

A

83. **RQ**. 1960. 4/yr. $42. Reference and Adult Services Division, American Library Association, 50 E. Huron St., Chicago, IL 60611.

This is the official publication of the Reference and Adult Services Division of the American Library Association and, therefore, many of its articles deal with problems and concerns involving reference work at various levels of service. However others include bibliographies in special areas including the regular feature, "The Alert Collector," which is a bibliography of reference materials on a particular topic. As well, in the "Sources" section, there are thorough reviews of current reference materials in three sections: databases, reference books, and professional materials. The reference book section reviews about 40 books per issue. Each issue ends with an unannotated list of "Books Received But Not Reviewed." This publication is useful in academic and large public libraries. *Reference Books*

A

84. **Reference and Research Book News**. 1986. 6/yr. $48 ($60 Canada). Book News, Inc., 5600 NE Hassalo St., Portland, OR 97213.

This relatively new periodical is intended as "a convenient source of information about new books from English language publishers worldwide." Books are selected for inclusion "that will be of interest to acquisitions librarians in academic, special and public libraries." Titles are arranged by their Library of Congress subject classification from A (General Works) to Z (Bibliography and Library Science). For each book, bibliographic data is included and a four or five line evaluative and descriptive annotation. There are author, title, and subject indexes. This is a concise and valuable guide to nonfiction scholarly books and should be of great help in collection building in academic and large public libraries. Two other companion series from the same publisher are also valuable in these types of libraries. They are *SciTech Book News* (1977,12/yr. $60.), a monthly publication that covers the fields of technology, engineering, computers, medicine, and the physical and biological sciences, and *University Press Book News* (1989, 4/yr. $18, $24 in Canada), a quarterly that introduces new books from the world's university presses. All three are distinguished additions to the literature of book selection.

Adult Books and Reading; Science; University Press Books

A

85. **Small Press Review**. 6/yr. $22. Greenfield Press, P.O. Box 176, Southport, CT 06940.

This periodical usually contains one article on some aspect of small press publication, but the emphasis is on reviews of important small press books. There are about 30 reviews of about 700 words each per issue. Academic and large public libraries will find this to be a valuable guide to the product of this important segment of American publishing. *Adult Books and Reading*

A

86. **World of Cookbooks**. 1987. 4/yr. $40. Grace Kirschenbaum, 1645 S. Vineyard Ave., Los Angeles, CA 90019.

This quarterly newsletter that averages 16 to 20 pages reviews cookbooks both from the U.S. and abroad. There are about 60 reviews per issues including reviews on general books on food and beverages. The annotations are lengthy and thorough. This will be of value in specialized collections. *Cookbooks*

Nonprint Media

A

87. **CD-ROM Librarian: The Optical Review Media Review for Information Professionals**. 1985. 11/yr. $79.50 ($33 Personal and School Rate). Meckler Publishing Corp., 11 Ferry Lane West, Westport, CT 06880.

In its articles, this periodical gives information on developments in the optical storage of information field and its applications to libraries and other information centers. The major feature of each issue is the section that reports on both new hardware and software products in authoritative, lengthy reviews. For larger libraries. *CD-ROM*

A

88. **CD-ROM Professional**. 1987. 6/yr. $86. Pemberton Press, Inc., 11 Tannery Lane, Weston, CT 06883.

Each issue of this periodical has general articles on the use of CD-ROM products, many of them dealing with library applications. There are also in each issue five or six new product reviews of about six or seven pages each. Such topics as installation, features and capabilities, sample screens (about five illustration per product to illustrate features), work station information, documentation, delivery, comparison with print versions, and suggestions for improvement are covered. There are also sections containing brief reviews called "CD-ROM in Brief" and one on reviews of books on CD-ROM. This periodical will be of value in large collections. *CD-ROM*

A

89. **database: The Magazine of Database Reference and Review**. 1978. 6/yr. $89. Online, Inc., 11 Tannery Lane, Weston, CT 06883.

This quality journal, a companion to *Online*, reviews databases and has review articles on various subjects as they are handled in various databases. For example, an August 1991 article, surveyed environmental information as covered in approximately 50 different databases. There is also news about new databases and services. This will be of value chiefly in academic libraries. Another valuable periodical that will also be of value in libraries where there is extensive online database base searches is *Database Searcher: The Magazine for Online Database Users* (1984, 10/yr. $95. Meckler, 11 Ferry Lane West, Westport, CT 06880). *Databases*

A*
90. **Fanfare: The Magazine for Serious Record Collectors**. 1976, 6/yr. $27 ($37 Canada). Fanfare, Inc., P.O. Box 720, Tenefly, NJ 07670.

There are approximately 350 reviews of classical CDs in each issue of this authoritative reviewing journal. Each review is about one half to a full page in length. They are arranged by composer with a separate section for collections. Preceding the review section there are many articles about individuals artists, record labels, and timely topics. In the Nov/Dec issue, each of their many reviewers choose their favorite records of the year and why. There are many advertisements in the front material but not in the review sections. Each issue closes with separate columns on recent recordings in jazz, film music, and laser discs, plus a section on books reviews. This is now the standard reviewing journal for classical music. Other highly regarded periodicals are *The American Record Guide* (1935. 6/yr. $36) from Record Guide Productions, 4412 Braddock St., Cincinnati, OH 45204, and the British *The Gramophone* (1923. 12/yr. $58.) from General Gramophone Publishers, 177-179 Kenton Road, Harrow, Middlesex HA3 OHA, England.

Compact Discs; Classical Music; Music

A
91. **Film Library Quarterly**. 4/yr. Film Library Information Center, Box 348, Radio City Station, New York, NY 10019.

This journal contains information pertinent to the management of film and video libraries. As well, it gives information about current happenings in the film world and reviews films and videos as well as books about films. *Audiovisual Materials; Videocassettes*

A
92. **Laserdisk Professional**. 1988. 6/yr. $86. Pemberton Press, Inc., 11 Tannery Lane, Weston, CT 06883.

This practical magazine is devoted to CD-ROM technology and its use. Each issue contains a number of articles on such subjects as setting up CD-ROM workstations, using CD-ROM products in various situations, choosing proper hardware, and other selection tips. As well, there are extensive in-depth reviews of CD-ROM products that total about 75 per year. Two compilations from the 1988 and 1989 issues of the magazine are *Practical Tips and Techniques for Using CD-ROM Systems* ($14.95) and a two volume collection of reviews, *Critical Reviews of CD-ROM Products, 1988-1989* ($24.95).

CD-ROM; Computer Software

A
93. **Laserlog**. 1986. 24/yr. $196. Trade Service Corporation, 10996 Torreyana Road, San Diego, CA 92121.

This is a loose-leaf index to all kinds of music recorded on compact discs. It includes thousands of listings in two sections, one for classical and the other for popular music. Each section features a section of "New Releases, Albums and Artists," while the "Singles" in the pop section and the "Composers" in the classical add two important access points. Though used most in commercial record outlets, this is found increasingly in libraries that have large CD collections. *Laserlog* is an offshoot of *Phonolog*.

Compact Discs

A
94. **Library Software Review**. 1981. 6/yr. $115 ($125. Canada). Meckler Corp., Ferry Lane West, Westport, CT 06880.

This periodical was formerly named *Software Review*. Each issue usually contains two or three general articles on software and its use in libraries and a section, "In the Literature," that consists of abstracts of articles on these subjects. The greater part of the magazine, however, is devoted to in-depth reviews of software products. There are about eight to ten per issue, each averaging three to six pages in length. In addition to many illustrations of "windows," the reviews include material on functions, features, content, ease of learning and use, documentation and support, and recommendations. There is also a book review section. This authoritative journal will be of value in large library systems. *Computer Software*

A

95. **Microform Review**. 1972. 4/yr. $125. R. R. Bowker, 121 Chanlon Road, New Providence, NJ 07974.

This quarterly scholarly publication devoted to micropublications for libraries and educational institutions is published by K. G. Saur in Munich but is available in this country through Bowker. Each issue contains several articles on microforms, their management and preservation, and microfilming. The review section contains about 10 in-depth reviews, first in narrative form and then in tabular format. Salient points covered include format, content, quality, hard copy availability, payment policy, replacement cost, and arrangement. Each review is about two pages in length, and there are also some book reviews on the subject.

Microforms

A

96. **Online: The Magazine of Online Information Systems**. 1977. 6/yr. $89. Online, Inc., 11 Tannery Lane, Weston, CT 06883.

This is a practical magazine with articles on how to improve online searches, new technologies, microcomputer applications, and news both of developments in the worlds of online and CD-ROM computerized information. In addition to these general articles, each issue has a section called, "Reviews/Product Tests" which reviews software, online sources, and books pertinent to the online industry and profession. In this section there is always a "Software Pick of the Month." This will be of value in academic and large public libraries. An online database from the publisher of *Online* that lists and reviews current software with an emphasis on library programs is *Buyer's Guide to Micro Software (SOFT)*. It is available both through DIALOG and BRS. *Computer Software; Online Databases*

A

97. **Phonolog**. 1948. 52/yr. $432. Trade Service Corporation, 10996 Torreyana Road, San Diego, CA 92121.

This is a complete guide to all forms of recorded music on records, compact discs, and audio cassette tapes. It is updated weekly in two main sections, pop and classical, with sections that list new releases and feature sections on titles, artists, and albums. The work involves about 6,000 pages in loose leaf format that give information on over 1,000,000 song titles categorized by such musical formats as pop, classical, Christmas, movie soundtracks, show tunes, sacred, band, and children's music. This is used primarily by record retailers but many larger public libraries find this is a valuable reference source to answer questions about recorded music of all types. *Phonorecordings; Audiocassettes; Compact Discs*

A

98. **Sightlines**. 1967. 4/yr. $20 ($30 Canada). American Film and Video Association (formerly EFLA), 8050 Milwaukee Ave., P.O. Box 48659, Niles, IL 60648.

This quarterly publication reviews association activities and concerns and reports on news about film and video libraries. There are about four or five general articles per issue and about six or seven lengthy reviews usually of videos. Of particular interest is an annotated section in each issue called "New Releases." This gives listings of new products on the market. Each entry includes such information as length, date, price, availability, and distributor. There is also a directory of names and addresses of the distributors mentioned in this section. For libraries with an extensive video and film collection. *Films; Videocassettes*

A

99. **Video Movies**. 1992. 12/yr. $42. Randy Pitman, P.O. Box 2725, Bremerton, WA 98310.

This new newsletter concentrates on reviewing forthcoming films and made-for-television movies on video that might go unnoticed at release date. Of course, the standard works are also included. For each review, production information, cast, a contents note, availability dates, distributors, running time, price, audience suitability, and a rating of four stars to one are given. This will be particularly valuable in libraries with medium- to large-sized video collections. *Videocassettes*

A

100. **Videolog**. 1981. 52/yr. $192. Trade Service Corporation, 10996 Torreyana Road, San Diego, CA 92121.

This loose leaf publication is updated weekly and lists all currently available retail videos. There are now over 30,000 entries categorized by title, star, director, and genre, such as adventure, musical, science fiction/fantasy, horror/suspense, and new releases. There are supplementary sections that deal with videos on recreation, education, closed-captioned material, and foreign videos. Though most used by video retailers, some large libraries have found this to be a useful guide for identifying videos. There is also a version available on diskettes for IBM and compatible PCs. *Videocassettes*

Children and
Young Adult
Sources

4 General Bibliographies

Basic and General Guides

C*

101. **Adventuring with Books: A Booklist for Pre-K-Grade 6.** Ed. by Julie M. Jensen and the Committee on the Elementary School Booklist of the National Council of Teachers of English. 10th ed. NCTE, 1993. 603p. $19.95 pap. 0-8141-0079-1.

This newest edition of an excellent bibliography describes and categorizes 1,800 of "the best" children's books published between 1988 and 1992; an increase of about 50 since the earlier 1989 edition. Fiction, nonfiction, and picture book titles are chosen on the basis of literary and artistic quality, as well as overall accuracy. This newer edition includes more titles for the very young. Each entry includes basic bibliographic information, recommended age and grade levels and a brief annotation. Books are arranged into 20 broad categories. Added bonuses include a chapter on book awards and booklists; a directory of publishers; and author, illustrator, title, and subject indexes. This outstanding standard bibliography belongs in every elementary school and public library. *Children's Literature; Picture Books*

C

102. **Becoming a Lifetime Reader.** American Library Association, 1991. $.50 (100 for $24).

This brief pamphlet contains an exciting list of books "guaranteed" to turn children on to books and become lifetime readers. Send a SASE along with your order to: ALA Graphics, 50 East Huron Street, Chicago, IL 60611. *Children's Literature*

C*

103. **Best Books for Children: Preschool through Grade 6**, by John T. Gillespie and Corinne J. Naden. 4th ed. Bowker, 1990. 1,002p. $44.95. 0-8352-2668-9.

This greatly expanded and updated 4th edition of highly selected books for children includes 11,299 fully annotated individual titles (more than 1,000 additional titles are mentioned in the annotations but not individually annotated). Entries are arranged under very broad subject or curriculum areas, then sublisted under more specific topics. Each entry includes author, title, grade level, illustrator, publisher, date, price, ISBN, and a brief annotation. Almost one-third of the book consists of extremely useful indexes: author, illustrator, title, and subject/grade level. This valuable basic tool is highly recommended for collection development and reading guidance for all libraries serving children or those who work with children from preschool through middle school. *Children's Literature*

C*

104. **The Best in Children's Books: The University of Chicago Guide to Children's Literature, 1985-1990**, by Zena Sutherland. Univ. of Chicago, 1991. 616p. $37.50. 0-226-78064-3.

Sutherland, former editor of the highly regarded *Bulletin of the Center for Children's Books*, has continued the high standards of reviewing in this most recent edition of *The Best in Children's Books ... 1985-1990*. Three earlier editions cover the time periods 1966-1972, 1973-1978, and 1979-1984 and are still useful and in print. This 4th edition includes almost 1200 titles all chosen on the basis of literary merit, and all originally reviewed in the *Bulletin....* Titles are arranged alphabetically by author. Each entry includes plot, type of illustration, reading level, and complete ordering information. Titles of special distinction are so identified. The six indexes are an added strength of this guide: title, developmental values, curricular use, reading level, subject, and type of literature. This well-known bibliography is highly recommended as a reading guidance, reference, and collection development aid for teachers, librarians, parents and others working with children. *Children's Literature*

C*; Y*

105. **The Best of Bookfinder: Selected Titles from Volumes 1-3,** by Sharon Spredemann Dreyer. American Guidance Service, 1992. $80. 0-88-671-440-0; $43.50 pap. 0-88-671-439-7.

Booklist states that *The Best of Bookfinder* "lays the foundation for bibliotherapy work with children. Highly Recommended." Over 675 fully-annotated titles from volumes 1-3 of *Bookfinder* (the time-tested standard aid for bibliotherapy, now in its 4th volume) are included in this relatively inexpensive and invaluable reference tool. The titles are arranged under the general areas of psychological, developmental, and behavioral topics. Complete author, title, and subject indexes are provided. This is particularly recommended as a selection tool for the smaller library that might not be able to afford most of the titles cited in the first three volumes of *Bookfinder.*

Bibliotherapy; Children's Literature; Young Adult Literature

C*

106. **The Best of Children's Choices,** Comp. by Lenore Nilson. Ottawa: Citizen's Committee on Children, 1988. 114p. $8.95. 0-9690205-5-4.

This brief work is a compilation of reviews by Canadian children of which Canadian children's books they liked the most. The titles which contain brief annotations, are arranged in three sections according to reading level. Also indicated are symbols denoting popularity and whether the book is available in a French edition. This list of "favorites" should be useful as a selection guide for both Canadian and United States libraries serving children. *Children's Literature, Canadian*

C*; Y*

107. **The Bookfinder 4: When Kids Need Books: Annotations of Books Published 1983 through 1986,** by Sharon Spredemann Dreyer. American Guidance Service, 1989. 642p. $75. 0-913476-50-1; $40. pap. 0-913476-51-X.

Published since 1977, and now in its 4th edition, *The Bookfinder* is becoming a basic guide for reading guidance and bibliotherapy. Its main intent is to match books to the special needs and problems of young people ages 2-15. Titles are arranged alphabetically by author; full bibliographic data, including in-print status, are given. This is followed by subject headings and a lengthy descriptive annotation and then a critical comment. The subject index includes about 450 psychological, behavioral, social, and developmental topics of real concern to young people and notes the age level of each book. A special bonus of this edition is a revised statement on bibliotherapy and an updated list of selection aids and professional books. Author and title indexes complete this useful guide. *Bookfinder 4* indexes and analyzes 731 titles published through 1986. *Bookfinder 2* and *Bookfinder 3* are still available and useful. This special aid is highly recommended for all libraries serving young people.

Bibliotherapy; Children's Literature; Young Adult Literature

C

108. **Bookmate.** Sunburst Communications, 1989. Apple II series (64K and printer). Disk, guide, backup. $65. #1631 Hard disk version.

This software program is aimed to motivate youngsters to read. Over 300 titles with reading levels ranging from grades 3-7 (ages 9-13) are included. Teachers and librarians can star items which are available in the library; youngsters can match their interest. This innovative program is recommended for all elementary schools and public libraries that have computers for kids to use. *Children's Literature*

C

109. **Books for Catholic Elementary Schools,** Comp. by Eileen F. Noonan. Rev. ed. Catholic Library Association, 1987. 16p. $5. pap. 0-87507-041-8.

This brief bibliography contains 145 basic books for grades Kindergarten through eighth in the areas of religion, fine arts, language arts, social studies, science and mathematics. All of the annotated titles were published between 1984 and 1987. Recommended for all elementary school libraries, but especially for those in Catholic schools. *Children's Literature; Catholics*

C

110. **BookWhiz Jr,** Educational Testing Service, 1990. Apple II series (64K, printer) 2 disks, guide, backup, $199.

This computer program for individual reading guidance is intended for youngsters in the intermediate grades (4-6). The 1000+ titles are arranged in broad categories, e.g., stories from the past, growing up, etc. Students can request a certain type of books, and the program selects up to 10 titles with annotations, and then the youngsters has a customized printed reading list of their own. The program can be localized by adding call numbers, etc. to titles that the library owns. The program expands on a similar program, *Bookmate*, which also is Apple II compatible, and, although more expensive, the additional titles and options make *BookWhiz Jr* a desirable purchase for all elementary school and public libraries that have Apple II computers available for use by youngsters. Also available from Educational Testing Service for the same price are: *BookWhiz* and *BookWhiz for Teens* which are similar in purpose and designated for grades 6 to 9 and 9 to 12 respectively. All programs are recommended for all libraries, school and public, that maintain records or develop reading guidance programs. *Children's Literature; Young Adult Literature*

C

111. **Canadian Books for Children: Guide to Authors and Illustrations**, by Jon C. Stott and R. E. Jones. Harcourt, 1988. 246p. $19.95. pap. 0-7747-3081-1.

With entries varying in length from a single paragraph to several pages, this guide profiles about 105 Canadian authors and illustrators of books for children. Each contains a complete bibliography of the author's works, and there is appended a selective list of recommended Canadian books for kindergarten through grade 8 plus a list of award winners. This is excellent for Canadian schools and libraries.

Children's Literature, Canadian; Canada

C; Y

112. **Canadian Books for Young People. Livres Canadiens pour la Jeunesse**, by Andre Gagnon and Ann Gagnon. 4th ed. University of Toronto Press, 1988. 186p. $18.95 pap. 0-8020-6662-3.

This update of the 1980 edition includes more than 2,500 titles in two sections—English and French. Each section is arranged by subjects such as picture books, fiction and science and covers material from preschool through senior high school. Age levels are assigned and brief annotation are given. There are author, title and illustrator indexes, plus information on awards and prizes. This will be extremely valuable in Canadian schools and libraries.

Children's Literature, Canadian; Young Adult Literature, Canadian; Canada

C

113. **Children's Booklist**, by the Children's Committee of the Theosophical Society. Theosophical University Press, [1991], 32p pap. $2.

This pamphlet lists 350 books for young people "chosen for literary and artistic merit as well as their contribution to the growth of the child as a human being." Copies can be obtained for $2 plus $1 for postage from Theosophical University Press, P.O. Bin C-RCB, Pasadena, CA 91109. *Children's Literature*

C*

114. **Children's Catalog**. 16th ed. Wilson, 1991. 1,370p. $90 0-8242-0805-6.

Now in its sixteenth edition, this is a mainstay for supplying authoritative material for collection development in elementary schools and children's rooms in public libraries. Compiled by specialists in children's library work from around the United States, the current volume lists and annotates over 6,000 titles. The first section lists nonfiction works arranged by Dewey Decimal numbers. Section two is for fiction books arranged by author's last name, and there are separate sections for story collections and easy books. Each entry contains full bibliographic and cataloging information plus (usually two) excerpts from reviews. The first is descriptive and the second critical. The second half of the books is given over to a huge author, title, subject, and analytical index. There are over 7,000 analytical references to short stories or specific parts of nonfiction books. Purchase of the main volume also entitles the owner to four annual paperback supplements listing over 500 titles each and covering the years 1992, 1993, 1994, and 1995. This is useful for evaluating collections as well as serving as a selection and purchasing tool. Highly recommended. *Children's Literature*

C

115. **Children's Literature for All God's Children**, by Virginia Coffin Thomas and Betty Davis Miller. John Knox, 1986. 107p. $11.99. 0-8042-1690-8.

This book proclaims the need for Christian children to read and enjoy reading. The first part addressed to Christian educators gives an overview of the importance of reading, and the second part is a selective list of books with positive values. The annotations stress content, themes, and values. This guide might be of value in public libraries serving church related schools and in the schools themselves.

Children's Literature; Values

C

116.   Children's Religious Books: An Annotated Bibliography, by Patricia Pearl. Garland, 1988. 316p. $45. 0-8240-8531-0.

This bibliography gives "an overview of children's religious literature" for preschool through sixth grade with a smattering of material for the junior high. The 1,123 fiction and nonfiction entries are annotated and entered in chapters under ten major subject headings. Eight are Christian and deal with topics like the Bible, religious denominations, fiction, and biography. Chapter nine is on Judaism (with a section on anti-Semitism). The last is on other religions like Baha'i, Hinduism, Islam, native American and cults. This will be of most value in large public or church libraries. A much shorter bibliography (just 350 entries) by the same author is *Religious Books for Children: An Annotated Bibliography.* This has sections of both the Old and New Testaments, Christianity, Judaism, Other Religions, and Holidays. Parochial schools and some public libraries will find this helpful.   *Religion; Children's Literature; Religious Literature*

C

117.   Choosing Books for Children: A Commonsense Guide, by Betsy Hearne. rev. ed. Delacorte, 1990. 228p. $21.95 0-385-30084-0; Dell, $9.95 pap. 0-385-30108-1.

In a direct, entertaining writing style, the author presents ideas on selecting and using books for children from preschool through the elementary grades, with a special chapter on young adult literature. The 13 chapters are arranged roughly by reader's age levels, and in addition to discussing reading interests at these various levels and ways of introducing books, a number of titles are cited and described. Each chapter has a list of recommended titles. Although most of the titles are recent, there is a chapter on classics. There are also sources for further reading listed. This lively book can by useful in collection development because of its many quality recommendations.   *Children's Literature*

C

118.   Choosing Books for Young People, Volume 2: A Guide to Criticism and Bibliography, 1976-1984, by John R. T. Ettlinger and Diana L. Spirt. Oryx, 1987. 152p. $43.50. 0-89774-247-8.

This, a continuation of this guide's first volume which covered 1945-1975 (ALA, o.p.), contains a listing of 415 alphabetically arranged works of 16 pages or more that deal with children's literature either critically or bibliographically. As well as complete imprint information, a descriptive and critical annotation is given to indicate the usefulness of each. Though now out of date, this still has historical importance in large children's literature collections.   *Children's Literature*

C

119.   Choosing Children's Books, by David Booth and others. Pembroke (Markham, Ont.), 1987. 175p $9.95 pap. 0-921217-12-9.

Three specialists in children's literature have pooled their talents and prepared a selective listing of the best in children's literature for audiences up to age 14. There is a division in the work by age groupings (birth-5; 5-8; 8-11; 11-14) followed by subdivisions according to genre or theme. There are short annotations for each listing as well as author and title indexes.   *Children's Literature*

C*; Y

120.   The Collection Program in Schools: Concepts, Practices and Information Sources, by Phyllis J. Van Orden. Libraries Unlimited, 1988. 347p. $27.50 0-87287-572-5.

This volume both combines and updates the author's earlier *The Collection Program in Elementary and Middle Schools* (1982) and *The Collection Development Program in High Schools* (1985) (both now out of print). This work is divided into three parts.

The first discusses theoretical aspects of collection building in school libraries, the second is on both general and specific criteria for evaluating various materials, and the third supplies details on administering the program. Of particular value is an appended 28 page annotated list of bibliographic and selection tools. There are also lists of associations and organizations, plus reprints of key documents. This is a highly respected textbook on collection development that is particularly useful for the beginner.

Libraries—Collection Development; School Libraries

C*; Y

121.   The Elementary School Library Collection: A Guide to Books and Other Media, by Lois Winkel. 18th ed. Brodart, 1992. 1149p. $99.95. 0-87272-094-2.

This highly respected, reliable selection aid for school library collection development now contains more than 10,000 print and nonprint titles and covers preschool through grade six. For each of these recommended titles, bibliographic information is given, plus cataloging and ordering information, a descriptive annotation, interest and reading levels, and acquisition priority (phase 1, 2 or 3). Titles available in large print and titles available from the National Library for the Blind and Physically Handicapped are also indicated. Selections are made with the help of a committee of specialists. The basic arrangement is first by Dewey call numbers for nonfiction titles, followed by fiction and easy books. Professional materials are included, and there are lists of media sources for preschool children, books for beginning readers, and recommended titles in publisher and author series, plus extensive author, title, and subject indexes. New editions appear every two years. This is an excellent, highly recommended source for basic collection development that is unique in the scope of material included and in its indication of priority purchasing.

Children's Literature; Audiovisual Materials

C

122. **Eyeopeners! How to Choose and Use Children's Books About Real People, Places and Things**, by Beverly Kobrin. Penguin, 1988. 317p. $10.95 pap. 0-14-046830-7.

This guide to about 500 nonfiction titles for grades K through eight also includes 150 tips on how they can be used interestingly to bring children and books together. The bibliography is preceded by a section on the importance of reading and suggestions on how to encourage quality reading. The books are organized by subjects such as dinosaurs, cars, and music, as well as by problem topics like death, sex, alcoholism and divorce. All materials are annotated and were in print in 1988. There is an index by authors and illustrators, titles, and detailed subjects. It is intended both for parents and teachers, as well as librarians and therefore contains material that experienced librarians might already be familiar with. However, the author's enthusiasm helps make this book a delight to read and it still has many uses including collection development. *Children's Literature*

C; Y

123. **Girls Series Books: A Checklist of Titles Published 1840-1991**. Children's Literature Research Collections, University of Minnesota Libraries, 1992. 347p. $22.25 pap.

This work, an expansion of *Girls Series Books 1900-1975*, was produced by the personnel of the Children's Literature Research Collections of the University of Minnesota. Only fictional series written by American writers for girls are included. They are arranged alphabetically by series with contents notes for each series. In addition to author, publisher and chronological indexes, there is a bibliography and a interesting introduction on the genre. This with be of interest in historical collections of children's literature.

Children's Literature; Young Adult Literature

C; Y

124. **Government Publications for School Libraries: A Bibliographic Guide and Recommended Core Collection**, by Donald J. Voorhees. New York Library Association, 1988. 35p. $7. pap.

This booklet identifies a core collection of U.S. government documents suitable for elementary and secondary school libraries. The entries are divided into 14 areas such as reference, careers, education, health and wildlife, with about 10 documents listed and annotated in each area. Ordering information is given, along with a set of order forms and a list of government bookstores. Some of the publications are free, others inexpensive. This pamphlet is available for $7 from the New York Library Association, 15 Park Row, Suite 434, New York, NY 10038. *United States—Government Publications*

C*; Y

125. **A Guide to Non-Sexist Children's Books, Volume II: 1976-1985**, by Denise Wilms and Ilene Cooper. Academy Chicago, 1987. 240p. $20.; 0-89733-161-3; $9. pap. 0-89733-162-1.

This is a sequel to the first volume that covered pre-1976 imprints (1976, $14.95; $5.95 pap. 0-915864-01-0; 0-915864-02-9 pap.). The present volume is divided into three main sections: pre-school to grade 3, grades 4-6, and grades 7-12. Each of these main sections are further subdivided into fiction and nonfiction titles. The nonfiction areas are heavy on female biographies. A total of about 700 titles are included, and they stress role-free characters both male and female. There are four indexes (author, title, and fiction and nonfiction subjects), plus a useful directory of small presses. A valuable tool for selection of materials and curricular use. *Sexism; Children's Literature; Young Adult Literature*

Y*; A*

126. **A Guide to Selected Federal Agency Programs and Publications for Librarians and Teachers**, by Carol Smallwood. Libraries Unlimited, 1986. 321p. $25. 0-87287-528-8.

This is a guide to the services and materials available from 227 federal organizations and agencies. There is an alphabetical arrangement by agency. For each, information is given on the objectives of the unit, national, state and regional offices, curriculum applications, special services and bibliographies of publications and audiovisual materials available. Prices are given for these, and there are brief annotations. In a series of useful appendixes, information is given on acronyms, federal information centers, land grant university film libraries, and the "Subject Bibliographies" available from the Superintendent of Documents. There is a subject index. This volume is a gold mine of information for high school teachers and librarians and will also be useful in public and college libraries. *United States—Government Publications*

C; Y
127. **Literature of Delight: A Critical Guide to Humorous Books for Children**, by Kimberly Olson Fakih. Bowker, 1993. 352p. $35. 0-8352-3027-9.

Fakih identifies about 1,000 humorous books which are useful as a bridge to literacy and learning in working with youngsters ages 3 to 14. Two thirds of the fiction and nonfiction titles were published within the past 10 years and most are readily available. The works are arranged within chapters which include: Nonsense and Absurdity; Satire; Parody; Spoofs and Send-Ups; Poetry and Rhyme; Just Plain Silly; and more. The useful volume is indexed by title, author, subject, character, and grade level. It is recommended for reference, reading guidance, programming, and collection building for most school and public libraries. *Children's Literature; Young Adult Literature; Humorous Stories*

C*
128. **More Exciting, Funny, Scary, Short, Different, and Sad Books Kids Like About Animals, Science, Sports, Families, Songs and Other Things**, ed. by Frances Laverne Carroll and Mary Meacham. ALA, 1992. 192p. $15. pap. 0-8389-0585-4.

It is the intended purpose of this volume to update and complement an earlier title, *Exciting, Funny, Scary...*, ALA, 1985 (still useful, but no longer in print). There is very little duplication with the older title, and as before, the list of titles "favored" by children was submitted to the editors by practicing librarians. This titles, which are intended primarily for youngsters in grades 2-5 (with a number stretching into junior high), are arranged under 75 popular topics, each containing about 4-12 titles. Books in each category are arranged in alphabetical order by title, and each contains a very brief annotation. An author-title and a subject index are provided. This inexpensive volume, which is useful for booktalks, reading guidance work and, of course, collection development is recommended for all libraries that serve children or those that work with children. *Children's Literature*

C
129. **Notable Canadian Children's Books: 1975-1979 Cumulative Edition.** National Library of Canada, 1985. 103p. $10.75. 0-660-53040-6.

Over the years, Canadian children's literature has emerged as a distinct body of literature with its own characteristics, no longer dependent on the influences of the United States. This bibliography discusses this movement and also provides us with 46 English-language and 55 French-language children's titles of outstanding quality, published from 1975 through 1979. All books are annotated in both English and French. Author, illustrator, subject, and geographical area indexes are provided. This brief but important bibliography of notable books is not only recommended for all Canadian libraries that serve children, but also for United States libraries interested in fostering a better understanding of other cultures with the children they serve. *Children's Literature, Canadian; Canadian Literature*

C
130. **100 Favorite Paperbacks 1989**. Children's Book Council and International Reading Association, [1990].

This list of favorite paperbacks for children 12 years of age and under was compiled by selecting the best from the several thousand books published in 1987 and 1988. Poetry, nonfiction, and fiction titles are all adequately represented. Single copies are available free by sending a SASE; multiple copies cost $8. per 100. Order from: International Reading Association, Attn: 100 Favorite Paperbacks 1989, 800 Barksdale Rd., P.O. Box 8139, Newark, DE 19714 *Children's Literature; Paperback Books*

C*; Y*
131. **100 World-Class Thin Books, or What to Read When Your Book Report Is Due Tomorrow**, by Joni Richards Bodart. Libraries Unlimited, 1993. 204p. $27.50. 0-87287-986-0.

Every school and many public librarians have been confronted with the problem of recommending a "good thin book" for a student who is desperate because of an impending deadline. Bodart, of booktalk fame, has provided librarians with a solution. All of the titles in this bibliography are 200 pages or less, and all are highly recommended and suitable for middle school and high school students. All entries contain bibliographic data as well as information on grade level, theme, genre, related subject area and whether or not a paperback is available (much of this data is also provided in the well-developed indexes). Subject areas chosen are timely and meant to catch the attention of students, particularly students who may be reluctant readers. This long-awaited bibliography is a must purchase as a quick reference tool and selection aid for all libraries working with young people.

Children's Literature; Young Adult Literature; Reading Guidance

C*

132. **Popular Reading for Children III: A Collection of Booklist Columns**, ed. by Sally Estes. ALA, 1992. 64p. $4.95. 0-8389-7599-2.

This short volume is a goldmine of retrospective bibliographies of popular books for children that have appeared in *Booklist* between 1986 and 1991. They are the "books kids want on the subjects kids care about," including dragons and dinosaurs, eerie reading, historical fiction, humor, and things that go bump in the night—it's all here. All titles listed have been checked in the 1991-1992 *Children's Books in Print*. This inexpensive and handy list is recommended for all libraries that work with children.

Children's Literature

C; Y

133. **Read! A Guide to Quality Children's and Young Adult Books**. Quebec Library Association, [1993].

More than 150 annotated titles published between 1980 and 1992 are included in this list that may be of interest to United States as well as Canadian libraries. The cost is only $3.00 (quantity rates are also available) and is available from: Quebec Library Association, READ! Booklet, C.P. 1095, Pointe Claire, Quebec, H9S 4H9 Canada. *Children's Literature; Young Adult Literature; Canada*

C; Y

134. **Reading for Young People**. American Library Association, 1979-1985. 11v. various editors and prices.

This is an 11-volume series of "annotated bibliographies of fiction and nonfiction titles, compiled for ... the primary grades through tenth grade and designed to focus on the history and character of each region of the United States." Each volume is organized into five genres (fiction, folktales, poetry/drama/music, biography, and informational books). Full bibliographic data and annotations are provided. The intent of this series was excellent, but unfortunately it has never been updated and now many titles are out-of-print. In fact there are only 10 volumes in the series (California was never completed). Despite the fact that all but two of the titles were published prior to 1985 (the cut-off date of this guide), the whole series, which is still available, is listed here because they are still useful because no other similar works exists. It is hoped that someday they may be revised and updated. All are available in paper editions in prices ranging from $5.50 to $8.75. *Reading for Young People* is the first part of every title. The prefix for each ISBN is 0-8389. Titles include:

The Great Plains. M. Laughlin, 1979. 0265-0.
Kentucky, Tennessee, West Virginia. B. Mertens, 1985. 0426-2.
The Middle Atlantic. A. Pennypacker, 1980. 0295-2.
The Midwest. D. Hinman, R. Zimmerman, 1979. 0271-5.
The Mississippi Delta. C. M. Dorsett, 1983. 0395-9.
New England. E. B. McCauley, 1985. 0432-7.
The Northwest. M. Meacham, 1980. 0318-5.
The Rocky Mountains. M. Laughlin, 1980. 0-0296-0.
The Southwest. E. A. Harmon & A. L. Milligan, 1982. 0362-2.
The Upper Midwest. M. F. Archer, 1981. 0339-8.

United States—Bibliography; Children's Literature; Young Adult Literature

C

135. **Reading Is Fundamental**.

RIF is a nationwide organization dedicated to the promotion of reading, especially for the very young in areas of our country that are considered disadvantaged. They have published a number of worthwhile pamphlets, reading lists, and guides. Four recent publications include:

Encouraging Young Writers
Building a Family Library
Family Storytelling
Summertime Reading

These lists are available for 50 cents each or $15 for 100. For these lists and other information write to: RIF, 600 Maryland Ave. SW, Ste. 500, Washington, DC 20024   *Children's Literature; Storytelling*

C; Y

136. **Sooner Gushers and Dusters: Book Reviews K-12**, Oklahoma State Department of Education, 1991. 179p.

This compilation of reviews by school library media specialists in Oklahoma is intended to help librarians in selecting books published in 1990. The fiction reviews are arranged alphabetically by author, and the nonfiction by the 10 major Dewey Decimal classes. This 179 page stapled booklet is free to Oklahoma librarians; others should inquire for prices from Bettie Estes-Rickner, Director, Library Media Section, Oklahoma State Department of Education, Oklahoma City, OK 73105-4599.

Children's Literature; Young Adult Literature

137. (This entry number not used.)

C

138. **What Kids Who Don't Like to Read—Like to Read**. Parents' Choice, 1989. free.

This exciting list of books in English and Spanish, has been selected by parents, librarians, and members of the Parents' Choice advisory board. Kids who don't like to read also helped select the titles. Parents' Choice is the nonprofit consumer guide of children's media. This list is available for a SASE sent to: Parents' Choice, Dept. R. R., Box 185, Newton, MA 02168. *Children's Literature*

C

139. **Who Reads What When: Literature Selections for Children Ages Three Through Thirteen**, by Jane Williams. Bluestocking Press, 1988. 60p. $3.95. 0-942617-01-0.

Williams compiled this bibliography of children's books by using literature recommendations of Russell Kirk of America's Future Textbook Evaluation Reports, private school recommended reading lists, and her own personal favorites. There are three detailed indexes which comprise almost half of the 60-page booklet: Age, Title, and Author. There are many more comprehensive lists of recommended children's books (most with annotations); however, *Who Reads What When...* is very inexpensive and it does contain an independent school focus with many titles not usually listed in other lists. Therefore, this slim bibliography is recommended as a supplement if additional reading lists are required for elementary school and public libraries. *Children's Literature*

Annuals and Continuations

C; Y

140. **Best Books 1991**. Cahners Reprint Services, 1992. 10p. $1.

This reprint of the top juvenile titles of the year selected by *School Library Journal* Book Review Editors "Best Books 1991" originally appeared in the December, 1991 issue of *SLJ*. Included are entries with full annotations for 54 children's books and 19 adult books recommended for young adults. This list, which appears annually, is helpful for reading guidance and for securing the "best of the year." The prices are: $1 each for 1 to 100 copies; $.85 for 101 to 500 copies. Prepaid orders only, with a minimum order of $25. For ordering or additional information write to: Cathy Dionne, Cahners Reprint Services, 1350 E. Touhy Ave., Des Plaines, IL 60017   *Children's Literature; Young Adult Literature*

C*

141. **Bibliography of Books for Children**, 1988-89 ed. Ed. by Helen Shelton. The Association for Childhood Education International (ACEI), 1989. 112p. $11. 0-87173-118-5.

This standard bibliographic reference tool has been published since 1937. In the current edition, entries are arranged into various sections by type, e.g., picture books, fiction, nonfiction, reference sources, and periodicals. Fiction titles are listed alphabetically by author; nonfiction are listed by Dewey Classification. Each entry provides full bibliographic information as well as a reading level and a brief annotation. This inexpensive work is highly recommended for all libraries that serve children and those working with children. There are annual updates. *Children's Literature*

C*

142. **Books for Children, No. 8,** by Margaret N. Coughlan. Children's Literature Center of the Library of Congress. U.S. Government Printing Office, current date. $1. Stock no. 030-001-00138-5.

With all the authority of the venerable Library of Congress, Coughlan, with a committee of children's book specialists from school and public libraries, has compiled this annual list of the "finest" in children's books. Actually each year about 100 are chosen out of 3 to 4 thousand considered. The books are arranged by approximate age group, then alphabetical order by title. A supplementary list of "Also Worthy of Note," books that are difficult to assign an age label to, is an added bonus. Any school or public library should consider purchasing this list in quantity and distributing it to parents, teachers, etc. Certainly, the titles are highly selective and the price is right. The lists for the past few years are available for $1. each from: Superintendent of Documents, U.S. Government Printing Office, Department 39-LC, Washington, DC 20402. *Children's Literature*

C

143. **Books to Share: Notable Children's Books of (year).** Office of Children's Services. Westchester (NY) Library System, annual.

This annual list of children's books is selected by a group of 11 children's librarians (approximately 90 titles are chosen per year). Titles are arranged under seven popular categories and have brief notes. The Westchester Library System also has available similar selected lists for nominal costs, e.g., *Reading for the Fun of It: A Guide to Books for Children with Learning Disabilities* ($3.50); and *Sharing the World's Magic: A Guide to Folk Literature for Children with Learning Disabilities* ($3.00). Above titles and a list of others currently in-print are available from: Judith Rovenger, Westchester Library System, 8 Westchester Plaza, Elmsford, NY 10523. *Children's Literature*

C; Y

144. **The Brookline Public Schools Reading List...** The Brookline (Mass.) Public Schools, 1991. $5.

The Brookline Public Schools have been producing and making available for many years a recommended reading list for young people. The current edition (1991-92) has been revised with particular attention to titles that reflect our multicultural diversity. The list includes over 1200 titles arranged by level and suitable for grades K-8. Titles include both fiction and nonfiction on a large variety of popular subjects and interests. Each title has been read by a team of teachers, and public and school librarians. The list is recommended as an excellent guide for reading guidance and collection development. The list is available for $5 (check or money order); $7 (purchase order or foreign). The price includes unlimited duplication rights within the school district. Send order to: The Public Schools of Brookline, Brookline, MA 02146.

Children's Literature; Young Adult Literature

C

145. **Children's Books (year): 100 Books for Reading and Sharing,** by the New York Public Library's Children Book Committee. New York Public Library, annual. 16p. pap.

This annual annotated listing of 100 outstanding new books is arranged by three levels of readers plus sections of picture books, poetry, and folk and fairy tales. The 1992 edition is available for $3 plus $1 postage from the Office of Branch Libraries, NYPL, 455 Fifth Ave., New York, NY 10016. Also available is a retrospective look at important children's books annotated and arranged by decade, *Children's Books, 1911-1986: Favorite Children's Books from the Branch Collections of the New York Public Library.* This is available from the same address for $5. *Children's Literature*

C*

146. **Children's Books of the Year**, by the Child Study Children's Book Committee. Bank Street College, annual. $4.

The Child Study Children's Book Committee is composed of educators, librarians, authors, illustrators, and other specialists. Each year since 1916, it has prepared a list of the year's recommended children's books suitable for readers from preschool through age 14. The works (usually about 600 per issue) are high in quality and grouped by age suitability or by special subjects (e.g., poetry). There are tips for parents and author, illustrator, and title indexes. This booklist can be obtained for $4 and $1 for postage. Back issues are available as are other specialized booklists such as *Books to Read Aloud with Children Through Age 8* and *Paperback Books for Children Through Age 14* (1988). Order or make requests for further information to Child Study Children's Book Committee, Bank Street College of Education, 610 West 112 St., New York, NY 10025. *Children's Literature*

C

147. **Children's Choices for [year]**, by the International Reading Association and the Children's Book Council Joint Committee. International Reading Association, annual.

The first *Children's Choices* appeared in the November, 1975 issue of *The Reading Teacher*. The list continues to appear annually in this periodical, but reprints are available from the International Reading Association. It is a preferential selection of newly published books selected by about 10,000 young people scattered around the United States in five teams. The hundred plus titles are arranged by broad age groups and are annotated with descriptive comments and quotes from young reviewers. There are no indexes. There are now two companion reprints. *Young Adults' Choices* (selected by the same team method) appears first in the September issue of *Journal of Reading* and contains approximately 30 well-annotated titles. *Teachers' Choices* is found in the November issue of *The Reading Teacher* and lists with annotations about 25 titles that teachers find to be very useful in curriculum use. These attractive pamphlets are available free from the International Reading Association, 800 Barksdale Road, Newark, DE 19714-8139 for a self-addressed stamped 9" by 12" envelope. Postage for the Children's Choices list is for four ounces first class and two ounces for the other two. Bulk copies are available. *Children's Literature*

C; Y

148. **Cooperative Children's Book Center Choices**, by Kathleen T. Horning and others. Cooperative Children's Book Center, annual. $5.00.

This "annual bibliography of the best books of the year" lists with annotations about 200 recommended titles. The titles for any given year are chosen by a group of specialists in the Cooperative Children's Book Center. Titles are grouped under such subjects as History, People and Places, and Fiction for Young Readers and for Teenagers. Annotations are given and suggested age levels. Copies can be obtained by sending a 9x12 self addressed envelope and a check for $5.00 payable to Friends of the CCBC, Inc. to Publications, Friends of the CCBC, Inc., Box 5288, Madison, WI 53705. *Children's Literature; Young Adult Literature*

C; Y; A

149. **The Nel and Sally Show**, comp. by Nel Ward and Sally Anne Thompson. Phoenix, AZ: Central High School and Orangedale School, 1991.

This 1991 edition of a popular reading list contains almost 550 juvenile/young adult novels and picture books. The titles were chosen by two practicing school librarians for their quality in writing and art and their appeal to young people. In addition to brief annotations, each entry includes complete bibliographic information and recommended age levels. Though subjective, this type of list of "Best Books" may serve a purpose in collection development and is available for $4.00 from: Seth Lansky, 8526 E. Via de los Libres, Scottsdale, AZ 85258   *Children's Literature; Young Adult Literature*

Awards and Award Winners

C; Y

150. **Award Winning Books for Children and Young Adults, 1990-1991**, by Betty L. Criscoe and Philip J. Lanasca. Scarecrow, 1993. 702p. 79.50 310p. $37.50. 0-8108-2336-5.

This annual guide lists 234 awards from around the world. The awards are listed alphabetically and most are annotated and contain bio/bibliographical information about the author. It can be assumed that the award winning titles are "the cream of the crop," and therefore listing becomes an excellent selection aid for building a collection of top literary quality. It meets its objectives, which were to identify award winning books, provide bibliographic and background information, and indirectly to encourage authors in their writing of outstanding literature for children and young adults. This promises to be a publication that will become a standard work in libraries. This edition complements Criscoe's earlier volume which listed 227 awards for 438 titles for the year 1989 winners and is still available: (*Award-Winning Books for Children and Young Adults: An Annual Guide, 1989*, Scarecrow, 1990. 0-8108-2336-5). These annual editions are highly recommended as a selection aid and reference tool for all collections serving children and young adults. *Children's Literature; Young Adult Literature*

C

151. **Children's Book Awards International: A Directory of Awards and Winners, from Inception to 1990**, by Laura Smith. McFarland, 1992. 649p. $75. 0-89950-686-0.

This guide is arranged by country, from Argentina to Yugoslavia, and lists 424 awards that are or have been given in the field of children's literature. Each award is described with such information as sponsor, date of inception, award provisions and conditions. There follows a listing of winners that supplies only bibliographic information. The four indexes allow for access by authors, awards, illustrators, and titles. A comparable title is *Children's Literature Awards and Winners: A Directory of Prizes, Authors and Illustrators* which lists 211 awards. *Newbery and Caldecott Medalists and Honor Book Winners* supplies better information on these two American awards but this international directory will be useful in libraries needing broad coverage on children's literature or where multicultural material is in demand.

Children's Literature

C*

152. **Children's Books: Awards & Prizes: Includes Prizes and Awards for Young Adult Books**. Children's Book Council, 1992. 404p. $85. 0-93363-01-7; $57.50 (pap.) 0-933633-02-5.

This important work has been updated regularly since its inception in 1969. This new edition (the first in six years) contains entries for 191 awards; each entry contains some back-ground information about the award as well as a chronological listing of the winners through 1992. The work is divided into four major sections: United States awards selected by adults; United States awards selected by young readers; Australian, Canadian, New Zealand, and United Kingdom awards; and selected international and multinational awards. Despite its rather steep price, most libraries that have serve children will want to consider this along with a similar work by Criscoe and Lanasa which covers only the 1990-1991 winners but in more depth: *Award-Winning Books for Children and Young Adults, 1990-1991.*

Children's Literature; Young Adult Literature

C

153. **Children's Literature Awards and Winners: A Directory of Prizes, Authors and Illustrators**, by Dolores Blythe Jones. 2nd ed. Neal-Schuman (Gale), 1988. 671 p. $94. 0-8103-2741-4.

This updating of the original 1983 edition describes awards for excellence in children's literature given in English speaking countries. Part I, the directory of awards, describes 211 awards and lists with full bibliographic material the winners and runners up as of 1987; Part II lists alphabetically authors and illustrators and the awards won; Part III is a bibliography of materials like books and articles about these awards; and Part IV consists of several indexes by author, illustrator, subject, title and award. This deserves a place in large public libraries where it can serve many purposes including evaluating collections for possible new acquisitions. *Children's Literature*

C

154. **Coretta Scott King Award and Honor Books**. American Library Association, 1989. 50 cents.

This pamphlet lists with annotations and illustrations the winners of the Coretta Scott King Award through 1989. This award honors distinguished works by African American authors and illustrators of children's books. A single copy can be obtained for 50 cents and a stamped, self-addressed #10 envelope sent to Office for Library Outreach, American Library Association, 50 E. Huron St., Chicago, IL 60611.

Children's Literature; African American Literature

C

155. **Dictionary of American Children's Fiction, 1859-1959: Books of Recognized Merit**, by Alethea K. Helbig and Agnes Regan Perkins. Greenwood, 1985. 640p. $69.50. 0-313-22590-7.

This alphabetically arranged reference work contains entries under author, title, and major characters for 420 award-winning children's books of more than 5,000 words (picture books are excluded) published between 1859 and 1959. The entries for titles are the longest and give plot summaries plus critical evaluations. Author entries give brief biographical information, and character entries describe the characters and their roles in the novel. There is an excellent extensive index section that includes characters not mentioned in the main body, settings by place and time, subjects, and themes. This is a valuable reference tool that can be helpful in developing historical collections of children's literature. There are continuation volumes by the same two authors that are similar in organization and presentation: *Dictionary of American Children's Fiction, 1960-1984: Recent Books of Recognized Merit* (1986, $75. 0-313-25233-5) and *Dictionary of American Children's Fiction, 1985-1989: Recent Books of Recognized Merit* (1993, $75. 0-313-27719-2). It is the publisher's intent to issue updates at five year intervals. Also of interest is the authors' *Dictionary of British Children's Fiction: Books of Recognized Merit.*   *Children's Literature*

C
156. **Dictionary of British Children's Fiction: Books of Recognized Merit**, by Alethea K. Helbig and Agnes Regan Perkins. 2 volumes. Greenwood, 1989. 1,632p. $135. 0-313-22591-5.

There are 1,626 entries in this work that analyzes 387 British prize-winning books published from 1687 to 1985. Only works of 5,000 words or more were included, thus omitting picture books. There are entries for authors, titles, and major characters with the title entry giving the greatest amount of information including and listing of both British and American editions, a plot summary, and critical comment. Author entries give biographical material and a bibliography of principal works. Character entries are for identification purposes. There is a lengthy index (over 200 pages) that includes subject and thematic references, plus listing of books by time and setting. This reference work will be valuable where historical information on children's literature is needed. It can also serve for collection development. This is a companion piece to the authors' *Dictionary of American Children's Fiction.*   *Children's Literature, British*

C
157. **Dictionary of Children's Fiction from Australia, Canada, India, New Zealand and Selected African Countries: Books of Recognized Merit**, by Alethea K. Helbig and Agnes Regan Perkins. Greenwood, 1992. 459p. $75. 0-313-26126-1.

This companion volume to the authors' *Dictionary of American Children's Fiction* and *Dictionary of British Children's Fiction* profiles 263 important books by 164 authors with entries that cover authors, titles with plot summaries, important characters, settings, and themes. About half of the books have appeared in American editions. Appendixes list the books by country and by prizes won. A fine volume for students of children's literature interested in its international aspects.   *Children's Literature*

C*; Y*
158. **The Newbery and Caldecott Awards: A Guide to the Medal and Honor Books, 1993 Edition**. American Library Association, 1993. 137p. $13. 0-8389-3429-3.

This publication, which is being issued annually, lists all Newbery and Caldecott award winners and runners-up from the inception of the awards (Newbery, 1922; Caldecott, 1938) to 1992. A brief descriptive annotation accompanies each title. As well, author, illustrator, and title indexes are provided. Obviously, these titles are considered the "cream of the crop" in children's literature and are recommended for all libraries. This handbook provides us with a great deal of reference information, in addition to the complete lists. Every library will want two copies, one for circulating and one for ready reference at the desk. Also available in quantity are leaflets listing the award winners for each year. This volume, the leaflets, and additional information are available by phoning 1-800-545-2433 or writing to: ALA Order Dept., 50 E. Huron St., Chicago, IL 60611.
   Children's Literature; Caldecott Medal Books; Newbery Medal Books; Young Adult Literature

C; Y
159. **Newbery and Caldecott Medal and Honor Books in Other Media**, by Paulette Bochnig Sharkey. Ed. by Jim Roginski. Neal-Schuman, 1992. 142p. $29.95. 1-55570-119-1.

This update of a 1982 directory of Newbery and Caldecott Award winners includes every Newbery and Caldecott winner or honor book since their inception. It also includes a listing in any format of all media about the awards in general, for example, media selections, a bibliography of resources such as reference books, journal and review sources, databases, a directory of producers, and distributors. It also serves as a companion volume to *Newbery and Caldecott Medalists and Honor Book Winners: Bibliographies and Resource Material Through 1991* (see next entry). Both of these volumes are recommended for reference and research and for all libraries where children's services are important.
   Children's Literature; Caldecott Medal Books; Newbery Medal Books; Young Adult Literature

C; Y

160. **Newbery and Caldecott Medalists and Honor Book Winners: Bibliographies and Resource Material Through 1991**, by Muriel W. Brown and Rita Schoch Foudray. Ed. by Jim Roginski. 2nd ed. Neal-Schuman, 1992. 511p. $59.95. 1-55570-118-3.

Brown and Foudray have updated and expanded Roginski's 1982 work of the same title which is no longer in print. The section on "Other Media" has been removed and is covered in a companion volume: *Newbery and Caldecott Medal and Honor Books in Other Media*, 1992 (see previous entry). This bibliography includes entries for 327 individual authors and illustrators which are arranged in alphabetical order by the recipients' names. Each entry includes date of awards, list of other works by awardee, a listing of important library collections, and a bibliography of background reading. A combined author-illustrator-title index is also provided. Both this volume and its companion title deserve to be in any library with an interest in children's literature.

Children's Literature; Caldecott Medal Books; Newbery Medal Books; Young Adult Literature

C

161. **Once Upon... A Time for Young People and Their Books: An Annotated Resource Guide**, by Rita Kohn. Scarecrow, 1986. 219p. $19.50. 0-8108-1922-8.

Rita Kohn has compiled a bibliographic resource guide of over 800 citations for materials on children's literature culled from both books and journal articles. Entries are arranged alphabetically by author, and each entry includes full bibliographic data and an annotation. Author, subject, and title indexes are also provided. This handy and rather complete list of important resources in children's literature is recommended for all libraries that serve children, as well as academic libraries that offer courses or programs in children's literature. *Children's Literature*

Guides for Parents

C

162. **Children's Books to Own**, by the Children's and Youth Services Department. Detroit Public Library, annual. 16p. pap. $1.

This booklet aimed chiefly at parents, annotates and gives age and interest levels for a select group of children's books suitable for the home library. Paperback editions are included. It is available for a check for $1 made out to Detroit Library Commission and sent to: Public Relations Department, Detroit Public Library, 5201 Woodward, Detroit, MI 48202. *Children's Literature*

C; Y

163. **Children's Classics: A Book List for Parents**. Horn Book, [1990] $3.

This 20-page pamphlet that recommends classics in the field of literature for both children and young adults is available for $3 and 50 cents postage to Horn Book, 14 Beacon St., Boston, MA 02108.

Children's Literature; Young Adult Literature

C

164. **How to Raise a Reader**, by Elaine K. McEwan. David C. Cook, 1987. 175p. $7.99 pap. 1-55513-211-1.

This is a bibliography aimed at parents to help them choose books for their children. Sections are devoted to various age groups: birth to 3, ages 4-7, ages 8-10, and reluctant readers who are 10-12. The commentary and selections are geared to Christian values and those titles are asterisked that contain Christian themes. *Children's Literature*

C*

165. **The New York Times Parent's Guide to the Best Books for Children**, by Eden Ross Lipson. Times Books/Random, 1991. 464p. $15. pap. 0-8129-1688-3.

According to the author, this revised and updated book "is for people who know and love particular children and want them to grow up loving particular books." Lipson, the Children's Book Review editor of the *New York Times*, has compiled a handy guide to almost 2,000 titles for every age group from preschool to middle school. They are indexed under 55 topics, such as picture books, religion, funny books, dinosaur books for babies, etc. It's popular, it's inexpensive, and it will help parents and their local libraries select good books for children. To that extent, this list, which is scheduled to be revised often, is recommended for all libraries that serve children. *Children's Literature*

C

166. **Reading for the Love of It: Best Books for Young Readers**, by Michele Landsberg. rev. ed. Prentice Hall, 1989. 350p. $10.95. pap. 0-13-755125-8.

This guide is intended for parents to guide them as they try to encourage youngsters to read books. Canadian journalist Landsberg, writing from a parent's point of view, has compiled a recommended list of over 400 books, for young people ages 4 to teenage. The work is divided by topics such as beginning reader, humor, fantasy, etc. The last section includes annotations of titles by age of readers. Bibliographic information is included. A list of books about children's reading is also provided. Recommended as another important guide for most school and public libraries that serve children and promote reading.

Children's Literature; Reading Guidance

C

167. **The RIF Guide to Encouraging Young Readers**, Ed. by Ruth Graves. Doubleday, 1987. 324p. $9.95. 0-385-23632-8.

This reading guide aimed at parents is "a fun-filled sourcebook of over 200 favorite reading activities of kids and parents across the country, *plus* an annotated list of books and resources." The booklists of recommended titles are annotated and contain adequate bibliographic data for ordering. This inexpensive list is recommended for all libraries that serve children. *Reading Guidance; Children's Literature*

Guides to Periodicals

C

168. **International Periodicals: The IYL Guide to Professional Periodicals in Children's Literature**. International Youth Library, [1990]. $5.

The International Youth Library in Munich has published a booklet listing 200 periodicals from 42 countries that deal with children's literature. Copies can be obtained by sending $5 in international postal coupons to the International Youth Library, Schloss Blutenburg, 8000, Munich 60, Germany.

Periodicals; Children's Literature

C

169. **Magazines for Children**, Ed. by Donald R. Stoll. International Reading Association/EDPRESS, 1989. 44p. $5.25. 0-87207-153-7.

This very brief booklet includes an introduction which discusses the advantages of using magazines to teach and promote reading. The list of magazines provides us with full bibliographic information, plus a brief annotation which includes level and content focus. Those publishers that will provide sample copies are also noted. *Magazines for Children* may be ordered for $5.25 (checks payable to IRA) sent to: Order Department, International Reading Association, 800 Barksdale Rd., P.O. Box 8139, Newark, DE 19714-8139. *Children's Periodicals; Periodicals*

C*

170. **Magazines for Children: A Guide for Parents, Teachers, and Librarians**, by Selma K. Richardson. 2nd ed. American Library Association, 1991. 139p. $22. 0-8389-0552-8.

This revised and updated edition includes 90 titles recommended for children from preschool through grade eight. Nearly a third of the titles are new since the 1983 edition. Detailed annotations describe the contents, interests, and special features of each selected magazine. Each entry also includes where indexed, grade level, and full bibliographic information. Appendices cover such areas as lists by age/grade level, magazines from religious affiliations, and editions for the visually-impaired. The subject index is by very broad topic. This very selective aid can stand side by side with Bowker's *Magazines for Young People* (1991) which evaluates over 1,000 magazines for young people through high school. Both are recommended for reading guidance, advice to parents, and collection development and evaluation.

Children's Periodicals; Periodicals

C*; Y*
171.   **Magazines for Young People: A Children's Magazine Guide Companion Volume**, by Bill Katz and Linda Sternberg Katz. 2nd ed. Bowker, 1991. $36. 0-9352-3009-0.

Formerly *Magazines for School Libraries*, this new and revised edition changed more than a title, which denoted a narrower scope. Also, as the subtitle indicates, an attempt was made to avoid a great deal of direct duplication—only about 100 of the 1,300 titles are for young children, preschool through age 14; the remaining include about 900 young adult, 14-18 years of age, and about 200 indicated as professional. Magazine titles are arranged alphabetically under 74 specific subject areas, which are further subdivided into three groups by level or audience. Typical entries might include founding date, frequency, price, editor, publisher and bibliographic data, other formats, such as microforms, whether online, where indexed, and the locations of book reviews. Annotations are both descriptive and evaluative and indicate a possible political leaning. Indexes by title, subject, and level complete this excellent resource. This is highly recommended for all secondary school libraries and all but the smallest elementary school libraries; it is also an important purchase for all public libraries not subscribing to *Magazines for Libraries*.
Young Adult Periodicals; Periodicals

Nonselective Lists
and Indexes

C
172.   **Children's Book Review Index**, by Barbara Beach and Beverly Baer. Gale, annual. $99.

Although this volume which annually lists about 18,000 review citations is not intended as a selection aid, it can be vital in locating reviews and other evaluative information that will determine acquisition. Reviews in about 450 periodicals are tabulated in this spinoff from *Book Review Index*. Children's books are defined as those suitable for children age 10 and under. There is a 5 volume cumulation available from Gale, *Children's Book Review Index: Master Cumulation, 1965-1984* (Gale, 1985, $350. 0-8103-2046-0).
Children's Literature

C
173.   **Children's Books in Print**. Bowker, annual. $139. 0-8352-3229-8.

This annual spinoff from *Books in Print* lists by author, title, and illustrator the children's books in print for a given year in the United States. Entries in the 1992-93 volume total more that 66,000 and deal with books for preschoolers through age 18. Full bibliographic information is given plus an indication of grade suitability. Introductory material contains a listing of children's literary awards and their winners. A companion volume is *Subject Guide to Children's Books in Print* (1992, $139. 0-8352-3262-X). Though not collection building tools per se, these bibliographies help determine availability of candidates for purchase. *Children's Literature*

C*; Y*
174.   **El-Hi Textbooks and Serials in Print 1993**. 121st ed. Bowker, 1993. 1,632p. $133. 0-8352-33344-8.

Though this is not an evaluative listing, it does indicate what textbooks and related material are currently in print in the United States. This annual publication (now over 100 years old!) contains about 42,000 materials from almost 1,000 publishers. They are arranged under 21 basic subjects like art, business, and literature, with 307 subcategories. Citations include basic bibliographic information plus grade levels and an indication of additional teaching materials. There are author, title, and series indexes and sections on professional books and serials for the educator as well as a directory of publishers. This is a valuable bibliographic guide in school libraries, but its price probably dictates that it can only be purchased for district-wide collections. *Textbooks; Periodicals*

C; Y

175. **Fiction, Folklore, Fantasy and Poetry for Children, 1876-1985**. 2 volumes. Bowker, 1986. 2,563p. $499.95. 0-8352-1831-7.

This massive labor of love provides bibliographic control for children's literature in the areas of fiction, folklore, fantasy, and poetry published or distributed in the United States from 1876 to 1985. There are four indexes in the work. The author and title indexes collectively give such information as birth and death dates, pseudonyms, variant spellings of the author's name, title, subtitles, publication dates, series, pagination, grade levels when known, and LC and ISBN numbers. The other two indexes are by illustrator and by book awards. Unfortunately because of its price, this massive retrospective trade bibliography will only be purchased by very large collections and those where there is intensive research done on the history of children's literature. *Children's Literature*

C

176. **Master Index to Summaries of Children's Books**, by Eloise S. Pettus. Scarecrow, 1985. 2v. 1,388p. $89.50. 0-8108-1795-0.

Pettus, a teacher of children's literature, has produced an exhaustive work, that is an index to summaries of more than 18,000 fiction and nonfiction titles, as a locational aid for teachers and librarians. More than 80 bibliographies, textbooks, and books of activities based on children's books contain these titles which are written for children from preschool to grade six. V. 1 contains the entries for book titles which are arranged by author and include title, publisher, date, grade level, and abbreviation symbol for the bibliography containing the summary. V. 2 contains title and subject indexes. This master index is recommended for all libraries that serve children or those that work with children for reference, reader's advisory, bibliography work, and of course for evaluating and building collections. *Children's Literature*

C; Y

177. **Select Annual Database: A Computer-Based Selection and Acquisitions Tool**. Select School Library Materials, annual. $70 per level.

This compilation and summary of reviews of curriculum related materials found in *Booklist, School Library Journal, Bulletin of the Center for Children's Books*, and *Book Report*, is available for three different levels, elementary (K-6), middle/junior (5-9) and senior high (9-12). Each contains records for over 1,300 items and is available on either an Appleworks or dBase III+ diskette. Both print and nonprint materials are included, but those items not recommended by the reviewers are excluded. A manual accompanies the diskette that explains how to generate either consideration lists or orders. For each item, standard bibliographic information is given plus a brief annotation, curriculum-based subjects, and then identifiers. Each diskette covers one year of reviews, from the April 1 through the March 15 issues of these periodicals. This service began in 1990. *Instructional Materials; Children's Literature; Young Adult Literature*

C*; Y*

178. **Young People's Books in Series**, by Judith K. Rosenberg. Libraries Unlimited, 1992. 350p. $27.50. 0-87287-882-1.

This is a new and completely up-to-date edition of a popular work which was last published in 1977. Most series published for young people from elementary through high school are identified and described. Fiction and nonfiction from 1976 through 1990 are listed. Each entry includes full bibliographic information, recommended grade level, and a brief descriptive annotation of the series. This guide is recommended for all school and public libraries as a reading guidance and collection development aid. *Series; Children's Literature; Young Adult Literature*

Reference Books

C

179. **Children's Reference Plus: Complete Bibliographic, Review, and Qualitative Information on Books, Reference Books, Serials, Cassettes, Software, and Videos for Children and Young Adults**. Bowker, 1992. $595.

This CD-ROM product covers the massive collection of Bowker's published works in the fields of children's and young adult literature. For example, there is *Children's Books in Print, El-HI Textbooks*, children's titles listed in *Bowker's Complete Video Directory*, and *Words on Cassette* for bibliographic information, plus 24 more specialized publications such as *Best Books of Children*, *Primaryplots*, *Books for the Gifted Child*, *High-Low Handbook*, and *More Notes from a Different Drummer*. This CD-ROM product runs on a IBM PC or compatible computer and is available on two 5 ¼-inch disks or a single 3-inch floppy. It is a companion to Bowker's *Books in Print Plus* and *Library Reference Plus*. *Children's Reference Plus*, though expensive, will find a place in very large collections where having all this material on a single database in a great convenience. *Children's Literature; CD-ROM*

C*; Y*

180.   **Guide to Reference Books for School Media Centers**, by Margaret Irby Nichols. 4th ed. Libraries Unlimited, 1992. 450p. $38.50. 0-87287-833-3.

This work identifies over 2,000 reference works that are in print and "designed specifically for the juvenile and young adult market." The titles are arranged in 54 subject categories. For each entry there is full bibliographic information, including price, a grade level indication, an annotation and review citations. In addition to standard print sources, this guide also covers review journals, nonprint and computer selection aids, library organizations and media skills material. There are subject and title indexes. This is an excellect selection guide particularly for junior and senior high school libraries.

Reference Books; Children's Literature; Young Adult Literature

C; Y

181.   **Index to Collective Biographies for Young Readers**, by Karen Breen. 4th ed. Bowker, 1988. 494p. $46. 0-8352-2348-5.

The latest edition of this popular work lists nearly 10,000 notables found in 1,129 collective biographies suitable for both elementary and junior high school readers. Most of the titles indexed in the first three editions have been retained, but there are almost 200 new volumes indexed. Out of print titles are marked. Inclusion of a title does not necessarily mean a recommendation; therefore, this volume should be used with caution for collection development. There is a key to indexed books at the beginning, followed by an alphabetical listing of biographees, with a list of the books in which each person's biography appears. The last major section lists individuals by subjects, i.e., area of renown, occupation, and nationality. The work also contains many aids to using the book, including a master list of subjects. This book is an excellent reference for public and school libraries with some peripheral use in book selection.

Biography; Children's Literature; Young Adult Literature

C

182.   **Reference Books for Children**, by Carolyn Sue Peterson and Ann D. Fenton. 4th ed. Scarecrow, 1992. 399p. $39.50. 0-8108-2543-0.

Over 1,000 annotated titles are included in this revised evaluative tool. All of the titles have been time-tested and are generally culled from recommended sources. Nonprint media are not included. Each entry has full bibliographic data and a brief descriptive annotation (50-100 words). Author, title, and subject indexes aid in easy access to the entries. It is intended as a guide to collection development; however, since the cut-off date is mid-1990, other sources may have to be checked for newer editions or new titles if used as a buying guide or evaluation checklist of an existing collection. Still, this guide, along with other sources such as *Children's Catalog*, will be useful for elementary school media centers and children's departments of public libraries. *Reference Books; Children's Literature*

C*

183.   **Reference Books for Children's Collections**, ed. by Dolores Volgliano. 2nd ed. New York Public Library, 1991. 79p. $7. 0-87104-696-2.

This slim bibliography lists over 420 reference book titles, ranging from the elementary level to adult materials used by children. Almost 25% of the listings are new titles. The books are current and are arranged by subject. Each entry contains a brief descriptive annotation and full bibliographic information. This list which is recommended for all elementary schools and children's departments of public libraries is available for $7 plus a mailing charge of $1 for one to five copies. Make checks payable to and send orders to: Office of Branch Libraries, The New York Public Library, 455 Fifth Avenue, New York, NY 10016.

Reference Books; Children's Literature

C*; Y*

184.   **Reference Books for Young Readers: Authoritative Evaluations of Encyclopedias, Atlases, and Dictionaries**, ed. by Marion Sader. Bowker, 1988. 627p. $49.95. 0-8352-2366-3.

This first entry in Bowker's new Buying Guide Series is aimed at librarians providing reference services to young people preschool through grade 12. Actually, this is not a general guide to reference books, but rather it very specifically limits itself to encyclopedias, atlases, and dictionaries (and large print books in the same categories). Extensive reviews (some several pages in length) of approximately 200 books are included. The selected titles are all published in the United States and were all available for purchase in 1987. There is an excellent introduction discussing the evaluation of reference books. Although there are several similar guides, e.g., *Guide to Reference Books for School Media Centers* and several Kister's guides for encyclopedias and atlases, there are special features of this new Bowker guide: the inclusion of online sources, the section listing large print materials, the ratings according to criteria, and the excerpts from published reviews. It is recommended that this guide be available for reference and as a buying guide in all school media centers and public library young people's departments.

Reference Books; Children's Literature; Young Adult Literature

5 Books for Beginners (Pre-school—Grade 3)

C*

185. **A to Zoo: Subject Access to Children's Picture Books,** by Carolyn W. Lima and John A. Lima. 4th ed. Bowker, 1993. 1,000p. $49.95. 0-8352-3201-8.

This greatly expanded and updated edition indexes more than 15,000 fiction and nonfiction picture books for youngsters, preschool through second grade. It has been chosen as an *ALA Outstanding Reference Source.* The selections are indexed under 700 subjects, author, title, and illustrator entries (an increase of thousands of titles since the still useful 1986 and 1989 editions). The book is designed to help librarians, teachers, and parents find the right book for children pre-school through second grade. The preface describes the purpose and organization of the book. This is followed by a brief history of children's books including a selected bibliography. The body of this useful index is divided into five parts: subject headings (with many cross references); a subject guide; a useful bibliographic guide (arranged by authors in most cases and including titles, illustrator, publisher, date, ISBN, and subjects); followed by complete title and illustrator indexes. Board books and popular books, as well as important out-of-print titles, are included. The authors, who are practicing librarians, have personally read almost every title. This new edition is recommended for all public libraries and elementary school libraries for use by all individuals working with the very young. *Picture Books; Children's Literature*

C

186. **Alphabet Books as a Key to Language Patterns: An Annotated Action Bibliography,** by Patricia L. Roberts. Shoe String Press, 1988. 263p. $32.50. 0-208-02151-5.

Roberts, an authority in the field of language patterns, has compiled a list of more than 500 alphabet books for use in "supporting a young child's developing language literacy, and learning skills." Each book is analyzed for language patterns, and the entries are arranged in alphabetical order by author under the specific patterns. Each entry is described with an annotation which indicates suggested age level and discusses the language pattern. Recommended titles are so indicated. An index of authors and titles is included. Recommended for most elementary school libraries and even some public libraries that work with the very young. *Alphabet Books; Picture Books; Children's Literature*

C

187. **The Art of Children's Picture Books: A Selective Reference Guide,** by Sylvia S. Marantz and Kenneth A. Marantz. Garland, 1988. 159p. $28. 0-8240-2745-0. (Garland Reference Library of the Humanities, 825).

This retrospective bibliography of 450 books, articles, theses, and some media items about children's picture books is grouped into six broad areas including the history, production, criticism, anthologizing, and further research of picture books. Each entry has a brief annotation and full bibliographic information. There are also artist, author, and title indexes. A major drawback in this otherwise useful bibliography is the lack of a subject index. Nonetheless, this relatively inexpensive book is recommended for elementary school and public libraries rounding out their collection of picture book bibliographies.

Picture Books; Children's Literature

C

188. **Beginning with Books.** Carnegie Library of Pittsburgh, 1991.

This family literacy program guide consists of three parts: (1), "Beginning with Books" a short pamphlet for parents on reading to children, (2), "Books to Begin With: Easy-to-Read Books for Family Reading" lists 51 children's books that can be read by parents with limited reading ability, and (3) "How to Set Up a Gift Book Program," which includes a step-by-step manual on conducting a gift book distribution program with sections on parent counseling for low-income families. The first two pamphlets cost $1.00

each and the entire package including the manual and other pamphlets costs $15 and is available from: Beginning with Books, The Carnegie Library of Pittsburgh—Homewood Branch, 7101 Hamilton Ave., Pittsburgh, PA 15208. *Children's Literature; Literacy Programs*

C*

189. **Beyond Picture Books: A Guide to First Readers**, by Barbara Barstow and Judith Riggle. Bowker, 1989. 336p. $41. 0-8352-2515-1.

Barstow and Riggle, two experienced children's librarians, have chosen more than 1600 first readers which they define as "books intended for children at a first or second grade level ... have a recognizable format and generally belong to a series." The titles were published between 1951-1989, and include books in-print and out-of-print, and fiction and nonfiction. Entries are listed in alphabetical order by author and are numbered sequentially. Each entry provides full bibliographic information, subject headings, reading level (using the Spache Readability Scale), and a brief annotation. A special feature of this work is the list of 200 in-print titles considered a core collection. The work concludes with five detailed indexes: subject, title, illustrator, readability, and series. This work complements Bowker's *A to Zoo*, and would be a welcome addition to all libraries serving young readers. *Children's Literature*

C

190. **Books, Babies, and Libraries: Serving Infants, Toddlers, Their Parents and Caregivers**, by Ellin Greene. American Library Association, 1991. 186p. $25. pap. 0-8389-0572-2.

Based on her experience as a library educator and project director for the New York Public Library's Early Childhood Project, Greene found little in the field related to library work with the very young. She designed a graduate course to alleviate this problem. This book is based on topics covered in this course. In addition to a full text on the library's role in early learning and in parent education, book and nonprint collection recommendations are included. Also included are other bibliographies, a discography, and suitable toys. Appendices include lists of professional articles and tools helpful in program planning. *Child Development; Children's Literature*

C*

191. **Books for Children to Read Alone: A Guide for Parents and Librarians**, by George Wilson and Joyce Moss. Bowker, 1988. 184p. $41. 0-8352-2346-9.

The authors have theorized that of the 2,500 books published each year for preschoolers to about third grade, the vast majority are written for a teacher, librarian, or parent to be read to a child, rather than for a child to read alone. They have isolated and described about 350 which they feel are in the best of the read-alone category. Each entry has an annotation that describes story and comments on the illustration and subject of the book. An appendix lists books by series and indexes by subject, title, author, and readability level. This bibliography is recommended for every elementary school and public library that serves children ages 4-8. *Children's Literature*

C

192. **Books for Early Childhood: A Developmental Perspective**, by Jean A. Pardeck and John T. Pardeck. Greenwood, 1986. 169p. $37.95. 0-313-24576-2 (Bibliographies and Indexes in Psychology, No. 3).

The Pardecks have stated that the purpose of this bibliography of almost 350 titles for pre-school children is to provide professional reading guidance information to social workers, psychiatrists, teachers, librarians, and parents as it relates to children's developmental needs. Further it serves as an aid to the bibliotherapy process as described in the introductory chapter. Additional chapters deal with specific developmental issues such as anger, attitudes, self-image, sex roles, single parents, etc. Each chapter provides background information, and an annotated bibliography dealing with each theme. All titles were published between 1980 and 1985. Similar titles which complement each other include: Dreyer's *The Bookfinder* and Lima's *A to Zoo*. This title despite its date is recommended for all libraries serving professionals working with young children. *Children's Literature; Bibliotherapy*

C*

193. **Books Kids Will Sit Still For: The Complete Read-Aloud Guide**, by Judy Freeman. 2nd ed. Bowker, 1990. 660p. $36. 0-8352-3010-4.

Freeman, a former elementary school librarian, now a professor of children's literature, calls her new edition "a manual of ways to fool around with books." She could well have added and to mix and match them with kids. This revised and updated 2nd edition is chock full of ideas on using books in reading aloud, booktalking, and storytelling programs. The second half of the book lists more than 2,000 fiction and nonfiction titles from pre-school to grade six. Each entry includes full bibliographic data and an annotation which includes titles of similar books and suggestions for activities. A bibliography of professional titles is an added bonus. The detailed index is divided by author, title, and subject. This book is highly recommended for all libraries offering services to young children. *Children's Literature; Read Aloud Programs*

C

194. **Books to Read Aloud with Children Through Age 8**, by Child Study Children's Book Committee at Bank Street College. Bank Street College, 1989. 59p. $4.00.

This little booklet contains a good mix of old and new books totaling 400 titles suitable for reading aloud to children from preschool to 8 years of age. This inexpensive but worthwhile bibliography is available for $4.00 plus .50 for p & h. Send check to: Child Study Children's Book Committee, Bank Street College, 610 West 112th Street, New York, NY 10025 *Children's Literature; Read Aloud Programs*

C

195. **Canadian Picture Books. Livres d'Images Canadiens**, by Jane McQuarrie and Diane Dubois. Reference Press (Toronto) 1986. 217p $21. 0-919981-12-7; $17. pap. 0-919981-09-7.

This is a comprehensive listing of over 700 French and English in- and out-of-print picture books published before July, 1985 that were written or illustrated by Canadians or residents of Canada. Brief annotations are given in the language of the books and outstanding titles are starred. Books are listed by general subjects and are indexed by author, title and detailed subjects. This is excellent for Canadian schools and libraries. *Children's Literature, Canadian; Canada*

C

196. **Counting Books Are More Than Numbers: An Annotated Action Bibliography**, by Patricia L. Roberts. Library Professional Publications/Shoe String Press, 1990. 270p. $32.50 0-208-02216-3.

The heart of this book is the annotated listing of nearly 500 counting books organized under four main sections: ABC and 1, 2, 3 rhyming books, collections of related objects, and collections of unrelated objects. For each book, full bibliographic information is given, summaries of the contents, grade and age recommendations, concepts featured, and hints for usage. This section is preceded by a scholarly introduction which describes the mathematical skills covered in the primary grades, difficulties encountered, how counting books can help, and their variety, plus a look at mathematics readiness activities. In an appendix, the appropriate books are listed under the various skills taught, and there is also a bibliography of professional readings on mathematics. An author, illustrator, and title index is supplied. For large children's literature collections. *Counting; Children's Literature; Mathematics; Picture Books*

C

197. **Mother Goose Comes First: An Annotated Guide to the Best Books and Recordings for Your Preschool Child**, by Lois Winkel and Sue Kimmel. Holt, 1990. 174p. $14.95. 0-8050-1001-7.

Two well-known authorities in children's literature have pooled their knowledge and produced a handbook of highly-selected and recommended titles for the preschooler. The titles are divided into general topics of interest, e.g., Mother Goose, Stories about growing up and families, etc. Each entry includes a bibliographic citation, a lively annotation, and an indication of age/grade level appeal. There is some concern with their emphasis on phonorecordings, since this format seems to be in a state of transition. However, the list is solid and certainly recommended for all libraries serving children and those who serve children. *Children's Literature; Phonorecordings; Picture Books*

C

198. **Mother Goose From Nursery to Literature**, by Gloria T. Delamar. McFarland, 1987. 314p. $29.95. 0-89950-280-6.

This isn't really a bibliography, but rather a long exposition on the role of the nursery rhyme in literature and in today's children's experience. However, the chronological bibliography of nursery rhyme collections of historical or artistic interest justify the listing in this guide and the cost of the otherwise handy handbook. An added bonus is the bibliography of secondary sources about the nursery rhymes. This is recommended not only for its research value but as a tool to evaluate and develop collections of nursery rhymes in public and school libraries. *Nursery Rhymes; Children's Literature; Picture Books*

C*

199. **Picture Books for Children**, by Patricia J. Cianciolo. 3rd. ed. American Library Association, 1990. 243p. $25. 0-8389-0527-7.

This revised and updated edition of a work that is becoming a standard in its field reflects the tremendous growth of the children's literature publishing field, especially in the 1980's. Most of the 213 titles chosen in this edition have been published recently. The stated purpose of this bibliography remains "to identify and describe picture books that will provide children with enjoyable, informative, and discriminating literary experiences." Titles chosen range from preschool to junior high school level. They are arranged by broad topical areas, e.g., Other People; The World I Live In; and the Imaginative World. The titles are then arranged alphabetically by author. Entries include full bibliographic data, illustrator, intended age level, and an annotation which describes the illustrations as well as giving a story summary. This work is intended for a wide audience, including teachers, parents, and of course librarians. It is highly recommended for all libraries that serve children and adults that work with children.

Children's Literature; Picture Books

C

200. **Play, Learn, and Grow: An Annotated Guide to the Best Books and Materials for Very Young Children**, by James L. Thomas. Bowker, 1992. 480p. $27. 0-8352-3019-8.
Intended as a guide for working with the very young child up to age six, this annotated list contains a full range of multimedia resources including books, videos, filmstrips, and audiocassettes. Over 1,100 items were chosen for inclusion from over 5,000 print and nonprint materials considered by "a panel of knowledgeable, highly-experienced specialists in child development who chose only those products judged to be the best in aiding the phases of child development." Each entry contains complete bibliographic information, age level, a brief annotation, and a "priority of purchase" ranking. This evaluative guide is recommended for all libraries that serve children and professionals who work with children.

Children's Literature; Audiovisual Materials

C; Y

201. **Pop-Up and Movable Books: A Bibliography**, by Ann R. Montanaro. Scarecrow, 1993. 559p. $59.50. 0-8108-2650-X.
Montanaro has provided us with both an unusual and a very extensive bibliography of books that literally have movable parts. More than 1,600 books published from the 1850s to the present are listed and described. An introduction traces the history of these fascinating books which are literally centuries old. The selected entries are arranged alphabetically by author. Each citation has complete bibliographic information as well as a brief descriptive annotation. Thorough indexes are provided, including indexes for series, author/illustrator, paper engineers and designers, and titles. The lack of a subject index is unfortunate, but does not limit the value of this very worthwhile bibliography which shows the great deal of time and research it took to produce. It deserves a place in most libraries, especially those that serve children, historians, and bibliophiles. *Book Collecting; Pop-Up Books*

C

202. **The Preschool Resource Guide: Educating and Entertaining Children Aged Two through Five**, by Harriet Friedes. Plenum/Insight, 1993. 245p. $27.50. 0-303-44464-9.
This work includes a rather detailed account of child development, as well as lists of useful resources for the preschool years. In addition to books, the author lists audio recordings, videocassettes, magazines, toys, games, and even software. A directory of professional organizations is also appended. In addition to the interesting information for pre-school children, the recommended lists will prove useful to libraries serving parents and teachers of the very young. *Education, Preschool; Child Development*

C*

203. **Primaryplots: A Book Talk Guide for Use with Readers Ages 4-8**, by Rebecca L. Thomas. Bowker, 1989. 392p. $41.95. 0-8352-2514-3.
This guide is intended "to serve as a guide for booktalks, story programs, and reading guidance." Geared for the very young, *Primaryplots* complements others in Bowker's series of guides for booktalks: Spirt's *Introducing Bookplots 3*, and Gillespie and Naden's *Juniorplots 3* and *Seniorplots*. The 150 early-reading and picture books chosen were published between 1983 and 1987. They are arranged in eight chapters under broad topics of literature, e.g., Enjoying Family and Friends, Developing a Positive Self-Image, Finding Humor in Picture Books, and Focusing on Folk-tales. Each entry includes full bibliographic information including reading level, a plot summary, notes on thematic material, suggested activities, audiovisual adaptations, and an annotated list of related titles. This guide is highly recommended for all libraries that serve the very young and those that work with the very young. A sequel is *Primaryplots 2* (Bowker, 1993, 0-8353-3411-8). *Children's Literature; Book Talks*

C

204.   **Read It Again**. Stone Center for Children's Books. The Claremont Graduate School, 1990. $5.

This handy list of 175 recent picture books was based on the choices of 500 children. This first edition ranks the books in order of preference and includes a brief review of each title. Copies of this list of picture books that kids like is available for $5.00 from: Stone Center for Children's Books, The Claremont Graduate School, 131 East 10th St., Claremont, CA 91711.   *Picture Books; Children's Literature*

C

205.   **Read to Me: Recommended Literature for Children Ages Two through Seven**. California Department of Education, [1992]. 144p. $5.50.

This inexpensive and illustrated bibliography contains over 460 titles recommended for the very young reader. It is available for only $5.50 from: California Department of Education, Bureau of Publications, Sales Unit, P.O. Box 271, Sacramento, CA 95812.   *Children's Literature; Picture Books*

C

206.   **Ready, Set, Read: Best Books to Prepare Preschoolers**, by Ellen Mahoney and Leah Wilcox. Scarecrow, 1985. 348p $25. 0-818-1684-9.

This book is intended to be a guide for parents who are interested in getting their very young children ready to read. The authors have drawn upon their extensive experience as teachers and librarians to develop a plan as well as an excellent bibliography for working with the preschoolers. The book is divided into the various developmental stages of children from infancy to five years of age which in turn are related to literature reading. Each chapter has a bibliography of titles discussed in the chapter as well as additional titles for that particular age group. Bibliographic information is included, and author, title, and subject indexes are provided. There are similar books aimed at the parent, but few are organized by developmental stages. This volume is recommended for public libraries serving the preschool child and those developing parenting collections.   *Children's Literature; Child Development*

C

207.   **Story Stretchers for the Primary Grades: Activities to Expand Children's Favorite Books**, by Shirley C. Raines and Robert J. Canady. Gryphon House, 1992. 256p. $14.95. pap. 0-87659-157-8.

The authors have provided us with a handy, inexpensive guide that suggests popular children's literature to enrich curriculum areas such as math, science, writing, creative dramatics, and art. Five fully-annotated titles are selected for each of the 18 thematic chapters. Indexes by author, illustrator, title, activity, and subject complete this useful little guide. This list of about 100 good children's books useful for curriculum enrichment is especially recommended for elementary school libraries, but it may also be useful for public libraries.   *Children's Literature; Early Childhood Education—Activity Programs*

C

208.   **Windows on Our World: A Guide to International Picture Books**, by Carol Hanson Sibley. Moorhead State University, 1991. $10.

This bibliography includes over 50 annotated international picture books representing about 20 different countries written in 18 languages. Also included are suggested teaching activities for the selected titles (which could be adapted for library progamming); addresses of foreign book dealers; and an added bibliography of related books and articles. To order send $10 plus $2 for postage and handling to: Moorhead State University, Curriculum Materials Center, Moorhead, MN 56563.

Children's Literature; Picture Books

C

209.   **Wordless/Almost Wordless Picture Books: A Guide**, by Virginia H. Ritchey and Katharyn E. Puckett. Libraries Unlimited, 1992. 223p. $27.50. 0-87287-878-3.

Ritchey and Puckett have compiled an extensive list of almost 700 wordless (or practically wordless) books intended for the very young. The titles are organized alphabetically by author. Each entry includes full bibliographic information, a short precis of the story, and descriptions of the illustrations. A special feature of this work is the inclusion of six indexes: title, format, use of print, series, illustrator, and subject.Another bonus is the resource list of articles and books that deal with wordless books intended for adults. This well-organized book is highly recommended for all libraries that serve the very young and those that work with this age group.   *Children's Literature; Picture Books; Stories Without Words*

6 Books About Children's Literature

C; Y

210. **Approaches to Literature through Subject**, by Paula Kay Montgomery. Oryx, 1993. 243p. $29.50 (pap.) 0-89774-774-7 (Oryx Reading Motivation Series).

This book outlines many methods that can be used to motivate middle grade and junior high youngsters to read by hooking them on books dealing with high interest subjects. Both fiction and nonfiction titles are used as examples, and some of the topics covered are people, things, and both historical and currents events. In the companion volume by Mary Elizabeth Wildberger, *Approaches to Literature through Authors* (Oryx, 1993, $29.50, 0-89774-776-3), various authors (and a few illustrators) like Beverly Cleary, Betsy Byars, Walter Dean Myers, Cynthia Voigt and even Shakespeare are used to interest prospective readers. Both books contains many examples of models to follow, plus extensive lists of students materials and resources, and aids for the teacher, all of which can be used for collection development. These books will be useful particularly in middle and junior high schools and, perhaps, in some children's rooms in public libraries.

Children's Literature; Young Adult Literature; Reading

C*

211. **Children and Books**, by Zena Sutherland and May Hill Arbuthnot. 8th ed. Harper, 1990. 751p. $45. 0-673-46357-5.

This has become a standard text on children's literature and rightly so because it gives a thorough and tasteful introduction to all aspects of this subject. It is now organized into four broad areas "Knowing Children and Books," "Exploring the Types of Literature," "Bringing Children and Books Together," and "Areas and Issues." All parts contain helpful bibliographies, but because the second part deals with specific authors and their works, the bibliographies here can serve as buying guides to the best in children's literature. There are also valuable bibliographies on selection aids and on recommended readings that explore special topics. Appendixes include a directory of publishers and children's book awards. There are author, title, illustrator, and subject indexes. Highly recommended for all children's literature collections.

Children's Literature

C

212. **Children's Literature: A Guide to the Criticism**, by Linnea Hendrickson. G. K. Hall, 1987. 696p. $38.50. 0-8161-8670-7. (Reference Publications in Literature).

This is a listing of critical writings on children's literature culled from periodicals, books, and dissertations mostly from the 1970's on. Material dealing with literature for preschoolers through age 16 is included in two parts. The first is a listing with annotations of criticism about some 600 authors and illustrators, and the second part is arranged by such subjects as censorship, comics, and fairy tales. There is a listing of periodical titles consulted and the books of criticism indexed. These lists might be of value in collection development. There are indexes by critics, authors, titles, and subjects. Of particular value in collections where there is a need for material on the study of children's literature. *Children's Literature*

C*

213. **Children's Literature in the Elementary School**, by Charlotte S. Huck et al. 5th ed. Harcourt, 1992. 775p $45. 0-03-047528-7.

This highly respected text on children's literature gives an excellent survey of the kinds of children's literature and ways of making it central to a school's curriculum. Every one of the chapters contain valuable bibliographies of books and materials about children's literature or lists of quality titles for children. These lists collectively can serve as a bibliography for a basic collection in a school and public library.

Children's Literature

C

214. **Children's Literature in the Reading Program**, ed. by Bernice E. Cullinan. International Reading Association, 1987. 171p. $18. 0-87207-782-9.

This is a collection of essays on how various types of literature can enrich the K-8 reading program in schools. In addition to many practical suggestions, nearly 500 quality children's books are referred to and listed along with several fine adult sources. *Children's Literature*

C

215. **Children's Literature Review: Excerpts from Reviews, Criticism, and Commentary on Books for Children**. Gale, 1976- . $95 per volume.

This extensive and expensive set (each volume is about $100) now numbers over 25 volumes. Each contains collective criticism on about a dozen authors and illustrators. Along with this extensive critical material there are bibliographies of books and other materials by and about the authors under discussion. This is a valuable set, but its price will probably limit its acquisition to large collections.

Children's Literature

C

216. **A Critical Handbook of Children's Literature**, by Rebecca J. Lukens. 4th. ed. Scott, Foresman, 1989. 300p. $20.50 pap. 0-673-38773-9.

This is an excellect guide to criteria for evaluating children's literature under such chapter headings as character, setting, plot, theme, and style. Each chapter ends with an unannotated list of recommended books, each of which can serve as a checklist and guide for purchasing quality titles. There are also extensive bibliographies in appendixes listing prize winning books. *Children's Literature*

C

217. **Experiencing Children's Literature**, by Alan C. Purves and Diane Monson. Scott, Foresman, 1984. 216p. $18.95 0-673-15348-7.

Using as a framework the theoretical ideas on literary criticism developed by Frye and Rossenblatt, the authors apply them to an analysis of children's literature. Each chapter lists literary research and critical works and gives a selected bibliography of children's books. This is not intended as a selection aid, but will help identify some important critical studies although it needs an update badly. *Children's Literature*

C

218. **An Introduction to the World of Children's Books**, by Margaret R. Marshall. 2nd ed. Gower, 1988. 250p. $38.95. 0-0566-05461-2.

This book's major strength is the breadth of its coverage on children's literature. Although there are some chapters that focus somewhat on British children's books, it is basically international in scope. Current and past trends are examined, practical criteria for choosing books are given, and suggestions are made on how to bring children and books together. Within each chapter there are many recommended titles, plus lists for further readings after each chapter, and a whole section on bibliographic aids.

Children's Literature

C

219. **Literature and the Child**, by Bernice E. Cullinan. 2nd ed. Harcourt Brace, 1989. 730p. $32. 0-15-551111-4.

In addition to the excellent lists of recommended children's books, this handbook updates recent research in children's literature for teachers, librarians, and others interested in the field. It also includes profiles of authors and illustrators, teaching ideas, and activity suggestions. This useful guide is recommended for all elementary school and public libraries. *Children's Literature*

C

220. **Mirrors of American Culture**, by Paul Deane. Scarecrow, 1991. 275p. $29.50. 0-8108-2460-4.

Deane has become an authority on children's series books. This analysis of the genre covers literary style, censorship, history, and children's taste and evaluates this literary form from 1899 to the present. He attempts to answer many questions that have puzzled librarians over the years, namely relating to why they are so popular with youngsters. The focus is an historical one; however, it does include some currently popular series such as *The Babysitters Club*. The volume is undoubtedly more useful to developing a philosophy of collection development in children's literature rather than in suggesting many worthwhile titles for purchase. Recommended for all librarians and others interested in children's services.

Children's Literature; Series

C

221. **More Creative Uses of Children's Literature: v. 1: Introducing Books in All Kinds of Ways**, by Mary Ann Paulin. Library Professional Publications/Shoestring Pr., 1992. 224p. $35.)-208-02202-3.

This update of Paulin's *Creative Uses of Children's Literature* (1982) focuses on titles published during the past 10 years, so consequently the vast majority of the titles listed are still readily available. In addition to many creative approaches to storytelling, booktalking, and multimedia presentations, the real value of this work lies in the many lists and annotated bibliographies which are arranged by subject and type. Almost half of the book is made up of bibliographic indexes. This creative volume is recommended for all libraries that work with children, especially those interested in using a multimedia approach to using children's literature. *Children's Literature; Creative Activities*

C; Y

222. **Publishers and Distributors of Paperback Books for Young People**, by John T. Gillespie. American Library Association, 1987. 188p. $7.50. pap. 0-8389-0471-8.

This inexpensive paperback is not a bibliography, but, nevertheless, it is a boon to library collection building. It is an excellent directory of paperback publishers and distributors of the United States and Canada. It supplements the useful paperback guides of the author: *The Elementary Paperback Collection*, *The Junior High School Paperback Collection*, and *The Senior High School Paper Back Collection* (all o.p.). The annotated entries contain such information as types of books published, available series, and backlists. The directory also contains a subject index that identifies publishers by subject strengths. Recommended for all libraries that are building up collections of paperbound books for children and young adults. *Paperback Books*

C

223. **Touchstones: Reflections on the Best in Children's Literature**, ed. by Perry Nodelman. Children's Literature Association, 1989. 3 v. $25. each or $60. for the set. 0-937263-01-X.

This three volume set contains approximately 30 essays about classic works of children's literature. V. 1 deals with children's novels; V. 2 is devoted to fairy tales, myths, and poetry; and V. 3 deals with illustration and how and why the books were selected; it also contains a listing of all books considered in the three volumes. The volumes may be purchased for $25 each or $60 for the 3 volume set, plus $1 per volume for shipping and handling from: Children's Literature Association, c/o 135 Edgebrook Dr., Battle Creek, MI 49015. *Children's Literature*

7 Programs and Activities

C

224. Beginning with Books: Library Programming for Infants, Toddlers, and Preschoolers, by Nancy N. DeSalvo. Library Professional Publications; Dist. by Shoe String, 1992. 186p. $29.50. 0-208-02318-6.

A professional librarian draws on her wide experience in library programming for preschoolers and shares many practical ideas and sample programming techniques involving librarians working with parents. Each sample program includes many annotated suggestions of books, music, games, etc. This brief account would be an important addition for reference, programming ideas, and collection development for all libraries and centers that work with the very young. *Children's Literature*

C; Y

225. The Book Report and Library Talk Directory of Sources, A Special Report, by Renee Naughton. Linworth, 1991. 110p. $15.95. 0-938865-09-9.

Naughton has truly compiled annotated bibliographies which serve as one-stop sources for supplies and products primarily for children's libraries and school libraries. The two final chapters: "Your Professional Library" and "Book Lists" are worth the price of this invaluable practical aid. This little goldmine is highly recommended for all libraries serving young people. *Library Supplies*

C

226. Books on Puppetry. Children's Library Services Section. Saskatchewan Library Association. 1990. 14p. $2.

In addition to a large number of practical guides on making and using puppets, this 14-page bibliography is loaded with books which offer suggested uses for puppets in storytelling, creative drama, and with special audiences, such as mentally retarded. To order send $2.00 made payable to The Saskatchewan Library Association to: SLA, P.O. Box 3388, Regina, Saskatchewan, Canada S4P 3HI. *Puppets*

C*

227. Booksharing: 101 Programs to Use with Preschoolers, by Margaret Mead MacDonald. Shoe-string, 1988. 264p. $32.50. 0-318-35043-2. $19.50. pap. 0-208-02314-3.

MacDonald has provided us with this excellent handbook on library programming with 2½ to 5-year-olds. More importantly, added to this gem is a bibliography of the titles to be used in the suggested programs plus a film list. This essential book is recommended for all libraries where children's librarians need program ideas. *Children's Literature*

C*; Y*; A

228. Booktalk! 5, by Joni Richards Bodart. Wilson, 1993. 282p. $32. 0-8242-0836-6.

This companion volume to the earlier *Booktalk! 4* (1992. $32. 0-8242-0835-8), *Booktalk! 3* (1988. $30. 0-8242-0764-5), and *Booktalk! 2* (1985. $30. 0-8242-0716-3) offers over 320 completely new booktalks with no duplication (though it does bring back some of the old popular titles). It also includes general chapters on instructions and advice on presenting booktalks to children, teenagers, adults, and senior citizens. In addition to this valuable information on booktalking, there are approaches by authors, titles, age level, and themes. These books are highly recommended for every library. *Book Talks*

C; Y

229. Collected Perspectives: Choosing and Using Books for the Classroom, by Hughes Moir. 2nd ed. Christopher Gordon, 1992. 296p. $38.75 0-926842-12-9.

This bibliography reviews nearly 1,000 books suitable for use with students in grades K through 12 and another 1,000 companion titles. There are about 1,000 class-tested teaching suggestions using these books and as many teaching topics. Although the bibliographies list works that are found in other more standard works, the teaching suggestions will be of some value in school collections.

Children's Literature; Young Adult Literature

C*

230. **Creative Fingerplays and Action Rhymes: An Index and Guide to Their Use**, by Jeff Defty. Oyrx, 1992. 255p. $29.50 0-89774-709-7.

Part one of this unique guide gives all sorts of background material that explains the history and use of finger plays and ways of integrating these activities into various stages of childhood development, types of development, and special needs. Part two is a index by subject and first lines to about 3,000 fingerplays and action rhymes found in 95 collections. Most of these sources are still in print and therefore can be acquired by libraries needing them. This is a practical handbook, highly recommended for elementary schools, nursery schools and children's rooms. *Children's Literature; Finger Plays*

C

231. **Creative Uses of Children's Literature**, by Mary Ann Paulin. Library Professional Publications/Shoestring Press, 1986. 730p. $55; 0-208-01861-1; pap. $35. 0-208-018620X.

This work, first published in 1982, is an extremely useful manual of hundreds of useful ideas for introducing various forms of literature to children. Scattered throughout the text are bibliographies of recommended books that can be useful for basic book-buying in this area. *Children's Literature*

C*

232. **For Reading Out Loud! A Guide to Sharing Books with Children**, by Margaret Mary Kimmel and Elizabeth Segel. Delacorte, 1988. $16.95 0-385-29660-6.

This guide on reading to children from preschool through the early elementary school grades, contains tips on how to hone one's techniques, plus an annotated bibliography of 300 child-tested winners. The annotations contains age suitability, length of reading time, and possible stopping points. They are arranged by subject and length. This work can be used for collection evaluation and as a selection guide.

Children's Literature

C

233. **Hey! Listen to This: Stories to Read Aloud**, ed. by Jim Trelease. Penguin, 1992. 414p. $11. 0-670-83691-5.

This is basically an anthology (with comments) of 48 tales arranged under headings like "Animal Tales," "Children of Courage," and "Classic Tales," that are suitable to be retold to children. As a bonus for collection builders, there are several bibliographies including one on outstanding anthologies and another on audio cassette producers. *Storytelling; Children's Literature*

C*

234. **Introducing Bookplots 3: A Book Talk Guide for Use with Readers Ages 8-12**, by Diana L. Spirt. Bowker, 1988. 352p. $41. 0-8352-2345-0.

Like the two earlier volumes in this series, *Introducing Books* (1970, $24.95 0-8352-0215-1) and *Introducing More Books* (1978, $24.95, 0-8352-0988-1), this book is intended as a manual on introducing good books to children in the middle grades. However, because there is a total of approximately 1,300 books and audiovisual sources listed and annotated in the "Additional Selections" sections that follow the detailed plot summaries of 81 books, this book can also be used as a selection aid. The books are arranged under categories that represent developmental goals for middle childhood, such as "Making Friends," "Getting Along in the Family," "Respecting Living Creature," and "Understanding Social Problems," and, in addition to a plot summary for each of the 81 highlighted titles, there are sections on thematic material found in the book, book talk material, and the aforementioned "Additional Selections." There are author, title, and subject indexes. This series has proven to be useful in both school and public libraries.

Book Talks; Children's Literature

Y*

235. **Juniorplots 4: A Book Talk Guide for Use with Readers Ages 12-16**, by John T. Gillespie and Corinne J. Naden. R. R. Bowker, 1992. 352p. $29.95. 0-8352-3167-4.

Although this is primarily intended as a manual to help librarians and teachers introduce books to junior-high age students, it can also be used for collection building in libraries serving this age group. The 80 basic titles included are arranged under such topics as "Teenage Life and Concerns," "Adventure and

Mystery Stories," "Biography and True Adventure," and "Guidance and Health." For each title a detailed plot summary is given, material on thematic content and methods of presenting the book is provided, followed by an annotated bibliography of about eight to ten additional recommended titles that are related in theme or content. All 700-odd titles are listed in the author and title indexes, though only the main titles are analyzed in the subject index. This volume was preceded by *Juniorplots* (Bowker, 1967), *More Juniorplots* (Bowker, 1977) and *Juniorplots 3* (Bowker, 1987). Each of these deal with different books but are essentially the same in arrangement and treatment of each title. This series has been highly recommended for public and school libraries. *Young Adult Literature; Book Talks*

C
236. Literature-Based Reading: Children's Books and Activities to Enrich the K-5 Curriculum, by Mildred Knight Laughlin and Claudia Lisman Swisher. Oryx, 1990. 168p. $29.95 0-89774-562-0.

This handbook offers practical suggestions and examples of using literature, rather than textbooks for elementary school classroom reading instruction. For each model unit, many activities such as role playing and art projects are suggested. Though not intended as a selection aid, the books suggested for use will make excellent additions to school libraries. There are two other similar guides by Laughlin for the same age group: *Literature-Based Art and Music* (1992, $29.92 0-89774-661-9) and *Literature-Based Social Studies* (1991, $27.50 0-89774-605-8). *Children's Literature*

C
237. Mother Goose Time: Library Programs for Babies and Their Care-givers, by Jane Marino and Dorothy F. Houlihan. Wilson, 1992. 172p. $30. 0-8242-0850-1.

This short but excellent work is really a handbook on programming for babies and their caregivers. However, in addition to many offering many ideas and material for setting up programs, it provides us with over 160 time-tested rhymes and songs and even more to the point, in part three, it lists musical arrangements, bibliographies of picture books, display books, resource books for adults, and indexes for quick access. Recommended for most public libraries and others offering programs for toddlers.
Children's Literature; Early Childhood Education—Activity Programs; Education, Preschool

C*
238. Musical Story Hours: Using Music With Storytelling and Puppetry, by William M. Painter. Library Professional Pub./Shoe String, 1989. 172p. $27.50. 0-208-022505-8.

This lively how-to guide is chock full of ideas on putting music and books together. Painter, an experienced youth services librarian, says "anyone interested in bringing books and stories to life creatively for children can experiment with thousands of variations on this basic theme." The work is intended for parents and teachers of preschool and elementary age children, as well as librarians. The real value for collection building is in the titles mentioned throughout the text, but especially those listed in a "Quick Reference Section" at the end of the book. This practical guide to programming and collection development is recommended for all libraries that serve children and those working with children.
Children's Literature; Storytelling; Puppets

C*
239. The New Read-Aloud Handbook, by Jim Trelease. Rev. ed. Penguin, 1989. 290p. $9.95. pap. 0-14-046881-1.

Though this book has a great deal of competition today, it has remained popular with teachers, librarians, and parents through its several revisions. Trelease devotes the first half of the book to a lively discussion of the virtues of reading aloud (even discussing the evils of television). The second half follows the usual pattern and lists about 300 annotated titles that are "predictable" winners. Each entry contains a recommended grade level and suggestions of other related titles. Bibliographic information and an author/illustrator index are also provided. There are no title nor subject indexes. This book is recommended for all libraries that serve children or those that serve children. It is recommended as a worthwhile complement to several other recommended and similar titles: *Books to Read Aloud with Children through Age 8*, *Books Kids Will Sit Still For,* 2nd ed., and *For Reading Out Loud,* 2nd ed.
Children's Literature; Read Aloud Programs

C
240. Nonfiction Books for Children: Activities for Thinking, Learning, and Doing, by Carol A. Doll. Teacher Ideas Press/Libraries Unlimited, 1990. 117p. $19.50. 0-87287-710-8.

Doll, a professor of library science at the University of Washington, has compiled a list of 57 carefully chosen and recently published nonfiction books for children. These were selected because it was felt they could be easily integrated into classroom activities to enrich the curriculum. For each book, Doll gives us a brief summary, recommended grade levels and curricular areas, and suggested activities. A list of 1989 titles selected from annual lists recommended by the National Council for the Social Studies and the National Science Teachers Association and indexes of grade levels and subjects are added bonuses for this useful book which is recommended for all elementary school libraries. Librarians may also want to consider Kobrin's *Eyeopeners*, a similar work, with more nonfiction titles suggested.

Children's Literature; Creative Activities

C

241. **Novel Experiences: Literature Units for Book Discussion Groups in the Elementary Grades**, by Christine Jenkins and Sally Freeman. Teacher Ideas Press/Libraries Unlimited, 1991. 231p. $23. pap. 0-87287-730-2.

Modeled after the Great Books/Junior Great Books literature discussion program, this guide includes 35 literary works for grades two through six. Each book unit includes a brief annotation, prereading activities for motivation, vocabulary, discussion questions, enrichment activities, and a list of related readings. A variety of genres, writing styles, cultural backgrounds, and reading levels are represented. This interesting program, designed to get youngsters to question and discuss reading, along with the many suggested tested titles, is recommended for elementary school and public libraries dedicated to creating lifelong readers. *Children's Literature; Reading Guidance; Book Discussion Groups*

C*

242. **Read for the Fun of It: Active Programming with Books for Children**, by Caroline Feller Bauer. Wilson, 1992. 372p. $45. 0-8242-0824-2.

This book of practical programming ideas aims to foster and support literature-based learning programs. It is intended for all who are interested in bringing books and children together—parents, librarians, and teachers. The strength of this book is the numerous lists arranged by age and interest; as well, there are lists for reading aloud, storytelling, and professional reading. This bibliography is recommended for all school and public library collections for ready reference, reading guidance, programming, and collection development. *Children's Literature; Reading Guidance*

C

243. **Stories: A List of Stories to Tell and Read Aloud**, ed. by Marilyn Berg Iarusso. 8th ed. New York Public Library , 1990. $6.

This booklet lists over 500 stories that are recommended for retelling or reading aloud by the members of the New York Public Library Stories Committee. Both traditional and modern tales are listed, along with some short stories and poetry. An alphabetical title arrangement is used, and for each entry there is a brief annotation that includes material on the plot, style and subject material. In-print sources are given for the stories. In a section called "For the Storyteller," there is a bibliography of books on storytelling, program planning, and basic reference tools, plus a listing of audiovisual sources.

Storytelling; Children's Literature

C*

244. **Storytelling: A Selected Annotated Bibliography**, by Ellin Greene and George Shannon. Garland, 1986. 183p. $31. 0-8240-8749-6.

From about 750 items located, the editors have chosen 262 for inclusion in this bibliography that includes entire books, chapters from books, and journal articles. They are arranged under such headings as "Beginnings," "Purposes and Values," "Art and Techniques of Storytelling," "Storytellers," "Library Story Hours," and "Bibliography and Indexes." Complete bibliographic information and a full descriptive annotation are given for each entry. There are author, title, and subject indexes. This is an excellent source for locating material on the whys and hows of storytelling and a help in building collections on this subject.

Storytelling

C

245. **The Storytime Sourcebook: A Compendium of Ideas and Resources for Storytellers**, by Carolyn N. Cullum. Neal-Schuman, 1990. 177p. $24.95 pap. 1-55570-067-5.

Using a subject arrangement from "alphabet" to "zoo," the author describes resources and activities for a variety of story hours. For each of the 100 topics, this guide suggests filmstrips, films or videos, books, crafts, fingerplays, and other activities. Additional lists include a title guide to each of the recommended filmstrips and videos that gives bibliographic information and publishers names, a directory of book publishers and media distributors, and indexes to recommended book titles, authors, crafts and activities. For children's rooms and primary school libraries. *Storytelling*

C*; Y*
246. **Tales of Love and Terror: Booktalking the Classics, Old and New**, by Hazel Rochman. American Library Association, 1987. 160p. $20. pap. 0-8389-0463-7.

Rochman demonstrates how to promote the pleasure of reading through booktalking, and, in a convincing introduction, she emphasizes the importance of booktalking. She contends: "The best booktalks are about those books I love and want to share ... always the emphasis is on pleasure." Rochman uses the thematic approach to booktalking and many titles are recommended throughout the text. As well, a series of lists are provided in the Appendix arranged by "Themes and Genres." Rochman's scope and style are quite different from Joni Bodart-Talbot's *Booktalk! 3*, but the two titles complement each other and both are recommended. Dorothy Broderick in *VOYA*, 10/87 stated: "*Tales of Love and Terror* belongs in every library." An accompanying videocassette (which can be used independently) is also available (see the following entry). *Book Talks; Children's Literature; Young Adult Literature*

C; Y
247. **Tales of Love and Terror: Booktalking the Classics, Old and New**, by Hazel Rochman. American Library Association, 1987. 25 min. VHS, Beta, ¾ inch U-matic, $135. 0-8389-2077-2.

This videocassette is meant to accompany the book by the same title (see above entry), but it can be used independently. It is based on the principle that many people can learn booktalking by watching someone else do it well. *Book Talks; Videocassettes; Children's Literature; Young Adult Literature*

C
248. **Those Bloomin' Books; A Handbook for Extending Thinking Skills**, by Carol Sue Kruise. Libraries Unlimited, 1986. 217p. $19.50. 0-87287-548-2.

Kruise applies the principles of Bloom's taxonomy to extend thinking levels in order to expand the uses of children's literature. Titles were selected for their diverse themes and include picture books, novels, and beginning to read books for children in grades K-6. This book, which is intended to introduce children to the critical thinking process, is recommended for all libraries serving children as a reading guidance tool and for building library collections. *Children's Literature; Bloom's Taxonomy; Critical Thinking*

C
249. **Using Children's Books in Reading/Language Arts Programs: A How-to-Do-it Manual for Library Applications**, by Diane D. Canavan and Lavonne Hayes. Neal-Schuman, 1992. 192p. $29.95. 1-55570-101-9.

This how-to-do-it manual also serves as a bibliography to enrich a whole-language classroom. The major sections deal with such topics as books with repetitive language, rhythm and rhyme, and rebus stories; books for developing vocabulary through word play, concepts, and literature; and books dealing with parts of speech, plot, setting, point of view, etc. The final chapter features titles dealing with reading, libraries, books, and writing. This short volume is recommended for all elementary school and many public libraries as a reference tool, programming guide, and guide to collection building.

Children's Literature; Language Arts; Reading

C; Y
250. **Using Picture Storybooks to Teach Literary Devices: Recommended Books for Children and Young Adults**, by Susan Hall. Oryx, 1990. 152p. $29.95. 0-89774-582-5.

Hall presents a convincing case for the use of quality picture storybooks to teach literary devices such as alliteration, allusion, and ambiguity. Following a number of brief introductory chapters are lists of picture storybooks alphabetically arranged under each literary device, which is also carefully defined. An index of authors and titles is provided. Recommended for school library media centers at all levels for use by teachers and as a library guide for reference and collection building.

Picture Books; Children's Literature; Young Adult Literature

8 Authors and Illustrators

C; Y

251. **American Writers for Children Before 1900**, ed. by Glenn E. Estes. Gale, 1985. 441p. $112. 0-8103-1720-6 (Dictionary of Literary Biography, 42).

This guide to 52 selected American authors of children's literature is really a bio-bibliography, but in addition to a well-written source of biographical and critical information, it serves as an excellent selection/buying guide. In addition to full bibliographic information on each author's work, each entry has a list of references about the authors or their works. The work is arranged alphabetically by the biographee. This is a recommended purchase for all public libraries and others that can afford its rather steep price.

Children's Literature; Authors, American

C; Y

252. **American Writers for Children Since 1960: Poets, Illustrators; and Nonfiction Authors**, ed. by Glenn E. Estes. Gale, 1987. 430p. $112. 0-8103-1739-7 (Dictionary of Literary Biography, 61).

Continuing the tradition of the excellent DLB series, this standard reference complements two other volumes in the series published by Gale and still in print: *American Writers for Children Before 1900* (see above entry) and *American Writers for Children, 1900-1960* (1983, $112, 0-8103-1146-1). This volume is also similar to others in the series in that it is arranged alphabetically by biographee. It also includes full bibliographical information of all books by and about the author. Its only real limitation is that only 32 authors and illustrators are included. Again, this work is recommended for all libraries that can afford it.

Children's Literature; Authors, American

C; Y

253. **Authors of Books for Young People**, by Martha E. Ward et al. 3rd ed. Scarecrow, 1990. 780p. $59.50. 0-8108-2293-8.

This revised and updated edition contains 3,708 entries and incorporates material from the 2nd ed. (1971) and its 1979 supplement, plus adding almost 300 new entries. Emphasis has been on authors whose biographies have been difficult to locate; therefore, this work tends to supplement rather than duplicate several standard juvenile authors biographical sources such as *Twentieth-Century Children's Writers* (St. James, 1989. $115. 0-912289-95-3). The information generally has been compiled from the files of the Quincy (Illinois) Public Library. The brief entries are arranged in alphabetical order by the author's last name. Each entry includes a brief biographical sketch and examples of the author's publications with bibliographic information. While this guide is more useful for reference work than collection building, it is still recommended for most school and public libraries because of the many authors included who are not found in other sources. *Authors; Children's Literature; Young Adult Literature*

C; Y

254. **Biographical Index to Children's and Young Adult Authors and Illustrators**, by David V. Loertscher. Libraries Unlimited, 1992. 225p. $45. 0-931510-40-6.

Over 13,000 international authors, illustrators, poets, filmmakers, and cartoonists from both collective and single biographies are included in this up-to-date index. Audiovisual resources are also included. More than 1,500 biographical works are indexed including the standard adult and juvenile reference sources: *Contemporary Authors* and *Something about the Author*, and the well-known Wilson author series. Each entry includes name, birth/death year, and country or state of birth, as well as a list of additional sources of information. This comprehensive guide is recommended for most school and public libraries as a handy reference tool and aid to collection development.

Authors; Illustrators; Children's Literature; Young Adult Literature

C*
255. **Black Authors and Illustrators of Children's Books: A Biographical Dictionary,** by Barbara Rollock. 2nd ed. Garland, 1992. 234p. $35. 0-8240-7078-X.

Rollock, a former Coordinator of Children's Services at the New York Public Library, has updated this much needed reference tool by adding 35 new entries to this second edition and revising most of the original 115 biographies to what is really a bio-bibliography. The authors and illustrators that are included in the "Bibliographical Sources and References" are added bonuses and helpful for both reader's advisory work and collection development. Of particular interest are the four appendixes: "Awards and Honor Books," "Publishers' Series," " Publishers and Bookstores," and "Distributors." A detailed index completes the work. This standard reference work is recommended for all school and public libraries serving children.
Children's Literature; Authors, African American; Illustrators, African American

C
256. **Children's Authors and Illustrators: An Index to Biographical Dictionaries,** by Joyce Nakamura. 4th ed. Gale, 1987 799p $150. 0-8103-2525-X.

This is not so much a collection building tool as a guide to locating biographical material on 25,000 children's authors and illustrators. However, the listing of the 450 reference books analyzed to find the 145,000 biographical entries included might be of some value in making children's librarians aware of the variety of biographical sources available in the field of children's literature.
Children's Literature; Authors; Illustrators

C; Y
257. **Major Authors and Illustrators for Children and Young Adults: A Selection of Sketches from** *Something about the Author*, by Laurie Collier and Joyce Nakamura. Gale, 1992. 6v. $265. 0-8103-7702-0.

The purpose of this work is simply to make data about authors known to patrons of small libraries that cannot afford the more extensive (and more expensive) *Something about the Author* series. *Major...* has selected 800 sketches of the better-known authors and illustrators of children's books whose works are widely read. Each entry includes a brief biographical sketch, a portrait, a list of writings, and a bibliography of additional information. This should prove to be a useful reference guide and selection aid for school libraries and smaller public libraries as a supplement/complement to the very familiar *Sixth Book of Junior Authors and Illustrators.* *Children's Literature; Authors; Young Adult Literature; Illustrators*

C; Y
258. **Photography in Books for Young People,** by Martha E. Ward and Dorothy E. Ward. Scarecrow, 1985. 93p. $20. 0-8108-1854-X.

The stated purpose of this bio-bibliography is to give due recognition to photographers as illustrators of books for young people. The authors note that no children's book using photographs has ever won a Caldecott Award. The first part of this slim book discusses the uses and history of photography in children's books. A list of more than 240 photographers arranged alphabetically make up the heart of this bio-bibliography. This work is a starting point in a field that is virtually ignored, and as such it is recommended for most libraries that serve children and young people and/or have special collections relating to photography. *Children's Literature; Photography; Illustrators*

C*; Y
259. **Sixth Book of Junior Authors and Illustrators,** by Sally Holmes Holtze. Wilson, 1989. 350p. $40. 0-8242-077-7.

Kunitz and Haycraft were responsible for the first *Junior Book of Authors* (2nd ed., 1951, $32. 0-8242-0028-4) over forty years ago. There have been periodic continuations that are similar in scope and coverage. This, the most current volume, provides detailed biographical sketches, autographs and portraits of 243 young adult and children's authors and illustrators, plus lists of their works. The latter is of some value in selection although the primary use of this classic series is to supply basic biographical information.
Authors; Illustrators; Children's Literature; Young Adult Literature

C; Y
260. **Something about the Author,** Ed. by Anne Commire. Gale, $79 per volume.

There are now almost 70 volumes in this set that covers over 7,500 authors and illustrators. Entries are of two kinds; the first gives only a brief introduction to the subject and his or her work, the second gives in-depth profiles that extend over several pages and are illustrated with photographs, dust jacket art and, when appropriate, examples of the subject's illustrations. In addition to career and personal data, these entries also include excerpts from letters and diaries, detailed chronologies, and author comments. For each of these entries there are two bibliographies, the first of primary sources, and the second of secondary biography and critical information. These can be of value in collection development. There are two other series that also contain bibliographic material, although each is primarily a source for biographical information. *Yesterday's Authors of Books for Children* ($82 per volume) series now contains two volumes and highlights authors and illustrators from early times to 1960, and *Something about the Author Autobiography Series* ($76. per volume), now has over a dozen volumes, each of which contains autobiographical essays by about 20 authors and illustrators of books for young people. Libraries should also consider *Major Authors and Illustrators for Children and Young Adults: A Selection of Sketches from Something about the Authors*. These excellent series are unfortunately often too expensive for many individual school or public libraries to acquire but perhaps they can be purchased for school district collections, public libraries and, certainly, academic institutions that support children's literature courses.

Children's Literature; Young Adult Literature; Authors; Illustrators

C

261. **They Wrote for Children Too: An Annotated Bibliography of Children's Literature by Famous Writers for Adults**, comp. by Marilyn Fain Apseloff. Greenwood, 1989. 202p. $37.95. 0-313-25981-X.

Included in this unusual bibliography are picture books, poetry, stories, drama, and nonfiction for children by famous authors who normally write for adults. For example, there are works by Faulkner, Menotti, Stein, Chaucer, Tennyson, Tolstoy, and over 100 others. In addition to exposing children to good literature, it is the compiler's hope "that this bibliography will spur renewed interest in some of the books and serve to bring them back into print." The volume is divided into three major parts: Pre-nineteenth, nineteenth, and twentieth-century literature. Within each section, the titles are arranged by form, e.g., picture books, poetry, biography, etc. Authors from many countries are represented, though the vast majority are American or British. About 400 different titles are included in over 500 entries. The work concludes with complete author/translator/reteller/ illustrator, title, and subject indexes. This work is recommended for most school media centers, public libraries, and other libraries serving children for reference and collection development. *Children's Literature; Authors*

C; Y

262. **Writers for Children: Critical Studies of Major Authors since the Seventeenth Century**, by Jane M. Bingham. Scribner, 1988. 661p. $95. 0-684-18165-7.

This critical guide examines 84 writers from the seventeenth to the early twentieth century whose books have become classics for young people. The entries are arranged alphabetically by author; each entry, which average about six or eight pages, includes biographical information as well as a critical essay. This is followed by a bibliography of primary and secondary works. A detailed index to the authors and all books and stories mentioned is provided. This well-written book is recommended for academic, public, and school libraries as reference book and as a guide to collection development.

Children's Literature; Authors

9 Nonprint and Vertical File Media

C

263. **All Ears: How to Use and Choose Recorded Music for Children**, by Jill Jarnow. Viking/Penguin, 1991. $19.95; $9.95 pap.

An annotated guide to recordings for children, intended for parents, teachers, and children's librarians. In addition to the list of recommended titles, the guide contains brief profiles of popular stars such as Rosenshontz and Sharon, and recognizes the contributions of such early leaders as Ella Jenkins and Pete Seeger. Entries are indexed by subject and age. Recommended for elementary school and public libraries serving children. *Music—Children; Phonorecordings*

C*; Y*

264. **American Library Association's Best of the Best for Children: Software - Books - Magazines - Video**, ed. by Denise Perry Donavin. Random House, 1992. 572p. $30. 0-679-40450-3; $20. pap. 0-679-74250-6.

This list of recommended titles representing a variety of media, uses as its basis various lists issued by the Association for Library Service to Children and the Young Adult Library Service Association both of the American Library Association. These, such as the many annual "notable" lists, are known for the high quality of the selections included. This master compilation has sections on various formats beginning with books (including basic reference sources for youngsters), followed by magazines, video cassettes, audio sources, computer software, toys, and travel. Subdivisions are used to indicate age level suitability, and each item is nicely annotated. Inserts on pages are often used to cover specific topics such as drugs. Although parents and teachers will find this bibliography of greatest use, librarians can also use it for reading guidance as well as a buying guide for basic materials for children and early adolescents.
Audiovisual Materials; Children's Literature; Young Adult Literature

265. (This entry number not used.)

C*; Y*

266. **Best Videos for Children and Young Adults: A Core Collection for Libraries**, by Jennifer Jung Gallant. ABC-CLIO, 1990. 185p. $39. 0-87436-561-9.

This list of about 350 nontheatrical videos produced during the past 15 years includes items especially useful for children and young adults from preschool through grade 12. Gallant, who is the AV editor of *VOYA*, based her selections on content, production quality, and potential use—curricular as well as recreational. All of the selected titles were reviewed favorably. The videos are arranged alphabetically by title, and each entry includes director, producer, distributor, release date, cost, etc. Also a brief annotation and suggestions for use and audience level are included. The work is well indexed by subject/title and information on distributors, and video sources are provided. This useful bibliography is a must purchase for all school and public libraries that have or are considering a video collection for children.
Videocassettes

C*; Y*

267. **Books and Films on Death and Dying for Children and Adolescents: An Annotated Bibliography,** ed. by Eva Murphy and the Good Grief Program Volunteer Staff. Good Grief Program, 1988. 30p. $4. 0-944364-02-0.

The Good Grief Program of the Judge Baker Guidance Center in Boston, Massachusetts, was established to help schools and other community groups that work with young people to serve as a support group for young people when a classmate or friend dies. This very brief bibliography contains fiction and nonfiction book and film titles for various age groups. Its available for only $4 from: The Good Grief Program, 295 Longwood Ave., Boston, MA 02115. *Death and Dying*

C

268. **Buy Me! Buy Me! The Bank Street Guide to Choosing Toys for Children,** by Joanne F. Oppenheim. Pantheon, 1987. 311p. $11.95 (pap.) 0-394-75546-4.

This guide, whose purpose is to help in the wise purchase of toys, begins with an overview of the toy industry, the types of toys marketed and the effects (often harmful) that these toys can have on children. The second section describes specific toys that are suitable for different types of children and at different developmental and age levels. Recommendations are made plus suggestions on making homemade toys. In the third section there are directories of catalog companies, manufacturers and parent action groups. This book will be useful in work with parents and teachers as well as supplying a fine buying guide for librarians.

Toys

C

269. **Children's Media Market Place,** by Dolores Blythe Jones. 3rd ed. Neal-Schuman, 1988, 397p. $45 pap. 1-55570-007-1.

About every five years a new edition of this directory of sources related to children's media appears. Although much of the material included will facilitate the acquisition process in children's collection, it is not primarily a bibliographic reference book (except for three sections on periodicals for children, parents and professionals, and an bibliography of selection tools). The first part, "Directory of Children's Media Sources" covers such areas as publishers, audiovisual and software producers, wholesalers, bookstores, book clubs, literary agents, museums, and appropriate personnel in state libraries and library organizations. In the second part, information for each entry in part one is given including names, addresses and related material. A fantastic collection of material principally related to preschool through ninth grade.

Children's Literature; Instructional Materials

C*

270. **Choosing the Best in Children's Video: A Guide for Parents and Everyone Who Cares about Kids.** ALA Video, 1990. 36 minutes, ½ VHS. $29.95 0-8389-2110-8.

This video cassette narrated by Christopher Reeve is an excellent guide to the best in children's video. Using many examples from existing videos, criteria for children's videos are explored, and ways in which children and parents can share viewing experiences are pointed out. An emphasis is placed on using television as a bridge to reading. Practical tips are given to assist in selection, such as identification of award winners. The tape ends with a list of sixty high-quality video titles, many of which had already been sampled within the film. This will be useful in many situations including in-service work and acquiring quality children's videos in libraries. *Videocassettes*

C*

271. **Creating Connections: Books, Kits and Games for Children: A Sourcebook,** by Betty P. Cleaver et al. Garland, 1986. 417p. $27. 0-8240-8798-4.

In addition to being an outstanding bibliography, this is a practical guide on integrating learning materials with the curriculum. Part I, called "The Process," shows how teachers from every discipline and a correspondingly large array of resources could be used in a sample unit on the topic of oceans. This section also includes a general resource guide to selection aids, bibliographies, and other basic titles. Part II is the largest section and consists of resource units on six topics: bodies, cities, monsters, mountains, oceans, and sound. After an introduction to each topic which incorporates material on approaches to studying the topic, there are extensive listings of materials that could be used. These are arranged by small topics and are for print as well as such nonprint media as slides, videos, models, kits, and games. Bibliographic information is given with annotations and grade range. There are almost 2,000 resources listed in the entire book. Most of the materials were published in the 1970s through 1985. There is an author/title index. Though an update would be welcome, this will still be very useful in elementary school libraries.

Children's Literature; Audiovisual Materials; Games

C*; Y*

272. **Educators Guide to Free Films**. Educators Progress Service. annual, $27.95 pap.

This is one of three paperbacks that list free materials in various audiovisual formats. The other two are *Educators Guide to Free Filmstrips and Slides* (annual, $20.50) and *Educators Guide to Free Videotapes* (annual, $24.95). The prices quoted are for the 1991-1992 editions. Orders should also include $1.75 per title for postage and handling. Each of the above titles have the same arrangement. The body of the work contains information on each title plus an indication of age suitability arranged under various subject area. This is preceded by a detailed table of contents and followed by several indexes: one by title, another by subject, and a third by source and availability. Here are given names and addresses of each of the organizations from which materials can be obtained and details concerning any limitation on use. Most of these films are available for free rental for limited periods of time and must be returned on a fixed schedule. Each of these section is printed on a different colored paper to facilitate use. These guides, like others in the series, have been in use for many years in America's schools and libraries and are available on a 15 day free approval basis. Enquiries and orders should be sent to: Educators Progress Service, 214 Center Street, Randolph, WI 53956. *Free Material; Films; Filmstrips; Slides; Videocassettes*

C; Y; A

273. **The Educators' Handbook to Interactive Videodiscs**, by Ed Schwartz. 2nd ed. Association for Educational Communications and Technology, 1987. 151p. $22.95. 0-89240-049-8.

The technology involved with interactive videodiscs is changing rapidly and therefore some of the material in this volume will need updating, but as a general introduction to the subject and the products available in 1987, this work still has value. The first section supplies general information on videodiscs, their technology, and uses in education. The remainder of the book is a guide to the hardware needed, including players, video monitors, and interfaces to connect to a computer, plus an extensive bibliography of the videodiscs available of interest to educators. This list is divided alphabetically by subject covered. The information given for each entry includes a description of the program, hardware needs, publisher, and price. This book will be used by teachers and librarians in schools and in academic institutions by their education departments. *Videodiscs—Education; Education*

C*; Y*; A*

274. **Educators Index of Free Materials**. Educators Progress Service, annual. $45.75.

This is one of the three guides produced by Educators Progress Service that lists only print material. This one covers material suitable for high school and colleges levels. For the elementary, junior high, and high school levels, there is *Educators Grade Guide to Free Teaching Materials* (annual, $43.75), and for elementary and middle school levels, there is the *Elementary Teachers Guide to Free Curriculum Materials* (annual $23.75). Each contains a listing of free pamphlet, picture, and chart materials, the first two in a loose-leaf format, and the third in a paperback book. Each contains a table of contents, a listing under subject headings of each of the materials with an annotation, a title index and subject index, and a source and availability index which provides names and addresses of the organizations from which materials can be obtained. Each of these bibliographies is revised annually. The prices quoted are for the 1991-1992 editions. They are available from Educators Progress Service, Inc., 214 Center Street, Randolph, WI 53956 for the above prices, plus $1.75 per guide for postage and handling. These are essential tools for building vertical file collections in school, academic, and public libraries. *Vertical File Materials; Free Material*

C; Y

275. **Free (and Almost Free) Things for Teachers**, by Susan Osborn. Perigee Books, 1990. $8.95 pap. 0-399-51635-2.

Although many of the 200 resources listed in this bibliography are print items, there are several nonprint items like a hand-held mini planetarium. Maximum cost is $5. In addition to descriptions of contents, complete ordering information is given in this useful little guide.

Free Material; Vertical File Materials

C

276. **Free Stuff for Kids**, by Ana Marie Gardner. Meadowbrook Press (Deephaven, MN), 1990. 130p. $6.25. 0-88166-182-1.

There are over 350 free or almost free (under $1) items listed here for youngsters, including booklets on pet care, a storybook cassette, and a hieroglyphics chart. The materials are offered by commercial firms, government agencies, and non-profit organizations. Instructions are given on how to obtain each item. This source book is available for $6.25 from Meadowbrook Press, 18318 Minnetonka Blvd., Deephaven, MN 55391. *Free Material; Vertical File Materials*

C; Y

277. **Free Things for Kids to Write Away For.** S. G. Kulka, [1990] $3.

This booklet lists about 300 free booklets, charts, maps, etc. that can be obtained for the asking. Full ordering instructions are supplied. A companion sourcebook is *A Few Thousand of the Best FREE Things in America.* The two booklets are available for $3 each from S. G. Kulka Co., Dept. 37, Warspite, Alberta, Canada T0A 3NO. *Free Material; Vertical File Materials*

C; Y

278. **From Page to Screen: Children's and Young Adult Books on Film and Video,** by Joyce Moss and George Wilson. Gale, 1992. 429 p. $35. 0-8103-7893-0.

This work covers 750 classic and contemporary works in children's and young adult literature that have been adapted into presentations on about 1,400 films, videos, or laser discs. This bibliography is organized alphabetically by the title of the book (some short stories, plays, poems, and folktales are also included). For each title, a brief summary and information is given on the author, publisher, and date. There follows a listing of screen adaptations, and for each of these, data such as title, production information, description of contents, awards, suitability, distributors, price, and format are given. Appendixes and indexes allow for access to this material by subject, age levels, film titles, distributors, and films for the hearing-impaired. An interesting additional feature is that each of the films is rated first by how closely it adheres to the plot and spirit of the original, and second by its over-all quality and appeal. Although some of these titles will also be found in *Best Videos for Children and Young Adults* and *Video Rating Guide for Libraries,* this listing is unique in its coverage and treatment. It is therefore highly recommended for both children's rooms and school libraries where there is need for this kind of material.

Children's Literature; Young Adult Literature; Motion Pictures; Videocassettes

C*

279. **Great Videos for Kids: A Parent's Guide to Choosing the Best,** by Catherine Cella. Citadel, 1992. 144p. $7.95 pap. 0-8065-1377-2.

This catalog of the best videos for children covers a variety of topics like animation, book-based videos, family topics, folk and fairy tales, holidays, and instructional films. Each is annotated, and in a preface the criteria used to judge these videos in outlined. The appendixes have interesting "the best" lists, like the best videos with positive black roles and the best with positive female roles. This will be useful in public libraries and elementary schools for use with parents and teachers and in collection building. *Videocassettes*

C

280. **Growing Up with Music: A Guide to the Best Recorded Music for Children,** by Laurie Sale. Avon, 1992. 256p. $10. pap. 0-380-76211-0.

This guide to recommended musical cassettes and CDs is organized into chapters that deal with such subject as lullabies, baby and toddler music, recordings for preschoolers, recordings for ages four through ten, holiday music, classical music, and recordings in French and Spanish. Recordings in each chapters are listed alphabetically by artist, and each citation is annotated. This be helpful in building collections in both children's rooms and elementary schools. *Music—Children; Compact Discs; Audiocassettes*

C*

281. **Guide to Videocassettes for Children,** by Diana Huss Green et al. Consumers Union, 1989. 270p. $13.95 (pap.). 0-89043-240-6.

Using twelve different subject headings like adventure, cartoon classics, folk and fairy tales, music, and dance, this valuable bibliography lists over 300 titles suitable for viewing by children. Professionals including teachers, psychologists, and librarians made the initial recommendations with television critics making the final decisions. Information supplied for each cassette cited includes date, director, producer, cast, age group suitability, and length. There are also annotations and suggestions of a book or two that could be used with the film. Additional lists include one of sources of videocassettes and another of the cassette titles arranged by age group. There is also a title index. This paperback volume will be of value in both public and school libraries where videocassettes are being purchased by librarians and parents.

Videocassettes

C
282. **High/Scope Buyer's Guide to Children's Software 1992: Annual Survey of Computer Programs for Children Aged 3 to 7.** High/Scope Press, 1992.

This volume contains over five hundred reviews, information about the software market, and descriptions of the High/Scope Award for Excellence winners. For each entry there are descriptions, evaluations, and producers' addresses, as well as screen samples given for the majority of the programs discussed. Additional features in this guide are a computer terminology glossary, a description of the evaluation process, and a directory of national software manufacturers. This will be very useful in elementary and preschool libraries. For information on price and ordering write: High/Scope Educational Research Foundation, 600 N. River St., Ypsilanti, MI 48198-2898. *Computer Software*

C
283. **The Kids' Catalog Collection: A Selective Guide to More Than 500 Catalogs,** by Jane Smolik. Globe Pequot Press (Chester, Conn.), 1990. 276p. $11.95 (pap.). 0-87106-433-2.

Anyone interested in shopping for children, including librarians and teachers in preschools, elementary schools, and public libraries, will be fascinated by this bibliography of catalogs for over 500 companies that specialize in all kinds of products for youngsters from toys and educational games to furniture and costumes. The catalogs are listed under 24 major categories that cover about 135 special areas of interest. Directory information is given for each company including telephone numbers and addresses and there are indexes by company name and by area of interest. Most of the catalogs are free—an additional reason for using this bibliography in situations where purchases of items for children are being made.

Products for Children; Catalogs—Commercial

C
284. **Kits, Games and Manipulatives for the Elementary School Class-room: A Sourcebook,** by Andrea C. Hoffman and Ann M. Glannon. Garland, 1993. 629p. $94. 0-8240-5342-7.

This unique sourcebook was produced by two librarians who recognized the importance of tactile and hands-on materials as classroom resources. About 1,400 available kits, games, and manipulatives are arranged within six subject categories: reading and language arts, mathematics, social studies, science and health, arts, and other subjects. Helpful information, such as grade level, price, format, source, etc., are provided under each entry. An extensive and useful descriptor index and author and title indexes are also provided. A directory of sources completes the work. This "catalog" should be available in every elementary school media center as well as academic libraries with elementary school education programs.

Games; Audiovisual Materials

C
285. **Notable Children's Films and Videos, Filmstrips, and Recordings, 1973-1986,** by the Association for Library Service to Children. American Library Association, 1987. 118p. $8.95 (pap.). 0-8389-3342-4.

Each year the Association for Library Service to Children compiles a list of the best films, videos, filmstrips, and recordings for children released that year. This list represents 14 years of these lists, from 1973 through 1983. This bibliography contains over 400 items arranged into three sections by format. For each entry, full citations are given, including length, grade level, price, and rental information. There are separate indexes by subject, author, illustrator, and producer. This list will be helpful (particularly if used with the subsequent annual lists) to children's librarians both for program planning and collection building.

Children's Films; Films; Videocassettes; Filmstrips; Children's Recordings; Phonorecordings

C*; Y*
286. **Only the Best, 1993: The Annual Guide to the Highest-Rated Educational Software, Preschool-Grade 12,** by Shirley Boes Neill and George W. Neill. Association for Supervision and Curriculum Development, 1993. $22.

Earlier editions of this guide were published by Bowker. The present volume is part of an annual listing of microcomputer software programs that have received the highest rating from many evaluation services in the U.S. and Canada. The entries are first listed alphabetically, serving as a title index. Then, annotated entries, which briefly describe noting system compatibility, usage tips, and grade level, are listed under broad headings such as Arts, Early Childhood Education, Foreign Language, Language Arts, Mathematics, Science, Typing, etc. Each entry also includes cost and ordering information. There is a cumulative guide, *Only the Best, 1985-93,* on disk (Mac or IBM) for $99. Details are available from the Curriculum/Technology Resource Center, Association for Supervision and Curriculum Development, 1250 N. Pitt St., Alexandria VA 122314. *Computer Software; Microcomputers*

C; Y

287. A Parent's Guide to Video Games: A Practical Guide to Selecting & Managing Home Video Games, by Jason R. Rich. DMS CA, 1991. $4.95. 0-9625057-7-3.

More and more libraries are acquiring video games for both in-library use and for circulating collections. This paperback reviews more than 40 video games. They are rated for overall content, educational value, quality of graphics, amount of violence, etc. The first part of the book presents criteria for choosing and also other hints on acquiring games. This is a helpful guide for libraries maintaining or developing collections of video games. *Games; Video Games*

C*; Y*

288. Recommended Videos for Schools, ed. by Beth Blenz-Clucas and Gloria Gribble. ABC-CLIO, 1991. 213p. $50. 0-87436-644-5.

The focus of this guide is the curriculum rather than entertainment or recreational videos. About 400 reviews were culled from approximately 2,000 reviews in the 1990 issues of *Video Rating Guide for Libraries* (a quarterly guide also published by ABC-CLIO). They represent the "best recently released educational videos for K to 12 audiences." Arranged by subject areas such as math, environment and ecology, performing arts, social issues, etc., the reviews include a content summary, recommended grade level, use policy, and price. Each entry also receives a rating from 3 to 5 ("good," to "must have"). Full imprint information useful for ordering and cataloging is also provided. This guide differs somewhat from a similar guide by the same publisher: Gallant's *Best Videos for Children and Young Adults* which lists 350 more public library oriented videos. *Recommended Videos...* is recommended for all school media centers for planning or maintaining a video collection. *Videocassettes*

C

289. Toy Buying Guide, by Judy Braiman-Lipson et al. Consumer Reports, 1988. 282p. $7 (pap.) 0-89043-8.

Based on surveys involving 12,000 households, this work rates about 400 toys in such areas as play value, educational value, and durability. The book is organized into 12 chapters each dealing with a specific kind of toy such as school toys, action toys, and construction playsets. In each entry, the toy and its uses are described and material is given on its numerical survey ratings. In an appendix, the top-rated toys are listed by category. This catalog will be of value in school or library settings where various toys are being purchased or where advice on the purchase of toys is requested. *Toys*

C

290. Toys for Growing: A Guide to Toys That Develop Skills, by Mary Sinker. Year Book Medial Publishers, 1986. 170p. $9.95 (pap.) 0-8151-7750-X.

This book, which concentrates on toys appropriate for children from birth through age six, was prepared from testing toys available at the National Lekotek Center in Evanston, Illinois. An introductory section deals with the various kinds of development that occurs during early childhood and the types of toys that are appropriate at each stage. There follows a large section in which specific toys are discussed under such headings as tactile toys, language play, puzzles, electronic toys, and books. Illustrations and text are used to describe the toys, evaluations are given, and there is information on manufacturers, availability and cost. This resource will be of great value in preschool institutions, elementary schools, and any academic or public library where information of this sort is needed by teachers, parents or students. *Toys*

10 Special Areas and Subjects

General and Miscellaneous

C
291. **Children and Gardens: An Annotated Bibliography of Children's Garden Books 1829-1988**, by Heather Miller. Council on Botanical and Horticultural Libraries, 1991. 60p. pap. $6. 0-9621791-1-6. (CBHL Plant Bibliography, 8).

There are descriptions in this bibliography of 300 fiction and nonfiction children's books that deal with gardens. The list is divided by four time periods. For specialized collections, this pamphlet is available for $6 plus $1 postage from The Council on Botanical and Horticultural Libraries, c/o The Library, New York Botanical Garden, Bronx, NY 10458. *Children's Literature; Gardening*

C
292. **Crafts Index for Young People**, by Mary Anne Pilger. Libraries Unlimited, 1992. $32.50. 1-56308-002-8.

Pilger has consulted more than 1,000 books in order to compile this index of craft projects; these are listed in the back of the work in numerical order. The individual craft entries are listed by subject in alphabetical order; each entry contains the number and page of the master list. The extensive list of craft books serves as a starting point for building up a collection of craft books for elementary school and children's departments of public libraries. *Handicraft*

C*; Y
293. **Dogs, Cats and Horses: A Resource Guide to the Literature for Young People**, by Charlene Strickland. Libraries Unlimited, 1990. 225p. $26.50. 0-87287-719-1.

This is a unique bibliography of the best of both fiction and nonfiction titles for youngsters in both the elementary and secondary grades on dogs, cats, and horses. Each of the three major sections is devoted to a single animal with further divisions by fiction and nonfiction. Each entry contains bibliographic information, subjects, suitability, setting, period, sequels, and an annotation. There is a subject, title, and author index. There are also, at about the same price as the print version, computerized data discs of this bibliography in versions for Apple, Macintosh, and IBM computers that allow it to be modified and adjusted to accommodate additions or deletions. This is recommended for both school (best at the elementary and junior high levels) and public libraries.

Dogs; Horses; Cats; Children's Literature; Young Adult Literature

C; Y
294. **Fun for Kids II: An Index to Children's Craft Books**, by Marion F. Gallivan. Scarecrow, 1992. 482 p. $42.50. 0-8108-2546-5.

Fun for Kids (Scarecrow, 1981, $25., 0-8108-1439-0), the original volume in this series, was published in 1981. This continuation of the parent volume indexes more than 300 craft books for youngsters in preschool grades through the eighth grade, published between 1981 and 1990. The first part of this book is a listing of the books indexed, and the second is a subject index with reference to the author of the book, appropriate page numbers, grade level suitability, and the material needed. Lastly, there is an index to the kinds of material used, e.g., burlap. This will be a great help to everyone responsible for providing craft activities for children and for librarians. It can also be used as an acquisition tool. *Handicraft*

C
295. **Glad Rags: Stories and Activities Featuring Clothes for Children**, by Jan Irving and Robin Currie. Libraries Unlimited, 1987. 276p. $22.50 0-87287-562-8.

This is basically a book of literature-enrichment activities for preschoolers and elementary school children centered on the theme of clothes, their care, and specific types of apparel like hats and shoes. The lists of children's books that can be used for these activities and the resource bibliography will both be helpful in collection development. *Clothing and Dress; Children's Literature*

C; Y; A
296. **Horse Stories: An Annotated Bibliography of Books for All Ages**, by Terri Wear. Scarecrow, 1987. 277p. $29.50 0-8108-1998-8.

This is an annotated bibliography of 1,537 books of fiction on horses and related animals like donkeys, toy horses, mules, and ponies. They are arranged by age groups: picture books, easy readers, juniors, young adults, and adults. In- and out-of-print titles are included, but in-print titles are indicated (about ⅓ are in-print). The annotations are descriptive but do not comment on the illustrations in picture books. Anthologies of short stories are included but not given analytics. There are title and subject indexes. It will be used more for advising readers than in collection development. *Horses*

C
297. **Introducing Children to the Arts: A Practical Guide for Librarians and Educators**, by Lea Burroughs. Hall, 1988. 306p. $35. 0-8161-8818-1.

For each of the seven arts (architecture, art, dance, music, poetry, story and theater), the author explains the basic structure and the history of the art form and how children react and experience it at various levels. Detailed ideas for workshops are given, plus hints for working with special children. For collection development, at the end of each chapter, there is an extensive bibliography of recommended books, films, discs, and videos. Many are acknowledged classics in the field, but others date from as late as the 1980s. This book will be of particular interest to children's rooms in public libraries as well as libraries in elementary schools. *Children's Literature; Audiovisual Materials; Education*

C
298. **Literature-Based Moral Education: Children's Books and Activities...**, by Linda Leonard Lamme et al. Oryx, 1992. 145p. $24.50 pap. 0-89774-723-2.

This timely and much-needed bibliography of children's books and instructional activities on moral education was compiled by university professors in elementary education. The books selected deal with self-esteem, responsibility, sharing, truthfulness, solving conflicts, perseverance, patience, and many other related topics; they are arranged in broad thematic chapters. Entries include an annotation which suggests possible classroom, library, or home use. Recommended grade levels are also suggested. The book is recommended for all children's and elementary school libraries for use by teachers, librarians, and parents.
Moral Education

Multicultural Resources

General and Miscellaneous

C; Y
299. **Cultural Diversity Videos**, by Phyllis Levy Mandell. Cahners Reprint Services. 1992. 4 parts. $2.50 each.

This series of bibliographies were compiled by the Audiovisual Review Editor of *School Library Journal* and originally appeared in that magazine. Part I, a 16-page pamphlet, deals with African Americans and includes annotations for 209 recommended videos for children and young adults; Part 2 lists 89 videos on Native Americans; Part 3 contains 105 videos on Asian Americans; and Part 4 lists 92 videos on the Hispanic American experience. The set succeeds in its purpose of helping children and young adult librarians in developing collections that reflect the cultural diversity of America. Each is available for $2.50 for up to 100 copies ($2 for more over 100) from Cathy Dionne, Cahneers Reprint Services, 1350 Touhy Ave., Des Plaines, IL 60017. Minimum orders are $25 and must be prepaid. Visa and Mastercard accepted. Telephone (800) 523-9654.

Videocassettes; African Americans; Asian Americans;
Multiculturalism; Hispanic Americans; Indians of North America

C; Y
300. **Developing Multicultural Awareness through Children's Literature: A Guide for Teachers and Librarians, Grades K-8**, by Patricia L. Roberts and Nancy Lee Cecil. McFarland, 1993. 216p. $24.95. 0-89950-879-0.

The authors have compiled an interesting bibliography of about 240 titles of multicultural fiction, folk literature, and biography suitable for elementary through junior high school youngsters and intended to portray positive cultural differences and "modify cultural stereotypes." The titles are listed under five major sections: African American, Asian American, European-American, Latino American, and Native American. Each section is further divided by grade levels, K-3 and 4-8. Each listing contains complete bibliographic information and a descriptive annotation. As well, many of the entries cite a target activity and possibly a list of related books-to-read activities. This relatively inexpensive work should prove to be a useful addition to most multicultural materials collections in schools and public libraries.

Multiculturalism; Children's Literature

C; Y
301. **The Human Family... Learning to Live Together: Books for Children and Adults**. National Council of Christians and Jews, annual.

Each of these annual booklists contains an annotated bibliography of approximately 50 recommended titles that successfully portray relationships among people of different origins, races, and religions. Some adult books are included as well as books written for children and young adults. This brochure is free with a stamped #10 envelope sent to National Conference of Christians and Jews, Inc., 71 Fifth Ave., Ste. 1100, New York, NY 10003   *Children's Literature; Young Adult Literature; Human Relations; Multiculturalism*

C
302. **Light a Candle! The Jewish Experience in Children's Books**. New York Public Library, 1993.

This annotated bibliography of 108 titles which celebrates Jewish life, past and present, was compiled by a committee of children's librarians at the New York Public Library. The work is divided into six sections: Celebrations and Observances; Tales of Tradition; Journeys—To a New Life; In Many Lands...; The Holocaust; and New Lives, New Hopes. Copies cost $4.00 plus $1.00 for shipping charges for 1-5 copies; $1.25 for 6-10 copies. Write to: Office of Branch Libraries, The New York Public Library, 455 5th Ave., New York, NY 10016   *Children's Literature; Jews*

C
303. **Literature for Children about Asians and Asian Americans: Analysis and Annotated Bibliography, with Additional Readings for Adults**, by Esther C. Jenkins and Mary C. Austin. Greenwood, 1987. 303p. $45. 0-313-25970-4. (Bibliographies and Indexes in World Literature, 12).

The authors state that "this volume ... is devoted to literature for young people of and about Asians and Asian Americans...." It includes Chinese, Japanese, Koreans, and various other culture groups. This guide is intended for teachers and librarians, and the criteria used for selecting books which are outlined in the introduction is a special bonus. The selected titles of books for children, young adults, and adults are arranged under each major cultural group; the number of titles varies from about 80 pages for the Japanese to just a few pages for Indonesians. Each entry has full bibliographic data, an annotation, and a suggested grade level. There also author/translator/illustrator, title, and subject indexes. This bibliography is particularly useful in developing collections to enhance the current curriculum in multiculturalism and is therefore recommended for all elementary schools and public libraries.

Asia; Asian Americans; Children's Literature

C; Y
304. **The Multicolored Mirror: Cultural Substance in Literature for Children and Young Adults**, Ed. by Merri V. Lindgren. Highsmith, 1992. 195p. $29. 0-917846-05-2.

Many questions were raised during a 1991 Conference of the Cooperative Children's Book Center. The papers presented by many noted authors are published in this series of essays edited by Lindgren and dealing with many aspects of our cultural heritage as portrayed in children's and young adult literature. Much of what is included in this brief account will be of value to both teachers and librarians as they get more and more involved in the role of multicultural literature in our changing society. Undoubtedly, the most valuable part of this book are the lengthy and detailed bibliographies of multicultural literature. They are useful both as reference and collection development aids, and perhaps they justify the acquisition of this interesting work. *Children's Literature; Multiculturalism; Young Adult Literature*

C; Y
305. **Multicultural Children's and Young Adult Literature: A Selected Listing of Books Published between 1980-88**, Comp. by Ginny Moore Kruse and Kathleen T. Horning. Cooperative Children's Book Center, [1989]. 38p. $3.

The Cooperative Children's Book Center at the University of Wisconsin, Madison is a noncirculating study and research center for children's and young adult literature, established for adults such as teachers, librarians, and other professionals. The titles in this bibliography of carefully selected and annotated books are recommended by the CCBC as being "high quality children's and young adult books innovative in style, important in theme, and/or unusual in insight." The books are arranged in alphabetical order by author under such subjects as Seasons and Celebrations, Issues in Today's World, Picture Books, etc. An index is provided. This oversized booklet is available free to Wisconsin residents or $3.00 to others from: Publications, Friends of the CCBC, Inc., Box 5288, Madison, WI 53705.

Multiculturalism; Children's Literature; Young Adult Literature

C

306. **Multicultural Folktales: Stories to Tell Young Children**, by Judy Sierra and Robert Kaminski. Oryx, 1991. $26.50. pap. 0-89774-688-0.

Twenty-five folktales from a number of cultures are contained in this collection which includes ideas for puppets, flannelboard presentations, and other practical ideas. The stories are arranged into two age categories: 2 ½ to 5, and 5 to 7. An added bonus to this idea book are the suggestions of stories/books with similar themes mentioned with each tale. An extensive bibliography list numerous collections and picture books that are also useful for storytelling or book talks. *Children's Literature; Multiculturalism*

C

307. **Multicultural Projects Index: Things to Make and Do to Celebrate Festivals, Cultures, and Holidays around the World**, by Mary Anne Pilger. Libraries Unlimited, 1992. 200p. $35. 0-87287-867-8.

At long last we have an index that provides teachers and librarians with sources of projects to make for festivals and holidays celebrated around the world and by the many ethnic groups in the United States. Pilger has done a tremendous job, and of course the list of more than 1,100 numbered titles from which the projects come is invaluable for collection development. The only real limitation to this otherwise goldmine, is the fact that many of the sources may be out of print because many go back as far as the 1960's. Still, this work, along with Pilger's other 1992 companion index, *Crafts Index for Young People*, should prove useful as a reference tool and selection guide for all libraries that serve teachers, librarians, and parents of young children. *Projects; Multiculturalism*

C*; Y*

308. **Our Family, Our Friends, Our World: An Annotated Guide to Significant Multicultural Books for Children and Teenagers**, by Lyn Miller-Lachmann. Bowker, 1992. 709p. $46. 0-8352-3025-2.

This very comprehensive guide claims to be global in scope; it deals with cultures, politics, geography, and pressing issues facing people from around the neighborhood to around the world. It includes books published in English from the U.S. and Canada since 1970. Each chapter includes a introductory summary, a map, and an annotated list of books for grades preschool through 12.

A similar work, but not much more than an oversized pamphlet, is Kruse and Horning's *Multicultural Children's and Young Adult Literature....* The publisher of *Our Family...* claims to have the first work of its kind; it certainly is the most extensive book currently available on a very timely topic. It is highly recommended for all school and public libraries building collections in this area.

Multiculturalism; Children's Literature; Young Adult Literature

C

309. **Rainbow Collection: Multicultural Children's Books**. Minneapolis Public Library, [1992].

Intended for children of all ages, this fully annotated list contains about 200 multicultural titles. The entries are arranged under broad and rather popular headings such as "People and Places," "Families Together," and "Seasons and Celebrations." This attractive booklet is available for $3.00 including postage and handling. For quantity discounts contact Kathleen Johnson (612 372-6532) or write to the address below. Make checks payable to the Minneapolis Public Library and send orders to: Children's Department, Minneapolis Public Library, 300 Nicollet Mall, Minneapolis, MN 55401-1992.

Children's Literature; Multiculturalism

C

310. **Reflections of the Rainbow**. Michigan Library Association, [1992].

Over 70 recent multicultural picture books are listed in this timely little pamphlet. The attractively illustrated work is divided into two sections: "Multicultural America" and the "Multicultural World." All titles have a brief annotation and enough bibliographic data for acquisition purposes. The cost is $5.00 for 50 booklets plus $1.00 for shipping. Order from and make checks payable to: Michigan Library Association, 1000 Long Boulevard, Suite 1, Lansing, MI 48911. *Multiculturalism; Picture Books*

C

311. **Religious Books for Children: An Annotated Bibliography,** by Patricia Pearl Dole. Church and Synagogue Library Association, 1993. 40p. $8.35. pap. 0-915324-21-0.

Pearl, a Presbyterian church librarian, has compiled this bibliography of 350 titles with the intention of having it serve "primarily as a guide for the selection of children's religious books and secondarily for the evaluation of this area in library collections." In other words, she has attempted to create a basic collection that would meet the needs of very diverse religious organizations, or perhaps even lay-organizations with collections of religious materials. The emphasis here is the Judeo-Christian faith (only three of the 36 pages are devoted to Buddhism, Islam, Hinduism, Native American faiths and Sikhism). Every entry has a brief annotation, recommended age level (preschool through grade six), and enough bibliographic information for ordering, including prices as of 1993. All entries are arranged by a specific subject, but author and title indexes are also provided. This slim, inexpensive, and well-done bibliography is recommended for many types of religious libraries and, because of its emphasis, especially Christian church libraries. *Children's Literature; Religious Literature*

C

312. **Teaching Multicultural Literature in Grades K-8**, ed. by Violet J. Harris. Christopher-Gordon, 1992. 296p. $31.95. 0-926842-13-7.

Harris, a member of the Center for Children's Books Advisory Committee, has edited this timely volume on multicultural literature. Noted authorities contributed chapters on the various aspects of concern, for example, Joel Taxel and Rudine Sims Bishop deal with the politics and selection of multicultural literature for children, and many others contribute chapters on specific cultures as depicted in children's books. Included are African Americans, Asian Pacific Americans, Native Americans, Puerto Ricans, Mexican Americans, and Caribbeans. Each chapter includes an extensive list of recommended titles. This handbook is more than a bibliography; it should prove useful for reference and reading guidance as well as collection development in elementary schools and public libraries working with children.

Multiculturalism

C; Y; A

313. **Venture into Cultures: A Resource Book of Multicultural Materials and Programs**, ed. by Carla D. Hayden. ALA, 1992. 166p. $25. pap. 0-8389-0579-X.

This multimedia-multicultural guide is organized around major cultural groups found in the United States, for example, African American, Arabic, Hispanic, Jewish, Native American, etc. Each chapter contains a brief overview of the cultural background and traits and availability of resources. Each section also has an annotated bibliography, many include audiovisual materials, ideas for programs, food preparation, games, crafts, and lists of resources and vendors. Although this is intended primarily for elementary and middle schools, it would also be useful for higher levels, and a bibliography of sources useful for adults is also included. An index by culture completes the work which is recommended for every school and public library. *Audiovisual Materials; Multiculturalism*

African Americans

C

313a   **The Black American in Books for Children: Readings in Racism,** by Donnarae MacCann and Gloria Woodard. 2nd. Scarecrow, 1985. 310p. $29.50. 0-8108-1826-4.

This updated second edition of critical essays on racist stereotypes examines the context of books about black Americans. In addition to special treatment of Twain's *Adventures of Huckleberry Finn*, MacCann and Woodard examine 20th century fiction and biography, picture books, and publishing in general for examples of racism and current trends. Recommended for most school and public libraries and academic institutions with library science and education programs.

Children's Literature; Racism; African Americans

C

314. **The Black Experience in Children's Literature**. 10th ed. New York Public Library, 1989. 64p. pap. $5. 0-87104-697-0.

More than 450 briefly annotated titles dealing with the African American experience are listed in this inexpensive guide. The titles, ranging in age from preschool to junior high school level, are divided into four geographical areas: The U.S., South and Central America and the Caribbean, Africa, and England. The titles are accessible through an author/title index. Copies are available for $5.00 plus a $1.00 shipping and handling charge (bulk orders are also available) from: *The Black Experience*, Office of Branch Libraries, The New York Public Library, 455 5th Avenue, New York, NY 10016.

Children's Literature; African Americans

C

315. **Black Is...** San Bernadino County Library. 1991.

A selected list of children's books featuring African Americans prepared by the Children's Services Department of the San Bernadino County Library. Free for one copy and a SASE; $5 for 25 copies sent to: Children's Services, San Bernadino County Library, 104 W. Fourth St., San Bernadino, CA 92415.

Children's Literature; African Americans

C; Y

316. **Books by African-American Authors and Illustrators for Children and Young Adults**, by Helen E. Williams. ALA, 1991. 270p. $39. 0-8389-0570-6.

Williams, a librarian and professor of children's literature, helps fill a void by providing background information on the contributions of African-Americans to children's and young adult literature. She states that her objective in this book is "to provide a representative identification of the books which are written and illustrated by black writers and artists." The book is divided into four chapters and includes descriptions of 250 books appropriate for children of pre-school to third grade; more than 350 descriptions of books considered appropriate for intermediate grades five through eight; over 700 books which should inform and challenge readers at the senior high level and above; and information about black illustrators and their works. The more than 1,200 books listed were published from the 1930's to 1990. The big difference between this work and *Black Authors and Illustrators of Children's Books* by Barbara Rollock is the arrangement by age group and the detailed annotations. The price is such that most school and public libraries that own the Rollock work will want both works despite the duplication of titles.

Children's Literature; Authors; African Americans;
Illustrators; Young Adult Literature

C

317. **Spin a Soft Black Song #2, A Selected List of Outstanding Children's Books That Reflect the Black Experience**. Boston Public Library, 1988. 17p. $3.50.

This seventeen-page pamphlet lists recent recommended children's books on black themes arranged under such subjects as folktales, the arts, black culture, picture books, stories for younger readers, fiction for older readers, and biographies. It is available for $3.50 and a self-addressed stamped #10 envelope from Children's Services, Boston Public Library, Copley Square, Boston, MA 02117.

Children's Literature; African Americans

C; Y

318. **Telling Tales: The Pedagogy & Promise of African American Literature for Youth**, by Dianne A. Johnson. Greenwood, 1990. 166p. $42.95. 0-313-27206-9. (Contributions in Afro-American and African Studies, 134).

This critically annotated work deals with the contributions of writers from 1920 to 1990 including works by W. E. B. DuBois, children's fiction by Langston Hughes and Arna Bontemps, and the writings and illustrations of John Steptoe and others. Recommended for most libraries, especially those supporting an African American or African studies program or those serving a large population of African Americans.

African Americans; Children's Literature; Young Adult Literature

Hispanic Americans

C

319. **Basic Collection of Children's Books in Spanish**, by Isabel Schon. Scarecrow, 1986. 230p. $22.50. 0-8108-1904-X.

This excellent bibliography of more than 500 titles in Spanish is intended for Spanish-speaking children from pre-school through grade six. It should prove immensely helpful as a buying guide for the busy school or public librarian (especially those not fluent in the Spanish language or familiar with the body of literature that exists and not reviewed in standard sources). Titles are arranged topically into nonfiction, fiction, easy books, reference books, and professional books. A brief descriptive note and a recommended grade level are provided. There are also author, title, and subject indexes, as well as an appendix of dealers of books in Spanish. This bibliography is a must purchase for all school and public libraries whether they have a large Spanish speaking population or are serving those studying Spanish as a second language. *Children's Literature, Spanish; Spanish Literature*

C*; Y*

320. **Books in Spanish for Children and Young Adults: An Annotated Guide, Series V,** by Isabel Schon. Scarecrow, 1989. 165p. $20. 0-8108-2238-5.

This much awaited up-date includes children and young adult books published in Spanish, bilingual and translated books, and titles published originally in Spanish. It is intended for teachers, librarians, and parents as an aid in selecting books in Spanish from preschool through high school. The titles are arranged by country and then by topic such as music, art, etc. Each entry contains full bibliographic information and a brief annotation. Earlier volumes, designated as Series II, III, and IV are also still available. Schon, a professor of library science at Arizona State University, is also the author of *A Basic Collection of Children's Books in Spanish* which includes about 500 titles arranged by subject. The titles complement each other and are recommended for all school and public libraries that support bilingual programs or serve a large Spanish speaking population.

Children's Literature, Spanish; Spanish Literature; Young Adult Literature, Spanish

C; Y

321. **A Hispanic Heritage, Series IV: A Guide to Juvenile Books about Hispanic People and Cultures,** by Isabel Schon. Scarecrow, 1991. 166p. $22.50 0-8108-2462-0.

This work lists over 200 juvenile books published from 1988 into 1990, suitable for readers in grades one through 12 that deal with the Hispanic people and their culture. The books are arranged in chapters with geographical divisions like Argentina, Spain, or the United States. Each entry contains bibliographic information, an evaluative and descriptive annotation, and grade and audience indicators, with specially recommended books marked with an asterisk. There in an author, title, and subject index. This is a fine collection development tool for school and public libraries that stress Hispanic studies. The three earlier volumes in the series are still available: *Series I* (1980. $20, 0-8108-1290-8), *Series II* (1985, $20. 0-8108-1727-6) and *Series III* (1988, $20. 0-8108-2133-8).

Hispanic Americans; Children's Literature; Young Adult Literature

C; Y

322. **Library Services for Hispanic Children: A Guide for Public and School Librarians,** by Adela Artola Allen. Oryx Press, 1987. 200p. $30. pap. 0-89774-371-7.

Fourteen individuals representing educators, language specialists, and librarians contributed articles and bibliographies to this practical guide for offering library services to Hispanic children. It is divided into three major parts dealing with history and approach, professional issues related to serving Hispanic children, and books and other resources. Part 3 is the most directly related and helpful for collection development in this area. Excellent annotated bibliographies include recommended children's books in English about Hispanics, noteworthy books in Spanish, and a list of nonprint materials and software. Although this guide could benefit from a more constant updating, it is recommended for most libraries, but especially those serving an Hispanic population. *Hispanic Americans*

Indians of North America

C; Y

323. **American Indian Reference Books for Children and Young Adults,** by Barbara J. Kuipers. Libraries Unlimited, 1991. 200p. $32.50. 0-87287-745-0.

Kuipers, an experienced library media specialist, has worked with native Americans for many years. This compilation of over 200 recommended and relevant nonfiction materials is intended for children and young adults in grades 3-12. Each entry provides full bibliographic data and indicates subject area and reading level. The annotations, which are lengthy, discuss the strong and weak points of each book and suggest possible curriculum use. A specially devised evaluation guide and checklist to ensure objectivity and avoid stereotypes is also provided. This much needed bibliography is recommended for most school and public libraries but especially those working with a native American population.

Indians of North America

C
324. **Books without Bias: Through Indian Eyes**, by Beverly Slapin and Doris Seale. 2nd ed. Oyate, 1988. 462p. $20. (no ISBN).

This work deals with the portrayal of native Americans in children's literature. It begins with a series of essays on stereotyping Native Americans in literature, ways of avoiding it, and methods of detecting it in books for children. Many examples are quoted to illustrate these points. Following this introductory material is the heart of the book, two sections that review children's books about Native Americans. The first gives lengthy descriptions of each book plus detailed analyses that both praise and condemn. The second contains a longer list of recommended titles with shorter annotations. There are author and title indexes plus a list of native American publishers and sources of teaching materials. This is a highly recommended selection tool for children's libraries. *Indians of North America; Children's Literature*

C; Y
325. **Through Indian Eyes**, ed. by Beverly Slapin and Doris Seale. New Society Publishers/New Society Educational Foundation, 1992. 336p. $49.95. 0-86571-212-3; $24.95. pap. 0-86571-213-1.

There are over 300 separate and diverse Native cultures in the United States, and the job of identifying and acquiring materials related to these cultures is oftentimes overwhelming. This handbook/bibliography is intended to make it possible for librarians, teachers, and parents to become familiar with and select quality children's books dealing with the Native American experience. This work is an expansion of the authors' earlier edition, which is still in print and still useful, *Books without Bias: Through Indian Eyes*. Of the present edition, over one-third of the text consists of book reviews from both standard sources as well as the less familiar presses. A resources section lists information on acquiring print and nonprint materials; curriculum materials; and periodicals, all ranging from levels pre-school through high school. Finally, a well-selected bibliography by and about Native Americans complete this volume which is recommended for every school and public library. *Indians of North America*

Science

C*
326. **Best Science Books & A-V Materials for Children: An Annotated List of Science and Mathematics Books, Films, Filmstrips, and Videocassettes**, by Susan M. O'Connell et al. American Association for the Advancement of Science, 1988. 335p. $20. 0-87168-316-4.

Over 1,200 books and audiovisual items are included in this excellent bibliography prepared under the aegis of AAAS. All of the titles originally appeared in the review journal *Science Books & Films* from 1982 through 1987, and all were rated as either recommended or highly recommended. Titles are arranged in classified order by topic; each entry contains full bibliographic data as well as the review from the above-mentioned journal. Despite the fact that many of the titles listed are over six years old, this is still perhaps the best bibliography of its type available today and is therefore recommended for all libraries serving children. *Children's Literature; Science; Mathematics; Audiovisual Materials*

C; Y
327. **Discovering Nature with Young People: An Annotated Bibliography and Selection Guide**, comp. by Carolyn M. Johnson. Greenwood, 1987. 468p $59.95 0-313-23823-5.

This is a guide to materials for young people on outdoor education that includes books, films, plays, poetry, special days, and program guides. For each listing, bibliographical information is given plus age suitability and a brief annotation. Recommended for elementary and junior high schools. *Outdoor Life*

C; Y
328. **E for Environment: An Annotated Bibliography of Children's Books with Environmental Themes**. Bowker, 1992. 306p. $39.95 0-8352-3028-7.

This bibliography contains 517 of the best fiction and nonfiction titles published in the past ten years for children from preschool through age 14. The major areas covered are fostering positive attitudes about the environment, ecology, environmental issues, people and nature, and learning activities. Each entry is helpfully annotated with material on contents and age suitability. There is also an appendix which lists the best titles for older students and adults. Access to this material is simplified by author, title, and subject indexes. This will be an extremely useful collection development tool in both elementary and middle schools. *Ecology; Environment*

C
329. **The Green Guide to Children's Books**. Books for Keeps, [1991]. 113p. free, pap.

This 113-page booklet, sponsored by the publisher HarperCollins and issued by the children's book reviewing periodical, *Books for Keeps*, describes over 450 children's books about the environment and how to conserve it. Books of fiction, poetry, and nonfiction are listed. It is a available from: Books for Keeps, 6 Brightfield Road, Lee, London SE12 8QF, England. *Ecology; Environment; Children's Literature*

C
330. **The Museum of Science and Industry Basic List of Children's Science Books, 1988**, comp. by Bernice Richter and Duane Wenzel. American Library Association, 1989. 72p. $11.95. 0-8389-0499-8.

This list is published annually for the Museum's Annual Children's Science Book Fair. The annotated titles (49 pages in this edition) are arranged by a wide range of topics, from animals, to technology/ engineering. Each entry also includes full bibliographic information and a suggested grade level. An author and title index is also provided. Some back editions that are still useful are available from the ALA. This authoritative list is highly recommended for all libraries needing to keep abreast of the newest and best in this genre. *Children's Literature; Science*

C*
331. **Outstanding Science Trade Books for Children in 1992**. Children's Book Council, 1993.

This list, which has been issued annually since 1973, is a project of CBC's joint committee with the National Science Teachers Association (NSTA). This year's list includes 87 outstanding books written for youngsters in grades prekindergarten to eight. They were chosen by science educators and librarians from almost 4,500 children's books published in 1990. This list appeared originally in *Science and Children*. In addition to being of high literary quality, the selections emphasize accuracy, consistency with current scientific knowledge, and readability. Each entry includes a recommended grade level, an annotation, and bibliographic information. This list is highly recommended, along with another fine list published by the CBC: *Notable 1992 Children's Trade Books in the Field of Social Studies*. Single copies are available for a SASE (75 cents) 6" x 9" envelope; also available in quantity. For more information and for ordering write to: CBC, 568 Broadway, Suite 404, New York, NY 10012. *Children's Literature; Science*

C*
332. **Read Any Good Math Lately?: Children's Books for Mathematical Learning K-6**, by David Whittin and Sandra Wilde. Heinemann, 1992. 206p. $18.50. 0-435-08334-1.

This bibliographic guide is intended to foster an understanding of a variety of mathematical concepts with elementary school children. Both children's fiction and nonfiction books are included. The basic mathematical operations, addition, subtraction, multiplication, and division, are treated in separate chapters. Other chapters deal with more complex concepts such as geometry, fractions, etc. Each chapter discusses how children's books can be used to present a specific math topic. Many very practical ideas are provided. This bibliography/handbook is highly recommended for every elementary school library and most children's departments of public libraries. *Arithmetic; Mathematics; Children's Literature*

C*
333. **Science and Technology in Fact and Fiction: A Guide to Children's Books**, by DayAnn Kennedy and others. Bowker, 1990. 331p. $36. 0-8352-2708-1.

This bibliography lists over 350 recommended juvenile titles suitable for youngsters ages three through twelve. Books are arranged in two principle sections, science and technology, with subdivisions for fiction and nonfiction titles. In each of these sections books are arranged alphabetically by author. Picture books and easy readers are included in the fiction sections. The selections have been made carefully and judiciously. Each entry contains grade level suitability, full bibliographic citations, and lengthy annotations that both summarize and evaluate the books' contents and usefulness. A few outstanding out-of-print titles are included. There are five indexes: authors, illustrators, titles, subjects, and readability. This will be useful in both elementary schools and children's rooms in public libraries.

Science; Children's Literature; Technology

C*
334. **Science Books and Films' Best Books for Children, 1988-91**, ed. by Maria Sosa and Shirley M. Malcolm, 1992. American Association for the Advancement of Science, 1992. 300p. $40. 0-87168-505-1.

This current bibliography is much-needed and can serve as an update for the ALA list of science books for children by Denise M. Wilms, *Science Books for Children: Selections from Booklist, 1976-1983* (A.L.A., 1985. $7.50. 0-8389-3312-2). All of the listed works were originally reviewed during the years 1988-1991 in *Science Books and Films*, a review journal of the highly regarded American Association for the Advancement of Science. Only those which received a highly recommended or recommended rating are included in this compilation; therefore, it can be assumed that this list represents the finest science books for children published recently. The citations are arranged first by broad subject areas such as Technology and Engineering, and then by more specific headings such as Aeronautics. Entries are alphabetically arranged under author within each subject category. Complete bibliographic data is provided as well as recommended interest/grade levels. An author and title index completes this fine bibliography which should prove very useful to all elementary school and public libraries serving children.

Children's Literature; Science

C; Y

335. **Science Experiments Index for Young People**, by Mary Anne Pilger. Libraries Unlimited, 1988. 239p. $35. 0-87287-671-3.

This is an index to the projects and experiments found in 694 books published for children in elementary and middle schools from 1941 through 1988. In addition to the pure physical sciences, books on topics related to the science, i.e., mathematics projects and those involving food and nutrition, are included. The main section is arranged by subject headings. Each experiment is briefly described, a book number is given, and the specific pages in the book provided. Grade levels are not given for the experiments. The second section lists by number the books analyzed and gives full bibliographic information. This section can be of value in developing library collections. In 1991 a companion volume, *Science Experiments Index for Young People, Update 91*, by the same author, was published (Libraries Unlimited, 1992, $19.50, 0-87287-858-9). It contains about 7,500 entries taken from 272 new books. Both books are also available in disc versions for use on IBM, Apple, or Mac computers at approximately the same price as the print version. These contain the same information but allow the library to tailor the index to individual library collections. The index is recommended for both elementary and middle school libraries. For an older group, *Science Fair Project Index* would be more appropriate. *Science—Experiments*

C; Y

336. **Science Fair Project Index, 1985-1989: For Grades K-8**, by Cynthia Bishop et al. Scarecrow, 1992. 555p. $47.50. 0-8108-255-4.

This index in intended for use by teachers, librarians, and students in grades five through high school to locate material on science fair projects found in about 150 books and in selected periodicals like *Science Teacher, Science and Children*, and *Scientific American*. An earlier volume, *Science Fair Project Index, 1981-1984*, is still available (1986, $47.50, 0-8108-1892-2). It indexes about the same number of books and six periodicals. Both are useful in school collections to locate material on science fair projects and for collection development of materials very much in demand. *Science—Experiments*

C

337. **Science Fare: An Illustrated Guide and Catalog of Toys, Books and Activities for Kids**, by Wendy Saul and Alan R. Newman. Harper, 1986. 295p. $20 pap. 0-06-091218-9.

The main purpose of this excellent guide for both parents and professionals is to suggest activities for kids that will turn them on to science. Separate chapters offer ideas for exploring biology, earth science, physics, chemistry, astronomy, and computers. Others discuss science education and various approaches to scientific enquiry. Of particular importance for collection building are the sections that discuss sources for such materials as books, equipment, games, and toys. Although some of these items are expensive, there are many references to sources of free and inexpensive services and materials like museums and government agencies. An update would be welcome, but this is nevertheless still a valuable book for elementary school libraries. *Science*

C*

338. **Science Through Children's Literature: An Integrated Approach**, by Carol M. Butzow and John W. Butzow. Libraries Unlimited, 1989. 234p. $24.50 pap. 0-87287-667-5.

This excellent work for teachers of preschoolers through the third grade shows how to integrate reading of trade books with the curriculum. Part one explains and gives examples of the successful use of the whole language approach in teaching and shows how it can be used in all subject areas to develop skills in both reading and writing. The other sections give sample science lessons based on the use of 30 outstanding children's books. Each lesson plan contains a list of content-related words, a variety of activities, and references to other books. This is primarily a professional tool for teachers and librarians that will help them to develop teaching methodologies, but it can also be used as a book selection aid.

Science—Study and Teaching; Children's Literature

Social Studies

C

339. **Adventures with Social Studies (Through Literature)**, by Sharron L. McElmeel. Teacher Ideas Press/Libraries Unlimited, 1991. 208p. $23.50. pap. 0-87287-828-7.

This work is not a bibliography as such, but rather an excellent collection of nine units of instruction in the field of history divided into four major parts. The third part, "Making Connections," includes a very comprehensive bibliography of current and retrospective materials and is the most useful part of the work for collection development. It is particularly recommended for use with teachers at the intermediate or middle school level who do not have a strong background in children's literature.

Children's Literature; Social Studies

C*; Y*

340. **American History for Children and Young Adults: An Annotated Bibliographic Index**, by Vandelia VanMeter. Libraries Unlimited, 1990. 350p. $32.50. 0-87287-731-0.

This important collection tool in American history lists almost 3,000 fiction, nonfiction and biographical titles arranged chronologically by time period and subject. Each entry includes full bibliographic data, as well as a brief annotation and a suggested grade level. Also very useful to school and public librarians are the author, title, subject, and grade level indexes.

United States—History; Children's Literature; Young Adult Literature

C; Y

341. **Directory of Central America Classroom Resources K-12**, by Mary A. Swenson and Kay Dunne. 2nd ed. Central America Resource Center, 1990. 172p. $12.95 0-9617743-3-9.

Under such subject headings as economics, culture, social conditions, history, and geography, this directory lists about 100 print and nonprint resources useful in teaching about Central America. All entries are annotated, and grade levels are given. The curriculum section, which lists units of study, and the directory section, which lists helpful organizations, are particularly valuable. To order this publication send $12.95 plus 75 cents postage to Central America Resource Center, 1701 University Ave. SE, Minneapolis, MN 55414 and ask for information about other publications. *Central America*

C; Y

342. **Eastern Europe in Children's Literature: An Annotated Bibliography of English-Language Books**, by Frances F. Povsic. Greenwood, 1986. 226p. $42.95 0-313-23777-8. (Biographies and Indexes in World Literature, 8).

This is a qualitative listing of 315 books for young people, published from 1900 through 1984, that deal with Albania, Bulgaria, Czechoslovakia, Hungary, Poland, Romania, and Yugoslavia. Fiction predominates, but there are entries for biographies as well. The annotations are lengthy, and there are author, title, and subject indexes. Unfortunately, because so many of the books are now out of print, this bibliography is of limited use for collection development; however, it will be of value in identifying ethnic literature. For large collections or those where this specialized material is needed.

Children's Literature; Young Adult Literature; East Europeans

C*; Y*

343. **Educators Guide to Free Social Studies Materials**. Educators Progress Service, annual. $27.95 pap.

This paperback is one of a series of six volumes divided by various curricular areas that list free films, filmstrips, slides, tapes, transcriptions, pamphlets and other printed available to schools, libraries and industries. Most of the audiovisual products available are for free loan not ownership. This book covers materials in the Social Studies field. The other five list similar materials in other areas. They are *Educators Guide to Free Science Materials* (annual, $26.95), *Educators Guide to Free Guidance Materials* (annual, $25.95), *Educators Guide to Free Health, Physical Education and Recreation Materials* (annual, $26.75), *Educators Guide to Free Home Economics Materials* (annual, $23), and *Guide to Free Computer Materials* (annual, $36.95). Prices quoted are for the 1991-1992 volumes. Orders should include an additional $1.75 per book for postage and handling. Each volume has six sections. First is a table of contents, followed by the body of the work which is a alphabetical listing of each item by title. There are three or four line annotations which describe contents and suitability by subject areas and give the source. There are title, subject indexes and one by source and availability. In the latter, names and addresses of sources are given plus any information concerning restrictions on use. For ease of use each section is color coded. These bibliographies have been found to be of great use in collection development in both schools and public libraries. They can be ordered from: Educators Progress Services, 214 Center Street, Randolph, WI 53956.

Vertical File Materials; Free Material; Social Studies; Science; Guidance; Health; Physical Education; Recreation; Home Economics; Computers

C; Y

344. The Indian Subcontinent in Literature for Children and Young Adults: An Annotated Bibliography of English-Language Books, by Meena Khorana. Greenwood, 1991. 392p. $49.95. 0-313-25489-3.

This bibliography of over 900 books for children and young adults concentrates on five geographical areas: India, Pakistan, Bangladesh, Sri Lanka, and the Himalayan kingdoms (like Tibet and Nepal). The author begins with a general introduction covering the differences in cultures of the area and ends with a short bibliography of works consulted. The body of the work is divided by country with subdivisions by genre, e.g., fiction, poetry, and biography. Full bibliographic data is supplied for each book, as well as a descriptive and critical annotation. All of the books were published between 1940 and 1989. There are author, title, illustrator, and subject indexes. This is a valuable book for both public and school libraries, particularly where there are children from these ethnic backgrounds.

Children's Literature; India; Pakistan; Bangladesh; Sri Lanka; Tibet; Nepal; South Asia

C; Y

345. Japan through Children's Literature: An Annotated Bibliography, by Yasuko Makino. 2nd ed. Greenwood, 1985 144p. $42.95. 0-313-24611-4.

This bibliography critically analyzes 450 children's and young adult works about Japan under seven broad areas like art, drama, music, and social studies. The latter is subdivided into specific topics like history, Hiroshima, and festivals. After bibliographic material, a grade level is given and an annotation. In spite of its age, this bibliography will be useful for book selection, particularly where there is a large Japanese American community or where there are curriculum units on Japan. *Children's Literature; Japan*

C

346. Japanese Children's Books at the Library of Congress: A Bibliography of the Postwar Wars, 1946-1985, by Tayo Shima. Library of Congress, 1987. 58p. $6.50 pap. 0-8444-0576-0.

This is an annotated bibliography of 300 children's books in Japanese held by the Library of Congress. They are arranged chronologically, allowing for comparison and tracing developments and trends. The work is nicely illustrated, and there is full bibliographic material given for each book, as well as an annotation. The booklet is available for $6.50 from the Superintendent of Documents, Government Printing Office, Washington, DC 20402. The stock number is 030-000-00197-4. *Children's Literature; Japan*

C

347. Learning Economics through Children's Stories, by Robert Hendricks et al. 5th ed. Joint Council on Economic Education, 1986. 119p. 44.95 (pap.).

Economics is one discipline that is often ignored in the general curriculum area known as Social Studies. This is a bibliography that uses recommended fiction and some nonfiction titles, written for children and published between 1976 and 1984, as a way of introducing concepts in economics to youngsters from kindergarten through sixth grade. Each of the 273 entries is annotated and a suitability level is indicated. The introductory material contains a key to the economic topics dealt with in the books, and in the middle there is a special section, "Research on Economic Education in the Elementary School." Appendixes contain lists of important periodical articles on teaching economics to this age group, plus a general bibliography on children's literature. In spite of its age, this is an interesting and still valuable selection aid for children's librarians. *Economics-Children's Literature; Children's Literature*

C*

348. Notable 1992 Children's Trade Books in the Field of Social Studies. Children's Book Council, 1993.

This list, which has been issued annually since 1972, is a project of CBC's joint committee with the National Council for the Social Studies (NCSS). This year's list includes 146 notable books written for youngsters in grades K-8. They were chosen by social studies educators and language arts specialists from almost 5000 children's books published in 1992. This annual bibliography appears first in *Social Education*. In addition to being of high literary quality, the selections "emphasize human relations; represent a diversity of groups and are sensitive to a broad range of cultural experiences." The list is divided into categories, e.g., World History, The American Frontier, Folktales, Biography, Peace, etc. Full bibliographic data, recommended grade levels, and an annotation are provided for each entry. Single copies are available by sending 75 cents and a six by nine inch envelope; also available in quantity. The CBC also has available for free with a similar SASE: *Outstanding Science Trade Books for Children in 1993*. For more information or to order write to: CBC, 568 Broadway, Suite 404, New York, NY 10012.

Children's Literature; Social Studies

C; Y

349. **Peoples of the American West: Historical Perspectives Through Children's Literature**, by Mary Hurlburt Cordier and Maria A. Perez-Stable. Scarecrow, 1989. 230p. $22.50. 0-8108-2240-7.

The focus of this annotated bibliography of almost 100 children's books is on the westward movement and the winning of the west during the latter part of the 19th century. There is some preliminary information on the importance of making history live through children's literature, but the heart of the book is the bibliographic entries which are divided into broad topics such as homesteading, overland journeys, immigrants and immigration, native Americans, and the American Southwest. Titles are further subdivided by grade level. This brief book is recommended for all elementary and middle school libraries and public libraries serving young people. *West (U.S.); Westward Expansion; Children's Literature*

C; Y

350. **The Soviet Union in Literature for Children and Young Adults: An Annotated Bibliography of English-Language Books**, by Frances Povsic. Greenwood, 1991. 284p. $45. 0-313-25175-4.

This is a bibliography of 536 books published from 1900 to 1990 that were either written originally in English or translated into English from Russian. A wide variety of genres are included, such as folktales, biographies, and both historical and contemporary fiction. Entries are arranged first by major geographical regions (all are now independent states) and then by genre. Annotations give plot summaries and astute evaluations. The bibliographic information includes grade level suitability. In an introduction the author describes the people of each region. The indexes are by author, title, subject, illustrator, and translator. This is a convenient guide, but unfortunately many of the books are now out of print which limits its use for collection development. *Children's Literature; Young Adult Literature; Soviet Union*

C; Y

351. **World History for Children and Young Adults: An Annotated Bibliographic Index**, by Vandelia VanMeter. Libraries Unlimited, 1992. 425p. $29.50. 0-87287-732-9.

This unique bibliography identifies and describes over 2,000 fiction and nonfiction books appropriate for children K through grade 12 dealing with world events. Each title has been reviewed favorably. The entries are arranged by time periods, then subdivided by subject. Full bibliographic data plus a brief annotation and recommended grade level are also provided for each entry. This reference guide is recommended for all libraries that serve young people or those that work with young people.

World History; Children's Literature; Young Adult Literature

Special Literary Forms

C

352. **Fairy Tales, Fables, Legends and Myths**, by Betty Bosma. 2nd ed. Teachers College, 1992. 200p. $15.95 0-8077-3134-X.

This is a handbook on how to use folk literature in the classroom in a variety of situations. It ends with a detailed example of combined fifth and sixth grade class activities in this area. Over 20 pages of the text are devoted to an annotated list of recommended books of folk literature for children which would be helpful in collection building in elementary schools and children's rooms. It can be obtained directly from Teachers College, Columbia University, 1234 Amsterdam Ave., New York, NY 10027 for $15.95.

Fairy Tales; Folklore; Fables; Legends; Mythology

C*; Y*

353. **Fantasy Literature for Children and Young Adults: An Annotated Bibliography**, by Ruth Nadelmen Lynn. 3rd ed. Bowker, 1989. 771p. $46. 0-8352-2347-7.

This is an annotated list of 3,300 English and American fantasy novels and collections of short stories for young people in grades three through twelve, published between 1900 and 1988. Part 1 lists them in 10 sections by type of fantasy such as ghost, time travel, and animal and then by author. Both in- and out-of-print books are included. There follows a one sentence annotation, some review citations, and, through the use of symbols, an indication of its quality. Part 2, the research guide, lists secondary sources for the use of adults. This is divided into four sections: "Reference and Bibliography," "History and Criticism," "Teaching Resources," and "Author Studies." There are author and illustrator, title, and subject indexes. This is a valuable tool for every elementary and high school, plus children's rooms in public libraries. *Fantasy; Children's Literature; Young Adult Literature*

C

354. **Index to Children's Plays in Collections, 1975-1984**, by Beverly Robin Trefny and Eileen C. Palmer. Scarecrow, 1986. 124p. $20. 0-8108-1893-0.

This is the third volume in this series (the first two are out of print) that systematically indexes collections of children's plays. The present volume covers a total of 540 plays found in 48 collections published between 1975 and 1984. Entries are of three types—author, title, and subject—in a single alphabet, the author entry supplying the major amount of information (including a cast analysis). There are 400 subject entries. These and the title entries simply give the author and the title of the anthology. The bibliography of collections analyzed, unfortunately, is of limited value in collection development because the anthologies were included nonselectively. However, for reference purposes, this is of value in elementary schools and public libraries. *Children's Plays*

C

355. **Index to Fairy Tales, 1978-1986: Including Folklore, Legends and Myths in Collection: 5th Supplement**, by Norma Olin Ireland and Joseph W. Sprug. Scarecrow, 1989. 575p. $49.50 0-8108-2194.

The *Third Supplement, 1949-1972* (1973, $45, 0-8108-2011-0) and the *Fourth Supplement, 1973-1977* (1979, $29.50, 0-8108-1855-5) of this respected index to collections of folk and fairy tales are still in print. The fifth supplement covers 262 collections published between 1978 and 1986. The main body of the work is a listing of titles and subjects in a single alphabet with the title entry containing the main information. This is preceded by a list of the collections analyzed. The work has an illustrious history that dates back over 60 years. It continues to be an important literature reference work for both school and public libraries. *Fairy Tales; Folklore; Mythology*

C*; Y

356. **Index to Poetry for Children and Young People, 1982-1987**, by G. Meredith Blackburn III. Wilson, 1989. 392p. $48. 0-8242-0773-4.

This series of poetry indexes began in 1942 with the original edition edited by John E. and Sara W. Brewton (1942, $43, 0-8242-0021-7). This was followed by the first supplement (1954, $30, 0-8242-0022-5) and second supplement (1965, $30, 0-8242-0023-3). Additional volumes cover the years 1964-1969 (1972, $30, 0-8242-0435-2); 1970-1975 (1978, $38, 0-8242-0621-5); and 1976-1981 (1983, $38, 0-8242-0681-9). The present volumes indexes over 100 poetry collections published between 1982 and 1987 that contain poetry suitable for young people from elementary through high school. About 8,500 poems are listed by title, first line, author, and subject with fullest information given in the title entry. There is a listing of the books analyzed with complete bibliographic materials and an annotation of the contents. Because the books analyzed were selected by 15 librarians and children's literature specialists, this list is valuable for selection purposes. This is an excellent reference book for libraries serving children and young adults. *Poetry; Children's Poetry; Young Adult Poetry*

C

357. **Nonsense Literature for Children: Aesop to Seuss**, by Celia Catlett Anderson and Marilyn Fain Apseloff. Library Professional Publications/Shoe String, 1989. 247p. $ 32.50. 0-208-02161-2.

In the first several chapters, Anderson and Apseloff praise the value of nonsense literature in promoting the love of literature and reading generally. Nonsense fulfills important linguistic, philosophical, and psychological needs of children. "Nonsense is not the absence of sense but the clever subversion of it that heightens rather than destroys meaning." In addition to examples throughout the text, at the end of the book, they also provide us with an extensive list of primary and secondary sources. There is enough here for the book to be useful as a basic handbook as well as a guide for collection development in this important but often neglected area. Recommended for all libraries that serve children. *Nonsense Literature; Children's Literature*

C*; Y*

358. **Plays for Children and Young Adults: An Evaluative Index and Guide**, by Rashelle S. Karp and June H. Schlessinger. Garland, 1991. 580p. $78. 0-8240-6112-8.

This index/guide identifies and evaluates over 3,500 plays written from 1975 to 1991 that may be produced by or for young people, ages 5 to 18. The word "plays" is broadly interpreted; coverage includes plays, choral readings, scenes, musicals, reader's theater, and skits. Many other indexes were screened in choosing plays for this index including, for example, Wilson's *Play Index* and *Index to Children's Plays in Collections*. Plays are arranged alphabetically by title. Each entry provides a grade level range for the audience as well as for the actors, a description of the set, playing time, royalty information, name of the playwright, and the original title if adapted. Full bibliographic information is provided for plays that appear as a single volume or part of an anthology or periodical. Five indexes facilitate use of this valuable collection-building aid which is recommended for most school libraries, public libraries, and academic libraries supporting theater/education/children's programs and programming.

Children's Plays; Drama; Young Adult Plays

C; Y

359. **Recommended Reading List**, comp. by The Los Angeles Science Fantasy Society, [1993]. Free.

In order to promote reading and to fight illiteracy, the Children's Literature Committee of the Los Angeles Science Fantasy Society has compiled a recommended reading list for young people ages 9 to teenage with an interest in imaginative literature (science fiction and fantasy). For more information on the work of this society write to Galen A. Tripp, Children's Literature Committee at the address below. For a free copy of this recommended list send a SASE to: Recommended Reading List, c/o LASFS Inc., 11513 Burbank Blvd., North Hollywood, CA 91601-2309.

Fantasy; Science Fiction; Children's Literature; Young Adult Literature

C; Y

360. **A Reference Guide to Historical Fiction for Children and Young Adults**, by Lynda G. Adamson. Greenwood, 1987. 401p. $65. 0-313-25002-2.

This historical fiction guide describes the work of 80 award-winning authors. All works were published between 1940 and the mid-1980's. Entries are arranged alphabetically by author. Each entry includes a bibliography of their works, honors, and lengthy plot summaries. There are a number of useful appendixes: a list of book titles by historical periods; readability levels from age 7 through 14 and interest levels; a bibliography on writing historical novels; and finally a list of secondary works on the 80 authors. The titles included here are more extensive than those found in the Standard Catalogs and much more recent than those found in Logasa's *Historical Fiction* (o.p.). This up-to-date reference guide is recommended for most school media centers and public libraries.

Historical Fiction; Young Adult Literature; Children's Literature

C; Y

361. **Subject Index to Canadian Poetry for Children and Young People**, by Kathleen M. Snow and others. Canadian Library Association, 1986 307p. $25. 0-88802-202-6.

This index to 120 collections of Canadian poetry available in hardcover covers the publishing years 1976 through 1983. They are listed by subject, without a title, author or first line index; there is, however, a listing of collections analyzed. This will be of value for reference and collection development in Canadian school and public libraries. *Poetry; Canadian Literature*

C

362. **Values in Selected Children's Books of Fiction and Fantasy**, by Carolyn W. Field and Jacqueline Schachter Weiss. Library Professional Pub./Shoe String, 1987. 298p. $29.50. 0-208-02100-0.

More than 700 books for preschoolers through eighth graders that have positive values in their story lines were identified for this practical selection tool. The ten values identified which served as reference points are cooperation, courage, friendship and love of animals, friendship and love of people, humaneness, ingenuity, loyalty, maturing, responsibility, and self-respect. Each chapter is devoted to one of the values in the form of a bibliographic essay; books are grouped and discussed in broad age ranges: preschool through 2nd grade; middle years, grades 3-4; and later years, grades 5-8. A paragraph-long essay is written for each title; included is a plot summary, main characters, and theme commentary dealing with value treatment. Full bibliographic citations are provided. This interesting book will be useful for reference as well as a selection tool for collection building of books with a positive treatment of values. Recommended for most elementary school libraries, district-wide libraries, and many public libraries. *Values; Children's Literature*

C

363. **Worlds Within: Children's Fantasy from the Middle Ages to Today,** by Sheila A. Egoff. American Library Association, 1988. 384p. $37.50. 0-8389-0494-7.

Egoff traces the fascinating development of English-language children's fantasy literature from the Middle Ages through Victorian and Edwardian times and on into the 1980's. The book will be of interest to the scholar as well as adults who simply enjoy reading fantasy, or in working with children who do. Egoff examines almost 400 novels, comparing and contrasting and commenting on the books' contributions and uniqueness. This work is highly recommended for all libraries working with children and those interested in working with children (including students of children's literature).   *Children's Literature; Fantasy*

Special Audiences

C; Y

364. **Accept Me As I Am: Best Books of Juvenile Nonfiction on Impairments and Disabilities,** by Joan Brest Friedberg et al. Bowker, 1985. 363p. $34.95. 0-8352-1974-7. (Serving Special Needs Series).

This bibliography of more than 350 nonfiction titles published between 1940 and 1984 serves as a companion volume to the earlier Baskin and Harris works *Notes From a Different Drummer* (Bowker, 1977, $34.95, 0-8352-0978-4) and *More Notes From a Different Drummer* (Bowker, 1984, $39.95, 0-8352-1871-6) which list fiction books dealing with handicaps and are also part of the excellent Bowker series on serving special needs. The first four chapters define and describe specific types of disabilities and discuss the value of using realistic nonfiction books in helping both youngsters and adults to understand and identify with "real" people with similar problems. The remaining sections of the book includes a comprehensive bibliography arranged by type of disability or impairment, such as physical, sensory, emotional and behavior. Suggested reading levels range from pre-school to grade twelve, including many adult books suitable for young people. There is also a professional bibliography and a very easy to use author, title, and subject index. This bibliographic guide is highly recommended for all librarians, teachers, and parents working with youngsters and trying to create a more tolerant view of the disabled.

Disabilities; Mental Handicaps; Physical Handicaps

C; Y

365. **Adoption Literature for Children and Young Adults: An Annotated Bibliography,** by Susan G. Miles. Greenwood, 1991. 201p. $39.95. 0-313-27606-4.

This work serves as a companion title to Melina's *Adoption: An Annotated Bibliography and Guide,* which lists books intended for adults. The approximately 500 titles are fully annotated and include full bibliographic data. They deal with topics such as age, sibling adoptions, step families, interracial and intercountry adoptions, surrogacy, and many other related areas. While most of the titles are currently available, some out-of-print titles are included. The work is divided into four broad areas by level: Preschool and Primary, Intermediate, Junior High, and Senior High Readers. Appended are a list of useful adult books as well as a list of adoption-related organizations. Three indexes—author and illustrator, title, and subject—are also included. This bibliography is recommended for all libraries serving a wide range of youth. *Adoption*

C; Y

366. **Books and Real Life,** by Nancy Polette. McFarland, 1984. 160p. $15.95. 0-89950-119-2.

Although this title by Polette, an education professor and authority on many books about the gifted, was published in 1984 and is beyond the normal scope of this guide, it is included because there are very few recent bibliographies dealing with the special interests of gifted children (see Hauser and Nelson, *Books for the Gifted Child v. 2,* which is a bit more current but covers only to grade 6). Polette also has a special focus on critical thinking for young people. It includes about 150 fiction titles from preschool through middle/junior high school interest comprehensibility level. Many of the titles delineated are still available; therefore this inexpensive title is recommended for most elementary and middle/junior high school and public libraries and especially those involved with special programs for gifted youngsters.

Gifted Children; Children's Literature; Young Adult Literature

C

367.   **Books for the Gifted Child. v. 2**, by Paula Hauser and Gail A. Nelson. Bowker, 1988. 244p. $46. 0-8352-2467-8. (Serving Special Needs).

This second volume expands and updates Baskin and Harris's 1980 volume one (1988. $34.95. 0-8352-1161-4). A list of 195 beginning, intermediate, and advanced titles, all published in the 1980s, has been selected for use by teachers, librarians, parents and others working with gifted children—preschool through grade six. The authors hope that this bibliography will serve as a "resource of cognitively challenging books recommended for intellectually gifted youngsters." Part 1 considers the definitions of gifted children and the importance of literature of various types. Part 2, "A Selected Guide to Intellectually Challenging Books," consists of bibliographic information, a detailed annotation, and appropriate level of the 195 titles which are arranged in alphabetical order by author. The volume is indexed by title, subject, and level. A similar work, but one that covers through 9th grade, is Polette's *Books and Real Life*. Both works may be considered for schools and libraries working with gifted children.

Gifted Children; Children's Literature

C

368.   **Books That Heal: A Whole Language Approach**, by Carolyn Mohr et al. Libraries Unlimited, 1991. 283p. $22. 0-87287-829-5.

This up-to-date book is intended to prepare teachers, counselors, librarians, and other professionals with the "whole language" approach to bibliotherapy. The authors define this important therapeutic skill as "using books to guide children toward problem solving and coping." Twenty-five well-known titles dealing with special and serious concerns of middle-grade children are arranged under such headings as coping, death, poverty, divorce, self-esteem, etc. Many practical suggestions for using books and suggested additional related titles are included in the annotations. This important book is recommended for all libraries serving children and those that work with children, especially those needing more suggestions for titles useful for bibliotherapy.   *Children's Literature; Bibliotherapy*

C*

369.   **Books to Help Children Cope with Separation and Loss: An Annotated Bibliography**, v.3, by Joanne E. Bernstein and Masha Kabakow Rudman. Bowker, 1989. 532p. $46. 0-8352-2510-0.

This bibliography of about 600 "real-life situation books" serves as a companion volume to the 1983 2nd edition (1983. $39.95. 0-8352-1484-2) which also included about 600 titles and is still in-print. The entries which include a detailed annotation and full bibliographic information are arranged under rather explicit and direct headings such as losing a friend, old age, prison, abuse, and suicide. There are a number of other recommended bibliographies that include books that are useful for applying bibliotherapeutic methods and strategies, for example, see *Books That Heal*. This comprehensive bibliography should be added to that list for all libraries working with children and serving teachers, parents, librarians, and counselors. A fourth edition (1993, $49. 0-8352-3412-6) covers 750 fiction and nonfiction books.

Children's Literature; Bibliotherapy

C; Y

370.   **Children Living Apart from Their Mothers: A Bibliography**, by Harriet Edwards, [1990]. 30p. pap. $6.50.

This pamphlet contains an annotated listing of fiction books for children and young adults dealing with children living without their mothers. Smaller sections contain fiction for adults, nonfiction for children, and a few periodical articles on the subject. For use in bibliotherapy situations. It is available for $6.50 from Mayflower Associates, Box 534, Hicksville, NY 11801.   *Broken Homes; Children's Literature*

C

371.   **Choices: A Core Collection for Young Reluctant Readers, Volume 2**, by Julie Cummins and Blair Cummins. John Gordon Burke Publisher, 1990. 544p. $45. 0-934272-22-0.

This continuation of the first volume of *Choices* (1984) covers material for second to sixth graders published between 1983 and 1988. A total of 275 titles are included that have appeal for the young reluctant reader and can also be used effectively in literature based curricula. The book is in two sections. In the first, each book is fully annotated under the author's name. In the second, a subject approach, the same annotations are repeated (sometimes several times) under a variety of subjects, including interest and reading levels, plus a heading for 'Group 2,' those youngsters who are able but unmotivated readers. In spite of the repetition, small print, and its price, this has many good choices and covers grade levels not usually included in bibliographies of hi-lo books.

High Interest-Low Vocabulary Books; Children's Literature

C; Y

372.　**Death and Dying in Children's and Young People's Literature: A Survey and Bibliography**, by Marian S. Pyles. McFarland. 1988. 173p. $25.95 0-89950-335-7.

This, an overview of death and dying in young people's books, is arranged by chapters on such topics as death in folklore; death of a friend, a pet, a relative; or one's own death. This is more of an interesting overview than a bibliography; however, a six page listing of the books discussed is appended and can be used as a checklist or a selection aid if more titles on this subject are needed in the library collection.

Young Adult Literature; Children's Literature; Death and Dying

C; Y

373.　**Discoveries: Fiction for Elementary School Readers**. National Library Service for the Blind and Physically Handicapped, 1986. 93p. free. 0-8444-0530-2.

This is the first of three bibliographies of recommended fiction titles that are on disc, audio cassette, or are a Braille book and are available from any of the cooperating network libraries that receive materials from National Library Service for the Blind and Physically Handicapped. This list covers titles suitable for children in kindergarten through grade six; the second, *Discoveries: Fiction for Intermediate School Years*, is for grades four through seven; and the last, *Discoveries: Fiction for Young Teens*, for grades four through nine, with a few titles for senior high schools. Using large, clear print, each of these bibliographies is arranged by subjects like mystery stories and historical fiction and then by format. There are also indexes for each format listing the entries by author and title. This is a fine work that will help school and public libraries provide library materials to young patrons who are blind or physically handicapped.

Blind; Physical Handicaps; Children's Literature; Young Adult Literature

C*

374.　**Growing Pains: Helping Children Deal with Everyday Problems through Reading**, by Maureen Cuddigan and Mary Beth Hanson. American Library Association, 1988. 208p. $22. pap. 0-8389-0469-6.

The authors focus on books for children ages two to eight that deal with problems and concerns of children today. They are organized into 13 topics plus subtopics that cover such situations as going to school, the death of a pet, foster care, lying, shyness, divorce, and sibling rivalry. Most were published between 1976 and 1986. For each title, there is a concise annotation, grade or age levels, and suggestions for use.

Bibliotherapy; Children's Literature

C

375.　**Helping Children through Books: A Selected Booklist**, by Patricia Pearl. Church and Synagogue Library Association, [1990]. $7.25.

This staple-bound booklet lists recommended books for elementary school age children that deal with such personal problems as divorce, remarriage, drugs, foster care, child abuse, sex roles, cancer, and death. It is available for $7.25 from Church and Synagogue Library Association, P.O. Box 19357, Portland, OR 97219. *Children's Literature*

C; Y

376.　**Portraying Persons with Disabilities: An Annotated Bibliography of Fiction for Children and Teenagers**, by Debra E. J. Robertson. 3rd ed. Bowker, 1992. 482p. $39.95. 0-8352-3023-6.

This selective annotated bibliography lists more than 650 fiction titles that help promote understanding and acceptance of the disabled. The selected titles are intended for young people between the ages of 5 through 18. This work updates the earlier editions by Baskin and Harris: *Notes from a Different Drummer...* (1977, $21.95, 0-8352-0978-4) and *More Notes from a Different Drummer...* (1984, $35. 0-8352-1871-6). This volume serves as a companion volume to *Portraying Persons with Disabilities: An Annotated Bibliography of Nonfiction for Children and Teenagers* (see next entry). This work is recommended for all school and public libraries as a tool for bibliotherapy, reading guidance, and collection development.

Disabilities; Children's Literature; Young Adult Literature

C; Y

377.　**Portraying Persons with Disabilities: An Annotated Bibliography of Nonfiction for Children and Teenagers**, by Joan Brest Friedberg et al. Bowker, 1992. 385p. $39.95. 0-8352-3022-8.

This work describes and evaluates 350 nonfiction titles about individuals with disabilities. It is written for youngsters ages two and up, and serves as a companion volume to the previous title: *Portraying Persons with Disabilities: An Annotated Bibliography of Fiction for Children and Teenagers*. This selective bibliography also updates the much earlier *Accept Me As I Am*. Both titles are highly recommended as guides to bibliotherapy, reading guidance, and collection building for all school and public libraries.

Disabilities; Children's Literature; Young Adult Literature

C
378. **Resources for Middle-Grade Reluctant Readers: A Guide for Librarians**, by Marianne Laino Pilla. Libraries Unlimited, 1987. 122p. $18.50. 122p. 0-87287-547-4.

Pilla devotes the first half of this book to describing the characteristics of reluctant readers and reading interests of students in grades 4-6. This is probably the first book to offer direct assistance to librarians in their work with this special group. The second half of the volume is an annotated bibliography of books, magazines, and software. The books are divided into popular subject categories such as adventure, humor, mysteries, sports, and science fiction. This volume, along with many of Pilla's unconventional ideas on working with reluctant readers or nonreaders, will be a welcome addition to most school and public libraries, especially those serving large numbers of such youngsters. *High Interest-Low Vocabulary Books*

C
379. **Sensitive Issues: An Annotated Guide to Children's Literature K-6**, by Timothy V. Rasinski and Cindy S. Gillespie. Oryx, 1992. 277p. $29.95. 0-89774-777-1.

This work is intended for teachers and librarians and suggests titles that deal with current and sensitive issues such as divorce, substance abuse, death, child abuse, prejudice, nontraditional home environment, and cultural differences, among others. All of the titles were published since 1975 and most are still in print. Indexes by author, title, and subject facilitate use. Librarians might also want to consider the slightly more expensive but more comprehensive Dreyer's *The Best of Bookfinder*. Most elementary school and public libraries will want both titles. *Bibliotherapy; Children's Literature*

C; Y
380. **The Single-Parent Family in Children's Books: An Annotated Bibliography**, by Catherine Townsend Horner. 2nd ed. Scarecrow, 1988. 339p. $35. 0-8108-2065-X.

This is an annotated bibliography of 600 primarily fiction titles published between 1965 and 1986 that deal with the single parent family. Most of the books are for grades five through nine but recommendations extend from kindergarten through the twelfth grade. The titles are grouped into the following areas: divorce/desertion/separation, widowhood, orphans, wards of the courts, protracted absence of a parent, and indeterminate cause.

Each entry contains a detailed annotation that gives the plot and a recommendation symbol (from exceptional to dated). There is a brief section on nonfiction works and indexes by author/subject and by title. The title index entries contain brief identifying annotations. This will be useful as a historical guide to the subject as well as a selection tool in both public and school libraries particularly those dealing with upper elementary school age children.

Children's Literature; Young Adult Literature; Family Life; Single Parent Family

C; Y
381. **Understanding Abilities, Disabilities, and Capabilities: A Guide to Children's Literature**, by Margaret F. Carlin et al. Libraries Unlimited, 1991. 114p. $20. 0-87287-717-5.

This innovative bibliography includes books, films, and other nonprint media covering more than 40 handicapping conditions. All of the items are appropriate for children ages 2-18. The entries include bibliographic information and an indication of readability and suggested age level. The annotations which are both descriptive and critical are quite lengthy and are useful for book talks. This current book on an important subject is recommended for all school and public libraries.

Disabilities; Mental Handicaps; Physical Handicaps

11 Young Adult Literature

General and Miscellaneous

Y*

382. **Beacham's Guide to Literature for Young Adults, Volume 5**, ed. by Kirk H. Beetz. Beacham Publishing, 1991. 610p. $63. 0-933833-25-3.

This is a major (perhaps first choice) source for young people when they need critical information on books that they have read from an assigned reading list or need help in choosing a book to read. This multivolume set includes over 200 novels, short story collections, general nonfiction, and biographies, all of which are fully described and analyzed. Titles are arranged in alphabetical order and each entry includes: type of work, a summary, an assessment of literary quality, brief biographical sketch of the author, suggestions for discussion or reports, and a list of criticisms. All of the text is written on a level and style that would appeal to young adults. There is also an author/title index. An earlier volume is also useful and still available: v. 4 (1990. $63. 0-933833-16-4). These very readable guides are highly recommended for use by students, teachers, and librarians in school, academic, and public libraries. *Young Adult Literature*

C; Y*

383. **Best Books for Junior High Readers**, by John T. Gillespie. Bowker, 1991. 567p. $39.95. 0-8352-3020-1.

Gillespie, a former junior high school librarian, professor of library science, and noted authority on young adult literature, has edited this as well as the *Best Books for Children* and *Best Books for Senior High Readers*. This important bibliography in his "Best Books" series lists almost 7,000 titles for young people, grades 7 through 9 (ages 12-15). Titles are arranged by broad subject areas—curriculum-oriented for nonfiction and interest categories for fiction. Each entry includes full bibliographic information as well as a brief descriptive annotation. All titles are recommended in at least two reviewing sources. Author, title, and subject/grade level indexes add to the value of this highly recommended tool. This is a basic reading guidance and collection development source for all libraries working with young people.

Children's Literature; Young Adult Literature

Y*

384. **Best Books for Senior High Readers**, by John T. Gillespie. Bowker, 1991. 931p. $44.95. 0-8352-3021-X.

This latest addition to the "Best Book" series (see preceding entry) maintains the high standards set in the others. Over 10,000 recommended books of high quality, geared to the 15 through 18 age group, are included. Entries include full bibliographic data as well as a brief annotation. Titles are arranged by broad subject area and then subdivided by specific topics, e.g., sports and games is followed by baseball, basketball, bowling, etc. As with the previous volumes in this trilogy, a detailed subject/grade level as well as separate author and title indexes are included. This resource is an excellent aid for collection evaluation and development, as well reader guidance, and is highly recommended for all secondary school and public libraries. *Young Adult Literature*

Y

385. **Best Books for Young Adults, 1993**. ALA Graphics, 1993. $24. for 100 copies.

This annual list of almost 100 fiction and nonfiction titles covers a wide range of interests and levels and includes several titles originally written for adults but of interest to young adults. The list is prepared for wide distribution and is available for $24. per 100 copies from: ALA Graphics, 50 E. Huron St., Chicago, IL 60611. *Young Adult Literature*

Y

386. **Books for Religious Education in Catholic Secondary Schools**, by Eileen Noonan. Catholic Library Association, 1986. 18p. $5.

This selective annotated bibliography of 95 titles is intended to serve as a core collection for libraries to support religious education programs in Catholic secondary schools. The list is divided into 16 sections by type or content, e.g., reference books, bibles, bible study, biographies, catechism, prayer, death and dying, literature, marriage, religions of the world, and saints. A directory of publishers and other sources is also provided. This brief list, which is still quite timely, is recommended for every Catholic secondary school library and perhaps should be considered as a selection guide for public libraries serving a sizable Catholic population. The list is available for $5.00 from: Catholic Library Association, 461 W. Lancaster Ave., Haverford, PA 19041. *Catholics*

Y

387. **Books for Teens: Stressing the Higher Values**, by Edith S. Tyson. Church and Synagogue Library Association, 1993. $10.35.

This annotated bibliography of recommended books for teenagers from grades seven through twelve stresses works that display positive values and promote a healthy self-image without being preachy or didactic. In addition to the presence of a value or values beyond self, each book must be of proven popularity and available in paperback. The few that are included in hardback are too current to be available in any other format. This list, though intended for volunteers working in church or synagogue libraries, can still be used as a checklist for possible acquisition activities or for reading guidance with young adult librarians. Copies are available by prepaying $10.35 and sending orders to: Church and Synagogue Library Association, P. O. Box 19357, Portland, OR 97280-0357. *Young Adult Literature*

Y*

388. **Books for the Teenage 1994**. New York Public Library, 1994.

This venerable bibliography, published annually by the Office of Young Adult Services of the New York Public Library, is now in its sixty-fifth edition. As stated in the introduction, this "list has been especially prepared for teenagers in New York City since 1929." The current list includes about 1250 titles which would be appealing to teenagers throughout the country, but especially for most urban youngsters. The titles are grouped into 77 subject categories and include a good mix of old time-tested titles and brand new 1993 titles. Each entry includes some bibliographic information (author, title, publisher) and a brief one-line catchy descriptive note. Copies are available free to teenagers at the various branches of the NYPL; copies are available to adults for $6.00. The additional charge for mailing and handling is 1 to 5 copies, $1.00; 6 to 10 copies, $1.25; bulk orders, $1.50. Copies can be ordered by mail from: Office of Branch Libraries, The New York Public Library, 455 5th Avenue, New York, NY 10016. *Young Adult Literature*

Y*

389. **Books for You: A Booklist for Senior High Students**, ed. by Shirley Wurth. 11th ed. National Council of Teachers of English, 1992. 2597p. $16.95. 0-8141-03650.

About 800 books arranged under 32 popular topics, all deemed to be appropriate and appealing to teenage readers, are listed in this the newest edition of *Books for You*, which has been prepared with the help of a committee of teachers, librarians, and school administrators appointed by the highly regarded NCTE. Each newly revised edition complements the older editions rather than replacing them. This edition includes titles published between 1988 and 1991, and is a good mix between fiction and nonfiction, and adult and young adult. Titles are arranged by popular subject categories ranging from "adventure and computer technology through romance, war and westerns." The annotations are written to appeal to young people. Author and title indexes are included. There are enough differences between this list and the NYPL's *Books for the Teenage* that most libraries will want to use both for collection development, reading guidance, and booktalking. This bibliography, which has been time-tested, is highly recommended for all libraries serving young adults. *Young Adult Literature*

Y*

390. **Fiction for Youth: A Guide to Recommended Books**, by Lillian L. Shapiro and Barbara L. Stein. 3rd ed. Neal-Schuman, 1992. 263p. $35. pap. 1-55570-113-2.

This third revised edition of an outstanding bibliography of twentieth-century novels lists and annotates over 600 titles for capable young adult readers. Literary quality and appeal were the two major criteria for inclusion. Most are adult novels, but a few better young adults titles are included. The books are arranged by authors with 10- to 12-line annotations describing the book and giving brief critical remarks. There are subject and title indexes and a directory of publishers. This is a valuable tool for reading guidance and collection development in senior high schools. *Fiction; Young Adult Literature*

C; Y

391.   **Fiction Index for Readers 10-16: Subject Access to Over 8200 Books (1960-1990)**, by Vicki Anderson. McFarland, 1992. 480p. $35. 0-89950-703-4.

This is an index by subject to books of fiction published from 1960 through 1990 for children ages 10 through 16. Over 225 subjects are listed, and there are detailed subject and title indexes. Although this is not evaluative or selective, it is a way of locating novels through the subject approach. For very large children's literature collections. *Children's Literature; Young Adult Literature*

C; Y

392.   **Fiction Sequels for Readers 10 to 16: An Annotated Bibliography of Books in Succession**, by Vicki Anderson. McFarland, 1990. 150p. $19.95 pap. 0-89950-519-8.

This listing of fiction sequels involves about 350 authors and 1,500 titles of books read in the upper elementary and junior high grades. Some of the title are out of print but are available in many libraries. There is an alphabetical arrangement by author, with each of the books in the author's series listed in order and annotated with a short annotation. There is no indication of grade or interest level, but there is a title index which supplies author names and the position of the title in the series. This work contains about twice as many authors as *Sequences* (o.p.). It will have value both in helping children's reading guidance and in collection development. *Children's Literature; Young Adult Literature; Sequels*

Y*

393.   **Genre Favorites for Young Adults**, ed. by Sally Estes. American Library Association, 1992. $7.50 pap. 0-8389-5755-2.

This paperback lists sure-fire reading hits with the young adult audience under reading interest categories like mysteries, science fiction, the supernatural, etc. The choices have been made judiciously, with many based on previously published bibliographies that have appeared from time to time in *Booklist*. This will be useful both for reading guidance and collection building in young adult collections, as well as junior and senior high schools. Enquiries for purchase should be addressed to: ALA Publishing Order Dept., 50 E. Huron Street, Chicago, IL 60611. *Young Adult Literature*

Y

394.   **Genre Title Lists**. Young Adult Library Services Association, 1992. free.

The Young Adult Library Services Association (YALSA) of ALA has prepared leaflets of favorite young adult reading in four genres: historical fiction, horror, mystery, and science fiction. Each list contains twenty recommended titles. For a free copy of these lists write: Baker and Taylor, 2709 Watger Ridge Parkway, Charlotte, NC 28217. *Young Adult Literature*

Y*

395.   **Junior High School Library Catalog**, by Juliette Yaakov. 6th ed. H. W. Wilson, 1990. 802p. $105. 0-8242-0799-8. (Standard Catalog Series).

This catalog was begun over 25 years ago to provide a basic selection tool for libraries serving young people in grades seven, eight, and nine, or roughly ages 12 to 16. Since that time, it has become a mainstay for building book collections for this age group. Like previous editions, this highly selective bibliography is divided into three parts. The first, the "Classified Catalog," is arranged by the Abridged Dewey Decimal Classification system for nonfiction and alphabetically by author's or editor's name for fiction and short story titles. Each entry contains full bibliographic and cataloging information, plus generous (usually two) excerpts from reviews. Part two is an extensive author, title, subject, and analytical index. Part 3 is a directory of publishers and distributors. There are 3,219 titles included in this edition and 3,600 analytical entries. Titles were chosen by committees of librarians and include listings of professional tools like other bibliographies, as well as the books for young adults. The purchase price includes four annual supplements (covering 1991-1994), each of which contains approximately 500 additional recommended titles in the same arrangement. This work continues to be extremely useful for building a basic collection for this age group, for evaluating existing collections, and for the preparation of bibliographies. *Young Adult Literature*

Y*

396. **Nonfiction for Young Adults: From Delight to Wisdom**, by Betty Carter and Richard Abrahamson. Oryx, 1991. 233p. $29.50. 0-89774-55-8.

Carter and Abrahamson, two noted authorities in young adult literature, have provided an invaluable aid for teachers and librarians. They discuss the role of nonfiction in literature-based curricula and very convincingly praise the merits of nonfiction: "We hope to show the literary qualities of nonfiction as well as define its importance for young adults. We suggest that the vital element nonfiction lacks is professional attention." Criteria for evaluating nonfiction are also dealt with. Finally, they include an extensive and excellent bibliography of nonfiction considered popular with young adults. This handbook, which will undoubtedly be used as a standard text for courses in young adult literature, is recommended for all libraries that serve young adults. *Young Adult Literature*

Y

397. **Olderr's Young Adult Fiction Index, 1990**, by Steven Olderr and Candace P. Smith, Jr., St. James, 1991. 450p. $50. 1-55862-091-5.

This index attempts to do for young adult fiction (for young people ages 11 to 18) what *Olderr's Fiction Index* does for adult fiction and in a sense serves as a companion volume. It indexes almost 1,000 titles that were previously reviewed in *Publishers Weekly, VOYA, Booklist,* and *School Library Journal,* and its purpose is "to connect young adult readers with material they are interested in reading." Actually, the purpose and format of the adult and young adult indexes are similar. There is some overlapping, e.g., adult books "suitable" for young adults are listed in both indexes. The 1988 and 1989 indexes are still available for $50 each. This title is recommended for every school and public library serving young adults. *Fiction; Young Adult Literature*

Y*

398. **Senior High School Catalog**, ed. by Ferne E. Hillegas and Juliette Yaakow. Wilson, 1992. 1,464p. $115. 0-8242-0831-5. (Standard Catalog Series).

The fourteenth edition of this basic selection aid for senior high school libraries and young adult collections in public libraries is the same in scope and treatment as previous editions. The approximately 6,000 entries suitable for readers in grades nine through twelve have been carefully chosen by practitioners from around the country. The nonfiction titles are arranged by Dewey Decimal numbers and the fiction by the author's last name. There is a separate section on short story collections. For each entry there is extensive bibliographic information given including complete cataloging information and subject headings. The annotations take the form of excerpts from reviews in reputable reviewing sources. There are usually two, the first is descriptive and the second critical. Professional tools are included. About one-half on the text consists of the single-alphabet index which includes entries for author, titles, subjects, and over 11,000 analytics. The last section consists of a directory of publishers and distributors. Purchase also includes the supplements for 1993, 1994, 1995, and 1996. A new edition will appear late in 1997. This is an indispensable tool for building core collections. *Young Adult Literature*

Y*

399. **Supernatural Fiction for Teens: More Than 1300 Good Paperbacks to Read for Wonderment, Fear and Fun**, by Cosette N. Kies. 2nd ed. Libraries Unlimited, 1992. 267p. $24.95 pap. 0-87287-940-2.

The 1,300 paperbacks recommended in this bibliography are arranged alphabetically by author. Full bibliographic information is given for each title plus an interest-catching annotation. Each entry is coded: A) written for teens, B) written for younger teens, C) written for adults, and D) a classic. There are both subject and authors indexes. This is a valuable sources for purchasing books as well as giving reader's guidance, preparing bibliographies, and preparing booktalks.

Young Adult Literature; Supernatural Fiction; Horror—Fiction

Y

400. **Teenage Perspectives Reference Series**. ABC-CLIO.

A series designed for young people with personal questions; this series of bibliographies are helpful for teens working on research papers, as well as for parents, teachers, and counselors who want additional information. Each work in the series includes chapter introductions to each broad topic; terms, definitions and statistics; fully annotated listing of organizations, hotlines, and print and nonprint resources; and listings of relevant young adult novels. Among the titles currently available at $35 each are:

Focus on School, by Beverly Haley. 1990, 250p.0-87436-099-4.
Focus on Physical Impairments, by Nicholas J. Karolides. 1990, 325p. 0-87436-428-0.
Focus on Sexuality, by Elizabeth Poe. 1990. 225p. 0-88436-116-8.
Focus on Careers, by Lynne Iglitzin. 1991. 200p. 0-88436-588-0.

Disabilities; Adolescence; Vocational Guidance; Sex Education

C*; Y*

401.   **U.S. Government Publications for the School Library Media Center,** by Leticia T. Ekhaml and Alice J. Wittig. 2nd ed. Libraries Unlimited, 1991. 172p. $22.50. 0-87287-822-8.

Updating the 1979 edition, this bibliography of U.S. government publications covers about 500 annotated items which are suitable for elementary and secondary school library media specialists, teachers, and students. The authors chose items that would generally reflect the school curriculum; included are books, periodicals, pamphlets, videos, and posters. Many of the items listed are free or inexpensive. Entries are arranged alphabetically by broad subject category. Each entry includes date, price, SuDocs classification number, stock number, title, issuing agency, number of pages, etc. Also included is a brief annotation and an indication of appropriate level. Some special features include a list of GPO indexes and selection aids; an alphabetical list of 240 subject bibliographies which are available free of charge; a core list of publications for a reference collection; and a selective bibliography on government publications. A title index and a subject index are also provided. Kelly's *Using Government Documents: A How-To-Do-It Manual for School Librarians* is very similar; however, it does not provide annotations. This book, and/or the Kelly book, provide valuable information for building collections in an area generally underutilized and both are recommended for all school library media centers.

United States—Government Publications

Y

402.   **Young Adult Annual Booklist,** by Young Adult Services, Los Angeles Public Library. $10.

This brief booklet, which has been published annually for the past seven or eight years, annotates and evaluates the fiction and nonfiction titles added to the young adult collection during the previous year. Also included is a list of "Adult Books Having YA Interest." An author and title index is also included. To order, send a check for $10. to: Young Adult Services, Los Angeles Public Library, Attn: Betty Lunn, 630 W. 5th St. , Los Angeles, CA 90071. *Young Adult Literature*

Y*

403.   **The Young Adult Reader's Adviser,** Bowker, 1992. 2v. 1798p. $79.95. 0-8352-3068-6.

Modeled after Bowker's *Reader's Adviser,* this two-volume set was designed to help students, teachers, and librarians find recommended reading material on subjects and authors for varying age groups ranging from middle school through senior high. Included are more than 17,000 bibliographic entries and biographical profiles of over 850 authors. Entries are arranged under four main subject categories reflecting the typical secondary school curricula: Literature and Language Arts; Mathematics and Computer Science; Social Science and History; and Science and Health. Noticeably missing from the main sections is the category for the Fine and Performing Arts. Entries include full bibliographic data. Each of the two volumes contains The Profile Index, an alphabetical listing of all individuals highlighted; the Author Index, a list of the authors of all books listed including editors and translators; and the Title Index; a complete listing of all books cited. Bibliographies with annotations are found in the profiles section and in specific subject areas. This "book finder" for young adults is highly recommended for all secondary school libraries and public libraries serving young adults. *Young Adult Literature*

C*; Y*

404.   **Your Reading: A Booklist for Junior High and Middle School Students,** ed. by Alleen Pace Nilsen. 8th ed. National Council of Teachers of English, 1991. 342p. $16.95. pap. 0-8141-5940-0.

This list of highly recommended books for the middle school/junior high age group has been published regularly since 1954. It is compiled by a committee made up of experienced teachers and librarians. The titles selected were all published between 1988 and 1990; since it is not cumulative, earlier editions of *Your Reading* are still useful. Each of the approximately 1,000 entries includes a complete citation and a 25 to 50 word descriptive annotation. Items that have been recommended by other "best books" sources are starred. Books are listed under six broad categories and over 25 subcategories, and are then arranged alphabetically by author. Popular series are listed at the end of subject chapters, e.g., Love and Romance. Author, title, and subject indexes are provided. Since this list is highly selective and only includes titles published during a three-year period, it cannot be fairly compared with several very extensive and cumulative lists such as Gillespie's *Best Books for Junior High Readers. Your Reading*, as with the other fine recommended reading lists published by the NCTE, is highly recommended for all libraries serving young people. *Children's Literature; Young Adult Literature*

Y
405. **Youth-to-Youth Books: A List for Imagination and Survival**, by the Enoch Pratt Free Library's Young Adult Advisory Board, 1989. $.30.

Sixty-seven titles have been selected for their "appeal and value to youth aged twelve to eighteen." The 67 titles published in 1988 are categorized in five groups: Young Adult Realistic Fiction; Mystery/Horror/Suspense; Adult Fiction; Science Fiction/Fantasy; and Nonfiction. The brochure is available for 30 cents and a SASE from: Publications, Enoch Pratt Free Library, 400 Cathedral Street, Baltimore, MD 21201-4484. *Young Adult Literature*

Authors

Y; A
406. **Author Profile Collection**. Linsworth Publishing, 1992. 100p. $24.95. 0-938865-12-9.

This compilation of materials first appeared in *The Book Report* and its partner *Library Talk*. Over 20 author and illustrator profiles are included in this looseleaf publication. Each profile contains a list of the author's works as well as selections for further reading. Though limited in number of titles, this should prove useful as a supplementary resource for information on authors for secondary school and public libraries. *Authors; Illustrators*

Y
407. **Authors and Artists for Young Adults, v. 9**, ed. by Laurie Collier. Gale, 1992. 258p. $63. 0-8103-7584-2.

This bio-bibliography maintains the level of excellence and bridges the gap between Gale's *Something about the Author* for children and *Contemporary Authors* which is designed for adults. Each volume includes material on 20-25 individuals and includes personal and professional biographical information, a portrait, a bibliography of writings and adaptations, a secondary bibliography, and sources for additional information. This is an important reference/selection source for school and public libraries serving young adults at the junior and senior high school levels and is highly recommended. New volumes usually appear two times a year. Volumes 1-8 are currently available at $63 per volume.

Authors; Young Adult Literature

C; Y; A
408. **The Neal-Schuman Index to Performing and Creative Artists in Collective Biographies**, comp. by Susan Poorman. Neal-Schuman, 1991, 250p. $35. 1-55570-055-X.

Poorman has indexed more than 1,200 individuals appearing in 127 collective biographies published between 1970 and 1989. The index is intended to be used by children and young adults, but it could also serve an older audience. Living and deceased artists are included from the fields of music, theater, film, television, visual arts, and literature. Entries are alphabetical by the biographee's professional name; also included are birth and death dates, country of birth, and profession. A coded list of sources also indicates special features such as photographs, length of biographical article, etc. Useful indexes by profession are provided. This useful reference tool to collective biographies can also serve as an aid to collection development, assuming that many of the 127 indexed titles are still available. Recommended for all school media centers and public libraries serving children and young adults. *Entertainers; Performing Arts*

Y
409. **Speaking for Ourselves: Autobiographical Sketches by Notable Authors of Books for Young Adults**, ed. by Donald R. Gallo. National Council of Teachers of English, 1990. 231p. $14.95

This is a collection of fascinating autobiographical sketches of 87 of the most popular writers of fiction for young adults as determined by a poll administered to past and present officers of the Assembly on Literature for Adolescents of the NCTE. Many describe how they became writers and how they regard their work. For each, there is a portrait and a selective bibliography of the major works with publication dates. The latter is a fine checklist for collection development. This is a useful item for any library that serves young adults. *Young Adult Literature; Authors*

Books About
Young Adult Literature

Y

410.   **The Adolescent in the American Novel Since 1960**, by Mary Jean DeMarr and Jane S. Bakerman. Ungar, 1986. 363p. $35. 0-8044-3067-5.

This new volume examines 600 novels published between 1961 and 1982, and serves as a follow-up to W. Tasker Witham's *The Adolescent in the American Novel, 1920-1960* (Ungar, 1979). All of the novels deal with teenagers or "American youth in American settings, and are written by American authors." The first two sections deal separately with male and female characters, but both cover similar concerns involving love and sexuality, family, crisis situations, friendships, environment, and fate. This is followed by an brief analysis of each of the novels vis-à-vis the common themes. Established authors as well as works of popular fiction are included, as are a number of adult novels read by teenagers. Although this is primarily a reference work for literary criticism, it can also serve as a useful selection guide.

Adolescence—Fiction; Young Adult Literature

Y

411.   **Characters from Young Adult Literature**, by Mary Ellen Snodgrass. Libraries Unlimited, 1991. 229p. $27. 0-87287-883-X.

In this work there is coverage on 71 old and recent books that have appeal to young adults. A sample would include *Great Expectations*, *Call of the Wild*, *Johnny Tremain*, *The Outsiders*, and *The Chocolate War*. Both fiction and nonfiction titles are analyzed. Under each title there is information on the author's dates, genre, setting, a brief plot summary, and a description of each of the major and minor characters. The books are arranged by title, but there are indexes by authors and characters. This is an unusual approach to some standard works in the field and should have value in both secondary school libraries and in public libraries.   *Young Adult Literature*

C*; Y

412.   **Comics to Classics: A Parent's Guide to Books for Teens and Preteens**, by Arthea Reed. International Reading Association, 1988. 121p. $9.95 pap. 0-87207-798-5.

Though intended for parents, this introduction to adolescent reading will be valuable for both librarians and teachers as well. This works covers stages of development for preteens (age 10 and up) and teens, reading patterns during this period, techniques for encouraging and sharing reading, and how to locate good books. The heart of this book is an annotated list of 300 recommended fiction and nonfiction titles divided into three age groups. Each section is subdivided by topic and coded for reading interest level. There is also a brief bibliography of books and magazines about adolescents. This booklet is available for $9.95, plus $2 postage from the International Reading Association, 800 Barksdale Road, PO Box 8139, Newark, DE 19714.   *Young Adult Literature*

Y*

413.   **Literature for Today's Young Adults**, by Kenneth L. Donelson and Alleen Pace Nilsen. 3rd. ed. Scott, Foresman, 1989. 620p. $43. 0-673-38400-4.

This updating of a basic study/textbook in young adult literature has placed a greater emphasis on adolescent psychology and the sections on short stories, television and movies, and YA magazines have been greatly expanded. In addition to many annotated lists of titles recommended, especially for young people, there are excellent bibliographies of further reading for teachers and librarians. The selection of titles runs the gamut from the historical/classical to the very current and popular, and little distinction is made between books for the teenager and those adult books suitable for the young adult. Author, title, and subject indexes are included. While the first and second editions are still useful, this revised and expanded third edition is recommended for all school and public libraries.   *Young Adult Literature*

Y*

414.   **Young Adult Literature: Issues and Perspectives, 1988**, by Mary Elizabeth Gallagher. The Catholic Library Association, 1988. 214p. $25. 0-87507-038-8.

This work was designed as a textbook for a young adult literature course. Following the detailed chapters on adolescent development and psychology; literacy in the information age; writers and publishers of young adult literature; and promotion of reading and programming, Gallagher includes a section on various categories of adult and young adult books and concludes with an annotated bibliography. This is less comprehensive, but covers essentially the same ground as Nilsen and Donnelson's *Literature for Today's Young Adults*, but the two texts could easily serve as companion volumes. Both are recommended for secondary school and public libraries. *Young Adult Literature*

Nonprint Media

Y

415. **Adventure Games for Microcomputers: An Annotated Directory of Interactive Fiction, 1991**, by Patrick R. Dewey. Meckler, 1991. 157p. $49.50. 0-88736-411-X.

This alphabetically-arranged list of computer adventure games is a revision of Dewey's 1988 *Interactive Fiction and Adventure Games for Microcomputers*. Like the earlier edition it should prove very popular with teenagers. Each citation includes title, vendor, cost, difficulty level, hardware requirements, type, and a brief descriptive annotation. Appendixes give dealer addresses, a list of reference books, and do-it-yourself game software. This list is recommended both for patron use and for building library collections of circulating software. *Computer Games; Computer Software*

Y

416. **Directory of Online and CD-ROM Resources for High Schools**, by Lynn S. Parisi and Virginia L. Jones. ABC-CLIO, 1988. 136p. $32.50 0-87436-515-5.

This selection guide describes both online and CD-ROM databases and their applications in the high school curriculum, particularly in the areas of English, social studies, and science. Charts that compare databases by content, formats, and courses for which they would be valuable are included and complement the written material on the databases. It is a useful guide for secondary school libraries. It is hoped that updates will follow. *Computer Software*

C; Y

417. **School Library Media Annual, 1993**, by Carol C. Kuhlthau. Volume 11. Libraries Unlimited, 1993. 290p. $42.50. 1-56308-099-0.

This annual volume summarizes for school library media specialists recent developments in the profession. Part 1 consists of specially written articles on topics of current importance in education, curriculum materials, and the school library media center. Part 2 reports on the year's happenings in international and national organizations, government affairs at both the state and national levels, library education, awards to people, and an almanac of general information. The third part is of direct value in collection development because here is listed current professional tools and award-winners in media, including software, plus those in children's and young adult literature.

This work supplies excellent background information in one handy source. Four back issues (for years 1989 through 1992) are still available. For school libraries at all levels. *School Libraries*

Y

418. **Selected Films for Young Adults**, American Library Association. Young Adult Services Division, annual.

This is an annotated and illustrated color brochure of recommended videos and 16m films released in the United States in a given year that are recommended for use in programs for young adults. The films were chosen on the basis of appeal, technical quality, contents, and use possibilities by a committee appointed by the Young Adult Services Division of ALA. It is compiled annually. Single copies are available for a stamped self-addressed envelope. In quantity the price is $20 per 100. Write to ALA Publishing Services, Order Department, 50 E. Huron St., Chicago, IL 60611. *Videocassettes; Motion Pictures*

Y*

419. **Selected Videos and Films for Young Adults, 1975-1985**, by Patsy H. Perritt and Jean T. Kreamer. American Library Association, 1986. 4101p. $5. pap. 0-8389-3327-0.

This is a retrospective cumulation of 10 years of the list, "Selected Films for Young Adults," that is compiled annually by ALA's Young Adult Services Division. There are about 200 films and videos listed, including entertainment films, documentaries, animation, and short story presentations. They are listed alphabetically by title. Each entry has extensive bibliographic information, a descriptive annotation, purchasing and/or rental information, plus data on available guides. There are several appendixes: one on authors whose works have been the sources for these films, and another that lists distributors, their addresses, telephone numbers, and films they distribute. There are also sections on program tips and an extensive bibliography of sources of information on films, programs, and review media followed by a subject index. This extremely valuable tool can be updated by consulting subsequent yearly lists. Recommended for both high school and public libraries. *Motion Pictures; Videocassettes*

Programs and Activities

Y*

420. **Book Bait: Detailed Notes on Adult Books Popular with Young People**, by Elinor Walker. 4th ed. American Library Association, 1988. 166p. $17.95. pap. 0-8389-0491-2.

Nearly 100 "kid-tested" titles are listed in this 4th edition of a basic book talk and reader's advisory tool. Most of the titles were published in the 1980's; only 17 have been used in the 1979 edition (which incidentally is still useful). All of the books written originally for adults can be recommended for young adults with complete confidence. It's so safe that even the few titles that contain explicit sex or violence are noted. The time-tested formula has been used in this edition: Details of plot or content are followed by comments on appropriateness and special uses, followed by a few suggestions of other books of related interest. This title is highly recommended for all school and public libraries that serve young adults.

Young Adult Literature; Book Talks

Y*

421. **Connecting Young Adults and Libraries: A How-to-do-it Manual**, by Patrick Jones. Neal-Schuman, 1992. 278p. $35. 1-55570-108-6.

This is primarily an extremely valuable guide to programming in libraries to attract young adult patrons. It is aimed at the thousands of public libraries that do not have a young adult librarian and includes ideas for promoting volunteerism, connecting with other groups, booktalking, program suggestions, censorship, etc. For the purposes of collection development, there is a YA core collection, lists of popular magazines, and addresses of major publishers. Its overall contents make it a must for both school and public libraries, and its bibliographies serve as an added bonus, though much of this material appears elsewhere.

Young Adult Literature

C; Y

422. **The Newspaper: A Reference Book for Teachers and Librarians**, by Edward F. DeRoche. ABC-CLIO, 1991. 216p. $32.50. 0-87436-584-8.

The first few chapters of this excellent handbook/bibliography describe how newspapers can be incorporated into the K-12 curriculum and the important role they can play as an untapped educational resource. The second half includes lists of articles and curriculum resources. The real meat of this reference work for librarians as an asset for collection development is the 57-page bibliography of curriculum resources available from newspapers, foundations, and publishers. Bibliographic and ordering information is provided for all materials listed. This resource is recommended for all school and academic libraries developing collections of curriculum resource materials. *Newspapers*

Y*

423. **Seniorplots: A Book Talk Guide for Use with Readers Ages 15-18**, by John T. Gillespie and Corinne J. Naden. Bowker, 1989, 386p. $39.95 0-8352-2513-5.

This aid to booktalkers contains detailed notes on eighty books recommended for reading by senior high-aged readers. For each book there is a general introduction, a detailed plot summary, a listing of thematic material, and a guide to ways of introducing the book. Of interest in collection building are the lists of eight to ten additional recommended titles after each book entry. Each title is briefly annotated and is on the same or related themes as the main entry. The main titles are arranged by subject content (e.g., science fiction and fantasy, teenage concerns, historical fiction), and there are author, title, and subject indexes. The introduction consists of a brief manual on how to booktalk. Recommended for senior high and young adult collections. *Young Adult Literature; Book Talks*

Y

424. **Storytelling for Young Adults: Techniques and Treasury**, by Gail de Vos. Libraries Unlimited, 1991. 169p. $24.50 0-87287-832-5.

This book on storytelling for young adults (ages 13-18) is divided into five sections which include a rationale for story telling at this level, a description of techniques, the types of tales that appeal, and sample stories. For particular value in collection development is an annotated bibliography of 120 stories with appeal for young adults that supplies locationary information. The stories are summarized and arranged by such subjects as folktales and fairy tales; myths and legends; ghost, horror, and suspense tales; and tales of love. This is the only book devoted entirely to storytelling at this age level and therefore should be of particular value in young adult collections and in junior and senior high schools. *Storytelling*

C; Y
425. **Supporting School Curriculum with U.S. Government Publications**, by Susan Lawrence. Manchester City Library, 1990. 42p. $5.

This brief guide is a list of both print and audio-visual materials available through the federal government that have use as learning materials in the school curriculum. They are organized under 35 subject headings, and each of the citations is annotated. Addresses and telephone numbers are included. This bibliography is available for $5 from: Manchester City Library, Carpenter Memorial Building, 405 Pine St., Manchester, NH 03104. *United States—Government Publications*

C; Y
426. **Using Government Documents: A How-To-Do-It Manual for School Librarians**, by Melody S. Kelly. Neal-Schuman, 1992. 176p. $29.95. 1-55570-106-X.

The first part of this handy little volume is chock full of practical tips for ordering and using free and inexpensive U.S. government documents. The main part of the text consists of a listing of recommended documents organized into broad subject (curriculum) areas with recommended grade level designations. The intended audience is elementary and middle schoolers; however, many of the ideas and manuals apply equally well for higher grade levels. Annotations are provided as in Ekhaml and Wittig's *U.S. Government Publications for the School Library Media Center*. However, the clearly divided curriculum areas do aid in accessing documents by subject. Also the Kelly work focuses on a younger level. Most school media centers may want to consider both for beginning and developing a collection of documents.
United States—Government Publications

Science and Social Studies

Y*; A
427. **America as Story: Historical Fiction for Secondary Schools**, by Elizabeth F. Howard. American Library Association, 1988. 156p. $22. 0-8389-0492-0.

More than 150 fiction works on American history are included in this highly selected bibliography useful for teachers and students in grades 7-12. The fully annotated titles are arranged in chronological order under broad topics from Colonial America to America in the Modern World. The titles were selected for literary quality and historical accuracy by Howard and a panel of curriculum specialists. Each annotation gives a plot summary, suggestions for follow-up activities, and recommended reading level. This well-developed bibliography is recommended as an important selection guide for all secondary school and public libraries. *United States—History—Fiction*

C*; Y*
428. **Best Science and Technology Reference Books for Young People**, by H. Robert Malinowsky. Oryx, 1991. 216p. $24.95. pap. 0-89774-580-9.

Malinowsky, a well-known authority of science reference books, has selected 669 reference books in the field of science and technology appropriate for elementary, middle, and high school libraries. The titles were selected from major review sources and include some out-of-print titles, though the vast majority of the titles were published within the past ten years. The books are listed in 12 broad subject area chapters, e.g., General Science, Astronomy, Biology, Chemistry, etc. Within each subject area, entries are arranged by type of reference source, e.g., bibliography, biography, dictionary, etc. Each entry includes complete bibliographic information and a brief annotation. Grade level recommendations are also provided. Finally, this useful aid has four indexes: title, author, subject and grade level. This comprehensive and current bibliography is highly recommended as a collection building and reference tool for all school and public libraries. *Reference Books; Science; Technology*

Y*

429. **Celebrating the Dream**. New York Public Library, 1990. $5 pap.

This annotated list of 260 outstanding books for teenagers about the black experience was prepared by the young adult librarians of the New York Public Library. Both old and new fiction and nonfiction are included in 12 categories such as poetry, art and photography, music, young love, and Africa. This is a revision of the 1985 list, *On Being Black*. It can be ordered from the Office of Branch Libraries, New York Public Library, 455 Fifth Avenue, New York, NY 10016 for $5 plus $1 postage and handling.

African Americans; Young Adult Literature

Y*

430. **Economics: A Resource Book for Secondary Schools**, by James E. Davis and Regina McCormick. ABC-CLIO, 1988. 354p. $39. 0-87436-479-5. (Social Studies Resources for Secondary School Librarians, Teachers and Students).

This is a resource guide that is an orientation to current information about economics. In the first four chapters there is an essay that defines economics and economic concerns, a chronology from 1500 to 1986, biographies of 16 famous economists, and basic tables of information. The next three chapters contain the heart of the book. There is a directory of economic organizations which list their purposes and publications, followed by lists of important reference books and a 150 page chapter that enumerates hundreds of classroom materials useful for teaching economics. This should be a great help to both teachers and librarians. Others in the series (many of which have their own entries) follow the same pattern of organization and should be of equal value. They are: *Geography* by A. David Hill and Regina McCormick (1989, $39. 0-87436-519-8), *Global/International Issues and Problems* by Lynn S. Parisi and Robert D. LaRue, Jr. (1989, $39. 0-87436-536-8), *U.S. History* by James R. Giese and Laurel R. Singleton (1989, 2 volumes, $39. each, 0-87436-505-8 and 0-87436-506-6), and *U.S. Government* by Mary Jane Turner and Sara Lake (1989, $39. O-87436-535-X). *Economics; Social Studies; Young Adult Literature*

Y*

431. **Global Beat: A List of Multi-Cultural Books for Teenagers**. Office of Young Adult Services, New York Public Library. 34p. $5.

This 32 page pamphlet lists multicultural books for teens under ten main headings such as, "The Far East," "Latin America and The Caribbean," "Native Americans," and "Coming to the U.S.A." Each is annotated with the teenager in mind. Copies are available for $5 plus mailing charges of $1 from: Office of Branch Libraries, New York Public Library, 455 Fifth Ave., New York, NY 10016.

Multiculturalism; Young Adult Literature

Y

432. **Hidden Treasure: An Annotated Bibliography of Women in History**. The Bronx High School of Science, [1990]. 255p. pap. $10.

This paperback volume lists books in the collection of the library at the Bronx High School of Science that deal with women's roles in history. It is arranged first by broad geographical areas and then by time periods. It is available for $10 per copy from The Bronx High School of Science, 75 W. Main St., Bronx, NY 10468. *Women*

Y; A

433. **The High School Mathematics Library**, by William L. Schaaf. 8th ed. National Council of Teachers of Mathematics, 1987. 83p. $7.80 (pap.). 0-87353-238-4.

This bibliography was first published in 1960 and is revised approximately every five years. The present volume contains about eleven hundred titles suitable for use by high school and community college students as well as teachers and librarians. About two hundred of the titles are new to this edition. The books are organized under 19 general subjects, such as history, philosophy, various branches of mathematics, biography, dictionaries, periodicals, and selected references for teachers. Those titles that are considered basic are given an star. There are about 300 starred entries in this edition. Each entry contains full bibliographic information and, when necessary, a brief annotation. This work is both a fine research guide as well as a valuable selection aid for librarians. *Mathematics*

C; Y

434.   **Literature for Young People on War and Peace: An Annotated Bibliography**, comp. by Harry Eiss. Greenwood, 1989. 131p. $35. 0-313-26068-0.

Almost 400 titles on all aspects of war and peace and related subjects are arranged alphabetically by author. A broad subject or type of literature arrangement might be less difficult to use; however, the author-title-subject index helps somewhat.

Criteria for inclusion are not given. Each entry contains full bibliographic data, and an annotation ranging from a one-liner to almost a full page. Despite the fact that the work is very expensive and some errors exist, there is no comparable list available and it is therefore recommended for most libraries.

Peace; War; Children's Literature; Young Adult Literature

C; Y

435.   **Nuclear Age Literature for Youth: The Quest for a Life-affirming Ethic**, by Millicent Lenz. American Library Association, 1990. 315p. $32.50. pap. 0-8389-0535-8.

The purpose of this interesting work is to identify and analyze books for children and young adults which deal with the fears and anxieties of nuclear war and its aftermath. Identification is also made of the development in literature of a new kind of hero, a biophile—a "lover of the total life system." Critical analyses and plot summaries are provided for many titles which will help teachers develop units on peace, and help librarians acquire related materials. This unique text is recommended for school and public libraries for reference and collection developments.   *Nuclear War; Arms Control; Peace*

Y*

436.   **Science and Technology in Fact and Fiction: A Guide to the Best Young Adult Books**, by DayAnn Kennedy and others. 1990, Bowker. 368p. $36. 0-8352-2710-3.

This is a guide to 380 trade books in science and technology suitable for junior and senior high school students. Both juvenile and adult books have been included if they meet the criteria involving literary quality, accuracy, quality of illustrations, appropriateness, and general suitability. A few outstanding out-of-print titles are included. There are two main sections in the work, one for science and the other for technology. These are subdivided into fiction and nonfiction. The emphasis is on nonfiction with only a total of 62 fiction titles included. Titles in each section are arranged by authors' last names. There are extensive annotations for each book, many a page in length. Each is divided into two sections, one for summary information and the other for evaluation. Full bibliographic material and grade level suitability is also given for each book. There are author, title, subject, and readability indexes. In the latter, using the Fry formula, the books are listed by level of difficulty from grade 3 to 12+. This is a valuable resource for both teachers and librarians.   *Science; Young Adult Literature; Technology*

Y

437.   **U.S. Government: A Resource Book for Secondary Schools**, by Mary Jane Turner and Sara Lake. ABC-CLIO, 1989. 317p. $39. 0-87436-535-X.

This handy quick-reference book is loaded with excellent information resources dealing with the U.S. Government. For example, the beginning chapters include the purposes and principles of the U.S. Government, the Constitution, political parties, a chronology of important documents, members of congress, all of the presidents, etc. The last third of the book contains a bibliography of reference works, including printed sources and online databases, relating to the U.S. Government and a list of classroom materials, which include print, audio, video, and computer sources. Each entry gives complete bibliographic information and a brief annotation. A detailed index of subjects, titles, and authors is also provided. Much of what is available here can be found in other readily accessible reference sources; however, the bibliographies are useful to both students and teachers; and can serve as a librarian's acquisition guide.

United States—Politics and Government

Y

438.   **U.S. History: A Resource Book for Secondary Schools. Volume 1: 1450-1865**, by James R. Giese and Laurel R. Singleton. ABC-CLIO, 1989. 347p. $39. 0-87436-505-8. (Social Studies Resources for Secondary Schools).

Y

439.   **U.S. History: A Resource Book for Secondary Schools. Volume 2: 1865-Present**, by James R. Giese and Laurel R. Singleton, ABC-CLIO, 1989. 340p. $39. 0-87436-506-6. (Social Studies Resources for Secondary Schools).

The two volumes cited above were designed to stand alone. While there is some duplication in the introductory pages, they include so much specifically suited to each volumes' inclusive dates, that both are necessary. They provide annotated listings of reference works on U.S. history, including atlases, dictionaries and encyclopedias, biographical sources, almanacs, periodicals, and online databases. AV materials, computer software, print material, and textbooks are listed by format with detailed descriptive annotations. This two volume set is recommended for all secondary school library media centers and other libraries serving secondary school teachers and students. *United States—History*

C; Y

440. **Using Literature to Teach Middle Grades About War**, by Phyllis K. Kennemer. Oryx, 1993. 209p. $29.95. pap. 0-89774-778-X.

This book is undoubtedly a one-of-a-kind. Kennemer has developed a series of study units around six wars involving the United States: Revolutionary and Civil Wars, World Wars I and II, Vietnam, and the Persian Gulf. The plan for each unit is similar: a selected chronology, a list of recommended books, a sample lesson plan, suggested activities, and a glossary. The recommended books include classics as well as current fiction and nonfiction (including biography) and picture books. Most of the titles are for grades six through 8; however, a number of titles for the more advanced reader as well as the reluctant reader are included. Author and title indexes complete this interesting work which is recommended for all school and public libraries. *Children's Literature; War; Young Adult Literature*

C; Y

441. **War and Peace Literature for Children and Young Adults: A Resource Guide to Significant Issues**, by Virginia A. Walter. Oryx, 1993. 171p. $27.50. 0-89774-725-9.

This resource guide is more than a bibliography. Walter devotes a great deal of the book discussing developmental needs of young people and relating them to problems evolving an under-standing of such events as holocaust, concentration camps, and the bombing of Hiroshima. Other issues discussed, all within the framework of a bibliography, include the futility and nobility of war, survival, heroism, and propaganda. The sections on peace and conflict resolution are especially well-developed. Bibliographic citations are adequate. Other strong features of this work include an annotated list of resources for adults and four complete indexes. It is interesting to note that Kennemer's book, *Using Literature to Teach Middle Grades About War*, another worthwhile resource on the same subject was published in 1993; however, it has a narrower focus both in level and in coverage. Nevertheless, both books are recommended as reference guides and as aids for collection development in school and public libraries.

Peace; War; Children's Literature; Young Adult Literature

Y*

442. **Women in the World: Annotated History Resources for the Secondary Student**, ed. by Lyn Reese and Jean Wilkinson. Scarecrow, 1987. 220p. $27.50. 0-8108-2050-1.

With the aid of the Women's Educational Equity Act Grant from the U.S. Department of Education, Reese and Wilkinson have compiled a much needed resource on the role and impact of women in the world. Materials are organized by chapters which cover all areas of the world. Within each chapter, the items are arranged under the following categories: Background/Reference; Anthology; Autobiography/Biography; First Person Accounts; and Fiction and Curriculum. Entries contain full bibliographical information and an annotation which includes reading level and possibly some suggested activities. Selected AV materials are also included. Finally, there is an appendix of publisher addresses and a title and place index. Highly recommended for all secondary school libraries as a reference and collection development tool.

Women; Developing Countries

Special Audiences

C*; Y*

443. **The Best: High/Low Books for Reluctant Readers**, by Marianne Laino Pilla. Libraries Unlimited, 1990. 100p. $11.50. 0-87287-532-6.

The 374 high/low titles included in this list were chosen on the basis of quality, reading level, and, most importantly, on how they would appeal to young people in grades three to twelve. Reluctant readers are defined by the author, an experienced children's librarian, as those reading 2 levels or more below grade level. Fiction and nonfiction titles are included; detailed criteria for inclusion are clearly stated in the well-written introduction. Titles are arranged alphabetically by author and numbered. Each entry includes full bibliographical data, a brief annotation, and grade and reading levels. Title, subject, and grade/reading level indexes complete this useful tool. This brief, inexpensive and up-to-date guide is recommended for all libraries serving children and young adults. *High Interest-Low Vocabulary Books*

Y*

444. The Best Years of Their Lives: A Resource Guide for Teenagers in Crisis, by Stephanie Zvirin. American Library Association, 1992. 122p. $18. pap. 0-8389-0586-2.

This excellent guide was compiled by the *Booklist* associate editor of Books for Youth. Her stated purpose is to "Give adolescents, ages 12-18, a better understanding of what growing up in a rapidly changing world is all about." Today's youth are faced with unimaginable problems and concerns such as drugs, AIDS, suicide, pregnancy, and abuse. This bibliography evaluates analyzes about 200 nonfiction self-help titles (a small number of fiction books and films are also included) that deal with these subjects. All of the titles are relatively recent and in-print and will undoubtedly be of interest to today's teens. Therefore this timely bibliography is highly recommended as both a reading guidance and selection aid for all school and public libraries serving today's adolescents. *Young Adult Literature*

Y

445. Bridges of Respect: Creating Support for Lesbian and Gay Youth, by Katherine Whitlock. American Friends Service Committee, 1989. 97p. $7.50. 0-910082-39-1.

This sensitively written book for young people under the auspices of the American Friends Service Committee (a Quaker organization) makes a strong case against homophobia (the fear or hatred of lesbians and gay males) which it indicates harms everyone. This straight-forward discussion of stereotypes, diversity, and differences, health, and sexuality is followed by a list of resources including publications as well as audiovisual materials. To order, send a check for $7.50 payable to AFSC to: American Friends Service Committee, 1501 Cherry St., Philadelphia, PA 19102-1479. *Homosexuality; Lesbianism*

C*; Y*; A*

446. Easy Reading: Book Series and Periodicals for Less Able Readers, by Randall J. Ryder and others. 2nd ed. International Reading Association, 1989. 90p. $8.75 pap. 0-87207-234-7.

This important resource for teachers, reading specialists and librarians gives thorough reviews for 44 recommended high interest-low vocabulary book series and 15 periodicals useful in work with poor readers in grades four through twelfth grades. This paperback is organized into five parts which cover bibliographic and ordering information, descriptive annotation plus thorough evaluations for each series and periodicals, lists of supplementary materials like filmstrips and workbooks, and individuals titles in each series. There are indexes that analyze contents under such subjects as romance or adventure, give the ethnic orientation of each series, and categorize each series by reading and grade and interest levels. This is an extremely valuable book for those working with both adults and young people with reading problems.

High Interest-Low Vocabulary Books

Y

447. Experiencing Adolescence: A Sourcebook for Parents, Teachers and Teens, by Richard Lerner and Nancy L. Galambos. Teachers College, 1987. 422p. $19.95 pap. 0-8077-2884-7.

This annotated selective bibliography lists books, periodical articles, audiovisual materials, and organizations under such subjects as puberty, sexuality, social relationships, substance abuse, health, careers, and handicapped adolescents. Each chapter begins with an overview and a report on research followed by the list of resources. This is still a fine book for development of professional collections and for identifying resources in junior and senior high schools, but is seriously flawed because of its age.

Adolescence

C; Y

448. Families with Young Adolescents: A Resource List. Center for Early Adolescence, [1988]. 55p. $5.

This update of a 1983 publication is divided into two sections, one for professionals and one for parents. It selectively lists and annotates print materials on such subjects as peer relationships; adolescent development; health and sexuality; and gender, racial, and ethnic issues. This very useful bibliography is available for $5 from the Center for Early Adolescence, University of North Carolina at Chapel Hill, 223 Carr Mill Mall, Carrboro, NC 27510. Also ask to be placed on their mailing list. *Adolescence*

Y

449.   **High-Interest Books for Teens: A Guide to Book Reviews and Biographical Sources**, by Joyce Nakamura. 2nd ed. Gale, 1988. 539p. $99. 0-8103-1830-X.

In an alphabetical listing by author, over 3,500 young adult and adult books that the editor believes have extensive appeal to adolescents are included with biographical sources given for the author and review citations for each book. Both fiction and nonfiction titles are included, but there is no indication of either interest or reading levels. There are both title and subject indexes. A number of factors limit the use of this book: its lack of consistent criteria for inclusion, its price, the lack of interest and reading levels, and the fact that over half of the titles included are now out of print. Nevertheless, large collections that need material on high interest books will find some value here.

Young Adult Literature; High Interest-Low Vocabulary Books

Y*

450.   **High Interest-Easy Reading: A Booklist for Junior and Senior High School Students**, by William G. McBride. 6th ed. National Council of Teachers of English, 1990. 133p. $8.95 pap. 0-8141-2097-0.

This bibliography contains about 400 fiction and nonfiction titles arranged by author under such broad topics as adventure, death, historical fiction, love and friendship, sports, and mystery. Each entry gives both bibliographical information and an interest-provoking annotation aimed at the teenager. The choices are well made and there is a subject index that allows finding works under specific topics like Vietnam War and AIDS. Only recently published books are included; therefore, librarians should continue to use earlier volumes (now unfortunately out of print) to supplement the present volume. One of the best titles on books for reluctant teenage readers.   *High Interest-Low Vocabulary Books; Young Adult Literature*

Y*

451.   **High/Low Handbook: Encouraging Literacy in the 1990s**, by Ellen V. Libretto. 3rd ed. Bowker, 1990. 304p. $41. 0-8352-2804-5. (Serving Special Needs Series).

This standard work on dealing with poor or reluctant readers is in three parts. The first is a series of essays on writing, publishing, and working with these special populations. The second, "Selecting and Evaluating High/Low Materials," deals with computers and reading, readability factors, and methods of determining reading levels. The third part, "The Core Collection," is an annotated bibliography of 312 high/low books that were published after 1985. Most are fiction, but there are some biographies and general nonfiction titles, and all are for students reading at first- to fifth-grade reading levels. There is an additional bibliography of about 100 titles suitable for youngsters at the fourth- to eighth-grade reading level. In appendixes there are annotated lists of other bibliographies and magazine sources, a directory of publishers and author, plus title and subject indexes. An extremely useful book for junior and senior high school libraries and public libraries.   *High Interest-Low Vocabulary Books; Young Adult Literature*

Y*

452.   **Out of the Closet and into the Classroom: Homosexuality in Books for Young People**, by Laurel A. Clyde and Marjorie Lobban. Bowker, 1992. 150p. $35. pap. 1-875589-02-3.

Over 120 titles are listed in this fully-annotated bibliography dealing with an important and timely topic. A discussion of sexual activity and awareness is treated in an incidental nature and is not explicit or over-emphasized. Entries are arranged alphabetically by author. Most of the books are intended for the pre-teen and young adult; however, six picture books for two to five year olds are also included. Also, while most of the titles are fiction and deal with male homosexuality (gay sex), almost 1/4 are concerned with lesbian sex. A special feature of the book are the seven appendices which include: stories with homosexual main characters; books that just mention homosexuality or use homosexual terms; and books by homosexual authors. This book is recommended for collection development and for reading guidance and reference use by teachers/librarians/parents. It is recommended for all school and public libraries.

Young Adult Literature; Homosexuality; Lesbianism

Y*

453.   **Outstanding Books for the College Bound**, Comp. by the Young Adult Services Division of the ALA. American Library Association, 1991. $.30 each; $20 for 100 (see below for more details).

Five newly revised and updated series are available for reading guidance to young people planning on college. They include a large variety of subjects and literary styles. Most of the titles listed are readily available in most school and public libraries. However, the lists are also useful for evaluating and filling in gaps in the existing collections. The available series include:

Fiction - 0-8389-5698-X
Biographies - 0-8389-5699-8
Fine Arts - 0-8389-5700-5
Theater - 0-8389-5701-3
Nonfiction - 0-8389-5702-1.

Single copies are available for $.30 and a SASE. Quantity orders are available at discounted prices: 50 for $11.25; 100 for $20.; 250 for $43.75, etc. Quantity discounts are based on single titles only, not total order quantity. Send orders to: ALA Graphics, 50 E. Huron St., Chicago, IL 60611.

Young Adult Literature

Y
454. **Quick Picks for Great Reading, 1993**. Young Adult Services Division. American Library Association, 1991. $24. per 100.
   This lively brochure contains 65 annotated titles that are intended to stimulate interest in reluctant teenage readers. All titles are at the sixth grade reading level or below, but have high interest appeal in terms of content, format, and artwork. All books are published since 1989. The list is available annually. Copies are available at $24. for 100 copies from: ALA Graphics, 50 E. Huron St., Chicago, IL 60611.

Young Adult Literature; High Interest-Low Vocabulary Books

Y; A
455. **Reading Lists for College-Bound Students**, by Doug Estell et al. Arco/Prentice Hall, 1990. 255p. $10. 0-13-756248-9.
   This is a compilation of nearly 100 lists of books recommended by various colleges. The intended purpose is to give college-bound students a head start on their reading as they prepare for college. The editors have compiled a composite list of "100 Most-Often-Recommended Works." This list is annotated, and each entry contains full bibliographic data. Perhaps most high school and public libraries would want to check their holdings against this list of 100. *Young Adult Literature; Adult Books And Reading*

Y
456. **Recommended Books for Reluctant Readers**. Recommended Books for Reluctant YA Readers Committee. American Library Association, annual.
   This ALA committee compiles a special list of hi/lo books each year. All titles are of young adult appeal and on the 6th grade or below reading level. They are aimed at teenagers who simply do not like to read. This list is available for 30 cents. Quantity discounts are available. For more information or to order send a SASE to: YASD/ALA, 50 E. Huron St., Chicago, IL 60611.

Young Adult Literature; High Interest-Low Vocabulary Books

Y
457. **Sex Guides: Books and Films about Sexuality for Young Adults**, by Patty Campbell. Garland, 1986. 374p. $27. 0-8240-8693-7 (Garland Reference Library of Social Science, Vol. 312).
   This exhaustive work on sex guides for young adults is divided into two parts: the first is an historical overview and the second, an analysis of contemporary publications on the subject. The first traces, decade by decade, publications on sex education from 1892 to the 1970s. Each chapter contains a bibliographic essay plus a list of the books discussed. There are about 400 books analyzed in these chapters. The second section covers sex guides, young adult fiction on the subject, religious sex books, films and books on specific sex topics such as pregnancy and diseases. The last chapter tells how professionals can provide reliable information and develop a good reference collection for adolescents. There are also lists of core materials for different age levels and for various library sizes. This is a book that is useful for reading guidance and collection building as well as being a fascinating document on social history.

Sex Education

C; Y
458. **Sexuality Education: A Resource Book**, by Carol Cassel and Pamela M. Wilson. Garland, 1989. 350p. $69. 0-8240-7899-3.
   This is basically a collection of articles for teachers of sexuality that deal with such aspects of the subject, such as those involving the family, human relationships, medicine, and biology. There are four sections, one each on the family, school, and community and the last a description of twelve model programs

and the issues involved in teaching sexuality to adolescents. Each section closes with an annotated bibliography, and within the chapters there are references to resources that can be valuable for building professional collections in this area. *Sex Education*

Y*

459. **Substance Abuse: A Resource Guide for Secondary Schools**, by Sally L. Myers and Blanche Woolls. Libraries Unlimited, 1991. 167p. $28.50 0-87287-805-8.

This extremely useful bibliography is divided into six chapters that deal with general reference items, teacher resources, materials for parents, free or inexpensive publications, a list of agencies, and a core collection of items considered to be essential in a secondary school library. All of the items are annotated and indicate journals where reviews have appeared, grade levels, and specially recommended items. The materials have either been examined or field-tested before inclusion and cover the use of drugs, alcohol, tobacco, and steroids, among other substances. Although aimed at high school libraries, this will also be useful in public library collections. *Drugs; Alcoholism; Steroids; Tobacco; Substance Abuse*

Adult Sources

12 General Reference Works

General and Miscellaneous

A

460. **American Book Publishing Record ABPR Cumulative...: An Annual Cumulation of American Book Production in .... Bowker**. annual, $200. (approx.)

An annual cumulation based on the 12 monthly issues of the *Record*. Recent years included over 35,000 titles published by American publishers; excluded are government publications, subscription books, dissertations, periodicals, and publications under 49 pages. Not truly a "selection guide," this compilation which is generally very accurate is useful for identifying publications and providing adequate bibliographical data for acquisition and technical services departments. See also *Forthcoming Books*. Recommended mainly for larger libraries or regional centers. *Books and Publishing*

A*

461. **Best Books for Public Libraries: The 10,000 Top Fiction and Nonfiction Titles**, ed. by Steve Arozena. Bowker, 1992. 1,024p. $75. 0-8352-3073-2.

This one-volume selective bibliography is based on positive reviews from highly-regarded sources such as *Library Journal, Booklist, Choice*, and *The New York Times Book Review*. According to the publisher, "this definitive, one-volume resource offers public library professionals a first-ever selective bibliography of the 'basic repertoire' of the 10,000+ best books in print." The titles are divided into fiction (arranged by genre) and nonfiction (arranged by Dewey class number), and identify award winners, best-sellers, and large-type editions. Each entry provides full bibliographic information, as well as a brief annotation. This "newcomer" compares very favorably with the old-standby: *Public Library Catalog* (now in its 9th edition). It is suggested that most public libraries have both titles on their reference/selection-tool shelf. *Adult Books and Reading*

A

462. **Bibliographic Index**. H. W. Wilson, current. Available in various formats: Subscription which includes two paperbound issues and a hardcover annual cumulation, Sold on the service basis (book budget); Online and tape; Not currently available in CD ROM. ISSN 0006-1255.

This bibliography of bibliographies has been a starting point for research for over 50 years. It includes bibliographies published in English and other Germanic and the Romance languages. It includes bibliographies of more than 50 citations found in books, pamphlets, or in more than 2,800 periodicals. Entries are arranged in alphabetical order by LC subject headings, and each provides complete bibliographic information on the bibliography indexed and indicates whether it is annotated. This basic index is useful for collection development and is recommended for all academic and public libraries. *Bibliography*

A*

463. **The Book Buyer's Advisor**, ed. by Bill Ott. Triumph Press, 1991. 408p. $49.95. 0-9624436-2-X. pap. $14.95. 0-9624436-1-1.

Intended as a reader's advisory guide, this listing of new books reprints recent reviews from ALA's *Booklist* and organizes them for browsing. Books that are expected to be popular are chosen, and nonfiction are arranged into 23 "interest appealing" categories, e.g., business, parenting, true crime, etc.; fiction titles are listed under general, mystery and espionage, and science fiction. Over 1,200 titles are included in this repackaged list of books that all librarians know were recommended by the *Booklist* staff. This list, which is updated annually, is more up-to-date and has a different focus than *The Reader's Catalog* and the highly-regarded *Reader's Adviser*. Author and title indexes aid in the use of this guide which is recommended for all public libraries as an aid to providing collections of good reading. *Note*: The 1992 edition is published under the title: *Booklist's Guide to the Year's Best Books: Definitive Reviews of Over 1,000 Fiction and Nonfiction Titles in All Fields*. *Adult Books and Reading*

Y*; A*
464. **Book Review Digest**, Annual. H. W. Wilson, 1905-present. Sold on Service Basis.

This standard reference tool, which has been published continuously for almost 100 years, provides excerpts from and citations to reviews of current adult and juvenile fiction and nonfiction. Currently, it covers over 6000 English-language books each year. Concise, critical evaluations are culled from about 95 selected periodicals. Entries are arranged alphabetically, and each entry includes full bibliographic information, a descriptive note, age or grade level, and review excerpts. A subject and title index is provided. A subscription provides 10 monthly paperbound issues, including cumulations in May, August, and October, plus a permanent annual bound cumulation. This is sold on a service basis, based on a library's annual book budget. *Book Review Digest* is also online and on CD-ROM (write to publisher for details). This guide is recommended for reference and collection evaluation and collection building for all but the smallest libraries. *Book Reviews*

A
465. **Booklist's Guide to the Year's Best Books: Definitive Reviews of Over 1,000 Fiction and Nonfiction Titles in All Fields**, ed. by Bill Ott. Triumph Books, 1992. 408p. $49.95. 1-880141-07-8; $14.95. pap. 1-880141-08-6.

The only real difference between this 1992 edition and its earlier edition is the title. It was first published in 1991 as *The Book Buyer's Advisor* which is still available. The aim and focus remain the same, to serve as a guide to quality adult book titles and an aid in collection development. All of the selected 1,000 titles previously appeared in *Booklist*. Fiction is arranged by popular headings such as, Mystery & Espionage, Science Fiction, etc. Nonfiction is arranged in 23 categories. This title and its predecessor is recommended for any public library as a handy reference tool and acquisition aid.

Adult Books and Reading

A
466. **Books for Adult New Readers: A Bibliography Developed by Project: LEARN**, by Frances Josephson Pursell. 4th ed. rev. New Readers Press, 1989. 210p. $14.95. 0-88336-599-5.

Project: LEARN, an adult literacy project developed by the Greater Cleveland Interchurch Council which is affiliated with Laubach Literacy Action soon discovered that there was a scarcity of adult interest/low level reading books. This bibliography of about 500 titles of books of high interest and 7th grade or below reading level is intended to identify those titles that fulfill that need. Each title has been evaluated against basic criteria such as appeal, unstereotyped characters, size of print, etc. All of the titles are in English and do not attempt to meet the special needs of handicapped or foreign language speaking adults. This bibliography is an essential resource for all public libraries developing collections for adult new readers or as an enrichment aid for library-sponsored literacy programs.

Literacy Programs; High Interest/Low Vocabulary Books

A*
467. **Books for College Libraries**, Ed. by Virginia Clark. 3rd. ed. American Library Association, 1988. 6v. $550. 0-8389-3353-X.

This much-needed new edition of a basic retrospective bibliography for academic libraries lists 50,000 titles designated as a core collection for academic libraries. The first five volumes are divided by broad disciplinary designations, and the 6th serves as a cumulative author and title index: v.1 Humanities; v.2 Language and Literature; v.3 History; v. 4 Social Sciences; v. 5 Psychology, Science, Technology, and Bibliography. Titles are arranged in each volume by LC Classification and entries appear as MARC records. This essential tool serves as a collection evaluation tool, an aid for collection development, and a guide for reader's advising and reference work, and is therefore recommended for all academic libraries.

Adult Books and Reading

Y; A
468. **Books in Print, 1992-93**. Bowker, 1992. 10v. $397. 0-8352-3205-0.

Books in Print and its various spin-offs are so widely known and used by librarians, book sellers, and the general public that it seems almost too obvious to list in this guide. However, this note will briefly describe the 1992-93 edition and merely list the bibliographic citations for the other titles in the "series."

The current edition contains over one million adult, juvenile, popular and scholarly titles, and other books considered trade books and usually available to the general public "books one might expect to find in a general bookstore." This would exclude most textbooks, serial publications, and government documents. Over 130,000 new titles are include in this new edition. The work is published in 10 volumes: 4 author; 4 title; 1 Out-of-Print/Out-of Stock Indefinitely, O.P./O.S.I; and 1 complete directory of publishers.

For each title, complete and current bibliographic and ordering information is provided, including pages, price, publisher, date, edition, and ISBN. *Books in Print* relies upon annual updating through Electronic Data Interchange. This database is also available online and on CD-ROM. See also in Periodical Section, *Forthcoming Books*. Related titles are *Subject Guide to Books in Print*. 5v. $281. 0-8352-3251-4; *Books in Print Supplement, 1992-1993*. 3v. $216. 0-8352-3220-4; *Paperbound Books in Print, Fall, 1992*. 6v. $187. 0-8352-3191-7. *Bibliographies, General*

A

469. **Books in Series, 1985-1989**. Bowker, 1989. 2v. $199.95. 0-8352-2679-4.

Undoubtedly, *Books in Series*, remains the most essential tool for keeping track of the many hard to locate titles published in series, both retrospectively from 1876 and currently.

The current edition maintains the high standards of accuracy of bibliographic searching. Five indexes, published in two volumes, "offer convenient access to full information on all original, re-printed, in-print, and out-of-print books published or distributed in the United States": Series and Book Entries for series titles; Series name heading, Author and title indexes, Subject Index, and Directory of Publishers. This tool is indispensable for filling inter-library loan requests, reference work, and for filling in gaps in areas of collection development for all academic and most public libraries. *Bibliographies, General; Series*

A

470. **Canadian Book Review Annual**, ed. by Joyce Wilson. 16th edition Simon and Pierre, 1991. 584p. $98.95. 0-88924-233-4.

This annual compilation, which is an evaluation of trade books of the previous year, involves the work of numerous subject specialists and will be of interest primarily in Canadian libraries.

Book Reviews—Canada

A

471. **Canadian Books in Print (year): Author and Title Index**, ed. by Marian Butler. University of Toronto Press, annual. approx. $125.

For Canadian libraries, this bibliography fills the gap between *Books in Print* and *British Books in Print* because it lists only the works currently being published by Canadian publishers. Information is collected from individual publishers who supply bibliographic information on current titles. At present, there are about 30,000 titles listed. As well as author and titles alphabets, there is a directory of publishers in the main volume. Quarterly updates are available in print and on microfiche. Also available annually in a hardcover edition is *Canadian Books in Print: Subject Index*. For Canadian libraries, this is an essential tool to determine availability of titles. *Bibliographies, General—Canada*

A

472. **Canadian Selection: Books and Periodical for Libraries**, by Mavis Cariou and others. 2nd ed. University of Toronto Press, 1985. 501p. $85. 0-8020-4630-4.

Geared to the special needs of small- to medium-sized Canadian public libraries, this second edition of this comprehensive bibliography lists 5,400 English language books for adults published in Canada, about Canada, or by Canadians through 1983. Part I is an annotated list arranged by the Dewey Decimal number, and Part II lists 255 basic Canadian periodicals. Other sections contain information on literary awards and author, title and subject indexes. Essential for Canadian libraries and large American libraries that need to build collections of Canadiana.

Canada; Canadian Literature; Bibliographies, General—Canada

A

473. **Covert Culture Sourcebook,** by Richard Kadrey. St. Martin's, 1993. $12.95 (pap.) 0-312-09776-X.

Richard Kadrey, who edits the "Whole Earth Catalog" column in the *San Francisco Chronicle*, has compiled a bibliography of 400 citations to unusual, off-beat items that represents unconventional tastes and trends. Each items is annotated and arranged under five different sections: books (with names of counter culture bookstores), magazines (some of them electronic journals), music (CDs and tapes), videos and "tools for living," which includes some software packages. This will be of value in libraries with selection aids similar in scope to the *Whole Earth Catalog*. *Subcultures*

A

474. **Cumulative Book Index**. Wilson, 1898+. service basis.

This is not a selection aid but instead can be used by acquisition to check publication dates and bibliographic records. Since 1898, it has served as an international bibliography of books published in the

English language. The print edition appears monthly except August with annual cumulations. Books are listed by author, title, and subject. This is found in academic, public, and larger school library collections only. *Bibliographies, General*

C; Y; A

475. **Current Issues Resource Builder: Free and Inexpensive Materials for Librarians and Teachers,** by Carol Smallwood. McFarland, 1989. 402p. $19.95 pap. 0-89950-388-8.

This comprehensive source book attempts to help in "locating many valuable, primary, and often scattered resources available for use in curricula, student and professional research and the library vertical file." In the first section, 280 social issues such as ozone layers, abortion, and bilingual education are listed alphabetically. Agencies offering material are then listed, plus the kinds of material offered and the grade and age suitability levels (kindergarten through adult). In section two, each of these agencies (2,000 in number) are listed alphabetically. For each, information is given on addresses, telephone numbers, purposes and services provided, format of material available, cost, selection aids available (like catalogs), age suitability, examples of materials and any regional offices of the agency. Inexpensive is defined as under $16. This will be particularly valuable for collection building in high schools and public libraries.

Free Material; Vertical File Materials

A

476. **Facts on File Bibliography Series,** ed. by Matthew Bruccoli. Facts on File, 1991-.

When complete, this sixteen volume series will span the entire field of American literature from 1588 to 1988. The volumes are arranged by period and genre including fiction, nonfiction, poetry, and drama. As of early 1992, three titles have appeared; they are *Facts on File Bibliography of American Fiction: 1588-1865* (1992, $75, 0-8160-2115-5), *Facts on File Bibliography of American Fiction: 1866-1918* (1991, $75. 0-81160-2116-3), and *Facts on File Bibliography of American Fiction: 1919-1988* (1991, 2 volumes, $145. 0-8160-2674-2). The latter is representative in scope and treatment of current and forthcoming volumes. It begins with two bibliographies: one on 100 basic references sources and 10 essential periodicals for the study of American literature, and the other a list of important general, historical, and critical sources on these topics. There follow entries for 219 writers born prior to 1941 whose first significant works were published after World War I. Representative writers include Faulkner, Mailer, Steinbeck, Updike, and Cheever. For each author, there is a brief biography, followed by a listing of published bibliographies of the author's works (both separately published bibliographies as well as those appearing as periodical articles or parts of books are included). All of the author's works are then arranged chronologically under type of publication like books or letters. The location of manuscript and archival collections related to the author are noted. Secondary works of significance are then listed also by type beginning with biographies and continuing with interviews and critical studies again found in entire books, parts of books, essays, special journals, or articles. Indexes include a chronology of noteworthy fiction and events. This is a significant new bibliographic tool that will be used in both academic and public libraries. *American Literature*

Y*; A*

477. **Free Resource Builder for Librarians and Teachers,** by Carol Smallwood. 2nd ed. McFarland, 1992. 352p. $24.95 0-89950-685-2.

This excellent guide to free library materials covers such formats as pamphlets, booklets, fliers, maps and charts that are available from businesses, government agencies, and nonprofit organizations. About 3,000 sources are identified. The book is divided into seven large sections covering the topics, business and finance, consumer affairs, government and legal affairs, health, library and archive usage, and travel and geography. Each has many subdivisions. There are additional sections on multiresource agencies which lists databases and clearinghouses, and special aids like film catalogs and curriculum guides, and a section called "Resource Management" that gives explicit directions on how to organize a vertical file including suggested subject headings. The listing of agency addresses is extremely valuable because, though many of the listed free materials may go out of print, these sources can be contacted for new publications. A valuable resource for both public, college, and high school libraries.

Free Material; Vertical File Materials

A

478. **Guide to Microforms in Print 1992.** Bowker/Saur, 1992. 700p. $258. 3-598-11082-0.

This annual compilation, once issued by Meckler, covers on an international basis both commercial and noncommercial publications in various microforms. All types of published material are included (e.g., books, journals, newspapers, government publications, and archival material) if available in a microform regardless of the format. Entries are arranged alphabetically and for each citation information includes author, title, volume, date, price, publisher, type of microform and ordering information. There is a separate publishers directory. In midyear a separate update, *Guide to Microforms in Print Supplement* is published at $135. and, as an important accompanying volume to the main title, there is *Subject Guide to Microforms in Print 1991* (1,000p, $265. 3-598-11005-7). For large collections. *Microforms*

Y*; A*
479. **Information America: Sources of Print and Nonprint Materials Available from Organizations, Industry, Government Agencies, and Specialized Publishers—Master Volume**, by Fran Malin and Richard Stranzi 2nd ed. Neal-Schuman, 1993. 900p. $150. 1-55570-078-0.

Three times per year, Neal-Schuman issues a periodical called *Information America* (from years 1977 through 1982, it was called *Sources)* that lists useful but often neglected sources of materials for libraries. This volume is a compilation of the 2,500 sources thought to be most important. Specifically, this directory lists "major public and private organizations, government agencies, associations, research centers, specialized and alternative publishers, grassroots and citizens' groups, cooperatives, political parties, volunteer groups, consultants, lobbyists, historical and literary societies and foundations actively involved in publishing in all formats and subjects." These agencies are organized under broad subjects like health, business, and recreation and leisure. For each entry, there is a great deal of background material supplied including information services like seminars, plus a rundown on the types of materials and catalogs available. There follows a specific title list of materials—books, pamphlets, periodicals, and nonprint items, all with prices. There are four indexes, one for free and inexpensive material (about 4,000 items are listed), one for periodicals, a third for specific subjects, and an alphabetical listing of the organizations. Both the parent volume and the periodical issues are wonderful selection aids, particularly for issue oriented materials. It will be valuable for collection development in public and academic libraries and should be available on a school district-wide basis for high school libraries.

Free Material; Vertical File Materials; Information Services

A
480. **International Books in Print, 1992: A Listing of English Language Titles Published in Canada, Continental Europe, Latin America, Oceania, Africa, Asia, and the Republic of Ireland**. 11th ed. Bowker, 1992. 4 vols. part 1: 2,500p. $350. 3-598-22121-5; part 2: 2,050p. $350. 3-598-22122-3; complete set: $650.

This four-volume set nicely complements *Books in Print* and *British Books in Print* because it lists English-language titles published outside the U.S. and U.K. In part one (2 volumes) the books are listed by author and title, and in part 2 (2 volumes) they are arranged in 134 broad subject groups plus belles lettres. Titles with a country focus and those about individuals are listed in separate indexes. There is also a list of participating publishers. Over 185,000 titles are listed in the entire set. This bibliography is also available on CD-ROM for $795. For large collections. *Bibliographies, General*

Y; A
481. **Lesko's Info-Power**, by Matthew Lesko. Information USA, 1990. 1,086p. $33.95. 1-878346-02-4.

Wow! Over 30,000 fee and low-cost sources of information. Although many of the items listed here are readily available, e.g., from your congressman, this is a very handy compilation and ideal for building up the vertical file. If one is selective, this can be useful for most school and public libraries.

Free Material; Vertical File Materials

A
482. **Microform Market Place, 1992-1993: An International Directory of Micropublishing**, ed. by Barbara Hopkinson. K. G. Saur, 1993. 260p. $59.95. pap. 3-598-11094-4.

This directory which has been published biennially since 1974-75 is a basic and comprehensive guide to micropublishing; it does not include micrographic equipment or supplies. One of the six major sections is titled: "Bibliography of Primary Sources." This core collection of 47 titles of monographs and serials on microforms is annotated and each entry includes full bibliographic information. The entire volume is an excellent reference resource; however, the bibliography alone is worth the cost for all libraries developing collections of microforms. *Microforms*

A*

483. **Public Library Catalog**, ed. by Paula B. Entin and Juliette Yaakov. 9th ed. H. W. Wilson, 1989. 1,338p. $180. 0-8242-0778-5.

This ninth edition represents a well-balanced collection of nearly 7,300 of the best adult, nonfiction English-language titles currently in print. The selections are chosen by a panel of public librarians, and the books listed encompass a wide range of subjects published through 1988. It includes journals, reference titles, and contemporary subjects such as AIDS, holistic medicine, problems of the aging, and environmental concerns. Classified by subject, the entries include complete bibliographic data and descriptive annotations. This standard guide is invaluable for book selection and purchasing, general reference, reader's advisory work, and collection development and is recommended for every public library, no matter how small.

Adult Books and Reading

A

484. **Publishers Trade List Annual 1992: A Buying and Reference Guide to Books & Related Products**. Bowker, 1992. 4v. $258. 0-8352-3241-7.

This is a time-saving, space-saving 4 volume set of reproductions in uniform size of the catalogs of the major publishers of the United States and Canada. Small publishing houses are listed in the "yellow pages," with entries varying from one or two to a number of pages. Helpful indexes include an index of publishers, a subject index, and an index to publisher's series. Recommended for all libraries that order enough volumes to need all publishers' catalogs but wish to avoid the nuisance of storing hundreds of them.

Publishers' Catalogs

Y; A*

485. **Reader's Adviser**, ed. by Fred Kaplan. 13th ed. Bowker, 1986-88. 6v. $411. (for set of 6). 0-8352-2428-7.

Begun in 1921 as *Bookman's Manual*, this reference source has become a standard tool in almost all libraries and it continues to be "a reflection of the current state of the best available literature in print in the United States." It provides basic material for the nonspecialist, student, and librarian. This greatly expanded 13th edition provides profiles of its authors plus annotated bibliographies of selected in-print works by and about them. Each volume has its own introduction which provides interesting background concerning the genre. The six volumes are available as a set or as individual volumes for $91 each. The titles of the six volumes are as follows:

V. 1.   *The Best in American and British Fiction, Poetry, Essays, Literary Biography, Bibliography, and Reference*, Ed. by Fred Kaplan. 1986 783p. 0-8352-2145-8.

V. 2.   *The Best in American and British Drama and World Literature in English Translation*, Ed. by Maurice Charney. 1986. 898p. 0-8352-2146-6.

V. 3.   *The Best in General Reference Literature, the Social Sciences, History, and the Arts*, Ed. Paula T. Kaufman. 1986 780p. 0-8352-2147-4.

V. 4.   *The Best in the Literature of Philosophy and World Religions*, Ed. by William L. Reese. 1988. 801p. 0-8352-2148-2.

V. 5.   *The Best in the Literature of Science, Technology, and Medicine*, Ed. by Paul T. Durbin. 1988. 725p. 0-8352-2149-0.

V. 6.   *Indexes to Volumes 1-5*. 1988. 511p. 0-2352-2315-9.

A revised and expanded 14th edition of the *Reader's Adviser* has been announced to be published in 1994 at the cost of $110 per volume, $500 for the set.   *Adult Books and Reading; Reference Books*

Y; A

486. **The Reader's Catalog: An Annotated Selection of More Than 40,000 of the Best Books in Print...**, ed. by Geoffrey O'Brien. dist. by Random House, 1989. 1382p. $24.95. pap. 0-924322-00-4.

Wow! 40,000 English-language titles in a one-volume list. The titles are arranged under 208 different subject areas. All of the titles were in-print at the time of publication. Two limitations are that the criteria for inclusion of "best" books are not stated, and most annotations are very brief notes. Still, the price is right and most public libraries will want this, if for no other reason than it would serve as a quick identifying checklist on so many subject areas; this would make it a convenient first step in filling gaps in the collection.

Adult Books and Reading

A

487. **Selection of Library Materials in Applied and Interdisciplinary Fields**, by Beth J. Shapiro and John Whaley. American Library Association, 1987. 352 p. $50. 0-8389-0466-1.

Like the other volumes that come from the Collection Management and Development of ALA's Research and Technical Services Division, this contains a series of bibliographic essays each written by subject specialists. The fields covered in this volume include agriculture, business and management, communication, criminal justice, education, engineering, environment, geography, health sciences, home economics, law, public administration, race and ethnic studies, political radicalism, social work, sports and recreation, urban planning, and women's studies. Each gives an introduction to the field and an introduction to the literature, plus practical tips on acquisition and selected sources of information. This is a fine basic introduction to collection development in these various areas and should be of value in both public and academic libraries. *Social Sciences*

A

488. **Selection of Library Materials in the Humanities, Social Sciences, and Sciences**, by Patricia A. McClung. American Library Association, 1985. 405p. $55. 0-8389-3305-X.

This book of twenty-four bibliographic essays written by subject specialists gives practical advice on collection development plus information on key resources. Following a general introduction which includes information on obtaining out-of-print material, there are separate chapters on such areas as English and American literature, history, philosophy and religion, art and architecture, music, anthropology, sociology, economics and political science, biology, chemistry, computer science, physics, and astronomy. Special formats like government documents, small press publications, microforms, nonprint media, and data bases are treated in separate chapters. Although dated, this excellent introduction to basic materials and their acquisition will be of value in public and academic libraries. *Humanities; Social Sciences; Science*

Y; A

489. **Spanish-Language Books for Public Libraries**, ed. by Fabio Restrepo. American Library Association, 1986. 169p. $6.25. pap. 0-8389-0448-3.

This product of the Library Service to the Spanish-Speaking Committee of ALA's Reference and Adult Services Division lists more than 600 works of fiction, nonfiction, biography, and young adult fiction that meet the criteria of "literary merit and wide general appeal" and include works of "great Spanish writers of all times and countries." The arrangement is by the Dewey Decimal system except for the sections on biographies, periodicals, and the 20 fiction titles for young adults that are cited. All items were in print as of 1984. High priority items are starred, which allows small libraries to begin a core collection using these recommendations. Each item is given a brief annotation in English. There is an appended list of 13 distributors of Spanish materials in the U.S. and a combined author-title and subject index. A very useful bibliography for libraries serving a Spanish speaking population. *Spanish Literature*

A

490. **University Press Books for Public and Secondary School Libraries**. Association of American University Presses, 1991. 114p. free ISSN 1055-4173.

This new annual bibliography is a combination of the two AAUP annuals of recommended university press titles, one for public and one for school libraries which were issued for many years. Since there was a certain amount of overlap, the combined catalog listing more than 500 university press titles makes good sense. Journals and serials are excluded. Each annotated entry is arranged in Dewey Decimal Classification order; they are annotated with quotes from the reviews. An author and title index is provided. Suggested for all public libraries and school libraries, but especially the smaller libraries which may need help in acquiring appropriate titles from the large output of the University Presses. Free to librarians by writing on library's letterhead to: Association of American University Presses, Publications Department, 584 Broadway, Suite 410, New York, NY 10012. *University Press Books*

Biographies

A

491. **ARBA Guide to Biographical Dictionaries**, ed. by Bohdan S. Wynar. Libraries Unlimited, 1986. 444p. $40. 0-87287-492-3.

The purpose of this useful guide is to bring together selected reviews of biographical resources that were previously published during the past 20 years in various editions of *American Reference Books Annual* (ARBA). More than 700 biographical dictionaries, encyclopedias, and other sources are included. Each title has full bibliographical information and an annotation or review of over 100 words. There are also author/title and subject indexes. Recommended for most libraries building or evaluating a retrospective collection of biographical reference resources. *Biography; Reference Books*

A
492. **Biographical Dictionaries and Related Works**, ed. by Robert B. Slocum. 2nd ed. Gale, 1986. 2v. 1,319p. $160. 0-8103-0243-8.

This standard and award-winning guide to biographical dictionaries, now in its 2nd completely revised and updated edition, contains about 16,000 entries arranged in three major sections: Universal Biography; National or Area Biography; and Biography: Vocations. Entries contain full bibliographic information. Author, title, and subject indexes are provided. This guide is recommended for all libraries which have extensive and growing collections of biographies. *Biography*

Y; A
493. **Biographical Sources: A Guide to Dictionaries and Reference Works**, by Diane J. Cimbala et al. Oryx, 1986. 146p. $35. 0-89774-136-6.

There are a number of authoritative bio-bibliographical sources. This one has as purpose "to assist researchers in identifying which sources are most likely to contain personal data about the persons they are interested in studying." Nearly 700 biographical dictionaries, indexes, and collective biographies are described and evaluated. Coverage has a cut-off date of 1984 and all works are in English and published in the United States or Canada. Entries have full bibliographic information as well as an annotation. Subject and title indexes complete the volume. There are two similar works: *ARBA Guide to Biographical Dictionaries* which has about the same number of titles but is to limited to recent publications, and Slocum's *Biographical Dictionaries and Related Works*, which is international in scope and has about 16,000 listings although it is not selective. However, Cimbala has an emphasis on works with personal data and includes a far larger percentage of juvenile titles, and is therefore recommended for purchase for school and public libraries. Many libraries will want to consider purchase of all three titles since they all perform a specific role. *Biography*

A
494. **Biography: An Annotated Bibliography**, by Carl Rollyson. Salem Press, 1992. 215p. $40. 0-89356-678-0.

Rollyson has compiled an extensive list of sources which deal with biography as literature. The first chapter covers biographers' comments on biography. This is followed by chapters that deal with the history and criticism of biography as well as an analysis of the works of well-known biographers and their contributions to the genre. The final chapters deal with new and special approaches to biography and the future of biography as a literary form. Coverage includes books, chapters of books, and articles from journals. Each entry has complete bibliographic data as well as a descriptive annotation. This work is recommended for all libraries that collect biographies as well as for those libraries serving institutions that offer programs in the study and writing of biography. *Biography*

Y; A
495. **Biography Index....** H. W. Wilson, current. Available in various formats, Subscription which includes four quarterly paperbound issues and a hardcover annual cumulation, $115; Online and on CD-ROM (inquire for prices). ISSN 0006-3053.

This basic reference tool, which has been published since 1946, indexes biographical material that has been published in more than 2,700 periodicals, more than 1,800 English-language books of individual and collective biographies, memoirs, obituaries, fiction, juvenile literature, and biographical material from otherwise nonbiographical sources. Biographical material is accessed in two ways: a "Name Index" which is arranged alphabetically by the name of the biography and includes date of birth and death, nationality, profession, and full bibliographic citation; and an "Index to Professions and Occupations" which names the biographies covered in that particular issue. The sources indexed become a recommended selection list for purchase or inter-library loans. *Biography Index* is recommended for all secondary school, academic, public, and other libraries that offer general reference services. *Biography*

A

496. **International Bibliography of Biography 1970-1987**. Bowker, 1988. 12 vols. 6,400p. $2,500 0-86291-750-6.

Though, because of its price, it is out of reach except to very large public library systems and cooperative bibliographic centers, it is valuable to know this extraordinary bibliography exists. It lists more than 100,000 biographies and autobiographies published throughout the world from 1970 through 1987. It is an amazing work and valuable for locating printed sources for thousands of historical and contemporary figures. *Biography*

Y; A

497. **St. James Guide to Biography**, by Paul E. Schellinger. St. James, 1991. 870p. $125. 1-55862-146-6.

This is a comparative guide to biographies written about 700 famous individuals from all walks of life and historical periods. Some sample entries are for Jesus, Mohammed, Mozart, John Lennon, and Judy Garland. Over 300 scholars are listed as contributors. The essays are arranged alphabetically by the name of the subject, and each analyses and compares existing biographies for scholarship, style, and quality of writing, among other points. Many current titles are included. Appropriate critical studies, histories, and articles are also referred to in the text. This will be useful for identifying biographical material in public libraries and some high schools with advanced placement courses. *Biography*

Dictionaries, Encyclopedias, and Atlases

C; Y; A

498. **Best Dictionaries**, by Kenneth F. Kister. Oryx, 1992. 448p. $39.50. 0-89774-191-9.

Kister's guides to atlases, encyclopedias, and dictionaries have been a mainstay of library service for many years. In this "Consumer's Guide" for dictionaries, Kister offers authoritative reviews, comparisons, and frank evaluations on hundreds of general English-language dictionaries, specialized or subject-oriented, and foreign language dictionaries. Dictionaries at all levels are described and rated as to coverage, accuracy, special features, and costs. This useful guide is recommended for academic, public, and all school libraries that can afford it as an advisement aid for patrons and a collection building tool. *Dictionaries*

C; Y; A

499. **Best Encyclopedias: A Guide to General and Specialized Encyclopedias**, by Kenneth F. Kister. 2nd ed. Oryx, 1993. 356p. $44.95. 0-89774-744-5.

In this successor to the *Encyclopedia Buying Guide, 3rd ed.* (1981), Kister has updated and expanded the scope and has, in effect, created the basic evaluation tool of encyclopedias; however, ALA's very inexpensive, *Purchasing an Encyclopedia: 12 Points to Consider*, does give concise evaluations of evaluations of 11 general multivolume encyclopedias. The review section of *Best Encyclopedias...* includes approximately 50 multivolume, single volume, and electronic English language general encyclopedias. Each entry includes background information, audience, format, currency, accessibility, purchasing information, and comparisons with similar works. As well, a comparative chart of 450 specialized encyclopedias is included. *Best Encyclopedias* provides more comprehensive facts and evaluations useful to librarians, teachers, and patrons. Therefore, it is a recommended purchase for all libraries. *Encyclopedias*

A

500. **Desk Dictionaries: A Consumer's Guide**, by Robert M. Pierson. American Library Association, 1986 32p. pap. $2.95 0-8389-3316-5.

This work evaluates 20 adult English language dictionaries, some considered desk dictionaries, others college-level, using such criteria as scope, suitability, number of entries, and unusual features. This is an update of an article from the *Reference Books Bulletin* of December 1, 1983. *Dictionaries*

C; Y; A

501.   **Dictionaries for Adults and Children**. Booklist Publications, 1991. $4.95 pap. 0-8389-7556-9.

This is a reprint of articles from *Booklist* that list the criteria that should be applied in reviewing dictionaries and gives reviews that cover a wide spectrum of English language dictionaries plus several ones on specialized areas. The reviews are thorough, perceptive, detailed, and up-to-date. Recommendations regarding purchasing are made. This pamphlet can serve two purposes in libraries, as a collection building tool in choosing the best in dictionaries and as a guide for patrons who want information and guidance before buying dictionaries for themselves or their children.   *Dictionaries*

A

502.   **First Stop: The Master Index to Subject Encyclopedias**, by Joe Ryan. Oryx, 1989. 1582p. $215. 0-89774-397-0.

This massive work is a subject index to over 400 subject encyclopedias, dictionaries, handbooks, yearbooks, and other reference sources. There has been an emphasis on current, in-print sources. General encyclopedias, and biographical dictionaries are not included. A key word approach is used for the index. The list of titles analyzed could help serve as a guide to acquiring new reference books in many public libraries.   *Encyclopedias; Reference Books*

Y*; A*

503.   **General Reference Books for Adults: Authoritative Evaluations of Encyclopedias, Atlases, and Dictionaries**, by Marion Sader. Bowker, 1988. 614p. $71.95 0-8352-2393-0.

In addition to evaluations of over 200 basic encyclopedias, dictionaries, and atlases, this work contains valuable background material. Section one is a 55-page history of reference books, with material on criteria, how librarians rate various general reference books, and a series of comparative charts. The other four sections are devoted to the three major types of reference books and large-print reference sources. Each of these sections list specific criteria for evaluation followed by lengthy (600 to 5000 words) reviews. There are 15 encyclopedias and 32 atlases discussed. The dictionary section includes 77 standard dictionaries, plus sections of etymological works, dictionaries of synonyms and antonyms, thesauri and usage manuals. This will be helpful as a buying guide for public librarians as well as an aid for patrons wishing evaluative material prior to home purchase. It will also be useful in senior high school libraries. A valuable resource.
Reference Books; Encyclopedias; Dictionaries; Atlases

C; Y; A

504.   **Kister's Best Dictionaries for Adults and Young People: A Comparative Guide**, by Kenneth F. Kister. Oryx, 1992. 438p. $39.95 0-89774-191-9.

After an interesting background introduction that covers 61 pages and such subjects as the history, evaluation, purposes, types, and contents of dictionaries, there follows an intensive, thorough review of 132 adult titles and 168 others suitable for children and young adults. Specialized dictionaries such as thesauri are not included. In the evaluations, there are many examples excerpted from the dictionaries as well as quotes from reviews. Tables and charts are often used for comparative purposes, and the final evaluations are frank and to-the-point. There are several appendixes including listings of reviews journals, publications on language, and a bibliography of books and articles on dictionaries. This book will be extremely valuable in all types of libraries when giving advice to patrons on purchasing a dictionary. It will also help in building the library's own component of dictionaries.   *Dictionaries*

C*; Y*; A*

505.   **Purchasing an Encyclopedia: 12 Points to Consider**, by the Editorial Board of *Reference Books Annual*. 2nd ed. American Library Association, 1988. 40p. $4.95. 0-8389-3341-3.

This brief pamphlet contains reviews of 10 general multivolume encyclopedias, with particular attention paid to the changes from their previous editions. Each is evaluated according to stated criteria such as age level, authority, arrangement, subject coverage, objectivity, recency, quality, style, bibliographies, illustrations, physical format, and special features. This handy guide cost only $4.95 and may be purchased from: American Library Association, 50 E. Huron St., Chicago, IL 60611.

Encyclopedias

Directories

A

506. **The Clearinghouse Directory: A Guide to Information Clearinghouses and Their Resources, Services, and Publications**, by Donna Batten. 2nd ed. Gale, 1993. 500p. $89.50 0-8013-8094-3.

This volume defined a clearinghouse as an institution that acquires material on a clearly defined subject and disseminates this material on request. This national directory lists over 6,000 clearinghouses in such areas as health issues (e.g., AIDS), women's issues (e.g., abortion), family issues (e.g., adoption), consumer issues (e.g., product safety), and community issues (e.g., homelessness). For each entry, information includes name, address, phone, contact, history, purpose, services resources, and publications. The latter and also audiovisual materials can be located through the alphabetical title index. Free publications are indicated in the text. There is also a name/keyword/sponsoring organization index. This is a useful reference tool for public and academic libraries. *Clearing Houses*

A

507. **Directories in Print 1991**, ed. by Charles B. Montney. 2 volumes. Gale, 1991. 2,059p. $250. 0-8103-7147-2.

This two-volume work supersedes two other Gale publications, *The Directory of Directories* and *International Directories in Print*. In this combined volume there are about 14,000 entries for individual directories arranged in 26 new subject chapters. Individual entries provide a great deal of bibliographic information, as well as the publisher's name and address, the scope of the work, language, arrangements, approximate number of listings and pages, frequency, editor, price, and whether it is available online. There are title/keyword and subject indexes. There is also available a *Directories in Print Supplement* (193p, 1991, $155. pap. 0-8103-71448-8) that contains about 1,000 new and updated entries. Also available from Gale is the *Directory of Directory Publishers 1991* (530p, 1990, $125. 0-913061-07-4). This companion to the work discussed above provides key facts about more that 7,000 directory publishers worldwide, plus listings of each publisher's titles and their markets. There are title, keyword, company, and geographical indexes. The information in this directory is aimed at the business sector. Both will be used in academic and public libraries where clients are involved in marketing or research and will be helpful to librarians in identifying directories for purchase. Directories of a more local nature are listed in *City and State Directories in Print* (Gale, 1989, 966p. $145; 0-8103-1848-2). *Directories*

C; Y; A

508. **The Complete Directory of Large Print Books and Serials, 1993**. Bowker 1993. annual. 320p. $140. pap. 0-8352-3299-9.

This annual guide to the large print field now contains about 6,800 titles of books arranged in three main sections on general reading, children's books, and textbooks. Each of these large sections is subdivided by such subjects as cooking, gardening, mystery and suspense, crossword puzzles and poetry. Full bibliographic information is given, but no annotations. There are now about 400 children's books and 150 textbooks listed. Also included are title and author indexes and a list of 65 large print periodicals and newspapers. Though this is nonselective, it gives an accurate picture of printed sources currently available in the field. *Large Print Books; Periodicals*

A

509. **Guide to American Directories**, by Barry T. Klein and Bernard Klein. 13th ed. Todd Publications, 1993. 600p. $95. 0-915344-22-X.

This listing of about 8,000 directories published by "business and reference book publishers, magazines, trade associations, chambers of commerce and by city, state and Federal government agencies" is organized into 200 categories. Most of the titles originate in the U.S. but there are some international listings. For each directory, title and publisher are given plus scope and contents notes and price. There is a title index. The Gale publications *Directories in Print, 1991* and *City and State Directories in Print* list considerably more publications (total about 20,000) but at a much higher price. *Guide to American Directories* is a useful reference tool and buying guide for small and medium-size libraries.

Directories

A
510.   **The Index and Abstract Directory: An International Guide to Services and Serials Coverage**.
2nd ed. EBSCO, 1990. 2,700p. $179. 0-913956-50-3.

The first part of this directory lists over 30,000 serials arranged under subjects and gives for each the publications in which they are indexed or abstracted. The second part lists each of the 700 indexes and abstracting services with the magazines they include. Formats of the abstract/index are noted (e.g., CD-ROM, print). There is also a complete alphabetical list of the periodical titles, a subject classification of the indexes and abstracts, and an ISSN index. This is a companion volume to EBSCO's *Serials Directory*. For large libraries.   *Periodicals; Indexes; Abstracts*

A
511.   **The Whole Again Resource Guide: A Periodical and Resource Directory, 1986/87**, by Tim Ryan and Patricia J. Case. SourceNet, [1988]. 359p. $24.95. 0-915051-01-X.

This interesting volume is a "directory to alternative and 'New Age' periodicals and resource books," and includes newspapers, magazines, newsletters, indexes, bibliographies, handbooks, directories, and other sourcebooks—many of which are not listed in standard sources. Entries are arranged alphabetically under about 40 different topics such as astrology, feminism, gays, peace and social justice, people of color, sex roles, and yoga. Each entry gives bibliographic data (including, in most cases, a telephone number) and a brief descriptive annotation. A geographic index and general index are provided. Perhaps reminiscent of the activist period during the 1960's, this guide may be a much-wanted addition to libraries anxious to acquire hard to locate, but often requested material. Recommended as a reference guide and an aid to collection building for most academic and public libraries.

Social Change; Lifestyles; Counter Culture

Indexes

Y; A*
512.   **Book Review Index ... An Annual Cumulation**, ed. by Barbara Beach and Beverly Baer. Gale.

The average annual edition of this index which began publication in 1963, reviews over 73,000 books and periodicals covered in more than 131,000 reviews which appeared in more than 470 reviewing periodicals. Almost every conceivable area in the general social sciences, the sciences, humanities, and the fine arts are represented. Most annual cumulations are still available, and for convenience a master cumulation including the years 1965 through 1984 is available in 10 volumes at $1250; 0-8103-0577-1. Gale has also published a number of BRI spin-offs. BRI is useful for reference as well as collection development and is recommended for all libraries that can afford it.   *Book Reviews*

Y; A
513.   **Essay and General Literature Index**. Wilson, annual (including one June paperbound issue). $100.

This comprehensive index to English-language books of essays and general nonfiction has given coverage to these areas from 1900 to the present. Each issue is arranged in a single alphabet with entries for both authors and subjects. Although a wide range of subjects is covered, the emphasis is on the humanities and social sciences. Issues appear with in one paperbound issue in June, followed by annual volumes and five-year cumulations. Because this is used not just for reference but also for collection development, there are monthly lists sent to subscribers of new titles elected for indexing in the next issue. This allows adequate time for acquisition librarians to order before books go out of print. Recommended for high school, academic and public libraries.   *Essays*

Y*; A*
514.   **Wilson Indexes**. H. W. Wilson.

The Wilson indexes have been a basic ingredient in reference services in libraries worldwide for about 100 years. Their important role as directional/locational tools for reference and research in a variety of subject disciplines and levels is unquestioned. Equally important, but not recognized or utilized fully, is their value as selection tools. All of the Wilson indexes have an appended list of "Sources Indexed," usually providing full bibliographic information. Many libraries use these lists to evaluate or build up their collections in particular subject areas or in certain types of materials (short stories, plays, periodicals, etc.). Also many libraries attempt to acquire as many of the sources as possible in order to alleviate patron frustration in seeking information. The major indexes currently available are listed below. It is suggested that the publisher be contacted (1-800-367-6770) for latest prices and availability in other formats, i.e., online, CD-ROM, MARC-tape, computer software. Those titles starred are also listed elsewhere in this guide with a more detailed annotation:

SERVICE BASIS—PERIODICAL INDEXES
The following indexes are priced according to the number of periodicals indexed that are held by the library:

Applied Science & Technology Index. 1958- ISSN 0003-6986
    391 periodicals
Art Index. 1935- ISSN 0004-3222
    223 periodicals, yrbks., and museum bulletins
Biological & Agricultural Index. 1964- ISSN 0006-3177
    225 periodicals
Business Periodicals Index. 1958- ISSN 0007-6961
    339 periodicals
Education Index. 1929- ISSN 0013-1385
    339 periodicals; yearbooks; monographic series
General Science Index. 1978- ISSN 0162-1963
    106 periodicals
Humanities Index. 1974- ISSN 0095-5981
    345 periodicals (published as *Social Sciences & Humanities Index* 1965-1974)
Social Sciences Index. 1974- ISSN 0094-4920
    342 periodicals (published as *Social Sciences & Humanities Index* 1965-1974); As
        (*International Index* 1907-1965)

SERVICE BASIS—BOOK INDEXES
The following indexes are priced according to the library's expenditure for books:

*Bibliographic Index. 1937- ISSN 0006-1255
    Bibliographies from books, pamphlets, and 2,800 periodicals
*Book Review Digest. 1905- ISSN 0006-24490
    Over 6,000 reviews from 95 selected periodicals annually
*Cumulative Book Index. 1928- ISSN 0011-300X
    Includes most English-language books published each year
*Library Literature. 1921- ISSN 0024-27468
    Indexes 223 journals and about 600 monographs each year

FLAT-RATED INDEXES
The following indexes are priced on an annual subscription at the rate indicated in catalog:

*Biography Index. 1946- ISSN 0006-3053
    Indexes about 2,700 periodicals and 1,800 books annually
*Essay and General Literature Index. 1900- ISSN 0014-083x
    Indexes collections and anthologies
Index to Legal Periodicals. 1952- ISSN 0019-4077
    Indexes about 570 legal periodical
*Play Index. 1949- ISSN 0554-1054
    Indexed over 26,000 plays since 1949
*Readers' Guide to Periodical Literature. 1900- ISSN 0034-0464
    Indexes about 200 periodicals
*Short Story Index. 1900- ISSN 0360-9774
*Vertical File Index. ISSN 0042-4439
    Issued 11 times a year; described under Periodicals

Reference Books

Y; A*
515. **American Reference Books Annual, 1994, v. 25**, Ed. by Bohdan S. Wynar. Libraries Unlimited, 1994. 897p. $90. 1-56308-177-6.

During the past 20 plus years, the *American Reference Books Annual*, more commonly referred to as *ARBA*, has established itself as perhaps the most comprehensive and highly regarded review source for English language reference books published or distributed in the United States (and Canada). The 1994 edition has more than 2,000 entries representing all major subject areas, e.g., general reference, humanities, science and technology, education, business and economics, etc. The hundreds of reviews are drawn from generalists and specialists from the library, information science, education, and college and university worlds. The reviews are evaluative and entries are included for nonrecommended items as well as those recommended. Most of the reviews are very lengthy and attempt to point out the strengths and weaknesses of each title. This is an excellent guide for developing and maintaining an up-to-date, quality reference collection. A must purchase for all libraries that can afford it.

ARBA titles also available:

93	$85	1-56308-076-1
92	$85	0-87287-964-X
91	$85	0-87287-885-6
90	$85	0-87287-825-2
89	$75	0-87287-758-2
88	$70	0-87287-681-0
87	$70	0-87287-595-4

A cumulative index to subjects, authors, and titles is also available: *Index to American Reference Books Annual, 1985-1989*. 275p. $55. 0-87287-793-0; and *Index to American Reference Books Annual, 1990-1994*. 350p. $60. 1-56308-272-1. *Reference Books*

Y; A
516. **Basic Reference Sources: A Self-Study Manual**, by Margaret T. Taylor and Ronald R. Powell. 4th ed. Scarecrow, 1990. 335p. $27.50. 0-8108-2244-X.

In reviewing the 2nd and 3rd editions, the Board of the *Reference Books Bulletin* "commended its arrangement by form of reference book, its well-selected questions, and its general commentary and good index are well-designed for student self-study." The 4th edition to this self-paced guide brings information about the sources up to date as of late 1988. This "bibliography" is recommended for all secondary school and public libraries as an acquisition aid as well as a useful guide to help students and other patrons work independently in the library. *Reference Books*

A*
517. **Best Reference Books, 1986-1990**, ed. by Bohdan S. Wynar. Libraries Unlimited, 1992. 450p. $65. pap. 0-87287-936-4.

Subtitled "Titles of Lasting Value Selected from *American Reference Books Annual*," this 5 year cumulation of about 1000 titles selected from almost 10,000 represents the finest in the judgment of the editor (who is a noted authority in reference books in his own right). Titles are arranged in four major subject areas: general, social sciences, humanities, and science and technology. All areas are further subdivided into more specific topics. The entries follow the same format as in ARBA. This compilation, along with the earlier *Best Reference Books, 1981-1985* (1986. $46. 0-87287-554-7), is recommended for all libraries than cannot afford or who do not regularly check the annual editions of ARBA. *Reference Books*

A
518. **Distinguished Classics of Reference Publishing**, ed. by James Rettig. Oryx, 1992. 356p. $55. 0-89774-640-6.

This fascinating collection of essays traces the history of 31 important reference books, such as Bartlett's *Familiar Quotations*, *Who's Who* and *Robert's Rule of Order*. Though this is not intended as an acquisition tool, it will supply good background material on some of the mainstays of the reference collection. Of value in larger collections. *Reference Books*

A*
519.   **Guide to Reference Books**, by Eugene Sheehy and others. 10 ed. American Library Association, 1986. 1560p. $50. 0-8389-0390-8.

This is a well-respected work that can serve several purposes in the library. It is a guide to research works in all phases of knowledge, a selection guide for reference collections, and a useful tool for collection evaluation and weeding. The 14,000 entries are arranged first by broad subject areas with many subdivisions by subcategory, and then by type of reference works and country of origin. There are a number of foreign titles included, and for each title there is extensive bibliographic information and an annotation. Coverage ends with titles published early in 1985. There are author and subject indexes. Medium and large public libraries and all academic libraries will want to have access to this basic reference source. Large libraries might also want Walford's multivolume English counterpart to Sheehy, *Guide to Reference Material.* In mid-1992, a first supplement to Sheehy was published under a new editor, Robert Balay. It lists over 4,800 reference books published between 1985 and the end of 1990: *Guide to Reference Books: Covering Materials from 1985-1990, Supplement to the Tenth Edition* (1992, $85. 0-8389-0588-9).   *Reference Books*

A
520.   **Guide to Reference Materials for Canadian Libraries**, by Kirsti Nilsen and Alanna Kalnay. 8th ed. University of Toronto Press, 1992. 596p. $50. 0-8020-6004-8.

This guide, prepared for library science/information science students at the University of Toronto, was never designed as a selection aid or buying guide for other libraries. Therefore, most of the almost 4,000 reference titles do not contain adequate data necessary for acquisitions, and many are no longer in print. However, despite these limitations, this guide which has a distinct Canadian emphasis is well-arranged and well-annotated and is recommended for most Canadian libraries and other academic and public libraries with an international, particularly a Canadian, interest.   *Canada; Reference Books*

Y; A*
521.   **Introduction to Reference Work; Volume 1; Basic Information Sources**, by William Katz. 5th ed. McGraw, 1987. 397p. $28. 0-07-033538-0.

In addition to introducing the scope and nature of reference work in libraries, this volume introduces basic reference sources in a variety of formats. Most of the chapters deal with individual types of materials such as dictionaries, encyclopedias, indexes and abstracts, biographical dictionaries, and selected subject sources. This is an excellent beginning place for a librarian-trainee to refresh one's knowledge of basic sources. It can also be used as a guide to collection evaluation and a blueprint for future purchases in the reference section of public libraries. There is great deal of interesting background information given on each type of reference book that also adds a new dimension to evaluating and using these materials.

Reference Books

A
522.   **The New, Completely Revised, Greatly Expanded, Madam Audrey's Mostly Cheap, All Good, Useful List of Books for Speedy Reference**, by Audrey Lewis. 5th ed. Saginaw, Mich., White Pine Library Cooperative, 1840 N. Michigan, Suite 114, Saginaw, MI 48602, 1992. 83p. $10. pap.

The title says it all! Lewis has compiled about 500 relatively inexpensive (as is the bibliography itself) titles organized in "loose Dewey arrangement." All entries are briefly and informally annotated. The emphasis throughout has been on securing the "cheapest" yet most useful reference sources when alternatives were available. As expected, the list is heavy on paperbound volumes. This popularly written, delightful short volume has a place in most public libraries, but particularly the small rural ones with limited funds. *Reference Books*

Y; A
523.   **The New York Times Guide to Reference Materials**, by Mona McCormick. NAL/Dutton, 1986. 320p. $4.95. pap. 0-451-14471-6.

This small, inexpensive handbook "is intended to assist students and general readers in their search for information by offering a strategy for searching and an introduction to basic reference sources." While this may be useful for lay researchers and young adults preparing to write a paper, there is little new information here for librarians. However, high school and small public libraries might benefit from comparing reference titles recommended in this guide to the library's holdings in order to acquire replacements or fill in gaps. *Reference Books*

C; Y; A*

524. Recommended Reference Books for Small and Medium-sized Libraries and Media Centers, 1994, ed. by Bohdan S. Wynar. Libraries Unlimited, 1994. 289p. $45. 1-56308-283-7.

This excellent guide is now in its 14th annual edition. This particular volume reviews almost 540 titles chosen by the editors as the most valuable reference books of the previous year. The number represents about a third of the titles which were originally reviewed in *American Reference Books Annual* (ARBA). RRB makes it convenient for librarians to locate new references in a given field because of its subject arrangement. All of the lengthy and generally well-written reviews are signed by the reviewer who is most likely a librarian, college professor, or subject specialist. They are also coded with a C, P, or S designating a recommendation for college, public or school library. This relatively inexpensive guide is highly recommended for all libraries for reference and collection development.

The following back volumes are still available and useful:

RRB 93	$39.50	1-56308-155-5
RRB 92	$38.50	0-87287-976-3
RRB 91	$38.50	0-87287-934-8
RRB 90	$37.00	0-87287-826-0
RRB 89	$32.50	0-87287-759-0

Reference Books

Y; A

525. Recommended Reference Books in Paperback, by Andrew L. March. 2nd ed. Libraries Unlimited, 1992. 300p. $37.50. 1-56308-067-2.

The more than 900 in-print paperback reference books chosen for this second edition have been selected on the basis of quality, availability, and economy. A variety of bibliographies, dictionaries, guides, and directories are included. The three dozen or more subject areas represented should appeal to a wide audience and include botany, business and economics, ethnic studies, mythology, sports/recreation, and zoology. Each entry contains full bibliographic information and a brief descriptive, evaluative annotation. Hundreds of unannotated, but recommended titles are also included. This completely revised and up-dated guide is recommended for all school, academic, and public libraries. *Reference Books; Paperback Books*

Y*; A*

526. Reference and Information Services: An Introduction, ed. by Richard E. Bopp and Linda C. Smith. Libraries Unlimited, 1991. 483p. $30. 0-87287-788-4.

This text is designed for a basic course in Information Services and Sources (Reference). The first 10 of 20 chapters cover the essential principles and procedures of reference services in a variety of library settings. The second half of the book deals with the selecting and evaluating of reference sources in the process of building (and using) a basic collection of reference materials. A number of titles are described under each chapter dealing with specific types of reference and information sources, including electronic sources. This text is similar in purpose and coverage to Katz's *Introduction to Reference Work; Volume 1: Basic Information Sources*, 1987. However, the Katz volume, while still useful, needs updating. Both are recommended for collection development in all school media centers and public libraries.

Reference Books

Y*; A*

527. Reference Books Bulletin 1991-1992, ed. by Sandy Whiteley. American Library Association, 1993. c240p. $25. 0-8389-3417-X.

The annual compilation of RBB has been available for almost a quarter of a century and has become a basic selection guide for reference books for many libraries. This cumulation contains almost 500 reviews and omnibus reviews which were originally published in the "Reference Books Bulletin" section of *Booklist*. The quality of the reviewing is unquestionable; the advantage of this particular work is that it pulls together a year's worth of reviews in one convenient place. Entries are arranged alphabetically under major subject classes, e.g., literature, language, science, medicine, history, etc. Subject, type of material, and title indexes are provided. Earlier annual compilations for 1988-89 and 1990-91 are still available at $25 each. Libraries Unlimited publishes a similar work: *Recommended Reference Books for Small and Medium-sized Libraries and Media Centers*, and while there may be some overlapping, many libraries would consider both guides to develop their reference collections. This guide is highly recommended for all libraries. *Reference Books*

Y*; A*

528.   **Reference Sources: A Brief Guide**, comp. by Eleanor A. Swidan. 9th ed. Enoch Pratt Free Library, 1988. 175p. $7.95. pap. 09-910556-26-1.

The first edition of this basic guide to reference sources appeared over 50 years ago, and since that time it has grown in size and in prominence. Part 1 covers general reference sources by type, e.g., encyclopedias, dictionaries, almanacs, etc. Part 2 includes reference sources in special subject areas, and this latest edition now includes bibliographic databases, which makes up Part 3. All of the more than 800 titles are annotated and include full bibliographic data. This mainstay of a basic bibliography of reference sources is recommended for all secondary school and public libraries as a handy source.

Reference Books

C; Y; A*

529.   **Reference Sources for Small and Medium-size Libraries**, ed. by Jovian P. Lang. 5th ed. ALA, 1992. 317p. $35. pap. 0-8389-3406-4.

This new edition of what is becoming a standard work was produced under Lang's editorial guidance and an ad hoc committee of ALA's Reference and Adult Services Division. With almost 2,000 entries, this newly revised edition contains an "approximate increase of 75 percent in number of new entries over the previous edition." This classified and annotated bibliography not only updates the standard sources, but it also includes "reference materials for children and young adults ... sources in other formats, such as microforms and databases...." The cut-off date is 1990; however, some newer editions have a 1991 imprint. Though the title is similar, Lang's work differs from an equally useful work by Wynar, *Recommended Reference Books for Small and Medium-sized Libraries and Media Centers, 1992*. Wynar's work is an annual edition with newer titles drawn from the best of *ARBA*; whereas, the Lang work is retrospective with irregular updates. Therefore, both titles are highly recommended for school media centers and public libraries. *Reference Books*

A

530.   **Spanish-Language Reference Books: An Annotated Bibliography**, comp. by Bibliotecas para la Gente Reference Committee. Chicano Studies Library Publications Unit, University of California at Berkeley, 1989. 45p. $10. pap. 0-918520-15-0. (Chicano Studies Library Publication Series, 15)

This annotated list of 117 works will help librarians find basic reference sources for their Spanish-speaking patrons. The works are arranged by headings like, "General Reference," "Library Science," "Religion," and "Economics and Business," and include such practical titles as a medical dictionary, etiquette guides, and auto-repair manuals. The detailed evaluative annotations are in English, and there is an index by names and titles. This highly selective bibliography will be of use in both public and academic libraries where there is a need for reference books in Spanish. *Reference Books—Spanish Language*

Y; A*

531.   **Topical Reference Books: Authoritative Evaluations of Recommended Resources in Special-ized Subject Areas**, ed. by Marion Sader. Bowker, 1991. 892p. $104.95. 0-8352-3087-2.

This third and last volume of Bowker's Buying Guide Series complements rather than duplicates the other two volumes: *Reference Books for Young Readers* (1988) and *General Reference Books for Adults* (1989). TRB lists more than 2,000 dictionaries, directories, handbooks, bibliographies, etc. in over 50 categories from advertising and current events, to library science, to zoology. Under each category are lists of core titles, out-of-print titles, supplementary titles, new and noteworthy releases, and special tips for collection development. A very useful special feature is a chart which notes the suitability of the core titles for a particular type of library. An appendix provides a directory of publishers for titles cited. Many detailed indexes complete this useful guide. Recommended for all academic and public libraries, many special libraries, and those high school libraries that can afford the rather steep price. *Reference Books*

A

532.   **Walford's Concise Guide to Reference Material**, by A. J. Walford. Ed. by Anthony Chalcraft et al. 2nd ed. Library Association: dist. by Unipub, 1992. 496p. $145. 1-85604-042-9.

Over 3,000 entries are included in this revised edition which "is a shortened version of the three-volume *Walford's Guide to Reference Materials*, 5th ed." A large variety of basic types of reference materials are included; in addition, microforms, online databases, and CD ROM sources are added. There is a duplication of many titles listed in other similar guides such as Sheehy's *Guide to Reference Books* and Lang's *Reference Sources for Small and Medium-sized Libraries*; however, this concise guide has a distinct British accent which may make this a desirable purchase if the larger three-volume Walford's is overwhelming.

Reference Books

A

533. **Walford's Guide to Reference Material**, Ed. by A. J. Walford et al. 5th ed. Library Association; distributed by American Library Association. 1989-1991.

This standard guide to reference material was first published in one volume in 1959. The second edition, in three volumes, began in 1966 and was completed in 1970. The standards of quality and authoritativeness have been maintained over the years. Its closest competitor is Sheehy's *Guide to Reference Books*, 10th ed., which is published in one volume and only contains about one-third the number of entries. There is some hope that new editions can be produced annually, by developing an electronically-based production system. Although there is some inevitable overlap between Walford's and Sheehy's guides, the exhaustive Walford guide is highly recommended for all academic and public libraries that are large enough to afford the high cost. Volumes currently available are:

> *Walford's Guide to Reference Material: Volume 1, Science and Technology.* 5th ed. $95. 0-85365-978-8.
> *Walford's Guide to Reference Material: Volume 2, Social and Historical Sciences, Philosophy and Religion.* 5th ed. 0-85365-539-1.
> *Walford's Guide to Reference Material: Volume 3, Generalia, Language and Literature, the Arts.* 4th ed. 09-85365-836-6.

Reference Books

Research Guides

A

534. **Find It Fast: How To Uncover Expert Information on Any Subject**, by Robert L. Berkman. Harper, 1990. 336p. $11. pap. 0-06-096486-3.

This handy beginner's guide to doing research is particularly good for business people and writers. After chapters on important library resources including databases, this book helps one identify resource people and outlines sample searches. The first sections lists basic reference books, many of which are found in even small and medium-sized public libraries. These bibliographies make good evaluative checklists of holdings. *Reference Books*

Y; A

535. **Guide to the Use of Libraries and Information Sources**, by Jean Key Gates. 6th ed. McGraw-Hill, 1989. 348p. $17.95 (pap) 0-07-022999-6.

This basic guide for the beginning researcher to using libraries has been a mainstay in collections for many years. The first two sections gives an introduction to libraries, their history, and how their collections are presented organized (DDC and LC). General reference sources like dictionaries and encyclopedias are then introduced and annotated in the third section, followed by similar coverage for basic research sources in the sciences, social sciences, and the humanities. Although primarily of use to students and patrons, the listings of resources can serve as a checklist for reference collections in public and college libraries, and perhaps in larger high school libraries with strong academic programs. *Reference Books*

A

536. **How to Look Things Up and Find Things Out**, by Bruce L. Felknor. Morrow, 1988. $22. 0-688-07850-8; pap. Quill, 1988. $10.95 pap. 0-688-07850-4.

This is a basic guide on using reference works with chapters devoted to various subject areas. This does not offer any new material for collection development, and for library patrons Robert Berkman's *Find It Fast* and Mona McCormick's *The New York Times Guide to Reference Materials* are superior.

Reference Books

A

537. **Knowing Where To Look**, by Lois Horowitz. Writer's Digest, 1988. 444p. $18.95 pap. 0-89879-329-7.

This revision of the book that first appeared in 1984, is a guide for nonlibrarians on how to do independent research. The nature of various types of library materials like encyclopedias, dictionaries, newspapers and microfilms is discussed, with many tips on how to use them plus annotated lists of major examples. Sections are also devoted to finding material on such subjects as addresses, quotations, legal topics, and statistics. An amazing number of resources are introduced. Sample search strategies are also given. If needed, this can serve as a checklist of reference resources in small libraries. *Reference Books*

Y; A

538.   **The New York Public Library Book of How and Where to Look It Up**, ed. by Sherwood Harris. Prentice-Hall, 1991. 382p. $30. 0-13-614728-3.

This convenient guide was designed for the lay researcher. The major divisions include reference books, government sources, picture sources, special collections, and electronic databases. These sources are then arranged under very broad subject areas such as education, health, ecology, etc. There is very little that would be new here for most medium-sized and large libraries; however, the list of over 800 annotated databases carried by such vendors as DIALOG, BRS, etc. might be of interest. Also the reference book chapter may prove useful to the high school or small public library as an evaluation and collection development guide. *Reference Books; Databases*

Y; A

539.   **Reference Readiness: A Manual for Librarians, Researchers, and Students**, by Agnes Ann Hede. Library Professional Publications; dist. by Shoe String Press, 1990. 232p. $29.50. hardcover. 0-208-02228-78; $21. paper. 0-208-02229-5.

The author states that this manual is intended for those who "wish to review the range of general, basic reference sources in the English language." The work is divided by type of reference work, e.g., encyclopedias, indexes, atlases, etc. Each chapter includes a great deal of basic information about criteria, use, etc., and concludes with a list of unannotated additional sources within the type. Annotations average about a page in length. Some children's reference works are also included under most chapters. The work is not nearly as comprehensive as Sheehy's *Guide to Reference Books* or even as Katz's *Introduction to Reference Sources*. Most large or medium-sized libraries might find this source too limiting; however, it is basic enough (inexpensive enough) to be recommended for collection development in the school library and small public library. *Reference Books*

A

540.   **Research Guides to the Humanities, Social Sciences and Technology: An Annotated Bibliography of Guides to Library Resources and Usage, Arranged by Subject or Discipline of Coverage**, by Martin H. Sable. Pierian Press, 1986. 181p. $35. 0-87650-214-1. (Basic Reference Guides Series, 1).

The long title actually describes the extensive coverage of this annotated bibliography of 161 guides to the literature of most disciplines. The guides are organized by major disciplines such as the "Humanities." Under each major field are listed general guides related to that discipline. This is followed by entries for guides for subjects within that field, e.g., art and music. Entries for all the guides listed are annotated fully with in-depth descriptions of purpose and criteria such as authority, arrangement, scope, indexes, and special features. Full bibliographic information is provided for each entry. Title and author indexes provide additional access to the guides listed. This bibliography is recommended for all academic and most public libraries as a reference tool, inter-library loan guide and collection-building aid. *Bibliography*

Y; A

541.   **Where to Find What: A Handbook to Reference Service**, by James M. Hillard. 3rd ed. Scarecrow, 1991. 333p. $35. 0-818-2404-3.

This unusual bibliography uses a completely new approach; it anticipates the reference question, then lists the book that will provide the answer. Hillard has selected and arranged alphabetically 607 subject headings that are commonly asked at the ready-reference desk, e.g., AIDS, Alzheimer's Disease, Toll-Free Numbers, etc. Recommended books are listed under each subject heading. For each title listed, bibliographic information is provided; descriptive annotations are also provided for many of the entries. This innovative idea is interesting and the titles supplied could serve as a starter reference collection, which individual libraries could then localize. Recommended for all school and small to medium-sized public libraries.

Reference Books; Reference Services (libraries)

Serials and Periodicals

A

542. **Albertsen's: 1991 International Edition.** 1st ed. 167p. Albertsen's, 1991. $45. 1-879338-06-8.

The first, of a planned annual undertaking, listing over 2,000 English language foreign magazines, newspapers, and news-letters published worldwide. Titles are arranged by five major regions and then subdivided by country. Each listing includes name, address, description, frequency of publication, subscription rates, telephone, fax numbers, and other information helpful for selecting and ordering. This relatively inexpensive and useful aid is available from: Albertsen's, P.O. Box 339, Nevada City, CA 95959.

Periodicals; Newspapers

A

543. **Canadian Serials Directory. Repertoire des Publications Seriees Canadiennes**, by Gordon Ripley. 3rd ed. Reference Press, 1987. 396p. $36. 0-919981-10-0.

A valuable work that lists all the periodicals and serials being published in Canada as of 1986. The approximately 4,000 entries also include daily newspapers, annuals and yearbooks, journals, and regularly published proceeding of societies and associations. The main body of the work lists the serials alphabetically by title. For each entry, information includes editor, publisher, address, frequency, general contents, advertising policy, circulation, ISSN, and price. The second section is a subject index in French and English, and the third, a list of the publishers and their publications. For Canadian libraries or American libraries needing a strong component of Canadiana, this is an important tool for identification and selection of serials.

Periodicals; Canadian Periodicals

Y; A

544. **Free Magazines for Libraries**, by Adeline Mercer Smith and Diane Rovena Jones. 3rd ed. McFarland, 1989. 228p. $19.95 pap. 0-89950-389-6.

This bibliography describes 500 free periodicals available from various private companies and agencies. Each publication meets basic standards of suitability and usefulness in libraries. They are arranged alphabetically by title in 62 topics such as folklore, forestry, law, geography, and sociology. There is complete bibliographic material for each entry plus an evaluative annotation and information on subscribing. Appendixes include one on magazines suitable for small and medium sized libraries, and a list of where (if any) place they are indexed. A valuable resource for both public and high school libraries. *Periodicals*

A

545. **Index to Free Periodicals: An Author, Title, and Subject Guide to Current Issues and the Research and Development Activities**, by C. Edward Wall. vol. 15 (1990) 2 issues per year, Perian Press, $35. 0-685-38317-2.

This index gives author, title, and subject access to the contents of 38 free periodicals. The work which appears twice per year is designed to act as a supplement to *Readers' Guide to Periodical Literature*. The list of publications indexed can be of value in building a library's periodical collection. For public and academic libraries. *Periodicals; Free Material*

Y; A*

546. **Magazines for Libraries**, by Bill Katz and Linda Sternberg Katz. 7th ed. Bowker, 1992. 1,160p. $139.95. 0-8352-3166-6.

Some bibliographic tools are venerable, and *Magazines for Libraries* is one of them. This revised and up-dated edition evaluates over 6,500 magazines from over 75,000 surveyed. Approximately 2,000 titles were dropped from the 6th edition, and an equal number of newer titles were added. The selected titles range from the general and popular to the scholarly and research-oriented, and from those recommended for young children to academicians. The entries are arranged by alphabetically by title under more than 130 subjects, including many newer headings such as Classroom Magazines, Animal Rights, Aquaculture, Comics, Food and Wine, New Age, and Philanthropy. Each entry includes information on publication, reviewing sources, other formats, audience level, and a critical as well as descriptive annotation. This bibliography is recommended for libraries for collection development and evaluation and as a basic reference source except, perhaps, the smallest which may want to consider a more targeted aid such as *Magazines for Children* or *Magazines for Young People*. *Periodicals*

A

547. **Newsletters in Print**, ed. by Brigitte T. Darnay. 6th ed. Gale, 1992. 1,397p. $175. 0-8103-7520-X.

Formerly titled *Newsletters Directory...*, this unique aid provides libraries with detailed entries to over 10,000 newsletters, bulletins, digests, and similar serial publications issued in the United States and Canada. A wide range of 31 topics are represented, arranged under seven broad categories. The lists lend themselves for browsing under headings of interest, such as business and industry; family and everyday life; information and communications; community and world affairs; and science and technology. Title, publisher, and subject indexes are provided. Appendixes list newsletters available online and also those that are free to the general public. This is an invaluable source of hard-to-locate information and recommended to many academic and public libraries, but unfortunately, the price will rule out all but the largest.

Newsletters; Serial Publications

A

548. **Serials for Libraries: An Annotated Guide to Continuations, Annual, Yearbooks, Almanacs, Transactions, Proceedings, Directories, Services**, by John V. Ganly and Diane M. Sciattara. Neal-Schuman, 1985, 441p. $85. 0-918212-85-5.

In the preface of this bibliography, serials are defined as "English-language titles which are available in the United States, published on an annual or other continuing basis (but not more often than once a year), and are suitable for collection by public, school, academic, and special libraries." The two thousand serials included are grouped under five broad categories (general works, business, humanities, science and social sciences) and by a total of 76 subjects. Bibliographic information is a given plus descriptive and evaluative annotations and an indication of audience level. This is selective and therefore can be used directly as a selection tool (unlike, for example, *Ulrich's*). The "When to Buy What" purchasing guide gives a month or season listing of when about 800 serials become available. There is also a section which gives information of 125 serials available online. This award-winning reference book now needs an updating but will still be of value in academic and larger public libraries. *Serial Publications; Periodicals*

A

549. **The Series Directory: An International Reference Book,** 5th ed. EBSCO, 1991, 4505p. 3 vol. $319 0-91356-51-1.

This directory, a reprint of the 1987 edition, gives bibliographic and ordering information on more than 113,000 serial titles published around the world. The first two volumes contain the serial listings arranged by 148 major subjects, and the third has the title index, a short ceased-title list, and an ISSN index. Although the coverage is essentially the same as *Ulrich's International Periodicals Directory*, there are unique titles in each. However, though slightly higher in price, *Ulrich's* is now more up-to date and now integrates material on both regular periodicals with irregular series and annuals. It is therefore preferable, though some very large collections might also benefit from the EBSCO volume. *Periodicals*

A

550. **The Standard Periodical Directory**. 15th ed. Oxbridge Communications, 1992. 1900p. $445. 0-917460-37-5.

This bibliography lists about 75,000 U.S. and Canadian titles having biennial or more frequent publication schedules. Entries are arranged under 230 major subjects. There is a complete title index and cross references to subjects that add to the book's usefulness. See also the entry under *Ulrich's International Periodicals Directory. Periodicals*

A

551. **Ulrich's International Periodical Directory, 1993-94**. 32nd ed. Bowker, 1993. 5v. $364.95. 0-8352-3320-0.

This standard reference tool, now in its 32nd edition, has been the leading serials directory for many years. Since 1986, a similar directory, EBSCO's *Serials Directory...*, has emerged. Each offers some special features, and each has some slight advantage over the other. The quantitative statistics of *Ulrich's* 32nd edition are: A listing of nearly 140,000 regularly and irregularly issued serials (11,000 titles new to this edition) and addresses and fax numbers for almost 70,000 publishers from 188 countries; Special features include an ISSN index, separate indexes for serials available online, a listing of serials available on CD-ROM, brief editorial descriptions for 34,000 titles, LC classification and Dewey numbers for nearly 24,000 titles, and more than 38,000 FAX numbers and over 16,000 Telex numbers. Subscribers also receive a free quarterly update listing new titles and title changes and cessations. Also, a toll-free hotline is available for research assistance and inquiries. *Ulrich's...* is also available on CD-ROM, online, and on microfiche (contact publisher for details). This indispensable resource is recommended for all libraries with sizable budgets. *Periodicals*

A

552. **Walford's Guide to Current British Periodicals in the Humanities and Social Science**, ed. by A. J. Walford. Library Association; dist. by American Library Association, 1986. 473p. $55. 0-85365-676-2.

Walford, a noted bibliographer, has compiled a list of more than 3,000 British periodicals in the humanities and social sciences. Entries are arranged under broad and narrow subjects using the Universal Decimal Classification (UDC). Entries include title, frequency, cost, publisher, ISSN, etc., and brief annotations. The volume is well-indexed by title, sponsoring groups, and subjects. There is very little here that cannot be found in *Ulrich's...*; however, the convenience of having all periodicals together will be appreciated by libraries that have strong British collections; this guide is recommended for academic and public libraries with such a collection. *Periodicals—British; Humanities; Social Sciences*

Genealogy

A*

553. **Ancestry's Red Book: American State, County & Town Sources**, ed. by Alice Eichholz. Ancestry, 1992. 858p. $39.95. 0-916489-47-7.

This handy guide to genealogy is not truly a bibliography, but it is such a rich identifying source to research material in the field (including bibliographic sources) that it cannot be ignored. The work is arranged alphabetically by state, and gives information on vital, census, land, probate, court, tax, church, cemetery, and military records. It also has many list of sources found in special collections. Special focus categories such as immigration, naturalization, and ethnic groups (African-American, Native Americans) are also included where appropriate. This is a must purchase for most public libraries. *Genealogy*

A

554. **Genealogical and Local History Books in Print**, ed. by Netti Schreiner-Vantis. 4th ed. Genealogical Books in Print, 1985. 1,733p. $35.

The purpose of this guide is to provide researchers with a knowledge of what books and services are available in the area of genealogy and to provide genealogical vendors with an inexpensive vehicle for marketing their products. In this edition, 4,200 family genealogies and many general source books are listed, which combined involve a total of 3636 vendors. There are also a number of helpful advertisements of services and supplies related to genealogy and listing of professional genealogists. A supplement of 434 pages was published in 1990 and is available for $19.95, plus $2. for postage. The second and third editions of the main title are also available. Each contains material unique to that edition. Enquiries and orders should be sent to: Genealogical Books in Print, 6818 Lois Drive, Springfield, VA 22150. *Genealogy*

A

555. **Genealogical Periodical Annual Index, 1988**, vol. 27, by Karen T. Ackermann. Heritage Books, 1990. $20. 1-55613-297-2.

This is a guide to approximately 300 genealogical periodicals. Citations include standard bibliographic information, and there is an index by surnames, localities, and subjects. This will be of value in tracking down specific serial publications in the area of genealogy. *Periodicals; Genealogy*

A

556. **Genealogical Research and Resources: A Guide for Library Use**, by Lois Gilmer. American Library Association, 1988. 64p. $15.95 pap. 0-8389-0482-3.

This practical guide is intended to act both as an introduction to the literature of genealogy and as a manual on doing research in the area. The material on genealogical references sources, primary and secondary sources, and specialized libraries and organizations will be helpful to librarians in building collections and identifying sources of new publications. There is a subject index. A useful guide both for librarians and beginning genealogists. *Genealogy*

A
557. **Generations Past: A Selective List of Sources for Afro-American Genealogical Research**.
Library of Congress, 1989. 105p. $4.50.

In this introductory guide to researching African-American genealogies, select basic material found in the Library of Congress is introduced. Types of materials discussed include guidebooks, bibliographies, local histories, and city directories. There is also a list of genealogical associations. This work is available from Dept. 36-EG of the Library. The stock number is 030-001-00129-6. This will be of value in any library that has a sizable number of African-American patrons. *African Americans; Genealogy*

A
558. **Passenger and Immigration Lists Bibliography, 1538-1900: Being a Guide to Published Lists of Arrivals in the United States and Canada**, ed. by P. William Filby. 2nd ed. Gale, 1988. 324p. $110. 8103-2740-6.

This second edition is a reprint of the bibliography found in the first edition and its supplements, plus several other lists on the subject. More than 2,500 published passenger and immigration lists, church records, naturalization date, military rolls, and other lists are included in this edition. Entries are arranged in alphabetical order by title or by compiler. Each entry contains full bibliographical information and an annotation which describes the contents of the list. The first edition, *Passenger and Immigration Lists Index* (1981), and supplements published from 1982-1991 are still available. Because of the cost of this very specialized tool it is obviously not a source for the smaller library; however, it is recommended as a reference tool and an aid for collection development for the special, academic, and public library serving clientele interested in genealogical research, immigration history, and ethnic studies.

Genealogy; Immigration; Ships—Passenger Lists; United States—History

A
559. **Researcher's Guide to Archives and Regional History Sources**, ed. by John C. Larsen. Library Professional Publications (Dist. by Shoe String, 1988. 167p. $29.50. 0-208-02144-2.

This researcher's guide is intended for beginning research in the field of genealogy. Fourteen respected archivists have contributed their expertise and discuss archives and manuscripts, reference tools, and types of sources, e.g., business, religious, maps, and public records. Except for basic reference sources in the field, most of the sources discussed are nonbook resources. This is recommended for undergraduate and public library collections needing additional material on the overall subjects of archives and genealogy.

Archives; Genealogy

CD-ROM and Online Products

A
560. **The CD-ROM Directory, 1992**, by Matthew Finlay and Joanne Mitchell. 7th ed., Omnigraphics, 1992. $159, pap. 10870889-26-6.

This directory lists over 2,000 titles available in the CD-ROM format arranged by title. There are also sections giving company information, hardware, software, and conferences, plus a listing of current periodicals and books on the subject. Indexes allow for retrieving information by subject, country of origin, and contact persons. This is an excellent guide, but it is much more expensive that the comparable *CD-ROMs in Print*. Useful in large public and academic libraries. *CD-ROM; Databases; Computer Software*

C; Y; A
561. **CD-ROM for Librarians and Educators: A Resource Guide to Over 300 Instructional Programs**, by Barbara Head Sorrow and Betty S. Lumpkin. McFarland, 1933. 155p. $24.905 (pap.) 0-89950-800-6.

This is a bibliography of 300 instructional CD-ROMs that range in intended users from kindergarten through college with some for a general adult audience. The packages are arranged by subject and for each entry the material that is supplied includes title, producer, format, subject, price, grade level, hardware and software needed, distributor, and a description of the contents. The annotations are not critical but inclusion in the bibliography suggests a recommendation. Introductory material contains a general explanation of CD-ROMs, a glossary, suggested reading list, policies for purchasing, and a review of search techniques. This is an excellent guide that will be particularly helpful in acquisition work.

CD-ROM; Education; Library Science

A

562. **CD-ROM Information Products: An Evaluation Guide and Directory**, by C. J. Armstrong and J. A. Large. Gower, 1990, 473p. $84.95 0-566-03626-6.

In this first volume of a planned series, there are lengthy reviews of 19 CD-ROMs, plus a brief listing of 508 others. The long reviews are by British librarians but include mostly American products like *Books in Print*, *Ulrich's Plus*, and three *Wilsondisc* titles. They are detailed and cover scope, installation procedures, value for money, use evaluation, and sample screen illustrations. The general classified directory gives only cursory information. There are indexes that provide addresses of publishers and distributors. *CD-ROM Information Products Volume 2* (1991, $84.95, 0-566-03645-2) contains a general commentary on CD-ROM publishing during 1990 and supplies an additional 25 in-depth reviews.

CD-ROM; Databases; Computer Software

A

563. **CD-ROM Market Place: An International Guide: 1992 ed.** Meckler, 1992. 200p. $30 pap. 0-88736-851-4.

This volume gives information on about 1,000 agencies that publish and/or distribute CD-ROM products. The body of the work is arranged alphabetically by organization. In each entry there is an address, names of contact people, a short title list of available CD-ROMs and a narrative about the company's history and publishing program. There is a geographical index (the list is international), plus a separate names and numbers index to facilitate contacts. The listing of available CD-ROM products is also found in Meckler's annual *CD-ROMs in Print* and also in the *Gale Directory of Databases, Vol. 2*. This directory will be of value in large public and academic libraries. *CD-ROM*

A

564. **CD-ROM Periodical Index: A Guide to Abstracted, Indexed, and Fulltext Periodicals on CD-ROM**, by Pat Ensor and Steve Hardin. Meckler, 1992. 420 p. $65. 0-88736-803-4.

This bibliography describes 77 CD-ROMs that abstract, index or give the full text of periodicals or books. For each entry, information includes publisher, price, years covered, contents, and software capabilities. The second half of this directory lists all of the titles contained in these 77 items. Although this is not exhaustive in coverage, it does included the most popular titles available. Useful in large collections. *CD-ROM; Databases*

A

565. **CD-ROM Research Collections: An Evaluative Guide to Bibliographic and Full-Text CD-ROM Databases**, by Pat Ensor. Meckler, 1991. 302p. $55. 0-88736-779-8.

This guide evaluates 114 bibliographic and full-text CD-ROM products that the author believes will be of particular value in research collections. Each entry contains information about the database including hardware and software requirements, versions, and licensing arrangements. For each there is a listing of reviews that have appeared in periodical literature. A wide range of CD-ROMs are included representing many disciplines, time periods, areas and formats. Most are American in origin, although a few are European and Canadian. This will be of use in large public library collections and in research and academic libraries at various levels. *CD-ROM; Databases*

A

566. **CD-ROMs in Print: An International Guide to CD-ROM, CD-1, CDTV & Electronic Book Products.** Meckler, 1987- (annual), approximately $95. (Inquire about hardware requirements which are constantly changing).

This annual disc guide lists commercially available CD-ROMs from around the world with several thousand titles arranged by title. For each entry, information is given on such topics as coverage and scope, demonstration discs available, cost, hardware and software, updates, and equivalent publications in other media. There are several indexes and directories appended: one for distributors, a publisher index, and another that lists the databases by type, format, and purpose. Though not evaluative, this is a fine listing of CD-ROMs currently available, and undoubtedly the most comprehensive. Somewhat comparable material is found in such publications as *CD-ROM Information Products* and *Gale Directory of Databases Vol. 2*. This reference source is recommended for all libraries acquiring CD-ROM products.

Computer Software; CD-ROM; Databases

A

567.   **Computer-Readable Databases: A Directory and Data Sourcebook**, by Kathleen Young Marcaccio. 9th ed. Gale, 1993, annual. 1,646p. $170. pap, 0-8103-7669-5.

This massive annual volume lists "all publicly available electronic databases, including online and transactional, CD-ROM, bulletin boards, offline files available for batch processing and databases on magnetic tape and diskette." The current edition supplies thorough descriptions of more that 6,000 publicly available databases. The six main sections are "Database Profiles," "Database Producers," "Database Vendors," "CD-ROM Product Index," a subject index, and a master index. The profile section is the largest. Each entry contains such information as general scope and type, language, time period covered, size, hardware, updates, print equivalents, plus the address, fax, and telex numbers of contact persons. The material is updated annually in the print version and quarterly in the online version on DIALOG. Several of the other database directories on the market, can be found under the subject heading Databases.

Databases

A

568.   **Database Directory**. Knowledge Industry Publications, 1992. 700p. $195. 0-86729-299-7.

This work consists of an alphabetical listing of approximately 2,000 databases. For each entry, information is given on names, addresses, and telephone numbers of producers; subjects covered; corresponding print products; time coverage; size and frequency; language; and the sources of original data. Methods of access for each database are also given. Vendors and prices are given, and new entries are indicated with a symbol. There are vendor, producer, alternate database names, and subject indexes. This will be of value in many public and academic libraries. *Databases*

A

569.   **Dial in 1992: An Annual Guide to Online Public Access Catalogs**, by Michael Shuyler. Meckler, 1992. 282p. $49.50. 0-88736-808-5.

This is a directory of about 250 libraries (mostly in United States with some in Canada) that have on-line catalogs that the public can access. There is a profile of each of the 187 academic and 73 public libraries represented with information on the collection, contact person, type of system, login/logout instruction, etc.—in short all that a person who has a modem and a PC needs to know to search their catalogs. Important for libraries who need this kind of information for researchers and for interlibrary loan.

Online Library Catalogs

A

570.   **Fulltext Sources Online: for Periodicals, Newspapers, and Newswires: Covers Topics in Science, Technology, Medicine, Law, Finance, Business, Industry, the Popular Press and More**, by Ruth M. Orenstein. BiblioData (Needham Heights, MA) 1992. $75. 1-879258-05-6.

Although this source directory is not directly applicable in acquisition work, it is sometimes valuable to know what periodicals and newspapers are available in full-text versions online. This publication does this for over 1,000 sources. There are two other publications that cover essentially the same areas but are more expensive and more complete in their areas of coverage. *Directory of Periodicals Online: Indexed, Abstracted and Full Text* (Federal Document Retrieval, Inc., Washington, DC) is broken into three separate volumes on (1) News, Law and Business, (2) Science and Technology, and (3) Medicine and Social Science. The other is Nuchine Nobari's *Books and Periodicals Online: The Guide to Business and Legal Information in Databases and CD ROM's* (Library Alliance, 1991, $49. 0-9630277-0-0).

Online Databases; Periodicals

A

571.   **Gale Directory of Databases. Vol. 1: Online Databases; Vol. 2: CD-ROM, Diskette, Magnetic Tape, Handheld, and Batch Access Database Products**, by Kathleen Young Marcaccio. 2 Vols. Gale, 1993. 2,300p $280. 0-8103-5746-1 (Vol. I, $199. 0-8103-8458-2; Vol. 2, $119. 0-8103-8439-6).

This massive work, which is updated semiannually, supersedes three other bibliographies published by Gale: *Directory of Online Databases*, *Directory of Portable Databases* and *Computer-Readable Databases*. Volume one covers over 5,400 worldwide databases arranged alphabetically by the name of the database. Information given includes addresses, telephones, fax numbers, database type, coverage, content notes, language, price schedule, time span, updating schedule, and alternate formats. There are two other directories in volume one. The first is an extensive list of producers and the second, a rundown of online services. Both list all of the databases available from each of these sources. There are, also, three indexes: one for producers arranged geographically, another by subject, and a third, the master index, an alphabetical listing of database names, keywords in these names, acronyms, former names, etc.

Volume two is similar in arrangement and organization to volume one, but covers 1,321 CD-ROM products, 676 diskettes, 584 magnetic tapes, 39 hand-held works, and 389 databases available through batch access. Jointly, these volume cover over 8,000 international databases, 3,000 producers, 800 online services and 760 vendors.

This directory is currently available online through several vendors, and a compact disc version will appear shortly. Unfortunately, the *Gale Directory of Databases* might prove to be too expensive for a small-medium sized library but, perhaps through cooperative acquisition, its contents could be made available to both patrons and librarians who need this valuable information on databases.

Databases; Online Databases; CD-ROM

A

572. Keyguide to Information Sources in Online and CD-ROM Database Searching, by John Cox. Mansell, 1991. 247p. $90. 0-7201-2093-4.

This is a guide to the literature on various facets of CD-ROMs and online technology and to searching databases through these media. Many of the items cited are either journal articles or conference papers, although other forms of print matter are also included. It is divided into three parts. The first surveys the literature in general and makes comparisons between similar sources. The second is an annotated listing of 450 entries arranged by subject. It includes indexes and abstracts, bibliographies, journals, journal articles, and directories. The third is a directory of online hosts, CD-ROM publishers, organizations, companies, and publishers and associations in the field. This is an up-to-date (1991) resource that is international in scope and should be useful in libraries where there is need for good bibliographies and resources information on these emerging technologies. *CD-ROM; Databases*

Government Documents

A

573. Access to U.S. Government Information: Guide to Executive and Legislative Authors and Authority, Comp. by Jerrold Zwirn. Greenwood, 1989. 158p. $39.95. 0-313-26851-7.

The author attempts to make the job of locating US government publications much less difficult by listing subject categories by various executive and legislative agencies and committees. Many familiar sources were used to compile this guide such as *U.S. Government Manual, U.S. Code*, etc. For full bibliographic citations on publications, standard sources such as *Monthly Catalog* will still have to be consulted; however this guide will make the retrieval process less overwhelming.

United States—Government Publications

A

574. Books in Print of the United Nations System. Comp. by Advisory Committee for Coordination of Information Systems. United Nations, 1992. 721p. $50. 92-1-100379-2.

Over 14,000 monographic publications currently available are listed in this long-awaited list of publications from the United Nations. The titles are from the main organization as well as its related and subordinate agencies, e.g., International Atomic Energy Agency (IAEA) and the General Agreement on Tariffs and Trade (GATT). Entries are listed by major categories such as agriculture, family planning, nuclear safety, etc. Each entry contains a full bibliographic citation, as well as a descriptive annotation and sales information. This much-needed guide is recommended for all academic and public libraries as a reference aid and buying tool. *United Nations Documents*

A

575. Directory of United Nations Documentary and Archival Sources, by Peter I. Hajnal. Academic Council on the United Nations System/United Nations, 1991. 106p. $12.50. 0-527-37321-4.

This directory supplies valuable information for librarians working with documents because it gives a guide to the documentation of the United Nations system of organization.

Arranged under seven subject headings, such as peace, human rights, and four groups of research resources like statistics and catalogs, there are 524 annotated citations to United Nations documents that give insights into UN system of librarianship. Using the author/title index, one can also trace documents by issuing agency. This directory will be useful in academic and large public libraries.

United Nations Documents

A

576. Easy Access to Information in United States Government Documents, by Julia Schwartz. American Library Association, 1986. 46p pap. $7. 0-8389-0456-4.

This pamphlet analyzes in alphabetical order 35 indexes to government documents, some published by the government, others from the private sector. An annotation for each index includes the subject, period covered, frequency, arrangement and scope, plus usage directions. There is also a comparative chart that gives quick access to the contents of each index and a closing publisher's directory. In addition to giving patrons and librarians information about locating federal documents, the list of indexes can be used as a guide for purchases. For large public libraries with an extensive collection of government documents.

United States—Government Publications

A

577. The Federal Data Base Finder: A Directory of Free and Fee-Based Data Bases and Files Available from the Federal Government, by Matthew Lesko and Claire Capretta. 3rd ed. Information USA, 1990, $125. 1-878346-03-2.

This is a guide to government-controlled databases and files in a variety of formats including disc, tape, on-line and CD-ROM. The arrangement is by agency, and there are descriptive annotations and contact names and addresses. There is also a detailed subject index. This is a valuable reference tool in academic and public libraries. *Databases; CD-ROM*

A

578. FEDfind: Your Key to Finding Federal Government Information: A Directory of Information Sources, Products and Services, by Richard J. D'Aleo. 2nd ed. ICUC Press, 1986. 480p. $17.95; 0-910205-03-5; pap. $7.95 0-910205-02-7.

This guide to information sources from and about our federal government contains two types of listings, one for products and services and the other for information sources. The book is divided into sections for each of the three branches of government, with a further breakdown by agency. Some independent agencies are also included. After a brief description of the agency, there are lists of sources and services and that include both print and nonprint materials and machine readable formats. SUDOC numbers are given for most GPO publications, and there is a subject, organization, and publisher index. This will be of use in most public libraries and can be obtained for the prices quoted above plus $2 for shipping from ICUC Press, P.O. Box 1447, Springfield, VA 22151. *United States—Government Publications*

Y; A

579. Free Publications from U.S. Government Agencies: A Guide, by Michael D. G. Spencer. Libraries Unlimited, 1989. 124p. $18.00 0-87287-622-5.

Instead of creating a bibliography of government publications which would rapidly become out of date, the author has supplied a guide to the publishing programs of over 50 U.S. government agencies. They are arranged under such subjects as public affairs, crime, education, energy, alcohol and drug abuse, and health. For each entry, there is information about the agency, the types of free publications available, evaluative comments, and a listing of typical examples. In one appendix, ordering information is given plus a list of bibliographies, and in another, an identification of some outstanding series. A valuable source for vertical file materials. *United States—Government Publications; Vertical File Materials; Free Material*

A

580. Government Reference Books 90/91: A Biennial Guide to U.S. Government Publications, by LeRoy C. Schwarzkopf. 12th biennial ed. Libraries Unlimited, 1992. 393p. $65. 0-87287-913-5.

This volume lists and describes over 1,300 reference documents published during 1990 and 1991. The works are arranged in four main sections, "General Reference," "Social Sciences," "Science and Technology," and "Arts and Humanities," with many subject subdivisions. Entry information is thorough and includes LC card numbers, classification and stock numbers, SuDocs classifications, OCLC numbers, prices, dates, and other descriptive information. There is a subject, author, and title index. Basic titles suitable for all libraries are indicated. This volume will be useful in public libraries for both reference and collection development. The previous volume, *Government Reference Books 86/87* (1988, $55. 0-87287-666-7), is still available. A companion volume is *Government Reference Serials.*

United States—Government Publications

A

581.   **Government Reference Serials**, by LeRoy C. Schwarzkopf. Libraries Unlimited, 1988. 344p. $48. 0-87287-451-6.

This companion to *Government Reference Books* lists and describes 583 government publications issued biennially or more frequently and distributed by the Government Printing Office to depository libraries. The publications are listed under four main headings: "General Library Reference," "Social Sciences," "Science and Technology," and "Humanities," with many subdivisions. Each entry contains full bibliographic material, a publishing history, and an annotation. There are indexes by title, author, subjects, and SuDocs class numbers. This will be useful in public and college libraries for both reference and collection evaluation.   *United States—Government Publications; Periodicals*

Y*; A*

582.   **Guide to Popular U.S. Government Publications**, by William G. Bailey. 3rd ed. Libraries Unlimited, 1993. 289p. $39.50. 1-56308-031-1.

This is a continuation of the *Guide* by Leroy C. Schwarzkopf that appeared in 1986 and is now out of print. The present guide contains 1,400 titles, most of which were published between July 1989, and December 1992. Some earlier publications such as popular serial titles and government best sellers are also listed. There is an introduction to government documents and how to obtain them, followed by the main body in which titles are arranged under broad subject headings with some subdivisions. Entries include issuing agency, date, stock number, price, SuDocs number, and a brief annotation. The choices are judiciously made and represent the needs of the general reader. There are title and subject indexes. This is a fine guide to free and inexpensive materials for school, college, and public libraries.

United States—Government Publications

A

583.   **Guide to U.S. Government Publications,** by John Andriot. Documents Index, annual. $295.

This complex guide to U.S. government publications first appeared in 1960 and has undergone numerous changes in format and contents. Among other things, it outlines the Superintendent of Documents classification system and gives a rundown on government agencies. For each agency there is material on its creation, authority, and history, plus information on the purpose and contents of selected series, serials, and monographs. There are agency and title indexes. Depository libraries and perhaps some public and college libraries with extensive documents holdings will want this volume. A companion volume is *Guide to U.S. Government Statistics* ($195). These volumes are available from: Documents Index, Inc., Box 195, McLean, VA 22101.   *United States—Government Publications*

A

584.   **Guide to U.S. Government Statistics**, by Donna Andriot. Documents Index, 1986. 686p. $215.

There are about 12,000 entries in this bibliography arranged by issuing agency in SuDocs order. For each statistical publication, complete bibliographical information is given, including ISSN, SuDocs number, OCLC, LC and Dewey numbers, stock number, and a useful annotation. Indexes are by agency, geographical area covered, subject, and title. This will be of value in large-sized collections with a good documents component.   *Statistics; United States—Government Publications*

A

585.   **Information, U.S.A.,** by Matthew Lesko. Viking Penguin, 1986. 1,253p. $24.95 pap. 0-14-046745-9.

This work supplies a wealth of information on U.S. government publications and services. The first part describes how to acquire material from the government. There is a sampling of the range of information available, plus a section called, "The Best of the Freebies." The main body of the work is a detailed directory of government agencies, boards, commissions, committees, corporations, plus entries for the judicial and legislative branches. For each, subdivisions are outlined, purposes and programs are described, and printed, online and other sources of information are given. There are subject and agency name indexes. This is a fine reference tool for most public libraries. Also useful, though less comprehensive, is *FEDfind*.

United States—Government Publications

Y; A

586.   **Informing the Nation: A Handbook of Government Information for Librarians,** ed. Frederic J. O'Hara. Greenwood, 1990. 560p. $49.95 0-313-27267-0.

This useful handbook reprints manuals and guides that provide access to government publications. It is in five sections and covers such areas as American government, Congress, depository libraries, the SuDocs classification scheme, the National Archives, NTIS, and the United Nations. Each section contains a brief introduction and an annotated list of selected readings. Although this is really an anthology of guides to documents, it will be of great help in building collections of U.S. government and U. N. publications in senior high schools as well as college and public libraries.

United States—Government Publications; United Nations Documents

A*
587.   **Introduction to United States Government Information Sources**, by Joe Morehead and Mary Fetzer. Libraries Unlimited, 1992. 4th ed. 450p. $32.50 pap. 1-56308-066-4.

This book, now in its fourth edition, gives an overall introduction to both the general and specialized sources of information and the bibliographic structure of the U.S. government and its publications. There are chapters on such areas as general catalogs, guides and bibliographies, the Presidency, research and technical report literature, geographic sources, government periodicals and serials, and statistical sources. Particular attention is paid to nonprint sources like CD-ROMs. This is an excellent resource for professional librarians that will serve as a guide to government documents and their acquisition. It will also be helpful to researchers. Recommended for both public and academic libraries.

United States—Government Publications

A
588.   **Monthly Catalog of United States Government Publications: Cumulative Index 1981-85**. Oryx, 1988. 12,000p. $654. 0-89774-380-6.

The United States government has been publishing 10 year and 5 year cumulations of the *Monthly Catalog*. In recent years this cumulation has been available on microfiche. Oryx has made them available in print copies. They are expensive, and the quality is not perfect; however, most libraries cannot consider housing the many paper editions without cumulative indexes. Many libraries will be considering other formats such as CD-ROM, or online. In the meantime, this type of cumulation is recommended for the nondepository academic or public library that wants to maintain some semblance of bibliographic control of U.S. government publications. *United States—Government Publications*

A
589.   **State Blue Books, Legislative Manuals and Reference Publications: A Selective Bibliography**, by Lynn Hellebust. Government Research Service (Topeka, KS), 1990. 142p. $30 spiral-binding. 0-9615227-7.

This is a guide to reference materials on state governments and their three branches of operation. For each of the states, plus Washington, D.C. and Puerto Rico, there are four categories of publications listed: (1) blue books and general references like manual and statistical abstracts, (2) legislative manuals and directories, (3) state government and politics texts (monographs on the history of the state, constitution, and legislative process), and (4) other sources such as telephone directories. There is also appended a selective list of general state government reference books and periodicals. Full bibliographic information is given for each entry plus an indication of frequency and price and a one sentence description of the contents. Updates of this material plus other data can be found in the more expensive ($135) *State Legislative Sourcebook*. Both are important sources for identifying and purchasing material dealing with state governments. *State Documents*

A
590.   **State Document Checklists: A Historical Bibliography**, by Susan L. Dow. William S. Hein, 1990 224p. $38.50. 0-89941-739-6.

For each of the 50 states, this bibliography lists all of the published document checklist titles in historical order. Each checklist is annotated, with material on the period covered, issuing agency, formats available, frequency of publication, and, when applicable, ordering information. There is also background material on the history of bibliographic control of state documents as well as an extensive bibliography of general sources on state publications. A title index in included. Public and academic libraries with extensive state document or local history collections will find this a valuable bibliographic tool. *State Documents*

A
591.   **State Legislative Sourcebook, 1992: A Resource Guide to Legislative Information in the Fifty States**, by Lynn Hellebust. Government Research Service, 1991. 520p. $135. looseleaf. 1-879929-02-3.

This looseleaf handbook is updated annually and is intended primarily for lobbyists and others who want detailed information on state legislative procedures. For each state, there is a brief description of the legislative structure and session times, financial disclosure and campaign finance regulations, and other pertinent information involving the legislative procedures. As well, there is a selective bibliography that lists such state reference materials as blue books, directories, biographical sources, legislative documents, bill status information, and general books and periodicals relevant to the state's politics and government. This bibliographic section is reprinted in a less expensive companion volume, *State Blue Books, Legislative Manual and Reference Publications*. The difference in coverage and price will determine purchase, but either will be helpful in collections where there is extensive research on state politics and legislation.

State Documents

Y*; A

592. **Subject Bibliographies**. U.S. Government Printing Office, various dates. free.

The Government Printing Office publishes a number of pamphlets listing what are considered to be the most useful government documents available on a variety of subjects including aging, accounting and auditing, economics, gardening, adult education, air pollution, poetry and literature, and transportation. They were once known as "Price Lists" and now total about 225 in number. They are revised periodically and usually include a listing of books, reports, and pamphlets that would be of general interest. These subject bibliographies are available free through the GPO, but first request a list of those that are available. The use of these pamphlets is a convenient way of building vertical file materials in public, high school, and college libraries with relatively inexpensive authoritative material.

United States—Government Publications

Y; A

593. **Subject Bibliographies of Government Publications: A Compilation of Books, Reports and Pamphlets Available for the U.S. Government Printing Office at the Time of Their Publication**, ed. by Pam D. Oliver. Omnigraphics, 1990. 932p. $75. 1-55888-813-6.

Since 1975, the US Government Printing Office has published *Subject Bibliographies* of basic publications for sale by the GPO. There are more than 200 of these leaflets available on a variety of subjects like aging and air pollution. These are available free by contacting the GPO. This volume reproduces in one volume those that were available as of June 1989. They are arranged alphabetically by title. There is a table of contents and a more precise index that lists 659 more precise subjects. Purchase of this volume depends on whether the convenience of having this material in a single volume outweighs the price and the fact that newer editions of some of these bibliographies are now available.

United States—Government Publications

A

594. **Subject Guide to Major United States Government Publications**, by Wiley J. Williams. 2nd ed. American Library Association, 1987. 257p. $11. 0-8389-0475-0.

This listing of publications that the editor believes are of permanent importance extends from the federal period to 1986. They are listed under 250 subject headings. Individual items are usually arranged alphabetically by title but sometimes in chronological order to reflect historical developments. Each entry has a bibliographic identification and a SuDocs classification plus annotations that vary from two sentences to a half page. Appendixes include one that is a bibliography of guides, catalogs, indexes, and directories of value in identifying government documents and one that lists the GPO subject bibliographies. There is a title index. This will be of greater use in reference work than in collection development.

United States—Government Publications

A

595. **Subject Guide to U.S. Government Reference Sources**, by Judith Schiek Robinson. Libraries Unlimited, 1985. 333p. $40. 0-87287-496-6.

This work contains 1,324 annotated entries divided into four broad areas: general, social sciences, science and the humanities. Each are amply subdivided by smaller topics. The annotations are brief, but there is excellent bibliographic material including stock numbers, Dewey and LC class numbers, and OCLC and LC card numbers. Both print and machine-readable databases are included in this volume designed to serve as a "handy one-volume guide to significant government resources on specific subjects." Most of the materials will be available through purchase, request, or loan from other libraries. It is therefore of use in collection building, as well as reference, but is now in serious need of updating.

United States—Government Publications

Y; A*

596. **Tapping the Government Grapevine: The User-Friendly Guide to U.S. Government Information Sources,** by Judith Schiek Robinson. 2nd ed. Oryx, 1993. 227p. $34.50. pap. 0-89774-712-7.

This extensive bibliography updates the 1988 edition of a very fine guide. It is intended to serve as a practical guide to locating federal, state, municipal, foreign, and international information sources. The book is arranged into chapters each covering a broad topic; some of the divisions focus on the distributors of information such as the Government Printing Office; others focus on types of information such as statistics and government regulations. The work is enhanced with detailed subject, title, and agency indexes. A similar work is Sears and Moody's *Using Government Publications*, a two volume work also published by Oryx that identifies government publications by broad topics. The two volumes are: v. 1, *Using Government Publications: Searching by Subjects and Agencies* (1985, $41.50, 0-89774-094-7) and v. 2, *Using Government Publications: Finding Statistics, Using Special Techniques* (1986, $41.50, 0-89774-124-2). Robinson's work, along with the two-volume Sears and Moody title, are recommended for purchase by most academic, public, special, and even secondary school libraries, where the subject coverage warrants. *United States—Government Publications*

A

597. **United States Government Publications Catalogs**. 2nd ed. Special Libraries Association, 1988. 292p. $20. pap. 0-87111-335-X.

Updated from the 1982 edition, this 2nd edition of an innovative reference guide contains over 370 titles of U.S. government agency publications catalogs. This unique guide includes catalogs that list printed publications, audiovisual materials, and machine readable as well as other nonprint materials. Entries are in Superintendent of Documents class number order and include name of issuing agency, title, frequency, depository item number, and a descriptive annotation. A number of catalogs that are not printed by the Government Printing Office are included; as well, many of the agency catalogs list items not found in depository libraries or not listed in the GPO's *Monthly Catalog* or other sources. This "bibliography of bibliographies" is recommended for all academic and public libraries.

United States—Government Publications

13 Social Sciences

General and Miscellaneous

A

598. **Advanced Research Methodology: An Annotated Guide to Sources**, by Barker R. Bausell. Scarecrow, 1991. 903p. $84.50. 0-8108-2355-1.

Bausell has designed this annotated guide for serious practicing researchers in all disciplines that conduct empirical investigations into the human conditions. Included are 401 citations to books and 2259 journal articles and book chapters. The purpose of this work is to give researchers a variety of methodological options. Many different topics are covered, for example, grantsmanship, experimental design, research ethics, statistical analysis and instrument design. This volume represents many different disciplines including psychology, medicine, education, sociology, nursing, political science, economics, and demography. This bibliographic guide is recommended for all academic libraries and other libraries needing basic guides to research. *Research Methodology*

A

599. **Assistance & Benefits Information Directory: A Guide to Programs and Printed Materials Describing Assistance Programs, Benefits, and Services Offered to Individuals by Federal and State Agencies, National Associations, and Other Organizations in the Areas of Cultural Affairs, Education, Employment, Health and Social Services, Housing, and Law. v. 1: Programs; v. 2: Publications**. V. 1 ed. by Kay Gill; v. 2 ed. by Mary Emanoil. Omnigraphics, 1992. 2v. $155. 1-55888-797-0. (v. 2 may be purchased separately for $75. 1-55888-756-3).

This convenient directory deals with both governmental and private financial assistance and other benefit programs. The two directories are arranged in six broad categories as the subtitle implies; these categories are further subdivided into 18 chapters covering more than 2000 entries. Volume 2 lists over 1200 publications issued by the agencies cited in volume 1. This directory is particularly strong in state directories. This work is recommended for special social work collections and medium-size to large public libraries. *Financial Aid; Social Work*

Y; A

600. **Contemporary Social Issues: A Bibliographic Series**. Reference and Research Services (Santa Cruz, CA). 1986+. 4 issues per year. 60 p. per issue. $15 per issue ($45 for an annual subscription).

Each of the bibliographies in this series is devoted to a single social issue and contains about 500 citations to books, journal articles from both scholarly and popular works, government documents, and pamphlets. Each booklet covers various authoritative points of view on the subject and contains a separate list of bibliographies and directories on the subject, plus a list of organizations. Bibliographies currently available include: *Investment and Social Responsibility* (1986), *Comparable Worth* (1986), *University Research: Social and Political Implications* (1986), *Domestic Violence* (1986), *Current Central American-U.S. Relations* (1987), *The Feminization of Poverty* (1987), *Pornography and Censorship* (1987), *Biotechnology and Society* (1987), *Reproductive Rights* (1988), *AIDS: Political International Aspects* (1988), *Toxic Waste* (1988), *The Homeless in America* (1988), *Glasnost: The Soviet Union Today* (1989), *International Debt and the Third World* (1989), *Eating Disorders* (1989), *Substance Abuse I: Drug Abuse* (1989), *Substance Abuse II: Alcohol Abuse* (1990), *The Greenhouse Effect* (1990), *Rape* (1990), *Food Pollution* (1990), *Animal Rights* (1991), *Environmental Issues in the Third World* (1991), *The Elderly in America* (1991), and *The Feminist Movement* (1991). These bibliographies supply timely, authoritative sources on current timely topics and will be of use in medium and large public libraries and some high schools.

Social Problems

Y; A

601. **Contemporary World Issues**. ABC-Clio, 1989+. $39.50 per volume.

This extensive series contains separate volumes on timely world topics, and each is intended to provide a convenient one-stop reference that supplies a variety of information. Included in each volume is an introductory essay on the subject, a historical and chronological overview, biographies of prominent people, a directory of agencies and organizations, plus annotated surveys of important books, magazines, audiovisual products, and documents on the subject and sources of information in databases and electronic bulletin boards. Titles in this series are: *American Homelessness* (1990) by Mary Ellen Hombs, *World Hunger* (1991) by Patricia L. Kutzner, *Health Care Crisis in America* (1991) by Linda Brubaker Ropes, *Abortion* (1991) by Mary Costa, *Space Exploration* (1991) by Mrinal Bali, *Environmental Hazards: Toxic Waste and Hazardous Materials* (1991) and *Environmental Hazards: Radioactive Material and Wastes* (1991) both by E. Willard Miller and Ruby M. Miller, *Human Rights* (1990) by Lucille Whalen, *Public Schooling in America* (1991) by Richard D. Van Scotter, *Nuclear Energy Policy* (1990) by Earl R. Kruschke and Byron M. Jackson, *Adult Literacy/Illiteracy in the United States* (1989) by Mary Costa, *Child Care* (1992) by Diane Lindsey Reeves, *Oceans* (1992) by Martha Gorman, *The Global Economy* (1992) By James A. Lehman, and *AIDS Crisis in America* (1992) By Mary Ellen Hoombs. Several of these have their own entries. These volumes have proven to be valuable in medium to large public libraries and some high school libraries. Another series of bibliographies that treats environmental problems is the Vance Bibliographies (P.O. Box 229, Monticelo, IL 61856). Also use *The Environment: Books by Small Presses* (Small Press Center, 1990. pap. $5, 0-9622769-8) available for the Small Press Center at 20 W. 44 St., New York, NY 10036. *Social Problems; Environment; Ecology*

Y; A

602. **Eating Disorders: Feminist, Historical, Cultural, Psychological Aspects: A Bibliography**, by Joan Nordquist. Reference and Research Services, 1989. 64p. $15. (pap.). 0-937855-29-4. (Contemporary Social Issues: A Bibliographic Series, No. 15)

A total of about 600 books and periodicals are cited in this unannotated bibliography that deals primarily with anorexia nervosa, bulimia, and obesity. The first three sections cover general information, treatments, and specific social, psychological, and feminist perspectives. There are subdivisions by various kinds of disorders and by format, such as books. The last two sections are on occurrence in men and the history of eating disorders. Unfortunately, there is no subject index; however, this one drawback does not prevent a recommendation for general collections, particularly because of the current demand for material on eating disorders. See the general entry under *Contemporary Social Issues: A Bibliographic Series* for other important bibliographies on current topics. *Eating Disorders*

A

603. **Finding the Source in Sociology and Anthropology: A Thesaurus-Index to the Reference Collection**, by Samuel R. Brown. Greenwood, 1987. 269p. $49.95 0-313-25263-7. (Finding the Source, 3)

A total of 578 reference books in sociology and anthropology are identified and annotated in the first part of this bibliography. In the second, they are referred to by entry numbers under an extensive thesaurus of terms. This selective list of books covers basic sources on a wide range of topics and were judiciously chosen. There are also title and author indexes. This is recommended for large library collections as both a fine guide to the literature and as a selection aid. *Sociology; Anthropology*

A

604. **A Guide to Journals in Psychology and Education**, by Wing Hong Loke. Scarecrow, 1990. 415p. $39.50 0-8108-2327-6.

This international bibliography supplies information from 356 periodicals in the fields of psychology and education. For each journal entry information is given including title, publisher, editor, the focus of the journal, content of articles and a typical issue, special features and recent topics covered. This title will be of value to prospective authors as well as librarians in academic and large public library collections.

Education; Psychology; Periodicals; Periodicals—Education

A

605. **Public Relations and Ethics: A Bibliography**, by John P. Ferre and Shirley C. Willihnganz. G. K. Hall, 1991. 127p. $29.95. 0-8161-7255-2.

This compilation of nearly 300 book and periodical articles comes close to the authors' goal which was "...to locate every published English language source on ethics and public relations, [published since 1922]." Even if this was not completely accomplished, it most certainly fills a gap in the professional literature dealing with ethics, a topic of increased public interest. The introduction presents an overview of the nature of public relations and ethics. The main body of text includes the citations which included both scholarly and popular works. Interestingly, almost half of the titles were published during the last ten years. The annotations are descriptive and quite brief. The entries are arranged alphabetically by author. A subject-keyword index completes the work. This bibliography on a timely topic will be of interest to public relations professionals, students, and the general, concerned public. Therefore, it is recommended for most academic and public libraries. *Business Ethics; Ethics; Public Relations*

A
606. **Public Relations in Business, Government, and Society: A Bibliographic Guide**, by Anne B. Passarelli. Libraries Unlimited, 1989. 129p. $32. 0-87287-741-8. (Reference Sources in the Social Sciences, 3).

The first part of this guide is a selective bibliography of over 600 annotated entries dealing with public relations. Included are handbooks, directories, periodicals, bibliographies, indexes, online databases, and a large number of monographs. Passarelli indicates that this is a selection of English-language sources most needed by researchers in the field. It was not intended to be comprehensive. Descriptive annotations are provided for each title, most of which were published after 1970. Author, title, and subject indexes are provided to facilitate access to the bibliographic entries. The latter chapters of this volume deal with public relations activities in government, the corporate world, and in nonprofit organizations; they are interesting for background and reference, but are not as pertinent for acquiring material. This bibliographic guide is recommended for most academic and public libraries having a business reference collection.

Public Relations

A
607. **Radioactive Waste as a Social and Political Issue: A Bibliography**, by Frederick Frankena and Joann Frankena. AMS Press, 1991. 668p. $67.50. (AMS Studies in Modern Society: Political and Social Issues, 21)

The Frankenas have compiled an extensive bibliography of over 6,000 entries dealing with the critical problem of nuclear waste and what to do about it. This up-to-date list includes federal and state government publications, NTIS reports, and newspaper and journal articles on the subject. Among the major aspects of the subject included are: ecological effects of radiation, federal regulations, transportation of waste, oceanic disposal, and even disposal in outer space. In addition to the series of bibliographies, the appendix list bibliographies on the technical aspects of the issue. Author and a title keyword index are also provided. This bibliography is recommended for academic and public libraries serving students, concerned citizens, and researchers on the public policy aspects of this still unresolved problem. *Nuclear Waste*

A*
608. **Social Science Reference Sources**, by Tze-chung Li. 2nd ed. Greenwood, 1990. 590p. $75. 0-313-25539-3. (Contributions in Librarianship and Information Science, 68)

In a series of bibliographic essays, the author gives an overview and history of the development of anthropology, business, economics, education, geography, history, law, political science, psychology, and sociology. For each, there is a description of the salient reference works and other sources of information. As well, in a special section "Bibliographical Needs and Usage of Social Scientists," traditional print sources are discussed with sections on CDs, microforms, databases, optical discs, and other multimedia formats. Though less comprehensive than Webb's *Sources of Information in the Social Sciences*, this is more selective in the basic titles discussed and gives better background information. For general public library collections and academic libraries. *Social Sciences; Reference Books*

A*
609. **The Social Sciences: A Cross-Disciplinary Guide to Selected Sources**, ed. by Nancy Herron. Libraries Unlimited, 1989. 287p. $36. 0-87287-725-6; $27.50 pap. 0-87287-777-9. (Library Science Text Series).

This highly selective bibliography includes entries for 790 reference sources in the social sciences. After a discussion of multidisciplinary materials and the social sciences in general, there are separate chapters on anthropology, business and economics, communications, education, geography, history, law and legal studies, political science, psychology, sociology, statistics, and demographics. Each chapter begins with the structure of the reference literature in the subject, followed by lengthy descriptions of the best, most used resources in the field, including nonprint materials and online databases. It is more selective and critical than Webb's *Sources of Information in the Social Sciences* (o.p.), and therefore could be considered a more basic ready reference tool for libraries. *Social Sciences*

Y; A
610. **World Hunger: A Reference Handbook**, by Patricia L. Kutzner. ABC-Clio, 1991. 359p. $39.50. 0-87436-558-9.

This detailed handbook makes a highly complex problem comprehensible to everyone. Obviously, Kutzner has a deep concern for the elimination of world hunger. The concern is reflected in a very comprehensive compilation dealing with all aspects of the problem and even suggesting possible solutions. An excellent bibliography of reference sources, core periodicals, monographs, and audiovisual resources is an added bonus. This timely and up-to-date work is recommended for secondary school, academic, and public libraries as a reference aid and as a guide to collection development in this crucial area. *Hunger*

Anthropology, Ethnic Studies, and Multiculturalism

Anthropology

A

611. **Anthropology in Use: A Source Book on Anthropological Practice**, by John Van Willigen. Westview, 1991. 254p. $32.50. 0-813-8250-5.

This work is an update of Van Willigen's *Anthropology in Use: A Bibliographic Chronology* (1980), which is no longer in print. The 210 new entries have been published in the journal, *Practicing Anthropology*, during the 1980s. Each entry deals with an individual work highlighting the application of anthropological information. Indexes include author, location of research, and subject. This work is recommended for academic and other libraries concerned with anthropological studies. *Anthropology*

A

612. **Anthropology of Aging: A Partially Annotated Bibliography**, Ed. by Marjorie M. Schweitzer. Greenwood, 1991. 338p. $45. 0-313-26119-9.

This work was compiled under the aegis of the Association for Anthropology and Gerontology. Schweitzer updates the Association's *Teaching the Anthropology of Aging and the Aged: A Curriculum Guide and Topical Bibliography* which is now out-of-print.

The vast majority of the items in this bibliography were published during the 1980's. Entries are arranged alphabetically within the 14 chapters which deal with such areas as: general, theoretical, and comparative works; demography, biology, and longevity; the medical aspects of aging; national cultures; ethnic and rural segments; and community organizations. Full bibliographic data is included, and annotations are provided for items deemed very important and subject not completely apparent by the title. An index is also provided. This scholarly and specialized work is recommended for academic and larger public libraries. *Aging; Gerontology*

A

613. **Cultural Anthropology: A Guide to Reference and Information Sources**, by Josephine Z. Kibbee. Libraries Unlimited, 1991. 300p. $57. 0-87287-739-6.

There are over 600 reference sources listed and critically annotated in this bibliography. Most of the works were published from 1970 to 1988. The work is divided into sections covering multidisciplinary works, related disciples, area studies, and cultural anthropology. Standard reference works like encyclopedias and dictionaries are included, as well as other resources like data bases, associations, and research collections. *Ethnology; Anthropology*

A

614. **Personal Names and Naming: An Annotated Bibliography**, comp. by Edwin D. Lawson. Greenwood, 1987. 185p. $42.50. 0-313-23817-0. (Bibliographies and Indexes in Anthropology, 3).

Onomastics, the study of names, has been increasing in interest in recent years. Lawson's bibliography really updates a much earlier work by Elsdon C. Smith: *Personal Names: A Bibliography* (o.p.), the basic source until the present work was published. Lawson groups by subject important books and journal articles on the general subject of personal names. About 1,200 items arranged under 48 subject categories are included. Some of the interesting categories include: Graffiti and Names; Obscenity and Names; and Identity, Self-Concept, and Names. Each entry includes full bibliographic information and a short annotation. Author and subject indexes complete the work. This is recommended for most academic and public libraries. *Names*

Ethnic Studies and Multiculturalism

General and Miscellaneous

A
615. **The Ethnic I: A Sourcebook for Ethnic-American Autobiography**, by James Craig Holte. Greenwood, 1988. 210p $39.95 0-313-24463-4.

This highly specialized work contains biographical, critical, and bibliographic material on 29 autobiographies by such ethnic American writers as Andrew Carnegie, Frank Capra, Emma Goldman, Booker T. Washington, Black Elk, Malcolm X, and Lee Iacocca. After an overview of ethnicity and writing, the accounts are presented alphabetically by author. Each entry contains material about the book and the author and a bibliography of further references. This unusual book can be useful for patrons interested in history, sociology or literature. For large collections. *Autobiographies; Ethnic Groups*

A
616. **The Immigrant Experience: An Annotated Bibliography**, by Paul D. Mageli. Salem Press, 1991. 183p. $40. 0-89356-671-3.

This bibliography about immigrants and related topics contains about 475 items that are mostly books, although there are some chapters from books and some periodical articles. These materials are arranged in 21 chapters chiefly on specific ethnic groups with a few devoted to particular themes like "Women and the Family," "Social Mobility," and "The Immigrant and Urban Ills." Most of the titles were published in the 1980s, and all are annotated. There is an author, but no subject index. Though limited in scope and size, this bibliography will have value in collections serving immigrant populations.

Immigration; Ethnic Groups

A
617. **The Immigrant Woman in North America: An Annotated Bibliography of Selected References** by Francesco Cordasco. Scarecrow, 1985. 231p. $27.50. 0-8108-1824-8.

This bibliography of 1,190 citations of chiefly books and periodicals articles deal with the literature on immigrant women to the United States and Canada with an emphasis of emigration from Europe. The entries are arrange under six broad headings, including "Bibliography and General Reference," "Autobiographies, Biographies and Reminiscences," and "The Family. Immigrant Child and Educational Influences." Annotations are brief and there is a title and subject index. For large library collections. Also see *Immigrant Women in the United States*. *Women Immigrants; Immigration*

A
618. **Immigrant Women in the United States: A Selectively Annotated Multidisciplinary Bibliography**, by Donna Gabaccia. Greenwood, 1989. 325p. $55 0-313-26452-X. (Bibliographies and Indexes in Women's Studies, 9).

This work covers somewhat the same subject matter as Francesco Corasco's *The Immigrant Woman in North America*. Gabaccia includes more citations (a total of over 2,000) but excludes coverage on Canada. It is arranged by chapters covering topics like bibliography, migration, family, work, cultural change, biography, and fiction. There are excellent multipurpose indexes. For large collections.

Women Immigrants; Immigration

C; Y; A
619. **Many Voices, Many Books...Strength Through Diversity: A Multicultural Catalog**. Baker & Taylor, [1991].

This brief catalog identifies and describes adult, young adult, and children's titles in major racial/ethnic groups. This bibliography would assist school and public libraries to develop and expand their collections in the very important and timely area. Copies are available free from a Baker & Taylor representative or by writing to: Baker & Taylor, P.O. Box 6920, Bridgewater, NJ 08807-0920. *Minorities; Multiculturalism*

A
620. **Multiculturalism in the United States: A Comparative Guide to Acculturation and Ethnicity**, ed. by John D. Buenker and Lorman A. Ratner. Greenwood, 1992. 280p. $55. 0-313-25374-9.

This handbook is an excellent overview of the history of ethnic groups in the United States. In addition to an examination of the acculturation of ten major groups commonly dealt with, Native Americans are also included. The strength of this volume, however, is found in the bibliographic essays at the end of each chapter dealing with each specific group. There is also a chapter dealing with the literature of ethnic acculturation. A detailed index completes the volume which is recommended as a basic reference tool as well as a selection guide for academic and other libraries with a special interest in this field.

Ethnic Groups; Multiculturalism

A
621.   **Racism in the United States: A Comprehensive Classified Bibliography,** by Meyer Weinberg. Greenwood, 1990. 682p. $75. 0-313-27390-1. (Bibliographies and Indexes in Ethnic Studies, No. 2).

In the introduction to this bibliography, the author states that, in addition to racism, he wanted to include coverage on other prejudices that "deny the equal humanity of large groups of people." Therefore, he includes material on sexism and anti-Semitism. The thousands of books, book chapters, articles, documents, dissertations, and reports are arranged alphabetically by author under 87 subject headings, such as affirmative action, blacks and Jews, mass media, and stereotypes. Annotations are supplied only when the title of the work is not self-explanatory. When they exist, there is a separate list of bibliographies at the end of each of these chapters. There is also a general author index. The breath and size of the coverage in this single volume would make it a valuable purchase for academic and some public libraries.

Racism; Sexism; Anti-Semitism

A
622.   **Women, Race, and Ethnicity: A Bibliography.** Univ. of Wisconsin., 1991. 202p. $7. pap.

This bibliography, the most recent one dealing with nonmainstream women, identifies almost 2,500 citations to books, articles, special issues of periodicals, and nonprint materials. The entries are arranged under 28 topics such as Education, Psychology, Religion, etc. They are further arranged under ethnic subsections, such as Asian and Pacific American Women, Black Women, Jewish Women, Latinos, etc. The table of contents serves as a detailed subject outline; in addition a subject index facilitates access. Each entry has full bibliographic information and a brief annotation. Audiovisual materials, located through filmographies and distributors' catalogs, are listed in separate section. This work which is very inexpensive and currently complements the two previous entries is recommended for all libraries. It may be purchased by sending $7 to: University of Wisconsin, System Women's Studies Librarian, 112A Memorial Library, 728 State Street, Madison, WI 53706.   *Women; Ethnic Groups*

A
623.   **World Racism and Related Inhumanities: A Country-by-Country Bibliography**, by Meyer Weinberg. Greenwood, 1992. 1,048p. $99. 0-313-281090-2.

Weinberg, former professor of Afro-American Studies at the University of Massachusetts and a compiler of an earlier title *Racism in the United States: A Comprehensive Classified Bibliography*, is most certainly an authority in the field. This bibliography is perhaps the most comprehensive work on worldwide racism with almost 12,000 citations of books, parts of books, journal articles and dissertations on the subject and on related topics such as anti-Semitism, sexism, slavery, etc. Over 135 countries are represented. The selected titles are in English, French, German, and Spanish from the 1980's through 1990. There are no annotations, but the thematic subject index is helpful in retrieving titles. As well, there is an author index. This international and very comprehensive work is recommended for any academic and public library for reference, research, and collection development on racism as well as other topics of related inhumanities.

Racism; Anti-Semitism; Sexism; Slavery

African Americans

A
624.   **African-American Traditions in Song, Sermon, Tale, and Dance, 1600-1920: An Annotated Bibliography of Literature, Collections, and Artworks,** comp. by Eileen Southern and Josephine Wright. Greenwood, 1990. 365p. $55. 0-313-24918-0.

The long title adequately describes the scope of this rather extensive bibliography of more than 2,300 entries of books, articles, sermons, and other formats. The work is arranged into four major periods, then subdivided into subject areas such as Social Activities, The Song, The Tale, etc. Each entry includes a very detailed annotation. There are also author, subject, and first-line indexes. This well-developed bibliography is recommended for all libraries supporting a black studies program or having a special collection in that field.   *African Americans*

A

625. African Americans: Social and Economic Conditions: A Bibliography, comp. by Joan Nordquist. Reference and Research Services, 1992. 72p. $15. pap. 0-937855-52-9. (Contemporary Social Issues: A Bibliographic Series, no. 27).

This classified bibliography of recent materials (published between 1986 and 1992) includes almost 900 entries to books, articles, and pamphlets listed under 22 topics in 5 chapters. Topics include health and housing, drug addiction, and affirmative action. There are also sections on directories, statistical sources, and bibliographies on the overall topic of African American social and economic conditions. The majority of the items are books, which is helpful for collection development. A major limitation is the lack of indexes, which makes retrieval of a specific work difficult. Still, because of the recency of the entries and the reputation of the overall series, this inexpensive and timely bibliography is recommended for most libraries.

African Americans

Y; A

626. Afro-American Reference: An Annotated Bibliography of Selected Resources, comp. and ed. by Nathaniel Davis. Greenwood, 1985. 288p. $55. 0-313-24930-X. (Bibliographies and Indexes in Afro-American and African Studies, 9)

An annotated bibliography of more than 600 titles which achieves the two purposes of providing a list of useful reference works for black studies and also those that are considered the best books on the many aspects of the black experience. The detailed and well-written annotations and the author, title and subject indexes add strength to this important, if slightly dated, but still useful, resource. Recommended for most senior high school and public libraries. *African Americans*

Y; A*

627. Black Americans Information Directory: A Guide to Approximately 4,500 Organizations, Agencies, Institutions, Programs, and Publications. 3rd ed., ed. by Darren L. Smith. Gale, 1993. 424p. $125. 0-8103-8082-X.

This excellent directory is really a complete African American sourcebook and many reference works under one cover. One may well consider acquiring this simply for the publications that are listed and consider all the other lists, i.e., organizations, agencies, institutions, and programs as bonuses. This is an excellent tool for reference, interlibrary loan, and collection development. It is highly recommended for most libraries, and especially for those serving a sizable African American community. *African Americans*

A

628. Black Authors: A Guide to Published Works in the Social Sciences and Humanities, by James Edward Newby. Garland, 1990. 720p. $80. 0-8240-3329-9. (Garland Reference Library of the Humanities, 1260).

This guide is intended as "a primary source for identifying some black authors who have contributed to the literary discourse in this country." Writers selected are mainly African Americans; however, some Africans and Caribbeans are considered. Included are approximately 3,000 titles mainly books, monographs, and essays. Entries, which span a 200 year period (1773-1990) in subject coverage, are arranged by subject using the LC classification. Though an author and title index are provided, the lack of a subject index and many titles without annotations are minor limitations. While there are several other guides to African American literature, they tend to present only a partial picture, e.g., children's literature, women writers, etc. Therefore, this comprehensive and up-to-date bibliography should be considered by most academic and all but the smallest public libraries.

African Americans; Authors, African American

A

629. A Guide to Research on Martin Luther King, Jr. and the Modern Black Freedom Struggle, by the staff of the Martin Luther King, Jr. Papers Project, Stanford, Calif. Stanford University Libraries, 1989. 185p. $14.50 (pap.). 0-911221-09-3. (Occasional Publications in Bibliography Series, No. 1).

This bibliography contains citations for all the known writings of Martin Luther King, Jr., as well as the most extensive listing of both popular and scholarly books and articles about King and the black freedom movement in existence. There are also separate sections on government documents, reference works, AV materials, special collections, and dissertations. Most of the entries contain brief but adequate annotations. Preceding the bibliographies is an introductory 23-page chronology of the life and times of Martin Luther King, Jr. Unfortunately there is no index but, in spite of this problem, this bibliography will be of help both in reference work as well as in collection development in public and college libraries.

King, Martin Luther Jr.; Civil Rights; African Americans

A
630. **Index to Afro-American Reference Resources**, by Rosemary M. Stevenson. Greenwood, 1988. 344p. $47.95. 0-313-24580-0.

This is a subject index to 190 reference works and standard titles dealing with African Americans principally in the United States but with some references included to Canada, the Caribbean, and South America. The body of the work is the detailed subject index, but it is complemented by shorter author and title indexes. For acquisitions librarians, a valuable part will be the list of works cited—a good current bibliography of books by and about African Americans and their experiences in the Americas.

African Americans

Y; A
631. **Malcolm X: A Comprehensive Annotated Bibliography**, by Timothy V. Johnson. Garland, 1986. 192p. $45. 0-8240-8790-9.

It has been almost 30 years since Malcolm X's assassination, yet his influence continues. Writings by and about this controversial man are being published and read as never before. This bibliography helps satisfy this thirst. An attempt was made to include references to all published works as well as tape collections of speeches by and bibliographies to the hundreds of books, articles, etc. about this prominent individual. The works about Malcolm X are divided into four sections by format, i.e., books and dissertations, articles, news reports, and FBI files. A collection of 84 book reviews is appended. Author and subject indexes complete this comprehensive bibliography. This work up-dates the 1984 work by Lenwood Davis: *Malcolm X: A Selected Bibliography*, and is recommended for most academic and public libraries. Larger libraries and those supporting African American studies collections will want both titles.

Malcolm X; African Americans

Y; A
632. **Martin Luther King, Jr.: An Annotated Bibliography**, comp. by Sherman E. Pyatt. Greenwood, 1986. 154p. $39.95. 0-313-24635-1.

This is a comprehensive and significant bibliography on a very significant person. Almost 1,300 article, books, dissertations, and even some declassified FBI documents are arranged under nine categories including works by Martin Luther King, Jr., marches and demonstrations, philosophy, assassination, and commemorations and eulogies; individual entries are subdivided by format. Full bibliographic citations and many brief annotations are provided. This bibliography is recommended for all levels of readers and belongs in every academic and public library for reference, interlibrary loans, and collection development.

King, Martin Luther Jr.; African Americans

A
633. **Negritude: An Annotated Bibliography**, by Colette V. Michael. Locust Hill, 1988. 315p. $35. 0-933951-15-9.

Collette Michael has compiled a bibliography of 495 items dealing with many aspects of Negritude— "the historical, cultural, and social heritage considered common to blacks collectively." The annotations for the 485 items are quite detailed; however, in a section titled: "For Further Study," there are 300 additional unannotated citations. The number of rather current titles included in this broad coverage of an important topic recommend it as an aid to collection development for academic and public libraries.

African Americans; Africans

Asian Americans

A
634. **The Asian American Media Reference Guide: A Catalog of More Than 500 Asian American Audio-visual Programs for Rent or Sale in the United States**, by Bernice Chu. Asian CineVision, 1986. 77p. $14.95 (pap.). no ISBN.

This bibliography contains approximately 500 films and video titles dealing with or produced by Asians or Asian Americans. Although some popular martial arts films are omitted, this bibliography contains a remarkable range of material, from locally produced videos to commercially available films. The items are arranged alphabetically by title and each entry contains the usual bibliographic information, including format, length, and availability, plus a summary of contents. Unfortunately, video cassettes are not listed. There are several indexes, including those by subject, ethnic groups, and distributors. This work will be of value in libraries serving a large Asian American population.

Asian Americans; Audiovisual Materials; Films

A

635. **Asian American Studies: An Annotated Bibliography and Research Guide**, ed. by Hyung-Chan Kim. Greenwood, 1989. 514p. $59.95. 0-313-26026-5. (Bibliographies and Indexes in American History, ll).

Kim has provided us with the most comprehensive bibliography of Asian American materials yet produced; it includes over 3,000 citations for both readily available "popular" materials and hard-to-find historical research items including articles, books and sections of books, and dissertations (government publications are excluded). Creative writing works are omitted in order to avoid duplication of Cheung's excellent bibliography (see entry: *Asian American Literature: An Annotated Bibliography*). The annotated entries have complete bibliographic data and are arranged by format under period, then topical headings.

This bibliography is suggested as a companion volume to *Asian American Literature...*, and it is recommended for all academic libraries and most public libraries, especially those serving an Asian American population. *Asian Americans*

Y; A*

636. **Asian Americans Information Directory: A Guide to Organizations, Agencies, Institutions, Programs, Publications, and Services Concerned with Asian American Nationalities and Ethnic Groups in the United States**, ed. by Karen Backus and Julia C. Furtaw, Gale, 1992. 461p. $75. 0-8103-8332-2.

This excellent directory of almost 5,000 listings deals with more than 20 Asian nationalities and ethnic groups in the United States. Within these divisions by nationality, complete contact information and often descriptive annotations are provided for associations, museums, and cultural organizations, embassies, consulates, government agencies, and much more, including publications. This directory is similar to, and does for Asian Americans, what two other Gale publications, *Black Americans Information Directory* and *Hispanic Americans Information Directory*, do for two other major American minority groups. This excellent tool is highly recommended for reference, interlibrary loan, and collection development in most libraries, especially those serving a large Asian American community. *Asian Americans*

C; Y; A

637. **Understanding Asian Americans: A Curriculum Resource Guide**, comp. and ed. by Marjorie H. Li and Peter Li. Neal-Schuman, 1990. 186p. $29.95. pap. 1-55570-047-0.

The intended purpose of this guide is to foster "a respect for cultural diversity and a sensitivity to cultural differences" with a focus on curricula dealing with Asians and Asian Americans from the elementary school through college years. There is a great deal included here, e.g., classroom activities, recommended programs, essays on attitudes, etc. However, of primary importance is the annotated listing of about 400 current fiction and nonfiction works for various levels of readers. Entries are arranged alphabetically by author and are briefly annotated. This timely resource guide is recommended for all school libraries and many public libraries, especially those serving a significant Asian American population.

Asian Americans

Hispanic Americans

Y; A*

638. **Hispanic Americans Information Directory, 1992-93: A Guide to Approximately 4,900 Organizations, Agencies, Institutions, Programs, and Publications...**, by Julia Furtaw. 2nd ed. Gale, 1992. 486p. $75. 0-8103-7536-2.

This guide covers a wide variety of approximately 5,000 information sources related to Hispanic life and culture in the United States. In its 16 chapters, there is coverage of organizations, associations, federal agencies and programs, and bilingual and Hispanic studies educational programs, as well as extensive coverage on the media. The later gives a guide to key publications, Hispanic publishers, library collections, videos, and radio and TV stations. This will be of value in collections serving a large Hispanic population where it will also have value in identifying publications and their sources for collection development.

Hispanic Americans

A

639. **Hispanic Resource Directory, 1992-1994: A Comprehensive Guide to Over 6,000 National, State, and Local Organizations, Agencies, Programs, and Media Concerned with Hispanic Americans**, by Alan Edward Schoor. Denali Press, 1992. 384p. $47.50 pap. 0-938737-26-0.

This is basically a listing of about 1,000 Hispanic associations (local, state and national), plus academic programs, museums, research centers, and other groups in the United States. Publications are also listed for the various agencies. Information is arranged by state, and for each entry extensive information is provided. There are many useful appendixes, including one on Hispanic-oriented publishers. This will be more useful for its directory information than its potential as a collection developing tool. It is not as comprehensive or as up-to-date as the *Hispanic Americans Information Directory*, but it is also only about half the price.

Hispanic Americans

A

640. **Latinos and Politics: A Selected Research Bibliography**, Comp. by F. Chris Garcia et al. Dist. by the Center for Mexican American Studies of the University of Texas Press, 1991. 288p. $34. 0-292-74654-7.

More than 700 entries are included in this first comprehensive bibliography on Latino politics. Journal articles, books, dissertations, occasional papers, and government documents are included. Most of the article and dissertation entries include abstracts. This bibliography is current and its topic continues to grow in importance in the United States; therefore, it is recommended for public and most academic libraries serving Hispanic populations. *Hispanic Americans*

A

641. **Latinos in the United States; A Historical Bibliography**, Ed. by Albert Camarillo. ABC-Clio, 1986. 332p. $49.50. 0-878436-458-2.

This guide to the literature by and about the Latino experience in the United States was compiled by a noted authority in the field from Stanford University. Camarillo defines Latino as "including people of Central and South America and the Spanish-speaking people of the Caribbean who reside in the U.S." This bibliography of almost 1,400 entries is taken from ABC-Clio's *America: History and Life* database for the years 1973-1985. The entries which are annotated are conveniently organized into topical chapters and arranged by country of origin. Subject and author indexes are also provided. This bibliography is recommended for all libraries interested in this minority group. *Hispanic Americans*

Native Americans

A

642. **American Indian Women: A Guide to Research**, by Gretchen M. Bataille and Kathleen M. Sands. Garland, 1991. 423p. $57. 0-8240-4799-0.

The authors continue with their important contributions to scholarship on Native American women with this annotated bibliography of almost 1,600 entries which covers "scholarly and literary work by and about Indian women in the U.S. and Canada." They were the authors of *American Indian Women: Telling Their Lives* in 1984 (which is beyond the scope of this guide but still in print). This undoubtedly is the most comprehensive, current bibliography on the subject, and it supersedes another important but older bibliography published in 1983: Rayna Green's *Native American Women: A Contextual Bibliography* (Indiana University, 1983. $25. 0-253-33976-6). The entries in this work are divided among major topical sections including: bibliographies and reference works; ethnography, cultural history, and social roles; health, education, and employment; autobiography and biography; the arts and literature, etc. Non-English language and juvenile materials are not included. A thorough index by time period, tribe, name, and subject is provided. Recommended for all academic and public libraries with Native American or women's studies collections. *Indians of North America; Women—Indians of North America*

A

643. **A Bookman's Guide to the Indians of the Americas: A Compilation of Over 10,000 Catalogue Entries with Prices and Annotations, Both Bibliographical and Descriptive**, by Richard A. Hand. Scarecrow, 1989. 750p. $72.50. 0-0-8108-2182-6.

This is a comprehensive bibliography complementing *American Book Prices Current* and aimed at a very special audience—the collector of books on the Indians of the Americas. Hand perused over 200 catalogs issued by book dealers to compile what is probably a definitive list of titles on the subject. Each entry provides full bibliographic information and cites references from 51 bibliographies listed in the beginning of the volume. Recommended for academic and public libraries collecting in this area and serving patrons as a guide to inter-library loan and collection development.

Indians of Central America; Indians of North America; Indians of South America

C; Y; A
644. **Native American Checklist**, Comp. by Barbara Beaver. Bookpeople, 1992. 20p. free.
This interesting checklist may be only 20 pages in length, but it lists over 900 titles dealing with almost every aspect of the life and contributions of Native Americans. Among the many topics included are art, history, literature, religion, travel, and women. Also separate lists of children's books and audio-visual materials are provided. This list which is free to schools and libraries can be requested by sending a S.A.S.E to: Bookpeople, 7900 Edgewater Dr., Oakland, CA 94621   *Indians of North America*

A
645. **Native Americans: An Annotated Bibliography**, by Frederick E. Hoxie and Harvey Markowitz. Salem Press, 1991. 325p. $40. 0-89356-670-5.
Over 1,000 books, most published since the 1960's, are included in this very comprehensive bibliography developed by two authorities connected with the D'Arcy McNickle Center for the History of the American Indian. The work is intended for both the beginning and more advanced student and the focus is on the historical and anthropological approaches to the study of the Native North Americans. The fully-annotated titles are divided into four parts: "General Studies and References," "History," "Culture Areas," and "Contemporary Life." These sections are also divided into more specific sub-sections. The annotations are succinct and descriptive, rather than evaluative. The work contains a detailed author index, but no subject index (perhaps a limitation since the work is divided and subdivided into many areas). However, this bibliography is highly recommended for all academic libraries and other libraries with a special need for additional material on the Native American.   *Indians of North America*

Y; A
646. **Reference Encyclopedia of the American Indian**, by Barry Klein. 6th ed. Todd Publications; dist. by ABC-Clio, 1992. 1,100p. $125. 0-915344-30-0.
This hefty volume is newly revised and updated. Actually, there are three distinct volumes in one: a directory of reservations in the United States and Canada, associations, Native American centers, etc.; a biographical dictionary of prominent American Indians and others related to Indians; and, most pertinent to this guide, an expanded bibliography of thousands of titles, with over 500 new ones added to this edition. The subject listing and the audiovisual lists make this extensive bibliography particularly useful. This important reference source is recommended for most academic and public libraries; unfortunately, most school libraries, where it would be used extensively, might have difficulty with the rather steep price.
Indians of North America

C; Y; A
647. **Resource Reading List, 1990: Annotated Bibliography of Resources by and about Native People**, Comp. by Catherine Verrall and Patricia McDowell. Canadian Alliance in Solidarity with the Native Peoples, 1990. 157p. $15. paper. 0-921425-03-1.
This annotated list of resources represents a wealth of information by and about the native heritage of Canada (with some obvious overlapping of border states of the United States). Included are Indians, the Inuit (Eskimos), and the Metis. The volume is intended to serve a many audiences, including the general public, schools, libraries, bookstores (for selection), and Native American cultural centers. The work is divided into four major sections: books for children; books and audiovisual teaching materials; books for young adults and adults; and directories and indexes. Most of the annotations are evaluative as well as descriptive. Full bibliographic information for ordering is also provided. While there is no subject index, sections are broken down quite specifically with subdivisions. Author and title indexes are provided. All Canadian and many American libraries, particularly those bordering Canada and those with strong interests in ethnic studies, will welcome this aid. It is available for $15. from: Canadian Alliance in Solidarity with the Native Peoples, P.O. Box 574, Sta. P. , Toronto, Ontario, M5S 2T1.
Indians of North America—Canada; Inuit—Canada

A
648. **Yakima, Palouse, Cayuse, Umatilla, Walla Walla, and Wanapum Indians: An Historical Bibliography**, by Clifford E. Trafzer. Scarecrow, 1992. 253p. $32.50. 0-8108-2517-1.
This bibliography contains close to 1,000 entries dealing with six little-known tribes of the Plateau Indians, or the Shahaptian tribes. The entries are arranged under 10 topical headings. Each entry has full bibliographical information and a detailed annotation. This bibliography, which fills a gap in Native American research, is recommended for all academic and other libraries which support programs or are building collections in this area. *Indians of North America; Plateau Indians; Shahaptian Indians*

Jewish Studies

A

649.   **Anti-Semitism: An Annotated Bibliography, Vol. 2, 1986-87**, by The Vidal Sassoon International Center for the Study of Anti-Semitism of The Hebrew University of Jerusalem. Ed. by Susan Cohen. Garland, 1991. 592p. $70. 0-8240-5846-1.

This work deals with anti-Semitism, "defined as antagonism towards Jews and Judaism," and it is intended to be a biannual bibliography of the works of international researchers and scholars. Almost half of the more than 2,000 entries in this volume are in non-English languages. Each entry has full bibliographic data plus a brief descriptive annotation. The work is divided into major sections: bibliographies and reference works, anti-Semitism throughout the ages, and anti-Semitism in literature and the arts. This bibliography, now in its second volume, is becoming the definitive current bibliography on the continuing and growing problem of anti-Semitism. Vol. l, covering the years 1984 and 1985 (1987, $56. 0-8240-8532-9), is still available. These bibliographies are highly recommended for all academic and public libraries.

Jews; Anti-Semitism

A

650.   **Jewish Heritage in America: An Annotated Bibliography**, by Sharad Karkhanis. Garland, 1988. 434p. $63. 0-8240-7538-2.

There are 323 books and 777 articles published from 1925 through 1987 in this bibliography that traces the Jewish experience in America. Selection of material was made on the basis of importance, although current publications have been favored. The works are arranged under seven major subjects like "Reference and Research," "Historical Perspectives," and "Anti-Semitism," with many subdivisions. The annotations are descriptive and vary in length, though the average one consists of several sentences. There are separate author, title, and subject indexes. This is a valuable work that will be useful in collections where there is research and interest in Jewish life and history. *Jews*

A

651.   **The Jewish World in Modern Times: A Selected, Annotated Bibliography**, by Abraham J. Edelheit and Hershel Edelheit. Westview/Mansell, 1988. 464p. $99.50. 0-8133-0572-1.

This highly selective bibliography of books, pamphlets and periodical articles covers the history of Jewish life in the past 350 years. The first part deals with broad topics like social history, religious trends, and the Holocaust; and second is arranged geographically with subdivisions by individual countries. There is a separate chapter on important reference books, such as bibliographies and guides to the literature. Each item is accompanied by brief critical annotations. There is a detailed table of contents, plus author, title, and subject indexes to provide easy access. This will be very useful in collections serving a population interested in Jewish studies. *Jews*

A

652.   **Soviet Jewish History, 1917-1991: An Annotated Bibliography**, by Yelena Luckert. Garland, 1992. 271p. $44. 0-8240-2583-0.

This bibliography covers material in ten different countries in ten languages published in books and articles on the history of Soviet Jews. There are almost 1,500 annotated citations organized into ten main sections that are chiefly chronologically arranged, e.g., chapters on the Revolution, followed by the Stalin period and emigration to Israel. There is an author but no subject index. Recommended for large collections.

Jews; Soviet Union

Area Studies

General and Miscellaneous

A

653.   **Indigenous Navigation and Voyaging the Pacific: A Reference Guide**, by Nicholas J. Goetzfridt. Greenwood, 1992. 294p. $55. 0-313-27739-7

Though this work, by its title, deals with the voyaging within the Pacific by natives, it actually touches on many more topics, including the history, sociology, and geography of the area. A total of 694 books and articles are cited, annotated, and organized by broad subjects. There are author, subject and geographical indexes. Recommended for academic libraries. *Pacific Ocean; Pacific Islands*

A*

654.   **Selection of Library Materials for Area Studies, Part I: Asia, Iberia, the Caribbean and Latin America, and the Soviet Union and the South Pacific**, by Cecily Johns. American Library Association, 1990. 446p. $65. 0-8389-5328-X.

This first volume of a set which describes acquisition of materials for specific geographical areas covers Hispanic countries in Europe, the Americas, Asia, and those countries that were once associated with the Iron Curtain. There are given, in a series of bibliographic essays written by specialists, which are arranged geographically, strategies for identifying, selecting, and acquiring materials from and about specific regions. Each chapter also contains a bibliography of sources, and a directory of book dealers or distributors for each region. An introduction covers the meaning of area studies, their interdisciplinary content, and prevailing documentation and distributions systems. Like the other volumes in the series, this book gives practical advice on the materials and techniques necessary for effective collection development in these areas. It will be of value in both academic and large public libraries.

Europe; Asia; Pacific Islands; Soviet Union; Latin America; Caribbean Islands

Africa

A

655.   **Africa Bibliography**, comp. by Hector Blackhurst in association with the International African Institute. St. Martin's, 1987- . Annual. $59.95. ISSN 0266-6731.

One of the most comprehensive bibliographies of up-to-date information on Africa in almost all fields, e.g., social sciences, environmental science, humanities, the arts (except fiction and poetry), and the sciences (particularly agriculture, nutrition, physical geography, and technology). Each annual compilation includes journal articles as well as monographs. Recommended for all libraries with special collections of Africana. *Africa*

A

656.   **Africa Since 1914: A Historical Bibliography**, ABC-Clio, 1985. 402p. $105. 0-87436-395-0. (Clio Bibliography Series, 17).

This is an extensive bibliography of over 4,000 books, articles, dissertations, and pamphlets of Africana published from 1973 to 1982. Broad subject headings, such as International Relations, African Culture, and Regional Divisions, make this a very useful aid. Entries include detailed annotations. Subject and author indexes add to the usefulness of this scholarly work which is recommended for all libraries with African collections. *Africa; Africa—History*

Y; A

657.   **African Studies Companion: A Resource Guide & Directory**, by Hans M. Zell. H. Zell (Dist. by K. G. Saur), 1990. 165p. $47.50. 0-905450-80-9. (Hans Zell Resource Guides, l).

In this guide to a large range of information sources on Africa, the almost 700 entries are arranged into 11 major sections including reference works, bibliographies, serials, etc. Each entry includes a brief annotation. Each entry is also indexed for fast retrieval. Recommended for all libraries having a special collection of African materials. *Africa*

A

658.   **African Studies Information Resources Directory**, comp. and ed. by Jean E. Meeh Gosebrink. H. Zell (Dist. by K. G. Saur), 1986. 572p. $88. 0-905450-30-2.

Under the auspices of the African Studies Association, the author has compiled an excellent identification tool to many resources, including publications, on Africa. Inclusion was based on a survey of institutions in the U.S. having special holdings related to Africa. The almost 450 entries are arranged alphabetically by the name of the institution, with a list of the holdings of each. Recommended for libraries having a special African studies collection. *Africa*

A

659.   **Bibliographies for African Studies, 1970-1986**, comp. by Yvette Scheven. K.G. Saur, 1988. 637p. $125. 0-905450-33-7.

This major contribution to the field of African studies updates several earlier editions, e.g., 1976-1979, and 1980-1983. Several thousand bibliographies published between 1970 through 1986 are included. The book is divided into two sections: one divides the material by major subject divisions, which are sub-divided into more specific topics; the second section is divided geographically by region and then by specific country, etc. Books, sections of books, and periodical articles are included. While most European languages are represented, most entries are in either English or French. Each entry includes full data for retrieval or ordering, and most are annotated with brief descriptive notes. One can hope that this very comprehensive and useful bibliography of bibliographies is continually updated. Recommended as an aid for collection development and as a guide for interlibrary loans for all academic and public libraries that serves patrons interested in African studies. *Africa*

A

660. **Bibliography of African Women Writers and Journalists: Ancient Egypt-1984**, by Brenda F. Berrian. Three Continents, 1985. 279p. $25. 0-89410-226-5; $14. pap. 0-89410-227-3.

This very specialized bibliography on African women writers is perhaps the only bibliography of its kind. Almost 500 writers are included. Entries are arranged by genre, i.e., fiction, drama, poetry, autobiography, etc. Appendixes group writers by country. This unique and ambitious work is recommended for libraries developing collections on Africana and/or women's studies. *African Literature; Authors, Women*

A

661. **Pan-Africanism: An Annotated Bibliography**, by Michael W. Williams. Salem Press, 1992. 142p. $40. 0-89356-674-8.

Williams has provided us with a bibliography of 360 items which cover many aspects of Pan-Africanism. Included are sections on the origin and historical development, organizations and movements, theoretical works, and cultural ties. As well, there is a biographical section with sketches of persons important to the movement. There are also many items that discuss the relationship of African-Americans in the movement. Citations include books, chapters from books, and journal articles. Unfortunately, government publications are not included. All items contain full bibliographic data, as well as extensive evaluative annotations. This work is recommended for all academic libraries with African studies programs as well as public libraries who serve patrons with an interest in the subject. *Africa*

A

662. **South Africa: An Annotated Bibliography with Analytical Introductions**, by Newell M. Stultz. Pierian, 1989. 191p. $40. 0-87650-254-0.

More than 1,100 scholarly books and periodical articles are included in this bibliography that concentrates on materials dealing with the last 30 years of South African history. The arrangement is by separate subject-oriented chapters, most of which deal with some aspect of the race problem. After brief introductions, the entries are listed, each with a descriptive annotation. There is a separate chapter of reference sources, plus a glossary of terms and author and title indexes. This bibliography will probably be of most value in academic institutions. *South Africa; Apartheid*

A

663. **South Africa under Apartheid: A Select and Annotated Bibliography**, by Jacqueline A. Kalley. Greenwood, 1989. 544p. $85. 0-313-28088-6.

One unique aspect of this bibliography is the inclusion of a large amount of material originally published in South Africa. Another is the breadth of the types of printed sources included, such as monographs, articles, theses, dissertations, surveys from independent agencies, and research reports for universities. There are a total of 1,100 well-annotated entries, plus author and subject indexes. Because of the nature of its contents, this will be useful chiefly in academic libraries. *South Africa; Apartheid*

A

664. **South Africa's Road to Change, 1987-1990: A Select and Annotated Bibliography**, ed. by Jacqueline A. Kalley. Greenwood, 1991. 432p. $65. 0-313-28117-3.

This 1,517 item bibliography contains entries primarily of periodical articles plus some books and compilations of documents. It updates the author's 1989 volume *South Africa Under Apartheid* (1989, $59.95 0-313-28088-6). The arrangement is in one alphabet by title with extensive author and subject indexes. There are descriptive annotations for all entries. The editor is a librarian at the South African Institute of International Affairs, and it is from this collection that most of these materials were found. Academic libraries will be the prime users of this bibliography. *South Africa; Apartheid*

Asia and the Middle East

A

665.   **Current Books on China, 1983-1988: An Annotated Bibliography**, by Peter P. Cheng. Garland, 1990. 268p. $38. 0-8240-3436-8. (Garland Reference Library of Social Science, 590)

This well-annotated bibliography includes 626 books in English about China published between 1983 and 1988, arranged under 25 broad subjects dealing with history, geography, foreign relations, government, and culture. There are also author and title indexes. This is a continuation of the author's earlier *China* (ABC-Clio, 1984, $55. 0-903450-81-X), which covered material published between 1970 and 1982. For large collections. *China*

A

666.   **Information Gathering on Japan: A Primer**, by Search Associates Incorporated. Search Associates, Inc. (Washington, DC), 1988. 90p. $50 pap. 0-9625460-0-3.

This guide to sources on the study of Japan primarily lists publications from US government offices and congressional committees and the Japanese government and corporations. They are arranged in 12 chapters, and for each agency there is usually a list of publications. This work is available from: International Research, 3422 Q Street, N.W., Washington, DC 20007. The audience for this is work is so specialized that it will probably be found only in large libraries. *Japan*

A

667.   **Japanese History and Culture from Ancient to Modern Times: Seven Basic Bibliographies**, by John W. Dower. M. Wiener, 1986. 232p. $39.95. 0-91029-20-7.

This selective bibliography on Japanese studies includes books, articles, chapters in books, encyclopedia entries, and microforms. There are seven chapters divided by broad subjects (e.g., "Ancient and Medieval Japan," "Occupied Japan and the Cold War in Asia") plus many subdivisions. The concluding two brief chapters list bibliographies and research guides and important serial publications. Unfortunately there are no annotations or subject index, however, this bibliography will be of use in large libraries where there is an interest in Japanese history and culture. *Japan*

A

668.   **Jerusalem, the Holy City: A Bibliography, vol. 2**, by James D. Purvis. American Theological Library Association/Scarecrow, 1991. 525p. $49.50. 0-8108-2506-6.

This, a continuation of the bibliography published in 1988 (Scarecrow, 1988, $42.50 0-8108-1988-6), contains books and articles published about Jerusalem since 1986. There are 40 topically arranged chapters with a list of important sources from volume one at the end of each chapter. Most of the works listed are in English. With the increased attention being paid to this troubled city, this bibliography will have value in academic and large public libraries. *Jerusalem*

Y; A

669.   **Middle East: A Directory of Resources**, Comp. and ed. by Thomas P. Fenton and Mary J. Heffron. Orbis Books, 1988. 144p. $12.95.

This brief bibliography deals with such currently important subjects as the Arab-Israeli conflict, Israeli and Arab peace movements, Zionism, Palestinian human rights, U.S.-Middle East relations, and Iran. Included are lists of organizations, books, periodicals, pamphlets, and audiovisuals on the Middle East. Many of the entries include long annotations and all have full bibliographic citations. This short and inexpensive resource is recommended for public, high school, and academic libraries. *Middle East*

A

670.   **Middle East Bibliography**, by Sanford R. Silverburg. Scarecrow, 1992. 564p. $69.50. 0-8108-2469-8.

This up-to-date bibliography contains almost 4,500 books published between 1980-1991 dealing with the Middle East.

The Introduction lists the major bibliographies and sources for research that were useful in compiling this bibliography, as well as additional titles for possible collection development. The chosen subject categories are arbitrary, and the author and subject indexes somewhat difficult to use. However, despite these minor limitations, this timely bibliography is recommended for most academic libraries and others with a special need for Middle East material. *Middle East*

A
671. Women in Japanese Society: An Annotated Bibliography of Selected English Language Materials, by Kristina Ruth Huber. Greenwood, 1992. 484p. $65. 0-313-25296-3. (Bibliographies and Indexes in Women's Studies, 16)

This is a very comprehensive bibliography on Japanese women. Almost every conceivable topic, as it relates to women, is included, for example, the arts, the home, economics, education, religion, recreation, etc. Included are books, parts of books, and periodical articles through 1990. Access to the specific items is facilitated through many indexes: author, title, translator, interviewee, and subject. This excellent volume is recommended for all academic and public libraries with a special interest or program in women's studies or Japan. *Japan; Women—Japan*

Europe and the Soviet Union

A
672. British Sources of Information: A Subject Guide and Bibliography, by Paul Jackson. Routledge, Chapman & Hall, 1987. 526p. $79.50. 0-7102-0696-8.

For the Anglophile, student, traveler, or general reader interested in Great Britain, this bibliography is a basic resource. It is divided into 4 major parts: Part 1, a Select Bibliography, which comprises about half the volume, is subdivided into 40 subject areas; Part 2, Periodicals, Journals and Magazines, lists names and sources of various titles under specific subject categories; Part 3, Sources of Information, lists addresses of organizations and institutions; and Part 4, Teaching Resources, is a directory of publishers, film distributors, etc.

It is hoped that this guide will be kept current; however, it is still quite useful and recommended for all academic and public libraries building collections in British history, culture, and society. *Great Britain*

A
673. Poland: An Annotated Bibliography of Books in English, by Gerald A. Kanka. Garland, 1988. 395p. $54. 0-8240-8492-6. (Garland Reference Library of the Humanities, 743).

This bibliography in effect updates several excellent but older bibliographies about Poland (e.g., Lewanski's *Poland* [ABC-Clio, 1984, $40. 0-903450-58-5] in the World Bibliographical Series which is four years older and includes only about half the number of entries found in this one) which identifies almost 1600 items. All entries contain well-written annotations which indicate whether they have illustrations or contain bibliographies. The volume is divided into two parts: General works and Special Works, with many specific subject headings (including a heading for additional Bibliographical Works). Author and title indexes are provided. This bibliography is recommended for all academic and public libraries, particularly those serving clientele with strong interests in Poland. *Poland*

A
674. Soviet Studies Guide, ed. by Tania Konn. Bowker/Saut, 1992. 237p. $75. 0-86291-790-5. (Area Studies Guides).

Each of the ten chapters in this guide covers a different aspect of Soviet history and culture and consists of a lengthy bibliographic essay followed by a core bibliography of 100 titles. There is an index to the works cited by author, title and subject. For large collections. *Soviet Union*

North America—Canada and the United States

A
675. American Studies: An Annotated Bibliography, 3v. Ed. by Jack Salzman. Cambridge, 1986. 2,058p. $230. 0-521-32555-2.

Salzman, director of the Columbia (University) Center for American Culture Studies, has edited one of the most comprehensive lists of informational sources concerning this country. The 7,500 plus entries are grouped into 11 areas of American studies, such as Anthropology and Folklore, Art, History, Literature, Religion, Popular Culture, etc.; because the areas are quite broad, many subdivisions have been included. The annotated entries are arranged in alphabetical order by author under each category.

Prices, ISBNs, and in-print status are not included. About 80% of the titles were published between 1965 and 1983. This is an excellent reference guide and an aid to collection development, but the cost will probably limit its purchase to large academic and public libraries or regional centers. *American Studies; United States—Civilization*

A

676. American Studies: An Annotated Bibliography, 1984-1988, Ed. by Jack Salzman. Cambridge, 1990. 1,000p. $95. 0-521-36559-7.

This bibliography updates Salzman's *American Studies...* (see above entry) by an additional 3,000 annotated titles published from 1984 to 1988. It is a recommended purchase if the basic set is available, or it can be purchased and used independently. *American Studies; United States—Civilization*

Y; A

677. The American West: A Narrative Bibliography and a Study in Regionalism, by Charles F. Wilkinson. Univ. Press of Colorado, 1989. 144p. pap. $9.95. 0-87081-181-9.

This introduction to the American West includes 488 readily available fiction and nonfiction entries included in the narrative under five thematic chapters: defining the West, events, people, terrain, and ideas. All entries in the text include author, title, and a number to the bibliography which is alphabetically/numerically arranged. This inexpensive and enjoyable work is recommended for all secondary school, academic, and public libraries not seeking research level material on the American West. *West (U.S.)*

A

678. The California Handbook: A Comprehensive Guide to Sources of Current Information and Action, with Selected Background Material, by Thaddeus C. Trzyna. 6th ed. California Institute of Public Affairs (Claremont, CA), 1990. 268p. $35. 0-912102-90-X. (California Information Guide Series).

Though this extensive source is primarily a listing of services, organizations, and agencies related to such aspects of information about California as natural resources, government, society, education, and the arts, each section contains a select bibliography. For large public library, academic and regional collections. *California*

A

679. Canada: A Reader's Guide. Introduction Bibliographique, by A.J. Senecal. International Council for Canadian Studies, 1991. 444p. $55. pap. 0-9691862-4-X.

Senecal has compiled a bilingual guide of about 1,500 items in print, microform, and machine-readable form, designed to meet the needs of those doing research in Canadian studies. Most of the titles have been published since 1985 and are still in-print. An advisory board of Canadian librarians, academicians, and other Canadiana experts aided Senecal in the selection of entries which represent many subject areas, including reference works, economy, political science, the arts, environment, geography, history, etc. Each entry contains full bibliographic data, as well as a descriptive annotation in both English and French. Complete author and title indexes are included. Though there are subject cross-references at the end of each section, subject access is limited. Despite this limitation and the paper binding, this well-developed bibliography is recommended for all Canadian libraries, as well as those elsewhere interested in Canada. *Canada*

A

680. Connecticut, A Bibliography of Its History, by the Committee for a New England Bibliography and Roger Parks. University Press of New England, 1986. 635p. $70.00 0-87451-361-8. (Bibliographies of New England History, 6).

This bibliography of printed works contains 9,778 entries arranged in three major sections: references to towns and cities, county listings, and a state section for references about more than one county. There is an extensive index by authors, subjects, and place. This is the last of the state bibliographies to appear. Others are *Maine, Vermont, New Hampshire, Massachusetts*, and *Rhode Island.* There are also two concluding volumes that cover New England topically. These bibliographies will have value in regional collections. *New England; Connecticut; Maine; Vermont; New Hampshire; Massachusetts; Rhode Island*

Y; A

681. New England, Additions to the Six State Bibliographies, v. 8, Prepared by the Committee for a New England Bibliography; ed. by Roger Parks. University Press of New England, 1990. 776p. $80. 0-87451-497-5. (Bibliographies of New England History, 8).

As the title indicates, volume 8 of this excellent series includes titles missed in the six original volumes as well as in volume 7 (see preceding entry). In this volume, biographies and autobiographies, and some masters theses are also included; also, many newer editions of titles cited in earlier volumes are indicated. The basic format in this volume is the same as in earlier volumes. New England libraries might want to consider all eight volumes, and the rest of the country will certainly want to consider volumes 7 and 8 of this excellent series—if only other regions had such excellent bibliographic control. Highly recommended for those libraries needing this regional material.

New England; Connecticut; Maine; Massachusetts; New Hampshire; Rhode Island; Vermont

A

682. New York: A Guide to Information and Reference Sources, 1979-1986, by Manuel D. Lopez. Scarecrow, 1987. 384p. $37.50. 0-8108-2018-8.

This book, which is an update of Lopez's 1980 volume (1980. $27.50. 0-8108-1326-2), includes over 1,000 titles intended for readers ranging from the general to the scholarly. The titles cover the years from 1979 to 1986 and include monographs, serials, guide-books, and some government publications. The book is about evenly divided between New York City and New York State. Its emphasis is on the "cultural, economic, political, and social life;" however, it does include some other diverse areas, such as geology and botany. Annotations are uneven in length and in quality; also, there are author and broad subject indexes. Despite its need for updating, the volume is recommended for all New York libraries, even the smallest, and for many other libraries throughout the country having collections of this type.

New York City; New York State

South and Central America and the Caribbean

A

683. Annotated Bibliography of Puerto Rican Bibliographies, by Fay Fowlie-Flores. Greenwood, 1990. 167p. $45. 0-313-16124-5. (Bibliographies and Indexes in Ethnic Studies, 1).

This bibliography of bibliographies includes works that deal with Puerto Rico in general, special topics or individuals related to Puerto Rico, or Puerto Ricans in the continental United States. Bibliographies range from slim mimeographed lists to full-length books; those published in either English or Spanish and compiled from 1877 to 1990 are included. Author, title, and subject indexes are provided. This work, which is printed in dot-matrix, is recommended for all academic and public libraries that have a special collection or serve a large Puerto Rican/Hispanic population. *Puerto Rico; Bibliography*

A

684. Brazil in Reference Books, 1965-1989: An Annotated Bibliography, by Ann Hartness. Scarecrow, 1991. 351p. $39.50. 0-818-2400-0.

Hartness has compiled the most definitive bibliography on Brazil, listing almost 1700 titles, " for those interested in the humanities, the fine arts, or the social sciences." The entries are arranged in 29 broad subject groups. Each entry includes full bibliographic information and a brief annotation. Also provided is a detailed subject index. This work is highly recommended as a reference tool, inter-library loan guide, and collection development aid for any library interested in Brazil. *Brazil*

A

685. Cuba: An Annotated Bibliography, by Lois A Perez. Greenwood, 1988. 301p. $45. 0-313-26162-8. (Bibliographies and Indexes in World History, 10).

This is a selective 1,120 entry bibliography that covers all aspects of Cuban history and culture for the generalist rather than the scholar. The arrangement is by 45 topical chapters like geography, mass media, and history (the largest section with 170 entries). Books and articles are included and annotated, and there is a combined author, title, and subject index. This volume will be useful particularly in libraries with large Cuban American patron populations. *Cuba*

A

686. Haiti: A Research Handbook, by Robert Lawless. Garland, 1990. 354p. $48. 0-8240-6543-3.

Past and contemporary writings on Haiti in books, articles, theses, and dissertations have been collected in this 2,041 entry bibliography. It is arranged historically and then topically with an overall author index. Each chapter begins with an introductory essay that highlights the major sources. This will be of value in large public libraries where there is a demand for works on Caribbean countries. *Haiti*

A

687. Haiti: Guide to the Periodical Literature in English, 1800-1990, Ed. by Frantz Pratt. Greenwood, 1991. 310p. $45. 0-313-27855-5.

This bibliography, which cites 5,045 periodical entries, is divided into nine broad subjects, such as physical setting, culture, economics, history, and bibliography. Subdivisions are by chronology. Though this is an important work for researchers on this topic, its value for collection development and enrichment in average sized libraries will be very limited. *Haiti*

A

688. Handbook of Latin American Studies, ed. by Dolores Moyano Martin. Vol. 51. University of Texas Press, 1992. 832p. $65. 0-292-75149-4.

This bibliography is the oldest continuing reference work in the field of Latin American studies. Beginning with volume 41 (1979), it has been published by the University of Texas Press. It is compiled by the Hispanic Division of the Library of Congress and annotated in either English or Spanish by about 100 specialists. The volumes alternate each year between social sciences and humanities. The 1991 volume, for example, is devoted to the humanities and covers such subjects as art, film, history, language, literature, music, and philosophy, as well as general works and bibliographies. The 1992 volume is on the social sciences. Each of the sections is preceded by an introductory essay that serves as a biannual evaluation of the literature and research in that area. This will be of value in large collections, particularly where there is a large population interested in Latin American studies. *Latin America*

Y; A

689. Latin America and Caribbean: A Directory of Resources, Comp. and ed. by Thomas P. Fenton and Mary J. Heffron. Orbis Books, 1986. 142p. $12.95. pap. 0-88344-529-8.

This brief and inexpensive compilation includes books, periodicals, pamphlets, audiovisual materials, and other curriculum materials available from many sources relating to Latin American and the Caribbean area. The emphasis of the compilers was to identify and cite *alternative sources* (alternative is defined as "sources that reflect the viewpoints of the powerless and the poor, in contrast to the mass media, which tend to rely on entrenched local governments and the U.S. government for information." [*Booklist*, 11/1/86]). This is an update and expansion of the "Latin America and Caribbean" section of the *Third World Resource Directory* (Orbis, o.p.). Each entry is fully annotated and includes complete ordering information. The strong feature of this directory is the extensive list of AV materials which will make this a particularly valuable collection building tool for high school and undergraduate library collections.

Caribbean Islands; Latin America

A

690. Latin America and the Caribbean: A Critical Guide to Resources, by Paula H. Covington. Greenwood, 1992. 924p. $115. 0-313-26403-1.

This extensive guide lists over 6,000 reference sources and identifies special research collections in the United States. It is an up-to-date, indispensable tool for the student, librarian, and scholar of Latin American studies. The work is divided into 15 chapters covering broad areas such as sociology, literature, etc. Most of the chapters are subdivided into more specific subjects. Detailed bibliographies follow a brief introductory essay for each chapter. Each entry has full bibliographic data, as well as a critical and descriptive annotation. While most of the titles are in English, some Spanish and Portuguese items are included. Complete author, title, and subject indexes are also provided. This work, along with Dolores Martin's annual *Handbook of Latin American Studies*, will allow for very complete bibliographic control of this part of the world. Both are recommended for academic and public libraries developing collections in this field. *Caribbean Islands; Latin America*

A*

691. Latin American Studies: A Basic Guide to Sources, Ed. by Robert A. McNeil and Barbara G. Valk. 2nd ed. Scarecrow, 1990. 470p. $42.50. 0-8108-2236.

This revised and enlarged second edition is an expansion of Hallewell's classic *Latin American Bibliography* which has been long out-of-print. Intended for the scholar, this work is also useful for the serious beginning undergraduate student. The detailed subject index and a "Reference Source Index" make this an excellent reference tool and aid for collection evaluation for academic and medium-sized public libraries. *ARBA* '91 states that: "This is the most helpful research guide for students of Latin American studies yet written." *Latin America*

Business and Economics

General and Miscellaneous

A*
692. **The Basic Business Library: Core Resource**, by Bernard S. Schlessinger et al. 3rd ed. Oryx, 1993. 2568p. $40. 0-89774-739-9.
This revised edition of a core collection of business books maintained the basic three part arrangement, but it has been expanded and updated. Part 1, "Core List of Printed Business Reference Sources," lists basic sources for the small library; Part 2, "The Literature of Business Reference and Business Libraries," identifies and annotates over 2,00 articles and books for librarians; and Part 3 is a series of essays on other types of business sources and business librarianship. There are a number of other useful guides to business literature, Lavin's *Business Information: How to Find It, How to Use It* and Strauss's *Handbook of Business Information: A Guide for Librarians, Students, and Researchers*; each lists about 700 to 800 sources. However, Schlessinger's Core List and the practical essays make this particularly recommended for smaller academic and public libraries. *Business*

A
693. **Better Said and Clearly Written: An Annotated Guide to Business Communication Sources, Skills, and Samples**, comp. by Sandra E. Belanger. Greenwood, 1989. 196p. $39.95. 0-313-26641-7.
The subtitle gives the full scope of this unique guide which is more than a bibliography. Listed are books, periodicals, databases, and workbooks designed to help "business and engineering students, faculty, librarians, and other working professionals... to communicate more effectively in school and the work-place." Over 1000 annotated entries are listed under such areas as technical writing, business style manuals, business plans, business letters, newsletters, resumes, reports, public speaking, etc. Also included are useful author, title, and subject indexes. While there are other bibliographies dealing with business research, e.g., Schlessinger's *The Basic Business Library*, this work contains more extensive coverage of sources on written and spoken communication. This comprehensive and up-to-date guide is recommended for all public, academic, and special libraries that serve those desiring to improve their communication skills in addition to business professionals and students. *Business Communication*

A
694. **A Bibliography of Historical Economics to 1980**, by Donald N. McCloskey and George K. Hersh. Cambridge University Press, 1990. 505p. $49.50. 0-521-40327-8.
The authors define historical economics as "the application of economic methods to historical facts...." About 4,300 books and journal articles are included in this, perhaps, most comprehensive bibliography in the area covering almost 25 years of publication and many nations. The work is divided into two major sections: Part 1 contains a classified listing in 17 categories, and Part 2 is an alphabetical list of all of the entries. Most large academic libraries supporting studies in historical economics might want to consider this scholarly and specialized work. *Economics; History*

A
695. **Business and the Environment: A Resource Guide**, ed. by Allison Penwell et al. Island Press, 1992. 364p. $55. 1-55963-159-7.
This up-to-date and well-developed guide is for those in the business field who are interested in the interrelationship of business with environmental concerns. Arrangement of the entries is alphabetical under broad categories such as accounting, finance, business, management, etc. Journals, books, reports, case studies, and videos are included. Detailed indexing is provided. This resource guide is recommended for academic libraries supporting business and natural resources/environmental programs and public libraries serving a clientele with like interests. *Business; Environment*

A
696. **Business Ethics and Responsibility: An Information Sourcebook**, by Patricia Ann Bick. Oryx, 1988. 216p. $38.50. 0-89774-296-6.
This extensive review of business ethics covers both corporate and individual issues in over 1,000 annotated citations and several useful lists of organizations. The major areas covered in the 13 chapters include: Corporate Social Responsibility; International Business; and Internal Corporate Affairs. Most of

the entries are selected from business publications rather than the more popular field. A special bonus is the core collection which lists the key works in each major section included. Recommended for reference and collection building for all academic, special and public libraries with collections in the field of business.

Business Ethics

A

697. **Business Information Desk Reference**, by Melvyn Freed and Virgil Diodato. Macmillan, 1991. 513p. $80. 0-02-910651.

This guide is intended as a reference source for students and business people; and as well, it can serve as an excellent bibliography for collection evaluation and development. However, there are other bibliographies that are more oriented toward business materials collection development; two are described below. The strongest feature of this particular guide is its currency. It is recommended for smaller academic and public libraries. *Business; Reference Books—Business*

A

698. **Business Information: How to Find It, How to Use It**, by Michael R. Lavin. 2nd ed. Oryx, 1992. 448p. $49.95. 0-89774-556-6. pap. $38.50. 0-89774-643-0.

Written by a staff member of a large metropolitan area library, this outstanding business handbook has two objectives, "to help the reader develop basic business research skills and to emphasize the need for a critical eye when using business information." However, an unstated objective that is most important for librarians is to serve as an aid for collection evaluation and development in the business information area. More than 750 sources are mentioned, and over a third are described in detail. However, despite the number and variety of sources, it is not as comprehensive as *Encyclopedia of Business Information Sources* with its (nonevaluated) list of 20,000 sources, nor as comprehensive as the 2,000 selected and annotated titles of Daniells' *Business Information Sources*. Still, the price is right and this well-written and multipurpose guide has its place in collection development alongside the other sources mentioned in an academic or public library serving those with business needs. *Business; Reference Books—Business*

A

699. **Business Information Sources**, by Lorna M. Daniells. Univ. of California, 1985. 673p. $47.50. 0-520-05335-4.

The use of this excellent bibliography is now seriously limited because of its copyright date. Daniells, an experienced business bibliographer and head of reference at the Baker Library Harvard University, has produced what is considered the standard or basic bibliography for libraries of all sizes. The first 8 chapters describe basic types of reference sources, e.g., bibliographies, indexes, directories, etc. The remaining chapters, 9-20, divide the book by different fields of management, e.g., Marketing, Insurance and Real Estate, Corporate Finance, etc. and in effect they become excellent subject bibliographies. A detailed author/title/subject index is provided. Lavin (see previous entry) describes *Business Information Sources* "as the undisputed classic in the field of business information guides."

It is hoped that this guide will soon be revised and up-dated, but in the interim, it is highly recommended for all academic and business libraries. *Business; Reference Books—Business*

A

700. **Business Journals of the United States**, Ed. by William Fisher. Greenwood, 1991. 318p. $59.95. 0-313-25292-0. (Historical Guides to the World's Periodicals and Newspapers).

This is a highly selected and annotated list of 111 journals considered by the author as the best in the field of business and related topics (*Ulrich's International Periodicals Directory* lists thousands of periodicals on business). Each of the 111 is described in detail in the form of an essay which includes a brief bibliography and publication history. This useful bibliography is recommended as a basic periodicals collection in the field of business for even the smallest academic and public libraries having business collections. *Business; Periodicals—Business*

A

701. **Business Serials of the U.S. Government**, by Priscilla C. Geahigan and Robert F. Rose. 2nd ed. American Library Association, 1988. 86p. $15. pap. 0-8389-3349-1.

This bibliography is intended to serve the small- or medium-sized public or academic library. Detailed annotations describe, compare, and evaluate 183 business serial publications. In addition to the annotation, each citation includes title, issuing agency, initial date of publication, frequency, and SuDocs number.

Arrangement is by broad subject categories. This slim publication is recommended for all libraries not receiving Andriot's *Guide to U.S. Government Publications* or the Government Printing Office's *Monthly Catalog.* *Business; Periodicals—Business*

A

702.   **The Catalog of Catalogs III: The Complete Mail-Order Directory**, by Edward Palder. Woodbine House. 1993. $19.95, pap. 0-933149-59-X.

This directory lists, under 650 subject headings, mail order companies that supply catalogs listing specialized goods that they sell. For each entry, information includes company name, address, toll-free numbers, plus other information on how to contact the supplier. There is also a subject\business index. This is more complete than Lowell Miller and Prudence McCullough's *Wholesale-by-Mail Catalog* (Harper, 1990, $19.95, 0-01-096545-2). Recommended for public libraries. *Mail-Order Catalogs*

Y; A

703.   **Consumer Information Catalog: An Index of Selected Federal Publications of Consumer Interest**. Consumer Information Center, quarterly, free.

In each of these pamphlets issued quarterly, there about 200 free or inexpensive government booklets and other publications covering such topics of interest to consumers as employment, safety, health, nutrition, housing, ways to save money, and federal benefits. Each is also a valuable source for building the vertical file collection in libraries serving both adults and young adults. Copies are available free from Consumer Information Center, Department LL, Pueblo, CO 81009. *Vertical File Materials*

A

704.   **The Directory of Business Information Resources, 1992**, by Leslie Mackenzie. Grey House Publishing, 1992. 681p. $120 pap. 0-939300-15-X.

This directory lists important research information on a total of 95 major industries such as aviation, garden supplies, mining, and travel. For each industry the main trade associations are profiled with information giving address, telephone numbers, contact persons, and membership data. Following this are lists of newsletters, magazines, and professional journals with annotations on frequency, price, contents, and circulation. Trade show information is also given with details on frequency, number of booths, and the nature of exhibits. There is a single easily-used index arranged by entry and company name. Much of this information is available, though scattered, in a variety of other sources such as *Encyclopedia of Associations*, Woy's *Encyclopedia of Business Information Sources*, Schwartz's *Small Business Sourcebook*, and *Newsletters in Print*, but, because of the convenience and accessibility of the material in this volume, it will be particularly useful in academic, business and large public libraries. *Business*

A

705.   **Economics Journals and Series: An Analytical Guide**, by Beatrice Sichel and Werner Sichel. Greenwood, 1986. 285p. $65. 0-313-23810-3. (Annotated Bibliographies of Serials, 5).

This bibliography of 450 English language journals in economics is international in scope and emphasizes scholarly publications. Titles are arranged alphabetically with excellent, detailed annotations that include indexing, abstracting, and database citations. There is a separate chapter on indexes and abstracting services, plus indexes by place, publisher, and subject. For large libraries with specialized business collections. *Economics; Periodicals*

A

706.   **Encyclopedia of Business Information Sources**, by James Woy. 9th ed. Gale, 1992. 1000p. $235. 0-8103-7489-7.

This is a bibliography of business sources rather than an informational encyclopedia. This extensive volume contains about 22,000 citations listed under 1,100 business subjects and further subdivided by content under such headings as general works, abstract services and indexes, encyclopedia and dictionaries, online databases, and statistical sources. Each listing includes title, editor and publisher, date, and price. About 20% of the entries are briefly annotated. There is unfortunately no title index. In large collections needing extensive business information, this can serve as both a reference source and as a guide for collection development. There is a supplement available which adds new subjects and updates information in the main volume (1993, $90. 0-8103-8232-6). *Business*

A

707. **Fast Facts Online: Search Strategies for Finding Business Information**, by Dan Ness. Dow Jones/Irwin, 1986. 548p. $37.50 0-87094-700-1.

This is a guide for business librarians and other information specialists to help the user identify appropriate databases and design search strategies to use them effectively. There is also a fine selective annotated bibliography. Unfortunately, because business databases change so rapidly, unless there is an updated edition, this title will be of limited use in evaluating and using current business databases.

Business; Online Databases

A*

708. **Handbook of Business Information: A Guide for Librarians, Students and Researchers**, by Diane Wheeler Strauss. Libraries Unlimited, 1988. 537p. $42. 0-87287-607-1.

This excellent guide to business information sources is divided into two sections. The first deals with basic references materials like literature guides, directories, periodicals, vertical file collections, and electronic sources including online, CD-ROMs, and data disks. The second section focuses on specific areas like marketing, accounting and taxation, money, credit, banking, insurance, and real estate. For each item listed, full bibliographic information is given and explanatory annotations provided (sometimes sample pages are reproduced). There are 12 appendixes including one each on free vertical file materials, key monthly federal periodicals, and business acronyms. The index gives access to the body of the work by author, title, and subject. Though somewhat more limited in coverage that Daniell's *Business Information Sources*, this work concentrates more on basic materials and is more up-to-date. In short, a fine reference work for medium and large public and academic libraries. *Business; Finance*

A

709. **Quick Check Directory of Online Business Databases**. W.B. McCarty, [1990]. $20.

This handy spiral-bound book lists data on more than 200 busniess/reference databases found through DIALOG, ORBIT, and BRS. Each database entry has codes for price, number of records, frequency of updates, search fields, sources used to compile database, and subjects covered. Monthly updates are planned. This directory is available for $20 plus $2.50 for postage and handling from: W. B. McCarty Assoc., Box 1537, Auburn, ME 04211-1537. *Business; Online Databases*

Human Resource Issues and Labor

A

710. **Black Labor in America, 1865-1983: A Selected Annotated Bibliography**, comp. and ed. by Joseph Wilson. Greenwood, 1986. 118p. $39.95. 0-313-25267-X. (Bibliographies and Indexes in Afro-American and African Studies, 11).

More than 580 titles of books, pamphlets, government documents, and privately funded studies and collections of papers have been identified and listed in this very specialized bibliography. There is no explanation as to why some professions and occupations are listed and others are not. Entries are arranged in alphabetical order by author and most are annotated. A title and subject index is provided, and are accurate if not complete. As well, there are reportedly many proofreading errors. Despite these limitations, this title is recommended for libraries that support research in the general area of labor or in the specific area of African American studies. *African Americans; Labor*

A

711. **Equal Employment Opportunity and Affirmative Action: A Sourcebook**, by Floyd Weatherspoon. Garland, 1986. 473p. $55. 0-8240-9158-2.

This is a selective listing of over 1,100 items that are mainly from legal, personnel, and labor journals or government documents on the subjects of equal employment and affirmative action. Each work is annotated, and there is a subject arrangement with author and detailed subject indexes. As well as the bibliography, this book contains a history of public laws on this subject, lists of black colleges and universities, government offices, and texts of important documents. For large collections.

Discrimination in Employment; Affirmative Action Programs

A
712. **The HRD Professional's Bibliography of Resources and References**, by Homer H. Johnson. University Associates, [1987]. 56p. $8.95.

This bibliography is aimed at people working in human resource development (HRD) and contains entries under such topics as conference and workshop planning, long-range planning, Japanese management, survey instruments and volunteer programs. This specialized listing of journals and books is available for $8.95 from University Associates, Inc., 8517 University Ave., San Diego, CA 92121.

Human Resources

A
713. **Meeting the Needs of Employees with Disabilities**. Resources for Rehabilitation, 1991. 167p. $42.95. pap. 0-929718-08-9.

This bibliography lists many publications and other sources of assorted devices for older workers and other employees with chronic disabilities, such as diabetes or epilepsy, and impairments in hearing, mobility, and vision. The publisher, Resources for Rehabilitation, is a nonprofit organization dedicated to providing resources for people with disabilities. In addition to the above title, they have recently published: *Resources for Elders with Disabilities*; *Living with Low Vision*; and *Rehabilitation Resource Manual*. To order or for additional information write to: Resources for Rehabilitation, 33 Bedford St., Lexington, MA 02173. *Disabilities*

A
714. **Mexican and Mexican-American Agricultural Labor in the United States: An International Bibliography**, by Martin H. Sable. Haworth, 1987. 429p. $89.95. 0-86656-542-6.

This volume which is a bibliography/directory attempts to fill the void in the important studies of migrant agricultural labor. Books, journal articles, dissertations, government publications, and research reports are included in the unannotated bibliography section of over 3,000 entries. The bibliography is divided into two major sections: popular and scholarly. Each of these, in turn, is divided into more specific subject categories, e.g., General Agricultural Labor, Mexican-American Farm Labor, Agricultural Labor Unions, etc. An appendix lists audiovisual materials on the topic; there is also a title index to the AV media. There is a special index to the bibliographies divided into author, book title, and periodical-title sections. Unfortunately, there is no subject index. Another limitation is that the emphasis is on California, while other important areas such as Texas receive slight attention. Despite these limitations, the volume is recommended for academic and public libraries that serve labor unions, government agencies, researchers, and others interested in the topic. *Mexicans; Mexican Americans; Agricultural Laborers; Migrant Laborers*

A
715. **Videos for Business and Training, 1989: Professional and Vocational Videos and How to Get Them**, Ed. by David J. Weiner. Gale, 1989. 501p $95. pap. 0-8103-7436-6.

Designed for use in training programs in business and industry, the 16,000 titles in this guide were culled from Gale's comprehensive *The Videosource Book*. Each entry is arranged in alphabetical order by title and includes information on the following: subject, release date, format option, credits, brief description, producer, and rental or purchase option. A subject index and a directory of distributors are also provided. This volume is recommended for those libraries supporting business and training programs, but not necessary for those libraries which have *The Video Source Book*.

Business Education; Employees—Training; Videocassettes

A
716. **Women and Work, Paid and Unpaid: A Selected, Annotated Bibliography**, by Marianne A. Ferber. Garland, 1987. 408p. $39. 0-8240-8690-2.

This selected, annotated bibliography of over 1,000 items deals with women's work both as part of the labor force and as an economic force in working in the home. The focus is on original, primarily scholarly works with an emphasis on the literature of economics; however, important references to the other social sciences are also included. The sources, most of which were published since 1965, are organized into nine chapters representing broad topics such as The Family, Discrimination, Occupational Distribution, and Women in Individual Occupations. Following a brief introduction for each chapter, the entries are arranged in alphabetical order; each has full bibliographic information and an annotation which is both descriptive and critical. An author and subject index are provided. This impressive bibliography serves well as a starting point to research and belongs in all libraries supporting a women's study program or a special collection in this area. *Women; Women—Employment*

A

717.   **Women in Administration and Management: An Information Sourcebook**, by Judith A. Leavitt. Oryx, 1988. 240p. $43.50. 0-89774-379-2.

This sourcebook of over 900 citations covers many aspects of the subject of women in the broad fields of administration and management, involving business, public service, communications, etc. The entries are grouped by 23 broad topics including salaries, mentors and networking, women bosses, etc. This work updates and complements Leavitt's earlier work: *Women in Management* (1982, $38.50. 0-89774-026-2) which is beyond the scope of this guide, but still available. A special feature of this 1988 work is the section "Core Library Collection" in which the most recommended titles are listed. The work provides complete author, title, and subject indexes. This volume is recommended for academic and public libraries that support a program of study or a special collection in business or women's studies.

Business; Women in Business

Industries

A

718.   **Hotel and Restaurant Industries: An Information Sourcebook**, by Judith M. Nixon. Oryx, 1988. 240p. $43.50 0-89774-376-8. (Sourcebook Series in Business and Management, 17).

This carefully selected bibliography begins with a recommended core collection of 100 books and journals on such topics related to hotels and restaurants as architecture, law, cookery, sanitation, marketing, and accounting. Following this general introduction, there are separate chapters on each of those topics, plus others that recommend additional less-essential materials. There are author, title and subject indexes plus appendixes on associations and educational programs. For large libraries.

Hotels, Motels, etc.; Restaurants, Bars, etc.

A

719.   **Inside U.S. Business: A Concise Encyclopedia of Leading Industries**, by Philip Mattera. Dow Jones-Irwin, 1991. $49.95. 1-55623-377-9.

In the 26 chapters of this book, leading companies are described in the fields of communications, entertainment, consumer products, retailing, computers, energy, utilities, finance, heavy industry, and transportation. The material in each area includes listings of trade associations and unions, directories, important periodicals. statistical yearbooks, and monographs. This is an interesting work for general collections that may also have value in collection development. *Business; Industry*

A

720.   **Public Utilities: An Annotated Guide to Information Source**, by Anne C. Roess. Scarecrow, 1991. 398p. $45. 0-8108-2443-4.

Roess, a professional librarian of a public utility, has compiled a guide of nearly 5,000 information sources. This one-of-a-kind volume serves as the standard guide in the field. Following the first chapter (which comprises about a third of the work) there are specific chapters focusing on a single public utility: natural gas, electric, telephone, and water. Each of the chapters, in turn, is subdivided by type of information source, for example, bibliographies and guides, dictionaries, abstracts and indexes, directories, databases, monographs, periodicals, and organizations and associations. A combined author/title/subject index completes the work. This comprehensive bibliography is recommended for all academic, public and special libraries which have a need for information on public policy and business. *Public Utilities*

A

721.   **The Real Estate Industry: An Information Sourcebook**, by Laura A. Harris. Oryx, 1987. 170p. $46.25. 0-89774-262-1. (Oryx Source-book Series in Business and Management, 5).

Harris has compiled a comprehensive annotated bibliography of books and periodicals dealing with the overall field of real estate. All of the 900 titles were published after 1980, and all are in English. Included are reference works, textbooks, government publications, and professional books which are listed by such topics as mortgages, appraisal, land economics, title industry, etc. The authors also includes in a separate chapter a list of more than 150 annotated periodicals related to the real estate industry. Author, title, and subject indexes are also provided. This slim book is expensive, but there isn't much available in this specialized area and therefore, it is recommended for all academic, special, and public libraries supporting clientele or programs involved in real estate. *Real Estate*

A

722. The Recreation and Entertainment Industries: An Information Sourcebook, by Norman F. Clarke. McFarland, 1990. 250p. $42.50. 0-89950-464-7.

This sourcebook focuses on the business and economics of the recreation and entertainment industries, a topic that, heretofore, was virtually ignored bibliographically. The work is organized into 30 sections that include such areas as fitness, boating, home amusements, and even gambling. Nearly 1,800 publications, databases, and organizations and associations that are involved in this industry are included. A list of reference sources and a list of publishers are appended. This work would be a useful addition to any academic or public library that supports a business collection. *Business; Recreation; Entertainment*

A

723. United States Corporation Histories: A Bibliography 1965-1990, by Wahib Nasrallah. 2nd ed. Garland, 1991. 511p. $67. 0-8153-0639-3.

Updated from the 1987 edition, this second edition lists more than 3,000 business histories arranged by corporate name from A&M Records to Zurn Industries. Included are books, periodical articles, dissertations, and corporate histories in annual reports. Titles range from the scholarly to the very popular. Also included are biographical accounts of prominent business leaders, such as Ford and Iacocca. Each entry contains full bibliographic information; however, the entries are not annotated. An industry index lists the various companies under type of industry category, such as Publishing, Auto Manufacturing, Aerospace, etc. This bibliography is recommended for most academic and public libraries, and especially those that have large business collections. *Business; Corporations*

Banking, Finance, and Marketing

A

724. Banking in the U.S.: An Annotated Bibliography, by Jean Deuss. Scarecrow, 1990. 164p. $22.50. 0-8108-2348-9.

This comprehensive and up-to-date bibliography reflects the more than 20 years experience of the author in working with banking collections. All areas of the banking industry are included, and there are chapters on commercial banking, savings institutions, investment banking, and the Federal Reserve System. The focus is on basic books published in English since 1984 on the history, organization, regulations, and management of U.S. banks. Reference tools such as compilations of statistics, bibliographies, dictionaries, encyclopedias, and serials are also included. Most entries are annotated, and there is an author and title index. This bibliography is recommended for academic libraries and for developing collections in public libraries with business departments. *Banks and Banking*

A

725. The Bibliography of Marketing Research Methods, by John R. Dickinson. 3rd ed. D.C. Heath, 1990. 1072p. $75. 0-669-21697-6.

This third and updated edition deals with the marketing research function, data collection methods, and data analysis techniques. It is possibly the best attempt of bibliographic control in the area of marketing research. Although a lack of detailed annotations, inconsistent indexing, and lack of stated criteria for inclusion of texts are serious limitations, this still remains an important bibliographic sourcebook for academic and public libraries serving business researchers. *Marketing Research; Business*

A

726. Financial Sourcebooks' Sources: A Directory of Financial Research, Marketing Surveys and Services. Financial Sourcebooks (Naperville, IL), 1987. 454p. $165. 0-942061-00-4.

Because of both its contents and price, this volume is designed for purchase by the corporate business library, but college and public libraries should be aware of its existence. It describes over 400 financial research reports, marketing surveys, and other services. Some of these, like the governement documents listed, are free or inexpensive, but others research services cost over $30,000. The chapters are divided into consumer areas, institutions like banks and credit unions, geographical areas, and international sources. The appendixes supply additional directory information and allow access to the listings in chapters by publisher and report name. *Business; Finance*

A

727. Findex: The Worldwide Directory of Market Research Reports, Studies and Surveys, ed. by Angela Hitti and Stuart Stern. 13th ed. NSA Directories (Bethesda, MD), 1991. 920p. $325. 0-942189-03-5.

This publication has semiannual supplements and a telephone service for updates. This service surveys both industries like utilities, as well as companies and specific products. In all, there are over 11,000 reports in this directory. Because of the detailed nature of their contents and the overall price of *Findex*, it is usually only purchased in large business libraries; however, as an identifier of current market research information it should be known to acquisition libraries. *Business; Finance; Marketing Research*

A

728. A Guide to Statistical Sources in Money, Banking and Finance, by M. Balachandran. Oryx, 1988. 119p. $45. 0-89774-265-6.

This is a selective, annotated guide to 480 serial publications dealing with money and banking. The chapter headings are: "State Sources," "Regional Sources," "National Sources," "Foreign Country Sources," "International Sources," and "Databases." Full bibliographic information is given, plus descriptive annotations. This will be of value in collection building in college and public libraries.

Statistics; Business; Finance

A

729. The Hulbert Guide to Financial Newsletters, by Mark Hulbert. 5th ed. Dearborn Financial Publishers, 1993. 633p. $27.95. 0-7931-0619-2.

This work carefully evaluates and describes over 120 of the most important financial newsletters currently available. The newsletters are arranged by such criteria as their total returns and risk-adjusted performances, in a series of charts and graphs, as well as written presentations. This work will be particularly useful in large libraries with active business collections. *Finance; Business*

A

730. Marketing and Sales Management: An Information Sourcebook, by Jean Herold. Oryx, 1988. 184p. $46.50 0-89774-406-3. (Oryx Sourcebook Series in Business and Management, 12)

This is an annotated listing of books (no articles) on marketing that have been published from 1980 through 1988. The arrangement is by topics related to marketing with subdivisions by such formats as dictionaries and encyclopedias. There are author, title, and subject indexes with a separate, very valuable index that lists titles for a core collection. *Marketing; Sales Management*

A

731. Marketing Information: A Professional Reference Guide, by Jac L. Goldstucker. 2nd ed. College of Business Administration, Georgia State University, 1987. 436p. $21.75. 0-8191-5588-8; $9.75 (pap.) 0-8191-5589-6.

This guide is divided into two parts. The first supplies directory information on organizations, research centers, special libraries, government agencies, and continuing education opportunities related to marketing. The second is a guide to current sources of print information, including books and periodicals on a variety of subjects associated with marketing such as advertising and retailing. There is also a final section on computer-related materials. This is a valuable, albeit somewhat dated, source of information on marketing for business people, researchers, and librarians identifying or building collections on this subject.

Marketing

A

732. The New York Stock Exchange: A Guide to Information Sources, by Lucy Heckman. Garland, 1992. 353p. $55. 0-8240-3328-0.

Following a brief history of the New York Stock Exchange, this volume lists and annotates about 500 English-language information sources on the NYSE. There are chapters covering the various types of sources, such as general histories, reference sources, and directories. Important events in the history of the exchange, such as the Crash of 1928 and 1987, are also covered. The bibliographic sources are listed in one numbered sequence throughout. Appendices also contain very useful information including lists of abstracts and indexes, a chronology, and online databases and CD-ROM products. A detailed subject index is also provided. This well-developed bibliography is recommended for all academic libraries and those public libraries with a special interest in this area. *New York Stock Exchange*

A

733. **Public Finance: An Information Sourcebook**, by Marion B. Marshall. Oryx, 1987. 287p. $52. 0-89774-276-1. (Oryx Sourcebook Series in Business and Management, 6)

Marshall, a research librarian for the Tax Foundation, has compiled a sourcebook on public finance (the fiscal policies of the public sector and expenditures and revenues of government at all levels). The focus of this work is on policy issues and theory rather than on the practical; yet the intended audience is the student and professional, as well as the researcher. Most of the more than 1,200 entries were published during the 1980's. Arrangement is by broad subject including such areas as federal, state, and local taxation; fiscal policy at all levels; inter-governmental relations; economic development; tax revenues; budgeting; etc. The annotated citations are arranged alphabetically under each subject. Typical entries include title, author, ordering information, and a short annotation. Also provided are excellent author, title, and subject indexes. Another bonus is a listing of a core library collection of basic sources in public finance. Since this bibliography can serve the general reader, as well as others noted, it is recommended for most public libraries, as well as academic libraries supporting a program in public finance. *Economics; Finance*

Small Business

A

734. **Mancuso's Small Business Resource Guide**, by Joseph R. Mancuso. Prentice Hall, 1988. 416p. $19.95. pap. 0-13-551888-1.

Most of this work deals with aiding persons considering or actually running a small business by supplying useful addresses and phone numbers and general advice on many related subjects, such as franchising, entrepreneurship, and personnel. However, more specifically, the section listing and describing books, periodicals, and other printed sources makes this a useful guide for libraries developing collections in this area. *Business; Small Business*

A

735. **Small Business: An Information Sourcebook**, by Cynthia C. Ryans. Oryx, 1987. 286p. $52. 0-89774-272-9. (Oryx Sourcebook Series in Business and Management, 1).

This book lists more than 1,500 publications in two parts. The first and largest, is called "Literature." Here the books are arranged under 38 subjects related to starting and maintaining a small business, such as "Accounting," "Growth," and "Venture Capital." The second is called "Core Library Collection" and here there are eight chapters that deal with general works like almanacs, dictionaries, handbooks, databases, and periodicals. No works are cited after 1985. The annotations are brief and descriptive. There are author and title indexes and appendixes that give directories of publishers, Small Business Administration offices, and related federal agencies. This will be of value in public libraries where this kind of information is needed. Also see *Small Business Sourcebook*. *Business; Small Business*

A

736. **The Small Business Information Source Book**, by Adrian A. Paradis. Betterway Publications, 1987. 136p. $7.95 0-932620-81-7.

This brief, inexpensive paperback tells where and how to find information on 150 subjects from absenteeism to yellow pages. Part two lists organizations and there is a glossary of business terms and a directory of publishers. Unfortunately the coverage is spotty and much valuable information is ignored. Both *Small Business: An Information Sourcebook* and *Small Business Sourcebook,* though much more expensive, give more complete and accurate information. *Business; Small Business*

A

737. **Small Business Sourcebook**, by Carol A. Schwartz. 6th ed. 2 vols. Gale, 1992. 2,304p. $210. 0-8103-8076-5.

This work is organized under type of business rather than topics and, as such, profiles about 200 different small businesses from bakery/doughnut shops and bowling alleys to medical and dental equipment manufacturing. For each, there is a variety of information included such as trade associations, franchise information, sources of supplies, trade shows, training, plus database information, and lists of key books and periodicals. There are separate sections on such topics as consultants, state agencies, and published sources of information like indexes and statistical information. Though expensive, this is a valuable source in public and academic libraries for reference and collection development. *Business; Small Business*

International Business

A

738. **Doing Business in and with Latin America**, by E. Willar Miller and Ruby M. Miller. Oryx, 1987. 128p. $35. 089774-308-3. (Oryx Sourcebook Series in Business and Management, 3).

The purpose of this work is "to provide up-to-date information to American businessmen who are now having economic relations with Latin America or plan to have such operations." There are a total of 741 sources cited in this work. They are divided into three major sections: an annotated core collection, the periodical literature (unannotated), and annotated reference sources. Appendixes list such agencies as banks, embassies, associations and organizations. *Business; Latin America*

A

739. **Information for International Marketing: An Annotated Guide to Sources**, by James K. Weekly and Mary K. Cary. Greenwood, 1986. 170p. $39.95. 0-313-25440-0. (Bibliographies and Indexes in Economics and Economic History, 3).

This guide for undergraduate students lists and annotates sources of information on world economic and political conditions, international statistics and business practice, and businesses involved in overseas production and trade. There are a number of obvious omissions, and therefore this is not as useful as the title would suggest. Daniell's *Business Information Sources* covers these and other subjects more thoroughly.

Marketing; International Business Enterprises

A

740. **Japan's Economy: A Bibliography of Its Past and Present**, by William D. Wray. M. Wiener, 1989. 303p. $39.95. 0-910129-79-7.

This extensive bibliography of books, chapters in books, articles and conference proceedings covers materials published in the last 100 years, with an emphasis on current material. The works are arranged under historical periods, with many subdivisions like business, finance, taxation specific industries, and social aspects. There are neither annotations nor a subject index. For very large collections.

Japan; Business

A

741. **Japan's High Technology: An Annotated Guide to English-Language Information Sources**, by Dawn E. Talbot. Oryx, 1991. 171p $45. 0-89774-528-0.

For anyone interested in doing research on Japanese business and technology, this is a fine guide to the literature. Beginning with two general chapters ("Guides to Sources of Japanese Information" and "Conferences and Reports on Access to Japans Information"), the author moves on to chapters on specific types of sources, such as bibliographies, dictionaries, handbooks, abstracts and indexes, periodicals, and online sources. Each item is annotated. There are author, title and subject indexes. *Japan; Technology*

A

742. **Protectionism: An Annotated Bibliography**, by James Lutz. Pierian Press, 1988. 270 p. $40. pap. 0-87650-249-4. (Resources on Contemporary Issues).

In this addition to an excellent series, over 800 articles, books, and government publications on protectionism are identified and described. The work is divided into chapters dealing with specific aspects of the topic. Each chapter includes a brief essay followed by an annotated bibliography arranged by author entries. There is no subject index, but a detailed table of contents outlines the specific topics covered in each chapter. This bibliography is recommended for most academic libraries and perhaps those public libraries that have a special collection in economics or other fields including protectionism.

Foreign Trade; Protectionism

A

743. **Through a Glass Clearly: Finding, Evaluating and Using Business Information from the Soviet Region**. Special Libraries Association, [1992]. 65p. $31.25. 0-87111-385-6.

Since the dismantling of the Soviet Union, each of the independent republics is exceedingly anxious to promote a closer business relationship with the West. This brief guide is intended for those from the West who are equally eager to become familiar with the business available in the 15 independent republics. This guide includes accessibility of sources, evaluative guidelines, and contacts for Soviet-produced publications. To order or obtain more information write to: Jane Taylor, Manager, Nonserial Publications, Special Libraries Association, 1700 18th St. N.W., Washington, DC 20009-2508.

Business; Business—Information Services; Soviet Union

A

744.   **The World Bank Group: A Guide to Information Sources**, by Carol R. Wilson. Garland, 1991. 322p. $45. 0-8240-4429-0.

Wilson cites books, articles, and other publications dealing with a number of agencies and organizations that make up the World Bank Group. Included are the International Bank for Reconstruction and Development, the International Development Association, and International Finance Corporation. The 1,000 plus entries were published from 1944 through 1988. Annotations are included for most entries which also include full bibliographic data. Appendices cite sources used to compile the bibliography as well as other information on the World Bank Group. Detailed author, title, and subject indexes round out the volume. The work is recommended for all academic libraries and special libraries interested in or offering programs in international banking.   *Banks and Banking; International Business Enterprises*

Careers and Occupations

C

745.   **Career Index: A Selective Bibliography for Elementary Schools**, by Gretchen S. Baldauf. Greenwood, 1990 212p. $37.95. 0-313-24832-X.

This is a listing of career materials consisting of over 1,000 books, filmstrips, cassettes, and videotapes for preschool through sixth grade, arranged under 20 broad career categories and 41 subcategories. Most of the material was published between 1970 and 1988. Though some outdated and therefore inaccurate material has been included, this list is particularly useful for the number of biographies of people who can serve as career role models.   *Occupations; Vocational Guidance*

A

746.   **Careers in Business and the Public Sector: An Annotated Bibliography**, by Michael Parrish. Ars Bibliographica, 1986, $8. 0-9617990-0-5.

This is a briefly annotated list of books alphabetically arranged by author that includes general topics such as job hunting plus material on specific careers in business and the public sector. Most books cover the period 1975 into 1986.   *Occupations; Vocational Guidance*

Y*; A

747.   **Careers in Fact and Fiction: A Selective, Annotated List of Books for Career Backgrounds**, by June Klein Bienstock and Ruth Bienstock Anolik. American Library Association, 1985. $9.95 pap. 0-8389-0424-6.

Intended to 'humanize' career counseling and give inside information for high school, college and adult readers, this annotated bibliography of basically adult materials consists primarily of fiction, biography, and plays with a few general nonfiction titles also included. The 1,000 items are arranged under broad subject categories like science and communication with subdivisions for approximately 150 specific occupations. Annotations are brief and descriptive. Author and title indexes are included. This volume, which supersedes the two earlier editions of *Vocations in Fact and Fiction*, will be useful in both high school and public libraries.   *Occupations; Vocational Guidance*

Y; A

748.   **Chronicle Career Index**, ed. by Paul Downes. Chronicle Career Publications (Moravia, NY), 1991. 159p. $14.25. 1-55631-149-4.

This bibliography on occupational and educational guidance materials includes hundreds of books, pamphlets, documents, and audiovisual materials all listed in groups according to producer, publisher, or sponsor. Many, but not all, are annotated. There are subject and keyword indexes, but unfortunately the work is awkward to use.   *Occupations; Educational Counseling; Vocational Guidance*

A

749.   **The Encyclopedia of Career Choices for the 1990s: A Guide to Entry Level Jobs**, by Career Associates. Walker, 1991. 862p. $75. 0-8027-1142-1.

This work provides information on entry level jobs to college students, concentrating on opportunities in the white-collar areas. There are 42 alphabetically arranged chapters which deal with various fields of employment ranging from accounting to television. Each contains information on such areas as job duties, qualifications, advancement possibilities, salaries, geographic areas where demand exists, and other essential basics about the occupation. Each also has a list of recommended readings which can also be used for collection development. There are many indexes, plus additional sections of background material such as "A Key to Match Your Fields of Study to Job Opportunities." *Vocational Guidance; Occupations*

Y*; A*

750. **The Encyclopedia of Careers and Vocational Guidance**, by William E. Hopke. 8th ed. Ferguson, 1990. 4 volumes. 2,800p. $129.95. 0-89434-117-0.

This four volume work contains a great deal of information on careers and for each supplies a bibliography of additional sources that be of help in building both regular and vertical file library collections. The set reviews major industries such as apparel, computers, and teaching; gives overviews of jobs, training required, and future possibilities; and lists sources for additional information. It also provides information on hundreds of specific careers. In the overview articles, there is material on the job outlook, training, working conditions, salaries, plus other related information including listings of further sources. It is hoped there will be updates, although many of the sources listed are still valuable.

Occupations; Vocational Guidance

A

751. **Great Careers: The Fourth of July Guide to Careers, Internships, and Volunteer Opportunities in the Nonprofit Sector**, ed. by Devon Cottrell Smith and James LaVecks. 2nd ed. Garrett Park, 1990. 605p. $35. pap. 0-912048-74-3.

This is a directory of source materials for job opportunities in the nonprofit sector in areas such as animal rights, women's issues, and homelessness. These careers are organized under 28 chapters. For each, there is an introduction to the field, a discussion of job opportunities, and annotated lists of books, directories, periodicals, organizations, and job listings. *Occupations; Vocational Guidance*

Y; A

752. **Job Hunter's Sourcebook: Where To Find Employment Leads and Other Job Search Resources**, by Michelle LeCompte. Gale, 1991. 1106p. $49.95. 0-8103-7717-9

The main body of this work contains sources of job-hunting information on 155 alphabetically arranged professions and occupations. Resources include help-wanted ads, employer directories, employment agencies, placement services, handbooks and manuals and network lists. In another section general employment topics are discussed such as how to use the library for job hunting and how to identify and use general employment information. There is an general index to sources cited. This hefty volume combines the 'how to' aspects of job hunting with directory information. The latter will be of value in helping public, academic and high school libraries in developing their career collections.

Occupations; Vocational Guidance

Y*; A*

753. **Professional Careers Sourcebook: Where to Find Help Planning Careers That Require College or Technical Degrees**, by Kathleen M. Savage et al. Gale, 1992. 1166p. $75. 0-8103-7573-7.

This up-to-date career planning sourcebook provides a wealth of current information. It serves as a companion volume to *Vocational Careers Sourcebook* which includes 125 careers not requiring a 4-year degree. The careers in this profession-oriented volume are arranged in career clusters such as writers, artists, engineers, etc. Individual career profiles includes a brief abstract taken from the well-known *Occupational Outlook Handbook*. Each career entry also includes information on general career guides and audiovisual materials, professional associations, standards and certification, basic reference handbooks related to the profession, professional and trade periodicals, etc. A master alphabetical index to all publications and other information sources is a "goldmine" for collection development. This sourcebook will be much used by high school and college students as well as professionals involved in career planning. The cost of this work which can quickly become outdated is of some concern; however, it appears evident that it will be revised regularly and is therefore highly recommended for all secondary school, academic, and public libraries.

Occupations; Professions; Vocational Guidance

Y; A

754. **VGM's Careers Encyclopedia**, Ed. by Craig T. Norback. 3rd ed. National Textbook Co./VGM Career Books, 1991. 464p. $39.95. 0-8442-8692-3.

More than 180 careers are included in this one-volume guide. Careers are listed in alphabetical order for quick reference. Following a brief description of the career, each entry contains more detailed information on places of employment, working conditions, education, training, expected income, and additional sources of information. An index is provided. This guide contains more information on fewer careers than the similar work edited by William E. Hopkke, *The Encyclopedia of Careers and Vocational Guidance*. Both volumes are recommended for high school, academic, and public libraries.

Occupations; Vocational Guidance

Y*; A*
755.   **Vocational Careers Sourcebook: Where to Find Help Planning Careers in Skilled, Trade, and Nontechnical Vocations**, Ed. by Kathleen M. Savage and Karen Hill. Gale, 1992. 1129p. $75. 0-8103-8405-1.
    This new career planning sourcebook provides information on 125 careers listed in the well-known *Occupational Outlook Handbook* which do not require a 4-year college degree. It serves as a companion volume to the *Professional Careers Sourcebook* which relates to 111 careers requiring a degree. Each career entry listed includes brief information about the career such as training, working conditions, etc., followed by information guides for additional information. This sourcebook will be much used by high school students as well as adults involved in career planning. Highly recommended for all secondary school and public libraries.   *Occupations; Vocational Guidance*

Y*; A*
756.   **Where to Start Career Planning: Essential Resource Guide for Career Planning and Job Hunting**, by Pamela L. Feodoroff and Carolyn Lloyd Lindquist. 8th ed. Cornell University/dist. by Peterson's Guides, 1991. 299p. $17.95. 1-56079-056-3.
    The eighth edition of this useful guide updates its predecessors and, like the earlier editions, is based on the career planning library at Cornell University's Career Center. Introductory information includes a great deal of valuable information on financial aid, planning a career, internships, etc. This is followed by a listing of more than 2,000 publications which are described and arranged under 21 broad career fields such as Agriculture, Biological Science, Education, Engineering, Health Services, etc. The appendix includes a list of audiovisual materials, periodicals which list job offerings, and periodicals related to careers. The regular updating, quality of the annotations, and the relatively low price make this a wise purchase for high school, college, and public libraries for developing or maintaining a career collection.

Occupations; Vocational Guidance

Education

General and Miscellaneous

A
757.   **A Bibliographic Guide to Educational Research**, by Dorothea M. Berry. 3rd. ed. Scarecrow, 1900. 500p. $49.50. 0-8108-2343-8.
    The 1,050 entries in this annotated bibliography are for works related to educational research. They are organized by form, i.e., there are sections on reference materials, books, periodicals, research studies, and government publications, with a separate section on special types of materials such as those covering children's literature or textbooks. All entries are annotated descriptively. This bibliography is a basic guide to beginning research in education and therefore will also have value as a collection-building tool in undergraduate collections, some public libraries, and teacher's resource centers in large school districts.

Education

A
758.   **Core List of Books and Journals in Education**, by Nancy Patricia O'Brian and Emily Fabiano. Oryx, 1991. 125p. $39.95 0-89774-559-0.
    This highly selective guide to the current literature in the field of education contains about 1,000 entries for books and journals. The book section is organized into 18 subject areas like special education and measurement. For each title, bibliographic information is given, plus a detailed evaluative annotation. There is also an unannotated list of basic periodicals and author, title, and subject indexes. This is recommended for large public libraries and others needing a guide to collection development in education.

Education; Periodicals

C*; Y*; A*

759. **Education: A Guide to Reference and Information Sources**, by Lois Buttlar. Libraries Unlimited, 1989. 258p. \$35. 0-87287-619-5. (Reference Sources in the Social Sciences Series, 2).

Both general and special references sources are listed in this bibliography that includes almost 900 selected titles on education and related fields, from the elementary school through college levels. The contents are arranged in 20 chapters covering such subjects as educational administration, career and vocational education, art education, bilingual and multicultural education, women's studies, special education, and higher education. Each contains critically annotated entries for major guides to the literature, bibliographies, indexes, abstracts, online databases, and other reference sources. Fifty major periodicals titles are listed. Most titles date from 1980 through 1988. There is a comprehensive index. This volume will be of value in school professional collections and in some public and academic libraries.

Education; Reference Books—Education

C*; Y*; A*

760. **The Educator's Desk Reference: A Sourcebook of Educational Information and Research**, by Melvyn N. Freed and others. American Council on Education/Macmillan, 1989. 536p. \$49.95 0-02-910740-7.

This handbook intended for educational professionals, particularly at the administrative level, is a combination of research manual, directory, and bibliography. There are six major sections. The first is useful for collection development and consists of an annotated list of important reference sources in education arranged by such types as encyclopedias, bibliographies, and statistical digests. There are also directories of leading publishers of books, journals, and software arranged by field; profiles of important standardized tests; and lists of professional organizations plus a great deal of material for would-be researchers and authors, including information on various types of research design and on where to submit manuscripts. This is a fine basic volume for professional collections in schools and colleges and will also be useful in any collection serving educators. *Education; Reference Books—Education*

A

761. **Encyclopedia of Educational Research**, 4 vols., ed. by Marvin C. Alkin. 6th ed. Macmillan, 1992. \$330. 0-02-900431-4.

This massive work is an important contribution to education literature. In volume one, all of the entries are grouped under large subjects, such as curriculum and organizational structure, but in the body of the work these entries are arranged alphabetically. Each subject entry contains a summary of pertinent research in the area, plus an extensive bibliography listing materials for each of these studies. There are many cross references plus comprehensive indexes. Before the index, there is an interesting section called "Doing Library Research in Education." Here there is a annotated listing of the standard basic reference works in education, both in print formats and non print, such as CD-ROMs. The bibliographies in the body of the work and this special research section contain valuable items for collection development. Recommended for public libraries needing material on education and any college that has an education department.

Education

A

762. **Guide to American Educational Directories**, by Barry T. Klein. 7th ed. Todd Publications, 1993. 350p. \$60. 0-915344-29-7.

This spin-off from the author's *Guide to American Directories* contains entries for about 5,000 directories, arranged under such broad subjects as art, communications, medical science, and travel. The word "educational" is defined broadly so that peripheral material is also included. Entries include title, name and address of publisher, contents notes, and price . There is a title index. Libraries owning any of the more comprehensive directory listings (like the parent volume) will probably not need this. *Directories*

A

763. **Handbook on Research in Teaching**, by Merlin C. Wittrock. 3rd ed. Macmillan, 1986. 1037p. \$75. 0-02-900310-5.

In this scholarly publication, there are 35 signed articles dealing with theoretical aspects of teaching, classroom dynamics, social and institutional aspects of teaching, specific groups of students, and individual grade levels and subjects. Each article contains extensive bibliographies that can help both researchers in identifying materials and librarians who are interested in collection development. There are author and subject indexes. For college, some public libraries and school district-wide curriculum centers. *Education*

A
764.   **Resources in Education (RIE) Annual Cumulation**. v. 26. Oryx, 1991. 2v. subscription rate, $315. ISSN 0197-9973.

RIE indexes educational research findings, speeches, unpublished manuscripts, and books identified by the ERIC (Educational Resources Information Centers) clearing houses. *RIE* serves as a companion volume to *CIJE*, which indexes current periodicals in education and is also under the auspices of ERIC.

The annual three volume sets of RIE cumulations include two volumes of abstracts and a one-volume index. Entries in the abstracts contain author, source, date, price, etc., and a 200 word description of the contents. The index permits searching of the abstracts by subject, author, or publication type. Back volumes are also available at $315 a year. This valuable index, which identifies thousands of documents that might otherwise go unused, is recommended for school district professional libraries, as well as academic and other libraries supporting programs in education.   *Education*

C; Y; A
765.   **The School Administrator's Resource Guide**, by Katherine Clay. Oryx, 1988. 104p. $25.95 (pap.) 0-89774-446-2.

There are 548 entries for books, articles, microfiche documents, and dissertations in this bibliography on various aspects of the present-day school administration. The citations are organized into nine chapters that cover topics like staff development, discipline, site management, school-community relations, and instructional leadership. Most of the material appeared first from 1982 to the beginning of 1987. Within each chapter the material is arranged by format. The annotations are thorough, and there are author, title, and subject indexes. The latter has been criticized for lack of completeness. This bibliography will be useful in professional collections in individual schools or district-wide curriculum centers.

Schools—Administration

C; Y; A
766.   **State Education Documents: A State-by State Directory for Their Acquisition and Use**. American Library Association, 1989. 45p. $19.95 pap. 0-8389-7327-2.

Most state education departments publish a variety of professional tools to guide teachers and administrators in their state. These publications often include curriculum guides, statistical sources, reports, directories, instructional materials, bibliographies, evaluation tools, and policy statements. Unfortunately, many of these documents go unreported. The Education and Behavioral Sciences Section of the Association of College and Research Libraries of ALA has tried to correct this in compiling this state-by-state guide to their education documents. Information given includes names and addresses of where to write for publications, types of material available, checklists, microformats available, and information about municipal education documents. This paperbound pamphlet will be useful in schools and other educational institutions trying to build a professional collection of state documents.   *Education*

Nonprint Media

C; Y; A
767.   **Audiocassette Finder: A Subject Guide to Educational and Literary Materials on Audiocassettes**, Ed. by Stephanie Korney. 3rd ed. Plexus-NICEM (National Information Center for Educational Media)), 1992. 925p. $95. 0-937548-22-7.

This massive identifying and locational tool contains descriptions of over 25,000 audiocassettes which focus on the spoken word and include educational, documentary, and recreation-al types. Each entry also provides useful information such as length, level, and source. This helpful finding tool is recommended for all libraries developing or maintaining audiocassette collections.   *Audiocassettes*

C*;Y*;A*
768.   **Educational Film and Video Locator**, by the Consortium of College and University Media Centers and R. R. Bowker. 4th ed. Bowker, 1990. 2 volumes. 3,361 p. $175. 0-8352-2624-7.

This is a union list of the film and video holdings of 46 members of the Consortium of University Film Centers. This listing contains information on 52,000 films and videos available for rental from one or more of the members. In the first volume there is a gigantic index by subject, title, and audience level plus names and addresses of producers and distributors. This is followed by the body of the work, a title listing through the letter H that gives for each title, such information as, running time, whether in color, format, production date, series notations, subjects, audience level, and rental sources. The remainder of the alphabet is found in volume two. There is also contact information given and lending terms for all participating media centers. It is updated every three years. Although this is an extremely valuable guide, its cost will limit its purchase to district-wide educational centers, state libraries, academic and very large public libraries.

Motion Pictures; Videocassettes

C; Y; A

769. **Educational Media and Technology Yearbook, 1993**, by Donald P. Ely and Barbara B. Minor. Volume 19. Libraries Unlimited, 1993. 369p. $60. 1-56308-153-9.

This yearbook is intended to give educators involved in educational technology up-to-date information on trends, research, and issues in the field. There are articles by specialists in educational media and technology, plus lists of media-related organizations in Canada and the United States and educational programs in colleges and universities. For collection development, there is a section called 'Mediagraphy' which is a comprehensive, annotated guide to reference sources, books, articles and ERIC documents arranged by subjects. There are directories of publishers, distributors, and producers, plus a general index. Back issues are also available from the publishers. This yearbook will be of value in large district-wide media collections and perhaps in some academic and large public libraries.

Education; Technology and Education; Instructional Materials

C; Y; A

770. **Film and Video Finder.** 3rd ed. 3 volumes, National Information Center for Educational Media, 1991. 3,700p. $295. 0-937548-20-0.

This huge three volume work now lists and gives information on 92,000 films and videos. Volume one allows access to the other two volumes by presenting a subject approach. First there is a subject heading outline and then an extensive subject section with each of the films and video listed under subjects by title (with grade level and distributor data). Volume I also contains directories to producers and distributors. In volumes two and three, films and videos are listed alphabetically by title. Each listing includes title, edition, physical format, running time, color code, a description of contents, recommended audience or grade level, year of release, and producer or distributor. This bibliography can be useful for identifying films and videos, whereas Bowker's *Educational Film and Video Locator* (which lists slightly more than half of these titles) can be used to find libraries that own them. As a companion paperback volume, NICEM has issued *Index to AV Producers and Distributors* (1991, 8th ed. 350p. $75.) which contains a directory of 20,000 producers and distributors of all kinds of nonprint media. Because of their expense and specialized content, these reference works are found only in collections that need extensive material on audiovisual sources.

Motion Pictures; Videocassettes

C; Y; A

771. **Media Resource Catalog**. National Audiovisual Center, 1991. $15.

The newly revised catalog lists over 600 titles of AV programs produced by a variety of federal agencies. Materials are useful at all levels, from elementary school to adult education programs. A wide range of media are listed including 16mm film, VHS video, filmstrips, slides, and multimedia kits. The catalog indexes media by subject, lists titles alphabetically, and includes complete ordering information. The subjects covered run the gamut including African-American studies, American history, drug abuse prevention, space, and World War II. The catalog costs $15 and may be ordered by calling the toll-free number 800-788-NAVC, or by writing to: National Audiovisual Center, 8700 Edgeworth Drive, Capitol Heights, MD 20743-3701. *Audiovisual Materials; Motion Pictures; Videocassettes*

C; Y; A

772. **National Information Center for Educational Media (NICEM)**, various publications and databases.

This omnibus entry will try to identify the various outputs available from the extensive NICEM database of nonprint materials. First located at the University of Southern California and later purchased by Access Innovations, Inc., of Albuquerque, New Mexico, NICEM covers in its huge database of over 360,000 bibliographical citations, the entire spectrum of nonprint media intended for use in the educational field from preschool to graduate and professional school levels. Current NICEM publications available from Plexus Publishing include the following printed volumes: *Film and Video Finder, Audiocassette Finder* (3rd ed., 1991, 925p. $75. 0-937548-22-7) and *Film and Slide Set Finder* (1990, 3 volumes, 1,863p. $225. 0-937548-15-4). The *Film and Video Finder* is typical in scope and arrangement of these bibliographies. It contains a total of 92,000 items. In volume one there is a subject heading outline, an index to subject headings, a subject section that lists films and videos by title with a distributor code, a producer's and distributor's directory by code, and a producer's and distributor's directory by full name. In volumes two and three each of the films and videos are listed alphabetically by title. Entries include coverage on physical format, running time, a brief description, recommended audience and grade level, producer and distributor, year of release and LC catalog numbers. NICEM also publishes an *Index to AV Producers and Distributors* (8th ed. 1991, 350p. $75. 0-937548-21-9), which gives directory information about producers and distributors of audiovisual materials and, in a separate section, lists them by the subjects in which they specialize. The entire NICEM database is also available electronically in two formats: on CD-ROM it is available from Silver Platter for $795, and it can searched online through DIALOG Information Services and Human Resources Information Network (HRIN).

Motion Pictures; Videocassettes; Audiovisual Materials; Audiocassettes; Filmstrips; Slides

Special Topics

A

773. **Artificial Intelligence and Instruction: A Selected Bibliography**, by William D. Milheim. Educational Technology, 1989. 51p. $14.95 pap. 0-87778-220-2. (Educational Technology Selected Bibliography Series, 1).

This is a very short, yet comprehensive, and interesting bibliography on a very specific topic. The work is divided into five major sections: general artificial intelligence, artificial intelligence and education, expert systems, intelligence tutoring, and knowledge systems. Within each section, the entries, which include books and journal articles, are arranged alphabetically by author. All titles are timely, being published between 1979 and 1989. This inexpensive bibliography is recommended for most academic and public libraries. *Artificial Intelligence*

A

774. **A Bibliography of Computer-Aided Language Learning**, by Vance Stevens et al. AMS Press, 1986. 140p. $32.50. 0-404-12666-9.

This bibliography deals with the use of the computer in the learning/teaching of English as a second language or as a native language. Over 1,700 books, research reports, articles, government documents, and reference sources are included. Sources were published in Western Europe, Canada, and the United States from 1965 through 1985. Nineteen languages are represented. Entries are arranged alphabetically by author and numbered successively. No annotations are included, though the general subject index with a reference number helps facilitate use somewhat. Since no similar work exists, despite the limitations of inadequate indexing and the need for an up-date, this will be useful for professionals working with language teaching, as well as independent learners.

English Language—Study and Teaching; Computer Assisted Instruction;
English as a Second Language

C; Y; A

775. **Computer Simulations: A Sourcebook To Learning in an Electronic Environment**, by Jerry Willis and others. Garland, 1987. 391p. $66. 0-8240-8539-6. (Source Books on Education, 11).

This book on computer simulation programs is divided into two parts. The first introduces computer use in schools and gives an overview of the concept of simulations, with guidelines for critiquing hardware and software. The second part is a collection of reviews of simulation programs that range in age suitability from preschoolers to adults. Each review gives thorough background information plus descriptive and critical comments. The copyright dates of the programs range from 1980 through 1986.

Computer Simulations; Computer Assisted Instruction

C; Y; A

776. **Computers in Education: A Research Bibliography**, by Richard A. Diem. Garland, 1988. 167p. $27. 0-8240-8541-8. (Garland Bibliographies in Contemporary Education, Vol. 8).

This bibliography of about 1,000 books and articles covers the literature reporting research on the use of computers in schools. The entries are presented in four main areas: preschool, elementary schools, secondary schools, and general computer use. The items cover the years 1975 through 1986 and each has a one sentence annotation. This will be helpful as a starting place to locate material on the various functions and results of using computers in public education. *Computers in Schools*

C; Y; A

777. **A Consumer's Guide to Tests in Print**, by Donald D. Hammill et al. 2nd ed. Austin Texas, Pro-Ed, 1992. 197p. $27. 0-89079-548-7.

More than 250 tests intended for use with K-12 students are reviewed by using a standardized evaluation form which makes the potential user's task less difficult. Group tests such as SAT's are not included, but rather there is "a focus on tests that are individually administered for diagnostic, screening, or identification purposes." The norm-referenced tests which are evaluated are given an A to F rating: highly recommended to not recommended. The tests are cited under 86 content areas and classified under four general types: achievement, aptitude, effect, and general intelligence. This guide is recommended for all academic libraries with education and psychology departments, as well as school and public libraries where there is an interest in tests. *Educational Tests and Measurements*

C; Y; A

778. **Cooperative Learning: A Guide to Research**, by Samuel Totten et al. Garland, 1991. 390p. $48. 0-8240-7222-7 (Garland Bibliographies in Contemporary Education, Vol. 12: Garland Reference Library of Social Science, Vol. 674).

Cooperative learning is an educational concept which, when applied, allows young people from elementary school through college to learn actively through a process of sharing and cooperating with their fellow students. This technique usually is applied to small groups where the participants study and work together. This bibliography reports on the progress of this movement through publications that appeared from the 1900s through 1991, with most of the 800 entries dating from the 1970s onward. There are several bibliographic essays included on cooperative education, its origin, and its present status, but the body of the work is the annotated bibliography that deals with various facets of the subject under broad headings. Books, journal articles, chapters in books, dissertations, and reports are included, and there are subject and author indexes. This bibliography will be useful in libraries serving education students and faculty or in school district-wide collections of professional materials. *Cooperative Education; Education*

C; Y; A

779. **The Evidence Continues to Grow: Parent Involvement Improves Student Achievement: An Annotated Bibliography**, by Anne Henderson. National Committee for Citizens in Education (Columbia, MD), 1987. 76p. $10 0-934460-28-0.

This is a compelling overview of the research done from 1966 to 1987 on the effects of parental involvement in their children's education. Both small and large studies are reported on with full research details given concerning size of samples, areas tested, and variables considered. The title summarizes the results found. For school district-wide collections and schools of education.

Education; Parent-Teacher Relationships

C; Y; A

780. **Home Education Resource Guide**, Ed. by Don Hubbs. Blue Bird Publishing/Quality Books, 1989. $11.95 0-933025-12-2.

This bibliography is primarily a listing by type of material of items that can be useful to parents who educate their children at home. There are sections on textbooks, correspondence courses, toys and games, and software, plus a list of books on the legality of home schooling and a directory of home schooling support groups. The entries on materials are all annotated. Somewhat specialized but of interest in large collections. *Home Instruction*

C; Y; A

781. **Multicultural Education: A Source Book**, by Patricia G. Ramsey et al. Garland, 1989. 177p. $27. 0-8240-8558-2. (Garland Reference Library of Social Science, 355).

Multicultural education as defined in this source book is "the process-oriented creation of learning experiences that foster awareness of and respect for the diversity of peoples within society and the world." Bilingual education, which is closely related to multicultural education, is excluded by design because an excellent book already exists in this equally important area: Melendez's *Bilingual Education: A Sourcebook* (o.p.). In scope, the Ramsey book includes theoretical, research, and practical information relating to multicultural programs in pre-school and elementary schools. All of the literature was published after 1976, and most of it was published in the United States. There is a separate chapter relating to the major issues, and following each essay is a bibliography of 30 to 50 annotated titles; also included is full bibliographic data helpful for acquisitions. This timely sourcebook on the topic of multiculturism is recommended for all academic, public and school libraries, and especially for those supporting a multicultural education program. *Ethnic Groups; Multiculturalism*

C; Y

782.   **Resources for Educational Equity: A Guide for Grades Pre-Kindergarten-12**, by Merle Froschl and Barbara Sprung. Garland, 1988. 266p. $47. 0-8240-0443-4.

The focus of this work is on educational equity; mainly gender equity, but disability and racial equity are also considered. The editors state that this "is the most comprehensive and up-to-date compilation of available resources to aid teachers locate the materials they need to create equitable curriculum and classroom environments." It appears to be the only work of its kind. Materials listed include curriculum guides, student texts and workbooks, audiovisual materials, and journal articles on the topic of educational equity. The various chapters are organized around themes which include early childhood, guidance counseling, sports, libraries, etc.; each is by a different contributor and each includes a lengthy essay and approximately a 50-item bibliography on the topic. The bibliographies are subgrouped by elementary, secondary, or professional levels. Each entry contains full bibliographical information as well as helpful annotations. Author and subject indexes are also provided. The comprehensiveness and uniqueness of this bibliography warrants it a place on the shelf of every curriculum, professional, and academic library for ready reference and collection development.

Educational Equalization; Instructional Materials; Sex Discrimination;
Discrimination in Education

C; Y

783.   **Resources for Teaching Thinking: A Catalog**, by Janice Kruse. Research for Better Schools (Philadelphia), 1989. n.p. $29.95 (pap.).

More than 500 different kinds of teaching materials are presented here that would be valuable in teaching thinking skills to youngsters from kindergarten through grade 12. They are presented by grade level but coded for curriculum area like art or mathematics. For each entry, material such as title, author, type of material, purpose, contents, publisher, and price are given. There is also cross referencing and indexing by the kind of thinking that the material promotes (e.g., critical thinking and creative thinking). This is a valuable resource guide and purchasing tool for librarians and teachers.

Thinking Skills; Education

C; YA; A

784.   **Robotics in Education: An Information Guide**, by Veronica Sexauer Pantelidis. Scarecrow, 1991. 435p. $47.50 0-8108-2466-3.

Pantelidis, a librarian, has compiled an excellent bibliography in an area where very little bibliographic control exists. Almost 1,600 items are included; they are intended for a very broad audience—from elementary school through college. The entries are arranged under nine categories including: reference sources, general information, educational robotics, noneducational robotics, social implications, economic implications, and a full array of nonprint media. Of the many appendices included, the listing of periodicals in the field is of particular interest. The range of materials and levels make this a useful reference and collection development aid for all libraries. *Robotics*

A

785.   **Teaching Social Studies to the Young Child: A Research and Resource Guide**, by Blythe S. Farb Hinitz. Garland, 1992. 164p. $24. 0-8240-4439-8.

Hinitz has compiled an excellent sourcebook of current ideas and resources for the teaching of social studies to students from kindergarten to third grade. In the form of a bibliographic essay, and with a focus on history, geography, and economics, many relevant citations are described that deal with how to present social studies skills, concepts, and principles. The work is intended for advanced education students and curriculum specialists, as well as practicing elementary school classroom teachers. This brief resource guide is recommended for professional education libraries as well as academic libraries supporting courses in education. *Social Studies—Study and Teaching*

C; Y; A

786.   **Textbooks in School and Society: An Annotated Bibliography and Guide to Research**, by Arthur Woodward et al. Garland, 1988. 176p. $31. 0-8240-8390-3. (Garland Reference Library of the Social Sciences, 405).

This is not a bibliography of textbooks, but rather a well-written specialized bibliography on textbooks. Its stated purpose is "to provide a comprehensive, up-to-date reference work for researchers and educators." The book is first divided into two main sections, "Textbook Producers and Consumers" and "Evaluation and Criticism of Textbooks," then there is a further subdivision of less-broad areas such as Textbooks and School Programs, Subject Matter Content Coverage, and Ideology and Controversy. Narrower and very specific topics are then arranged under the broad areas, e.g., treatment of ethnic and minorities and women, content areas, censorship, and evolution and creationsism. In addition to full bibliographic information, most entries include a brief annotation. This bibliography is highly recommend for all academic libraries, many public libraries, and other libraries directly or indirectly involved in teacher education programs.

Textbooks

Special Populations

C; Y; A

787.   **Educating the Gifted: A Sourcebook**, by M. Jean Greenlaw and Margaret E. McIntosh. American Library Association, 1988. 468p. $50. 0-8389-0483-1.

This is a comprehensive overview of the subject as well as extensive bibliography of approximately 2,000 background sources. There are chapters on historical background, definitions and methods of identifying the gifted, ways school districts supply education for this special group, training programs for teachers, needs of parents of the gifted, and programs for specific subject areas. Each chapter concludes with extensive bibliographies subdivided by topics. Appendixes include one on state agencies for the gifted and another on evaluations of materials for the gifted. There are copious indexes. This volume is highly recommended for school, college, and public libraries where there is a particular interest in the subject.

Gifted Children

C; Y; A

788.   **Gifted, Talented and Creative Young People: A Guide to Theory, Teaching and Research**, by Morris I. Stein. Garland, 1986. 465p. $94. 0-8240-9392-5. (Garland Reference Library of Social Science).

This annotated bibliography includes books, chapters in books, and periodical articles dealing with gifted and talented students. Topics covered include theory, characteristics, counseling, tests, and programs. This excellent resource will be helpful for both professional people and parents in identifying materials that were published mainly during the 1970s on this topic. There are author and subject indexes.

Gifted Children

Y; A

789.   **Materials and Strategies for the Education of Trainable Mentally Retarded Learners**, by James P. White. Garland, 1990. 368p. $40. 0-8240-6345-7.

White's guide has two purposes: first, he provides the goals and strategies of working with the retarded; second, he identifies and describes the materials that would be useful in achieving these goals. The work is divided into 15 chapters on specific areas of the challenge, such as assessment, spoken language, home skills, vocational skills, reading, behavior, and working with parents. Following a brief summary of the problem, each chapter contains 20-50 annotated resources which are numbered sequentially. Included are handbooks, periodicals, kits, and even computer software. An author, title, and subject index with references to the numbered items of each bibliography completes the useful handbook, which is recommended for school district professional libraries, academic libraries, and larger public libraries that serve patrons working with retarded learners. *Mental Retardation*

A

790.   **Resources for Educating Artistically Talented Students**, by Gilbert A. Clark and Enid D. Zimmerman. Syracuse Univ. Press, 1987. 176p. $22. 0-8156-2401-8.

This work is not a bibliography, but it contains such an invaluable array of instructional materials on the subject of gifted young artists that it must be considered as a purchasing guide. The book serves as a complement to an earlier text by the same authors: *Educating Artistically Talented Students* (o.p.). Teachers and administrators often "reinvent the wheel"; the bibliographies in this volume will prevent this by providing them with resources and materials to guide them in their work with artistically talented students. Recommended for academic, public, and school district libraries working with teachers of these special students.   *Gifted Children*

C; Y; A

791.   **The Specialware Directory: A Guide to Software for Special Education**, by LINC Associates. Oryx, 1986. 160p. $24.75 0-89774-192-7.

This bibliography lists more than 300 software programs that have been released from 1981 and 1985 and are designed specifically for the handicapped or have applications in special education programs. The works are listed in alphabetical order by title, and for each there is copious material including publisher, format, price, release date, types of compatible hardware, academic and curriculum areas for use, grade, reading and interest levels, and a list of review sources. The many indexes allow access to the title section by curriculum area, type of handicap, hardware needed, input-output options, and academic level from infant to postsecondary. Appendixes include lists of publishers and distributors, product titles, and reviewing sources. Though now in need of an update, this work is still of value for those working in special education. *Disabilities; Special Education*

Adult Education and Literacy

Y; A

792.　**Adult Basic Education Collection: An Annotated List of Titles.** Martin Luther King Memorial Library (Washington, D.C., 1989. 195p. $5.

This bibliography lists easy-to-read material found in Washington, D.C.'s public libraries that would be useful when working with inner-city young adults and adults in literacy programs. The reading levels range from 0 to grade 8, and the topics in the books reflect the interests of a racially mixed, big city environment. The entries are arranged by subject and include many nonfiction titles, as well as a number of books geared for leisure reading. As well as bibliographic information, each entry contains clear annotations with candid evaluations to help prospective readers and librarians choose suitable books. A reading level is given for each book. There are also lists of instructional materials for reading programs with suggestions on how to use them effectively. This is an important tool for giving reading guidance to poor readers as well as for building relevant materials for this population.

Literacy; Illiteracy; Adult Education

A

793.　**Adult Basic Education English as a Second Language Collection: An Annotated List of Titles.** Adult Basic Education Office, Martin Luther King Memorial Library (Washington, D.C.), 1991. 65p. $3. (pap.).

This companion to the library's earlier *Adult Basic Education Collection* (entry 792) supplies information on books suitable for adults who are learning to speak and read English as a second language. The titles are annotated, current (most were published in the 1980s), and arranged in broad categories that take into consideration both practical and recreational reading needs. Difficulty levels are also indicated. Titles were chosen on the basis of their general appeal, their cultural value, and their usefulness in various teaching situations. There is appended a list of resource materials in various formats for teachers or tutors of these adults, plus a directory of publishers and a title index. This bibliography will be a valuable addition to the collection of public libraries who sponsor these literacy programs or who work with other agencies that do community work in this area. *Adult Education; English as a Second Education; Literacy; Illiteracy*

A

794.　**Adult Literacy: A Source Book and Guide**, by Joyce French. Garland, 1987. 435p. $58. 0-8240-8574-4.

This extensive bibliography on all aspects of adult literacy in the United States is divided into two parts. This first is a narrative bibliography in which topics covered include basic definitions, issues involved in literacy, different types of populations, and learning theory. The second is an annotated list of the sources previously cited plus additions. Materials include books, journals, and reports, chiefly from 1980 to 1987. There are also subject and author indexes. This source book is of value to anyone interested in the current literacy problem and possible solutions. *Literacy; Illiteracy*

A*

795.　**Education for Older Adult Learning: A Selected, Annotated Bibliography**, by Reva M. Greenberg. Greenwood, 1993. 219p. $65. 0-313-28368-0.

Greenberg, a well-known authority in gerontology, has compiled an excellent bibliography. The more than 700 entries include books, journal articles, government publications, dissertations and other research reports, and curriculum materials of a variety of types. The recommended items are arranged under two broad sections: general issues and instructional techniques. All of these entries have full bibliographical information and succinct annotations. In addition there is a list of journals cited, online databases, federal laws and regulations, and an extensive lists of professional organizations which can provide additional information. This basic bibliography is recommended for all public libraries and others that are involved in learning programs for the older adult. *Adult Education; Senior Citizens*

A*

796. **The Independent Learners' Sourcebook: Resources and Materials for Selected Topics**, by Robert M. Smith and Phyllis M. Cunningham. American Library Association, 1987. 308p. $40. 0-8389-0459-9.

This boon to libraries where adult education is important is organized into three parts. The first is an introduction to lifetime learning, with an annotated bibliography and a locator grid that links related topics. The second part is the body of the work and contains a listing of "Thirty-Four Popular Subjects for Inquiry," such as art appreciation, foreign languages, history, drugs, parenting, photography, and bird watching. For each, there are lists of materials and information sources that cover key references and useful books, government documents, magazines, online databases, and organizations. Full bibliographic information is given and, in most cases, an annotation. In the third part, there are annotated listings of directories of postsecondary education programs, libraries, museums, and bookstores and publishers, plus a further bibliography of general sources. Several indexes, including those by author and title, are included. Though specialized in scope, this is an excellent handbook both for readers' guidance and collection development. *Independent Study; Adult Education; Continuing Education*

A

797. **Learning Independently**, by Steven R. Wasserman, et al. 3rd ed. Gale, 1987. 437p. $220. 0-8103-0362-0.

In this very interesting resource guide to almost 4,000 programs designed for independent learning (not requiring a class-room or teacher), more than 400 subjects are represented on tapes, cassettes, programmed instruction, simulations, games, books, etc.. Entries are arranged by title, and complete ordering information is provided; also, many entries have descriptive notes. This is a rather expensive guide, and possibly only larger libraries or those with many independent (self-study) learners will consider it, though it is undoubtedly, the most comprehensive in the field. *Independent Study*

Y; A

798. **Reader Development Bibliography: Books Recommended for Adult Readers**, by Vickie L. Collins. 4th ed. Free Library of Philadelphia; dist. by New Readers Press, 1990. 194p. $14.95. pap. 0-911132-13-9.

This book is designed to assist librarians and adult teachers in the task of choosing interesting and easy-to-read books for new adult readers. The list contains 390 entries of printed literacy materials, including books and workbooks for adult basic education and English as a second language instruction. The list is divided into ll categories, including Leisure Reading (fiction), Biography, Science, Religion, and Materials for Tutors. Books chosen are for adults and young adults 14 years of age or older having a reading level below 8th grade. Brief annotations and bibliographical information are included with each entry. Two indexes are also provided: author and title/series. A similar work is Project Learn's *Books for Adult New Readers* (New Readers Press, 1989, 210p. $14.95. 0-88336-599-5) which has about 300 more titles, and serves a similar purpose. Larger libraries will want both titles. This bibliography is recommended for most public libraries building a comprehensive collection of literacy materials. *Literacy; Illiteracy; Adult Education*

Higher Education

A

799. **College Admissions: A Selected Annotated Bibliography**, Comp. by Linda Sparks. Greenwood, 1993. 187p. $47.95. 0-313-28483-0.

This selective bibliography deals with college admission at community colleges, four year colleges, and universities. The more than 900 entries include books, book chapters, journal articles, dissertations, and ERIC documents. Both older titles useful for historical research and current titles are included. Each entry includes bibliographic data and a brief descriptive annotation. Author and subject indexes complete the work. This specialized bibliography may prove useful to all academic and other libraries with education collections. *College and Universities—Admissions*

Y*; A*

800. **How to Find Out about Financial Aid: A Guide to over 700 Directories Listing Scholarships, Fellowships, Loans, Grants, Awards, Internships**, by Gail Ann Schlachter. Reference Service Press (Los Angeles, CA), 1987. 334p. $35. 0-918276-05-5.

This is a bibliography of over 700 commercially available directories of financial aid published from 1980 to 1987. Entries for each directory contains full bibliographic material, plus annotations on purpose, arrangement, limitations, and special features. There are separate chapters on scholarships, fellowships, grants, awards, loans, internships, databases, and search services, with subdivisions by disciplines like social science, by special populations like ethnic groups, and by geographical areas. Addresses and telephone numbers of publishers are given, and there are indexes by name, title, place, and subject. A thorough work that will be of great value in developing financial-aid collections in high schools, college and public libraries. *Financial Aid; Scholarships, Fellowships, etc.*

A

801. **Key Resources on Community Colleges**, by Arthur M. Cohen and James C. Palmer. Jossey-Bass, 1986. 522p. $49.95. 1-55542-020-6.

This selective bibliography contains 680 books, articles, and research reports related to the history, administration, recent developments, and current concerns involving two-year community colleges. After a general overview of the topic, there are eleven chapters dealing with such topics as students, career education, and the collegiate function. Each of these chapters contains a brief introduction, followed by the entries, each of which has a complete bibliographic citation plus an annotation.

This is an excellent choice for anyone interested in a selective guide to the literature on community colleges. *Community Colleges; Colleges and Universities*

A

802. **Library Services for Off-Campus and Distance Education: An Annotated Bibliography**, by Sheila Latham et al. American Library Association, 1991. 272p. $40. 0-8389-2158-2.

This guide to the literature of library service to off-campus students is both timely and unique. The work contains 535 entries that are arranged under 14 major headings which include: guidelines and standards; collection management; document delivery; types of media; and technological innovations. The entries date from 1930 to 1990 and contain full bibliographic information and detailed annotations. Author, institution, and subject indexes are provided. This practical bibliography is recommended for all academic libraries faced with the concerns of off-campus library services.

Colleges and Universities—Library Services

A

803. **The Multicultural Education Debate in the University: A Bibliography**, comp. by Joan Nordquist. Reference and Research Services, 1992. 63p. $15. pap. 0-937855-48-0.

Nordquist has compiled a very selective list of about 500 books, pamphlets, journal articles, and government publications dealing mulicultural education as it applies to the university setting. All sources are recent, published in late 1980's and early 1900's. The citations are arranged under six broad areas: the political correctness argument, the intellectual and political climate at the university, academic freedom, multicultural education in the university, Eurocentrism in the curriculum, and women in the curriculum. Entries are arranged alphabetically (usually by author for books and journal articles) under each of the above sections. Each entry has adequate bibliographic data. However, there are no annotations, nor are there author and title indexes. Despite these limitations, which effect ease of use, this very timely and up-to-date bibliography is recommended for all academic libraries and even public libraries where the debate on the various aspects of multiculturism is prevalent. *Multiculturalism; Colleges and Universities*

A

804. **Research in Higher Education: A Guide to Source Bibliographies**, by Richard H. Quay. 2nd ed. Oryx Press, 1985. 133p. $37.50. 0-89774-194-3.

This revised and expanded second edition cites 932 references relating to higher education. Many were published as recently as the year this guide was published, 1985. Entries are arranged in alphabetical order by author under 15 chapters, each dealing with a broad area of higher education. Many of the entries are ERIC documents, for which the guide provides document numbers for easy retrieval. Most entries are not annotated unless the title is ambiguous. An author index is provided. The *Thesaurus of ERIC Descriptors* serves as a subject index. This bibliography though published in 1985 is still very useful and recommended for most academic libraries. *Colleges and Universities*

Folklore, Mythology, and Popular Culture

Y; A

805. **Big Footnotes: A Comprehensive Bibliography Concerning Big Foot, the Abominable Snowman & Related Beings,** by Daniel E. Perez. D. Perez Publishing, 1988. 189p. $10. pap. 0-9618380-0-0.

This unusual bibliography is the most extensive published that deals with materials relating to the study of "elusive" creatures including Bigfoot, Sasquatch, Yeti, and the Abominable Snowman. More than 5,000 entries are included and arranged by format: books, magazine and newspaper articles, reference books, audiovisual materials, etc. Publication dates range from 1556 to 1983. Citations include scholarly and popular sources. Unfortunately, annotations are not included, but comprehensiveness and the nature of the sources make this a fascinating bibliographic source for the folklorists as well the students of popular culture. It is recommended for all libraries serving such clientele. *Abominable Snowman; Bigfoot*

A

806. **Celebrations: Read-aloud Holiday and Theme Book Programs.** Wilson, 1985, $40. 301p. 0-8242-0708-4.

Though not intended as a selection tool this collection of ideas, suggestions and literature suitable for celebrating a variety of holidays contains helpful bibliographies that can be used for collection building.

Holidays

A

807. **Etiquette: An Annotated Bibliography of Literature Published in English in the United States, 1900 through 1987** by Deborah Hodges. McFarland, 1989, 182p $45. 0-89950-429-9.

About 1,1000 important pamphlets, books, government documents and periodical articles dealing with etiquette and published in the twentieth century are cited in this bibliography that is arranged by author and indexed by title and subject. Each is annotated, some with wit and humor. For large collections. *Etiquette*

C; A

808. **A Guide to Folktales in the English Language: Based on the Aarne-Thompson Classification System,** by D. L. Ashliman. Greenwood, 1987. 384p. $59.50. 0-313-25961-5. (Bibliographies and Indexes in World Literature, 11).

Using a classification system that uses basic plot devices as subject headings, the author has analyzed hundreds of folktales with emphasis on those of European and Near-Eastern origins. There are two useful bibliographies for building collections: one is the listing of collections cited in the book and the other is a bibliography of books about folk literature. This will be of value in libraries serving children and adults who are students of folklore. *Folklore*

A

809. **Handbook of American Popular Culture,** by Thomas Inge. 3 vols. 2nd ed. Greenwood, 1989. $165. 0-313-25406-0.

The 46 aspects of American popular culture that are explored in this book cover such topics as advertising, the automobile, computers, magazines, the occult, death, television, and women. Each topic is covered by introductory and historical essays, plus lists of basic reference works, names of research collections, a rundown on historical and critical sources and a general bibliography. This is a fine place to identify sources on these important aspects of contemporary American life. Literature is covered in a companion volume, *Handbook of American Popular Literature.* Both sets will be useful in large libraries.

Popular Culture

A

810. **Italian Folklore: An Annotated Bibliography,** by Alessandro Falassi. Garland, 1985. 438p. $60 0-8240-9041-1. (Garland Folklore Bibliographies).

This is a 3,000-item bibliography of books and articles on Italian folklore. Though much of the material is in Italian, the annotations are in English. This highly specialized work will be considered for purchase in only very large libraries; however, some of the other volumes in the series might be of interest. For example *Folklore and Literature in the British Isles,* by Florence E. Baer (1986, $43, 0-8240-8660-0), and *Jewish Folklore,* by Eli Yassif. *Folklore*

A
811. **Jewish Folklore: An Annotated Bibliography**, by Eli Yassif. Garland, 1986. 341p. $77. 0-8240-9039-X. (Garland Reference Library of the Humanities 450).

This bibliography of about 1,300 books and articles about Jewish folklore emphasizes scholarly contributions made in the past 100 years. Each item is arranged alphabetically by author and is accompanied by detailed evaluative annotations that describes themes and motifs discussed. There is a combined index by personal names such as authors and editors and by subjects taken from key words in the titles. This is recommended for large collections. *Folklore*

Y; A
812. **Mythical and Fabulous Creatures: A Source book and Research Guide**, Ed. by Malcolm South. Greenwood, 1987. 393p. $49.95. 0-313-24338-7.

A professor of English, South, and a host of contributors have compiled a series of fascinating bibliographic essays. The work is "designed as a reference and research guide that describes fabulous creatures and their appearance in history, literature, and art." The introduction to the volume is a bibliographic essay which identifies the literature in the field, including general books, bibliographies, anthologies, and other reference sources. There are 20 chapters, each dealing with an individual creature; they are arranged under four major categories: "Birds and Beasts," "Human-animal Composites," "Creatures of the Night," and "Giants and Fairies." Each chapter is written as an essay incorporating references to the wide variety of sources. The sources are listed in a selected bibliography at the end of each chapter. This very readable volume will appeal to the beginning creature buff as well as the scholar on the subject, and it is recommended for all academic and public libraries for collection development, reference, and inter-library loan work. *Monsters; Creatures; Animals, Mythical*

Geography and Travel

Geography

A
813. **A Bibliography of Geographic Thought**, by Catherine L. Brown and James O. Wheeler. Greenwood, 1989. 520p. $55. 0-313-26899-1.

Brown and Wheeler's comprehensive bibliography lists over 6,500 English-language citations from journal articles and books dealing with geographical history, philosophy, and methodology. Entries are listed under ten broad categories based on both type of work and subject orientation, e.g., books, bibliographies, geography in various countries, applied geography, educational geography, and geography and other disciplines. While bibliographic data is provided, indexing is inconsistent, though there are biographical, author, and subject indexes. Still, because of the extent of the coverage in this area where there is a dearth of bibliographic control, this bibliography is recommended for all academic and larger public libraries. *Geography*

A
814. **Encyclopedia of Geographic Information Sources: United States Volume**, by Jennifer Mossman. Gale, 1987. 437p. $105 0-8103-0410-4.

This huge compilation of information about states and cities contains over 11,000 citations that will be of interest, not only to tourists, but also to businessmen and economists. Beginning with a brief introduction to basic resources on the entire U.S. and large regions, there is coverage on each state, followed by material on each of its cities of 50,000 or more population (about 400 are included). The headings used for the citations are: General Works, Geographical Sources, Gazetteers and Guides, Government Publications, Handbooks, Newspapers and Periodicals, Organizations, Statistical Sources, and Other Sources. When the title is not self-explanatory, a brief annotation is given.

This is an important reference book and a boon for collection development. There is a companion volume, *Encyclopedia of Geographic Information Sources: International Volume* (1988. $130. 0-8103-0415-5) which gives similar data on 75 major countries and 81 major cities.

United States—Geography; Geography

A

815. **Geographical Bibliography for American Libraries,** by Chauncy D. Harris. Association of American Geographers/National Geographic Society, 1985. 437p. $20.45 0-89291-193-X.

This bibliography of almost 3,000 citations on geography includes books, maps, atlases, periodicals, reference works, biographies and dissertations published since 1970. Various aspects of the discipline of geography are explored, including physical and human geography, history, philosophy, and methodology; however, nearly half of the entries are on regional geography. Annotations are clear, and there is an author and title index. Useful in medium and large collections. *Geography*

Y*; A

816. **Geography: A Resource Book for Secondary Schools,** by A. David Hill and Regina McCormick. ABC-Clio, 1989. 387p. $39. 0-87436-519-8. (Social Studies Resources for Secondary Schools).

This manual is part textbook and part bibliography. The first section introduces the discipline of geography, its methodology, and history. Another section is devoted to a directory of key agencies and organizations and their publications. Also for collection development there is chapter on key reference works and another on important classroom instructional materials. Included are both print and nonprint material and software products. All are annotated, and grade levels are given. This will be useful in senior high school libraries as well as in some public libraries. *Geography*

A

817. **Information Sources in Cartography,** by C. R. Perkins and R. B. Parry. K. G. Saur, 1990 540p. $96. 0-408-02458-5. (Guides to Information Sources).

This work by 34 contributors consists of a series of bibliographic essays on cartography that cover subjects like general information, history of cartography, map production, map librarianship, types of mapping, and map use and promotion. There are appendixes on periodicals, publishers and organizations and indexes by subjects and authors. This is a somewhat specialized bibliography for large collections.

Maps

A

818. **Keyguide to Information Sources in Cartography,** by A. G. Hodgkiss and A. F. Tatham. Facts on File, 1986. 253p. $50 0-8160-1403-5. (Keyguide to Information Series).

The first section of this extensive work on cartography surveys the field of maps and map making, gives a brief history, explain divisions in the discipline, and discusses major current references, plus listing major map-producing sources and important collections. The main body of the work is divided into two annotated bibliographies of books and articles. The first of 333 items is on the history of cartography with many subcategories including a geographical breakdown. The second of 463 entries deals with contemporary concerns in the field such as map librarianship and types of maps. A third section of 601 entries describes major map collections, associations, and publishers. This series is British in origin but gives good coverage on American sources. For large library collections. *Maps*

Y*; A*

819. **The Map Catalog: Every Kind of Map and Chart on Earth and Even Some Above It,** Ed. by Joel Makower. 2nd ed. Random House/Vintage, 1990. 364p. $18. 0-679-72767-1.

It is the intention of this guide to list in one volume maps of all kinds, atlases, and other geographic information, then to describe them and indicate how to acquire them. In this time of concern about geographic literacy, this is a difficult but important task. This source identifies hundreds of "items," even some software programs on maps and map-making. The volume is divided into four parts: land maps, sky maps, water maps, and map products. A section titled "Et Cetera" describes educational and recreational games and puzzles, accessories, organizations, etc. This "catalog" is simply loaded with hundreds of items on maps and related ephemera. This inexpensive guide is recommended for all libraries except the very large where there is a map department with professional staff. *Maps*

Y; A

820. **Treasure Hunting Bibliography and Index to Periodical Articles,** by John H. Reed. Research and Discovery Publications, 1989. 425p. $29.95 pap. 09-940519-04-6.

This bibliographic guide contains over 5,200 citations to articles on lost, buried, or sunken treasure. The titles were collected from a search of 50 periodical indexes, various books, and hundreds of popular adventure magazines. Entries are arranged in alphabetical order by the author (those without authors are arranged by title in a separate section). Full bibliographic information is provided. A brief explanatory note is given if the title is not self-explanatory. Two indexes are included, one is by periodical title which indicates by number the citation(s) cited, the other by very detailed subjects (about 2,000 subject headings are used). This bibliography is recommended as a reference tool and collection-building aid for all libraries that serve "treasure hunters, researchers, writers, historians, folklorists, and lovers of adventure." *Treasure Hunting*

Y; A

821. **Women into the Unknown: A Sourcebook on Women Explorers and Travelers,** by Marion Tinling. Greenwood, 1989. 356p. $69.95. 0-313-25328-5.

This fascinating compilation highlights the lives of 45 nineteenth and twentieth-century American and European women who ventured into remote areas of the world sometimes to study little-known societies and tribes on archaeological or anthropological studies, or sometimes just for plain excitement and adventure. Their published travel accounts remain to this day an inspiration to other women and men. For each of the 45 women selected, there is a detailed biographical essay, a bibliography of their works, and a listing of articles and books written about them. This bio-bibliography is recommended for all secondary school, academic, and public libraries as a reference and collection-building guide. *Women; Explorers*

A

822. **World Bibliographical Series,** Ed. by Robert Neville. ABC-Clio.

This outstanding bibliographical series on individual countries or areas now numbers more than 120 volumes, with more scheduled to be published in 1993. They include annotated entries to books, periodicals, newspapers, and important documents. Each volume is compiled by an authority in the country. Call the publisher for a full catalog of The World Bibliographical Series titles currently available (1-800-422-2546). As an example of the works in this series, the volumes published during the 1990-1991 year include the following:

Bhutan, by Ramesh C. Dogra. 123p. $49.50. 1-85109-128-9.
Canada, by Ernest Ingles. 393p. $92. 1-85109-005-3.
Cape Verde, by Caroline S. Shaw. 192p. $68.50. 1-85109-119-X.
Colombia, by Robert H. Davis. 204p. $60. 1-85109-093-2.
Djibouti, by Peter J. Schaeder. 242p. $80.50. 1-85109-084-3.
Dominican Republic, by Kai Schoenhals. 212p. $62.50. 1-85109-110-6.
France, by Frances Chambers. 175p. $72.50. 1-85109-082-7.
Grenada, by Kai Schoenhals. 179p. $59. 1-85109-126-2.
Guinea-Bissau, by Rosemary E. Galli. 180p. $57. 1-85109-108-4.
Hong Kong, by Ian Scott. 248p. $71. 1-85109-089-4.
Japan, by Frank Joseph Shulman. 876p. $139.50. 1-85109-074-6.
Monaco, by Grace Laird Hudson. 200p. $70. 1-85109-117-3.
Nepal, by John Whelpton. 296p. $75. 1-85109-68-2.
Pakistan, by David Taylor. 258p. $70. 1-85109-081-9.
Suriname, by Rosemarijn Hoefte. 277p. $65. 1-85109-103-3.
Switzerland, by Heinz K. Meier. 409p. $98. 1-85109-107-6.
Taiwan, by Wei-chin Lee. 247p. $69. 1-85109-091-6.
Venezuela, by D.A.G. Waddell. 208p. $59. 1-85109-106-8.
Wales, by Gwilym Huws and D. Hywel E. Roberts. 330p. $77.50. 1-85109-118-1.
Yugoslavia Rev. ed. by John J. Horton. 282p. $71. 1-85109-105-X.

Geography

Travel

A

823. **Before You Go to Great Britain: A Resource Directory and Planning Guide,** by James W. Brown and Shirley N. Brown. Shoe String, 1986. 201p. $29.50. 0-208-02088-8.

This work, which sounds like a typical travel guide, is really also a rich bibliography of sources to help one prepare for a trip to Great Britain. The comprehensive sourcebook is divided into nine major chapters which deal with such topics as: history of Great Britain, planning the trip, food and drink, sports and arts, etc. Each chapter also includes an annotated list of books, pamphlets, maps, AV resources, and addresses of additional sources. This comprehensive guide is useful for reference work and collection building for most academic and public libraries. *Great Britain—Description and Travel*

A

824.   **Going Places: The Guide to Travel Guides**, by Greg Hayes and Joan Wright. Harvard Common Press, 1989. 606p. $26.95 1-558-32007-5; pap. $17.95 1-558-32003-2.

Using a geographical arrangement, this bibliography describes and evaluates about 3,000 titles in English. There are also sections on various series, phrase books, travel bookstores, and publishers. This will be a useful guide for libraries that have extensive travel collections.   *Travel*

A

825.   **Good Books for the Curious Traveler: Asia and the South Pacific**, by Theodora Nelson and Andrea Gross. Johnson Books, 1989. 312p. $12.50 pap. 1-55566-040-1.

This guide to about 350 in-print travel books focuses on those that deal with archaeology, history, folklore, cuisine, and culture, rather than the usual fare like listings of hotels and restaurants, etc. There are separate sections on each country including Australia, China, India, Japan, Korea, New Zealand, the Pacific Islands, and Southeastern Asia countries. Also included are books for children. The annotations are evaluative and informative. This will be helpful for both reader's advisory work as well as in collection development. There is a companion work, *Good Books for the Curious Traveler: Europe.*   *Travel; Asia*

A

826.   **Good Books for the Curious Traveler: Europe**, by Theodora Nelson and Andrea Gross. Johnson Books, 1989. 300p. $12.95 pap. 1-55566-038-X.

This bibliography of about 400 in-print books on European countries covers background cultural topics like anthropology, archaeology, architecture, the arts, history, and geography. There are also entries for children's books. The arrangement is by country from England to Russia. The annotations are extensive in length. This will be helpful for reader's guidance work as well as collection building. A companion volume is *Good Books for the Curious Traveler: Asia and the South Pacific.*   *Europe; Travel*

A

827.   **Recreational Vehicles and Travel: A Resource Guide**, by Bernard Mergen. Greenwood, 1985. 221p. $38.95. 0-313-23672-0.

Over 1,000 items are cited in this unusual guide which is directed to "students of popular culture, history, travel, and any field in which movement of people from place to place plays a part." Mergen, a professor of American civilization, is a recreational travel maven, and his love of the topic is reflected in this resource guide which he hopes will encourage further research in the field. This work is a series of bibliographical essays. Chapter 2 concerns itself with travel in general and includes bibliographical guides, research aids, histories, primary sources, and periodicals. Throughout the work, critical and descriptive comments are made on each title cited. Mergen also provides a "Checklist of Books and Articles," which places all references in alphabetical order and includes full bibliographic information. Periodical listings also include publication information. A list of major research collections, a selected list of movies on the subject, and a detailed index are appended. The nature of this guide is such that, even though published in 1985, it is still not outdated and therefore recommended for academic libraries supporting American studies programs and public libraries serving the travel-bound.

Travel; Recreational Vehicles; United States—Description and Travel

A

828.   **The Traveler's Reading Guide: Ready-Made Reading Lists for the Armchair Traveler**, Ed. by Maggy Simony. Rev. and expanded ed. Facts on File, 1993. 510p. $50. 0-8160-2648-3.

A popular guide to travel information, this is "an informal, 'derivative' bibliography consisting largely of data collected from standard bibliographic sources." It is intended to provide reading lists for librarians, teachers, travel professionals, and of course armchair travelers of all types. Included are guidebooks, novels, background reading, and travel articles arranged by continent, then by country and city. This is especially useful for identifying travel guides not included in the popular series. Under each geographic area, the suggested readings-generally organized by type, e.g., guidebooks, novels, etc. Each entry has bibliographic information and a one or two line descriptive note. An author index is included. This guide is useful for reference and collection development, but it is hoped that it will be updated on a regular basis. Recommended for most public libraries.   *Travel*

History

General and Miscellaneous

A

829.   **The Living History Sourcebook**, by Jay Anderson. American Association for State and Local History, 1985. 469p. $14.95. pap. 0-910050-75-9.

This outstanding directory/sourcebook includes among its 360 annotated entries 43 books and 30 periodicals and is a useful bibliography on the fascinating subject of "living history." The book is divided into ten major sections, and the entries on museums, organizations, films, simulation games, etc. are all added bonuses to collection development and reference services. The author admits that this sourcebook is a "subjective selection and not a complete listing." However, this work is a good start and is therefore recommended for most public libraries. *History; Museums*

A

830.   **Oral History: A Reference Guide and Annotated Bibliography**, by Patricia Pate Havlice. McFarland, 1985. 140p. $29.95. 0-89950-138-9.

Havlice's guide to oral history is a fresh approach to historical research. She lists and annotates 773 items on the subject (which has become one of the major sources of data for historical research—e.g., Haley's *Roots*). All of the entries were published from the 1950's to 1983. The first part of this slim work includes a brief survey of oral history and basic information sources on the topic. The bibliography is alphabetically arranged by author. Brief annotations and bibliographic information are included with each entry. Subject and title indexes facilitate use. This useful guide is recommended for all libraries supporting oral history. *Oral History; Research Methodology*

A

831.   **Reference Sources in History: An Introductory Guide**, by Ronald H. Fritze et al. ABC-Clio, 1990. 319p. $55. 0-874365-164-8.

Compiled by an historian with the assistance of two history-oriented librarians, this selective, annotated bibliography describes nearly 700 major reference and information sources from all periods of history. The 14 chapters are organized by type of source and include entries for monographs, reference books, periodicals, dissertations, indexes and abstracts, bibliographies, government publications, and microforms. Entries include lengthy critical and descriptive annotations and full bibliographic information. The chapters are further divided by geographic location. Some titles are considered to be of timeless value, but many were published as recently as 1990. A special feature is the core list of journals in the field of history. Webb's *Sources of Information in the Social Sciences* is geographically more inclusive, but slightly more dated. As an introductory reference work in the field of history, which was its intention, this is highly recommended for most academic and public libraries. *Reference Books—History; History*

A

832.   **Serial Bibliographies and Abstracts in History: An Annotated Guide**, by David Henige. Greenwood, 1986. 220p. $42.50 0-313-25070-7. (Bibliographies and Indexes in World History, 2).

This is an annotated guide to about 900 bibliographies in the field of history. The emphasis is on listings of journal articles. Bibliographies that list only books are excluded. The entries are arranged by title and there is a subject index. The annotations are evaluative and describe the scope, size and time-span of the bibliography. This will be of value primarily in academic libraries. *History*

A

833.   **The Study of History: A Bibliographical Guide**, by R. C. Richardson. Manchester University (St. Martin's), 1988. 98p. $59.95 0-7190-1881-1.

This is a selective bibliography of books and articles that introduce the discipline of historiography. There are about 2,100 entries, each well identified and each described in a brief annotation. There are nine chapters: the first is on general works, and the other eight are organized by chronological periods like medieval history and the nineteenth century. The emphasis is on British writings. It will be of value particularly in undergraduate libraries. *History*

Archaeology

A

834. **Keyguide to Information Sources in Archaeology**, by Peter Woodhead, Mansell, 1985. 219p. $39. 0-7201-1745-3. (Keyguide to Information Series).

This useful guide to the literature of archaeology consists of three parts. The first defines the discipline and its scope, its relation to other fields, its organization, and the kinds and nature of archaeological information. Major reference sources are listed here. The main bibliography is in part two, which contains annotated listings arranged geographically. Parts one and two contain a total of 759 sources. Part three is a list of worldwide organizations. There is an author, title and subject index. This will be of use in larger library collections. *Archaeology*

World History

General and Miscellaneous

Y; A

835. **Agent Orange and Vietnam: An Annotated Bibliography**, By Caroline D. Harnly. Scarecrow, 1988. 401p. $37.50. 0-8108-2174-5.

This expanded version of the author's earlier work, *Agent Orange and the Vietnam Veteran* (1985), contains citations for books, articles, and technical reports. The bibliography is divided into six major sections including: General Discussions; Ethical and Political Issues; Effects on Vietnam's Ecology; Health; and Effects on Vietnam Veterans. Recommended for libraries having a need for additional information on this controversial topic. *Agent Orange; Vietnam War Veterans; Vietnam War, 1961-1975*

A

836. **Columbus: An Annotated Guide to the Scholarship on His Life and Writings, 1750 to 1988**, by Foster Provost. John Carter Brown Library/Omnigraphics, 1991. 225p. $48. 1-55888-157-3.

In the year 1992, at the time of the 500th anniversary of Columbus' first voyage to the New World, there was considerable reassessment of the explorer's role in world history. Although this bibliography precedes that flurry of writing, it does supply a guide to the important publications on Columbus that appeared between 1750 through 1988. The 780 items cited are arranged in seven sections under such headings as collective works, editions of primary documents, studies of Columbus' life, bibliographies, and historiography. In addition to extensive bibliographic information, each entry has a descriptive annotation, some of which are quite lengthy. Many of the items are in foreign languages. There are extensive indexes including those by subjects, authors, titles, persons, and places. A more popular bibliography called *Bibliografica Columbiana 1492-1990* was published in 1990 by the National Parks Service and edited by Joseph P. Sanchez. It lists 2,600 items in three sections: books, juvenile literature and periodical articles. Both of these bibliographies complement each other nicely, one being scholarly and the other more popular in scope. Both could be valuable in acquisition of materials on this controversial explorer.

Columbus, Christopher

A

837. **The Korean War: An Annotated Bibliography**, by Keith D. McFarland. Garland, 1986. 463p. $82. 0-8240-9068-3. (Wars of the United States, 8).

This selective bibliography contains brief annotations for over 2,300 citations to books, reference materials, personal accounts, articles, government publications, and theses. The work is divided into 23 chapters including "Reference Works," "General Accounts of the War," "The United Nations and the War," and "The Truman-MacArthur Controversy," with many subdivisions. All items are in the English and cover both scholarly and popular writings. There are subject and author indexes. This is a fine bibliography on an important topic in American history, but the high price will probably limit this book's purchase to large libraries. *Korean War*

A

838. **Modern Italian History: An Annotated Bibliography**, Comp. by Frank J. Coppa and William Roberts. Greenwood Press, 1990. 226p. $49.50. 0-313-24812-5. (Bibliographies and Indexes in World History).

This selective bibliographic essay of current books, journal articles, and dissertations covers the period of modern Italian history from the 18th century to the late 1980's. It serves to complement Coppa's 1985 work by Greenwood: *Dictionary of Modern Italian History* (1985. $65. 0-313-22983-X). The titles cover Italian and English-language materials published from about 1970 to the present. Included are reference works, monographic studies, and works representing various periods of Italian history from the 18th century to the present. Full bibliographic information, plus a brief annotation accompany each entry. This bibliography is recommended for academic libraries or any other library that supports a special collection in Italian history. *Italy*

Y*; A*
839.   **Nazism, Resistance & Holocaust in World War II: A Bibliography**, by Vera Laska. Scarecrow, 1985. 183p. $20. 0-8108-1771-3.
This is more than a bibliography; Laska, a survivor of three concentration camps has presented us with a vivid and horrific picture of the Holocaust and the resistance movement. The bibliography includes about 2,000 titles, the vast majority of which are annotated. Arrangement is under 13 subject categories such as War Crimes, Jews, Anti-Semitism, Holocaust, Women, etc. Another section, entitled Literature, includes plays, poetry, and novels related to the topic. An author index is provided; however, a subject index would have been desirable, especially since the subject headings are very broad. This book is useful for reference, interlibrary loans, and especially collection development, and deserves to be in all high school, academic, and public libraries. *Nazism; Holocaust; World War II*

A
840.   **The Normandy Campaign, 1944: A Selected Bibliography**, by Colin F. Baxter. Greenwood, 1992. 167p. $45. 0-313-28301-X.
This bibliography is really a handbook which includes a series of bibliographical essays on various aspects of the Normandy campaign. There is enough here to satisfy both the beginning student as well as the scholar of this very crucial campaign of World War II. It is, therefore, recommended to both the academic library and general public library, as well to those libraries specializing in the military generally.
Normandy Campaign, 1944; World War II

Y; A*
841.   **Research Guide to European Historical Biography: 1450-Present**, vols. 1-4, Ed. by James Moncure. Beacham Publishing, 1992. 2,138p. in 4v. $299. 0-933833-28-8.
Nearly 200 "prominent men and women who shaped European civilization since 1450" are profiled in these first four volumes. The set is projected to be eight volumes when complete. These initial volumes include explorers, heads of state, diplomats, military leaders, and social reformers. Volumes five through eight will include scientists, philosophers, political theorists, theologians, artists, writers, and musicians. The format and arrangement is similar to *Research Guide to American Historical Biography* (1991). Entries include a chronology of the person's life, a brief annotated listing of biographies of the individual, an overview of writings by the person, and a list of other sources dealing with the contemporary period. This excellent set of bio-bibliographies is recommended as a reference resource and as a guide to collection development for all libraries from the secondary school level through undergraduate academic libraries.
Biography; Europe—Biography; Europe—History

A
842.   **The Rise and Fall of the Soviet Union: A Selected Bibliography of Sources in English**, Ed. by Abraham J. Edelheit and Hershel Edelheit. Greenwood, 1992. 430p. $65. 0-313-28625-6.
Over 2,000 highly selected, English-language references are included in this timely volume. The entries are arranged in topical chapters; some of the entries are annotated. A separate title and subject index are provided. Most of the works were published between 1970 and the early 1990's. The strength of the coverage is in history, politics, and the economy. Its coverage is limited in culture and literature, and almost nonexistent in art and music. Recommended for undergraduate and public libraries as a much needed work, despite its limitations. *Russia; Soviet Union*

A
843.   **A Subject Bibliography of the First World War: Books in English, 1914-1987**, by A. G. S. Enser. Gower, 1990. 412p. $69.95 0-566-05619-4.
This is a comprehensive bibliography of English-language books on World War I published between 1914 and 1987. Only adult, nonfiction is included. There are about 6,800 entries listed under 350 subject

headings arranged alphabetically from addresses and speeches to Zimmerman. There are no annotations, but each entry receives full bibliographic treatment. There are author and subject indexes and an index of the books that have only titles. This will be of value in academic and large public libraries. *World War I*

A

844. **A Subject Bibliography of the Second World War and the Aftermath: Books in English, 1975-1987**, by A. G. S. Enser. 2nd ed. Gower, 1990. 287p. $59.95 0-566-05736-0.

This, a revision of the first edition which appeared in 1985, serves as a companion to the author's earlier *A Subject Bibliography of the Second World War: Books in English 1939-1974* (London Stamp Exchange, $90. 0-317-932187). It includes books written in English from all over the world in thousands of entries arranged by subjects. The entries are not annotated, but full bibliographic information is given. There are author and subject indexes and an index to those books that are listed only by title. These volumes are suited to large public and academic libraries. *World War II*

A

845. **Victorian Studies: A Research Guide**, by Sharon Propas. Garland, 1992. 334p. $50. 0-8240-5840-2.

One of the major purposes of this guide was to complement and update an earlier existing guide (long out-of-print) by Lionel Madden, *How to Find Out about the Victorian Period* (Pergamon, 1970). Both works list general reference works, but Propas lists the resources by discipline rather than a specific topical arrangement. Further, Propas has provided useful annotations. The major flaws of the newer title are the inclusion of many outdated editions of reference works and also the limited subject access. However, because there is a dearth of current bibliographical material in this area, the work should be considered by libraries supporting collections on the Victorian era. *Victorian Period*

A*

846. **The Vietnam War: Handbook of the Literature and Research**, by James S. Olson. Greenwood, 1993. 500p. $65. 0-313-27422-3.

Fourteen contributors under the editorial leadership of Olson compiled this comprehensive review of the literature of the Vietnam War. It covers many facets of the conflict, including military, political, cultural, and social aspects. A large array of both popular and scholarly materials are included, for example, nonfiction and fiction books, films and videos, and even comic books. Much of the material is published as recently as 1992. This volume is an excellent reference, research, and collection development handbook/guide that deserves to be in all academic and public libraries. *Vietnam War, 1961-1975*

A

847. **The War Against Japan, 1941-1945: An Annotated Bibliography**, by John J. Sbrega. Garland, 1990. 1050p. $109. 0-8240-8940-5. (Wars of the United States, 10).

Over 5,200 English-language items on the 1941-1945 Pacific War published through 1987 are included in this detailed bibliography. The entries include reference books, histories, biographies, periodical articles, fiction works, and even some official reports. All aspects of the war are considered, e.g., biography, religion, battles, and even demographic aspects. The citations are complete, and the annotations are both descriptive and evaluative. Also included are a list of 400 periodicals consulted. Author and subject indexes are also provided. This is recommended for libraries at all levels, and is essential for U.S. history, World War II, and Japanese studies collections. *World War II—Pacific; World War II—Japan*

A

848. **World War II at Sea: Bibliography of Sources in English, 1974-1989**, by Myron J. Smith. Scarecrow, 1990. 314p. $32.50. 0-8108-2260-1.

This bibliography of almost 3,500 entries serves as an up-dating to Smith's earlier three-volume set *World War II at Sea*, (o.p.) which covered the same topic for materials published between 1939 and 1973. This volume covers material from 1974 to early 1989 (plus some items published earlier and not included in the basic set). Books, articles, theses, dissertations, and research reports are the types of sources listed. Material is both popular and scholarly. This is recommended for all libraries that have the original bibliography and for libraries that do not, since they can be used independently of one another and especially since the items in the current update are more readily available. *World War II—Naval Operations*

A

849.   **Writing about Vietnam: A Bibliography of the Literature of the Vietnam Conflict**, by Sandra M. Wittman. G. K. Hall, 1989. 385p. $40. 0-8161-9083-6.

Wittman has compiled an impressive, comprehensive bibliography of over 1,700 citations covering English-language literature written between 1954 and 1988 and relating to the Vietnam War. Works dealing with the French involvement are also included, as are the antiwar movement, refugee problems, and post-war veterans' concerns. A wide variety of types of literature is included, e.g., personal narratives and biographies, novels, poetry, drama, short stories, literary criticism, other bibliographies, dissertations, teaching materials, periodicals, and even books for young people. The entries are arranged alphabetically within the categories aforementioned, and the majority contain brief annotations. Author and title indexes are also provided. This work is the most comprehensive bibliography on the subject to date. A similar and also an excellent bibliography is Newman's *Vietnam War Literature*. Wittman's excellent bibliography is recommended as a reference guide and aid to collections for most secondary school, academic, and public libraries. *Vietnam War, 1961-1975*

Genocide and Holocaust

C; Y; A*

850.   **Bibliography of the Holocaust Memorial Resource and Education Center of Central Florida**, Comp. by Eva L. Ritt and Tess Wise. Holocaust Memorial Resource and Education Center of Central Florida, 1990. 399p. $10. pap.

To the extent that the collection of the Holocaust Memorial Resource and Education Center of Central Florida represents a comprehensive and up-to-date resource, this bibliography, which is based on its catalog, becomes an excellent collection evaluation and development guide. The collection consists of books, audio-tapes, films, and videotapes. The bibliography is divided into over twenty major subject areas including: After the Holocaust, Anti-Semitism and Prejudice, Children's Literature, and Terrorism. Entries include author, title, and imprint information. There are also brief annotations. Although the focus is on the Holocaust, information on Jewish history, discrimination, hate groups, and related topics is not excluded. This work is not as scholarly as Edelheit's *Bibliography on Holocaust Literature*, but it is more current and lists more titles than Cargas' *The Holocaust: An Annotated Bibliography* (1985). Therefore, this inexpensive and useful bibliography is particularly recommended for school, synagogue and public libraries.

Holocaust; Jews

A*

851.   **Bibliography on Holocaust Literature**, ed. by Abraham J. Edelheit and Hershel Edelheit. Westview, 1986. 842p. $132. 0-8133-7233-X.

The Edelheits have spent more than ten years of research in compiling this comprehensive bibliography on the Holocaust which is intended to serve the scholar and general reader. More than 9,000 books, pamphlets, periodicals, and dissertations are included. This is more than a list of items on the Holocaust; it also includes Jewish life in prewar Europe, anti-Semitism, fascism, World War II in general, and the aftermath and implications of the Holocaust. This is reflected in the four main sections of the work: Before the Storm, The Perpetrators, The Crucible, and Aftermath, which are in turn subdivided into more specific topics. Each numbered item includes full bibliographic information, and some entries without descriptive titles are annotated. Subject access is through the table of contents and there is an author index. A supplement has also been published (1990. $94.50. 0-8133-0896-8). This work, along with the ... *Supplement*, will undoubtedly become the standard bibliography on the Holocaust for some time to come and is therefore recommended for all libraries developing or maintaining a collection is this area. *Holocaust; Jews*

C, Y, A

852.   **Facing History and Ourselves: Holocaust and Human Behavior: Annotated Bibliography**, by Margaret A. Drew. Walker, 1988. 124p. $15.85 0-8027-9411-4.

This bibliography of recommended books deals primarily with the Jewish World War II Holocaust but also contains some coverage on the Armenian and Cambodian attempted genocides. The book is divided into two main sections: one for children's and young adult books, and the other for adult works. Each of these sections is subdivided into areas such as general works, fiction, biographies, and historical works. Following bibliographic information there are both descriptive and evaluative annotations. This is an excellent bibliography for librarians in schools, as well as public or academic libraries, who wish to evaluate and build their collections in this vital area. *Holocaust; Jews; World War II*

A

853.   **First-Person Accounts of Genocidal Acts in the Twentieth Century: An Annotated Bibliography**, by Samuel Totten. Greenwood, 1991 351p. $55. 0-313-26713-8.

Totten has compiled an interesting bibliography of first-hand accounts of persons who witnessed or experienced genocidal acts. All of the accounts are in the first-person and include diaries, oral histories, newspaper articles, archives, and other items generally not available for purchase, but rather they may be available for research and inter-library loans. On the other hand, many films, microfilm collections, bibliographies, and autobiographies are available for acquisition. All of the more than 1,250 numbered items are annotated. The accounts are arranged by type of material, for example, films, reports and studies, etc. Bibliographic data is adequate and subject and author indexes are provided. This unusual bibliography may prove useful for most academic and public libraries.   *Genocide*

A

854.   **Genocide: A Critical Bibliographic Review**, by Israel W. Charny. Facts on File, 1991. 288p. $65. 0-8160-1903-7.

In 13 chapters. various aspects of genocide are explored, from the mass annihilations of ancient times through the slaughter of the Armenians in World War I, the planned starvation by Stalin of the Ukraine during the 1930s, the World War II Holocaust and the recent horrors in Cambodia. Various facets of the topic and a variety of academic disciplines such as sociology, psychology, political science, and the arts are represented. The bibliographies are current, selective, and well-annotated. There is an author, title and subject index. Volume Two (1990, $65. 0-8160-2642-4) focuses on the legal literature, international law and current genocide studies. These volumes are highly recommended for most academic and public libraries.   *Genocide*

A

855.   **Genocide in Our Time: An Annotated Bibliography with Analytical Introductions**, by Michael N. Dobkowski and Isidor Wallimann. Pierian, 1992. 183p. $40. pap. 0-87650-280-X.

Cambodia, Uganda, and Bosnia remind us that genocide did not cease with the tragic Holocaust. This work focuses on the Holocaust, the Armenian genocide, and the Ukrainian famine under Stalin. However, current genocidal and ethnocidal acts are included in the eight chapters of analytical essays and critical annotated bibliographies. In a detailed chronology 25 genocides are listed. Author and title indexes are also provided. While this work is highly recommended, libraries that have the earlier but similar work *Genocide: A Critical Bibliographic Review*, may not want both.   *Genocide*

Y; A

856.   **The Holocaust: An Annotated Bibliography**, by Harry James Cargas. 2nd ed. American Library Association, 1985. 196p. $13.75 0-8389-0433-5.

This highly selective bibliography of the 500 titles was intended for undergraduate students, interested adults, or better readers in senior high schools. It contains a wide variety of literary types including histories, fiction, biographies, poems, memoirs, and plays. The annotations both describe and evaluate the works. They are arranged by subjects like the arts, Jewish resistance, and the camps. There is a section on researching the Holocaust that lists basic reference works. This excellent bibliography is unfortunately now in need of an updating.   *Holocaust; Jews*

Y; A

857.   **Holocaust in Books and Films**, ed. by Judith Herschlag Muffs. Hippocrene Books, n.d. 64p. $6.50 0-686-95068-2.

This is a selected annotated guide to 400 books and audiovisual materials on the Holocaust and related topics. Some of the subjects covered are war criminals, the camps, Third Reich, ghettos, European Jews, survivors, and anti-Semitism. There is an author, title, and AV index. This is a valuable collection building tool for secondary schools, junior colleges, and public libraries. It can be obtained for $6.95 plus $2.50 for postage from the Anti-Defamation League of B'Nai B'Rith, 823 United Nations Plaza, New York, NY 10017.   *Holocaust; Jews*

A

858.   **Holocaust Studies: A Directory and Bibliography of Bibliographies**, by Martin H. Sable. Penkevill (Greenwood, Fla.), 1987. 115p. $20. 0-913283-20-7.

This unusual sourcebook is in two main sections. The first is a bibliography of bibliographies published about the Holocaust that appeared through 1985. The second is a directory of associations, government organizations, survivor groups, and related agencies, plus additional sections of archives, research centers, museums, memorial parks, statues, and other constructions related to the Holocaust. For large collections where material on the Holocaust is needed. *Holocaust; Jews*

A

859. **The Jewish Holocaust: An Annotated Guide to Books in English**, by Marty Bloomberg. Borgo, 1991. 248p. $29.95; $19.95 pap. 0-89370-160-2; 0-89370-260-9.

This useful bibliography lists more than 800 books arranged by subjects that cover such areas as pre-war Jewish civilization, anti-Semitism, the Holocaust, and war-crime trials. All kinds of books are included, from reference sources to first-person accounts, though nothing after 1986 is listed. For each entry, there is full bibliographic information and a brief annotation. In an appendix, the editor chooses the contents of basic collections for public, academic, and high school libraries. This will have value in general collections. *Holocaust; Jews*

United States

Y; A

860. **America on Film and Tape: A Topical Catalog of Audiovisual Resources for the Study of United States History, Society, and Culture**, Ed. by Howard B. Hitchens. Greenwood, 1985. 392p. $55.95. 0-313-24778-1. (Bibliographies and Indexes in American History).

This highly-selective bibliography of more than 1,500 titles is intended to support an American Studies curriculum. Its inclusion of films, videotapes, slides, filmstrips, and audio-cassettes is its strongest feature. Entries are arranged in alphabetical order under title in subsections under 14 very broad categories such as Anthropology, History, Political Science, etc.

Each entry includes title, suggested grade level, audiovisual format, length in time or number of frames, date, producer/distributor, and a brief annotation. Materials included were produced from the 1930's (some classic films) to 1983. There is no subject index, and the "Subject Category Outline" is a bit confusing and difficult to use. Despite its flaws, because there is very little available in this much needed area of selection, it is recommended for most school libraries and many public libraries.

American Studies; United States—History

A

861. **American History: A Bibliographic Review. Volume V: 1989**, Ed. by Carol Bondhus Fitzgerald. Meckler, 1990. 250p. $59.50. 0-88736-583-3.

Each volume of this bibliography has a theme of current publications in some area of American historical research. In addition to a survey of the outstanding publications of each year's theme, with detailed reviews, there is a summary of major bibliographic projects, awards, databases, political thought, and publishing awards and prizes in American history for the year. This is a recommended addition for any academic or public library attempting to keep current with important United States history topics.

United States—History

A

862. **A Bibliography of American County Histories**, Comp. by P. William Filby. Genealogical Publishing Co., 1985. 449p. $24.95. 0-8063-1126-6.

Filby has compiled an extensive bibliography of about 5,000 items that draws heavily on the county history collections of the Library of Congress and New York Public Library. Cut-off date was 1984; however, it does cover the transition of counties from rural to urban and suburban societies since it reaches back into the late 19th century. Alaska and Hawaii are not included in this project. Entries are arranged first by state, then chronologically by county. Each entry provides full bibliographic data. Filby has fulfilled his intention "to produce a work that is more scholarly, accurate, and complete than the other major work in this area: Peterson's *Consolidated Bibliography of County Histories in the Fifty States* (1963, $12.50, 0-8063-0563-0)." This volume is highly recommended for all libraries serving genealogists and maintaining state and local history collections. *United States—History, Local*

A

863. **Books About Early America: 2001 Titles**, Comp. by David L. Ammerman and Philip D. Morgan. Institute of Early American History and Culture, 1989. 126p. $25. 0-910776-03-2. pap. $25. 0-910776-04-0.

In this 5th edition of a work that first appeared in 1954, the high standards of bibliographic accuracy have been maintained by a reputable and authoritative organization. This up-to-date core bibliography of over 2,000 titles is arranged by subject; included are thematic and narrative works, biographies, primary sources, and reference works. Author and title indexes are provided. Summary and headnotes are also included in place of detailed annotations. This bibliography is intended for the serious student of Colonial American history and the list is recommended for every academic and many public libraries.

United States—History—Colonial Period

A

864. **Civil War Eyewitnesses: An Annotated Bibliography of Books and Articles, 1955-1986**, by Garold L. Cole. University of South Carolina, 1988. 351p. $34.95 0-87249-545-0.

This reference work lists 1,395 items published between 1955 and 1986 on the United States Civil War. Using a subject approach, each of the books and articles cited is annotated, and there is a title and subject index. This scholarly work deserves a place in large public libraries as well as in libraries where information on this topic is in demand. *United States—History—Civil War*

A*

865. **Handbook for Research in American History: A Guide to Bibliographies and Other Reference Works**, by Francis Paul Prucha. University of Nebraska, 1987. 289p. $21.95; $9.95 pap. 0-8032-3682-4; 0-8032-8719-4 pap.

This general guide to reference sources in American history is divided into two main sections. Section 1 contains 17 chapters on various categories of works like government publications and databases, and the second section contains works arranged by broad subjects like social history, travel accounts, and political history. Citations are well identified and there are good descriptive annotations. Its reasonable price and the basic nature of the material included help make it an attractive and useful addition to any college and medium to large public libraries. *United States—History*

A

866. **Index to America: Life and Customs, 20th Century to 1986**, by Norma Ireland. Scarecrow, 1989. 361 $37.50 0-8108-2170-2. (Useful Reference Series, 107).

This is a subject index to 180 books (most published in the 1970s and early 1980s) that deal with American history and culture. The subject headings cover such topics as Theodore Roosevelt, television, Woodstock, Henry Ford, skyscrapers, and Elvis Presley. This affords analytics to many of the general surveys and biographies found in many library collections and can serve as a selection guide for smaller collections. There were three previous volumes, each covering one century of our history. Of these, only the third, *Index to America: Life and Customs, 19th Century* (1984, $35, 0-8108-1661-X), is still in print.

United States—History

A

867. **New Day/New Deal: A Bibliography of the Great American Depression, 1929-1941**, Comp. by David E. Kyvig and Mary-Ann Blasio. Greenwood, 1988. 306p. $49.95. 0-313-26027-3.

According to the book's preface, this bibliography of 4,600 unannotated items is the most extensive bibliography of the depression decade. Included are books, journal articles, and dissertations. The work is arranged by topics in 13 chapters which are in turn subdivided into 44 additional subtopics. All aspects of the Depression/New Deal are considered, e.g., the Hoover and Roosevelt Administrations; Foreign Relations; The Economy; Society; and even Biography (with entries for 167 individuals). There is an author index, but no subject index, which is a draw-back, despite the number of topic and subtopic divisions. Still this bibliography will be most welcome to historians and researchers alike and should be considered for collection development by most academic and many public libraries.

Depressions, Economic; New Deal; United States—History—1933-1945

Y; A

868. **New England, A Bibliography of Its History, v.7**, Prepared by the Committee for a New England Bibliography; ed. by Roger Parks. University Press of New England, 1990. 259p. $40. 0-87451-496-7. (Bibliographies of New England History, 7).

Volume 7 incorporates lists of materials for the New England region as a whole. Bibliographies of the six individual states were published over a 15 year period preceding this volume. This volume and v. 8 (see entry 681) follow the guidelines; they are comprehensive in scope and include citations for books, pamphlets, journal articles, dissertations, and biographies and some genealogies (no government publications or newspaper articles are included). Organization is by broad subject area. High bibliographic standards are maintained throughout. Each entry indicates one New England holding library. This excellent regional bibliography deserves to be in every academic and public library in the country, especially in New England libraries (there, even school libraries should consider it) for reference and collection development.

New England; Connecticut; Maine; Massachusetts; New Hampshire; Rhode Island

Y; A*
869. **The 1960s: An Annotated Bibliography of Social and Political Movements in the United States**, by Rebecca Jackson. Greenwood, 1992. 237p. $49.95. 0-313-27255-7. (Bibliographies and Indexes in American History, 24).

Jackson has provided us with a bibliography of almost 1,400 books that really capture the phenomena of the hard-to-explain events that occurred in the United States during the 1960's and early 1970's. The protest movements, the cultural revolution, religion, music, drugs, hippies, presidencies, and radicalism are all included and are the major sections of this important work.

Bibliographic data is provided, and all of the citations are briefly annotated. Author, title, and subject indexes complete the work. This handy reference tool is recommended for all academic, public, and larger secondary school libraries as a research aid and selection guide for this exciting period.

United States—History—1961-1974

A
870. **Pearl Harbor, 1941: A Bibliography**, by Myron J. Smith. Greenwood, 1991. 197p. $55. 0-313-28121-1.

The 50th anniversary of the World War II era has fostered an increased interest in books of all types dealing with this period in U.S. history. This volume focuses on the attack on Pearl Harbor, which led to the United States' direct involvement in World War II. The events leading to the attack, the attack itself, and our military activity immediately after December 7, 1941 are included in this bibliography. Smith has compiled a list of reference works, periodical articles, and monographs that should be of interest to the student, general reader, and scholar. Books and other materials for young readers are excluded. The bibliographies are preceded by an introduction which discusses the overall organization of the work and cites the criteria used to select the titles for inclusion. This bibliography is recommended for all academic libraries, as well as those public and special libraries with patrons interested in Pearl Harbor specifically, or World War II generally. *Pearl Harbor, Attack on, 1941; World War II*

Y*; A*
871. **Research Guide to American Historical Biography**, Ed. by Suzanne Niemeyer. Beacham Pub., 1991. 5 vols. $63. per vol. or $315 per set. 0-933833-24-5.

Another biographical dictionary? This set not only has complete biographical coverage of prominent Americans, but for each entry, there are extensive and diverse bibliographic sources for additional information (from very basic to quite specialized). The work was designed both for secondary school and undergraduate students working on papers, as well as graduate students and faculty working on research. Further and most importantly, it was also designed to serve librarians as both a ready-reference and as an acquisitions checklist. Volumes 1 through 3 include individuals in a wide-range of fields, e.g., politics, business and labor, education, and religion. On the other hand, v. 4 emphasizes women, Native Americans and minorities; and v. 5. concentrates on entertainers, Civil War personalities, and additional minorities. Each volume, especially v. 4 and 5, stands alone and can be purchased separately. In addition to biographies and autobiographies, many primary sources are cited. A section titled: "Fiction and Adaptations" describes novels, films, plays, and other creative works about the individual. A cumulative index to all five volumes is included in v. 5. This excellent resource is recommended for all secondary school, academic, and public libraries. *Biography; United States—Biography*

A
872. **The Spanish-American War: An Annotated Bibliography**, by Anne Cipriano Venzon. Garland, 1990. 255p. $40. 0-8240-7974-4. (War of the United States, 11).

Like other works in this series on American wars, this bibliography gives coverage to the major monographs and articles in a subject arrangement. The present topic is the 1898 war with Spain, and the material is divided into 17 separate chapters like "General Works," "Foreign Relations," "Expansion,"

"Fiction," "Music," and separate geographical sections for Cuba, Puerto Rico, and the Philippines. Also included are major War and Navy Department reports. The cutoff date for inclusion was the end of 1986. The annotations are brief and sometimes critical. There are many useful cross-references in the text. This bibliography will be useful primarily in academic institutions.

Spanish-American War; United States—History—War of 1898

A

873.   **U.S. Reference-iana: (1481-1899) A Concise Guide to Over 4000 Books and Articles**, by Thomas Truxtun Moebs. Moebs Publishing, Williamsburg, VA, 1988. 826p. $85.

Moebs, an antiquarian and publisher, has compiled a guide to Americana. Included are citations for over 4,000 books and articles representing a variety of subjects such as art, newspapers, military, travel, and state and local history. Entries are arranged in alphabetical order under subject. Many, but not all, of the entries are annotated. This guide is recommended for academic and public libraries for reference, interlibrary loans and collection development. *American Studies; United States—History*

Law, Criminology, and Civil Liberties

Law

A

874.   **The American Constitution: An Annotated Bibliography**, by Robert J. Janosik. Salem Press, 1991. 254p. $40. 0-89356-665-9.

Janosik indicates that this selective, annotated bibliography "is an effort to encourage the serious study of the American Constitution" within all levels of academia. The citations are arranged under four broad headings: general studies, which include reference sources; the text of the U.S. Constitution; institutions of the federal government; and the individual and the Constitution. Entries contain full bibliographic information, as well as a detailed annotation which discusses the primary focus of the work and its unique characteristics. There is no other similar work published within the past 10 years, and therefore, this well-developed bibliography is recommended for all academic and law libraries, and many public libraries with a strong interest in this area. *United States—Constitution*

A

875.   **American Legal Literature: A Guide to Selected Legal Resources**, by Bernard D. Reams et al. Libraries Unlimited, 1985. 229p. $27.50. 0-87287-514-8.

This highly selective guide to legal resources is intended for the serious researcher as well as laypersons interested in the American legal system. It contains monographs, reference materials, and some primary sources. The 550 titles, published between 1969 and 1984, are arranged in three chapters: Current Primary Legal Materials; Selected Reference Sources; and the most important for the general reader, Subject Bibliographies of Law-related Monographs. This third chapter contains more than half the entries, all with descriptive annotations. Despite its age, this guide is recommended as a buying guide for most public libraries, particularly those with a law or legal reference focus. *Law*

A

876.   **The Dynamic Constitution: A Historical Bibliography**, by Suzanne Robitaille Ontiveros. ABC-Clio, 1986. 343p. $49.50. 0-87436-470-1. (Research guides, 19).

This volume brings together 1,370 citations for books, articles, and dissertations published in ninety countries between 1974 and 1985 on the U.S. Constitution. There is an introductory chapter listing overviews and general reference works, followed by four chronologically arranged chapters ending with one covering 1900 to 1985. For each of the periodical articles, there is an abstract, but not for books or dissertations. A supplementary section outlines constitutional history, and there are author and subject indexes plus a reprint of the Constitution. Middle to large public libraries and academic libraries should find this of value. *United States—Constitution*

A
877. **Encyclopedia of Legal Information Sources**, by Paul Wasserman et al 2nd ed. Gale, 1992. 700p. $165 0-8103-7439-0.

Using a topical arrangement involving over 450 subject headings like bail, bankruptcy, consumer credit, and lawyer's fees, this work lists a total of 19,000 unannotated citations involving many types of media, including encyclopedias, law books, periodicals, statutes, loose-leaf services, databases, organizations, and audiovisuals. Although there is no index there are many cross-references and a good introductory outline of the contents. Only a few of the resources were published before 1980. This will be a very useful guide to resources for public libraries. *Law*

A
878. **Feminist Legal Literature: A Selective Annotated Bibliography**, by F. C. DeCoste and others. Garland, 1991. 499p. $65. 0-8240-7117-4.

This annotated bibliography of journal articles concerns women's issues as they pertain to the law and legal matters. The coverage is approximately the decade of the 1980s, and the entries are primarily in English (although some French articles are included from French-Canadian periodicals). The subjects covered in separate chapters include criminal law, constitutional law, labor and employment, pornography, prostitution, and feminist theory. There are separate chapters on bibliographies and annotated book reviews, plus author, subject, and journal indexes. The work is recommended for libraries requiring material for women's studies programs. *Law; Women's Studies; Feminism*

A
879. **Find the Law in the Library: A Guide to Legal Research**, by John Corbin. American Library Association, 1989. 496p. $65. 0-8389-05020-1.

After an introduction on how U.S. law is organized, the author proceeds through the steps in collecting legal information ending with the final preparation of reports. Each section of this handbook contains bibliographies that can be of value in building collections on legal literature. Another useful guide to basic legal publications is *Fundamentals of Legal Research* (Foundation Press, 1990, $29.95 0-88277-794-7), a 709-page textbook that is now in its fifth edition. *Law*

A
880. **How to Research the Supreme Court**, by Fenton S. Martin and Robert U. Goehlert. Congressional Quarterly, 1992. 140p $13.95 pap. 0-87187-697-3.

This selective annotated bibliography about the Supreme Court is divided into three parts. The first part deals with reference sources such as encyclopedias, biographical dictionaries, indexes, bibliographies, newspapers, and non print sources such as CD-ROM products and online databases. The second part contains such primary sources as digests of court decisions and government publications, with information on how to use them. The third part, which is not annotated, lists more general material like biographies of court judges up to and including Judge Thomas. General tips on doing research are given in the introduction and, before the author and title indexes, there is a legal term glossary. This will be useful in large public library collections and in academic libraries. *United States Supreme Court; Law*

A
881. **Law for the Layman: An Annotated Bibliography of Self-Help Law Books**, by Frank G. Houdek. Fred B. Rothman, 1991. n.p. $42.50 0-8377-0685-8.

This annotated bibliography offers a guide to recommended books about the law that are understandable to laypeople. The work is divided into two parts: the first, and shorter, lists books that are general and comprehensive in nature. The second lists more specialized sources under such headings as adoption, bankruptcy, copyright, and immigration. In addition to lengthy, helpful annotations, there are author, title, and jurisdiction indexes, plus a directory of publishers. This will be of value both as a reference work for patrons and a buying guide for acquisition librarians in public and small academic libraries. *Law*

A
882. **The Law Library Reference Shelf: Annotated Subject Guide**, by Elizabeth W. Matthews. William S. Hein, 1988. 127p. $37.50. 0-89941-645-4.

This guide is based on a compilation of approximately 350 selected reference works held by the Southern Illinois University School of Law Library, a medium-size law library. This bibliography deals primarily with national and international works; individual state materials are excluded, thus making this guide of immediate use to any law library in the country. The briefly annotated entries are arranged under

38 subject categories. The work also contains an author/title index. However, despite the subject arrangement, the lack of a subject index is a big drawback. Still, this bibliography is recommended as a core law library for most academic and public libraries with a special law section or collection. *Law*

A

883. The New American Immigration: Evolving Patterns of Legal and Illegal Immigration: A Bibliography of Selected References, by Francesco Cordasco. Garland, 1987. 418p. $64. 0-8240-8523.

More than 2,300 entries from books, articles, and government reports were culled in order to present this overview of past and present U.S. immigration policies and practices and its many aspects. Most of the entries are in English; however, some are in Spanish. Part 1 includes 73 works on U.S. policy prior to 1965 (1965 was the year that a long-standing U.S. immigration policy was modified and restrictions placed on nonwestern immigration were lifted); Part 2 deals with general works on immigration after 1965; Part 3 concerns itself with illegal immigrants in 850 entries (more than $\frac{1}{3}$ of the total); and Part 4 is miscellanea. All entries in each part are arranged in alphabetical order by author, and basic bibliographic data is included. Annotations are not always provided if titles are considered self-explanatory, and even then, they are only brief notes. The lack of a subject index is a serious limitation with so many entries listed under rather broad headings. Still, the source is recommended for academic and public libraries serving a clientele with a serious interest in the topic. *Immigration; Aliens, Illegal*

A

884. The U.S. Supreme Court: A Bibliography, by Fenton Martin and Robert U. Goehlert. Congressional Quarterly, 1990. 594p. $175. 0-87187-554-3.

This extensive bibliography on the U.S. Supreme Court includes books, articles, dissertations, government documents, and other publications. Entries are organized by topic, time period, and by individual justice. Entries are not annotated. The introduction gives some suggestion for conducting legal research and discusses materials available for studying the U.S. Supreme Court. Subject and author indexes are provided. Recommended for law libraries, academic, and public libraries that have a need for extensive research in this area. *United States Supreme Court*

Crime and Criminal Justice

A

885. Capital Punishment in America: An Annotated Bibliography, by Michael L. Radelet and Margaret Vandiver. Garland, 1988. 243p. $36. 0-8240-1623-8. (Garland Reference Library of Social Science, 466).

This is an alphabetically arranged bibliography of over 1,000 English language books and articles an capital punishment, with emphasis on material published in the 1970s and 1980s. Additional sections include Congressional publications, Supreme Court decisions, plus a subject index. For large collections. *Capital Punishment*

A

886. Comparative Criminology: An Annotated Bibliography, by Piers Beirne and Joan Hill. Greenwood, 1991. 144p. $42.95 0-313-26572-0. (Research and Bibliographical Guides in Criminal Justice, 3).

This bibliography of comparative crime studies lists about 500 entries consisting of books, journal articles chapters, proceedings, and unpublished material from 1960 to the present, all in English dealing with criminal theory in various countries. Each entry has a descriptive annotation and is arranged into broad subject areas, such as comparative criminology, with author and subject indexes. This work is recommended for collections in college libraries with strong criminal justice programs. *Criminal Justice*

A

887. Crime and the Elderly: An Annotated Bibliography, by Ron H. Aday. Greenwood, 1988. 118p. $42.95. 0-313-25470-2. (Bibliographies and Indexes in Gerontology, 8).

This 361-item bibliography of books and periodical articles is in ten chapters—five dealing with crimes against the elderly, such as abuse and neglect, and five about the elderly as criminals involving topics like crime patterns, causes, and rehabilitation. All items are annotated with approximately 10 lines each. Materials were published in the 1970s and 1980s. There are appendixes of organizations and programs, plus an author and subject index. Useful in large collections, particularly in libraries serving a population of the elderly. *Aging; Senior Citizens*

A

888.   Criminal Justice Documents: A Selective, Annotated Bibliography of U.S. Government Publications since 1975, by John F. Berens. Greenword, 1987. 236p. $45. 0-313-25183-5. (Bibliographies and Indexes in Law and Political Science, 7).

Because the U.S. government is so active in the study of crime and its prevention, it is also an important publisher in these areas. This bibliography of 1,098 documents published between 1975 and October, 1986, is divided into eight major subject areas, such as the courts, the criminal justice system, crime and criminals, and juvenile justice. The annotations are brief but adequate and full bibliographic information is given for each item including its SuDocs number. There are four indexes: by author, title, geographical area, and organization. Useful in large collections.   *Criminal Justice; United States—Government Publications*

A

889.   Criminal Justice Ethics: Annotated Bibliography and Guide to Sources, by Frank Schmalleger. Greenwood, 1991. 113p. $39.95 0-313-26791-X. (Research and Bibliographical Guides in Criminal Justice, 2).

After an introductory essay that defines and gives historical information on ethics in criminal justice in the United States, there is a bibliography of 231 items primarily published after 1988. They include articles, books, chapters in books, reports, videocassettes and government publications. The book is organized into chapters that deal with such divisions of the criminal justice system as the law, the police, the courts, and victims' rights. Each entry is descriptively annotated. There are many separate lists, such as those on important libraries, organizations, indexing and abstracting services, and other research sources. The book ends with subject and author indexes. This will be used in academic and large public libraries.
Criminal Justice

A

890.   Criminal Justice Research in Libraries: Strategies and Resources, by Marilyn Lutzker and Eleanor Ferrall. Greenwood, 1988. 177p. $47.50 0-313-24490-1.

This is a fine introduction to sources in the study of criminal justice and the techniques and approaches necessary to make effective use of them. The first part introduces the ways information is communicated in criminal justice and tips on how to do profitable research in this area. The second section introduces basic sources such as encyclopedias, dictionaries, bibliographies, guides to the literature, indexes and abstracts, newsletters, periodicals, newspapers, documents, and library catalogs. The bibliographic information is full, as are the helpful annotations. A short third section discusses some of the special problems involving research in this area. There are useful appendixes of LC subject headings, directories, and major government reports, as well as author, title, and subject indexes. This is a good basic volume on the subject that will be useful for collection development.   *Criminal Justice*

A

891.   Homicide: A Bibliography, by Ernest Abel. Greenwood, 1987. 169p. $45. 0-313-25901-1 (Bibliographies and Indexes in Sociology, 11).

This 1,919 item bibliography of books, articles, and dissertations is arranged in a single alphabet by author. There are no annotations, but there is a 12-page subject index. Most of the titles included were published from the 1950s to the mid 1980s and are in English. There is also an introduction on the topic of homicide in the United States with accompanying statistics. For large collections.   *Homicide*

A

892.   Rape: A Bibliography 1976-1988, by Dorothy L. Barnes. Whitson, 1991. 326p. $38.50. 0-87875-261-7.

This updating on a much earlier work by Barnes includes works published between 1976 and 1988. Citations are drawn from books, periodical articles, pamphlets, and dissertations on many aspects of rape. Entries are listed alphabetically by author (or title) under such diverse subject headings as capital punishment, rape in literature, and parking garages. Full bibliographic data. A list of journals cited is appended. Recommended for most academic and public libraries.   *Rape*

Civil Liberties

A
893.   **American Civil Liberties Union: An Annotated Bibliography**, by Samuel Walker. Garland, 1992. 304p. $50. 0-8153-0047-6.

This very comprehensive and scholarly bibliography traces the history of this important libertarian organization from its beginning in 1914 to the present time. About 1450 books, articles and other publications are included in the six major chapters which cover history, leaders, policies, important issues dealt with, constitutional law, and resources of the ACLU. Detailed subject and name indexes are included. This easy-to-read reference source will prove useful to most academic and public libraries despite its rather expensive price. *American Civil Liberties Union*

A
894.   **The Freedom to Lie: A Debate About Democracy**, by John Swan and Noel Peattie. McFarland, 1989. 206p. $21.95 0-89950-409-4.

Two experts with opposing viewpoints debate in print whether or not there should be limits on freedom of speech. Each also has produced a very useful bibliography on this subject which could be of value in large collections. *Free Speech*

A
895.   **Human Rights: A Reference Handbook**, by Lucille Whalen. ABC-Clio. 1989. 218p. $39.50 0-87436-093-5. (Contemporary World Issues).

Following introductory material that includes a chronology of human rights events from 1941 on, brief biographies of 15 rights leaders and an annotated directory of human right organizations, there is a extensive bibliography of print and nonprint materials related to human rights published between 1983 and 1988. Print material listed are general books, directories, periodicals, document sources, and reference books; nonprint sources include films, filmstrips, videos, computer networks, and databases. All are annotated. A concluding section contains the texts of important documents involving world human rights. There is a subject index. This is a useful collection development tool for medium and large public libraries, academic libraries and senior high schools where there are advanced courses needing this sort of material.

Civil Rights

Y; A
896.   **Intellectual Freedom: A Reference Handbook**, by John B. Harer. ABC-Clio, 1992. 328p. $39.50. 0-87436-669-0.

After introductory sections which give an overview of intellectual freedom, the First Amendment, citizen rights, censorship, and current issues, the author outlines important court cases and gives biographies of people involved in intellectual freedom issues. Of particular use to librarians are the listings which follow. After a directory of organizations which includes a mention of their publications, there are annotated bibliographies of print materials, including reference works, like indexes, bibliographies, yearbooks, and directories, followed by general important monographs and periodicals. The nonprint section lists films, videos, filmstrips, online databases, CD-ROMs, educational software, and games. While the book has great overall value, these bibliographies will be particularly useful in both public and academic libraries, as well as high schools that need material on this subject. *Intellectual Freedom; Censorship*

Y; A
897.   **Intellectual Freedom and Censorship: An Annotated Bibliography**, by Frank Hoffmann. Scarecrow, 1989. 244p. $27.50 0-8108-2145-1.

This 900-item bibliography lists books, articles in professional journals and newspapers, plus government reports. These are organized into five parts: theoretical foundations, important court cases, professions concerned with censorship, pro and anti censorship groups and individuals, and cases of censorship in the mass media. Most of the citations are from the 1970s and 1980s. The concise annotations are evaluative. There are subject and author indexes. The author intended this as a general introduction to the fields of intellectual freedom and censorship for both senior high school students, as well as adults. Because of the topic's pertinence in both school and public libraries, it should be useful in both.

Censorship; Intellectual Freedom

Library Science

General and Miscellaneous

A

898. **American Library History: A Comprehensive Guide to the Literature**, by Donald G. Davis and John Mark Tucker. ABC-Clio, 1989. 471p. $125. 0-87436-142-7.

This bibliography is, without a doubt, the most comprehensive currently available dealing with the history and development of libraries in America. Each of the 15 chapters is introduced with a well-written essay which precedes the bibliography which contains subject, period, and geographic subdivisions. Each entry contains full bibliographic information and an annotation.

This definitive guide is recommended for all library science collections as well as other libraries that have special collections on education and libraries. *Libraries—United States*

A

899. **Collection Development for Libraries**, by G. E. Gorman and B. R. Howes. K. G. Saur, 1989. 432p. $47.50. 0-408-30100-7. (Topics in Library and Information Studies).

This overview of important aspects of collection development in libraries also deals with related topics like weeding and conducting users studies. Each of the chapters contains an overview of the topic and an extensive bibliography for further readings. Its usefulness in public libraries is somewhat limited by the fact that the selection aids that are mentioned are often British in orientation, and case study examples are frequently on academic libraries. However this is a good overview of the subject.

Libraries—Collection Development

A

900. **Developing Library and Information Center Collections**, by G. Edward Evans. Libraries Unlimited, 1987. 443p $38; $29.50 pap. 0-87287-463 X; 0-87287-546-6.

This textbook covers all major concerns in developing collections in libraries, such as criteria, evaluation, assessing user needs, and developing policies, plus special areas like series, government documents, and automating acquisitions.

There are many extensive bibliographies in the text that cover basic selection aids as well as listing further readings on each of the subjects. This has become a basic text on the subject and would be a useful guide for acquisition librarians in public libraries. *Libraries—Collection Development*

A

901. **Library and Information Science Journals and Serials: An Analysis Guide**, Comp. by Mary Ann Bowman. Greenwood, 1985. 140p. $37.50. 0-313-23807-3.

This handy little guide identifies and describes over 300 journals and serials in the field of library and information science; also included are the related areas of bibliography, publishing, and archives. The scope is international, but all journals are printed in English. The entries are annotated and contain full bibliographic information. They are arranged alphabetically by title. The publishers, classified title, and geographic indexes facilitate use of this guide. Though there is undoubtedly a need for an updating, this guide is recommended as part of the professional collection for all libraries. *Library Science; Information Science*

A

902. **Library and Information Service for Handicapped Individuals**, Keith Wright and Judith F. Davie. 3rd ed. Libraries Unlimited, 1989. 142p. $28. 0-87287-632-2.

This helpful handbook on specialized library services is not a bibliography, but is listed here because it identifies and recommends sources of information for working with the handicapped. The appendix has an annotated list of important selection aids for collection building. Recommended for all libraries.

Library Services; Disabilities

Y; A

903. **Library Instruction: A Bibliography, 1975 through 1985**, Comp. by Tian-Chu Shih. McFarland, 1986. 112p. $14.95. 0-89950-236-9.

Shih has compiled an extensive list of almost 1,100 publications on the topic of library instruction. The entries are arranged alphabetically within major sections: Libraries in General; Academic Libraries; School Libraries; and Public Libraries. An author and a title key-word index are provided. This handy bibliographic guide is recommended to all secondary school, academic, and public libraries having library instruction programs and not having access to other bibliographic tools listing such programs, such as *Library Literature* or *Education Index*. *Library Instruction*

A
904. **Library Service to Children: A Guide to the Research, Planning, and Policy Literature**, by Phyllis Van Orden. A.L.A., 1992. 141p. 425. pap. 0-8389-0584-6.

Van Orden has pulled together a wealth of information relating to library service to children; included are "policy literature, historical works, research studies, reports, and conference proceedings..." The items date from the early 1900's to the present. Types of materials included are periodical articles, books, governmental and private reports, and theses. Each entry includes complete bibliographic information, a descriptive annotation and notes on funding source, type of literature, and research method. This list should prove useful to library school students and those doing library planning among children's librarians and elementary school librarians. *Children's Libraries*

A
905. **Planning Library Facilities; A Selected, Annotated Bibliography**, by Mary Sue Stephenson. Scarecrow, 1990. 259p. $25. 0-8108-2285-7.

Stephenson has identified and described about 800 entries from 1970-1988 related to the library facility design literature. The bibliography is arranged by type of library and then by specific facility topics, e.g., children's department. Author and subject indexes are provided. This work is recommended for all libraries interested in library building design or renovation. *Library Architecture*

A
906. **Prison Librarianship: A Selective, Annotated, Classified Bibliography, 1945-1985**, by Fred R. Hartz et al. McFarland, 1987. 155p. $19.95. pap. 0-89950-258-X.

Prison librarianship has long been considered the "unwanted child" of the library world; certainly, little has been known to the outside world of librarianship. To this end, Hartz has performed a real service by selecting 185 items that cover the full gamut of prison librarianship. Collectively, they present a total view of the organization, administration, services, and programs of libraries in penal institutions. This much-needed bibliography fills a void in library literature and is therefore recommended for professional collections in library education programs, public libraries, and of course in institutional libraries.

Prison Libraries Service

A
907. **Reference Work in the University Library**, by Rolland E. Stevens and Linda C. Smith. Libraries Unlimited, 1986. 436p. $37.50. 0-87287-449-4.

This work is actually a handbook or text for basic instruction in reference services for students involved in reference work in university libraries. It is not intended for the scholar involved in serious research. However, to the extent that it covers typical holdings found in a large university library, the brief overviews of general reference sources and sources in the subject specializations can serve as a collection evaluation and development guide, and many acquisition/reference librarians will welcome it. *Reference Books*

A
908. **Serials Reference Work**, by Joseph A. Puccio. Libraries Unlimited, 1989. 228p. $34.50. 0-87287-757-4.

This excellent text explores many facets of reference service as it relates to periodicals, newspapers, annuals, and irregular serials. For acquisition and library loan purposes, there is also extensive coverage on all major serials reference sources including directories, union lists, abstracting and indexing services, and guides to microforms and databases. The annotations are both descriptive and critical. Information is current to 1988. *Serial Publications; Periodicals*

A
909. **Tools of the Profession**, 2nd ed. Special Libraries Association, 1991. 135p. $19. 0-87111-378-3.

This collection of bibliographies is intended to aid the librarian and other professionals seeking information in special subject areas. The work is divided into chapters covering many broad subjects and includes books, journal, software, etc., under each category; many of the entries are annotated. Among the subjects included are: advertising, aerospace, business and finance, chemistry, engineering, agriculture, nuclear science, physics/astronomy/mathematics, social science, and telecommunications. In addition to special libraries, this volume is recommended for all libraries conducting research or evaluating and building a collection in a particular subject area. *Bibliography; Reference Books*

Computers and Library Technology

A

910. **A Directory of Library and Information Retrieval Software for Microcomputers**, by Hilary Dyer and Alison Gunson. 3rd ed. Gower, 1988. 75p. $41.95 pap. 0-566-05586-4.

The largest section of this book enumerates microcomputer software programs (listed by name) dealing with the handling of information particularly in a library setting. Unfortunately the details given for each program are only descriptive and so this can be used best as a source for identifying available software. There are useful indexes by supplier, functions, and hardware involved. *Computer Software*

A

911. **Essential Guide to the Library IBM PC. Volume 15: Utility Software**, by Blaine Victor Morrow. Meckler, 1990, 235p. $34.95. 0-88736-529-9.

This directory lists software utility programs that have potential use in libraries in such areas needing backup and data compression utilities, display utilities, virus protection utilities, or printer utilities. Many of the programs listed are in public domain or are shareware products. None costs more than $100. The programs are arranged under specific functions and for each citation there is full bibliographic information plus a description and critique of the program. There is also a glossary of terms and information on how each type of utility could be used in a library. This is an interesting directory that opens up the possibility of all sorts of computer applications in both academic and public libraries.

Computers; Computer Software; Libraries—Software

A

912. **Information Sources in Information Technology**, ed. by David Haynes. K. G. Saur, 1990. 320p. $80. 0-408-03285-5.

This is a selective and evaluative guide to the most important sources on information technology including books, journals, conference proceedings, microforms, online databases, and CD-ROMs. Part I deals with subject areas in the field including input and output technologies, computer software and hardware, information transmission and applications. Part II looks at such sources as those that are machine readable, secondary sources and reference works, periodicals, conferences and organizations. An interesting overview of the information in this field. *Information Technology*

C; Y; A

913. **The Integrated Library: Encouraging Access to Multimedia Materials**, by Jean Weihs. Oryx, 1991. 168p. $27.50 pap. 0-89774-658-9.

This is essentially a handbook that shows how to organize and get maximum use out of video and audio tapes, computer discs, film materials, and other nonbook items in a library. There are, however, suggested readings at the end of each chapter and extensive bibliographies of selection aids.

Audiovisual Materials; Videocassettes; Motion Pictures; Audiocassettes

A

914. **Library Hi Tech Bibliography, Vol. 7**, Ed. by C. Edward Wall. Pierian Press, 1991. $45. 0-87650-297-4.

Each volume in this series contains a number of bibliographies dealing with various aspects of library technology. The number of entries in each bibliography is small, but the annotations are lengthy and evaluative. Back volumes are still available for about $45. each. Most volumes are also available on a disk or in the CD-ROM format. This source is recommended for large many libraries, but especially for those where the use of more technology is being considered. *Library Technology*

A

915. **The Library Microconsumer: MRC's Guide to Library Software**, Ed. by Robert M. Mason. Metrics Research Corp., 1986. 322p. $34.50. pap. 0-932393-03-9.

This is one of a growing number of aids to current software on library operations and management. This lists and describes about 200 currently available programs. They are arranged by function, e.g., circulation, cataloging, etc., thus making it easier to do comparative shopping to select a program to meet specific needs. Date of issue and current prices are not always provided, still this is a much needed guide and one recommended for even small libraries considering some type of computerization, even on a small scale. *Computer Software; Microcomputers*

A

916. **Microcomputers and Libraries: A Bibliographic Sourcebook, 1986-1989,** by Thomas L. Kilpatrick. Scarecrow, 1990. 1100p. $89.50. 0-8108-2392-6.

This volume supplements and updates the original volume which was published by Scarecrow (1987. $49.95. 0-8108-1977-5). Together, these present the most comprehensive guide to library microcomputing to date. Topics covered by over 5,300 entries include "microcomputer selection, implementation, applications, management, software, and hardware for libraries from 1986 through 1989." This sourcebook is recommended for all libraries involved with, or planning microcomputer services. *Microcomputers*

C; Y; A

917. **101 Software Packages to Use in Your Library: Descriptions, Evaluations, Practical Advice,** by Patrick Dewey. American Library Association, 1987. 160p. $25. pap. 0-8389-0455-6.

In this slim volume, Dewey has provided us with recommendations for over 101 computer software packages. Many are for direct library applications, e.g., acquisitions, cataloging, children's services, and circulation. There are also a number that are general purpose packages that can be used for library management, e.g., word processing, database management, and spreadsheets. Each entry includes information on the title, vendor, price, hardware requirements, possible uses, grade level (if needed), similar or related programs, and a brief description. Because the field is changing so rapidly, there is a tendency for a work like this to be outdated as soon as it is published, with many packages obsolete or no longer available. However, for the cost of only $25, this guide is recommended, even if only a few of the packages are still useful and available. Recommended for any library involved with using microcomputers for library applications. *Computer Software; Microcomputers*

Y; A

918. **Online and CD-ROM Databases in School Libraries: Readings,** by Ann Lathrop. Libraries Unlimited, 1989. 372p. $29.50. pap. 0-87287-756-6.

The beginning of this volume contains descriptions of active online database programs and the problems of integrating them into an established curriculum. Also described are several model district and state projects. This is followed by a directory of online and CD-ROM programs of particular interest to schools, a bibliography, and a useful glossary of terms. This work is recommended for secondary school and district/regional centers. *Online Databases; CD-ROM*

A

919. **Online Inc.'s Top 500 Library Microcomputer Software Application Programs.** Online Inc./Eight Bit Books, 1992. 350p. $44.95. pap. 0-910965-09-9.

The online database *Buyer's Guide to Micro Software* (also known as *Soft*) served as the basis for this compilation of micro-computer software. *Soft* is also available through Dialog and BRS. The software chosen for this volume was selected specifically for its importance to libraries and thus the work is divided into two major sections: "Library-Specific Software" and "Library-Related and/or Support Software." The software packages are then arranged alphabetically under specific topics, such as cataloging, graphics, etc. Each entry contains full data helpful for acquiring such information as version, date, cost, vendor, producer, and hardware requirements. Descriptive notes are very informative and may also list bibliographies cited and excerpts from reviews. This volume is similar to Elsevier's *Software Catalog: Microcomputers* (1990, 2 vols., $250. pap. 0-44001554-X), but it lists more library-specific software, is easier to use, and is updated more frequently. This relatively inexpensive guide is recommended for all libraries, the *Soft* version for libraries with online capabilities, and the print version for all other libraries with microcomputers.

Computer Software; Online Databases

Parapsychology, Magic, Cults, and the Occult

A
920. **Channeling: A Bibliographic Exploration**, by Joel Bjorling. Garland, 1992. 363p. $5.7. (Sects and Cults in America, 15).

In occult terms, channeling involves the medium through which a spirit guide communicates with the physical world. This bibliography contains 2,715 items divided into such areas as "Predecessors of Modern Channeling," and UFO channeling. Essays introduce each section and the bibliographic material on each book listed is accurate and complete. For use in large collections or where there is a special demand for material on the occult. *Channeling; Occult Literature*

Y; A
921. **Magic: A Reference Guide**, by Earle J. Coleman. Greenwood, 1987. 214p. $42.95. 0-313-23397-7. (American Popular Culture).

About half of this fascinating volume is in the form of several bibliographic essays on the literature, history, psychology, techniques and aesthetics of magic. The other half, in a chapter titled "The Creation of Illusion," is a list of over 650 titles on magic and a chapter titled "Biographies and Autobiographies," which lists and annotates over 100 books by and about magicians. There is also an appendix which includes a list of periodicals dealing with the topic and a listing of dealers, directories, and special collections. There are no indexes to the bibliographic citations. This interesting resource (with references to almost 1,000 titles on the topic of magic and related areas) is recommended for most public libraries and many secondary school libraries. *Magic*

A
922. **Magic, Witchcraft, and Paganism in America: A Bibliography**, by J. Gordon Mwelton and Isottas Poggi. 2nd ed. Garland, 1992. 408p. $65. 0-8153-0499-4.

The second edition of this interesting work has added over 1,000 new entries for over 2,500 total, perhaps reflecting the growing interest in witchcraft in the United States. This bibliography includes information on a number of minority religions such as Wiccan, Druid, Shamanistic, Hoodoo-Conjureman, Voodoo, Macumba, and Huna movements. A number of American witchcraft periodicals are cited as well as several foreign titles. This esoteric bibliography is recommended for any library collecting materials on American religions. *Religious Literature; Witchcraft*

A
923. **The Occult in the Western World: An Annotated Bibliography**, by Cosette Kies. Shoe String, 1986. 233p. $32.50. 0-208-02113-2.

Kies has compiled a basic bibliography of 890 citations on the occult intended primarily for the uninitiated in the field. There are several bibliographies in the field, but they all pre-date the scope of this guide and also they are intended more for the sophisticated, e.g., Thomas C. Claire's *Occult/Paranormal Bibliography*, (o.p.). The background material to the Kies work is also of an introductory nature. Each entry in the bibliography contains a well-written, but brief, annotation. Bibliographic data is also included. This work, which emphasizes reference works, is recommended for academic and public libraries that are beginning collections on the occult. *Occult Literature; Parapsychology*

A
924. **On Being Psychic: A Reading Guide**, by Rhea A. White and Rodger I. Anderson. 2nd ed. Parapsychology Sources of Information Center, 1989. 154p. $18. 0-944446-17-5.

This comprehensive listing of over 1,000 titles dealing with the psychic experience including scholarly works and popular works for the general reader. Included are books, parts of books, and journal articles from the late 19th century to 1989. Many sources listed are not easily available; however, the publisher makes an unusual offer: they claim to make photocopies available up to 60 pages for a nominal fee. This interesting and inexpensive guide is recommended for most public libraries as a reference, inter-library loan, and collection-building aid. *Psychical Research; Parapsychology*

A

925. **Parapsychology: New Sources of Information, 1973-1989**, by Rhea A White. Scarecrow, 1990. 699p. $67.50. 0-8108-2385-3.

This is a continuation of the author's 1973 edition (1973, $22.50, 0-8108-0617-7) that updates previous information and adds 800 new information sources. White defines parapsychology in the introduction as a "field which uses the scientific method to investigate phenomena for which there appear to be no normal (that is, sensory) explanations." The work is arranged in chapters covering books, journals, organizations, general sources, U.S. government reports, and theses. Entries are arranged alphabetically by author within each chapter. The chapter including books is divided into major topic subdivisions, e.g., Near-Death Experiences and Applications of Psi. *Choice* indicates that "All academic libraries (and possibly many public libraries) will find this a handy volume that receives a good amount of use." It certainly would be useful in collection building in this fascinating area. *Parapsychology*

A

926. **Social Science and the Cults: An Annotated Bibliography**, by John A. Saliba. Garland, 1990. 694p. $91. 0-8240-3719-7. (Sects and Cults in America: Bibliographic Guides, 17).

This companion to the author's *Psychiatry and the Cults* (1987, $71. 0-8240-8586-8) in the same series includes 2,219 annotated entries from the literature of the social sciences. Entries are arranged by broad categories like general works, historical studies, and specific groups. Each section is subdivided into smaller subjects. Within these sections works are arranged by author. Books, chapters in books, and articles are included; all in English and published between 1970 and 1989. The annotations are brief and descriptive. As well as author and subject indexes, there is a an index to sects, cults, and movements. This will be useful in public and academic libraries. *Cults*

Political Science and Government

General and Miscellaneous

A

927. **Information Sources of Political Science**, by Frederick L. Holler. 4th ed. ABC-Clio, 1986. 417p. $89.50. 0-87436-375-6.

This is a listing of 2,423 annotated sources on political science. The guide is divided into three sections: the first is a discussion of political theory, the second and largest is a listing of the reference sources under such topics as general references, the social sciences, American government, politics, public law, international relations and organizations, political theory and public administration. Works included are books, periodicals, radio and television broadcasts, newspapers, micropubications, electronic sources, and government documents. The third section is a four part index, by author, title, subject and type of material. There is extensive coverage on databases and online services. This will be valuable in public library research collections. *Political Science*

A*

928. **Political Science: A Guide to Reference and Information Sources**, by Henry E. York. Libraries Unlimited, 1990. 250p. $38. 0-87287-794-9. (References Sources in the Social Sciences, 4).

York, a social sciences and history librarian, has compiled an excellent bibliography which is somewhat more recent than a similar work: Holler's *Information Sources of Political Science*. It also differs from Holler's work in that the annotations are critical as well as descriptive. It contains over 800 major resources for the study of political sciences and related fields. It is divided into many chapters which include general political science reference works, social science disciplines other than political science, international and comparative politics, American government and politics, other nations, political ideology and theory, and public policy. Most of the titles were published from 1980 to 1987; they are arranged by type of work under each chapter heading. Author/title and subject indexes complete the book. This up-to-date, selective bibliography is highly recommended for all academic and many public libraries as a reference tool and a collection evaluation and development guide. *Political Science*

Ideologies

Y; A

929.   **Apartheid: A Selective Annotated Bibliography, 1979-1987**, by Sherman E. Pyatt. Garland, 1990. 169p. $25. 0-8240-7637-0.

Pyatt has compiled a selected list of writings which deal with the "effects of apartheid on the people of South Africa and its indirect effect on the world." This bibliography of more than 800 items covers the period 1979-1987 and thus updates Peter Potgeiter's outstanding historical work: *Index to Literature on Race Relations in South Africa* (1979, o.p.). The entries, which include books, periodical articles, and United States and United Nations documents, are grouped according to format within the general subject chapters: Economics and Labor Conditions; Politics and Government; Religion; World Views; and Anti-Government Resistance. Each entry has a short descriptive annotation. An author index and a much too general subject index are also provided. Because popular as well as scholarly titles are included, this bibliography is highly recommended for all types of libraries including those in many secondary schools.

Apartheid; South Africa

A

930.   **Communism and Anti-Communism in the United States: An Annotated Guide to Historical Writings**, by John Earl Haynes. Garland, 1987. 321p. $56. 0-8240-8520-5.

In a 2,086-item bibliography of books, periodical articles, reviews, and dissertations, the author chronicles the history of the Communist party in the United States with emphasis on the period from 1917 to its disintegration in the mid 1950s. This thorough review of the literature is divided into 37 subject-oriented chapters with many subsections. Most entries are annotated, and there is a thorough author index. For large public libraries.   *Communism*

A

931.   **Communism in the World Since 1945: An Annotated Bibliography**, by Susan K. Kinnell. ABC-Clio, 1987. 450p. $99.50 0-87436-169-9.

This extensive bibliography of 4,151 items includes books, articles, and dissertations culled from databases produced at ABC-Clio. It is arranged in geographically oriented chapters such as one on Asia and another on the Soviet Union. Subdivisions are used, and the final chapter deals with overviews and other miscellaneous entries. All items are annotated or abstracted and can be accessed by author and subject indexes. There are also lists of acronyms, abbreviations, periodicals cited, and abstracters. For academic and large public library collections.   *Communism*

A

932.   **From Radical Left to Extreme Right: A Bibliography of Current Periodicals of Protest, Controversy, Advocacy, or Dissent, with Dispassionate Content-Summaries to Guide Librarians and Other Educators**, by Gail Skidmore and Theodore Jurgen Spahn. 3rd ed. Scarecrow, 1987. 491p. $59.50 0-8108-1967-8.

The subtitle of this bibliography describes the work accurately—it is a listing of periodicals from extremist organizations. They are arranged under 21 different subject headings such as: "Marxist-Socialist Left," "Anti-Communist," and "Race Supremacist." Excellent bibliographic information is supplied, plus lengthy annotations and evaluations. There are geographic, subject, title, editor, and publisher indexes. Large collections will need this information on radical and conservative publications. A work of somewhat similar scope is *Spectrum*.   *Periodicals; Radicals and Radicalism; Right and Left (Political Science)*

A

933.   **Guide to the American Right: Directory and Bibliography, 1992**, by Laird Wilcox. L. Wilcox, 1992. $29.95 pap. 0-933592-67-1.

Like its companion volume, *Guide to the American Left, 1992* (1992, $29.95 pap. 0-933592-68-X), this volume appears annually and consists of six parts: a list of organizations with addresses, a bibliography of serials and presses, the organizations and publications arranged by zip code, a section on Canadian organizations and serials, and an overview essay, plus a general bibliography on the American Right (or Left). Collectively, the two volumes represent over 7,500 organizations and publications. These volumes will have some value in large libraries. A work of somewhat comparable scope is *From Radical Left to Extreme Right*.   *Conservatism; Radicals and Radicalism; Right and Left (Political Science)*

A

934.   **Sources in European Political History, Volume One: The European Left**, by Chris Cook and Geoff Pugh. Facts on File, 1987. 237p. $40. 0-8160-1016-1. (Sources in European Political History).

This particular volume provides an "outline guide to the surviving personal papers of over 1000 individuals active in the socialist, labor, radical and revolutionary movements in Europe." The emphasis is on the period between 1848 and 1945. The work is arranged alphabetically by personal names with content notes on the collections and their locations. The scope and purpose of this bibliography will limit its usefulness to large academic institutions. The two other volumes in this series are *Sources in European Political History, Volume Two: Diplomacy and International Affairs* (1989, $40. 0-8160-1756-5) and *Sources in European Political History, Volume Three: War and Resistance* (1992, $40. 0-8160-1757-3).

Europe—History

International Relations

A

935.   **American Intelligence, 1775-1990: A Bibliographical Guide**, by Neal H. Petersen. Regina, 1992. 406p. $49.50. 0-941690-45-8. (The New War/Peace Bibliography Series, No. 2).

The subtitle of this bibliography is "published sources on espionage, covert action, counter intelligence, domestic intelligence, technical collection, cryptology, research and analysis, policy and process, organization and oversight, and other aspects of U.S. intelligence operations since the American Revolution." This practical guide draws on unclassified material and covers books as well as articles from both scholarly and popular journals. After an introductory essay on intelligence scholarship and the literature associated with it, the remainder of the book is arranged chronologically into 13 chapters, each with topical subdivisions. There are cross-references by author and subject. Because of the wide scope of the period covered and the high selectivity used to produce the contents, this bibliography will be useful in both academic libraries as well as some public libraries with a demand for materials on American history.

United States—History; Intelligence Operations; Espionage

A

936.   **The American Peace Movement**, by Charles F. Howlett. G. K. Hall, 1991. 416p. $40. 0-8161-1836-1.

Howlett surveyed a number of collections and hundreds of books on the peace movement in the United States in order to compile this very comprehensive, annotated bibliography of 1,600 entries. The work is divided into 12 major sections which include general reference works, historical accounts, leaders and thinkers, women and peace, religious pacifism, disarmament, etc. In addition to an introduction to each chapter, primary sources, books, articles, biographies, anthologies, and government documents are included. Author and subject indexes complete this useful work which is recommended for most academic libraries and those public libraries which have a particular interest in the topic.   *Peace*

A

937.   **Global/International Issues and Problems**, by Lynn S. Parisi and Robert D. LaRue, Jr. ABC-Clio, 1989. 222p. $39. 0-87436-536-8. (Social Studies Resources for Secondary Schools).

This volume covers an enormous amount of material on current international issues. After an introductory essay, plus chronologies, biographies of important people, and other background information, there are lists of agencies and organizations and their publications, plus annotated bibliographies of both key reference works, as well as print and nonprint classroom materials and resources. Excellent for both the librarian and social studies teachers in senior high schools. Some public libraries might also find it useful.   *International Relations; Social Problems; International Agencies*

A

938.   **Global Terrorism: A Historical Bibliography**, by Susan Robitaille Ontiveros. ABC-Clio, 1986. 168p. $49.50. 0-87436-453-1. (Research Guides, 16).

This guide includes almost 600 abstracts of periodical articles published from 1965 to 1985 on the topic of global terrorism. Divided geographically, this work includes both English language and foreign publications. This is primarily a research tool, although the references to various periodicals can give acquisition guidance in large libraries.   *Terrorism*

A
939.   **A Guide to the Sources of United States Military History: Supplement III**, ed. by Robin Higham and Donald J. Mrozek. Archon\Shoe String, 1992. 530p. $47.50. 0-208-02214-7.

The first two supplements to the original guide that appeared fifteen years ago are still available. Supplement I (Archon\Shoe String, 1981, $42.50, 0-208-01750-X) and II (Archon\Shoe String, 1986, $45. 0-208-02072-1) each cover about five years of publication, as does supplement III. In a series of bibliographical essays on various subjects, the writings of the period on the history of the U.S. military forces are reviewed and commented on. Books, articles, and scholarly publications are included. Each chapter ends with a listing of the materials discussed. There are author and title indexes. For large collections.

United States—Armed Forces

A
940.   **International Negotiations: A Bibliography**, by Amos Lakos. Westview, 1989. 417p. $54.50 0-8133-7558-4.

Using sources such as books, journal articles, conference papers, government documents, and dissertations, the author has collected 5,400 citations on international negotiations published in the twentieth century and arranged them in 12 subject chapters covering topics like: negotiation processes and theories, psychological and sociological aspects, arms control negotiations, summit meetings, American diplomacy, and international trade negotiations. Chapter divisions are by type of material. Unfortunately, the works are not annotated but there are subject, author and title indexes.   *International Relations*

A
941.   **International Terrorism: A Bibliography**, by Amos Lakos. Westview, 1986. 481p. $65. 0-8133-7157-0.

This bibliography covers the period from the late 1960s through early 1986 with a total of 5,622 English-language entries for periodical articles, books, chapters in books, U.S. and U.N. publications, conference papers, and dissertations. The material is arranged by broad subjects like reference works, theories of terrorism, psychological and social aspects, counter measures, and media and terrorism. There are further breakdowns by type of material and geography. The works are not annotated but there are excellent author and subject indexes. This is more comprehensive than ABC-Clio's *Global Terrorism*, but the latter is annotated.   *Terrorism*

A
942.   **Military and Strategic Policy: An Annotated Bibliography**, Comp. by Benjamin R. Beede. Greenwood Press, 1990. 334p. $59.95. 0-313-26000-1. (Bibliographies and Indexes in Military Studies, 2).

Beede has compiled an interesting bibliography of almost 2,000 English-language items on U.S. military and strategic policy during the 1950's through the 1970's. All of the sources were published before 1988 and include books, journal articles, and government publications, such as Papers of the Presidents from Eisenhower to Reagan and Department of Defense reports. Special attention is paid to certain events such as the Cuban missile crisis and the Vietnamese conflict. This bibliography, while not comprehensive, is broad in scope and level. It would be of interest to undergraduate students as an introduction and to researchers as a review of the subject. Recommended for most academic libraries and many public libraries with special collections in the subject.   *United States—History, Military*

A
943.   **Military History of the United States: An Annotated Bibliography**, by Susan K. Kinnell. ABC-Clio, 1986. 333p. $85. 0-87436-474-4. (Clio Bibliography Series, N. 23).

Drawing on the huge database prepared by ABC-Clio, *America: History and Life*, this bibliography contains about 3,300 entries for books and articles that deal with the military history of the United States. Using a chronological approach, the material is divided in to sections such as "1860 to 1900" and "1901 to 1945." There is a final chapter on the post World War II era. The sources cited are international in scope, and each entry is annotated briefly. There are author and key word indexes. This will be useful in American history reference collections in public and college libraries.

United States—History; Military History—United States

Y; A

944.   **The Nuclear Arms Race: A Digest with Bibliographies,** by William Gay and Michael Pearson. American Library Association, 1987. 289p. $25. 0-8389-0467-X. (Last Quarter Century, 1).

Although 1991 saw many developments which led to a lessening of the threat of a nuclear war between the superpowers, the nuclear threat remains, particularly through the proliferation of nuclear armaments in third world nations. This work presents an excellent overview in the first eight chapters of the book. This narrative is followed by a bibliography of books, articles, and reports. Many of the entries are fully annotated. All provide complete bibliographic data. As well, there is a 26-page appendix which provides additional references to the literature in the field. This comprehensive guide is recommended for reference and as an aid to collection development on an important topic for all secondary school, academic, and public libraries.   *Nuclear War; Nuclear Weapons; Arms Control*

A

945.   **The Nuclear Present: A Guide to Recent Books on Nuclear War, Weapons, the Peace Movement, and Related Issues, with a Chronology of Nuclear Events, 1789-1991,** by Grant Burns. Scarecrow, 1992. 633p. $69.50. 0-8108-2619-4.

This topically arranged bibliography includes works published between 1984 and 1991. Citations include books, government publications, periodicals, and newsletters and covers all aspects of the nuclear issue, including nuclear weapons, testing, the arms race, proliferation, and strategic defense. Also included are related titles on such topics as ethical and religious issues and peace and disarmament. Even with the ending of the Cold War, the concerns are still very much present.

Bibliographic data is provided, and all entries have a brief annotations. Access is facilitated by four indexes: author, title, subject, and a separate index for the very last chapter: "A Nuclear Chronology." This well-balanced bibliography updates Burns' earlier work *Atomic Papers...* (1984. $27.50. 0-8108-1692-X) and complements a similar work with a more singular focus: *The Atomic Bomb* by Hans Graetzer. *The Nuclear Present* is recommended for all types of libraries and will be useful for reference as well as collection development.   *Arms Control; Nuclear War*

A

946.   **Ocean Politics and War: An Annotated Bibliography,** by James C. F. Wang. Greenwood, 1991. 243p. $49.95. 0-313-27925-X.

Wang has provided a timely overview of recent literature (from the 1960's to late 1980's) on ocean and maritime law. Included is a variety of sources such as reference sources, articles from popular and specialized periodicals, monographs, and yearbooks. Among the topics covered in this bibliography are basic/general principles, technological developments, environmental concerns, pollution, exploitation of natural resources, international law, and oceanography. Even related areas are included, such as UN activities and scientific research. Only a limited number of the more than 200 entries are annotated; however, a detailed subject index helps in identifying and accessing sources. This bibliography is recommended for academic and special libraries with a need for general and specific material in this field.

Maritime Law; International Law; Ocean

A

947.   **Peace Resource Book 1988-1989: A Comprehensive Guide to the Issues, Organizations, and Literature,** Ed. by Carl Conetta. Ballinger/Harvard Business, 1988. 440p. $17.95. 0-88730-289-0.

Concern for world peace has not ended with the termination of the Cold War. This revised and updated edition lists about 300 national peace advocacy groups; describes peace-oriented educational programs; and indexes about 7,000 national and local peace groups in the United States, both alphabetically and by zip code. The final section, "Guide to Peace-Related Literature," arranges published resources, including reference works, books, pamphlets, etc. by subject headings and includes full bibliographic information for ordering (unfortunately, annotations are not included). This timely and inexpensive sourcebook is recommended for reference and collection building for all public libraries.   *Peace; Arms Control*

A

948.   **The Reader's Guide to Intelligence Periodicals,** by Hayden B. Peake. National Intelligence Book Center, 1992. 250p. $19.95. pap. 1-878292-00-5.

Hayden, an ex-CIA and Defense Intelligence Agency official, has compiled this interesting and comprehensive bibliography of periodicals reflecting a broad spectrum of views on intelligence, from the extreme right to the extreme left. The work is divided into eight sections reflecting the various types of journals in the field, for example, there are sections on intelligence-specific journals, out-of-print journals, and limited distribution journals. Entries include scope, kind of article, addresses, and price. A title index completes the work. This rather esoteric bibliography is recommended for academic and special libraries supporting intelligence programs as well as large public libraries. *Intelligence Operations*

A

949. **Terrorism: An Annotated Bibliography**, by Susheela Bhan et al. Concept Publishing/South Asia Books, 1990. 338p. $44. 81-7022-256-7. (Concepts in Communication Informatics & Librarianship, 9).

A number of well-done bibliographies have been produced during the 1980's on terrorism. This bibliography's best feature is that its 2,800 sources have been taken from several large online databases and print resources such as *CIS, PAIS,* and *Sociological Abstracts*. This means it can be updated easily online. About a third of the entries include abstracts. Full bibliographic information is provided throughout. Also, subject and author indexes conclude the work. Similar bibliographies on the topic include: Lakos', *International Terrorism*, and Mickolus and Fleming's, *Terrorism, 1980-1987* (see next entry). The Bhan bibliography is recommended for medium to large collections depending on other bibliographies held.

Terrorism

A

950. **Terrorism, 1980-1987: A Selectively Annotated Bibliography**, Comp. by Edward F. Mickolus and Peter A. Fleming. Greenwood, 1988. 314p. $65. 0-313-26248-9. (Bibliographies and Indexes in Law and Political Science, 8).

This continuation of Mickolus's *Literature of Terrorism* (1980, $75. 0-313-222654-7) is another valuable addition to the bibliographic literature on terrorism. This compares favorably with Lakos' excellent *International Terrorism*, but there are several differences worth mentioning: Lakos includes publications back to 1960, has only English-language publications, and has a detailed subject index. This bibliography includes publications from 1980 through 1986, includes non-English citations, and has no subject index. On the other hand, Bhan's *Terrorism* is similar to both and includes slightly more sources and many sources which are several years more recent. Smaller libraries may want any one of the three bibliographies, whereas larger libraries may want all three. *Terrorism*

A

951. **Terrorism, 1980-1990: A Bibliography**, by Amos Lakos. Westview, 1991. 443p. $55. 0-8133-8035-9.

Lakos cites almost 6,000 English language publications on terrorism, most published between 1986-1990. Actually, this volume might be considered an update of his *International Terrorism: A Bibliography* (1986) which included works published from the 1960's to the mid-1980's. The items are arranged by type of publication, such as, encyclopedias, periodicals, etc.; by topic, such as psychological and social implications; and by geographic area. As with his earlier work, the selected titles are not annotated; however, there is a detailed index, as well as a detailed table of contents facilitating subject access. Terrorism is spreading worldwide, and as a result there is a proliferation of publications on the subject. Other bibliographies that might be considered are: Bhan's, *Terrorism: An Annotated Bibliography* (1990), and Mickolus and Flemming's, *Terrorism, 1980-1987* (1988). Still, despite the lack of annotations, Lakos' work is the most comprehensive and up-to-date and should receive special consideration, especially for advanced undergraduate and graduate academic libraries. *Terrorism*

Government and Public Administration

Y; A

952. **The American Presidency: A Bibliography**, by Fenton S. Martin and Robert U. Goehlert. Congressional Quarterly, 1987. 506p. $75. ($160 with companion volume cited below). 0-87187-415-6.

Martin and Fenton have designed this bibliography of more than 8,000 citations to serve as a companion to their *American Presidents: A Bibliography* (see entry below). However, these bibliographies do not have duplicate entries, have separate indexes, and can be used independently of one another. The entries in this bibliography deal with "the office of the presidency, including its history, development, powers, and relations with other branches of the federal government." Like its companion, this guide is intended for librarians for collection development, researchers, students, and the general reader, and includes scholarly as well as popular works. *Presidents—United States*

Y; A
953.   **The American Presidents: An Annotated Bibliography**, by Norman S. Cohen. Salem Press, 1989. 202p. $40. 0-89356-658-6. (Magill Bibliographies).

This addition to the Magill Bibliographies intended for the general reader, continues the long-standing emphasis on quality and scholarship. The more than 750 books include biographies, autobiographies, and studies of the presidents' positions in United States History. The works are divided into three sections: bibliographies about the presidents and presidency, general studies on the presidency, and then titles related to the individual presidents. The title entries, which include annotations of 50 to 100 words, are arranged within each section alphabetically by author. This bibliography would be particularly useful for secondary school and undergraduate student reports. It is recommended for all libraries serving that audience as well as the general reader.   *Presidents—United States*

Y; A
954.   **American Presidents: A Bibliography**, by Fenton S. Martin and Robert U. Goehlert. Congressional Quarterly, 1987. 756p. $145. ($160 with companion volume cited above). 0-87187-416-4.

Compiled by two university library bibliographers, this bibliography of about 13,000 citations, along with its companion volume *The American Presidency* (entry 952), constitute perhaps the most ambitious project of its kind covering the American presidents and the presidency. This work includes books, articles, and dissertations arranged in chronological order by president under several major headings: biographies, private life, public career, presidential years, and writings; for many of the presidents, these categories are subdivided into more specific areas. The titles, which are not annotated, include titles for both the scholar and the general reader. Though useful to high school students, the cost will undoubtedly relegate its purchase to the larger public and academic library.   *Presidents—United States*

A
955.   **Encyclopedia of Public Affairs Information Sources**, by Paul Wasserman et al. Gale, 1988. 550p. $145. 0-8103-2191-2.

This guide to information sources lists about 8,000 items under 290 subjects such as atomic power, religion, roads, climate, collective bargaining, and other topics related to public affairs and social issues. There are 12 kinds of sources listed, including abstracts and indexes, annuals and reviews, encyclopedias and dictionaries, periodicals, databases, institutes and organizations, and statistical sources. There are neither annotations nor indexes, but the book has good cross-referencing and an introductory section that gives details about the contents. This is a unique source in the field of public affairs and should have value in public libraries.   *Public Affairs; Social Problems*

A
956.   **Ethics and Public Policy: An Annotated Bibliography** by Peter J. Bergerson. Garland, 1988. 200p. $30. 0-8240-6632-4 (Public Affairs and Administration, Vol. 20; Garland Reference Library of Social Science, Vol. 414).

Questions involving ethics and various areas of public administration are always examined, particularly when tales of corruption in government are exposed. This fine bibliography explores many facets of this question in citations to 330 scholarly books, dissertations and articles. The work is organized into nine sections covering topics like state and local governments, health care issues, codes of ethics, foreign policy, and decision making. Entries are annotated descriptively, and there are indexes by subject and author. Academic libraries and some specialized public library collections will find this useful.

Ethics; Public Policy

Y; A
957.   **The Presidency: A Research Guide**, by Robert U. Goehlert and Martin S. Fenton. ABC-Clio, 1985. 341p. $49.50. 0-87436-373-X.

The focus of this guide is the American presidency as an institution; however, the president as an individual is also considered. Both popular and scholarly primary and secondary sources are considered. The work is intended for both the researcher and the general reader. The sources are annotated in terms of their relevancy to the study of the presidency. This comprehensive guide is recommended for some high school libraries, most academic, and many public libraries.   *Presidents—United States*

A
958. **Public Administration Desk Book**, by James R. Coleman and Robert E. Dugan. Government Research Publications, 1990. 175p. $35. 0-931684-12-9.

Coleman and Dugan have compiled a practical annotated bibliography on public administration. The work is divided into seven parts generally by type of resources included in this very diverse bibliography, for example, directories, statistical sources, indexes, handbooks, encyclopedias and dictionaries, periodicals, and online and CD-ROM databases. Each entry is annotated with both descriptive and critical notes. Full bibliographic information is also provided. There are detailed author/title and association indexes and a very specific subject index. There is an appendix listing a core reference library in public administration and another listing other useful guides. This bibliography is intended for a diverse audience from beginning students, to researchers to practitioners of public administration. It is recommended for all libraries serving such a clientele. *Public Administration*

A
959. **Public Administration Research Guide**, by Virginia R. Cherry and Marc Holzer. Garland, 1992. 253p. $35. 0-8240-7643-5.

Cherry and Holzer provide us with a fine bibliography of over 750 items related to public administration. Each of the 15 chapters deals with a particular aspect of research in public affairs/public administration and annotated guides to the literature are included. The work is recommended for academic libraries serving public administration programs as well as public libraries with special collections in public affairs and public administration. *Public Administration; Public Affairs*

A
960. **The Speakers of the U.S. House of Representatives: A Bibliography, 1789-1984**, by Donald R. Kennon. Johns Hopkins, 1986. 323p. $48. 0-8018-2786-8. (Studies in Historical and Political Science).

This is a guide to materials on the institution of the Speaker of the House of Representatives and the careers of the 46 men who held this office from 1789 through 1984. There are references to books, articles, dissertations and manuscript collections. Following a section on general works, the bibliography is divided into four major historical periods again with an opening chapter on general works followed by coverage for each individual Speaker. Within each of these sections, the works are arranged by type of material (e.g., books, periodicals articles, speeches, correspondence). A total of 4,280 items are cited. Annotations are given only for works written by the Speakers or items of exceptional importance. There is an excellent table of contents and a detailed subject index. This is a unique and important tool on the study of the Congress and will be particularly valuable in academic libraries.

United States—Congress—House of Representatives

Sociology

General and Miscellaneous

A
961. **Discrimination and Prejudice: An Annotated Bibliography**, by Halford H. Fairchild and others. Westerfield Enterprises, 1991. 312p. $89.95; $59.95 pap. 0-942259-03-0; 0-942259-02-5.

In this work, there are over 3,000 bibliographical entries that deal with discrimination and how it affects the major ethnic groups in America. About half deal with African Americans and another 600 are on Hispanics. Other major chapters are on Asian and Native Americans with a last one that deals with other ethnic groups. In each of these chapters the materials are subdivided by such topics as bias, criminal justice, education, women, housing, and health. Both the citations and annotations are brief. Unfortunately, most of the entries date before 1985 and so already this bibliography needs updating. It will, nevertheless, have value in academic and public libraries or those libraries serving large minority groups.

Prejudices; African Americans; Hispanic Americans;
United States—Race Relations; Minorities; Discrimination

A
962. **Rural Sociology: A Bibliography of Bibliographies**, by Judy Berndt. Scarecrow, 1986. 177p. $20. 0-8108-1860-4.

Berndt has compiled an impressive number of 434 bibliographies on the literature of rural sociology. All of the works were published since 1970 and all are in the English-language. Several large collections and databases were scanned including the National Agricultural Library and the RLIN database of the

Research Libraries Group in order to make this bibliography of bibliographies as comprehensive as possible. The volume is divided into 16 chapters by broad topic, e.g., "Overview" and "Rural Development." Some of the bibliographies are quite brief; however, almost all are readily available from sources such as ERIC or NTIS. Many are foreign imprints and much more difficult to acquire, but probably only needed by the very large research library. This bibliography of bibliographies is recommended as an important tool for research, as an inter-library loan aid, and as a guide to collection development for most academic libraries and all but the small public libraries. *Sociology, Rural*

A

963. **Sociology: A Guide to Reference and Information Sources**, by Stephen Aby. Libraries Unlimited, 1987. 231p. $36. 0-87287-498-2. (Reference Sources in the Social Sciences).

This guide to the literature of sociology lists and annotates a total of 650 important works in three sections. The first lists general reference works in social science that have good coverage on sociology, and the second describes important sources in related disciplines like education, social work, and anthropology. In these sections, works are arranged by type of reference source such as guides to the literature, indexes and abstracts, encyclopedias, dictionaries, and handbooks. The third and largest section deals first with general sociology and then with 23 subdivisions such as gerontology, marriage and the family, women's studies, and the sociology of sports. In the general section, there is a list of 60 important journals in the field. Annotations are thorough and both descriptive and evaluative. There is material on databases, lists of publishers, professional organizations, societies, and research centers, as well as author/title and subjects indexes. An excellent guide for public libraries and colleges. Two other introductory guides that contain good bibliographies are Pauline Bart's *The Student Sociologist's Handbook* (McGraw, 1986, $10.12 0-07-554884-4) and T. B. Bottomore's *Sociology: A Guide to Problems and the Literature* (Unwin, 1986, $39.95 0-04-300108-4). *Sociology*

A

964. **Welfare Reform: A Bibliographic Guide to Recent Sources**, Comp. by Richard Hug and Timothy Sutherland. Vance Publications, 1988. 22p. $6.25. 1-55590-747-4.

This bibliography of 115 citations is on a timely topic and it provides a comprehensive list that can serve as a "starting point for persons wishing to become well informed about welfare reform." A variety of information sources, books, articles, bibliographies, and government documents, are arranged alphabetically by author or title. Full bibliographic data is provided. To order, send $6.25 to: Vance Publications, PO Box 229, Monticello, IL 61856 *Welfare—United States*

A

965. **Women in Sociology: A Bio-Bibliographical Sourcebooks**, Ed. by Mary Jo Deegan. Greenwood, 1991. 468p. $75. 0-313-26-85-0.

Deegan, a feminist scholar, has edited the most current bio-bibliographic source documenting the work of women in the field of sociology. All sociological eras from 1840 to the present are represented with the 51 women included in this volume. As well, an attempt was made to include women throughout the world and to represent ethnic, political, and ideological diversity. The lengthy entries are arranged alphabetically and include summaries of achievements, short biographical sketches, sources for critiques of individual's works, and selective bibliographies. Name and subject bibliographies are also provided. This scholarly work is recommended for most academic and public libraries as a reference source and guide to collection building in both sociology and women's studies. *Sociology; Women in Sociology*

Abortion

A

966. **Abortion**, by Marie Costa. ABC-Clio, 1991. 300p. $39.95. 0-87436-602-1. (Contemporary World Series)

Like the other titles in this excellent series, this timely book presents a balanced overview of issues concerning this "controversial" topic. It deals with the historical and social aspects of the subject, and it includes a chronology of events, biographical sketches, and a directory of organizations (including their major publications). However, its importance for collection development are the up-to-date and annotated lists of print and nonprint sources for further study. Recommended for all libraries from the secondary school level up as both a reference and selection resource. *Abortion*

A

967. **Pro-Choice/Pro-Life: An Annotated , Selected Bibliography (1972-1989)**, Comp. by Richard Fitzsimmons and Joan P. Diana. Greenwood, 1991. 251p. $45. 0-313-27579-3.

This timely bibliography covers both sides of the very controversial topic of abortion drawing largely from book and periodical literature. Entries are arranged alphabetically by author or title. While full bibliographic information is provided, only brief descriptive annotations are included. This important bibliography prepared for the general reader is recommended as a companion volume to Winter's more academically-oriented *Psychological and Medical Aspects of Induced Abortion*. Recommended as a guide to interlibrary loans and collection-building for academic and public libraries. *Abortion*

A

968. **Psychological and Medical Aspects of Induced Abortion: A Selective, Annotated Bibliography, 1970-1986**, Comp. by Eugenia B. Winter. Green-wood Press, 1988. 162p. $45. 0-313-26100-8. (Bibliographies and Indexes in Women's Studies, no. 7).

Winter defines induced abortion as "elective (voluntary) abortion." Books, parts of books, articles, dissertations, and audiovisual materials are included among the more than 500 selected items listed in this bibliography. Recognizing the emotional and controversial aspects of this topic, the author attempted to present items with impartiality. The annotated entries are arranged alphabetically under broad topics related to induced abortion, including general works, counseling, and abortion techniques. Full bibliographical information is included. An author/subject/title index is also provided. This bibliography on a very timely and important topic is recommended for all academic and public libraries for reference, interlibrary loans and collection development. *Abortion*

Aging

A

968a. **Aging with Style and Savvy: Books and Films on Challenges Facing Adults of All Ages**, by Denise Donavin. ALA, 1990. $27.50. pap. 0-8389-0526-9.

A listing of more than 250 books, films, and videos on the concerns and challenges of aging, arranged under such topics as Health, Housing, Travel, Finance, and Family. A variety of literary forms are included such as fiction, poetry, and drama. An excellent source for selection as well as programming with senior citizens, or with those working with senior citizens. *Aging; Senior Citizens*

A

969. **Building Library Collections on Aging: A Selection Guide and Core Collection**, by Mary Jo Brazil. ABC-Clio, 1990. 174p. $45. 0-87436-559-7.

Brazil, a former gerontology librarian, has provided us with an excellent guide to collection development on a timely and growing concern, i.e., providing adequate and appropriate library services to our growing senior population. Criteria for selecting, as well as basic selection aids for this special audience are cited. In addition, 500 annotated titles making up a core collection of nonfiction books, periodicals, newsletters, documents, films, videocassettes, and databases makes up the heart of this much needed tool. This guide and bibliography is highly recommended for all public libraries as an evaluative tool and aid in collection building. *Aging; Senior Citizens*

A

970. **Choices and Challenges: An Older Adult Reference Series**. ABC-Clio, 1990- . $45. per volume.

This is a series of sourcebooks on concerns and issues facing the elderly today. Part I of each book analyzes the topic in narrative form, and Part II lists organizations that seniors can contact for help and information. Also in this part are bibliographies of books, periodicals, government documents, films and videos, and databases. The latter section will be of help in public libraries in collection building. The first titles in this series are Elizabeth Vierck's *Paying for Health Care after Age 65* (1990, $45. 0-87436-095-1), *Housing Options and Services for Older Adults* (1990, $45. 0-87436-144-3) by Ann E. Gillespie and Katrinka Smith Sloan, *Travel and Older Adults* (1991, $45. 0-87436-573-2) by Allison St. Claire, *Older Workers* (1990, $45. 0-87436-259-8) by Sara E. Rix, *Volunteerism and Older Adults* (1990, $45. 0-87436-562-7) by Mary K. Kouri, and Gregory A. Hinrichsen's *Mental Health Problems and Older Adults* (1990, $45. 0-87436-240-7).

Senior Citizens; Health Care; Housing; Travel; Work; Voluntarism; Mental Health

A

971. The Encyclopedia of Aging, by George L. Maddox and others. Springer, 1987. 890p. $96. 0-8261-4840-9.

Using contributions from over 200 scholars, the editors have compiled a popular encyclopedia that explores about 500 terms and concepts associated with the topic of aging. Of importance in collection building is the large bibliography of 2,000 references to various kinds of printed sources. This will be of value in large collections particularly where a large percentage of the patrons are elderly.

Aging; Senior Citizens

A

972. Encyclopedia of Senior Citizens Information Sources, by Paul Wasserman et al. Gale, 1987. 505p. $155. 0-8103-2192-0.

Under a total of 300 subject headings such as Alzheimer's disease, social security benefits, adult education, diets, Keogh plans, and medical ethics, hundred of resources are listed under various forms such as associations and societies, abstracts and indexes, conferences, bibliographies, legal works, databases, and statistical sources. This is both a fine starting point for research and a good collection-building tool for public libraries. *Senior Citizens*

A

973. Families and Aging: A Selected Annotated Bibliography, by Jean M. Coyle. Greenwood, 1991. 208p. $45. 0-313-27211-5.

This scholarly bibliography covers materials published in gerontology from 1980 to 1990. The 700 items cover chiefly books, articles, and dissertations and are organized into eleven chapters on such topics as grandparents, widowhood, adult children and living arrangements. Each citation is annotated. Because of the nature of the material included, this volume will be most useful in academic libraries.

Aging; Gerontology

A

974. Federal Public Policy on Aging Since 1960: An Annotated Bibliography, by William E. Oriol. Greenwood, 1987. 141p. $42.95. 0-313-25286-6.

This specialized bibliography is in two sections. The first lists and annotates 162 entries for books and journal articles on federal policy in general, and the second with 589 listings deals with specific programs and polices like housing, health and minorities. Most of the items are from the 1970s through 1986. There is an appendix on organizations and federal agencies and author and title indexes. For large collections that serve a substantial elderly population. *Aging; Senior Citizens*

A

975. A Guide to Research in Gerontology: Strategies and Resources, by Dorothea R. Zito and George V. Zito. Greenwood, 1988. 130p. $39.50 0-313-25904-6.

This manual describes how to do research in gerontology and covers such areas as how to design a search strategy, how to evaluate sources, and where to locate various kinds of information. For collection development purposes, there are four useful appendixes: one that lists and annotates reference books, another on indexes and abstracts, and others on journals and databases. There is a brief subject index. For large public libraries. Another bibliography in this area is Diana K. Harris' *The Sociology of Aging* (Harper, 1990, $41.50 0-06-042655-1). *Gerontology*

A

976. The Image of Older Adults in the Media: An Annotated Bibliography, by Frank Nuessel. Greenwood, 1992. 181p. $47.95. 0-313-28018-5. (Bibliographies and Indexes in Gerontology, 18).

Nuessel has compiled an interesting bibliography of more than 550 items primarily covering the past 20 years. The increase of literature about the aged is directly related to the increase in the number of aged and to the increase of our awareness and concern for aging as a social issue. The resources listed are from print and nonprint sources which are divided into 21 chapters covering attitudes about and portrayals of older adults in humor, television, art, literature, and even in cartoons. Under each chapter, the annotated entries are arranged alphabetically. The number of citations within each chapter varies from 2 to over 150. Specific subject and author indexes are also provided. This work is recommended for all academic libraries with collections in gerontology, as well as public libraries with a particular concern for the aged.

Senior Citizens; Gerontology

A

977.   **Retirement: An Annotated Bibliography**, by John J. Miletich. Greenwood, 1986. 147p. $39.95. 0-313-24815-X. (Bibliographies and Indexes in Gerontology).

As our population gets older, our society becomes more concerned with the impact of this population on health, economics, social welfare, recreation, and education. This bibliography is the second in the series on gerontology. The first, *Elder Neglect and Abuse: An Annotated Bibliography* (Greenwood, 1985, 223p. $45. 0-313-24589-4), set the stage; this volume on retirement deals with the same above mentioned concerns but more so on the impact on individuals as they face retirement, rather than on society as a whole. The main part of this work is divided into nine sections including: Planning and Counseling for Retirement; Retirement Adjustment; Health and Leisure; Financial Aspects; Work and Retirement; Old Age and Death; etc. Each of the 633 complete bibliographic citations is numbered and has a 10- to 50-word descriptive annotation. This comprehensive bibliography of books, articles, theses, and government publications is international in scope, though all items are in the English-language and cover a ten-year time span, from 1975 through 1985. Many of the sources cited would be useful to individuals planning and coping with retirement. It is highly recommended for all libraries supporting a gerontology collection or serving an increasingly large senior population. *Retirement; Gerontology*

A*

978.   **Retirement Sourcebook: Your Complete Guide to Health, Leisure, and Consumer Information**, by Edward L. Palder. Woodbine House, 1989. 521p. $14.95. pap. 0-933149-24-7.

The focus of this sourcebook is on the elderly, but much of information will be of interest to persons of all ages. The volume deals with most concerns of retirees or soon-to-be retired individuals. The work is divided into four major parts: Consumer Information; Home and Family Life; Travel and Leisure; and perhaps the topic of greatest concern to those facing retirement, Health. Each of these categories is subdivided into many, many topics. Health, for example covers more than 50 topics such as asthma, allergies, incontinence, Medicare, hearing problems, and senility. Books, brochures, and leaflets are listed under each topic; many are free, and addresses are given and in many cases toll-free numbers are provided. There is also a 5th part which lists organization and other resources of interest to retirees. A detailed subject index is also provided. This volume offers a "gold mine" of valuable information and is highly recommended for even the smallest public library for reference and collection building. The price might suggest two copies, one for reference, one for circulating. *Retirement*

A

979.   **Women and Aging: A Selected, Annotated Bibliography**, Comp. by Jean M. Coyle. Greenwood, 1989. 163p. $35.95. 0-313-26021-4. (Bibliographies and Indexes in Gerontology, no. 9).

Recognizing the dearth of information on the subject, Coyle states: "It is only during the past decade that publications on the subject of middle-aged women in the United States have begun to appear in significant numbers." To identify and describe this insufficient but growing body of literature is the purpose of this bibliography. Each chapter deals with a broad aspect of the subject including: economics; roles and relationships; employment; health; sexuality; religion; middle age; housing; retirement; etc. Entries are arranged in alphabetical order by type and format under each of the various categories. Included are books, articles, films, government publications, and dissertations. Each entry has full bibliographic information and a descriptive annotation. This volume is recommended for most academic and public libraries, but especially those having a special program or collection in the areas of women or aging. *Aging; Women*

Childhood and Adolescence

Y; A

980.   **Black Adolescence: Current Issues and Annotated Bibliography**, by the Consortium for Research on Black Adolescence. Hall, 1990. $29.95. 0-8161-9080-1.

This survey of the issues and problems involved with black adolescence is divided into separate subject-oriented chapters, each written by a different person. Topics covered are psychosocial development, psychological health, physical health, drug abuse, suicide, academic performance, education and occupational choice, employment, family-adolescent relationships, sexuality and contraception, and teen parenting. Each chapter begins with a summary of the research and findings in the area plus a fine annotated bibliography of basic readings in books and periodicals on the subject. This book will be of value in high schools and public libraries that serve a substantial African American population.

Adolescence—African American; African Americans

C; A

981.   **Child Abuse and Neglect: An Information and Reference Guide**, by Timothy J. Iverson and Marilyn Segal. Garland, 1990. 220p $36. 0-8240-7776-8. (Garland Books on Family Issues, 15).

The topic of child abuse is covered in six chapters that explore such areas as cultural and historical factors, characteristics of abusive parents, kinds of child maltreatment, intervention procedures, and prevention programs. Each chapter contains a selective bibliography that can be used to identify additional materials for library collections.   *Child Abuse*

C; A

982.   **Child Care: An Annotated Bibliography**. International Labor Office, 1990. 71p. $10.50 92-2-107275-4.

Although the majority of citations are for English language publications, this selective bibliography of over 100 items published on child care from 1978 through 1988 has some international coverage. The main thrust is on scholarly materials that deal with problems faced by working mothers and contains sources like conference proceedings, professional journals, and some monographs. For large collections.

Child Care

C; A

983.   **The Child Care Catalog: A Handbook of Resources and Information on Child Care**, by Randy Lee Comfort and Constance D. Williams. Libraries Unlimited, 1985. 203p. $23.50 0-87287-458-3.

This catalog lists and describes resources dealing with current day care options such as kinds of day care available, what type is best in various situations, how to run a center, and government regulations and legal aspects. The age range dealt with is from birth to school age. Each chapter contains an extensive annotated bibliography of popular and scholarly books, articles, and documents on the subject. This book is basic enough in scope to be of use in any public library, and the bibliographies, though now dated, can supply information on available resources.   *Child Care*

C; A

984.   **Child Molestation: An Annotated Bibliography**, by Mary de Young. McFarland, 1987. 176p. $29.95 pap. 0-89950-243-1.

This bibliography contains 527 entries from professional journals from the early 1960s through 1986 in twelve chapters on such topics as prevention, pedophile groups, and homosexual child molestation. Annotations are 50 to 100 words in length. For collection development there is a separate chapter that recommends 30 basic books on the subject. They explore the topic from various viewpoints including social, medical and legal aspects.   *Child Molesting*

C; A

985.   **Childbirth: An Annotated Bibliography and Guide**, by Rosemary Cline Diulio. Garland, 1986 203p. $31. 0-8240-9220-1. (Reference Library of Social Science, 358).

The 174 selected and annotated titles in this bibliography explore various aspects of the subject of childbirth. Some of the annotations are lengthy and there is a title and subject index. For large collections.

Childbirth

C; A

986.   **Childhood Information Resources**, by Marda Woodbury. Information Resources (Herder and Co.), 1985. 593p. $45. 0-87815-051-X.

This useful book lists over 1,100 recommended sources of information representing a variety of disciplines on the childhood years between conception and age 12. There are chapters on research methods, printed reference works, periodicals, directories, nonprint sources, tests, statistics, children's literature and compendiums. Each chapter contains a two to five page overview followed by annotated entries arranged alphabetically. There is a 60 page author, title, subject index which leads readers to the 789 books, 150 periodicals, 40 online databases and 173 organizations included in the main body of the work. This is an excellent source for both school and public libraries. It can be ordered directly for $45 plus $2.75 postage form Information Resources Press, 1700 N. Moore St., Arlington, VA 22209.   *Children; Child Care*

Y; A

987.   **Focus on Teens in Trouble: A Reference Handbook**, by Daryl Sander. ABC-Clio, 1991. 182p $39. 0-87436-207-5. (Teenage Perspectives).

Some of the teenage problems dealt with in this handbook are gangs, violence, substance abuse, runaways, and the juvenile justice system. Each chapter cover a different problem, and like other volumes in this series contains an introduction to the topics that gives background information, definitions of terms, and important statistics. This is followed by annotated lists of fiction, nonfiction, and nonprint sources for further study. All are suitable for young adults. There is a single index for authors, titles, and subjects. This is a useful addition to young adult collections in schools and public libraries. Two other recommended titles in this series for the same audience are: *Focus on Physical Impairments* by Nicholas J. Farolides (1990, 325p. $39. 0-87436-428-0) and *Focus on Sexuality* by Elizabeth Ann Poe (1990, 225p. $39. 0-87436-116-8).

Adolescence; Disabilities; Sexual Behavior

A

988. **Infancy: A Guide to Research and Resources**, by Hannah Nuba-Scheffler. Garland, 1986. 182p. $43. 0-8240-8699-6.

This specialized work mingles text about the characteristics and findings concerning infancy with a bibliography on topics related to the development of babies. It has a chapter that might interest children's librarians on books and babies, but otherwise it will be found only in large library collections. *Infants*

C; A

989. **One-Parent Children, the Growing Minority: A Research Guide**, by Mary Noel Gouke and Arline McClarty Rollins. Garland, 1990. 494p. $54. 0-8240-8576-0. (Reference Books on Family Issues, 14); (Garland Reference Library of Social Science, 344).

The number of children living in single-parent households has increased to staggering proportions during the past ten years. This has led to a host of psychological, social, and educational concerns that are reflected in an increase in the literature on the subject. This bibliography contains 1,000 entries. Each item is arranged in alphabetical order and numbered in sequence. Annotations are primarily summaries of the research cited. The book is useful as a starting point for beginning research by students, teachers, or parents, and therefore may be important for academic as well as public libraries. *Family Life; Single Parent Family*

C; A

990. **Parent-Child Attachment: A Guide to Research**, by Kathleen Pullan Watkins. Garland, 1987. 255p. $33. 0-8240-8465-9. (Garland Reference Library of Social Sciences).

This work focuses on the literature relating to parent-child attachments, and is intended for a wide audience of parents, teachers, and health and social services professionals. The first chapter of the book presents an overview of the topic. Each succeeding chapter deals with an important aspect of parent-child attachment, such as relationships with fathers, adoptive families, single parents, etc. At the end of each chapter is an annotated bibliography relating specifically to the topic. Annotations are brief. All of the titles are in English, and most were published during the past 20 years. An author index and a detailed subject index are also provided. This research guide is recommended for all academic libraries and special libraries (including some public libraries) supporting research in the field of attachment behavior in children.

Parenting; Parent and Child; Family Life

C; A

991. **Research Guide for Studies in Infancy and Childhood**, by Enid E. Haag. Greenwood, 1988. 430p. $57.95. 0-313-24763-3. (Reference Sources for the Social Sciences and Humanities, 8).

The emphasis of the two parts of this research guide is in creating many annotated bibliographies. Section 1 has, in addition to an introduction on search strategy, a chapter on databases and one on general reference works. Section 2, the heart of this book, contains specialized subject bibliographies on almost every aspect of infancy and childhood, e.g., child care; families; behavior; physical development; and creativity. Each area is further subdivided into very specific topics, e.g., adoption and siblings are under families. Descriptive annotations are provided for every entry. Bibliographic information is also provided for all of the entries which are generally very recent. The work is similar to Woodbury's *Childhood Information Resources*, which is more extensive (it even includes nonprint media) but not as content-laden. Actually the two excellent sources complement each other. Haag's work is not aimed at parents, but it is recommended for most academic libraries and other libraries serving professionals who work with children.

Child Development; Children; Infants

C; A

992. **Resources for Middle Childhood: A Source Book**, by Deborah Lovitky Sheiman and Maureen Slonim. Garland, 1988. 138p. $31. 0-8240-7777-6.

The purpose of this sourcebook is to "help the parent, teacher, and student of child development gain a better understanding of the growth and needs of the six to twelve year old child." The work is arranged in eight broad themes including physical, psychological, and cognitive development; play; peer relationships;

school; and society. Each thematic chapter includes a five- to eight-page essay on the topic, followed by an annotated bibliography of 30 to 50 sources. Some classics are included, but most of the sources are from the late 1970s to mid-1980s. There are author and title indexes, but lack of a subject index is a serious limitation. Still, this work can be used topically, and is recommended for professional collections and many public libraries. *Child Development*

C; A

993. **Resources on Child Sexual Abuse**. Memphis Shelby County Public Library, [1987]. 14p. $1.

The Memphis Shelby County Child Sexual Abuse Council donated a collection of materials on child sexual abuse to the Memphis Shelby County Public Library and Information Center. From this library, the staff and council members compiled a bibliography of 60 items which forms the nucleus of this bibliography. The collection of items for both adults and children includes videocassettes, curriculum guides, coloring books, and even comic books. They are willing to share this important and timely bibliography. For their latest edition send $1 and a SASE to: Memphis Shelby County PL and Information Center, 1850 Peabody, Memphis, TN 38104. *Child Abuse; Sexual Abuse; Child Molesting*

Y; A

994. **Youth Information Resources: An Annotated Guide for Parents, Professionals, Students, Researchers, and Concerned Citizens**, Comp. by Marda Woodbury. Greenwood, 1987. 371p. $49.95. 0-313-25304-8.

Woodbury, an experienced librarian, administrator, and author has compiled an annotated bibliography of nearly 700 citations on adolescence (which she defines as those transitional years between childhood and adulthood: 13 to 19). In addition, several hundred youth-related organizations are listed in an appendix. Emphasis is on resources about American and Canadian youth and on authoritative sources readily available. This is a cross- and multidisciplinary work, and entries are arranged by format rather than subject, e.g., abstracting and indexing services, dictionaries, bibliographies, directories, periodicals, etc. Subjects included are as varied as education, religion, drugs, sex, sports, vandalism, employment, and violence. Complete bibliographic information is included with each entry, and the annotations are both descriptive and evaluative. Two indexes are provided: an author/title, and organization index, and a subject and format index. This guide is recommended for secondary school professional collections, and public, academic, and special libraries with collections in the social sciences or youth services. *Adolescence*

Death and Dying

A

995. **Affairs in Order: A Complete Resource Guide to Death and Dying**, by Patricia Anderson. Macmillan, 1991. 256p. $21.95. 0-02-501991-0.

A detailed manual on an important topic of current interest, which deals with the practical concerns in preparing for the inevitable. The book is divided into three major parts—before, during, and after death—and includes details on such matters as wills, life support systems, funerals, and administering estates.

While not a bibliography as such, the complete resource listings, which include annotated bibliographies, make this an excellent selection tool and it is therefore highly recommended for most public libraries. *Death and Dying*

A

996. **The Challenge of Euthanasia: An Annotated Bibliography on Euthanasia and Related Subjects**, by Don V. Bailey. University Press of America, 1990. 395p. $47.50 0-8191-7711-3.

The author, a hospital chaplain, has compiled a list of 949 annotated entries for books, articles, and audiovisual materials mostly from the 1970s and 80s that represent a cross-section of thinking on this controversial subject. Using broad subjects for each chapter, entries are then arranged alphabetically by author. There is unfortunately no specific author index. A 43-page introduction gives an emotional overview of the subject and there is a title index. For academic and larger public library collections. *Euthanasia*

A

997. **Death and Dying: A Bibliographical Survey**, by Samuel Southard. Greenwood Press, 1991. 514p. $55. 0-313-26465-1.

This multidisciplinary work, which stresses material on counseling, contains over 2,225 entries from the literature on death and dying found in such media as periodicals, books, parts of books, and reports. Each is critically annotated. There are eight subject-oriented chapters, the last of which describes 54 bibliographies in the field. In each chapter, the entries are listed alphabetically by author. The work ends with title and subject indexes. Academic and public libraries should find this a valuable reference work and one that will be of value in collection development. *Death and Dying*

C; Y; A
998.   **The Dying Child: An Annotated Bibliography**, by Hazel B. Benson. Greenwood, 1988. 270p. $42.95 0-313-24708-0.
This annotated bibliography of more than 700 print sources deals with various aspects of the death of children. Both scholarly and popular books and articles from about 1960 through 1987 are cited in six major areas including "general aspects," "the young child," "the adolescent," "the family," "the caregivers," and "physical care" with many subdivisions. There are author and subject indexes and appendixes that list 25 suitable children's books and 50 recommended audiovisual materials. This is recommended for large library collections. *Death and Dying*

A
999.   **Dying, Death and Grief: A Critical Bibliography**, by Michael Simpson. University of Pittsburgh Press, 1987. 280p. $29.50 0-8229-3561-9. (Contemporary Community Health Series).
This update of the 1979 edition covers 1,700 nonfiction and fiction titles published since that date that deal with death and related areas. This is a selective, critical bibliography with the main section arranged by title. After imprint information, there is an evaluation annotation and a rating of zero to five stars. Books for children are also listed and indicated as such.
There are also additional sections that update the main section for books published in 1985 and 1986 and lists of titles under broad headings like murder, terrorism, and nuclear holocaust. There is also an author and subject index. This should prove useful to most public libraries. *Death and Dying*

A
1000.   **Near-Death Experience: An Annotated Bibliography**, by Terry K. Basford. Garland, 1990. 182p. $28. 0-8240-6349-X. (Garland Reference Library of Social Science, 481).
The personal experiences of people who were near death has always been fascinating. The curiosity in it has been increasing in recent years, since more and more accounts have been written. Basford has compiled an extensive bibliography of over 570 books and articles written from 1847 through 1989. The entries are arranged chronologically in two sections: deathbed visions and analogs of near death experiences. Annotations are succinct, and many include pertinent quotations. Only an author index is provided, making the bibliography somewhat difficult to use without skimming through hundreds of entries. Still, this bibliography should prove useful for reference and collection development on a interesting topic for academic and public libraries. *Death and Dying*

Family, Marriage, and Divorce

A
1001.   **American Families: A Research Guide and Historical Handbook**, Ed. by Joseph M. Hawes and Elizabeth I. Nybakken. Greenwood, 1991. 435p. $75. 0-313-26233-0.
The bulk of this excellent handbook on the American family deals with a series of bibliographic essays on the history and development of families from preindustrial times to the present. Included are chapters on women and the family; African American families; Native American families; and immigrant working-class families. A bibliography of more than 1,000 entries is included at the end of the volume. A detailed author and subject index is also provided. This is a must purchase for all academic and many public libraries for patrons doing serious research and for library collection building. *Family—United States*

A
1002.   **Adoption: An Annotated Bibliography and Guide**, by Lois Ruskai Melina. Garland, 1987. 292p. $42. 0-8240-8942-1. (Garland Reference library of Social Science, 374).
A selective guide to almost 850 entries of adoption literature from books and journal articles published since 1974. All entries, which are readily available, include full bibliographic citations and brief annotations. All aspects of adoption, i.e., social, legal, medical, psychological are included. The works are intended for professionals dealing with adoption, but can be used by interested laypeople. The thirteen chapters are arranged by type or special aspects of adoption, for example, preadoption issues, adoption of minorities, international, sealed records, and search and reunion. There are also chapters about books for children on adoption, education and training materials for professionals, and lists of audiovisual resources. This

comprehensive and useful bibliography updates Elizabeth Wharton Van Why's *Adoption Bibliography and Multi-Ethnic Sourcebook* (Open Door Society, 1977, $7.50, 0-918416-02-7) and should be added to all public and academic library bibliography collections. *Adoption*

A
1003. **Black American Families, 1965-1984: A Classified, Selectively Annotated Bibliography**, Ed. by Walter R. Allen et al. Greenwood, 1986. 480p. $49.95. 0-313-25613-6. (Bibliographies and Indexes in Afro-American and African Studies, 16).

This selective bibliography includes about 1,100 entries drawn from journal articles, books, dissertations, government documents, and university publications. The main part of this bibliography is a listing of entries arranged alphabetically by author which include brief descriptions and subject headings. A subject index and a keyword-in-title index complete the volume. While this volume is quite extensive in its coverage and recommended for most public libraries and academic libraries, libraries should also consider Davis' *The Black Family in the United States* which covers a broader time span (1939-1985) and was also published by Greenwood in 1986 in a revised edition. *African Americans; Family Life*

A
1004. **The Black Family in the United States: A Revised, Updated, Selectively Annotated Bibliography**, Comp. by Lenwood G. Davis. Greenwood, 1986. 234p. $47.50. 0-313-25237-8. (Bibliographies and Indexes in Afro-American and African Studies, 14).

Davis, a professor of history and compiler of dozens of bibliographies in the area of black studies, has done it again. This revised and updated edition includes 722 books, articles, and dissertations and is arranged first by format and then by subject such as the black family and sex, slavery, poverty, education, housing, and health. Most titles listed are from the past 30 years. Each entry includes a bibliographic citation and a brief annotation. This work is very similar to Allen's *Black American Families*; however, all entries in the Davis work are annotated and there are many titles that do not overlap. Therefore, many libraries will want to consider both bibliographies, especially those academic and public libraries serving a large African American constituency. *African Americans; Family Life*

C; A
1005. **Children and Adjustment to Divorce: An Annotated Bibliography**, by Mary M. Nofsingser. Garland, 1990. 282p. $40. 0-8240-4297-2.

The greater part of the bibliography of 747 books, articles, and other material is intended for professionals who wish to explore the topic of children's adjustment to divorce. The items are arranged by author and are given extensive annotations. Two shorter sections supply material for parents and for children and young adults and another section annotates appropriate audiovisual sources. All materials listed were produced from 1981 through 1988. For larger collections. *Divorce; Children*

A
1006. **Families in Transition: An Annotated Bibliography**, by Judith DeBoard Sadler. Archon Books/Shoe String, 1988. 251p. $32.50. 0-208-02180-9.

The various recent changes affecting the structure of the American family are reflected in this bibliography of about 900 hundred books, articles, and research studies published roughly from 1975 through 1987. There are 16 chapters on such subjects as single-parent families, stepfamilies, divorce and remarriage, and working parents. All entries are annotated, and about 100 of them are for books for children. There are indexes by subject, author, and title. Both popular and scholarly works are included, and there is a separate chapter that lists about 40 audiovisual sources. This will be useful in public libraries.
Family Life; Single-Parent Family; Divorce

C, Y, A
1007. **Family Literacy: A Bibliography**, by Amanada S. Rudd. Baker and Taylor, 1989. 54p. free.

This bibliography is aimed at families where reading difficulties exist both with the parents and the children. It is divided into four parts. In the first, "Breaking the Cycle," books and materials are suggested that could increase adult basic skills and job skills and help in other everyday life situations. The second, "Home Affairs," suggests easily-read books that deal with such topics as teenage pregnancy, drugs, alcohol, schools, and helping with homework. The third, "Reading for Pleasure," covers high interest/low vocabulary books of fiction and nonfiction, plus a section on simple books to read aloud to children. The last, "English as a Second Language," deals with information sources on citizenship requirements and various academic achievement tests. For each of the books listed, there is full bibliographic information, an annotation, and a reading level code. All of the materials are available from Baker and Taylor. This free publication can serve as both a collection-building tool as well as a useful resource for giving reading guidance to families with reading problems. *Literacy; Illiteracy*

Y; A

1008. Focus on Families: A Reference Handbook, by Ruth K. J. Cline. ABC-Clio, 1990. 233p. $39. 0-87436-508-2. (Teenage Perspectives).

This handbook gives current information on a variety of family issues for teenagers as well as adults. The work is divided into nine chapters covering such topics as family, stepfamilies, and divorce. Each contains an introduction to the topic with definitions and explanations of terms followed by an annotated bibliography of nonfiction, fiction, and nonprint materials suitable for young adults. Most chapters also have listings of important organizations and hotlines. There is an author, title, and subject index. This will be useful in both high school and public libraries. Two other similar titles in this series are *Focus on School* by Beverly A. Haley (1990, 250p $39. 0-87436-099-4) and *Focus on Careers* by Lynne Iglitzin (1991, 200p. $39. 0-87436-588-0). *Social Problems; Divorce; Adolescence; Occupations*

A

1009. The Influence of the Family: A Review and Annotated Bibliography of Socialization, Ethnicity and Delinquency, 1975-1986, by Alan C. Acock and Jeffrey M. Clair. Garland, 1986. 315p. $47. 0-8240-8567-1. (Garland Reference Library of Social Science, 9).

The materials listed in this bibliography deal with young adults and how they are influenced by their families. Some books are included, but most of the references are to journal articles from 175 different periodical titles. The works are arranged in three main sections on family influence, ethnicity, and delinquency, and there are author and title indexes and a subject index by key words. This work will be of value to people working with adolescents and therefore should be found in both high school library professional collections and large public libraries *Adolescence; Family Life*

A

1010. Research on Men Who Batter: An Overview, Bibliography, and Resource Guide, by Edward W. Gondolf, ed. by Lee Joiner. Human Services Inst., 1988. 104p. $11.95. 0-943519-05-5.

This work delves into the causes, characteristics, and disposition of batterers. Gondolf devotes the first 10-15 pages to an overview of the topic. This is followed by about 1,000 unannotated citations arranged in four chapters: Dynamics of Wife Beating; Roots of Wife Battering; Men Who Batter; and Intervention with the Batterer. There is also a chapter of Program Resources which includes entries for many self-help books for both victim and batterer; also included in this chapter are program manuals for professionals, films, periodicals, resource centers, and reference books on the topic. This guide is intended primarily for social workers, therapists, researchers, and other professionals. Its price and the excellent lists of resources make this a wise purchase for public libraries, as well as academic libraries supporting abuse programs.

Spouse Abuse; Family Violence

A

1011. Spouse Abuse: An Annotated Bibliography of Violence Between Mates, by Eugene A. Engeldinger. Scarecrow, 1986. 317p. $29.50 0-8108-1838-8.

In this bibliography there are 1,783 citations from many types of sources including popular and scholarly books, periodical articles, theses, conference papers, reference books, pamphlets, and government documents. All are in English and date from the nineteenth century through 1983, with most from the late 1960s on. They are arranged alphabetically by author and, in addition to having bibliographic information, are annotated with descriptive notes. There is an index by name (for persons and corporate bodies that are subjects) and subjects. This will be of use in large public and academic libraries chiefly as a location device, rather than as a collection-building tool. *Spouse Abuse*

A

1012. Stepfamilies: A Guide to the Sources and Resources, by Ellen J. Gruber. Garland, 1986. 122p. $28. 0-8240-8688-0. (Garland Reference Library of Social Science, Vol. 317).

After a general introduction that comments on the present structure of the American family and the many stresses and changes it is currently undergoing, this bibliography lists alphabetically by author 213 books and journals that deal with stepfamilies and related topics. Most of the entries are annotated. Additional lists include books of special value to children, young adults, and parents, plus a directory of organizations and a list of audio visual sources. Title and subject indexes are included. A major limitation, however, is that the coverage is limited to the years 1980 through 1984. This subject, however, is of increasing importance in both public and academic libraries. *Stepfamilies*

Homelessness

Y; A
1013. **American Homelessness: A Reference Handbook**, by Mary Ellen Hombs. ABC-Clio, 1990. 190p. $39. 0-87436-547-3. (Contemporary World Issues).

This relatively brief handbook gives a great deal of background information on the problem of homelessness in America today, including a chronology of major events and a biographical sketch of individuals making major contributions in this area. Also included are documents, organizations, and major print and nonprint reference sources. The reference materials are listed under specific categories, e.g., children, alcohol, AIDS, etc. Each entry provides adequate information for ordering. This handbook is recommended as a timely reference and selection guide to an important, timely topic for secondary school and public libraries. *Homeless People*

A
1014. **Homelessness: An Annotated Bibliography**, by James M. Henslin. Garland, 1993. 2v. 1,092p. $125. 0-8240-4115-1.

Henslin has compiled a very timely and much-needed bibliography of over 3,000 entries. The inclusions represent historical as well as a global aspects of the issue. However, most of the entries are from recent sources, and there is a definite focus on homelessness in the United States. The annotated entries are arranged alphabetically by author in the first volume. In volume two, the citations are arranged under 41 subject categories. While a variety of resources are included, the vast majority of entries are articles from newspapers and popular and scholarly journals, thus making the set more useful for research than collection development. Nevertheless, this up-to-date bibliography is recommended for all academic and public libraries, and special libraries serving patrons that are studying or are actively involved with the very real problems of homelessness. *Homeless People*

Homosexuality

A
1015. **The Alyson Almanac: A Treasury of Information for the Gay and Lesbian Community**. Rev. ed. Alyson, 1990. 284p. $8.95. pap. 1-55583-019-6.

As the title implies, this "almanac" is chock-full of a great deal of information for and about gays and lesbians. Areas covered include, for example, history, books, periodicals, films, organizations, sports, hotlines, health, slang, travel, religion, famous gays, etc. Because of this coverage, this is an important reference tool. Particularly useful for selection and acquisition purposes are the many bibliographies "for more reading" that follow many sections. Therefore, this inexpensive source is highly recommended for most public libraries. *Homosexuality*

A
1016. **Gay and Lesbian Library Service**, ed. by Cal Gough and Ellen Greenblatt. McFarland, 1990. 355p. $36.50 0-89950-535-X.

This work offers both bibliographic and directory information chiefly in a series of useful appendixes that follow several essays on various aspects of library service to gays and lesbians. The appendixes include a core list of nonfiction books, a filmography, a discography, a bibliography of AIDS-related materials, directories of publishers and mail-order houses, and other helpful lists. This will be valuable in large and specialized collections. *Homosexuality; Library Services*

A
1017. **Gayellow Pages: USA and Canada for Gay Women and Men: National Edition**. 20th ed. Renaissance House (NY), 256p. $12. pap. ISSN 0363-826-X.

This directory was first published in 1973. There are separate sections for Canada and the United States that contain entries for national organizations, services, and publications, followed by state and local listings that include information on telephone switchboards, groups, services, bars, accommodations, bookstores, etc. Whenever appropriate, publications are also noted. This book is updated annually and, in addition to this national edition, there are also local editions for New York/New Jersey, the South, and the Northeast. *Homosexuality*

A

1018. **The Homosexual and Society: An Annotated Bibliography**, by Robert B. Marks Ridinger. Greenwood, 1990. 444p. $49.95 0-313-25357-9. (Bibliographies and Indexes in Sociology, 18)

This bibliography of over 1,500 sources is arranged in seven areas such as homophobia, the military, censorship, religion, and employment discrimination and then organized in chronological order. Many of the entries are for articles in the popular gay and lesbian press, rather than scholarly publications. The items are well annotated and there are author and subject indexes. For large collections. *Homosexuality*

A

1019. **Homosexuality: A Research Guide**, by Wayne R. Dynes. Garland, 1987. 853p. $56. 0-8240-8692-9. (Garland Reference Library of Social Science, 313)

This bibliography on male and female homosexuality contains about 5,000 items arranged in 24 broad headings like history and area studies, philosophy and religion, lifestyle, the family, and violence with about 150 subdivisions. There are introductions to each section, and both English and foreign language materials are included. The annotations are objective, and there are subject and name indexes. Useful for research and material identification in large collections. *Homosexuality*

A

1020. **International Directory of Gay and Lesbian Periodicals**, by H. Robert Malinowsky. Oryx, 1987. 226p. $25. pap. 0-89774-297-4.

This international directory contains almost 2,000 entries arranged alphabetically by title. Full bibliographic information is given for the titles where this information was supplied by the publisher, others contains only whatever information was volunteered. There are two indexes, one by subject and place and the other by editors and publishers. The scope is wide and this could be used in very large libraries to identify available material and perhaps act as a selection guide. *Homosexuality*

A

1021. **Lesbianism: An Annotated Bibliography and Guide to the Literature, 1976-1991**, by Dolores J. Maggiore. Scarecrow, 1992. 265p. $32.50. 0-8108-2617-8.

The subject of lesbianism is represented in this bibliography which is an update of Maggiore's earlier work which stopped at 1986. Two hundred additional titles were added to the more than 300 books, articles, theses, dissertations, and other sources listed in the first edition. The annotated entries are listed under five major categories, including the individual lesbian, minorities, lesbian families, oppression, and health. Also included are author and title indexes. This is a useful selection tool and the cost places it within the range of most academic and public libraries. *Lesbianism*

Sexuality and Sex Education

Y; A

1022. **Adolescent Pregnancy and Parenthood: An Annotated Guide**, by Ann Creighton-Zollar. Garland, 1990. 244p. $42. 0-8240-4295-6. (Reference Books on Family Issues, v. 16).

This annotated guide to the serious problem of teenage pregnancy was sorely needed by social workers, persons in health and education, and counselors, as well as students in these fields. The guide is arranged by broad topics relating to many aspects of the problem, e.g., adolescent sexuality, contraception, sex education, risk factors, as well as the social, medical and legal concerns. The entries from journals and books are well annotated and current. This will be an important addition to all libraries serving interested professionals and students. *Pregnancy, Adolescent; Parents, Adolescent*

Y; A

1023. **Adolescent Sexuality**. Planned Parenthood Federation of America, [1989] $3.25.

A useful guide in building up a collection of information to enhance a sex education curriculum. Recommended as a selection aid for both school and public libraries. Available from: Planned Parenthood Federation of America, 810 Seventh Avenue, New York, NY 10019 *Adolescence; Sex Education*

C; Y; A

1024. Educator's Guide to Preventing Child Sexual Abuse, by Mary Nels et al. Network, 1986. 250p $19.95 0-941816-17-6.

This book is a compilation of information about child sex abuse written by a number of experts in the field and covering such subjects as issues, guidelines for prevention education, and considerations with special or ethnic populations. There are bibliographies at the end of each chapter, plus an appendix that contains an extensive bibliography of books, pamphlets, and audiovisual materials for both adults and children. These bibliographies will by helpful in developing collections and programs on this subject.

Child Abuse; Child Molesting

A

1025. Prostitution: A Guide to Sources, 1960-1990, Ed. by Vern L. Bullough and Lilli Sentz. Garland, 1992. 369p. $56. 0-8240-7101-8.

Nearly 2,000 books and periodical articles are cited in this interesting and unique compilation. Though the title implies that the sources are written from 1960 on, a number of reprints of earlier works are included. Also, the index of personal names is really an author index. However, these minor limitations aside, this one-of-a-kind collection will be of interest to many academic libraries for research needs as well as collection development. *Prostitution*

A

1026. Studies in Human Sexuality: A Selected Guide, by Suzanne G. Frayser and Thomas J. Whitby. Libraries Unlimited, 1987. 442p. $47.50 0-87287-422-2.

The subject scope of the 627 monographs that have been selected for inclusion in this bibliography on human sexuality covers a variety of disciplines including biology, sociology, anthropology, religion, psychology, and art. Most of the books were published since 1970 with about half bearing imprint dates in the 1980s. The work is in three parts. The first lists reference works and historical and statistical studies. The second is a topical guide to sexual functioning and disorders divided into a number of narrow subjects. Part 3 lists bibliographies by subjects like incest and sexual abuse. Complete bibliographic information is followed in each entry by lengthy descriptive annotations. Each title is coded for use suitability, i.e., professional, layperson, popular, young adult, and children. There is an extensive analytical subject index, as well as author and title indexes. Patron and acquisitions librarians in public and academic libraries will find this work useful. A second edition is forthcoming. *Sexual Behavior; Sex Education*

Social Work

A

1027. A Guide to Information Sources for Social Work and the Human Services, by Henry Neil Mendelsohn. Oryx, 1987. 144p. $33. 0-89774-338-5.

The purpose of this book is "to systematically present pertinent sources that social work practitioners, educators and students can use to locate information in libraries." The work is organized around various formats and types of information sources, such as reference books, professional journals, books, databases, statistical works, etc. There is a combined title and subject index, plus a list of the 100 most important journals in the field. For large collections. *Social Work*

Substance Abuse

A

1028. Biomedical and Social Aspects of Alcohol Use: A Review of the Literature, Ed. by Dirk G. van der Heij and Gertjan Schaafsma. Pudoc, 1991. (Dist. by UNIPUB) 273p. $75. 90-220-1051-1.

This bibliography is concerned with moderate and excessive alcohol abuse. Many aspects of alcohol use (abuse) are included; for example, there are chapters on alcohol metabolism, effects on different organ systems, cancer, pregnancy, driving, etc. The authors introduce each chapter with an overall discussion of the topic and a general review of the related literature. The citations included in each chapter are arranged alphabetically by author. While most of the entries deal with journals, many books, dissertations, and proceedings are also included, adding to the volumes usefulness as both a reference guide and an aid in collection building. Although international in scope, more than 90% of the 1,600 plus titles were written in English. This is recommended for most upper-division, graduate school and research libraries with an interest in the subject. *Alcoholism*

Y; A

1029.   **Prevention Education: A Guide to Research**, by William J. Derivan and Natalie Anne Silverstein. Garland, 1990. 282p. $36. 0-8240-3716-2.

Prevention of substance abuse has been a high priority concern of our country for quite some time. This bibliography lists over 600 citations to literature on the prevention of abuse of alcohol and drugs. Included are citations "related to primary prevention: education prior to abuse; secondary prevention; education during early stages of abuse; and tertiary prevention: education during the later phases of abuse." Major topics considered are school-based prevention programs, reports on model programs, curricula for prevention programs, community-based prevention programs, and the family and prevention. An important chapter includes the list of the literature; each entry is annotated with a brief description. Included are books, articles from journals, government publications, research reports, pamphlets, and curriculum guides. Author, title, and subject indexes are provided. The major limitation of this otherwise excellent guide is that most of the literature cited was published between 1974 and 1983 (although this guide was published in 1990). Still, because the subject is important and there is a crucial need for more bibliographic identification, this bibliography is recommended for all libraries supporting research and programs on the topic of substance abuse. *Alcoholism; Substance Abuse; Drugs*

A

1030.   **Substance Abuse among Ethnic Minorities in America: A Critical Annotated Bibliography**, by Howard Rebach et. al. Garland, 1992. 469p. $72. 0-8153-0066-2. (Garland Library of Sociology, 20).

This bibliography of 168 periodical articles published from 1980 to 1991 lists materials that deal with substance abuse and African Americans, Asian Americans, Native Americans, and Alaskan Indian/Pacific Islanders. Each citation contains full bibliographic material, a summary, and a critical analysis. There are several comparative tables and an index to authors. For academic and large public libraries.

Drugs; Substance Abuse; African Americans; Asian Americans;
Indians of North America; Pacific Islanders

A

1031.   **Work and Alcohol Abuse: An Annotated Bibliography**, Comp. by John J. Miletich, Greenwood, 1987. 263p. $49.95. 0-313-25689-6.

Miletich, a reference librarian at the University of Alberta, has compiled a very comprehensive bibliography of over 1,000 citations covering the years 1972-1986. Although many countries are mentioned in the work, most were published in the United States, Canada, or Great Britain, and all are in the English language. The volume is arranged in seven topic chapters, including Definitions, Identification, and Diagnosis; Companies and Management; Unions, Safety, and Employee Dismissal; and Counseling and Treatment. Entries are arranged alphabetically by author within each chapter. Annotations, which range from one sentence to a paragraph, are both descriptive and evaluative. Full bibliographical information is provided. There are separate author, subject, and company-name indexes as well. The work, though specialized in scope, is recommended for public as well as academic libraries and libraries serving businesses, personnel staff, health services professionals, and social workers. *Alcoholism*

Disabilities

A

1032.   **Complete Directory for People with Disabilities, 1993...**, Ed. by Leslie Mackenzie. Grey House, 1993. 539p. $125. pap. 0-9239300-24-9.

This directory is arranged in four sections. The first lists associations, camps, housing, and libraries prominent in work with the disabled. The second (of value for reference and collection development) is a bibliography of books, newsletters, videos, and important conferences. The third covers special devices, clothing, and computer product sources. The fourth and largest section gives material of educational and rehabilitation programs, travel opportunities, and other forms of recreation. Excluding the print sources, there are about 6,000 directory entries with indexes by name, state, and specific needs or disabilities. Access is made possible through an entry index and a subject index listed by disability. This will be of value in public, academic, and other professional libraries serving a substantial population of disabled people.

Disabilities

A

1033. International Directory of Periodicals Related to Deafness. Gallaudet University, 1987. 114p. pap. $6.

This bibliography lists over 500 domestic and foreign titles on deafness alphabetically by title. For each, information like frequency, price, name and address of publisher and country are given. This bibliography is available for $6 from Gallaudet University Press, 800 Florida Ave. NE, Washington, DC 20002. *Deafness*

A

1034. Meeting the Needs of People with Disabilities: A Guide for Librarians, Educators, and Other Service Professionals, by Ruth A. Velleman. Oryx, 1990. 288p. $37.95. 0-89774-521-3.

This excellent resource is a completely revised and updated version of Velleman's *Serving Physically Disabled People* (o.p.). It examines the information needs of the physically or mentally disabled, blind/visually-impaired, and the deaf/hearing-impaired. It includes current information sources, new technologies, and publications. This well-written book is recommended for all public and academic libraries for reference use and as an aid in library collection development. *Disabilities*

C*; Y*; A*

1035. A Reader's Guide for Parents of Children with Mental, Physical, or Emotional Disabilities, by Cory Moore. 3rd ed. Woodbine House, 1990. 248p. $14.95. pap. 0-933149-27-1.

This guide to up-to-date information about disabilities has several focuses: first, it is designed to help parents find current information about living with a disabled child as well as information about specific conditions; second, it is intended to supply a list of books written for children and young adults for librarians and other professionals to use in bibliotherapy work. For each disability discussed in the second section of the book, there is a list of basic readings and sources for additional information. The volume concludes with publishers addresses and indexes of organizations and agencies (good source for vertical file information), authors, and editors, titles, and subjects. Most of the sources cited are dated in the 1980's. All include full bibliographic information and a concise annotation. There are several similar sources on the topic, but none as current or as broad-based. Friedburg's, *Accept Me As I Am*, is an excellent bibliography, but deals only with nonfiction titles and is five years older. Moore's book is inexpensive and it deserves to be in every school and public library as a reference tool and as a selection aid.

Disabilities; Mental Handicaps; Physical Handicaps

A

1036. Resource Directory for the Disabled, by Richard Neil Shrout. Facts on File, 1991. 392p. $45. 0-8160-2216-X.

This resource directory covers a wide-ranging array of resources including appliances, aids, and devices; travel; recreation, sports, and social opportunities; education; computer products; organizations; and of course publications. The work is divided into four main parts. The first covers resources for all types of disabilities; this is followed by sections for those who are impaired by mobility, hearing, or visual defects. While the use of annotations is inconsistent, complete explanatory text is provided when necessary. As well, a detailed table of contents and a name-subject index are provided. There are fewer services and products listed than in a similar work: Mackenzie and Lignor's *The Complete Directory for People with Disabilities*. However, the arrangement of the *Resource Directory* makes it easier to use, and it is recommended for most smaller to medium-sized public libraries as a reference tool for patrons and buying guide for libraries. Larger libraries may want to consider both titles. *Disabilities*

Philanthropy

A

1037. Philanthropy and Volunteerism: An Annotated Bibliography, by Daphne Niobe Layton. Foundation Center, 1987. 308p. $18.50. pap. 0-87954-198-9.

It is noted in the foreword that "until now there has been no comprehensive bibliography of philanthropy and volunteerism, with the result that students, scholars, and the general public have no systematic aid to understanding the field." This work by Layton fills that void. Over 1,600 books and articles on the subjects are listed, and 244 titles, deemed of exceptional value, are given extensive treatment through long annotations. Most annotations are descriptive rather than critical. An author and subject index complete this much needed bibliography. Recommended for all libraries that serve users interested in this field. Useful for reference and for collection development. *Philanthropy; Voluntarism*

A

1038. **Volunteerism and Older Adults**, by Mary K. Kouri. ABC-Clio, 1990. 197p. $39.50. 0-87436-562-7.

The purpose of this book is to give older adults and others involved in volunteerism an overview of volunteerism as a source of activity for the elderly, plus a rundown of the many varieties and opportunities it involves. In addition, this book supplies lists of the kinds of opportunities available; major local, national and international organizations and agencies; and directories of state offices. Following this material there is also an excellent bibliography of books, periodicals, newspaper articles, films, and computer databases on aging and volunteerism that can be useful for identifying and selecting materials for library collections serving senior citizens. *Voluntarism; Senior Citizens*

A

1039. **Volunteerism: The Directory of Organizations, Training, Programs and Publications**, by Harriet C. Kipps. 3rd ed. Bowker, 1991. 1164p. $104.95. 0-8352-2739-1.

This unique directory compiles valuable practical information on 5,300 volunteer organizations whose work deals with today's most critical concerns, including AIDS, homelessness, and senior citizens. The first two parts deal with the administrative and organization resources, such as addresses, objectives, services, etc. Part three, on the other hand, consists of an extensive fully annotated bibliography. This guide is intended to serve a wide audience such as volunteer directors, governmental official at all levels, and actual and potential volunteers and therefore belongs in all public libraries that can afford it for reference and for collection development. *Voluntarism*

Sports, Recreation, and Leisure

Y; A

1040. **Adventurers Afloat: A Nautical Bibliography: A Comprehensive Guide to Books in English...**, By Ernest W. Toy, Jr. Scarecrow, 1988. 2v. 1179p. $89.50. 0-8108-2189-3.

The complete subtitle clearly indicates the full scope of this thorough compilation: "A Comprehensive Guide to Books in English Recounting the Adventurers of Amateur Sailors upon the Waters of the World in Yachts, Boats, and Other Devices and Including Works on the Arts and Sciences of Cruising, Racing, Seamanship, Navigation, Design, Building, etc. from the Earliest Writings Through 1986." Most of the almost 5,600 entries are annotated and are arranged in interesting topical chapters, e.g.: cruises, surfing, rowing, etc. There are also complete author and title indexes. This selective bibliography is recommended for all libraries used by sailors and landlubbers alike. *Sailing and Boating*

Y; A

1041. **Baseball: A Comprehensive Bibliography**, by Myron J. Smith, Jr. McFarland, 1986. 915p. $55. 0-89950-222-9.

This exhaustive bibliography on baseball is the most comprehensive available. More than 21,000 entries for books and articles in 365 journals are arranged by subject categories which include every imaginable aspect of the subject such as the World Series, baseball cards, minor leagues, each of the individual teams, and biographical information on most players and others involved with this American pastime. Many entries include annotations and all include data for locating or ordering items.

There are also author and title indexes. Despite the fact that it may have to be updated periodically, this ambitious work will serve as the basic bibliography on baseball for years to come and is recommended for most public and academic libraries. *Baseball*

Y: A

1042. **Baseball: A Comprehensive Bibliography: Supplement 1 (1985-May 1992)**, Comp. by Myron J. Smith, Jr. McFarland, 1993. 422p. $45. 0-89950-799-9.

This bibliography of more than 8,000 sources about baseball updates the author's earlier work which was published in 1986—See above entry. *Baseball*

Y; A

1043.   **The Baseball Research Handbook**, by Gerald Tomlinson. Society for American Baseball Research, 1987. 120p. $6. pap. 0-910137-29-3.

This slim and inexpensive volume is really a guide, with many practical tips, to doing research on the subject of baseball. Chapter 3, "A Checklist of Sources," identifies important published and unpublished sources. This "invaluable little book" is recommended for secondary school, undergraduate, and public libraries of all sizes. *Baseball*

Y; A

1044.   **Basketball Resource Guide**, Ed. by Jerry V. Krause and Stephen J. Brennan. 2nd ed. Leisure Press, 1989. (c1990) 238p. $25. pap. 0-88011-369-3.

This guide to the literature on basketball is really an up-date of Krause's *Basketball Bible* which was published in 1982. The book is divided into six major chapters by format, and the most useful for collection development lists books and monographs. Entries are arranged in alphabetical order by author. There are other brief chapters which list periodicals, visual resources and pamphlets. Though there is a subject index, it is quite general, which makes it difficult to retrieve titles on specific subjects. Despite this limitation, this up-to-date guide is a standard comprehensive bibliography of the subject of basketball and is recommended for all libraries supporting a physical education program, including academic and public libraries.

Basketball

A

1045.   **Chess: An Annotated Bibliography, 1969-1988**, by Andy Lusis. Mansell, 1991. 320p. $90. 0-7201-2079-9.

This survey of the literature on chess supplements the massive work by Douglas Betts *Chess: An Annotated Bibliography of Works Published in the English Language, 1850-1968* (o.p.). The present volume covers a twenty year period of books and articles in English in 2,601 entries. A total of 600 chess periodicals are referred to in these entries. The citations are divided into eight subject-oriented chapters with name, title, series, and subject indexes. This will be of value in large and specialized collections. *Chess*

A

1046.   **Diamond Classics: Essays on 100 of the Best Baseball Books Ever Published**, by Mike Shannon. McFarland, 1989. 464p. $29.95 0-89950-320-9.

In this survey of baseball literature, the editor of *Spitball* magazine has chosen his 100 favorite books including fiction, biographies, histories, essays, anthologies, and pictorial works. For each entry, information about the author and a summary of the contents are given, plus critical remarks by both the author and others. This book can be used for recreational reading, reference, as well as in selection and collection evaluation. *Baseball*

Y*; A*

1047.   **The Drug File: A Comprehensive Bibliography on Drugs and Doping in Sport. Dossier Dopage**, by Richard W. Stark et al. Gloucester, Ont., Sport Information Resource Centre, 1991. 179p. $45. 0-921817-10-X.

All aspects of the use of drugs in sports are included in this comprehensive bibliography of about 4,000 citations. Most of the titles were published between 1984 and 1991 (a few earlier titles listed are helpful for historical background information). There are listings for specific drugs such as steroids and growth hormones. Rules and regulations, testing, detection methods, and ethical, psychological, and sociological concerns are also well represented. This is a must item for all academic, public and high school libraries as a reference tool and selection aid. *Drugs; Sports*

A

1048.   **A Guide to Sources in Leisure Studies, Fitness, Sports and Travel**, by Nancy Herron. Libraries Unlimited, 1992. 181p. $28.50 1-56308-062-1.

This guide to 283 book sources is divided into four chapters, one each for leisure studies, fitness, sports and travel. Each citation is annotated, and there are essays describing each of the disciplines. Appendixes list college degree programs, organizations, and publishers, and there are author, title, and subject indexes. For academic and large public libraries. *Sports; Fitness; Travel; Leisure*

A
1049. **Information Sources in Sports and Leisure**, ed. by Michele Shoebridge. Bowker, 1991. 350p. $95. 0-86291-901-0.

This is a subject-arranged international bibliography of material in various formats on the subjects of sports, recreation, and leisure. Allied disciplines like medicine, physiology, psychology, and history are also included when they relate to the central topics. This will be used only in large specialized collection in academic and public libraries. *Sports; Recreation; Leisure*

Y; A
1050. **The Martial Arts: An Annotated Bibliography**, by Randy F. Nelson with Kathleen C. Whitaker. Garland, 1988. 436p. $71. 0-8240-4435-5. (Garland Reference Library of Social Science, 451).

With almost 2,400 works on the martial arts, this bibliography is probably the definitive work. All works are written in English and most were published from 1921-1987. The book is divided into various related topics including general reference materials, Akido, Jujitsu, Karate, Kung Fu, Sumo, etc. All entries have full bibliographic data, but only about half are annotated and even those only with brief notes. The volume does have complete author and subject indexes. This very comprehensive bibliography should find its place in many academic and public libraries for interlibrary loan and collection development purposes. *Martial Arts*

Y; A
1051. **Motorcycle Books: A Critical Survey and Checklist**, by Kirby Congdon. Scarecrow, 1987. 135p. $20. 0-8108-1985-6.

Motorcycling is becoming increasingly more popular, even with the general public. The number of newer books on the subject reflects this increased interest. This annotated bibliography covers 117 newer titles on the subject, arranged in alphabetical order by author. The entries are numbered sequentially, and each has full bibliographic information. The descriptive and evaluative annotations are helpful for individuals to choose a book on the subject or for librarians to select for their collection. The second part of the book offers two bonus lists: a comprehensive list of additional books covering biography, children's books, history, racing, reference, restoration, riding, travel, touring, and a list of videos; and a supplementary list of books catalogs, and handbooks by make. This bibliography would be useful for high school, public, and college libraries to develop collections for their patrons who are motorcycle enthusiasts. *Motorcycles*

C; Y; A
1052. **The Neal-Schuman Index to Sports Figures in Collective Biographies**, Comp. by Paulette B. Sharkey. Neal-Schuman, 1992. 180p. $35. 1-55570-055-X.

This index to sports figures in collective biographies is very similar in purpose, format, and level to *The Neal-Schuman Index to Performing and Creative Artists in Collective Biographies*. In this volume, 1,600 athletes in 255 collective biographies published between 1970 and 1988 are included. The three indexes list the athletes by 34 different sports, by country, and women athletes. Basically, the index is a handy reference tool for the many youngsters who are sports enthusiasts; as well, to the extent that most of the collective biographies indexed are still available, it is useful for collection development in school media centers and public libraries serving children and young adults. *Athletes; Sports—Biography*

Y; A
1053. **The Pro Football Bio-Bibliography**, by Myron J. Smith. Locust Hill Press, 1989. 289p. $25. 0-933951-23-X.

In order to "draw attention to many of the thousands of titles available on various football figures," Smith has compiled quite a fascinating bibliography; the statistics are amazing: About 6,600 citations are included for more than 1,400 players from the 1920's through 1988. Books, periodical articles, and team publications were screened for biographical information on players, broadcasters, coaches, executives, and others directly involved with professional football. The biographies are listed in alphabetical order, and each entry gives brief biographical data such as nickname, positions, teams played with, etc. This is followed by bibliographic entries listed by author; entries are not annotated. The introduction of this work has some useful information for collection development such as a list of important reference works and a list of the 167 journals cited. This bio-bibliography is recommended for most libraries serving football fans, which includes most high school and public libraries. *Football*

A

1054. **Sports Ethics in America: A Bibliography, 1970-1990**, by Donald G. Jones and Elaine L. Daly. Greenwood, 1992. 230p. 0-313-27767-2.

Arranged in five sections which include a separate chapter on reference works, this unannotated bibliography of about 2,900 entries includes citations for books and articles in journals, magazines and newspapers that explore many aspects of ethics in sports such as drugs, gambling, violence, women, and the media. There is an author and an extensive subject index. For use in academic and large public library collections. *Ethics; Sports*

A

1055. **Sports Fan's Connection: An All-Sports-in-One Directory to Professional, Collegiate, and Olympic Organizations, Events, and Information Sources**, ed. by Bradley J. Morgan and Peg Bessette. Gale, 1992. 584p. $59.95 0-8103-7954-6.

This comprehensive source contains almost 5,000 entries that cover about fifty different sports arranged in three sections by professional, collegiate, and Olympic sports. This includes all of the obvious sports as well as less known ones like rodeo events, lacrosse, and tractor pulling. In each of the three sections, there are subdivisions by the name of the sport with general information on organizations and teams with address and telephone numbers. This is followed by additional material including radio and television station coverage, magazines, newsletters, newspapers, reference sources, important books, and videos. The book and video entries are annotated. There is a general master name and keyword index. This will be useful in both public and academic libraries both as a research tool and a collection development aid. *Sports*

A

1056. **Sports Law and Legislation: An Annotated Bibliography**, comp. by John Hladczuk et al. Greenwood, 1991. 324p. $55. 0-313-26499-6. (Bibliographies and Indexes in Law and Politival Science, 15).

This bibliography contains 1,367 entries divided into 35 chapters, some of which deal with individual sports. A few of the subjects covered are discrimination, drug abuse, broadcast rights, and antitrust regulations. Coverage includes books, domestic and foreign legal journals, and law reviews. Popular periodicals are excluded. There are author, case, and subject indexes. The use of this book is probably restricted to libraries where law is an important research subject. *Law; Sports*

Y; A

1057. **Teaching, Coaching, and Learning Tennis: An Annotated Bibliography**, by Dennis J. Phillips. Scarecrow, 1989. 178p. $19.50. 0-8108-2254-7.

Though not indicated by the title, this annotated bibliography of over 500 entries is limited to the teaching, coaching, learning, and playing of lawn tennis. Books, periodical articles, theses, and dissertations are included; entries are arranged alphabetically by authors. Most of the works were published from 1968 through 1988. Some foreign titles written in English are also included. Entries include full bibliographic information and a brief annotation or abstract. A title and subject index are provided. This bibliography is recommended for all academic and public libraries with strong sports collections. *Tennis*

A

1058. **Women in Sport: An Annotated Bibliography and Resource Guide, 1900-1991**, by Mary L. Remley. G. K. Hall, 1991. 210p. $35. 0-8161-89977-3.

This work is more than an update of a 1980 work by Remley titled *Women in Sport: A Guide to Resources* (o.p.). The number of entries has increased considerably, and interesting subjects such as body-building, football, and Alaskan dogsled racing have been added. The work is arranged chronologically into four time frames: 1900-30; 1931-60; 1961-75; and 1975-90. Perhaps not surprisingly, only one book is listed for 1901, and only 88 of the 700 monographs were published before 1961. Most of the resources are American, with a few British and Canadian titles included. Each entry contains full bibliographic information, as well as a very brief annotation. In addition to the bibliography, a section on other information sources includes a list of periodicals that deal exclusively with women's sports, and a list of national sports organizations exclusively for or open to women. Author, title, and subject indexes are provided. This unique source will be a useful addition to women's studies and sports programs and collections.

Women in Sports; Sports

Statistics, Demography, and Urban Studies

A

1059. City and State Directories in Print, 1990-1991 edition, by Julie E. Towell and Charles B. Montney. biennial. Gale, 1989. 966p. $145. 0-8103-18848-2.

This bibliography, a companion volume to Gale's *Directories in Print*, lists 4,500 city and state directories in a geographical arrangement, first by state and then by city. The directories listed cover such areas as manufacturers, chambers of commerce, minority businesses, educational institutions, museums, banks and savings and loan agencies, and various kinds of organizations. Entry information includes title, address, plus telephone and fax numbers of publishers, scope of the directory, content and arrangement, frequency and price. There are subject, title, and keyword indexes. Though not complete, this listing will help identify and simplify procurement of regional directories for public libraries.

State Directories; City Directories; Directories

A

1060. Guide to Statistical Materials Produced by Governments and Associations in America, by Juri Stratford and Jean Slemmons. Chadwyck-Healey, 1987. 279p. $100. 0-85964-127-9.

This unusual bibliography cuts across conventional boundaries and lists about 700 statistical publications from both federal and state government agencies, as well as private membership associations. Each must be published at least at two-year intervals. Full bibliographic data and acquisition information is given for each publication, and there are subject and title indexes, plus a directory of agencies and a glossary. For large library collections. *Statistics*

A

1061. The Industrial Belt: An Annotated Bibliography, by Thomas J. Schlereth. Garland, 1987. 256p. $40. 0-8240-8812-3. (Garland Bibliographies in American Regional Studies, 1).

The areas considered in the industrial belt for this bibliography are western Pennsylvania, Ohio, Indiana, Michigan, western New York and northern Illinois. The works cited were published mainly from 1965 to 1986 and deal with the industrialization of this area during the nineteenth and twentieth centuries from many points of view. Some of the book's ten sections are on specific sources of information like bibliographies or libraries, while others cover subjects like the physical environment, politics, cultural expression and rural/urban issues. Books, periodical articles, and dissertations are included. There are three indexes, by author, place and subject. This will be of value in public libraries particularly those in the regions discussed. *Industrialization; United States—Industries*

A

1062. Mexican Americans in Urban Society: A Selected Bibliography, Comp. by Albert Camarillo. Floricanto Press, 1987. 296p. $29.95. 0-915745-12-7.

Floricanto Press specializes in bibliographies and research works which help in the development of collections for and about Chicanos and other Hispanics living in the United States. Camarillo's work lists publications published up to 1983. Items are arranged first by subject and then alphabetically by author. Materials dealing with agricultural or other aspects of rural society are excluded. A title and author index is provided. Despite the need for an up-dating, this volume is recommended for all academic and public libraries, particularly those that serve Hispanic users. *Mexican Americans; Urbanization*

A

1063. New York City, the Development of the Metropolis: An Annotated Bibliography, by Alan Burnham. Garland, 1988. 366p. $58. 0-8240-9133-7. (Garland Bibliographies in Architecture and Planning, 5); (Garland Reference Library of the Humanities, 408).

Burnham has compiled a rather specialized bibliography of over 600 items dealing with the history and development of New York City. The annotated entries are arranged into sections mixed by type and topic, e.g., general histories, guidebooks, monographs, government materials, pictorial and literary material, New York society, banking and commerce, architecture, sculpture, etc. There are even sections that deal with boroughs, neighborhoods, and parks. Author, title, and subject indexes are also provided. This work will be of particular interest to libraries in and around New York; however, other libraries supporting programs in urban planning and architecture may also want to consider it for reference and collection building. *New York City; Architecture; City Planning*

A

1064. A Retrospective Bibliography of American Demographic History from Colonial Times to 1983, comp. by David R. Gerhan and Robert V. Wells. Greenwood, 1989. 474p. $75. 0-313-23130-3. (Bibliographies in American History, 10).

Gerhan and Wells have identified over 3,800 items for this very comprehensive guide to the field of American demographic history. Citations to books and journal articles covering references to 1983 are arranged into six sections: general; marriage and fertility; health and death; migration; family; and population, economics and society. Entries are subdivided within each section into early America, the nineteenth century, and recent history. Because the focus was on historical aspects, materials, particularly journal articles of the 20th century "have been used sparingly." Author, place, and broad subject indexes are provided. This rather scholarly work with a specialized focus will be well-received by academic librarians for reference and collection development. Larger public libraries with strong historical collections may also want to consider it. *Demography; United States—History; United States—Population*

A

1065. Rural Development: An Annotated Bibliography of ILO Publications and Documents, by Evelyn Schaad. Geneva: International Labour Office, 1991. Dist. by ILO. 338p. $28. 92-2-106451-4.

This brief and rather specialized bibliography of publications on rural development will be of particular interest to those concerned with a major problem of the developing nations. All of the items are authored, issued, or sponsored by the International Labour Office. Each entry includes standard bibliographic data as well as an indication of availability and an English language abstract. Indexes for author, corporate author, and subject are provided. Recommended for academic and other libraries with a special interest in this area or in the Third World generally. *Developing Countries*

A

1066. State and Local Statistics Sources 1990-1991: A Subject Guide to Data on States, Cities and Locales, by M. Balachandran and Sarojini Balachandran. Gale, 1990. 1,124p. $135. 0-8103-2798-8.

This companion volume to *Statistics Sources*, which gives information on national and international levels, contains approximately 40,000 citations that deal with state, city, and local statistic sources. Publications have been culled from a variety of sources, including state and local government agencies, local, state and national associations, universities and related organizations, commercial producers of statistical data, and federal agencies. Included are data on industrial, business, social, educational, and financial topics. The material is arranged in 54 chapters on states and territories. There is an annotated bibliography of all the sources cited that contains information on the geographic scope and coverage of each source and an appendix of state data centers and databases. This sourcebook will be of value in identifying state statistical documents and in building collections in this area.

United States—Statistics; Statistics

A

1067. Statistical Sources 1992: A Subject Guide to Data on Industrial, Business, Social, Educational, Financial, and Other Topics for the United States and Internationally, by Jacqueline Wasserman and Steven R. Wasserman. 15th ed. Gale, 1991. 3,800 p. 2 vols. $325. 0-8103-7378-5.

Wherever detailed statistical data are required at the national or international level, this comprehensive guide will be a help in locating sources. The two-volume work is basically arranged by 20,000 subjects, including geographical headings for countries. For each subject, source documents are listed in which statistical information can be found. There are a total of 95,000 citations to over 2,000 print and nonprint sources, and published and not published statistical sources. In a separate section each of the publications cited as sources are cited with addresses plus listings of names and addresses of organizations and agencies, federal statistical telephone contacts, and federal statistical databases. This is an important source for academic and large public libraries. *Statistics; United States—Statistics*

A

1068. The Urban South: A Bibliography, by Catherine L. Brown. Greenwood, 1989. 455p. $49.95. 0-313-26154-7.

Brown treats the word urban very broadly in this work and includes any "gathering of people and buildings," not just cities. In the rural south, this could include some rather small hamlets. The entries are organized first by type of material, that is, dissertations, periodical articles, and monographs. Then, they are further divided into major subject areas. There is no author index; however, a geographic index and a limited subject index facilitate some ease in retrieval. This rather specialized bibliography is recommended for public libraries (particularly those in the southern states), and academic libraries supporting courses in urban or southern studies. *City Life; Urbanization; Southern States*

Women's Studies

A

1069. An Annotated Critical Bibliography of Feminist Criticism, by Maggie Humm. G. K. Hall, 1987. 240p. $40. 0-8161-8937-4.

The purpose of this multidisciplinary bibliography of over 900 entries is "to provide a core collection of women-centered materials which can support feminist research, policy, and studies." All titles are in English and published in either Great Britain or the United States between 1950 and 1985—however, the work has a distinct and strong British accent. The entries are chronologically arranged and numbered within each major subject category, e.g., theory and sexual politics; literary criticism; sociology; psychology; history; anthropology; education; and women's studies. A detailed subject index is also provided. This bibliography includes many titles not found in a similar work, Catherine Loeb's *Women's Studies: A Recommended Core Bibliography, 1980-1985*. Most public and academic libraries will want to consider this inexpensive guide, particularly if the Loeb book is unavailable or if additional titles are needed.

Feminism; Women Studies

Y; A

1070. Biographies of American Women: An Annotated Bibliography, by Patricia E. Sweeney. ABC-Clio, 1990. 290p. $67.50. 0-87436-070-6.

This comprehensive and informative bibliography of biographies "examines 1,391 biographies of American women that comprise at least 50 pages and are written in English." Sweeney says of the 700 women included in this work: " Most are famous, many are noteworthy, and a few are notorious." Entries are arranged in alphabetical order with cross references from maiden names to married names when necessary for identification. The annotations are critical and rather brief. An appendix lists biographies by profession, and an author/title index is provided. This guide would be useful as a reference/reader's advisory aid and as a tool for collection development in most secondary school, academic and public libraries.

Women—United States

A

1071. Building Women's Studies Collections: A Resource Guide, ed. by Joan Ariel. Choice, 1987. 48p. $12. (pap.), 0-914492-07-1. (Choice Bibliographical Essay Series, no. 8)

This guide to developing libraries collections in the area of women's studies concentrates on general sources rather that individual titles. The material is divided into 18 different sections such as bibliographies, review sources, publishers' series and catalogs, bookstore catalogs, organizations with strong publishing record, dissertations, important book dealers, databases, and AV materials, plus a listing of books for children and young adults. Entries are annotated with both descriptive and evaluative comments. Only English language material is included chiefly from United States and Canada. A selected bibliography of further readings on developing women's studies collections and general indexes complete this work that will be useful in public and academic libraries interested in strengthening their collections in this area.

Women's Studies

Y; A

1072. The Continuum Dictionary of Women's Biography, by Jennifer S. Uglow. Crossroad/Continium, 1989. 621p. $39.50 0-8264-0417-0.

The main body of this biographical dictionary is a 600-page section on the lives and accomplishments of 1,750 famous women of history. Preceding it is a section called "Additional Reference Sources" which is an impressive list of sources of biographical information about women starting first with general encyclopedias and biographical dictionaries and moving onto specific sources. This is a valuable reference tool for both public, academic and high school libraries. *Women—Biography*

A

1073. **The Equal Rights Amendment: An Annotated Bibliography of the Issues, 1976-1985**, by Renee Feinberg. Greenwood, 1986. 151p. $39.95 0-313-24762-5.

In this 700 item bibliography of books, articles, and documents, the editor chronicles the last futile struggles to have ERA ratified. The items are arranged in 11 chapters under such headings as 'Education,' 'Family and Religion,' 'Boycott,' and 'Defeat.' There is an introduction that gives the historical background, and some entries for television news coverage, plus a list of organizations and subject and author indexes. *Equal Rights Amendment; Women*

Y; A

1074. **Feminist Resources for Schools and Colleges: A Guide to Curricular Materials**, by Anne Chapman. 3rd ed. Feminist Press, 1986. 190p. $12.95 pap. 0-935312-35-8.

This is a guide to 310 print publications and 136 audiovisuals that are recommended nonsexist curricular materials published between 1975 and 1984. They are arranged principally by academic subject areas like art and music, but also have sections on bibliographies and reference works. The annotations are extensive and indicate ages and reading levels. There are author, title, and subject indexes. This will be of value in professional collections in high schools, colleges, and public libraries. *Feminism*

C; Y; A

1075. **Her Way**, by Mary-Ellen Siegel. 2nd ed. American Library Association, 1984. 430p. $10. pap. 0-8389-0396-7.

This work lists recommended biographies of 1100 historical and contemporary women. Each is annotated with age and grade level suitability indicated. Literary merit, accuracy, and freedom of bias were criteria used in selecting the titles. Though now considerably out-of-date, this will still be of some value in collection development in elementary and junior high schools. *Biography; Women—Biography*

A

1076. **Index to Women of the World From Ancient to Modern Times: A Supplement**, by Norma Olin Ireland. Scarecrow, 1988. 774p. $79.50 0-8108-2092-7.

This work is a supplement to the original volume that analyzes many collective biographies for their material on women (1970, $32.50, 0-8108-2092-7). The present index covers an additional 380 collections that appeared from the 1970s to the mid 1980s. The main body of the work lists the women alphabetically and gives a list of sources in which pertinent material can be found. The books indexed are listed in the front with full bibliographic information. Most are popular rather than scholarly. Some references sources (like *Current Biography*) are included as well as general nonfiction. This list might be helpful in collection building. The index itself will be a welcome addition for large libraries. *Women*

A

1077. **Introduction to Library Research in Women's Studies**, by Susan E. Searing. Westview, 1985. 257p. $41. pap. 0-86531-267-2.

This guide to research in women's studies begins with a section called "Using the Library," which gives general information on women's studies, and how to do research in the area. The second part, "The Tools of Research" is the body of the work and gives annotated bibliographies of reference works, indexes, handbooks, catalogs, etc., plus sections on specific works on such subjects as the arts, business, education, health, law, lesbian studies, literature, political science, religion, and science. There are indexes by title, author, and subject. This excellent bibliography and research guide is unfortunately marred by its coverage cutoff, 1985. For large libraries. *Women; Women's Studies*

A

1078. **Journal of Women's History: Guide to Periodical Literature**, ed. by Gayle V. Fischer. Indiana University, 1992. 501p. $39.95 0-253-32219-7; $18.95 pap. 0-253-20720-7.

Under 40 different subjects, citations to over 5,000 periodical articles from 789 journals are listed. The subjects are either topical (e.g., politics, health) or geographical (e.g., Asia) and are subdivided. Unfortunately there are no subject or author indexes. However, apart from its reference value, the names of periodicals indexed might help serials librarians in the acquisition process. For academic libraries.

Women Studies; History

A

1079. **The National Women's History Project's Catalog**. [1992] 48p.

This 48-page catalog lists a wide variety of multicultural, multimedia materials dealing with women's history. It includes over 300 posters, videos, pamphlets, books, and miscellaneous items. A copy is available for only $1.00 from: National Women's History Project, 7738 Bell Rd., Windsor, CA 95492, (707) 838-6000. *Multiculturalism; Women; Women Studies*

Y; A

1080. **Personal Writings by Women to 1900: A Bibliography of American and British Writers**, Comp. by Gwenn Davis and Beverly A. Joyce. University of Oklahoma, 1989. 294p. $65. 0-8061-2206-4.

This work, which deals with women's " feelings and pursuits in their own words," includes diaries, autobiographies, correspondence, and other personal writings. All the books included in this bibliography were published prior to 1900, and translated works and journal articles are not included. Almost 5,000 entries are included; they are arranged in alphabetical order by author. Each entry includes bibliographic data, source where found, and notes when necessary for explication. A similar work that complements *Personal Writings...* is Goodfriend's *The Published Diaries and Letters of American Women: An Annotated Bibliography* (o.p.). Even smaller academic and public libraries will want both sources if they support research in women's studies. *Authors, Women*

A

1081. **Sources: An Annotated Bibliography of Women's Issues**, by Rita L. McCullough. Knowledge Issues and Trends, 1991. 320p. $24.95 pap. 1-879198-28-2.

The 1,500 entries for books in this annotated bibliography are arranged alphabetically by author under broad subjects like age and aging, bibliographies, and women of color. the books are as current as 1990, and most were published in the 1980s. The editor has tried to include many titles from small publishers and university presses. The annotations are brief but sometimes evaluative. However, because of the large number of titles included, this bibliography will be used to identify publications rather than as a selection tool. There is a directory of publishers included and author and title indexes. For large collections.

Women; Women's Studies

A

1082. **Violence Against Women: A Bibliography**, by Joan Nordquist. Reference and Research Services, 1992. 68p. $15. 0-937855-50-2.

Nordquist has compiled a list of about 600 titles dealing with the serious issue of violence against women. The titles selected include: books, pamphlets, parts of books, journal articles, and government publications. All entries in this up-to-date list were published from 1986 to 1991. The list is divided into six sections: Section 1-5 are the sources listed alphabetically by author under format, e.g., books, articles, etc.; Section 6 lists type of resources, e.g., bibliographies, statistics, directories, and organizations. The major limitations of this otherwise excellent list are the lack of annotations and indexes. Still, this very inexpensive and current list is recommended for all libraries with an interest in women's issues.

Violence; Women Studies

A

1083. **WAVE (Women's AudioVisuals in English): A Guide to Nonprint Resources for Women's Studies**, Compiled by the Office of the Women's Studies Librarian. University of Wisconsin-Madison, 1993. 88p. $2.00. pap.

More than 800 nonprint titles are included in this annotated bibliography compiled at the University of Wisconsin-Madison. This fine list is organized by 22 broad subjects, including: law, history, sports, anthropology, and sexuality. Many of the brief entries include excerpts from reviews. Films, audio-cassettes, videocassettes, and filmstrips, all produced by and about women are included. Names and addresses of distributors to contact for purchase or preview are also provided. Title and subject indexes complete the work. The bibliography is available for a check of $2.00 payable to UW-Madison and sent to: Women's Studies Librarian, UW-Madison, 430 Memorial Library, 728 State St., Madison, WI 53706.

Audiovisual Materials; Women's Studies

A

1084.   Women: A Bibliography of Bibliographies, by Patricia Ballou. 2nd ed. G. K. Hall, 1986. 349p. $35. 0-8161-8729-0.

This revised and updated 2nd edition has been expanded from 557 entries to 906, perhaps reflecting the growing body of literature in this important field. Ballou selected the bibliographies on the basis of their scope, availability, organization, and commentary. Included are books, parts of books, pamphlets, journal articles, documents, and microforms. Entries are arranged by broad topics (some newer subjects added to this edition include peace, comparable worth, and traditional arts). The table of contents with almost 200 headings listed reflects the subject focus of this bibliography. Entries provide full bibliographic information and most are annotated. Subject, title, and author indexes are also provided. This work is recommended as a reference guide and an aid for collection development for all libraries supporting a women's studies program or collection.   *Women; Bibliography*

A

1085.   Women of Color and Southern Women: A Bibliography of Social Science Research, 1975-1988, Ed. by Andrea Timberlake et al. Center for Research on Women, Memphis State University, 1988. 264p. $17. pap. 0-9621327-0-5.

This is an extensive bibliography of almost 1,500 citations on women of color drawn from the online database of the Center for Research on Women, Memphis State University. It represented 56% of the database as it existed in 1988. Articles, dissertations, conference proceedings, and books are represented. The work is divided into six major categories: Culture, Education, Employment, Family, Health, and Political Activism/Social Movements which in turn are subdivided by ethnic groups, including African Americans, Latinos, Asian Americans, and Native Americans. Two special categories, Women of Color and Southern Women, are used to list items that deal with more than one group. A regional bibliography of this size is quite uncommon; however, it is important because the collection of the Center for Research on Women has been used as a model collection throughout the country. Annual supplements have been issued for 1989 and 1990 costing $10. each and containing about 1,000 entries each. This extensive bibliography is recommended for larger libraries and those libraries supporting programs or collections on women's studies or racial/ethnic studies.   *Women; Minorities; African American Women*

A

1086.   Women of Color in the United States: A Guide to the Literature, by Bernice Redfern. Garland, 1989. 156p. $27. 0-8240-5849-6. (Garland Reference Library of Social Science, 469)

Redfern has compiled this much needed bibliography of over 600 items from scholarly books, parts of books, articles, and dissertations published from 1975. There have been many guides to the literature on white, middle-class women; this volume fills the void and helps redirect the focus to black women and women of other ethnic groups. The work is divided by major groups of women of color: Afro-American Women; Asian-American Women; Hispanic-American Women; and Native American Women. The entries are organized within each group under a further subdivision, e.g., bibliographies, general works, education, employment, etc. Author and subject indexes refer to the numbered entries. This work emphasizes scholarly works and excludes the popular unless they are very significant. This bibliography is not as extensive as *Women of Color and Southern Women...*(see previous entry) which has about three times as many entries; however, they are not annotated, nor does the work have the useful background essays relating to each chapter. There is a need for both; and the price is such that all libraries purchasing one will want both. Recommended for all libraries supporting programs or having collections in women's studies or racial/ethnic studies.   *Women; Minorities; African American Women*

A

1087.   Women in the Third World: A Directory of Resources, Comp. and ed. by P. Fenton and Mary J. Heffron. Orbis, 1987. 141p. $12.95. pap. 0-88344-530-1.

Since the editors admit that the resources chosen for inclusion are "by and large 'partisan and biased' in favor of a 'radical analysis' of Third World affairs," the books, organizations, periodicals, journal articles, and audiovisuals include many not found in more traditional sources. They also partially update Fenton and Heffron's earlier work: *Third World Resource Directory* (Books on Demand, 1984, $82.70 0-8357-2674-6). Many, but not all, of the sources are annotated. This inexpensive, slim, and more unusual directory is recommended for most public and academic libraries; however, it is not a substitute for the more scholarly and comprehensive 1986 ABC-Clio bibliography edited by Byrne and Ontiveros: *Women in the Third World: A Historical Bibliography*. (See next entry).   *Developing Countries; Women*

A

1088.   **Women in the Third World: A Historical Bibliography**, Ed. by Pamela R. Byrne and Suzanne R. Ontiveros. ABC-Clio, 1986. 152p. $45. 0-87436-459-0. (ABC-Clio Research Guides, 15).

This bibliography of 600 citations and abstracts was pulled from the 2,000 journals in ABC-Clio's *Historical Abstracts* database. All of the entries were published between 1970 and 1985. The articles included cover women from all areas of the Third World. The work is divided geographically by chapters. Complete bibliographical information is given for all of the citations, and most have extensive abstracts. The editors point out that when there is an unevenness in coverage as reflected in the size of chapters, that this was not an editorial decision, but rather it says a great deal about what has not been written. This comprehensive bibliography is recommended for all academic and most public libraries. Another work on the same topic, but not as extensive, and representing a more radical point of view is Fenton and Heffron's *Women in the Third World: A Directory of Resources*. (See previous entry).   *Women; Developing Countries*

A

1089.   **Women's Issues: An Annotated Bibliography**, by Laura Stempel Mumford. Salem, 1989. 163p. $40. 0-89356-654-3.

This bibliography of 163 pages is one of the many bibliographies on women published in recent years, perhaps reflecting the amount of scholarship on the topic where heretofore was a dearth of information. The bibliography is organized into nine broad issue-oriented sections, including economics, history, politics, education, the women's movement, health issues and sexuality, and violence against women. These areas are further divided into subsections. Entries include a well-written annotation. Unfortunately, indexing is by author only; a subject index would enhance its usefulness. Still, despite this flaw and the relatively high cost for a 163-page publication, the emphasis on issues makes this a recommended purchase for high school library collections as well as for many academic and public libraries. Similar bibliographies published in recent years include: Loeb, Searing, and Stineman's *Women's Studies...*; Timberlake's *Women of Color and Southern Women...*; and Redfern's *Women of Color in the United States....* Libraries already holding one or more of these more extensive bibliographies on women may not need this more limited work.   *Women*

A

1090.   **Women's Studies: A Guide to Information Sources**, by Sarah Carter and Maureen Ritchie. McFarland, 1990. 278p. $39.95. 0-89950-534-1.

Carter and Ritchie have compiled one of the most comprehensive guides to the literature dealing with women. It not only updates, but it is more international in scope, than two similar bibliographies in the field: Searing's *Introduction to Library Research in Women's Studies* and Loeb, Searing, and Stineman's *Women's Studies: A Recommended Core Bibliography*. The 1076 annotated entries focus on the 1978-1988 time period (an era when great strides in women's studies were being made). The book is divided into three broad sections dealing with: general reference sources; geographic areas; a treatment of special areas of women's studies, e.g., black women, arts and media, lesbians, and women in the work force. A combined author-title-subject index is provided. This work, with a slight British accent, is one of the most well-developed and current bibliographies in the field and is highly recommended for all academic and public libraries offering programs or supporting collections in women's studies.   *Women; Women's Studies*

A

1091.   **Women's Studies: A Recommended Core Bibliography, 1980-1985**, by Catherine R. Loeb et al. Libraries Unlimited, 1987. 538p. $55. 0-87287-472-9.

This bibliography is an updating, through 1985, of the earlier volume by Stineman which was published in 1979. The more than 1,200 citations are organized by academic disciplines. Lengthy and well-written annotations describe, evaluate, and compare the selected works and often mention related works and other books by the same author. An added bonus is the chapter which lists and describes about 60 feminist periodicals. There are many bibliographies dealing with women, which compare very favorably with this update (many are identified and described in this guide). The strong feature of this guide, as compared with others, is the quality of its annotations. This is recommended as a starting point to building a core collection in women's studies for academic and public libraries. For collections in high school and small libraries use the abridgment: *Women's Studies, 1980-1985: A Recommended Core Bibliography. Abridged Edition* (Libraries Unlimited, 1987. $23.50. 0-87287-598-9).   *Women; Women's Studies*

A

1092.   **Women's Studies Index, 1990**. G. K. Hall, 1991. 502p. $135. per year. 0-8161-0510-3.

This index, which made its debut in 1989, offers breadth in that it indexes 78 titles on a regular basis. Included are the popular magazines such as *Family Circle* and *Ladies Home Journal* as well as the academic and scholarly feminist journals. Many of the 78 journals listed could serve as a checklist to evaluate the library's holdings in periodicals of this genre. This index is recommended for those libraries that can afford it, but most certainly for those academic and public libraries that support women's studies programs and collections.   *Women; Women's Studies*

14 Humanities

General and Miscellaneous

A

1093.   **Blacks in the Humanities, 1750-1984: A Selected Annotated Bibliography**, by Donald Franklin *MSU*
Joyce. Greenwood, 1986. 209p. $39.95. 0-313-24643-2. (Bibliographies and Indexes in Afro-American
and African Studies, 13).

Joyce, a black historian and librarian, has compiled a bibliography documenting and annotating over
200 pages of print materials by and about African Americans spanning more than two centuries. The
citations were culled from bibliographies, indexes, union lists, encyclopedias, biographical dictionaries,
library catalogs, journal articles, and general works. The book is arranged by major subject divisions, e.g.,
art, science, literary criticism, history, music, etc. The entries are then subdivided by format. In addition to
full bibliographic citations each entry includes an informative annotation. Detailed subject and name
indexes complete this fine bibliography which is recommended for all academic and public libraries.

African Americans; Humanities

A

1094.   **The Fifth Directory of Periodicals: Publishing Articles on American and English Language** *Ref*
and Literature, Criticism and Theory, Film, American Studies, Poetry and Fiction, by Richard Barlow.
Swallow/Ohio University, 1992. 349p. $49.95 0-8040-0958-9; $19.95 pap. 0-8040-0962-7.   *PE9*
.D57

This is an updating of *The Fourth Directory*, which was published in 1974. It is primarily meant for
scholars in the humanities who are interested in knowing about publications in their area of expertise,
usually with the object of submitting manuscripts. This volume contains an eight-page introduction to help
the novice get his or her work published and continues with a listing of 611 journals in six sections: literature
journals, criticism and theory journals, film journals, and language and linguistics journals. Entries include
such information as fields of interest, editorial address, price, and information on submitting manuscripts.
There is also a subject index. Much of this same information is also available in the more pricey *MLA
Directory of Periodicals* (Modern Language Association, 1993, $130. 0-873-52650-3) which appeared in
its seventh edition in mid-1993. Another useful source in this area is the *International Directory of Little
Magazines and Small Presses* (Dustbooks, 1991, $41.95, 0-916685-24-1; $25.95, 0-916685-23-3), now in
its 27th edition.   *Periodicals; Literature*

A*

1095.   **The Humanities: A Selective Guide to Information Sources**, by Ron Blazek and Elizabeth *4th ed*
Aversa. 3rd ed. Libraries Unlimited, 1988. 382p. $28. pap. 0-87287-594-6. (Library Science Text Series).   *AZ221*
.Z99853
The humanities are defined liberally in this bibliographic guide. They include literature and language,
the visual arts, applied and decorative arts, the performing arts, philosophy, religion, mythology, and   *1994*
folklore (no history). As in previous editions, each discipline has a two-chapter coverage: the first is an
introduction to the subject, its subdivisions, a rundown on how its information is organized and used, details
on computer use in the discipline, and the major organizations in the field. The second chapter consists of
listings of principal information sources classified by types of material. Annotations are included for each
work, many of them giving comparisons with other similar works. The choices are well made and cover
each of the fields admirably. A total of 973 titles are included (fewer than in the last edition because coverage
of periodicals has been dropped). There are also author, title and subject indexes. This is used as a library
school text and also has value in public libraries for reference and collection development.

Humanities; Reference Books

CC, MSU

A

1096.   **Images of the Blacks in American Culture: A Reference Guide to Information Sources**, by Jessie Carney Smith. Greenwood, 1988. 390p. $55. 0-313-24844-3.

Ten specialists have written separate chapters on the image of blacks in literature, theater, music, film and television, the graphic arts, children's literature, and cultural artifacts such as toys and dolls. After each essay, there is a extensive bibliography and other reference material. This interesting work will be of value in many public library collections. *African Americans*

A

1097.   **Where Do We Come From? What Are We? Where Are We Going? An Annotated Bibliography of Aging and the Humanities**, by Donna Polisar et al. Gerontological Society of America, 1988. 150p. $15. pap. 0-929596-01-3.

This annotated bibliography produced under sponsorship of the Gerontological Society of America is a highly selective guide to humanities literature on aging. Included are almost 1,100 books, parts of books, articles, and dissertations written from 1975-1987. The entries are arranged in alphabetical order by author in six broad topic chapters: Ethics and Philosophy; History; Literature and Art; Religion; Jurisprudence; and Interdisciplinary Humanities. Bibliographic data is provided with each entry; most annotations are about a paragraph in length. Detailed subject and author indexes are also included. This well-developed bibliography is recommended for all academic and public libraries that support programs or collections on aging. *Aging*

Communications and Mass Media

General and Miscellaneous

A

1098.   **Alternative Publications: A Guide to Directories, Indexes, Bibliographies and Other Sources**, Ed. by Cathy Seitz Whitaker. McFarland, 1990. 96p. $18.95. pap. 0-89950-484-1.

This guide is the work of the American Library Association's Social Responsibilities Round Table Task Force on Alternatives in Print. An earlier edition, *Field Guide to Alternative Media*, was published by the ALA in 1984. Alternative press is defined in this guide as meeting the following criteria: the publisher is noncommercial; the subject should pertain to "social responsibility;" the publisher should define itself as a publisher of alternative media; and the work is published by a small press poetry or literary publisher. The work begins with a selective bibliography on alternative media in general. This is followed by a number of chapters on abstracts, review sources, and subject and trade bibliographies covering a wide number of topics—peace, minority rights, health and human services, and small press and little magazines. There are 160 citations included; they are arranged alphabetically by title within each section. Each entry contains full bibliographic information and a brief descriptive annotation. A subject index is provided. This slim publication is recommended for academic and public libraries having a need for more information of this type. *Press; Underground Press*

A

1099.   **Blacks and Media: A Selected, Annotated Bibliography, 1962-1982**, Comp. by J. William Snorgrass and Gloria T. Woody. University Presses of Florida, 1985. 150p. $17.95. 0-8130-0810-7.

Almost 750 entries dealing with African Americans in media are arranged under the areas of focus: Print Media, Broadcast Media, Advertising and Public Relations, and Film and Theater. Entries include books, parts of books, and journal articles. In addition to bibliographic information, concise descriptive annotations are provided. There is also an author/title index, but unfortunately no subject index. One should also consider Hill's *Black Media in America* ... (o.p.), which, though a year older, is much more comprehensive and covers a great deal of the same information. Still, despite its limitations, it does complement Hill and is recommended for libraries with either media or African American collections if additional sources are desired. *African Americans; Mass Media*

A

1100.   **Cable Television: A Reference Guide to Information,** by Ronald Garay. Greenwood, 1988 192p. $45. 0-313-24751-X.

This series of bibliographic essays lists a total of approximately 400 books, government documents and periodical articles published between 1980 and 1987 that cover such topics related to cable television as program content, viewing habits, laws and regulations, cable businesses, economics and consumer criticism. An extensive index is included. For academic and larger public collections.   *Cable Television*

A

1101.   **Celebrity Sources**, by Ronald Ziegler. Garland, 1990. $57. 0-8240-5946-8.

To help satisfy the public's constant need for information on celebrities, the author has compiled this bibliography of 2,000 citations to biographical sources, series, nonprint materials, and fan clubs in four sections: general biographical sources, film and TV stars, music celebrities and sports figures. Though nonevaluative, this is a valuable source for biographical searching and collection building in pop culture.

Celebrities

A

1102.   **Comic Books and Strips: An Information Sourcebook**, by Randall W. Scott. Oryx, 1988. 152p. *MSU* $32.95 pap. 0-89774-389-X.

This 1,033 entry sourcebook serves as a guide to the study of comic books and strips, an important part of our popular culture. It is divided into five parts with each entry in these parts identified with citation material and a descriptive annotation. The first part lists a core collection of the 100 most important titles for researching this topic. There follows a longer, general list of books that are recommended but are not as essential as those in the first part. There is a listing of books that have reprinted comics in part three, and an annotated bibliography of 53 periodicals on the subject in part 4. The last part lists 43 important library collections. Extensive indexes by author, title, and subject are appended. Valuable for public libraries with extensive pop culture collections.   *Comic Books, Strips, etc.; Popular Culture*

A

1103.   **Communication and the Mass Media: A Guide to the Reference Literature**, by Eleanor S. Block *P90* and James K. Bracken. Libraries Unlimited, 1991. 198p. $40. 0-87287-810-4.   *.Z99B54*
1991

Subjects like communication theory, rhetoric, speech, applied linguistics, mass communication, telecommunication, group communication, and new communication technologies are covered in this selective bibliography of about 500 English language reference sources published since 1970. The arrangement is by type of work and includes sections of bibliographies, biographical sources, dictionaries, and encyclopedias. In addition to complete bibliographic information, there are annotations that are evaluative. Separate chapters deal with CD-ROM databases, a list of 91 core periodicals, research centers and archival collections, as well as societies and associations. There are subject and author/title indexes. This is a good source both for reference and collection development in academic and public libraries.

Reference Books; Communication; Mass Media

A

1104.   **Control of Information in the United States: An Annotated Bibliography**, by James R. Bennett. Meckler, 1987. 587p. $69.50 0-88736-082-3.

Using the thesis that information is spread or withheld by the action of a power cartel consisting of such elements in the establishment as government, big business, the media, and education, the author has compiled a fascinating annotated bibliography on censorship and the control of information in the United States. The 3,000 entries are on books and periodical articles and organized under such topics as corporations, the Pentagon, and intelligence agencies. There are indexes by author and subject. Over 250 journals were consulted and the work is current up through 1986. For use in academic and large public libraries.

Censorship; Freedom of Information

A

1105.   **Control of the Media in the United States: An Annotated Bibliography**, by James R. Bennett. Garland, 1992. 819p. $125. 0-8240-4438-X (Garland Library of Social Science, 456).

This bibliography of 5,000 items contains both books and periodical articles; the latter from about 450 journals. Each is briefly annotated and in general support the thesis that the American media are controlled directly or indirectly by a combination of business and government. This specialized bibliography would be of particular interest in universities having strong journalism programs. *Journalism; Media Studies*

A

1106. Encyclopedia of American Humorists, by Steven H. Gale. Garland, 1988. 557p. $85. 0-8240-8644-9.

There are 135 articles in this reference work, each dealing with the life and work of famous American humorists both past and present. Some contemporaries included are Woody Allen, Erma Bombeck, Garrison Keillor, and Andy Rooney. In addition to biographical and critical material, there are bibliographies of works by the humorist and secondary sources about him or her. An interesting acquisition for many libraries.

Wit and Humor; Humorists

A

Ref
Z6951
.A97

1107. Gale Directory of Publications and Broadcast Media, 1991, by Karin E. Koek and Julie Winklepleck. 123rd ed. Gale, 1991 (annual). 3 vols. 3,441 p. $265. (includes updates) 0-8103-7185-5.

This annual directory of newspapers, periodicals, radio and television stations, and cable companies was first published over 100 years ago as *Ayer's Directory of Publications*. For a brief period in the 1980s it was also known as *IMS Directory of Publications*. Over 35,000 periodicals published in the United States, Canada, and Puerto Rico are included, plus about 10,000 radio and TV stations in the same geographical areas. The arrangement is geographical, first by state or province and then by city. Each state section begins with a statistical profile on population, manufacturing, industry, and agriculture. Periodical and newspaper entries include title, publisher's name and address, telephone numbers, frequency, circulation numbers, price, political affiliations, advertising rates, and special notes. Comparable information is given for the broadcast media including areas covered, important local programs, key personnel, and advertising rates. Indexes provide access through lists arranged by title and by subjects and special interests. This directory is valuable in large library collections where there is a need to identify media particularly for businesses involved in advertising. *Periodicals; Newspapers; Radio Stations; Television Stations*

A

P90
.P46
1992

1108. Human Communication Behavior and Information Processing: An Interdisciplinary Sourcebook, by Donald E. Phillips. Garland, 1992. 938p. $128. 0-8240-3531-3.

This impressive bibliography of books covers all aspects of communication roughly from 1970 to the beginning of the 1990s. The scope is so broad that not only are books on speech, writing, television, news media, etc. are covered, but also material on information science, data processing and computer languages. The nearly 6,000 entries are arranged in three main sections and some are briefly annotated. Unfortunately the arrangement and the meager subject index (only 50 headings) make is difficult to access the material easily. For large collections. *Communication; Mass Media*

A

1109. Information Sources in the Press and Broadcast Media, ed. by Selwyn Eagle. Bowker, 1991. 250p. $70. 0-89291-900-2.

Librarians and other information specialists from North America, Europe and the United Kingdom contributed to this volume, which is a comprehensive listing of sources on newspapers and news-oriented periodicals, radio, and television. For large collections.

Newspapers; Periodicals; Radio Broadcasting; Television Broadcasting

A

PN4731
.Z99C38
1990

1110. Journalism: A Guide to the Reference Literature, by Jo Cates. Libraries Unlimited, 1990. 214p. $38. 0-87287-716-7 (Reference Sources in the Humanities).

This bibliography deals with both print and broadcasting journalism in 728 selective entries covering the period from the late 1960s to 1989. There are separate chapters for various types of reference sources like bibliographies, encyclopedias, abstracts, and dictionaries, plus sections on core periodicals, databases, libraries, associations, and government bodies. Annotations are both descriptive and critical. A useful work for large public libraries with collections where there is research in journalism. *Journalism*

A

P 90
.Z99B55
1990

1111. Mass Media Bibliography, by Eleanor Blum and Frances Wilhoit. University of Illinois Press, 1990. 344p. $49.95. 0-252-01706-4.

The stated purpose of this bibliography on mass communications is "to serve as a reference tool; to suggest materials for research or reading; and to act as a checking or buying list." The nearly 2,000 monographs, films, journal articles, journals, indexes, bibliographies, etc., help attain the authors' goals. The emphasis of the selected titles is more on theory and research, rather than on technique or methodology. The entries are arranged alphabetically under nine chapters, which are divided by subject or by format. Full bibliographic data is provided, and annotations are given for many (but not all) titles. Detailed subject, author, and title indexes are also provided. This work is especially recommended for academic libraries supporting programs in mass communications, but may also be considered by many public libraries.

Mass Media; Communication

Y; A

1112.   **Mass Media Sex and Adolescent Values: An Annotated Bibliography and Directory of Organi-** *CC* **zations**, Comp. by A. Odasuo Alali, McFarland, 1991. 138p. $19.95. pap. 0-89950-518-X.

The stated purpose of this research-oriented bibliography is "to reflect the current research findings, discussions, articles, and analyses of mass media products and their impact, or lack of it, on adolescent's sexual attitudes, values, and behavior." Alali has compiled an annotated bibliography of 227 articles and books that deal with media sex role stereotypes, media use and frequency, influence of sexual media, and attitudes, knowledge, and beliefs of adolescents toward contraception, pregnancy, etc. This rather esoteric bibliography is recommended for academic libraries supporting research in the area of adolescent's values and mass media sex.   *Mass Media; Adolescence; Sexual Behavior; Values*

A

1113.   **Violence and Terror in the Mass Media: An Annotated Bibliography**, Comp. by Nancy *MSU* Signorielli and George Gerbner. Greenwood, 1988. 264p. $49.95. 0-313-26120-2.

This bibliography developed from a UNESCO survey of published sources on terrorism and violence. The authors, both university professors surveyed the field through 1987 and drawing from the initial UNESCO survey, they have compiled this bibliography of 784 numbered entries which includes scholarly and popular journal articles, conference papers, governmental publications and dissertations. The work is arranged in four main sections: violence and mass media content, violence and mass media effects, terrorism and the mass media, and pornography (only slightly more than 100 items deal with the last two categories). Entries are arranged in alphabetical order under author and numbered sequentially. Each entry contains full bibliographic information and about one-paragraph annotation. Author and a detailed subject index are also provided for easy access. Recommended for academic and public libraries.

Mass Media; Terrorism; Violence

Print Media

A

1114.   **American Women's Magazines: An Annotated Historical Guide**, by Nancy Humphreys. Gar- *O.P.* land, 1989. 320p. $46. 0-8240-7543-9. (Gar-land Reference Library of the Humanities, 789).

Nancy Humphreys has provided us with a much needed guide to the bibliographical and critical information on most of the important women's magazines published from the 18th century to the present day. The bibliography is divided into two major parts. Part one, "Alternative Publications," includes a great deal on the women's rights and feminist periodicals. Part two, "Main-stream Publications," includes chapters from the 18th to the 20th centuries, including confession/romance magazines. The entries for the hundreds of titles included are annotated with descriptive contents notes. This bibliography is designed for the scholar and the general reader of popular culture and is recommended for the general public library and libraries having special collections in women's studies or journalism.   *Periodicals; Women*

A

1115.   **Bestsellers 1895-1990**, by Daisy Maryles. Bowker, 1992. 465p. $39.95. 0-8352-2730-8.

In this completely updated edition of an old standby, *80 Years of Bestseller, 1895-1975*, Maryles identifies almost 100 years of bestsellers from *Prisoner of Zenda* (1895) to *The Bourne Ultimatum* (1990). Maryles, *Publishers Weekly*'s bestseller editor, offers a year-by-year lists of bestsellers plus important books in other areas such as mysteries, science fiction, cookbooks, etc. Special criteria for "choosing" books of bestseller quality are also provided. This interesting guide is recommended for all public libraries that can afford it.   *Best Sellers*

A

1116.   **Corporate Magazines of the United States,** by Sam G. Riley. Greenwood, 1992. 281p. $75. 0-313-27569-6 (Historical Guides to the World's Periodicals and Newspapers).

This bibliography highlights 51 important in-house publications with three- to five-page essays that discuss history, editorial policies, availability, and indexing. There is a wide range of subjects dealt with and most of these periodicals are currently still being published. In an appendix, there is brief information given on an additional 300 titles. For a more extensive listing of this type of publication one could use volume five of *Working Press of the Nation* (National Research Bureau, 1990, $290., 0-912610-25-5) which is called *Internal Publications Directory*. *Corporate Magazines* will be of some value in collection building in many public and academic libraries. *Periodicals*

A

1117. The Directory of Humor Magazines and Humor Organizations in America (And Canada), by Glenn C. Ellenbogen. Wry-bred Press, 1992. 3rd ed. 288p. $34.95 0-9616190-5-4.

This authoritative guide is in two parts. The first lists in detail 80 current humor magazines, newsletters, newspapers, and organizations that are of key importance in the present day humor industry. All sorts of material is provided such as subscription or membership information, descriptions, and sample articles. The second part is about 80 additional humor resources not considered as important as those listed in part one. There are a number of useful appendixes and indexes. Though very specialized, this resource will be of value in some public and academic collections. *Humor*

A

MSU **1118. Editing: An Annotated Bibliography,** by Bruce W. Speck. Greenwood, 1991. 295p. $49. 0-313-26860-6.

This annotated bibliography includes 637 citations to books and periodical articles published between 1959 and 1989 that deal with "the process of acquiring and preparing texts for publication." The work is divided into three main sections: one on general editing, another of technical editing and a third on references to material of specific types such as manuals, newsletters and abstracts. There is an extensive index by author, title and subject. This is suited to academic and public libraries. *Editing; Journalism*

A

1119. Gale International Directory of Publications, by Kay Gill and Darren L. Smith. 1st ed. Gale, 1989. 573p. $100. 0-8103-4255-3.

This companion volume to *Gale Directory of Publications and Broadcast Media*, lists over 2,000 newspapers and about 2,700 periodicals published in 132 countries. The body of the work is arranged alphabetically by country. For each publication entry, there is information in such areas as title, address, phone and Telex numbers, descriptive notes, frequency, advertising rates, language, ISSN, price, and key personnel. There are title and keyword indexes. This work is a selective guide to much of the material covered more extensively in *Ulrich's International Periodicals Directory*, *Benn's Media Directory* and *Editor and Publisher International Yearbook*. *Periodicals; Newspapers*

A

1120. The Independent Publisher's Bookshelf, by John Kremer. Ad-Lib Publications, 1986. 90p. $3.95.

This is an annotated bibliography of about 150 current books on book publishing, marketing, and production. There are also reviews of 30 magazines about publishing and information on publisher's associations. This paperback has author, title, and association indexes and can be obtained for $3.95 from Ad-Lib Publications, P.O. Box 1102, Fairfield, IA 52556. For large collections needing a great deal of information on publishing. *Publishers and Publishing*

A

Ref
Z6944
.L5 D5 **1121. The International Directory of Little Magazines and Small Presses,** by Len Fulton. 27th ed. Dustbooks, 1991. 891p. $41.95. 0-916685-24-1; $25.95 (pap.) 0-916685-23-3.

This work contains about 5,000 entries for both domestic and foreign small presses and little magazines. Full bibliographic information is given for magazines, including advertising costs. Important directory material is given for each of the publishers. Of particular value both to writers looking for markets and collection developers searching for material on specific topics is the 120 page subject index which allows easy access to the main part of the volume. This is a work that will have a number of uses in both public and academic libraries. *Publishers and Publishing; Periodicals*

Y; A

7th ed @
PN4731
.Z99 J6
this ed @
MSU **1122. The Journalist's Bookshelf: An Annotated and Selected Bibliography of United States Print Journalism,** by Roland E. Wolseley and Isabel Wolseley. 8th ed. R. J. Berg, 1986. 400p. $38.50. 0-89730-139-0.

This 2,427 item bibliography of books that deal with print journalism updates the 1961 edition of this work. The book is divided into 34 sections on such topics as: "Freedom of the Press," "Biography," "Sportswriting," and "Women in Journalism." Most of the categories include children's and young adult books, as well as popularizations. "High School Journalism," and "Journalism as a Vocation" are two sections useful for the general reader. There are evaluative annotations for each item and indexes by title and personal names but not by subject. Annual supplements are planned. This will be of value in school, academic and public libraries serving clients interested in journalism. *Journalism*

C; Y; A

1123. Magazines: A Bibliography for Their Analysis, With Annotations and Study Guide, by Fred *cc, MSU* K. Paine and Nancy E. Paine. Scarecrow, 1987. 698p. $62.50. 0-8108-1975-9.

Over 2,200 periodical articles, theses, books, and book chapters dealing with every imaginable aspect of the magazine industry have been selected for this annotated bibliography. Among the topics included are editorial and advertising, editing process, audience, design, production, history, ethics, publishing, electronic publishing, and censorship. A wide variety of magazine types are included, e.g., black, women's, adventure, men's, children's, sports, fashion, news, etc. The entries are arranged alphabetically by author under 17 sections. Academic and special libraries supporting programs or collections in communications, journalism, or mass media (and some larger public libraries) will want to consider this interesting bibliography. *Periodicals*

A

1124. Periodical Directories and Bibliographies: An Annotated Guide to Approximately 350 Directories, Bibliographies, and Other Sources of Information about English-Language Periodicals, from 1850 to the Present, Ed. by Gary Tarbert. Gale, 1986. 195p. $60. 0-8103-1474-6.

The sub-title provides an accurate description of this book. It includes all of the well-known and many little known directories and bibliographies of periodicals, and therefore should be very useful to acquisition librarians and all others interested in bibliographic control of periodicals, newsletters, magazines, and other serial publications. Recommended for academic and larger public libraries.

Periodicals; Directories; Bibliography

A

1125. Small Press: An Annotated Guide, ed. by Loss Pequeno Glazier. Greenwood, 1992. 138p. $49.95 0-313-18310-9.

This is a bibliography that supplies listings of material for anyone wishing to research the literature on small presses. The 173 items are arranged into three main sections: current information sources such as directories, indexes, and guides; sources that deal with issues involving small presses; and supplementary materials like lists and bibliographies. A fine bibliography for anyone interested in this important segment of publishing. *Small Presses*

A

1126. Small Press Record of Books in Print, Ed. by Len Fulton. 21st ed. Dustbooks, 1992. 1400p. *Ref* $42.95. 0-916685-35-7 (Small Press Information Library, 4). *Z1215 .F8*

This suitable companion to *Books in Print* lists approximately 20,000 in-print titles published by small independent presses and presently appears annually. The material is indexed by author, title, publisher, and subject. The author/title entries often contain brief descriptive annotations. Standard bibliographic information is given for each entry. Although it is nonevaluative, this bibliography is useful in large collections to identify hard-to-trace publications. *Bibliographies, General*

A

1127. Sources on the History of Women's Magazines, 1792-1960: An Annotated Bibliography, by *cc, MSU* Mary Ellen Zuckerman. Greenwood, 1991. 297p. $49.95 0-313-26378-7. (Bibliographies and Indexes in Women's Studies).

For each of the thousands of books and magazine articles cited, each is annotated and each pertains to the history of women's magazines from 1792 through 1960 (with some references dated much later). The works are divided into ten subject chapters with separate sections for the most important magazines. Both secondary and primary sources are described and there are subject and author indexes. For large collections.

Periodicals; Women's Magazines

Y

1128.   Spectrum: A Guide to the Independent Press and Information Organizations, Ed. by Laird Wilcox. 21st ed. L. Wilcox (Olathe, KS), n.p. pap. $19.95 0-9335592-66-3.

This is a directory of organizations and publications that are involved in extremist, controversial, or political viewpoints. The work is organized into chapters that cover types of publications, specific topics, and geographical areas. For each entry, only the publication or organization and address are given with very brief descriptive comments. There is no index. Because this work tries to include as many sources as possible and is nonevaluative, it will be used chiefly for identification purposes to supplement standard reference sources. For large libraries that need material on these little-known and often controversial organizations and publications.   *United States—Politics and Government; Right and Left (Political Science); Periodicals*

A

1129.   Words to the Wise: A Writer's Guide to Feminist and Lesbian Periodicals and Publishers, by Andrea Fleck Clardy. Rev. 3rd ed. Firebrand Books, 1990. 54p. $4.95. 0-932379-16-8.

This annotated guide lists more than 100 feminist and lesbian presses and periodicals. The work is divided into presses; periodicals; and academic and trade presses. Entries have brief statements about each publisher and provide addresses, contact persons, and descriptions of the types of materials accepted. The periodical lists could serve as a checklist for collection evaluation and development. Two copies are recommended, one for reference and one for the circulation collection; recommended for all academic and public libraries.   *Women's Studies; Feminism; Lesbianism; Periodicals*

Radio

A

1130.   Radio: A Reference Guide, by Thomas Allen Greenfield. Greenwood, 1989. 172p. $45. 0-313-22276-2.

This guide, which includes a bibliography of about 500 items, is intended for the scholar and student of popular culture alike. Greenfield, a professor of English, has included many dissertations and theses, as well as monographs and journal articles. The first part of the work is a brief overview on radio and its role in American life. This is followed by a a series of bibliographic essays on many aspects of radio as a popular culture medium, including network and station histories, drama programs, news, music, comedy, sports, women, and religious programs. A few chapters deal with important personalities of radio, e.g., Edward R. Murrow, and Jack Benny. Bibliographic citations are complete throughout the text. The two major limitations are that the indexing is inconsistent, and many of the titles cited are out of print. Still, this aid is recommended for most academic and public libraries as a reference tool, interlibrary loan guide, and also as a selection aid for titles.   *Radio Broadcasting*

A

1131.   Radio Broadcasting from 1920 to 1990: An Annotated Bibliography, by Diane Foxhill Carothers. Garland, 1991. 564p. $70. 0-8240-1209-7. (Garland Reference Library of the Humanities, Vol. 967).

Though the topic is specialized, this is a fascinating collection of citations about all aspects of radio broadcasting from its beginnings to 1990. This listing of over 1,700 books covers such topics as the history of radio, biographies of famous personalities, programming, regulations, educational broadcasting amateur radio, women and minorities, and general reference sources. The annotations are interesting, and there are author and title indexes. This will be of value in specialized collections where material on the mass media is needed.   *Radio Broadcasting*

A

1132.   Radio Soundtracks: A Reference Guide, by Michael R. Pitts. 2nd ed Scarecrow, 1986. 337p. $32.50. 0-8108-1875-2.

This is a revised edition of an extensive list of radio soundtracks of mainly pre-1972 radio programs. The main part of this book is a list of over 1,000 radio programs available on tape recordings. These numbered entries are arranged alphabetically by title. Most are annotated: some quite lengthy, most merely brief notes. Shorter lists include: radio programs available on LP records; radio specials on tape; and LPs of performers' radio appearances on LPs. There is also an appendix which lists tape and record resources and an index to titles and performers. This is more of an identification guide rather than a buying guide.

Individuals or libraries must first contact possible sources found in the appendix to determine availability and cost. Still, this extensive identifying list is a "gold mine" for the radio buff or researcher in this area, and it is therefore recommended for academic and public libraries serving this clientele.

Audiocassettes; Phonorecordings; Radio Programs

Audio and Audiovisual

C; Y; A

1133. **AudioVideo Review Digest**, Ed. by Susan L. Stetler. Gale, 1990. 350p. $150. 0-8103-2992-3.

Every media specialist has been waiting for this much needed guide to Audiovisual materials. Here in one place are cumulated reviews of videos, films, filmstrips, audiocassettes from several hundred review periodicals. Each entry provides excerpts, bibliographic data, suggested audiences, subject descriptors, etc. Entries are arranged in alphabetical order by title, and three indexes make for easy retrieval—media, subject, and credits (producer, author, star, director). This guide is available in a three issue per year subscription or in an annual hardcover cumulation. Recommended for medium-sized to large libraries developing and maintaining collections of nonbook media. *Audiovisual Materials*

A

1134. **AV Market Place, 1992: The Complete Business Directory...**, Bowker, 1992. 1390p. $119.95 pap. 0-8352-3155-0.

As the subtitle states, this work is intended to be the complete business directory of audio, audiovisual, computer, film, video, and programming systems. It has achieved its stated purpose beyond a doubt and unquestionably is an important aid to purchasing materials and equipment in most libraries. Also pertinent to collection building, are the excellent annotated lists of periodicals and reference books related to the audiovisual field, making this a recommended guide for most libraries building a professional collection that answers questions involving who, what, when, and where in the AV industry. *Audiovisual Materials*

A

1135. **British Words on Cassette, 1992**. 2nd ed. Bowker/K. G. Saur, 1992. 170p. $45. 1-85739-085-7.

Over 6,200 titles from about 140 publishers are included in this very comprehensive listing of spoken word materials produced in the United Kingdom. This expanded and revised edition of *British Words on Tape, 1991* includes popular and classical literature, poetry, drama, children's books, and educational materials. Each entry includes full bibliographical data including author, reader, length, purchase price information, and publisher/producer. Entries are indexed by author and title. This interesting reference source is recommended for academic libraries and other libraries developing an audiocassette collection.

Audiocassettes; English Literature

C; Y; A

1136. **Media Review Digest, 1991...**, Ed. by C. Edward Wall et al. Pierian Press, 1992. annual. 852p. $245. 0-87650-0-207-9.

Close to 50,000 citations to reviews from over 130 periodicals has justifiably made this the *Book Review Index* of the nonprint media world. These reviews include films, videocassettes and videodiscs, filmstrips, phonorecords and tapes, slides, charts, media kits, games, etc. Both educational and entertainment media are included and divided into major sections according to format. The introduction offers an explanation of the scope and arrangement, subject cataloging, audience levels, ratings, and sources. A major feature are the detailed indexes for general subject, alphabetical subject, geographic, and reviewers. This important reviewing tool which is helpful for developing and maintaining collections of media is recommended for medium-size to large academic, public, and school district libraries that have media collections; unfortunately, the cost would rule out most small public libraries and school building libraries.

Audiovisual Materials; Motion Pictures; Audiorecordings; Videocassettes

A

1137. **Powerful Images: A Women's Guide to Audiovisual Resources**. Isis International; dist. by Inland Books, 1990. 220p. $12. pap. 0-942317-00-9.

The purpose of this guide is to share "women's experiences as makers and users of audiovisual media" (particularly women in the Third World) and to make it possible to secure their work. The heart of this volume is an annotated list of more than 600 films, videos, and slideshows from more than 50 countries arranged in 17 topical chapters including: reproductive rights, sexual violence, women in prisons, migrants and refugees, against apartheid and racism, prostitution, etc. The last part does contain lists of distributors, guides, and periodicals. One major flaw in this interesting guide is the lack of an index, but the "diversity of coverage and excellent annotations make this a valuable resource." Recommended for academic and public libraries serving those involved in women's studies and in libraries with collections of AV media.

Audiovisual Materials; Developing Countries; Women's Studies

A

1138.   **The Spoken Audio Source Guide**. Williamson Distributors, 1991. $99.95.

This software product requires the use of an IBM-compatible computer with 512K RAM and a hard drive but not CD-ROM capabilities. It lists over 40,000 titles of audio tapes available from hundreds of publishers. For each title entry the information supplied includes subject/category, the abridged or un-abridged status, author, narrator, annotations and reviews, copyright date, price, number of cassettes and publisher. Ordering information can be found in a separate publisher and distributor section. The software and instruction manual is $99.95 or $199.95 per year which includes quarterly updates. Order from Williamson Distributors, Inc., 4305-J Norman Bridge Road, Montgomery, AL 36105.   *Audiocassettes*

Y; A

1139.   **Words on Cassette**. Bowker, 1993. 1500p. $135. 0-8352-3298-0.

Words on Cassette made its debut in January, 1992 with the merger of Bowker's *On Cassette* with the recently acquired Meckler publication, *Words on Tape*. This new publication is the most comprehensive guide to commercially available spoken-word audio cassettes, which is one of the fastest growing segments in the publishing/media production industry. Titles on spoken-word cassettes currently are available on every conceivable topic and audience level, covering fiction and nonfiction, contemporary works and classics, entertainment, education and business in more than 30 languages. This edition provides easy access to information on more than 50,000 audiocassettes from over 1,100 producers. There are five indexes: title, author, readers/performer, subject, and producer/distributor. Therefore, it is recommended for all academic and public libraries with audiocassette collections as well as those school district libraries that can afford it.   *Audiocassettes*

Fine Arts, Photography, Crafts, and Hobbies

Fine Arts

A

1140.   **Architecture and Women: A Bibliography Documenting Women Architects, Landscape Architects, Designers, Architectural Critics and Writers and Women in Related Fields Working in the United States**, by Lamia Doumato. Garland, 1988. 269p. $46. 0-8240-4105-4.

Lamia Doumato has compiled a comprehensive bibliography on a very significant and specialized topic. As stated in her introduction: "the primary motivation for compiling this volume was to encourage research on the history of women in architecture." Among the many formats included in this bibliography are monographs, dissertations, and journal articles, all published from the 19th century through 1987. Entries are arranged alphabetically by the name of the women architects and related areas. While there are some brief notes under each entry, they are not truly annotated. The work should be of interest to all academic and public libraries supporting an art (architecture) or women's studies program.

Architecture; Architects, Women

A

1141.   **Art Books: A Basic Bibliography of Monographs on Artists**, by Wolfgang M. Freitag. Garland, 1985. 351p. $90. 0-8240-8763-1. (Garland Reference Library of the Humanities, 574).

Freitag, Chief Art Librarian of the Fine Arts Library of Harvard University has compiled this very extensive unannotated bibliography of more than 10,000 books representing more than 1,800 individual artists. Actually, this is a long awaited up-date, with many new titles, of E. Louise Lucas' *Art Books: A Basic Bibliography* (o.p.). The entries are arranged alphabetically by artist and include biographies, exhibition catalogs, and other items related to the artist. While the work is intended to have an international art focus, there is a heavy emphasis on European and American artists, and two-thirds of the titles are in the painting-drawing area. Publication dates of the included titles range from the 18th century to the 1980's. This important reference work is very useful as a guide for collection building and evaluation. It is also highly recommended for the academic and public libraries with special art collections. *Art*

A

1142. **Art on Screen: A Directory of Films and Videos on the Visual Arts**. Program for Art on Film Joint Venture Staff, G. K. Hall, 1992. 350p. $35. 0-816-0538-3.

This guide lists over 900 films and videotapes dealing with the visual arts. It is the first English language directory of films produced since 1976. The titles were selected from the *Art on Film* database, which is a joint project of the Metropolitan Museum of Art and the J. Paul Getty Trust. Entries are indexed by the names of the artists as well as by selected subject headings such as art forms, materials, etc. The Art on Film Program also publishes a free newsletter three times a year. (for more information write to Program for Art on Film, 980 Madison Ave. New York, NY. 10021. This guide is recommended for all academic and public libraries with special programs on art films. *Art Films*

A

1143. **Arte Chicano: A Comprehensive Annotated Bibliography of Chicano Art, 1965-1981**, by Shifra M. Goldman and Tomas Ybarra-Frausto. Univ. of Calif., Chicano Studies Lib. Publications, 1986. 778p. $90. hardcover, 0-918520-11. $35. pap. 0-918520-09-6.

This computer-generated bibliography is very extensive and comprehensive, representing art from colonial times to the present. The citations are for works drawn from the University of California at Berkeley's Chicano Periodical Indexing Project and its *Chicano Database* and include both books and periodicals. Each numbered entry has full bibliographic data, is indexed by subject, and has a brief annotation. This massive bibliography is recommended as an identification and selection guide for academic and public libraries with a special emphasis or need for Chicano materials. *Art, Chicano*

A

1144. **artsAmerica Fine Art Film and Video Source Book**. artsAmerica, Inc., [1987] $12.95.

This very specialized catalog advertises itself as "the first nationally distributed catalog listing documentary film and videotapes on fine art." Canadian, European, British, and Australian, as well as American film makers are represented. Each entry describes the production and provides information for ordering. This catalog is particularly recommended for those libraries building up collections of art films and videos. The catalog is available for $12.95 from: artsAmerica, Inc., 125 Greenwich Ave., Greenwich, CT 06830, Supplements for 1988 and 1989 are also available at $3 each. *Art Films; Films; Videocassettes*

A

1145. **Contemporary Artists**, by Colin Naylor. 3rd ed. St. James Press, 1989. 1,059p. $135. 0-912289- *C,M* 96-1

There are biographies of 849 contemporary artists from around the world in this volume. Entries include a variety of information including detailed biographies, listings of exhibits, honors, collections holding the artist's work, sometimes a black and white reproductions, and a statement by the artist about his or her work. Important for collection building are the accompanying lists of books and articles by and about each artist. This is a reference volume that will be useful in public libraries and perhaps also in some high schools. *Artists*

A

1146. **Fine Arts: A Bibliographic Guide to Basic Reference Works, Histories and Handbooks**, by *N5300* Donald L. Ehresmann. Libraries Unlimited, 1990. 373p. $55 0-87287-640-3 *.Z99E47*

This classified selective bibliography of 2,051 entries covers the combined fields of painting, archi- *1990* tecture, and sculpture. The works included were published from 1840 to 1988 with emphasis on the current. Although most are in English, important works in foreign languages are also cited. Part I deals with reference works and Part 2 with histories and handbooks. All entries are annotated, many critically. There are author, title and subject indexes. Academic and public libraries can use this excellent source for both collection development and for helping researchers. *Art*

A

1147. Guide to Research in Classical Art and Mythology, by Frances Van Keuren. American Library Association, 1991. 307p. $35. 0-8389-0564-1.

This well-annotated guide is both a bibliography and a guide to research in classical art and mythology. The work is divided into three major parts. Part one deals with general references on Greek, Etruscan, and Roman art and architecture; part two describes references dealing with mythology in art and literature of Classical times; and part three deals with specific art forms like Athenian vases and Etruscan mirrors. Each part is divided into separate chapters where bibliographical essays on the authors start with general works and progress to more specific titles. Both reference and monographic books are listed. There are author, title, and subject indexes. Another bibliography in the same area but lacking the excellent annotations of this volume is Coulson and Freiert's *Greek and Roman Art, Architecture and Archaeology: An Annotated Bibliography* (Garland, 1987, $46. 0-8240-8756-9).   *Greek Art; Roman Art; Mythology, Classical*

Y; A

1148. National Gallery of Art Color Reproduction Catalog. National Gallery of Art. free

This catalog of one of America's finest art museums lists postcards, plaques, and reprints of paintings in their large collection. Included are reproductions of many of the greatest, from Botticelli to Renoir to Whistler. Each painting is illustrated in color; each entry details what kind of reproductions are available. Recommended (along with catalogs of other famous museums, e.g., New York's Metropolitan Museum of Art) for school and public libraries to develop their collection of art reproductions. *Art; Paintings*

A

1149. Old Master Print References: A Selected Bibliography, Comp. by Lauris Mason et al. Kraus International, 1986. 279p. $70. 0-527-62196-X.

More than 3,000 citations to more than 900 old masters were screened from checklists, articles, museum and dealer catalogs, and exhibit catalogs. Artists are listed in alphabetical order. Publications about each artist are then arranged in chronological order. No indexes are included, which could be a limitation if one is looking for a particular work, or even for a particular artist with a variation of name. Art museum libraries, public libraries with art collections, and academic libraries supporting art history programs will want to consider this rather comprehensive work. *Art—History; Artists*

A

1150. Picture Researcher's Handbook: An International Guide to Picture Sources-and How to Use Them, by Hilary Evans and Mary Evans. 4th ed. Van Nostrand, 1989. 464p. $69.50. 0-7476-0038-4.

Following introductory materials on the scope of this directory and how to use it, this work lists hundred of international sources for pictures. The collections are arranged alphabetically, and for each, information is given on areas like addresses, services, fees, number of items in the collection, plus a description of the holdings. Most museums are excluded and should be contacted directly. Although this work has a strong European focus, many sources from Canada and the United States are included. There is a useful subject index. This book will be helpful in developing picture collections in both public and academic libraries where this kind of material is needed. *Pictures*

C, M

A

1151. Slide Buyers' Guide: An International Directory of Slide Sources for Art and Architecture, by Norine D. Cashman. 6th ed. Libraries Unlimited, 1990. 190p. $30. pap. 0-087287-797-3 (Visual Resources Series).

This is the standard work for use by anyone involved in developing slide collections. It identifies 308 international sources, both commercial and nonprofit, for slides useful in the study of art and architecture. The arrangement is, first by country, then alphabetically by commercial vendor. Each entry contains information on scope, photographic methods, the nature of identifying citations, prices, quality, and service. Information was obtained by questionnaire, catalogs, and first-hand use of the materials. There is an appendix that lists the 121 vendors who did not answer the questionnaire and another that gives sources of sides that are coordinated with specific texts. Detailed subject and name indexes plus many cross references give good access points to the entries. This is the primary source of information for any library, public or academic, that deals with slides. *Slides*

A

1152. **Twentieth-Century Artists on Art: An Index to Artists' Writings, Statements, and Interviews,** *NX456*
by Jack Robertson. G. K. Hall, 1985. 488p. $40. 0-8161-8714-2. *.R59*
1985

This index is a guide to the verbal commentary of approximately 5,000 artists of the 20th century. Robertson contends that: "Frequently, an artist will speak and write about not only his art, but also about his life and training, his influences and associates, his tastes and aesthetic theories, and technical procedures ... that things otherwise unknown ... are revealed." A total of 14,000 citations from 495 published sources are included. Each citation gives full bibliographic information. Nearly 500 sources were examined personally by Robertson. A 41-page bibliography gives adequate information for retrieval. While this work is an important contribution to the field, many of the entries are unavailable for acquisition, but are still useful for reference and interloan purposes. This volume is recommended for all libraries which support art or art history collections. *Artists; Art, Modern*

A

1153. **Visual Arts Research: A Handbook,** by Elizabeth B. Pollard. Greenwood, 1986. 165p. $42.95. *CC, MSU*
0-313-24186-4.

Pollard, a university librarian, has created a concise guide intended to provide "guidance in research methods and resources for art students and other scholars." Each of the chapters is in the form of a bibliographic essay; each reference is numbered and keyed to a bibliography of about 400 items. The beginning chapters are rather general, dealing with the basic elements of research and library use. Chapters 4 through 8 contain discussions on biographical information, art history sources, specific works of art, techniques and materials, and art education, all with bibliographic references. Chapter 9 is a listing of visual-arts periodicals. Full bibliographical data and a brief annotation are provided for each numbered item. A detailed author, title, and subject index is also provided. This bibliographic guide which updates and includes a great deal of the same sources as an older work, Jones' *Art Research Methods and Resources* (o.p), is recommended for academic libraries and those public libraries which support art collections or art research programs. *Art—Study and Teaching; Research Methodology*

C; Y; A

1154. **Visual Literacy: A Selected Bibliography,** by Rebecca Clemente and Roy M. Bohlin. Educational Technology, 1990. 50p. $14.95

This bibliography distinguishes between verbal literacy and visual literacy, with coverage on such topics as art appreciation, film study, aesthetic education, nonverbal communication, perceptual development, semiotics, and television viewing. Books and magazine articles are included. Unfortunately, there are no annotations, but all citations have been selected on the basis of both material covered and the quality of the coverage. This will be a good starting place for teachers at all levels to locate material on this important and often neglected area. *Visual Literacy*

A

1155. **Women Artists in the United States: A Selective Bibliography and Resource Guide on the Fine** *MSU*
and Decorative Arts, 1750-1986, by Paula Chiarmonte. G. K. Hall, 1990. 997p. $65. 0-8161-8917-X.

This exhaustive bibliography includes approximately 3,000 women in American art from 1750 to mid-1980's and is the most comprehensive on the subject currently available. It includes every category in the fine and decorative arts except needlework, (and a future volume on that topic is planned). The work is divided into two parts: Part 1 deals with feminist art critics, art organizations, and directories; followed by an extensive bibliography of reference works and periodicals. Part 2, the larger section, lists the citations to items on women's art and artists, arranged by medium and then by name. Each entry is numbered sequentially. In both parts, entries have full bibliographic information and most have brief descriptive annotations. Author/title and artist indexes are also provided. As indicated, this work is far more comprehensive than similar bibliographies on women artists which have been consulted and acknowledged. The most similar is the work by Tufts, *American Women Artists, Past and Present*, which has about one-third the entries. Researchers might want to consult both. The Chiarmonte work is recommended for all libraries which have programs or collections on women's studies or art. *Women Artists; Artists*

A

1156. **Women in the Fine Arts: A Bibliography and Illustration Guide,** by Janet A. Anderson. *MSU*
McFarland, 1991. 362p. $49.95. 0-89950-541-5.

Both general and specialized materials on women in the fine arts are included in this bibliography. Women from the Renaissance to modern times are included. The work is divided into four major parts: General Reference; Periodicals; Exhibition Catalogs; and Newspapers. Within each section entries are listed in alphabetical order by author (title if no author listed), rather than by the name of the artist. The special feature of this work is the large number of exhibition catalogs included. A complementary work is Chairmonte's *Women Artists in the United States: A Selective Bibliography and Resource Guide on the Fine and Decorative Arts, 1750-1986.* There is some duplication in the reference section; however, both contain many unique artists. This volume is recommended as an additional source for libraries building collections in fine arts or women's studies. *Women Artists; Artists*

Photography

A

1157. Black Photographers, 1840-1940: An Illustrated Bio-Bibliography, by Deborah Willis-Thomas. Garland, 1985. 141p. $48. 0-8240-9147-7.

This oversized book provides an interesting collection of the works by and about 70 black photographers who were important during the first century of photography. Public, academic and special libraries with collections on photography will want to consider this and the next entry.

Photography—History; African Americans; Photographers, African American

A

1158. Black Photographers, 1940-1988: An Illustrated Bio-Bibliography, by Deborah Willis-Thomas. Garland, 1989. 500p. $95. 0-8240-8389-X.

This work updates and expands the previous entry while maintaining the same high standards of research and quality.

The more than 300 pages of beautifully reproduced photographs add immensely to the well-researched contents. This useful reference, along with the basic volume, is recommended for all libraries with photography or black studies programs.

Photography—History; African Americans; Photographers, African Americans

MSU **A**

1159. Films and Videos on Photography, by Nadine Covert et al. Program for Art on Film, 1990. 114p. $14.95 0-87099-573-1.

Using two databases—one French and the other American—the authors have compiled an impressive listing of 500 titles of films and videos on photography. The list is arranged alphabetically by title. There is extensive bibliographic information on each film (e.g., running time, date, producer, distributor, series), plus a content synopsis and critical citations. There are also subject and name indexes. Excellent for courses on photography or large audiovisual collections in libraries. It is available for $14.95 from The Metropolitan Museum of Art, Institutional Sales, Middle Village, NY 11381.

Photography—Motion Pictures; Motion Pictures

A

1160. History of Photography: A Bibliography of Books, by Laurent Roosens and Luc Salu. Mansell, 1989. 446p. $72. 0-7201-2008-X.

This extensive bibliography on the history of photography contains over 11,000 entries on books and theses dealing with the history of photography. The materials are arranged under 3,000 subject headings and span the entire twentieth century through the mid 1980s. There is an author index. For large collections.

Photography

CC **A**

1161. An Illustrated Bio-Bibliography of Black Photographers, 1940-1980, by Deborah Willis-Thomas. Garland, 1989. 483p. $85. 0-8240-8389-X.

This is a continuation of the author's earlier *Black Photographers, 1840-1940* (1985, $45. 0-8240-9147-7). This supplementary volume contains biographies of 32 black photographers. Accompanying each biography is a bibliography that includes exhibition catalogs, monographs by and about the photographer, and citations to articles and reviews of their work in magazines and newspapers.

African Americans; Photography

A
1162. **Stock Photo Deskbook,** by Fred W. McDarrah. 3rd ed. Photographic Arts Center (New York, NY), 1989. 312p $29.95 pap. 0-913069-20-5.

Stock photos is a term that refers to photographs that can be reproduced usually for a fee and are available from such sources as Bettmann Archive. This directory lists 7,090 sources in eight sections. The first seven deal with American sources and are divided by such sources as stock-photo agencies, businesses, museums and other educational institutions, government sources, photo researchers, and television and press services. Within these sections there is a geographical breakdown by state and zip code. For each agency listed, information is given that includes name, address, contact person, and subject specializations. The eighth (international) section is arranged by country. Besides a detailed table of contents, there are name and subject indexes to help access this vast amount of material. This work is found in very large collections. A more selective listing of about 980 agencies in Canada and the United States is found in *Picture Sources* (Special Libraries Association, 1983, $35.), but this is now about ten years old and the contents are dated. *Photographs; Pictures*

Crafts and Hobbies

A
1163. **The Crafts Supply Sourcebook: A Comprehensive Shop-by-Mail Guide,** by Margaret A. Boyd. Betterway Publications, 1989. 286p. $14.95 1-55870-121-4.

This is an omnibus item that contains material on 2,600 suppliers of craft products plus coverage for information sources. Part I lists suppliers under such subject areas as stained glass craft, jewelry making, sculpture, wine and beer making, model railroading and photography. Part II does the same for every variety of needlecraft. The third section called "Resources" contains general information about crafts and gives a useful list of books, other publications and associations. This volume will have many uses in public libraries.
Handicraft

A
1164. **Embroidery and Needlepoint: An Information Sourcebook**, by Sandra K. Copeland. Oryx, 1989. 150p. $48.50 0-89774-442-X.

This unique annotated bibliography of books published since 1950 is arranged under specific sewing techniques such as crewel and needlepoint. There are author, title and subject indexes. Of particular value are the author's list of 91 titles for a core collections and a list of periodicals. For large libraries.
Needlework

A
1165. **Handweaving: An Annotated Bibliography**, by Isabel Buschman. Scarecrow, 1991. 250p. $29.50. *CC*
0-8108-2403-5.

This bibliography contains over 550 book and periodical article citations to works on the history and techniques of weaving. The first and largest part is devoted to references involving materials, tools, processes and products involved in handweaving. Other sections cover a history of weaving (with special attention to the weaving of Native Americans), reference works, and a bibliography of important journals. As well as full bibliographic information, each entry is annotated with a clear description of contents. There are author, title, and subject indexes. This will be useful in collections where craft books and periodicals are important. *Weaving; Handicraft*

Y; A
1166. **Hobbyist Sourcebook,** by Denise M. Allard. 2nd ed. Gale, 1993. 459p. $49.95. 0-8103-7614-8.

This unique reference work collects a variety of useful information about 50 popular hobbies including amateur radio operation, antique dolls, crafts. painting, sports card collecting, and woodworking. After an introduction to each hobby, there are 15 subcategories of information that cover associations, learning opportunities, catalogs and sources of supplies, basic guides and reference books, periodicals and magazines, juvenile literature, nonprint materials, conventions, special libraries, data bases and other information sources. Most entries have brief annotations and there is an extensive index. This is a useful reference book as well as one that can be used to evaluate and develop collections in both high school and public libraries.
Hobbies

A

1167. Index to Handicraft Books, 1974-1984, by the Staff of the Science and Technology Department, Carnegie Library of Pittsburgh. University of Pittsburgh/Harper, 1986. 411p $31.95. 0-8229-3532-5.

The editors describe this volume as a craft index that "is a subject guide to projects in how-to-do-it books." Approximately 1,000 books published between 1974 and 1984 are analyzed. They are listed with full bibliographic information by author in the first part of the book. The main part of the book is a listing by subject of the projects found in these books. They include entries on techniques, materials, and equipment, as well as specific projects. The bibliography section can be helpful in reference work as well as in collection development and for interlibrary loan. Public libraries and some school libraries will find this to be a useful source. *Handicraft*

Y; A

1168. Make It—II: An Index to Projects and Materials, 1974-1987, by Mary Ellen Heim. Scarecrow, 1989. 552p. $42.50. 0-8108-2125-7.

Heim has produced an interesting index to over 35,000 projects culled from 450 English-language titles published from 1974-1987. This work includes "handicraft projects in needle-working, electronics, woodworking, toy-making, fence-building,..." This practical guide which would be helpful for reference, as well as for building a library collection in this very practical area, is recommended for all public and many school libraries. *Handicraft*

A

1169. Numismatic Bibliography, by Elvira E. Clain-Stefanelli. K. G. Saur, 1985. 1,848p. $125. 3-598-07507-3.

This work is an impressive undertaking; it has to be the definitive bibliography in the field of numismatic literature currently in-print. With 18,000 citations, it is four times the size of the author's 1965 *Select Numismatic Bibliography* (o.p.), which was, heretofore, considered the standard bibliography in the field. About one third of the entries deal with related topics such as counterfeiting, paper money, tokens, etc. Most of the titles are monographs; however, journal articles, catalogs, and some pamphlets are also included. Bibliographic data and five indexes add to the value of this comprehensive, if not exhaustive, work, which is recommended for special libraries and other libraries having a special collection in the field of numismatics. *Coins; Numismatics*

A

1170. Stamps, Coins, Postcards and Related Materials: A Directory of Periodicals, by Doris Robinson. Peri Press, 1991. 151p. $29. pap. 0-9617844-7-4.

There are 700 periodicals listed in this bibliography in three separate sections, one for stamps, another for coins, and the third for postcards and related materials. All but two of the entries are for English language periodicals, but the scope is definitely international. For each entry, full bibliographic information is given including frequency and price, plus a contents note on a typical issue, name and nature of the sponsoring agency when applicable, and publication policies. There are several indexes which allow access to these entries by title, subject, country of origin, publisher, and organization. This title should have value in academic and large public libraries. *Postage Stamps; Coins; Postcards; Periodicals*

Language and Literature

General and Miscellaneous

A

CC, MSU

1171. The Bloomsbury Guide to Women's Literature, Ed. by Claire Buck. Prentice Hall, 1992. 1,171p. $40. 0-13-689621-9; $20. pap. 0-13-089-665-9.

More than 5,000 biographical, bibliographical, and critical entries are included in this comprehensive one-volume guide to women authors and fiction by women of all countries and time periods from ancient Greece to modern times. The first 250 pages or so is an overall survey of women's contributions to literature throughout the world. This is followed by an extensive alphabetically-arranged section of brief notations of over 6500 entries which contain name, work, and theme. While the focus is on fiction, poetry and dramatic works are included; however, Nonfiction is not included. The editor has attempted to stress lesser known authors as well as non-Western writers. The scope of this exhaustive work makes it an essential resource to academic and larger public libraries. *Women Authors; Women in Literature*

A
1172.   **The Catholic Lifetime Reading Plan,** by John A. Hardon. Doubleday, 1989. 299p. $22.95.
0-385-23080-X.

This lavishly annotated bibliography contains a guided tour of the great Roman Catholic writers from historic times to the present day. The selection spans history from Dante, Aquinas and Thomas More to Evelyn Waugh and Sheen. For each author, brief biographical information is given plus a selection of important books, their synopses, and a generous handful of quotations. This list of the great books of the Catholic Church will be of interest to patrons and to acquisition librarians in libraries where there is a active interest in religious writings, history and/or the Catholic faith.   *Authors, Catholic*

A
1173.   **Critical Surveys,** by Frank N. Magill. Salem Press, 1981+. prices vary.

There are nine series in this massive set which supplies an in-depth analytical survey of the major writers in world literature. Each entry consists of a listing of major works, a discussion with critical comment of the most important works, a biography and a short bibliography of critical works. The bibliographies can be of help in collection building, although this is obviously not the main purpose of these books. The series with number of volumes, publication dates and prices are: *Critical Survey of Short Fiction* (7 volumes, 1981, $330.), *Critical Survey of Long Fiction: English Language Series* (8 volumes, 1991, $475.), *Critical Survey of Poetry: English Language Series* (8 volumes, 1992, $475.), *Critical Survey of Long Fiction: Foreign Language Series* (5 volumes, 1984, $275). *Critical Survey of Poetry: Foreign Language Series* (5 volumes, 1984, $275.), *Critical Survey of Drama: English Language Series* (6 volumes, 1985, $350.), *Critical Survey of Drama: Foreign Language Series* (6 volumes, 1986, $350.), *Critical Survey of Literary Theory* (4 volumes, 1988, $300.), *Critical Survey of Mystery and Detective Fiction* (4 volumes, 1989, $300.). There are now also supplements to the short fiction (1987) and the drama (1987) volumes. For large libraries.   *English Literature; American Literature; Literature*

A
1174.   **Facts on File Bibliography Series,** Ed. by Matthew Bruccoli. Facts on File, 1991-.

When completed, this sixteen volume series will span the entire field of American literature from 1588 to 1988. The volumes are arranged by period and genre, including fiction, nonfiction, poetry, and drama. As of early 1992, three titles have appeared: *Facts on File Bibliography of American Fiction: 1588-1865* (1992, $75, 0-8160-2115-5), *Facts on File Bibliography of American Fiction: 1866-1918* (1991, $75. 0-81160-2116-3) and *Facts on File Bibliography of American Fiction: 1919-1988* (1991, 2 volumes, $145. 0-8160-2674-2). The latter is representative in scope and treatment of current and forthcoming volumes. It begins with two bibliographies: one of 100 basic reference sources and 10 essential periodicals for the study of American literature, and the other of important general, historical and critical sources on this topics. There follows entries for 219 writers born prior to 1941 whose first significant works were published after World War I. Representative writers include Faulkner, Mailer, Steinbeck, Updike, and Cheever. For each author, there is a brief biography, followed by a listing of published bibliographies of the author's works (both separately published bibliographies as well as those appearing as periodical articles or parts of books are included). All of the author's works are then arranged chronologically under type of publication like books or letters. The location of manuscript and archival collections related to the author are noted. Secondary works of significance are then listed also by type beginning with biographies and continuing with interviews and critical studies, again found in entire books, parts of books, essays, special journals or articles. Indexes include a chronology of noteworthy fiction and events. This is a significant new bibliographic tool that will be used in both academic and public libraries.   *American Literature*

Y*; A*
1175.   **Good Reading: A Guide for Serious Readers,** by Arthur Walhorn and others. 23rd ed. Bowker, 1990. 465p. $41. 0-8352-27070-3.

Since its first appearance in 1932, this guide to world literature from ancient times to the present has become a mainstay in both high school and public libraries, both for reader's advisory work and collection building. There are now about 3,000 annotated titles included under five different sections, "Historical Periods," "Regional and Minority Cultures," "Literary Types," "Humanities and Social Sciences," and "Sciences," with many subdivisions in each section. Each division has an introductory essay. Special features of this edition include a core list of 101 significant books, a special section on reference books and separate lists of books to read before entering college, while on vacation, and after retiring. This work is updated regularly.   *English Literature; American Literature; Literature*

1985
edtn@
Ref
Z1035 .C6

① MSU   ② CC, MSU

C; Y; A

1176. **Masterplots II**, Ed. by Frank N. Magill. Salem Press, various dates.

The original masterplots began in the late 1940's and were constantly updated until about 1976. At first, they were primarily plot summaries, but with the introduction of *Masterplots: Definitive Revised Edition* (1976), they evolved into volumes of brief summaries with more analyses. Then came the *Masterplots II* series which covered titles not covered in any other series and also eliminated the plot summaries and expanded the analyses. Salem Press also publishes the *Critical Survey...* series which is arranged by author rather than title. Each of the *Masterplots II* series consists of 4 to 6 volumes covering from about 300 to 500 titles (except the short story series which has 6 volumes and includes over 700 stories). This massive long-standing publishing enterprise has become a mainstay in libraries for reference, reader's advisory work, and of course collection evaluation and development. They are recommended for most academic, secondary school, and public libraries. The *Masterplots II* series currently available are listed below in chronological order by publication date; they are all edited by Frank N. Magill and published by Salem Press:

Masterplots II   *[handwritten: Ref PN846 .M37 1986]*
(American Fiction Series) 1986 4v. $350. 0-89356-456-7. (Short Story Series) 1986 6v. $425. 0-89356-461-3. *[handwritten: Ref PN3326 .M27 1986]*
(British and Commonwealth Fiction Series) 1987 4v. $350. 0-89356-468-0. *[handwritten: cc, MSU]*
(World Fiction Series) 1988 4v. $350. 0-89356-473-7. *[handwritten: Ref PN3326 .M28 1987]*
(Nonfiction Series) 1989 YA 4v. $350. 0-89356-478-8. *[handwritten: Ref PN44 .M345 1989]*
(Drama Series) 1990 4v. $350. 0-89356-491-5. *[handwritten: Ref PN6112.5 .M37 1990]*
(Juvenile and Young Adult Literature Series) 1991 4v. $350. 0-89356-579-2.
(Poetry Series) 1992 6v. $425. 0-89356-584-9. *[handwritten: cc, MSU]*

All of the above series are also available on CD-ROM as of 1992: *Masterplots II CD-ROM*. CD-ROM. EBSCO, 1992. full set approx. $1,295. 1-882248-00-7.

Literature; American Literature; Fiction; Children's Literature;
Young Adult Literature; Drama; English Literature; Short Story; Poetry

A

[handwritten left margin: 2d ed / on order / 3/14/95]

1177. **MLA Directory of Periodicals: A Guide to Journals and Serials in Languages and Literatures: Periodicals Published in the United States and Canada, 1988-89 ed.**, Comp. by Eileen M. Mackesy and Dee Ella Spears. Modern Language Association, 1988. 300p. $30. pap. 0-87352-472-1.

Almost 1,200 journals and serials published in the United States and Canada dealing with languages and literatures are included in this paperbound, abridged version of the biennial *MLA Directory of Periodicals*. The entries are listed alphabetically by title and assigned a sequential number. Each entry (which is identical to the unabridged edition) includes publication and subscription information, such as editor, address, frequency, microform editions, subscription price, advertising, etc. A number of indexes, including a subject index, complete the volume. While much of the information provided in this directory is available elsewhere, e.g., in *Ulrich's International Periodicals Directory*, the specificity and cost of this directory make it desirable for smaller academic and public libraries for whom it is recommended.

Periodicals; Languages, Modern; Literature

A

1178. **The Peters Third Black and Blue Guide to Current Literary Journals**, by Robert Peters. 3rd ed. Dustbooks, 1987. 164p. $5.95 pap. 0-916685-03-9.

This is Peters' third compilation of guides to contemporary literary journals. Several dozen titles are listed and reviewed. The useful index to several hundred small-press authors is an added bonus. This useful little guide will be appreciated by researchers in this genre. This is recommended for most academic and many public libraries. *Literary Journals; Periodicals*

Y; A

[handwritten left margin: Ref PN44 .P58 1991]

1179. **Plot Locator: An Index to Summaries of Fiction and Nonfiction**, by the Reference Department, John Davis Williams Library, University of Mississippi. Garland, 1991. 704p. $110. 0-8153-0145-6.

This guide to plot summaries for poems, plays, and books of fiction and nonfiction indexes 82 plot summary sources published between 1902 and 1990. Most of the sources are readily available in academic, public, and some high school libraries. They include the well-known Magill Masterplot series to one-volume titles, such as *Stories from Shakespeare*. An author and title indexes are included; the author entries include information on source, volume, and page numbers. There is some duplication between this volume and

①

Kolar's *Plot Summary Index* (o.p.); however, a number of newer sources published since 1981 are included. This rather expensive index is recommended only for libraries that do not have Kolar's index and have a need for such a guide to plot summaries as well as an acquisition guide to the 82 plot summary sources.

Fiction; Literature—Stories, Plots, Etc.; Poetry; Drama; Adult Books and Reading

Language and Writing

A

1180. **Linguistics: A Guide to the Reference Literature**, by Anna L. DeMiller. Libraries Unlimited, 1991. 256p. $45. 0-87287-692-6. (Reference Sources in the Humanities).

DeMiller has compiled a useful guide to the literature of linguistics for the student, researcher, and librarian. Emphasis is on monographs and serial reference works. All aspects of the topic are included, such as historical and comparative linguistics; morphology; phonetics; phonology; semantics; and syntax. She has also included material of interest to linguists in other disciplines. Citations include full bibliographic information and lengthy and critical annotations. All material was published after 1957. This well-organized, current, and thoroughly researched guide is recommended for all academic libraries and other libraries for reference and collection building. *Linguistics*

P121
.299D45
1991

A

1181. **Research in Basic Writing: A Bibliographical Sourcebook**, Ed. by Michael G. Moran and Martin J. Jacobi. Greenwood, 1990. 241p. $55. 0-313-25564-4.

This bibliography on basic writing (sometimes considered remedial writing) is intended for the undergraduate student. There are ten chapters, each by a different contributor, on some aspect of basic writing. Topics include writing labs, computer software, teaching of E.S.L., methodology, etc. Each chapter has an extensive bibliography of recent sources (about half date from the 1980's). This title is recommended for all academic libraries, with the text for reference and the bibliographies for collection evaluation and development. *Writing*

cc

A

1182. **Resources for Writers: An Annotated Bibliography**, by R. Baird Shuman. Salem, 1992. 167p. $40. 0-89356-673-X.

Shuman, a professor of English provides us with a bibliography of more than 530 titles. The entries are arranged into a number of major chapters covering various types of writing, for example, plays and poetry, etc.; writing for commercial publication, for juveniles, and for magazines and journals; and preparing and marketing manuscripts. Most of the entries are for monographs or parts of books, and the vast majority are published from 1930 to the 1990's. As with other titles in the Magill Bibliography series, entries are arranged alphabetically by author. Each has full bibliographical data and a brief annotation of about 50 to 100 words. An author and title index conclude the volume. This bibliographic guide is recommended for academic and public libraries. Large secondary school libraries may also want to consider its purchase. *Authorship; Writing*

A

1183. **Writer's Advisor**, Comp. by Leland G. Alkire. Gale, 1985. 452p. $70. 0-8103-209-3-2.

MSU

Alkire has compiled a very comprehensive bibliography of over 4,000 books and articles for this sourcebook, which is intended (according to its long sub-title) as: "*A Guide to Books and Articles about Writing Novels, Short Stories, Poetry, Dramatic Scripts, Screenplays, Magazine Articles, Biographies, Technical Articles and Books, as Well as a Guide to Information and Literary Agents, Marketing, and a Wide Range of Legal and Business Materials of Interest to Full- and Part-Time Writers.*" The entries are organized under 34 sections, most of them on genres. The 800 book titles are annotated, some with very lengthy notes; the articles are simply listed. All entries have full bibliographic information. Three indexes are provided: authors of items listed or mentioned, book titles, and subjects. While still very useful, let's hope the work is updated soon. In the interim, this work is recommended for most academic and public libraries both as a reference tool and aid to collection development. *Writing*

① Ref PN44 .K64 1981

Bio-Bibliography

Y; A

1184.   **Black Writers: A Selection of Sketches from Contemporary Authors,** Ed. by Linda Metzger. Gale, 1989. 619p. $80. 0-8103-2772-4.

Black Writers is really a spin-off of the familiar *Contemporary Authors* with an added advantage. Of the 400 entries, 300 are updated from *Contemporary Authors*; however, about 100 were written specifically for this bio-bibliography. Entries are arranged alphabetically and include biographical information, lists of writings and works in progress, comments from writers themselves, and lists of secondary sources for additional information. This volume is highly recommended for all libraries because of its single volume convenience, addition of new writers, and cost. It is especially recommended for those smaller libraries that have a particular interest in black culture and lack *Contemporary Authors.*

African Americans; Authors, African American

A

1185.   **Contemporary Authors: A Bio-Bibliographical Guide to Current Writers in Fiction, General Nonfiction, Poetry, Journalism, Drama, Motion Pictures, Television, and Other Fields,** by various editors. Gale, various dates, about $90. per volume.

This extensive set now numbers well over 130 volumes. Each contains information on about a thousand contemporary writers. There is a cumulative index of entries in even numbered volumes. A typical entry contains basic information on the writer's personal and professional life, a listing of works, and a bibliography of biographical and critical sources. The latter two areas of coverage can be useful in collection development, but because of its size and price, this set is found only in colleges and universities and large public library collections.   *Authors*

A

1186.   **Contemporary Authors: Bibliographical Series,** by various editors. Gale, 1986+ , about $50. per volume.

This companion set to *Contemporary Authors* supplies in-depth critical information on major writers since 1950. Each volume deals with a particular genre and geographic area and contains entries on approximately a dozen very prominent writers. The first three volumes deal with American novelists, American poets and American dramatists. In a typical entry, there is a bibliography of the author's work, followed by a section of works about the writer and, lastly, a lengthy analytical bibliographical essay in which the critical works are discussed. This set will be of value in many public libraries as well as in colleges and universities.   *Authors*

C; Y; A

1187.   **Contemporary World Writers.** St. James, 1993. $130. 750p. 1-55862-200-4.

This update of the 1984 volume, *Contemporary Foreign-Language Writers*, profiles 358 important living writers of fiction, drama, and poetry who write in languages other than English and whose works have been translated into English. Each entry contains a who's who style biography, a complete bibliography citing English translations of the works, a list of critical studies, and a critical essay of up to 1,000 words. This will be a valuable asset in some high school libraries, as well as public and college libraries.

Literature; Authors

A

1188.   **Dictionary of Literary Biography.** Gale, 1978- . $108. per volume.

This extensive set now totals over 100 volumes and covers American, British, Canadian, Austrian, French, German, and Spanish writers. These are not intended for selection purposes, but each entry in every volume contains extensive listings of both primary and secondary sources on the author being highlighted. These lists can be helpful particularly for identifying materials for interlibrary loans. Of the many volumes in the parent set that deal with American authors, there is a six volume abridgment, the *Concise Dictionary of American Literary Biography* (1989, $350. 0-8103-1818-0), which covers writers from the colonial period to the present.   *American Literature; Canadian Literature; English Literature; Literature*

A

1189. **An Encyclopedia of Continental Women Writers**, Ed. by Katharina M. Wilson. Garland, 1991. *CC, MSU*
2v. 1,401p. $175. 0-8240-8547-7. (Garland Reference Library of the Humanities, 698).

Signed bibliographies of 1,800 Continental women writers from ancient Greece to contemporary Europe are included in this two volume set. The entries are usually a half to a full page in length and contain both biographical and critical material. There is a two-part bibliography at the end of each entry: the first lists the author's works and the second, principal critical publications. These can help in identification of sources for both acquisition and loan. This work is a companion to *An Encyclopedia of British Woman* *CC, MSU* *Writers*. *Women Authors; Literature; Authors, Women*

A

1190. **Magill's Survey of World Literature**, Ed. by Frank N. Magill. Marshall Cavendish, 1992. 6v. $389.95. 1-85435-482-5.

Articles on 215 writers from ancient times to the present are included in this excellent reference tool. This is similar to *Magill's Survey of American Literature* in purpose and format, but its focus is on all countries except the United States. It is difficult to understand why some authors were selected and many equally well-known were not, e.g., Hans Christian Andersen is excluded and yet the Brothers Grimm and included. Still, despite these obvious shortcomings, this major undertaking should be considered as a supplement to other similar tools as a reference aid and selection guide for secondary school, undergraduate, and public libraries. *Literature—History and Criticism; Literature—Bio-Bibliography*

Y; A

1191. **Major 20th Century Writers**, Ed. by Bryan Ryan. Gale, 1991. 4v. 3,300p. $295./set. 0-8103-7766-7.

This reference work includes novelists, poets, playwrights, and other authors of the twentieth-century which are most often studied in high schools and colleges (according to librarians and educators in the United States and Great Britain who were surveyed). This newer reference set is designed for the smaller library which doesn't really need (or is unable to afford) the more extensive *Contemporary Authors*. While international in scope, Authors chosen for inclusion have written in English or their works have been translated into English. All sketches taken from *Contemporary Authors* have been reviewed and updated. All entries follow the familiar CA format and include personal biographical facts, bibliographies of complete works, and a bibliography of biographical/critical sources for additional, more extensive research. This bio-bibliographic set is recommended for all secondary school, academic, and public libraries that do not presently hold *Contemporary Authors*. *Authors; Literature—Bio-Bibliography*

Y; A

1192. **Nobel Laureates in Literature: A Biographical Dictionary**, Ed. by Rado Pribic. Garland, 1990. 473p. $95. 0-8240-7541-4. (Garland Reference Library of the Humanities, 849).

The Nobel winners in literature are arranged in alphabetical order, which makes this handy reference source easy to use. There is also a chronological list of awardees. Each entry includes a biographical sketch and a select bibliography. An appendix includes a list of secondary sources. Much of the information in this bio-bibliography is found elsewhere, but it would be convenient for students and others working specifically on Nobel winners in literature. Recommended for most academic libraries and large public libraries needing additional resources in this area. *Nobel Prizes; Literature*

A

1193. **Scribner's Writers Series**. Scribner, 1974- .

This extensive, multivolume set contains many subsets each containing many volumes. Though not intended for selection purposes, author entries contain lists of both primary and secondary sources and can be useful for collection development and identifying sources for interlibrary loan. Some of the recent titles have been given separate entries. The parts of this series at present are: *American Writers, Ancient Writers: Greece and Rome, British Writers, European Writers, Science Fiction Writers, Supernatural Fiction Writers, Writers for Children, African American Writers, Latin American Writers,* and *Modern American Women Writers.* Two other extensive series from other publishers that will be useful for the same purposes are *Ungar's Library of Literary Criticism* and *Chelsea House Library of Literary Criticism*.

American Literature; English Literature; Literature

① Ref PS129 .A55   ② CC, MSU   ③ PR85 .B688 (Supplements @ CC, MSU)   ④ CC, MSU   ⑤ Ref PS374 .S35 S36 1982
⑥ CC, MSU   ⑦ CC, MSU   ⑧ CC, MSU   ⑨ CC, MSU

Y*; A*

1194. **Wilson Author Series**. H. W. Wilson. 1938-1991.

This time-tested bio-bibliographic series now consists of 11 volumes covering writers from 800 B.C. into the mid-1980's. Earlier volumes, which have not been revised, are still useful. Each volume follows a similar pattern: "Sketches describe their subjects' lives and careers, literary significance, and critical evaluations, and include lists of the author's principal works with date first published, lists of major critical works, and a portrait or photograph, where available." This series is highly recommended for all secondary school, academic, and public libraries. Titles currently available in this bio-bibliographic series include:

American Authors, 1600-1900. Ed. by Stanley J. Kunitz and Howard Haycraft. 1938. $65. 0-8242-0001-2. Ref PS 21 .K8

British Authors Before 1800. Ed. by Stanley J. Kunitz and Howard Haycraft. 1952. $53. 0-8242-0006-3. Ref PR 105 .K9

British Authors of the Nineteenth Century. Ed. by Stanley J. Kunitz and Howard Haycraft. 1936. $55. 0-8242-0007-1. Ref PR451 .K8 1936

European Authors, 1000-1900. Ed. by Stanley J. Kunitz and Vineta Colby. 1967. $68. 0-8242-0013-6. ①

Greek and Latin Authors, 800 B.C.—A.D. 1000. By Michael Grant. $60. 0-8242-0640-1. Ref PA 31 .G7

Twentieth Century Authors. Ed. by Stanley J. Kunitz and Howard Haycraft. 1942. $85. 0-8242-0049-7. ②

Twentieth Century Authors: First Supplement. Ed. by Stanley J. Kunitz and Howard Haycraft. 1955. $75. 0-8242-0050-0. ②

World Authors, 1950-1970. Ed. by John Wakeman. 1975. $95. 09-8242-0429-0. Ref PN451 .W3

World Authors, 1970-1975, Ed. by John Wakeman. 1980. $78. 0-8242-0641-X. Ref PN451 .W67

World Authors, 1975-1980. Ed. by Vineta Colby. 1985. $80. 0-8242-0715-7. Ref PN451 .W672 1985

World Authors, 1980-1985. Ed. by Vineta Colby. 1991. $90. 0-8242-0797-1. cc, MSU

Index to the Wilson Author Series. 1991. $25. 0-8242-0820-0.

Authors

Literary Criticism

Y; A

MSU

1195. **Black Literature Criticism: Excerpts from Criticism of the Most Significant Works of Black Authors over the Past 200 Years**, Ed. by James P. Draper. Gale, 1992. 3v. 2100p. $250. 0-8103-7929-5.

This latest addition to Gale's Literary Criticism Series follows the same general format as others in the series. Over 150 black writers of the 18th, 19th, and 20th centuries from the U.S., Nigeria, South Africa, Jamaica, "and over a dozen other nations" are included. Each author entry consists of a biographical/critical introduction that concludes with references to other Gale works. Also included are a list of principal works and excerpts from criticism that present an overview of critical commentary on the author. Finally, each entry contains a bibliography of additional sources. Author, nationality, and title indexes for the whole set are included in v. 3. This set, while relatively expensive, is recommended for public, academic, and high school libraries. The overlap with Gale's Literary Criticism series will have to be considered, especially for the smaller libraries. *Authors, African American*

A

1196. **Chelsea House Library of Literary Criticism**, by Harold Bloom. 37 volumes. Chelsea House, 1985-87. $55. and $60. per volume.

This extensive 37-volume series is not a selection aid per se; however, each of the entries for authors contains a bibliography of critical writings that could be checked for possible acquisitions. The series is divided into five sets that cover various literary periods. They are *The Critical Perspective* (10 volumes), *The Major Authors Edition of the New Moulton's Library of Literary Criticism* (5 volumes), *The New Molton's Library of Literary Criticism* (10 volumes), *Twentieth-Century American Literature* (5 volumes), and *Twentieth-Century British Literature* (7 volumes). Collectively, the sets cover about 2,000 major authors and give often lengthy excerpts from critical works. A typical entry is two pages in length, but for very important writers like Chaucer, they are frequently around 100 pages. For large libraries.

American Literature; English Literature

① Ref PN 451 .K8   ② Ref PN 451 . K84/Suppl

A

1197.   **Classical and Medieval Literature Criticism**. Gale, 1988- . $95. per volume.   *MSU*

There are now seven volumes in this set that encompasses literature from pre-Biblical epics through the middle ages. Each volume covers between four and six authors. There are extensive bibliographies for each entry that will be useful chiefly for interlibrary loan purposes in academic libraries. Another important set from Gale is *Shakespearean Criticism*. There are now 16 volumes in print; each priced at $110.

Classical Literature; Literature, Medieval; Shakespeare, William

A

1198.   **Comedy: An Annotated Bibliography of Theory and Criticism**, by James E. Evans. Scarecrow, 1987. $37.50 0-8108-1987-2.

This three-part bibliography contains more than 3,000 books, articles, and other items that deal with various aspects of comedy from Aristotle to Woody Allen. Part 1 deals with theoretical writings, part 2 (the largest) with comedy in various literary forms in English, and part 3 with related subjects, such as farce, jokes and satire. Annotations are one-liners. Useful in large collections.   *Comedy*

Y; A

1199.   **Contemporary Literary Criticism**. Gale, about $100 per volume.   *Ref PN771 .C59*

This set, which now numbers over 70 volumes, is a collection of critical excerpts and bibliographic entries that analyze many important authors' works. It is therefore of very limited use in collection development. There is a *Contemporary Literary Criticism Yearbook* and, of interest to young adult librarians, is volume 30 of the main set, which is devoted to authors of young adult material.   *Literature*

A

1200.   **Gale Literary Criticism Series.** Gale, various dates.

This multivolume conglomerate offers several series that collectively study critical receptions to authors of all time periods, genres, and nationalities. Each set is added to periodically and now averages over $100 per volume. The sets are not intended as collection development tools, but nevertheless contain extensive bibliographies that can be of value for acquisitions or interlibrary loan in large collections. The sets are *Contemporary Literary Criticism* (authors who are now living or died after December 31, 1959; now about 70 volumes; see separate entry), *Children's Literature Review* (authors who write for young people; about 25 volumes; see separate entry), *Classical and Medieval Literature Criticism* (authors who lived from antiquity through 1399; now about eight volumes), *Literature Criticism from 1400 to 1800* (authors who died between 1400-1799; about 20 volumes), *Nineteenth Century Literature Criticism* (authors who died between 1800-1899; over 30 volumes), *Twentieth-Century Literary Criticism* (authors who died from 1900-1959; over 40 volumes), *Shakespearean Criticism* (over 15 volumes), *Poetry Criticism* (3 volumes), *Short Story Criticism* (about 10 volumes) and *Encyclopedia of Literature and Criticism* (first volume, 1991). 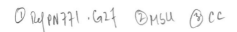 *English Literature; American Literature; Literature*

A

1201.   **Literature Criticism from 1400 to 1800**, Ed. by James P. Draper and James E. Person. Gale, 1984- . v. 1-17 currently in print. $104. per volume.

This major reference set which began in 1984 and is continuing to date has 17 volumes in print as of 1991. The purpose of this work is to provide excerpts from criticism of the works of novelists, poets, playwrights, philosophers, and other writers who died between 1400 and 1800. Each volume includes criticism on about 8 to 10 writers; for example, volume 17 includes entries on William Caxton, Geoffrey Chaucer, Stephen Hawes, and Jean de La Bruyere. Each extensive entry includes author portraits and illustrations (where possible), facsimile pages, and biographies, in addition to the annotated critical excerpts. A selected bibliography of additional sources of information on the writers is also provided. This major reference work is recommended for reference/research and collection development for all academic and public libraries as an essential complement to world literature courses.

Literature—History and Criticism

Y; A

1202.   **Nineteenth-Century Literature Criticism**. Ed. by Laurie DiMauro. Gale, 41 volumes in print. $104. per volume.

This set, published since the early 1980's, fills the need for a source of critical comment on those authors who died during the nineteenth century. About three or four new volumes are published each year. This series provides extensive excerpts from published criticism of the major novelists, poets, playwrights, and other writers during the period. Each volume is about 500 pages in length and covers about 10 authors.

Entries contain biographical information, bibliographies for the critical selections, and sources of additional information. This set is recommended for all academic libraries and for those public and secondary school libraries that can afford it. *Literature—History and Criticism*

A

1203. **Twentieth-Century Literary Criticism**, Ed. by Paula Kepos. Gale, new volumes published regularly; 41 volumes in print. $104. per volume; separate ISBN # for each volume.

This extensive reference tool includes critical evaluations of the major novelists, poets, and playwrights of 1900-1959. There is no duplication between this work and Gale's *Contemporary Literary Criticism* which includes criticism and evaluations of authors who are living and died after 1959. Each entry begins with an introductory biographical and critical essay; critical excerpts follow in chronological order. An annotated list of further reading concludes each entry. This major reference tool is recommended for all libraries that can afford it. *Literature—History and Criticism*

Y; A

1204. **World Literature Criticism, 1500 to the Present: A Selection of Major Authors from Gale's Literary Criticism Series**, Ed. by James Draper. Gale, 1992. 6v. 4,209p. $360. 0-8103-8361-6.

"Specially compiled to meet the needs of high school and college students...," this work covers 225 authors. The selected titles represent many nations and a broad selection from 1500 to the present. This work was probably intended to serve those libraries unable to afford the huge Gale Literary series..., "and most of the sources cited are available in typical small and medium-sized libraries." Each entry contains a biographical sketch, excerpts of selected criticism, and a short bibliography of secondary sources. Author, nationality, and title indexes complete the volumes. This "one-stop" guide is recommended for all libraries, but especially for smaller libraries with tight budgets or smaller collections.

Literature—History and Criticism

Poetry

A

1205. **The Columbia Granger's Guide to Poetry Anthologies**, by William Katz and Linda Sternberg Katz. Columbia, 1991. 231p. $45. 0-231-07244-9.

The venerable guide to locating individual poems, *The Granger's Index to Poetry* (Columbia University Press, 1990), is now in its ninth edition. It analyzes and indexes the contents of about 400 anthologies. Using this list, the authors have provided a qualitative and descriptive guide to these anthologies. They are arranged in 60 categories by such topics as Afro-American, love, nature and children's poetry. Citations include bibliographic information and evaluative comments about the contents of each. There is also an index of editors and titles, plus a list of the 10 must-purchase anthologies and 34 other highly recommended ones. This will be useful both for reader's advisory work in public libraries and for collection development. Large high school libraries might also find it helpful. *Poetry*

A

1206. **Contemporary Poets**, by Tracy Chevalier. 5th ed. St. James Press, 1991. 1,179p. $115. 1-55862-035-4.

There are entries for about 800 living poets in the fifth edition of this standard work. In addition to biographical material, each entry contains a signed critical essay and, as a help in collection development, a complete list of separately published books and a list of works about the poet. This will be of value in most medium and large public libraries and, perhaps, in high schools with advanced English classes. *Poets*

Y; A

1207. **Granger's Index to Poetry**, by William F. Bernhardt. 8th ed. Columbia University Press, 1986. 2,014p. $150. 0-231-06276-1.

This volume indexes a total of 405 anthologies of poetry published through June 30, 1985. There is a combined title and first-line index plus one by author and another by subject. Approximately 50,000 poems are indexed. Although this book is used primarily for reference purposes, the listing of books indexed can be helpful as a purchasing guide for both high school and public libraries. For more information on them see *The Columbia Granger's Guide to Poetry Anthologies* by Bill Katz and Linda Sternberg Katz. *Poetry*

Y; A

1208. **Poetry Criticism**, Ed. by Robyn V. Young. Gale, 1991- open. 3 v. $75. per volume. v. 1, 0-8103-5450-0; v. 2, 0-8103-5539-6; v. 3, 0-8103-5440-X.

Poetry Criticism is the newest addition to Gale's highly-regarded series on literary criticism sources. Each volume of this fully-illustrated guide to poets contains critical excerpts on 12 to 15 major poets most frequently studied in high schools and undergraduate college courses. Added volumes are tentatively planned to be issued biannually. Entries are arranged in alphabetical order by poet. Each entry contains a biographical sketch, excerpts of critical analyses; and sources of additional readings. Author, title, and subject indexes are provided. This bio-bibliographical source is recommended for reference and collection development in secondary school, academic, and public libraries. *Poetry—History and Criticism*

Y; A

1209. **Poetry Index Annual 1990: A Title, Author, First Line and Subject Index to Poetry in Anthologies**. Roth Publishing, 1992. 300p. $54.99. 0-89609-321-2.

Do libraries that have *Granger's Index to Poetry* really need another index to poetry? The editors of this annual index which has been published since 1982 claim it to be "the first and only work to systematically index all poetry anthologies as they are published." One might quibble with the word *all* since only about 50 to 60 anthologies are indexed each year; however, the strong case made for this index is recency. English language poetry anthologies are included, no matter where published, though most are published in the United States. This title is recommended for those libraries that need more currency, an international flavor, and additional anthologies that the standard indexes do not provide. It is recommended as a complement to rather than a substitute for such basic indexes as *Granger's ...* or Brewton's *Index to Poetry for Children and Young People....* *Poetry*

Drama

A

1210. **Contemporary Dramatists**, by D. L. Kirkpatrick and James Vinson. 4th ed. St. James Press, 1988. 785p. $115. 0-912289-62-7.

The fourth edition of this valuable work supplies information on about 400 living English language writers for the stage, screen, radio, and television. As well as biographical information, there is a signed critical essay for each author, a full bibliography of written works, plus a listing of critical sources. It is the latter two sections that can be helpful in collection development. A good public library addition.

Dramatists

A

1211. **Drama Criticism, Volume 3**, Ed. by Lawrence J. Trudeau. Gale, 1993. 600p. $75. 0-8103-7959-7.

This is the third of a new subseries that is part of a larger literary criticism series from Gale. Subsequent volumes are planned to appear annually. Like others in this series (see below and individual titles) this volume will be more useful for research than collection building, but its bibliographies will be of some value in satisfying both needs. Approximately 15 playwrights are covered in each volume, with brief biographical summaries, portraits, critical essays, excerpts from reviews and critical writings, and two bibliographies, one of primary works and the other of secondary sources. There are title and nationality indexes and a cumulative author index to all the Gale Literary Criticism titles. They are *Short Story Criticism* (now about 9 volumes), *Classical and Medieval Literature Criticism* (about 8 volumes), *Literature Criticism from 1400 to 1800* (18 volumes), *Shakespearean Criticism* (17 volumes), *Nineteenth Century Literature Criticism* (34 volumes), *Twentieth-Century Literary Criticism* (65 volumes), *Contemporary Literary Criticism* (65 volumes) and *Encyclopedia of Literature and Criticism* (1st ed, 1991, $125. 0-81038331-4).

Drama—History and Criticism

Y; A

1212. **Drury's Guide to Best Plays,** by James M. Salem. 4th ed. Scarecrow, 1987. 488p. $39.50. 0-8108-1980-5.

The first edition of this bibliographic guide to nonmusical full-length plays in English appeared in 1953. The present volume contains listings for 1,500 plays written from 400BC to 1985, arranged by author. Listed for each play are title and date, the publisher or the collection in which the play is included, a cast and setting analysis, and given plus an annotation. There are many supplementary appendixes and indexes, such as lists of prize winning plays, collections cited, and those popular with high school groups plus cast and title indexes. This is a fine addition to high school and public library reference collections which also has value in collection development. *Drama*

A

1213. **500 Plays: Plot Outlines and Production Notes,** by Theodore Shank. Drama Book Publishers, 1988. 450p. $15. pap. 0-89676-102-9.

This is a reprint of a 1963 title that lists and analyzes 528 plays in 11 chapters organized under nationalities such as Greek drama or American drama. For each play there is a brief plot summary, plus production hints on sets, number of characters, costumes, etc., and a list of recommended editions. Although this should be updated it can serve as a guide to the best in the history of drama. *Drama*

C; Y; A

1214. **Index to Plays in Periodicals, 1977-1987**, by Dean H. Keller. Scarecrow, 1990. $42.50. 0-8108-2288-1.

This is a supplement to *Index to Plays in Periodicals* (1979, $60, 0-8108-2288-1). The present volume lists 4,605 plays that have appeared in 104 periodicals that were published between 1977 and 1987. The body of the work arranges the plays alphabetically by author, with references from titles to authors. There is no subject index. Many of the plays are from teaching journals and therefore are suitable for young people. *Drama*

A

1215. **Major Modern Dramatists, v. 1, British, American, and German Dramatists**, Comp. and Ed. by Rita Stein et al. Ungar, 1984. 550p. $75. 0-8044-3267-8. (Library of Literary Criticism).

This is the first in the new Library of Literary Criticism series whose primary aim "is to give an overview of the critical reception of the dramatist from the beginning of his career up to the present time by presenting excerpts from reviews, articles, and books." Obviously these sources are helpful bibliographic sources for reference, interloan, or library development centered on a particular dramatist. This volume includes 35 American, British, Irish, German, Austrian, and Swiss dramatists from the late 1800's to the mid-1980's. Dramatists are grouped by language, then alphabetically by name. A bibliography with full citations follows each biographical and critical commentary. This volume and the following are recommended for all academic, most public libraries, and many larger high school libraries. *Drama; Dramatists*

A

1216. **Major Modern Dramatists, v. 2, Norwegian, Swedish, French, Belgian, Italian, Spanish, Russian, Czech, Hungarian, & Polish Dramatists**. Comp. and ed. by Rita Stein et al. Ungar, 1986. 572p. $75. 0-8044-3268-6. (Library of Literary Criticism).

This is a companion volume to v. 1; the aim, format, and period of coverage are identical. (See above entry.) *Drama; Dramatists*

Y; A

1217. **Modern Drama Scholarship and Criticism, 1966-1980: An International Bibliography**, by Charles A. Carpenter. University of Toronto Press, 1986. 587p. $80. 0-8020-2549-8.

This international bibliographic checklist contains the staggering number of over 27,000 entries, culled from over 1600 journals and thousands of monographs and reference works. As the author states, it is "a bibliographical précis of the entire discipline of modern drama." The emphasis is on plays and playwrights, rather than on actors or performances. The basic bibliography is arranged by nationality or language, e.g., American drama, British and Irish drama, Canadian drama, Hispanic drama, etc. Playwrights are listed alphabetically under each major group, followed by works by and works about. This comprehensive bibliography is recommended for reference, interloan work, and collection building for all academic and public libraries and larger secondary school libraries. *Drama*

A

1218. **Ottemiller's Index to Plays in Collections: An Author and Title Index to Plays Appearing in Collections Published between 1900 and 1985**, by Billie M. Connor and Helene G. Mochedlover. 7th ed. Scarecrow, 1988. 564p. $42.50. 0-8108-2081-1.

This 7th edition of a standard index covers plays published between 1900 and 1985 anywhere in the English-speaking world. Over 2,500 authors are cited, including a number of contemporary playwrights, such as Harvey Fierstein and David Mamet. Over 1,350 collections are analyzed. These collections of course are to receive serious consideration for collection building. Three main indexes are provided: author, title, and list of collections analyzed. This basic reference, interlibrary loan, and collection evaluation and development aid is recommended for all secondary school, academic, and public libraries. *Drama*

Y*; A*
1219. **Play Index 1983-1987**, Ed. by Juliette Yaakov and John Greenfieldt. Wilson, 1988. 522p. $55. *Ref*
ISSN 0554-3037.

PN 1655
.P53

This basic index has been a standard reference tool for nearly 40 years for students, teachers, librarians, and those involved with or interested in theatre and drama. This new 1983-1987 volume indexes nearly 4,000 new and previously published plays appearing in new collections published during this five year period. All plays have been written in or translated into English. The word plays is interpreted broadly; also included are puppet plays and TV and radio plays. The standard format, familiar to all librarians, is used in this work, e.g., plays can be accessed by author, title, subject, or dramatic style. However, only the author entry provides a full bibliographic citation, descriptive annotation, and make-up of cast; symbols are used to indicate suitability for children or young people. The special section, "List of Collections Indexed" is an invaluable bibliography useful for collection development. All seven volumes (from 1949-1952 to present) are still available, with prices ranging from $20 to $55. *Play Index* is recommended as a reference tool and aid for collection building for all school, academic, public, and special libraries involved in theater/drama.
Drama

Y; A*
1220. **Research Guide to Biography and Criticism: World Drama**, Ed. by Walton Beacham. Beacham Publishing Co., 1986. 742p. $69. 0-933833-06-7.

This work which deals with dramatists is almost identical in purpose and format to the editor's *Research Guide to Biography and Criticism: Poetry and Fiction* of poets and writers of fiction and prose. The entries for each of the 144 dramatists include brief chronologies; selected bibliographies; overviews and evaluations of biographical and critical sources, and additional references. This volume which serves as a companion to the volumes on fiction is highly recommended for all libraries for reference and collection building in the field of dramatic criticism. *Drama; Drama—History and Criticism*

Fiction

General

Y; A
1221. **All the Other Voices: An Annotated Bibliography of Fiction by African, Asian and Latin American Women**, by Elizabeth Gray. [1988]. $3.50.

"This bibliography can serve as a buying guide for libraries serving these population, for honors English courses, for social and political studies courses, and for good general reading.... Gray deserves our thanks for this excellent compilation in an all too neglected area." (*VOYA*, 4/88) Available for $3.50 prepaid from: Elizabeth Gray, 88 North Road, Bedford, MA 01730. *Authors—Women; Women Authors*

Y; A
1222. **Classic Cult Fiction: A Companion to Popular Cult Literature**, by Thomas Reed Whissen. Greenwood, 1992. 319p. $65. 0-313-26550-X.

This work consists of essays on fifty books that the author feels in each case "touches the nerve of its time with uncanny accuracy." It begins with *The Sorrows of Young Werther* (1774) and ends with Douglas Adams' *The Hitchhiker's Guide to the Galaxy* (1979). More than half have been published since 1960. Each essay contains a brief bibliography, and there are lists of other cult titles and books for further reading. Though many may disagree with some of the inclusions and wonder why other titles have not been included, this is an interesting book for browsing and for ideas related to collection development in large high school and public libraries *Popular Culture; Fiction on order*

Y*; A*

1223.   Fiction Catalog. 12th ed. Wilson, 1991. 951p. $98. 0-8242-0804-8.

This standard reference and bibliographic tool now lists over 5,000 the best English language in-print (and a few out-of-print) fiction titles. They are chosen by a select committee of libraries from across the United States and include books from different periods and languages if translated into English. The main section is arranged by author and gives plot summaries and often a short critical annotation for each book, plus a list of contents for each story collections. There is a title, thematic and subject index. Subscribers to the main volume also get annual paperback updates (covering 1991, 1992, 1993, 1994) which usually contains an additional listing of 500 books each. This is a basic selection aid in academic and public libraries and can also be used in many high schools.   *American Literature; English Literature; Fiction*

*PS374
.P63R67
1991*

Y*; A*

1224.   Genreflecting: A Guide to Reading Interests in Genre Fiction, by Betty Rosenberg and Diana Tixler Herald. 3rd ed. Libraries Unlimited, 1991. 300p. $33.50 0-87287-930-5.

Following an introduction on the nature of genre fiction, the authors deal with such major areas as westerns, thrillers, romance, science-fiction, fantasy and, supernatural/horror. Each area is broken down into subdivisions, e.g., the western section contains subheadings like mountain men, mining, the Indian, and railroads. This is not intended to be an exhaustive bibliography, but instead gives representative titles and popular authors. For each genre there is also a selective annotated bibliography on its history and criticism plus material on bibliographies, clubs, associations and conventions. There are indexes by author and themes. Although the lack of annotations somewhat limit its value in book selection, this is still a useful book to familiarize librarians with popular reading tastes and to supply them with guidance for collection building. Although young adult titles are not included, its coverage for adult material will make it valuable in senior high schools as well as public libraries.   *Fiction; Popular Culture*

Y*; A*

1225.   A Handbook of Contemporary Fiction for Public Libraries and School Libraries, by Mary K. Biagini. Scarecrow, 1989. 247p. $25. 0-8108-2275-X.

This handbook is a guide to various genres in popular fiction. Part I covers areas like romance, spy stories, mystery and detective stories, science fiction and fantasy, westerns, historical fiction, and "trash." In each section there is an overview and basic list of references, followed by lists of authors with their books and their publication dates. Other pertinent information (e.g., pseudonyms) are given, and there are many cross references. In part II, the authors that don't fit into these genre classifications are listed in separate sections for American, British, and world authors. There is an over-all author index. This is a fine companion to Rosenberg's *Genreflecting*. Both will be useful for collection development and reader guidance in high school and public libraries.   *Popular Culture; Fiction*

MSU

Y; A

1226.   Heroines: A Bibliography of Women Series Characters in Mystery, Espionage, Action, Science Fiction, Fantasy, Horror, Western, Romance and Juvenile Novels, by Bernard A. Drew. Garland, 1989. 400p. $55. 0-8240-3047-8 (Garland Bibliographies on Series and Sequels; Garland Reference Library in the Humanities, 878).

This guide contains entries to about 1,200 series published between 1900 and 1988 that feature women as protagonists in the various genres (e.g., mystery, western, etc.) listed in the subtitle. Each entry includes the name of the series, the author, names of characters, brief descriptions of each series, and books in the series arranged chronologically. There are many appendixes that include a list of titles by genre, a bibliography of reference works, and a title index. This will be useful for both reader's advisory work and collection development in large libraries.   *Series; Women in Literature*

A

1227.   Of a Certain Age: A Guide to Contemporary Fiction Featuring Older Adults, by Rhea Joyce Rubin. ABC-Clio, 1990. 308p. $39.50. 0-87436-547-3.

This bibliography of fiction focuses on the older adult, defined here as over 55 years of age. For this detailed analysis, Rubin identifies 904 novels and short stories which present a realistic portrayal of the older adult. Of these, she includes almost 200 novels and a little more than 100 short stories, published between 1980 and 1989, and a wide variety of novels and short stories, for example, romances, mysteries, science fiction, and black humor were represented. Entries are arranged in alphabetical order by authors surname, and numbered sequentially. Each is assigned a subject heading related to aging, such as family relationships, retirement, death and dying, widowhood, etc. Full bibliographic data is presented. Special features, such as large print, audiocassette, visually-handicapped materials are indicated. This important and timely guide is recommended for all public libraries for reference and collection development.

Aging; Senior Citizens—Fiction

Y; A

1228. **Olderr's Fiction Index, 1990**, by Steven Olderr. St. James, 1991. 600p. $50. 1-55862-090-7.   MSU

This index of almost 2,000 books published during the pre-ceding year was first produced in 1988 to cover the year 1987 and it is proposed as an ongoing annual project. Titles chosen were reviewed in standard reviewing media: *Booklist, Library Journal, Publishers Weekly,* and in a few cases, *School Library Journal.* Entries are arranged in one alphabet, with author, title and up to nine subject headings integrated. Each main entry (author) includes full bibliographic information, subject headings, and locations of reviews. Another interesting feature is the rating of reviews from 1 to 4 stars. Any title with 4 stars is included in a "Best Books" section. The ... *Fiction Index* for 1987, 1988, and 1989 are still available for $50. each. This index is recommended for all public libraries and secondary school libraries with large fiction collections where it will serve as a complement to *Book Review Index* and *Book Review Digest* as a reference tool and as a selection guide. *Fiction*

Y; A

1229. **Popular World Fiction, 1900-present**, Ed. by Walton Beacham and Suzanne Niemeyer. Beacham Publishing, 1988. 4v. 1842p. $250. 0-933833-08-3.

This work serves as a companion volume to *Beacham's Popular Fiction in America* (1986). Included in this volume are 176 authors whose reputations were established from 1900-1987 and who are considered world authors by having works translated into English. The vast majority of the authors included are American. Examples of this eclectic group of world authors include Edgar Rice Burroughs, Joseph Conrad, Elie Wiesel, William Faulkner, Margaret Mitchell, and Sidney Sheldon. Most entries are over seven pages long and include the publishing histories, critical reception, and analyses of selected titles. Each entry includes two bibliographies, one for additional works by the author and the other for secondary sources about the author with a very brief note. Author and title indexes appear in the 4th volume. "This set provides information on authors and novels not found in standard reference works such as *Masterplots ....*" This set is recommended for high school, academic, and public libraries where additional information on popular fiction is needed; it would be helpful for both reference and collection development.

Fiction—20th Century; Literature

A

1230. **Postmodern Fiction: A Bio-bibliographical Guide**, Ed. by Larry McCaffery. Greenwood, 1986. *ce, MSU* 604p. $79.95. 0-313-24170-8. (Movements in the Arts, 2).

This guide to postmodern fiction is divided into two major parts: a number of articles that present the major themes and styles of this period, and entries of individual authors which present a brief biographical sketch, critical survey of his or her works, and a selected bibliography of both primary and secondary sources. A great deal of what is covered here can be found in other sources such as *Contemporary Authors* and *Contemporary Literary Criticism.* Because of the additional authors included, the updating of many of the entries, the detailed index, and the background information, this work is recommended for academic and public libraries where postmodern fiction is part of the curriculum or a collection in this area is supported. *Fiction—20th Century; Literature*

Y; A

1231. **The Prentice Hall Good Reading Guide**, by Kenneth McLeish. Prentice Hall, 1988. 310p. $12.95. 0-13-712775-X.

More than 3,000 fiction books are selected for this list of recommended reading. Books date from very ancient times to the present. All books are written in English or are translated into English. About 300 authors and over 70 topical entries are interspersed in one alphabetical arrangement. Bibliographic information, synopses of major works, background information, and lists of the authors' other principal works are found under author entries. A complete author and title index is provided. Despite the fact that the work has a strong British accent (it was originally published in Great Britain under the title *Bloomsbury Good Reading Guide*), this volume is recommended for reader's advisory work and for filling in gaps in a libraries fiction collection. *Literature; Fiction; Adult Books and Reading*

Y; A

C C

1232.   **Read All Your Life: A Subject Guide to Fiction**, by Barbara Kerr Davis. McFarland, 1989. 286p. $24.95. 0-89950-370-5.

This book is intended as a selection guide for adults (or young adults) looking for a good book to read or choosing a serious book for discussion groups. The book is organized into five broad categories: self, family, society and politics, religion, and philosophy. These categories are further subdivided into 43 more specific areas. Each of these subsections contains a brief essay on the topic and about eight recommended titles. Title entries include excerpts, discussion questions, and additional recommended titles on the subject. A total of over 500 books are included in this excellent list of quality fiction. This excellent guide includes an appendix on holding book discussion groups and a complete index. It is recommended for all libraries that have readers needing help in choosing a good book to read. The material on book discussion groups is an added bonus.   *Fiction; Reading Guidance; Book Discussion Groups*

Y; A

*PN3353
Z99H37
1988*

1233.   **Themes and Settings in Fiction: A Bibliography of Bibliographies**, Comp. by Donald K. Hartman and Jerome Drost. Greenwood, 1988. 238p. $45. 0-313-25866-X. (Bibliographies and Indexes in World Literature).

Over 1,400 citations to bibliographies to specific subject areas in literature and literary criticism are included in this comprehensive bibliography of bibliographies. The volume is divided into five parts: sources that cover more than one theme or setting, including 29 standard literary reference tools; themes and settings in fiction; an appendix of recent publications; a joint author index; and a subject index. The major part, the section that deals with themes and settings in fiction, is arranged alphabetically by author; each entry includes full bibliographic information and a brief annotation. All of the bibliographies included are in the English-language and all were published between 1900 to 1985. This well-written bibliography is recommended for all academic and public libraries and larger school libraries for reference purposes and collection building.   *Fiction; Bibliography*

Y; A

1234.   **What Do I Read Next?: A Reader's Guide to Current Genre Fiction**, Ed. by Neil Barron et al. Gale, 1991. 525p. $75. 0-8103-7555-9.

This volume, which is planned to be an annual publication, is designed to help librarians and patrons locate new titles in the popular fantasy, western, romance, horror, mystery, and science fiction genres. Each area has an introduction written by an editor who is well-informed in that area. Titles are arranged by author within genre sections. Nearly 1,500 recent titles are included in this 1991 volume. Each entry includes publisher and date; series name and number if appropriate; main characters; time and geographical setting; story type and brief a plot synopsis; review citations; other works by the author; and similar books by different authors. Most of the titles will have been reviewed within 11 months of the publication date of each volume. A very special feature of this innovative work is the inclusion of eight indexes: title; series name; names of main characters; time setting; geographic setting; type of story; and author. This work is well thought-through and is highly recommended for all public libraries that do extensive reader's advisory work and can afford the cost.   *Fiction; Popular Culture*

Romance and Westerns

A

1235.   **Romance Reader's Handbook**, by Melinda Helfer et al. Romantic Times, 1989. 353p. $12.95. pap. 0-940338-25-4.

As long as there are readers of romances, there is an important need for this bibliography. It complements *Twentieth-Century Romance and Historical Fiction Writers* (which is an update of *Twentieth Century Romance and Gothic Writers* (o.p.). An interesting and useful bonus in this handbook is the very thorough list of pseudonyms, needed because, in this genre, pseudonyms are widespread. The list of "Recommended Reads" is particularly useful for expanding a paperback collection. This handbook/bibliography is recommended for public libraries that serve a large flock of romance readers.

Romances—Fiction

A
1236.   **Twentieth-Century Romance and Historical Fiction Writers**, Ed. by Lesley Henderson. St. *M SU*
James Press, 1990. 856p. $95. 0-912289-97-X.
   This volume is an expanded and updated edition of a basic reference source. It provides essential
biographical, bibliographical, and critical information on this century's important historical and romance
fiction writers. With an expansion of over 60 per cent, this new edition includes more than 500 British,
American, Canadian, New Zealand and Australian writers. While there may be a British focus, American
writers are well-represented. After a rather brief introductory section which includes a selected reading list,
the major part of the volume deals with the individual authors and their works. Each entry includes brief
biographical information, a complete bibliography of the writer's works, a critical essay, and in many cases,
authors' comments. A title index is also provided. This bio-bibliography is recommended for all academic
and public libraries for reference, interlibrary loan, and collection development.
                                                                                Historical Fiction; Romance Literature

A
1237.   **Twentieth-Century Western Writers**, by Geoff Sadler, 2nd ed. St. James Press, 1991. 848p. $105.
0-912289-98-8.
   This title, now in its second edition, joins other titles in St. James's Twentieth-Century series of fine
bio-bibliographies, such as *Twentieth-Century Crime and Mystery Writers* (1991) and *Twentieth-Century
Science-Fiction Writers* (1991). More than 450 authors are included, and many of the authors added are
women, including Jessamyn West and Bess Streeter Aldrich. Each entry consists of a brief biography,
followed by a bibliography and a signed critical essay. Pseudonyms are cross-referenced. A title index is
also provided. Most of the authors included are covered in *Contemporary Authors* and other biographical
sources; however, there are a number of advantages for reader's advisory work, reference, collection
evaluation, etc. to having all works of one genre together. Despite the cost, this biobibliography is
recommended for all public libraries with sizable budgets.   *West (U.S.)—Fiction; American Literature*

Crime and Espionage

Y; A
1238.   **Action Series and Sequels: A Bibliography of Espionage, Vigilante, and Soldier-of-Fortune
Novels**, Garland, 1988. 328p. $54. 0-8240-8396-2.
   This comprehensive guide to 18 types of actions series is arranged alphabetically by title or by last
name of major characters (e.g., Nick Carter series is arranged under Carter). Each entry for the 750 series
included gives type, characters, and a chronological listing of all of the titles in the series. The two useful
appendices give series categories and special lists of series designed especially for young people. As well,
there are author and title indexes which refer the user to the series number. Recommended for those libraries
with popular series fans and those who have found earlier Garland titles on science fiction and mystery
series useful.   *Adventure Stories*

A
1239.   **Crime and Mystery: The 100 Best Books** by H. R. F. Keating. Carroll and Graf, 1987. 219p. *CC MSU*
$15.95 0-88184-345-8; $8.95 pap. 0-88184-441-1.
   The author who is a famous mystery story writer has written entertaining two-page critiques for each
of what he considers to be the 100 best mystery stories ever written. The arrangement is chronological from
Poe to P. D. James, and, although many of the standard titles are here, there are several surprises. This can
be used in public libraries as a checklist and possible buying guide as well as an entertaining book to read.
                                                                                Mystery and Detective Stories

A
1240.   **Crime Fiction, 1749-1980: A Comprehensive Bibliography**, by Allen J. Hubin. Garland, 1984.
1,000p. $70. 0-8240-9219-8.
   In this massive unannotated bibliography, 60,000 books are listed by author with title, series and
settings indexes included. The parent volume covers publications through 1980; a *Supplement* covers the
field from 1981 through 1985 (Garland, 1988, $32. 0-8240-7596-X) in the same manner. In addition to
updating the main volume, it gives additional information on 4,300 titles and 270 series in the original
work. For large collections.   *Mystery and Detective Stories*

A

1241. **Index to Crime and Mystery Anthologies**, by William G. Contento and Martin H. Greenberg. G. K. Hall, 1991. 736p. $60. 0-8161-8629-4.

This index analyzes about 1,000 English language anthologies of crime and mystery stories published from 1975 to the beginning of 1990. Single author collections are not included. The body of the work is in three parts: listings of the stories by author and title, and of the contents of each anthology. This latter bibliography can be of some help in checking holdings and in collection development. There is no subject index. This is a useful index for large libraries. *Short Stories; Mystery and Detective Stories*

Y; A

c c

1242. **Masters of Mystery and Detective Fiction: An Annotated Bibliography**, by J. Randolph Cox. Salem Press, 1989. 281p. $40. 0-89356-652-7.

Cox, a reference librarian, mystery buff, and critic has compiled an annotated bio-bibliography of 74 well-known and popular mystery and detective writers (spy story writers and mystery writers who also write in other areas are excluded). The authors are arranged in alphabetical order. Each entry contains a separate section on biography and commentary. Bibliographic information and an index are also provided. This brief sampling of a popular genre is recommended for college, high school and public libraries for reading guidance and collection development. *Mystery and Detective Stories*

A

MSu

1243. **Murder by Category: A Subject Guide to Mystery Fiction**, by Tasha Mackler. Scarecrow, 1992. 470p. $52.50. 0-8108-2463-9.

Mackler, the owner of a bookstore called Murder Unlimited which specializes in mysteries, felt there was a need for a bibliography which identified mysteries by subject. This volume lists about 1,600 titles under 90 headings; some of the unusual headings include Academics, Bees, Crossword Puzzles, and Writers and Their Conventions. Most titles are readily accessible, having been published between 1985 and 1991 (a few older classic mysteries are also included). Each entry provides bibliographic information and a brief annotation. A list of reference books on mysteries and an author index are also provided. There is very little overlap with Hubin's *Crime Fiction 1749-1980* and its 1981-85 supplement. However, there is more overlap with Menendez's *The Subject Is Murder,* which includes 6,000 titles but provides no annotations. Still, *Murder by Category,* because of the annotations, unusual subject headings, and recency of titles is recommended for most public libraries where mystery fans abound.

Mystery and Detective Stories

Y; A

1244. **Mystery Index: Subjects, Settings, and Sleuths of 10,000 Mystery Novels**, by Steven Olderr. American Library Association, 1987. 506p. $40. 0-8389-0461-0.

This bibliography of 10,000 novels may seem exhaustive; however, compared with Hubin's *Crime Fiction* (Garland, 1983. $60. 0-8240-9219-8), which includes a variety of subgenres and 60,000 titles, it is still just "scratching the surface." Olderr defines a mystery book as one that "has as its focus the detection or solution of a crime." Therefore, despite the fine line of distinction, he excludes many suspense, espionage, and gothic novels. He also limits his work to 20th-century works published in English. With these limits in mind, he still includes 10,000 titles. Each entry includes bibliographic information, names of principal character(s), and a number representing the order of appearance of recurring characters within a series (aimed at readers who read sequels). The work provides four indexes: author (main entry), title, subject and setting, and character. Because of the five year recency in titles and its comprehensive subject access, this bibliography is recommended for most public libraries, even if they already have Hubin's *Crime Fiction.* As well, the price makes it accessible for all libraries who cater to mystery fans, which is most.

Mystery and Detective Stories

A

1245. **A Reader's Guide to the American Novel of Detection**, by Marvin Lachman. G. K. Hall, 1993. 435p. $45. 0-8161-1803-5. (Reader's Guides to Mystery Novels).

Lachman has compiled an interesting list of over 1,300 novels of detection by amateur detectives. All of the novels were written by American and Canadian writers and were published between 1878 and 1991. In the main body of this book, the authors are arranged alphabetically with brief plot summaries of their major works. Special features of this work include a list of authors' pseudonyms, series characters, and stories taking place during holidays. Another special feature which could serve as a buying guide is the author's personal recommendations of "One Hundred Notable Novels of Detection." This unusual volume is especially recommended for all libraries that have fervent mystery fans among their readers.

Mystery and Detective Stories

A

1246.   **A Reader's Guide to the Classic British Mystery,** by Susan Oleksiw. G. K. Hall, 1988. 585p. $35. *CC* 0-8161-8787-8.

Oleksiw, a free-lance writer and mystery-lover has compiled a guide to more than 1,400 mystery novels written by 121 British authors from the early 1900's to 1985. The authors are arranged alphabetically, with their works listed chronologically by series character, to make it possible for readers "to follow the biography of their favorite characters." The author does not define "classic British mystery," but her interpretation is evidently broad because included are police procedurals, romances, novels of detection, and thrillers. All of the novels are annotated with a descriptive note (without giving away any clues). As well, all include full bibliographic information. Access is through a series of indexes including setting of story, time period, occupation of main character, etc. Though, there are a number of bibliographies of mystery novels, the focus on British mysteries in this volume and the unusual arrangement by character, make this guide unique and therefore recommended for reference and collection development for all libraries that serve mystery lovers.   *Mystery and Detective Stories; English Literature*

A

1247.   **Silk Stalkings: When Women Write of Murder. A Survey of Series Characters Created by Women Authors,** by Victoria Nichols and Susan Thompson. Black Lizard Books, 1988. 522p. $16.95 (pap.) 0-88739-096-X.

Using chapters headings, such as private eyes, lawyers, bankers, and authors, the largest part of this book identifies and gives background material on about 600 of the leading characters created by women mystery writers, plus some biographical information on the authors themselves. Collection builders will be more interested in the next 170-pages which are organized by authors names and gives book titles and dates of publication. There is additional appended material on author's pseudonyms, and chronological listings of characters' first and last appearances. This book will be helpful in public libraries for reader's guidance and collection development.   *Women Authors; Mystery and Detective Stories*

A

1248.   **Spy Fiction: A Connoisseur's Guide,** by Donald McCormick and Katy Fletcher. Facts on File, 1990. 352p. $23.95 0-8160-2098-1.

The main body of this work is an alphabetical listing of more than 200 authors, mostly English and American, who are known as writers of spy stories. Entries include basic biographical material, titles written in this genre with publisher, date and place, major characters, versions in film, etc., and a critical analyses from six lines to three pages that evaluate the authors' work and often supply quotes from reviews. There is an introductory essay on characteristics of spy fiction, plus eight other essays on such topics as a history of American spy fiction, real events depicted in novels, screen adaptations and the future of the genre. The work ends with a glossary of terms, a bibliography of background readings, and an index. This work will be of help in medium and large public libraries, both for reader's advisory work and as a checklist for book selection.   *Spy Stories; Authors*

A

1249.   **The Subject Is Murder: A Selective Subject Guide to Mystery Fiction, Volume 2,** by Albert J. *CC, MSU* Menendez. Garland, 1990 216p. $29. 0-8240-2580-6.

Volume one of *The Subject Is Murder* (1986, $29. 0-8240-8655-4) classified about 4,000 British and American mystery novels published from 1890 through 1984. The present volume updates this bibliography with 2,000 additional titles published from 1985 into 1989. As before, the titles are arranged under broad subjects. There are now 48 different categories like boats and ships, fashion, and gardening. Titles are unannotated, but there are title and author indexes. This will be of greater use as a tool to identify books rather than a selection guide.   *Mystery and Detective Stories*

A

1250.   **Twentieth-Century Crime and Mystery Writers,** Ed. by Lesley A. Henderson. 3rd ed. St. James *MSU* Press, 1991. 1,294p. $115. 55862-031-1.

Included in this exhaustive work of almost 1300 pages are short biographical sketches of crime and mystery writers followed by their publications. Also included are signed essays of more than 700 writers (American and foreign) and bibliographies of their books in this genre. More than authors have been added to this new edition, including Clancy, Sue Grafton, and Scott Turow. Included are lists of nineteenth century writers and their works and foreign writers. The title index includes names of series characters. A similar work with much longer entries is *Magill's Critical Survey of Detective Fiction*. The two guides are recommended for libraries serving mystery fans and for reference and collection building purposes.

Mystery and Detective Stories

A

1251.   What About Murder? 1981-1991: A Guide to Books About Mystery and Detective Fiction, by Jon L. Breen. Scarecrow, 1993. 376p. $39.50. 0-8108-2609-7.

This guide is an update and continuation of Breen's 1981 volume by the same title and publisher and an Edgar Allan Poe Award winner, which is still useful and in print (1981, $20. 0-8188-1413-7). Breen also happens to be a mystery writer in his own right and a recognized authority of the genre. There are 565 titles in the current volume, including histories, reference books, collected essays and reviews about mystery literature, bio-bibliographic works, anthologies of mystery stories, and special subjects, e.g., mystery stories and Christmas, and technical manuals for would be writers of mysteries. Bibliographic information and lengthy annotations are provided for each entry. An extensive index completes this authoritative reference source. This work is recommended for all academic and public libraries that cater to patrons who read, write, or study in this area.   *Authorship; Mystery and Detective Stories*

Science Fiction, Fantasy, and Horror

A

1252.   Anatomy of Wonder: A Critical Guide to Science Fiction, Ed. by Neil Barron. 3rd ed. Bowker, 1987. 874p. $44.95. 0-8352-2312-4.

Librarians involved in selecting or recommending science fiction have found this to be a basic tool in the field. This third edition includes over 2,500 fully evaluated and annotated titles in three major sections: English-language science fiction; Foreign-language science fiction; and Research aids (which includes such bonuses as general reference works, magazines, film and television and a core collection checklist). There are also author, title and subject indexes. "This book is indispensable for any public/school/academic collection, even if the previous editions are owned" (*VOYA*, 5/88).   *Science Fiction*

Y; A

1253.   Fantasy: The 100 Best Books, by James Cawthorn and Michael Moorcock. Carroll and Graf, 1989. 216p. $15.95 0-88184-335-0.

This highly selective list of fantasy fiction begins with *Gulliver's Travels* (1726) and continues chronologically to the present. The lengthy annotations are both witty and erudite. This book will interest fantasy fans and librarians who can use it for reader's guidance and as a checklist for possible collection development.   *Fantasy*

A*

1254.   Fantasy Literature: A Reader's Guide, by Neil Barron. Garland, 1990. 586p. $49.95 0-8240-3148-2.

This excellent guide to fantasy literature is divided into two sections: a survey of the genre, followed by a survey of research aids about the genre. Each section contains individual chapters written by subject specialists, consisting of overview essays and critically annotated bibliographies. These are selective, with very important works starred. The second section includes material on reference works, history and criticism, library resources, films, awards, art and illustration, and periodicals and related topics. There are author, title, and theme indexes. This volume can be used in public libraries (and perhaps in some high schools) for both research and collection development purposes. It's companion is *Horror Literature*. There is a some overlapping in material (about 10% of the same text appears in both volumes), but both are valuable for acquisition purposes.   *Fantasy*

A

1255.   Gothic Fiction: A Master List of Twentieth Century Criticism and Research, by Frederick S. Frank. Greenwood, 1987. 193p. $42.95. 0-303-27671-4. (Bibliographies on Science Fiction, Fantasy and Horror, 3).

This extensive bibliography of works about Gothic fiction covers English, American, German, and French Gothic fiction, each in a separate section, with an additional one for other countries. Each section has different chapters, e.g., one on general reference works, another on histories, and a third on individualwriters. Coverage ends with 1985 and the work of Stephen King. There are indexes by critics and authors. This thorough listing of critical writing will have value in large collections. *Horror—Fiction*

A

1256. **The Gothic's Gothic: Study Aids to The Tradition of the Tale of Terror**, by Benjamin Franklin Fisher. Garland, 1988. 485p. $72. 0-8240-8784-4.

PN3435 .Z99F57 1988

For very large collections, this is a bibliography of about 2,500 critical studies on Gothic literature published before 1978. The first part deals with studies on individual British and American writers, and the second deals with specific topics like drama and comedy. Annotations are short but adequate, and there are several indexes. Another similar bibliographic aid is Frederick S. Frank's *Guide to the Gothic: An Annotated Bibliography of Criticism* (Scarecrow, 1984. $34. 0-8108-1669-5). *Horror—Fiction* *PN3435.F7 1984*

Y; A

1257. **Horror: A Connoisseur's Guide to Literature and Film** by Leonard Wolf. Facts on File, 1989. 262p. $27.95 0-8160-1274-1; $17.95 pap. 0-8160-2197-X.

CC

After an introductory overview of the horror genre and its history, the author presents his favorite 400 examples of horror as found in novels, short stories, poems, and movies. All are presented alphabetically by title, and there are extensive critical evaluations and complete bibliographical information. Black and white stills are presented for most of the movies. There is a complete, unannotated list of sources and an index by names. Most medium to large public libraries (and perhaps some high schools and colleges) will find this interesting and useful. *Horror—Fiction; Horror—Motion Pictures*

Y ; A*

1258. **Horror Literature: A Reader's Guide**, by Neil Barron. Garland, 1990. 596p. $55.95 0-8240-4347-2.

PN3435 .Z99H67 1990

This books is divided into two main sections. The first surveys the genre with chapters on such aspects of horror literature as Gothic romance and contemporary horror fiction. The second section is a survey of research aids like reference works, history and criticism, films, and television programs. Each of the chapters is written by an expert, and begins with a critical essay and ends with an extensive annotated bibliography with recommended titles starred. This is a companion piece to *Fantasy Literature: A Reader's Guide*, and there is a certain amount of overlap in the material involving 6 of the 13 chapters, or about 10% of the text. Both books have author, title and theme indexes. Both books will be useful for research, reader's advisory and collection development in medium and large public libraries and many colleges and high schools.

Horror—Fiction

Y; A

1259. **Horror: 100 Best Books**, by Stephen Jones and Kim Newman. Carroll and Graf, 1990. 256p. $8.95 pap. 0-88184-594-9.

A number of authors have contributed to this survey of the best in horror literature from 1592 (*Doctor Faustus* by Christopher Marlowe) to the mid 1980s. For each book there is a summary and a review essay. Appendixes include biographies of contributors and a bibliography of important readings about horror fiction. *Horror—Fiction*

Y; A

1260. **Modern Fantasy: The Hundred Best Novels; An English Language Selection, 1946-1987**, by David Pringle. Peter Bedrick, dist. by Harper, 1989. 278p. $17.95. 0-87226-328-2.

CC

British SF Magazine editor, Pringle, lists his 100 favorite fantasy books. The titles are arranged in chronological order by date from 1946 to 1987 (which causes some problems with several series published over a period of years). Each entry includes a brief synopsis of the story, some critical comments, followed by a brief publishing history. Most titles have a British accent and many are on the adult level, according to one reviewer on the soft porn category. However, the list is imaginative and worth considering. Secondary school librarians might also want to consider Lynn's *Fantasy Literature for Children and Young Adults*. Still, the 100 titles are recommended for most public libraries and many secondary school libraries.

Fantasy

C; Y*; A*
1261. Reader's Guide to Twentieth-Century Science Fiction, Comp. and ed. by Marilyn P. Fletcher. American Library Association, 1989. 786p. $63. 0-8389-0504-8.

The 130 major science fiction writers included in this volume are arranged alphabetically from Adams to Zelazny. This work probably has everything one ever wanted to know when researching a prominent 20th century science fiction writer. Under each author's name is included a brief biographical sketch, a discussion of themes and writing style of author, and plot summaries of selected works. Entries average about five pages per author. A title index lists all books and short stories which have a plot summary in the text. There are several other bibliographies of science fiction books, for example, Barron's *Anatomy of Wonder*, but none include both plot summaries and biographical information. In this work science fiction for children and young adults are also represented. *VOYA* states that "this stunning contribution... is essential for all but the poorest of libraries." *Science Fiction*

A
CC
1262. Reference Guide to Science Fiction, Fantasy, and Horror, by Michael Burgess. Libraries Unlimited, 1992. 403p. $45. 0-87287-611-X.

Burgess has provided us with one of the best and most complete guides to the popular genres of science fiction, fantasy, and horror. A wide variety of reference sources are cited, such as encyclopedias and dictionaries, yearbooks, reader's guides, atlases, magazine and anthology indexes, and bibliographies of all types. Full bibliographic data, included with each entry, is followed by an extensive annotation in most cases. An added bonus is the section on "Core Collections," which will be useful in building or evaluating an existing collection for any type of library. This relatively inexpensive guide is highly recommended for all libraries serving science fiction, fantasy, or horror buffs. *Fantasy; Horror—Fiction; Reference Books; Science Fiction*

A
1263. Science Fiction and Fantasy Book Review Annual, 1990, by Robert A. Collins and Robert Latham. Greenwood, 1991. 728p. $75. 0-303-28150-5.

This annual began in 1988 with the aim of providing "critics, teachers, researchers, librarians, students and fans with a comprehensive critical overview of the genres of science fiction, fantasy and horror" for the year covered. The opening chapters, written by recognized experts, supply overviews of the year's publications in these genres and important research and criticism. The heart of the book is the review section which contains separate divisions for adult fiction, young adult fiction, and nonfiction. Each volume contains about six to seven hundred reviews by approximately 100 reviewers. Though only "significant" books are supposedly included, this section contains a high percentage of the total output of a given year. These entries contain both plot summaries and astute critical analyses. There is also an exhaustive list of prizes and their winners and an author and title index. This is a helpful bibliographic tool for large collections. *Science Fiction; Fantasy; Horror—Fiction*

A
MSU
1264. Science Fiction and Fantasy Literature, 1975-1991: A Bibliography of Science Fiction, Fantasy, and Horror Fiction Books and Nonfiction Monographs, by Robert Reginald. Gale, 1992. 1,512p. $199. 0-8103-1825-3.

This exhaustive bibliography which lists over 22,000 titles, published in English from 1975-1991, *PN3433.5* serves as a continuation and supplement to Reginald's *Science Fiction and Fantasy Literature: A Checklist,* *.R42* *1700-1974* (1979, 2v. $260. 0-8103-1051-1), which is still in print. The main body of the work is arranged in alphabetical order by author; fiction and nonfiction are interfiled. Complete bibliographic data is provided. An alphabetical guide to series of the various genres is helpful. This checklist and its master volume serve as companions to Hal W. Hall's *Science Fiction and Fantasy Reference Index, 1878-1985*, (see next entry). This comprehensive work is recommended as a reference and selection tool for most academic and many public libraries, especially those that have avid science fiction buffs and those that have the first volume; however, the price may be prohibitive to the smaller libraries with limited budgets. *Science Fiction; Fantasy; Horror—Fiction*

A
1265. Science Fiction and Fantasy Reference Index, 1878-1985: An International Author and Subject Index to History and Criticism, by Hal W. Hall. Gale, 1987. 2 vols. 1,460p $185. 0-8103-2129-7.

This is a comprehensive guide to the secondary literature about science fiction, fantasy and horror found in books, articles, essays, newspaper articles and dissertations. Most of the material is from 1945-85. There are about 19,000 items indexed in the two volumes. Volume one lists the material alphabetically under a total of 16,000 authors; volume two uses a subject approach with a total of 27,000 entries. This massive publication is updated by the author's annual *Science Fiction and Fantasy Research Index*. Both would be suitable for very large library collections where there is considerable interest in this field.

Science Fiction; Fantasy; Horror—Fiction

A

1266. Science Fiction and Fantasy Research Index, Volume 9, by Hal W. Hall. Borgo, 1992. 167p. $25. 0-8095-6112-3.

This annual compilation is an index to books, articles, chapters in books, and newspaper articles dealing with science fiction and fantasy. Each volume is divided into two sections, the first is an author listing and the second, which is the body of the index, lists all of these works under hundreds of subject headings. Early volumes were cumulated into *Science Fiction and Fantasy Book Review Index, 1980-1984*. Annual volumes covering the subsequent years are still available. This is not primarily a selection aid although the citations might give some direction for collection development. For very large collections.

Science Fiction; Fantasy; Horror—Fiction

A

1267. Science Fiction, Fantasy and Horror, 1991, by Charles N. Brown and William G. Contento. Locus Press, 1992. 237p. $60. 0-9616-6299-9.

This annual publication, which was begun in the mid '80s, is a comprehensive bibliography of English language science fiction, fantasy and horror novels, and short stories published within a given year. Organized into several parts, this book contains separate sections that list the books under author and then by title. The author listing is the more complete with full bibliogaphic data and contents notes. Stories are also listed in separate author and titles sections. A subject list classifies entries under such headings as "Juvenile/Young Adult," "Reference," and "Horror." Supplementary material includes a list of recommended fiction and nonfiction reference titles which can be of some help as a checklist for collection development, but this publication is essentially used to identify materials and is found only in large collections. *Science Fiction; Fantasy; Horror—Fiction*

A

1268. Science Fiction, Fantasy and Horror Reference: An Annotated Bibliography of Works about *MSU* **Literature and Film**, by Keith L. Justice. McFarland, 1989. 226p. $35. 0-89950-406-X.

The publication dates of the 304 references sources contained in this excellent bibliography range from 1968 to 1987. They are included in nine chapters on such topics as bibliographies, biographies, and general reference works. There are separate chapters on "Television, Film and Radio," and "Comics, Art and Illustration." In addition to full bibliographic information, each entry contains a lengthy critical annotation. Appendixes analyze the output of series publishers, list the titles in each series, and, as a great help for acquisition librarians, list core collections of reference material at three different levels of development. This is a useful acquisition tool in both medium and large public libraries, as well as academic libraries.

Science Fiction; Fantasy; Horror—Fiction; Reference Books

A

1269. Science Fiction: The 100 Best Novels; An English Language Selection, 1949-1984, by David Pringle. Carroll and Graf, 1987, $7.95 pap. 0-88184-346-6.

Many might quibble with some of the choices because this is a highly subjective list of the author's choice of the best in science fiction, beginning with George Orwell's *1984*, published in 1949, and ending with William Gibson's *Neuromancer*, first printed in 1984. Each of the 100 titles is arranged in chronological order and has a one or two page essay that contains both a plot summary and a critique. There is an author/title index. This bibliography can be used for reader's guidance and, to a limited degree, as a selection aid. *Science Fiction*

A

1270. Supernatural Fiction Writers: Fantasy and Horror, Two Volumes by E. F. Bleiler. Scribner, 1985. 1,169p. $160. 0-684-17808-7.

This is a companion to the author's earlier *Science Fiction Writers: Critical Studies of the Major Authors from the Early Nineteenth Century to the Present Day* (1982, $65. 0-684-16740-9). The present volume contains bio-bibliographies on 148 writers contributed by a number of literary specialists. They are grouped by nationality and by genre and extend chronologically from Apulius of the second century A.D. to today's Stephen King. Each entry is five to ten pages in length and includes a biography, a critical evaluation which often includes plot summaries of important works plus two bibliographies, the first of primary works and the second a list of sources about the author and his or her output. This is an interesting set primarily for reference work but the bibliographies can also be used in acquisition work.

Supernatural Fiction; Fantasy; Horror—Fiction

A

1271.   **Through the Pale Door: A Guide to and through the American Gothic,** by Frederick S. Frank. Greenwood, 1990. 338p. $45. 0-313-25900-3. (Bibliographies and Indexes in American Literature).

Frank, in his introduction, states that the American gothic novel "rapidly diverge[d] from the European model just as our country had broken away from England." To test this thesis, the author analyzes over 500 titles of many well-known writers from Hawthorne and Poe to Shirley Jackson and Stephen King. The annotations are well-written. Detailed indexes are provided. This unusual bibliography is recommended for all libraries supporting a strong literature program. It would serve as an excellent companion volume to the author's *The First Gothics* (Garland, 1987, $60. 0-82409-8501-9) which analyzes 500 English gothic novels. *Literature—History and Criticism; Gothic Fiction*

A

1272.   **Twentieth-Century Science-Fiction Writers,** Ed. by Noelle Watson. 3rd ed. St. James Press, 1991. 1,000p. $115. 0-685-51990-7.

This third edition of perhaps the most comprehensive biobibliography of science-fiction writers includes revisions and updates for the original 600 and adds an additional 50 writers. English-language writers since 1895 is the basic scope of this work. A feature to this edition is a title index to all novels and short story collections listed in the "Science Fiction Publications" bibliography for each individual author. Each entry includes a biographical sketch, a list of works by the author, and a critical and evaluative essay. A five-page reading list of books on science-fiction history and scholarship is provided in addition to a extensive title index. This work is similar to several other bio-bibliographies, but is the only major one published since 1985. Though expensive, this bibliography is recommended for all but the smallest libraries

Science Fiction

Y; A

1273.   **The Ultimate Guide to Science Fiction,** by David Pringle. Pharos/World Almanac, 1991. 407p. $24.50. hardcover. 0-88687-537-4; $14.95. pap. 0-88687-536-6.

Pringle, in consultation with other science fiction authorities, has compiled a list of 3,000 novels, anthologies, and collections. Excluded are children's titles, fantasy, non-English, and works published prior to 1970. The entries are arranged alphabetically by title, necessitating the use of the author index to access all listings by a given author. Each title is rated by the author from 0 to 4 (4 being the highest rating). Each entry has a three- or four-line story summary and evaluation. Also noted are date of first publication, type of work, sequels, related titles, and film adaptations. A similar critical guide with almost as many entries is Barron's *Anatomy of Wonder*. Pringle's guide may not be the ultimate guide; however, it is a very useful guide for collection development and reference work and is recommended for most public, school, and even academic libraries where there are science fiction fans. *Science Fiction*

A

1274.   **Uranian Worlds: A Guide to Alternative Sexuality in Science Fiction, Fantasy, and Horror,** by Eric Garber and Lyn Paleo. 2nd ed. G. K. Hall, 1990. 286p. $35. 0-8161-1832-9.

This is a greatly expanded edition of a bibliography of gay and lesbian science fiction and fantasy. It identifies homosexual themes found in books and films from ancient times to 1989. Following an introduction which presents an overview of the subject is an alphabetical listing of entries. Each entry includes full bibliographic information, a descriptive annotation, and a code indicating whether the work deals with lesbian or gay male sexuality. A list of selected films and videos is appended. A chronological index and a list of titles are also appended. This guide is recommended for all libraries with collections in feminism, gender studies, and science fiction as a reference tool and as an aid in collection development.

Fantasy; Science Fiction; Homosexuality; Lesbianism

Novel

Y; A

1275.   **Contemporary Novelists**, by Lesley Henderson. 5th ed. St. James, 1991. 1100p. $115. 1-55862- *CC, MSU*
036-2.

This volume supplies information on over 600 contemporary novelists that are published in the English language. Each entry includes biographical material about the author, a bibliographical listing of the author's writing, and a selection of secondary sources about the author and his or her work. Medium sized and large public libraries and some high school libraries will find this work valuable.   *Literature*

Y; A

1276.   **Novels of World War Two: An Annotated Bibliography of World War Two Fiction**, by Michael Paris. Library Association, UK (distributed by American Library Association), 1990. 184p. $35. 0-85365-918-4.

More than 2,000 novels dealing with World War II are arranged chronologically in this annotated bibliography (although most of the "annotations" are mere two or three word notes). However, a detailed subject index does lessen the difficulty of locating a title on a specific aspect of the war. There are also author and title indexes. Though this is a rather large list, it still might best be used with other lists such as the World War II section of *Fiction Catalog* in order to get a more comprehensive list. Still, because there is a desire by many to identify fiction by subject, this list would be useful to secondary school and public libraries needing additional titles in this area.   *World War II—Fiction*

A*

1277.   **Sequels: An Annotated Guide to Novels in Series** by Janet Husband and Jonathan F. Husband. *1st ed e*
2nd ed. American Library Association, 1990, 576p. $45. 0-8389-0533-1. *Ref PN 3448*

This helpful guide in identifying sequels in fiction is arranged alphabetically by author with titles *.S47H87* listed in the preferred order of reading. Only series where there is some development of plot or characters *1982* or where the books were conceived as a series are included. For each author, general information on the series is given, and for each individual title, the date of first publication is given plus a one-sentence plot *2d ed e* annotation. There are title and subject indexes. The latter also gives access by genre and main characters. *cc* For sequels in children's and young adult literature, there is a companion volume, *Sequences*, which was published in 1985 and is now out of print. Both are of great help in giving reader guidance and in book selection.   *Sequels*

Short Story

Y; A*

1278.   **Short Story Index, 1984-1988** Wilson, 1989. 1,300 pages. $125. 0-685-45834-2. *Ref*

This is the latest installment of this invaluable index which indexes stories that are published as part *PN6120.2* of collections of books or separately in magazines. The basic volume covers the years 1900-1949, and the *.C62* subsequent continuations each cover about five years of publications. This volume offers, in one alphabet, author, title, and subject access to about 21,400 stories published in 1,250 anthologies and collections, plus hundreds of periodicals. The list of collections analyzed is useful for collection development and interlibrary loans. There is also a separate "Directory of Periodicals." A separate volume, *Short Story Index: Collections Indexed 1900-1978* published in 1979, is also valuable for these purposes.   *Short Stories*

Y; A

1279.   **Twentieth-Century European Short Story: An Annotated Bibliography**, by Charles E. May. *CC*
Salem Press, 1989. 178p. $40. 0-89356-656-X.

This is a well-written annotated bibliography on 32 well-known European writers of the twentieth-century. Only English-language criticism is included, and the titles included have been written or translated into English. General biographical information and critical studies are listed for each author. Annotations are generally concise and information-laden. Walker's *Twentieth Century Short Story Explication, 1900-1975* (Shoestring, 1977, $69.50, 0-208-01570-1) and 4 supplements (see later entry) still remain the basic reference tool in this area; however, May's work may still be desired because of its more specific focus and well-written annotations; therefore, it is recommended for most academic libraries.   *Short Stories*

A

Ref
PN6120.2
.W33
1993

1280. **Twentieth-Century Short Story Explication: New Series: v.1: 1989-1990; With Checklists of Books and Journals Used**, by Warren S. Walker. Shoe String Press, 1993. 366p. $49.50. 0-208-02340-2.

This updated volume continues the coverage of short story explications from books and journals through 1990. References to short stories published since 1800 are included. Explications are explanations or interpretations of meaning, therefore, biographical sources, or background information sources are not included in this work. More than 5,650 citations on more than 800 short story writers are included in this volume, reflecting a large increase in women writers. Coverage is international, but limited to those published in the major Western languages. Entries are arranged in alphabetical order by author, followed by authors and short titles of works explicated (full publication data is given in a checklist of books used). This work along with the other supplements is recommended for all undergraduate academic and many public libraries. *Short Story*

English-Speaking Countries

A

CT25
.Z99H38
1987

1281. **And So to Bed: A Bibliography of Diaries Published in English**, by Patricia Pate Havlice. Scarecrow, 1987. 698p. $62.50. 0-8108-1923-6.

This unusual and much needed reference guide lists more than 2,500 diaries published in English and updates William Matthews' important but long outdated bibliographies: *American Diaries* (Canner, 1945. $32.50. 0-910324-05-0), *British Diaries* (Univ. of California Press, 1950. $42.50 0-5200-05358-3), and *Canadian Diaries and Autobiographies* (Books on Demand, 1950. $36. 0-8357-7994-7). All of the diaries listed by Havlice were published as books, journal articles, or dissertations. They are arranged in chronological order by year of the first entry in the diary (838 to 1983). Full bibliographic data and brief annotations are provided. This relatively inexpensive bibliography is recommended for libraries owning the Matthews' bibliographies and for other academic and public libraries building up collections of primary resource materials. *Diaries*

A

PR111
.B57
1990

1282. **The Feminist Companion to Literature in English: Women Writers from the Middle Ages to the Present,** Ed. by Virginia Blain, Patricia Clements, and Isobel Grundy. Yale, 1990. 1,231p. $49.95. 0-300-04854-8.

This is predominantly a biographical dictionary of about 2,700 women writers, from about 1300 to the present, who have written significant works in English. The entries are arranged chronologically by birthdate and are brief in nature. The books mentioned in these entries might, in some cases, be of value in collection development in large libraries. *Women Authors; Authors*

A

1283. **International Literature in English: Essays on the Major Writers**, Ed. by Robert L. Ross. Garland, 1991. 762p. $95. 0-8240-3437-0. (Garland Reference Library of the Humanities, 1,159).

This bio-bibliography focuses on 60 little-known or neglected writers in English outside of the U.S. and Great Britain. Most are twentieth century writers and include such writers as V. S. Naipaul, Margaret Atwood, Salman Rushdie and Christina Stead. Each entry includes a brief biography plus a critical essay on the author's work. There are also bibliographies of both primary and secondary works that will be of value particularly in academic collections to build collections by and about these writers. A subject and title index is provided. *Authors; Literature*

A

PR83
.Z99H34
1993

1284. **Literary Research Guide: A Guide to Reference Sources for the Study of Literatures in English and Related Topics**, by James L. Harner. 3rd ed. Modern Language Association, 1993. 766p. $37. 0-87352-558-2.; $19.50 pap. 0-87352-559-0. *2nd*

This revised and up-dated guide includes 1,194 entries, 1,248 other works, and 745 reviews. It is intended for the serious researcher and is the most scholarly-oriented of two similar guides: Baker's *Research Guide for Undergraduate Students,* the most basic which serves the needs of beginning undergraduates, and Bracken's *Reference Works in British and American Literature* with only about 500 references and in the middle on the difficulty spectrum. The entries in Harner's *Literary Research Guide* are arranged in 21 chapters in two parts. Part 1 is by type, e.g., manuscripts, biographical sources, etc. Part 2 is organized by particular literatures, e.g., American, English, Scottish, etc. Most entries have lengthy

CT214 .M37

annotations which are critical, as well as descriptive. Despite the fact that Harner's may be overwhelming to all but the seasoned scholar, the price is right and it is recommended for purchase for all academic and many public libraries. *Literature—History and Criticism*

Y; A
1285. The New Moulton's Library of Literary Criticism: British and American Literature to 1904. 11 v., Ed. by Harold Bloom. Chelsea House, 1985-1988. $70. volume; $770. set. 0-87754-778-5.

The original work of this standard biographical work has been updated by the addition of some authors and the deletion of others who were not considered as relevant by Bloom. Coverage begins with Beowulf and concludes with Kate Chopin. The last volume of this set (and other sets in the Moulton series) includes an extensive bibliography and an index; it may be purchased separately and would serve well for reference, interlibrary loan, and collection development. Most academic and public libraries would consider the entire set; secondary schools and smaller public libraries might consider only v. ll.

American Literature; English Literature

A
1286. A Reference Guide for English Studies, by Michael J. Marcuse. Univ. of California, 1990. 790p. $120. 0-520-051561-0.

folio
PR56
.M37
1990

More than 2,700 entries are arranged under 24 subject headings in this guide which "aims to provide more help to more people than any single reference guide" to English studies, defined by the author as "all those subjects and lines of critical and scholarly inquiry presently pursued by members of university departments of English language and literature." Listed and annotated are bibliographies, guides, reviews of research, encyclopedias and dictionaries, journals and reference histories. This guide is intended for the advanced student or scholar in English studies. A similar, but less ambitious and much less costly guide that is geared more for the beginning student is Harner's *Literary Research Guide*. Larger libraries, however, will want both. *English Literature*

A
1287. Reference Guide to English Literature, Ed. by D. L. Kirkpatrick. 2nd ed. St. James Press, 1991. 3v. 2,143p. $285. 1-55862-080-X.

This scholarly set of biocritical essays includes "writers from Britain, Ireland, Australia, Canada, New Zealand, and English-speaking Africa, Asia, and the Caribbean." The first two volumes contain biographical entries for almost 900 writers. Each entry contains a brief biographical sketch, a complete list of publications by the author, a list of bibliographies on the author, a bibliography of critical studies, a signed critical essay on the author, and references to essays on specific works dealt with in volume 3. There are several reference works which cover similar ground without necessarily overlapping, e.g., Scribner's *British Writers* and Salem's various Critical Survey titles. Libraries that have extensive literature reference collections may not need this new edition. However, smaller academic and public libraries may wish to consider this rather comprehensive work if they feel they need added material *English Literature*

A
1288. Reference Works in British and American Literature, Ed. by James Bracken. 2 vols. Libraries Unlimited, 1990-1991. v. 1, 252p. $38. 0-87287-699-3; v. 2, 310p. $55. 0-87287-700-0.

PR83
.Z99874
1989

This two-volume set of reference works in British and American Literature is intended for a wide audience, ranging from undergraduate students to graduate students undertaking more sophisticated research. Each volume which is described below may be purchased separately:

Volume I, *English and American Literature*, includes 512 annotated entries with extensive subentries for research guides, dictionaries, indexes, biographical sources, core journals, etc. Annotations are both descriptive and critical. Author/title and subject indexes are provided.

Volume II, *English and American Writers*, describes and evaluates about 2000 bibliographies, chronologies, dictionaries, indexes, and scholarly journals for some 500 English and American writers.

Reference Books; English Literature; American Literature

A
1289. A Research Guide for Undergraduate Students: English and American Literature, by Nancy L. Baker. 3rd ed. Modern Language Association of America, 1989. 70p. $8.50. pap. 0-87352-186-2.

PR56
.B34
1989

This slim work, now in its third edition, is considered a basic guide for undergraduate students undertaking literary research. Its all here: bibliographies, handbooks, guides, special encyclopedias and dictionaries, and even a great deal on online systems such as DIALOG and BRS. Though not as ambitious nor as expensive, this work compares favorably with Harner's *Literary Research Guide,* which, perhaps, places a greater emphasis on English literature. Professors of freshman English and composition will want both. Baker's is recommended for all undergraduate college libraries.

American Literature; English Literature; Reference Books

Y; A*

1290. **Research Guide to Biography and Criticism: Volumes 5 and 6**, Ed. by Walton Beacham et al. Beacham Publishing Co., 1991. 914p. $125. 0-933833-27-X.

Nearly 130 English language (and mainly contemporary American, Canadian, and British) authors have been added to the 325 authors included in the base set and 1990 update. The format and purpose of volumes 5 and 6 are similar to the set; therefore, each presents a chronology of the author's life, a selected list of the author's works, evaluative annotations of selected criticism, an overview of biographical, autobiographical, and critical sources, and citations to treatments in other reference books. These two volumes are recommended for all secondary school and undergraduate academic libraries, as well as public libraries, and are a must for all libraries having the earlier volumes.

American Literature—History and Criticism; Canadian Literature—History and Criticism;
Literature—History and Criticism

Y; A*

1291. **Research Guide to Biography and Criticism: 1990 Update**, Ed. by Walton Beacham et al. Beacham Publishing Co., 1990. 590p. $65. 0-933833-23-7.

This supplement to the excellent 2-volume set by the same title updates the bibliographies for nearly all the British, American, and Canadian authors with additional references to 3,300 titles published since 1985 in the fields of British and American literature (1,900 are fully annotated). One useful change is the addition of symbols indicating academic level. Obviously, for those owning the earlier volumes, this update is a must.

Literature—History and Criticism; American Literature—History and Criticism;
Canadian Literature—History and Criticism

Y; A*

1292. **Research Guide to Biography and Criticism: Poetry and Fiction**, Ed. by Walton Beacham. Beacham Pub. Co., 1985. 2 v. 1,362p. $99. 0-933833-00-8.

Beacham designed this research guide to "assist students in narrowing and researching topics for term papers... and to provide librarians with a tool which will help them lead students to valuable, accessible resources." Approximately 300 British and American poets, novelists, and prose writers from the Middle Ages to 1985 are included in this guide. Each biographical entry contains a brief chronology of the writer's life, a selected bibliography, overviews of biographical and critical works, and a few biographical references found in most libraries. This 2 volume set is highly recommended for all secondary school, undergraduate college and public libraries.

Literature—History and Criticism; American Literature—History and Criticism;
Canadian Literature—History and Criticism

British and Irish Literature

General and Miscellaneous

A

1293. **British Women Writers: A Critical Reference Guide**, Ed. by Janet Todd. Crossroad/Ungar/Continuum, 1989. 762p. $59.50. 0-8044-3334-8.

This reference guide can serve as a companion volume to *American Women Writers.* Included are almost 450 critical essays on British women writers from the Middle Ages to the present. Entries are arranged alphabetically by last name and each includes a biographical profile and a list of works by and about the writer. A similar work, Garland's *An Encyclopedia of British Women Writers*, has about the same coverage, but each has a number of unduplicated entries. This guide is recommended for most academic and public libraries, but most will not need both titles. *English Literature; Authors, Women*

A
1294. **British Writers: Supplement II**, Ed. by George Stade. Scribner's, 1992. 626p. $90. 0-684-19214-4.

Twenty-six lengthy critical essays focus on the author's works and include biographical information, as well as selective bibliographies of primary and secondary sources dealing with the writer. Important "British" authors of the past 100 years are included. "British" here includes English language writers of Great Britain as well as of her former colonies. The detailed index is cumulated with the base set and first supplement. This volume is recommended for all libraries that have the previous volumes (which are still-in-print). *Authors, English; English Literature*

A
1295. **The English Library**, by Nigel Farrow et al. 6th ed. Gower, 1990. 385p. $29.95 0-566-05818-9.

This highly selective bibliography from England is somewhat similar in scope to the American, *Good Reading*. There are 15 subject sections, including fiction, world literature in English, children's literature, poetry, drama, and biography. This is a well-annotated survey of the best in literature from an English point of view. *English Literature; Literature*

A
1296. **English Romantic Poetry: An Annotated Bibliography**, by Bryan Aubrey. Salem Press, 1991. 296p. $40. 0-89356-661-6.

This bibliography, intended for undergraduates and general readers, deals primarily with 14 poets: six major ones such as Keats, Blake and Wordsworth, and eight minor like Leigh Hunt and Robert Southey. The bibliography is selective and excludes material in scholarly journals in favor of more general, accessible items. There are also citations for writings on individual poems. Entries are annotated, and there is an index to the authors and titles of the more than 1,500 books cited and annotated. There is also a general introduction on the Romantic Period and its importance in English literature. This work is recommended for collections in both public and college libraries. *English Poetry; Romantic Poetry; Poetry*

A
1297. **Modern Irish Literature**, Comp. by Denis Lane and Carol McCrory Lane. Ungar; dist. by Harper, 1988. 736p. $95. 0-8044-3144-2.

George Moore and Paul Muldoon are among the 87 writers included in this addition to the Library of Literary Criticism. Essays, plays, poetry, short story, and the novel are all included in this overview of modern Irish literature. Bibliographies relating to each author are found in the back of the volume, arranged in chronological order; these include both primary and secondary sources. An index of the critics is also included. This resource, with its bibliographic references, is recommended only for the academic library with strong majors in this area or in larger public libraries where there is an expressed interest in Irish literary history. *Irish Literature*

A
1298. **Restoration Drama: An Annotated Bibliography**, by Thomas J. Taylor. Salem Press, 1990. 155p. $40. 0-89356-657-8. (Magill Bibliographies).

This bibliography on the Restoration period includes 13 major dramatists active from 1660 to 1700. The selections are aimed at "the undergraduate...and lay person seeking introductory information." The annotations are very informative. Bibliographic information is provided. This brief well-focused volume is recommended for all academic libraries and many public libraries.
English Drama; Drama—History and Criticism

Y; A
1299. **The Victorian Novel: An Annotated Bibliography**. by Laurence W. Mazzeno. Salem Press, 1989. 222p. $40. 0-89356-653-5.

This bibliography focuses on only 13 Victorian novelists, including Anne Bronte and Charles Dickens. Even then, only critical works (books or parts of books) considered easily accessible are included. Entries are arranged in alphabetical order by author and title of author's works. A "general studies" section is followed by citations to specific novel titles. Annotations to the critical works are mainly descriptive. A detailed index of authors and editors of secondary works is provided. While this bibliography is intended primarily for the undergraduate, it would also be useful to many secondary school students doing initial research on Victorian novels, and is therefore recommended for most academic and public libraries and larger high school libraries for both reference work and as a guide to collection development.
Fiction—History and Criticism; English Literature; Victorian Period

Shakespeare

Y*; A*

1300. The Essential Shakespeare: An Annotated Bibliography of Major Modern Studies, By Larry S. Champion. G. K. Hall, 1986. 463p. $65. 0-8161-8731-2.

This highly recommended bibliography, which lists 1511 items published between 1900 and 1984, aims "to provide a convenient and annotated checklist of the most important criticism on Shakespeare in the twentieth century." It includes books, chapters, and journal articles arranged first under general works (334 entries) and then under types of plays (tragedies, etc.) and a further breakdown by individual plays. There are clearly written annotations and a detailed index by author and subject. Excellent for both research guidance, sources identification, and collection building. *Shakespeare, William; Drama*

A

1301. Shakespeare, A Bibliographical Guide, by Stanley Wells. Oxford, 1990. 431p. $65. 0-19-871036-4; $19.95 pap. 0-19-811213-0.

This work contains a series of chapters that cover such topics as the general study of the Bard, the text, Shakespeare in performance, the poems, the plays (there are individual chapters on the most popular plays), and English history of the period; and it supplies a critical analysis of the available texts, a summary of critical studies, and a bibliography of general references. The works cited are both current and retrospective. This will be of value in public library collections as well as academic libraries.

Shakespeare, William

A

1302. Shakespeare: A Selective Bibliography of Modern Criticism, by Linda Woodbridge. Locust Hill, 1988. 266p. $20. 0-933951-14-0.

This is an unannotated bibliography of 2,460 articles, books, chapters in books and pamphlets on Shakespeare and his works published between 1900 and 1985. Items are numbered and include full bibliographic information. Chapters are divided by general topics, with separate chapters for the poems and individual plays. The index is by authors only. This will be of use in public library collections and academic libraries. *Shakespeare, William*

Y; A

1303. Shakespeare: An Annotated Bibliography, ed. by Joseph Rosenblum. Salem, 1992. 307p. $40. 0-89356-676-4.

This annotated bibliography of Shakespeare criticism emphasizes books published in the twentieth century. It is organized in a series of subject oriented chapters that includes headings such as bibliographies, reference works, biographies, the Shakespearean stage, comedies, histories, and tragedies. There are also separate chapters for each of the plays. Each of the entries is annotated, and there is an author index. This is a basic, practical bibliography that should be useful in public and the college libraries, as well as some high schools. *Shakespeare, William*

A

1304. Shakespeare and Feminist Criticism: An Annotated Bibliography and Commentary, ed. by Philip C. Kolin. Garland, 1991. 420p. $55. 0-8240-7386-X. (Garland Reference Library of the Humanities).

The 439 items in this bibliography were published between 1975 and 1988 and include books, essays, articles and dissertations. All deal with feminist views of Shakespeare's plays and poems. The items are arranged first by year of publication and then alphabetically by author with author, play or poem, and subject indexes. *Shakespeare, William*

A

1305. Shakespeare Index: An Annotated Bibliography of Critical Articles on the Plays, 1959-1983, Ed. by Bruce T. Sajdak. Kraus, 1992. 2 vols. $295. 0-527-78932-1.

This bibliography lists 7,116 English language articles from periodicals published between 1959 and 1983 that deal specifically with various aspects of Shakespeare's plays. Reviews of staging or articles on teaching Shakespeare are examples of the kinds of material omitted. The 48 chapters are organized by subjects and the names of individual plays. Each citation is annotated, and there are indexes by play title, general subjects, characters, and scenes. *Shakespeare, William*

American Literature

General and Miscellaneous

Y*; A*

1306. American Ethnic Literature: Native American, African American, Chicano/Latino, and Asian American Writers and Their Backgrounds, by David R. Peck. Salem Press, 1992. 218p. $40. 0-89356-684-5.

Peck has compiled a bibliography of writers of the four major ethnic groups in the United States—Native American, African American, Latino, and Asian. The first four chapters serve as an overview and general picture of ethnicity with an indication of availability of resources, etc.: Chapter 1 is an annotated listing of important reference works for ethnic studies; Chapter 2 presents major studies that deal with the social and historical aspects of a diverse society; Chapter 3 deals with "Teaching Ethnic Literature;" and Chapter 4 lists general studies of ethnic literature and is subdivided into sections on biography, fiction, and theater. The main body of the volume are the remaining chapters on each major ethnic group. These include an introductory section dealing with the history and background of the ethnic group, this is followed by the listing of resources and finally a list of major critical studies. Peck's work is a real contribution to the field of multicultural materials and is recommended for reference and as a buying guide to all secondary school, academic and public libraries.

Multiculturalism; Multicultural Literature; African Americans; Indians of North America; Hispanic Americans; Asian Americans

A

1307. American Literary Magazines: The Twentieth Century. Ed. by Edward Chielens. Greenwood, 1992. 474p. $89.50. 0-313-23986-X.

Eighty twentieth-century literary magazines are included in this bibliography. Each entry includes an overall evaluation, comments on editorial policies and changes, controversies dealt with over the years, noteworthy authors, and financial and other administrative adjustments. A detailed index is also included. This detailed listing is recommended for most academic libraries as a reference guide and selection aid.

Literary Journals; Periodicals

Y; A

1308. American Women Writers: A Critical Reference Guide from Colonial Times to the Present. Abridged ed. Ed. by Langdon Lynne Faust. Ungar; dist. by Harper, 1988. 944p. $59.50. 0-8044-3157-4.

This one volume hardcover is really a reprint and some updating of the 1983 two-volume paperback edition, which was in turn an abridgment of the original four-volume set published in 1972 with over 1,000 articles. Some bibliographies have been updated, and other minor revisions have been made. However, this guide, though useful as a selection aid for school and public libraries, does not add enough significant new material and, therefore, is only recommended if the library has neither of the earlier editions cited above.

Authors, American; Authors, Women; Women Authors

A

1309. Biographical Dictionary of Contemporary Catholic American Writing, Ed. by Daniel J. Tynan. Greenwood, 1989. 364p. $55. 0-313-24585-1.

This specialized reference work is a collection of essays on about 135 American Catholic writers, rather than a bibliography. However, the appended bibliographies list works by the authors and indicate useful sources for further research, including critical studies and other biographical works. There is an author and title index and an appended "Bibliographical Note" that surveys research on Catholic American writing. One should also consider *The Catholic Novel: An Annotated Bibliography*. This basic biographical dictionary, with its useful bibliographical sources, should be considered by most Catholic institutions, other academic and many public libraries. *Catholic Literature; Authors, American; Authors, Catholic*

A

1310. Concise Dictionary of American Literary Biography. Gale, 1987+. 6 volumes. $350. 0-8103-1818-0.

This six volume set is a spin-off from the massive *Dictionary of American Literary Biography* which contains entries for 2,300 American writers of fiction, poetry, and plays. The present six-volume set is limited to about 200 major writers. In addition to biographical information and a critical analysis, entries include awards and prizes, a chronological list of works, and an extensive secondary bibliography of works involving the author such as books, articles, letters, interviews, papers, and location of manuscripts. This set is intended for purchase by high school, junior college, and public libraries. There is also an eight volume companion set *Concise Dictionary of British Literary Biography* (1991-2. $395 0-8103-7980-5).

American Literature; English Literature; Authors, American; Authors, English

A

1311. Contemporary Lesbian Writers of the United States: A Bio-Bibliographical Critical Sourcebook, by Sandra Pollack and Denise D. Knight. Greenwood, 1993. $99.50. 0-313-28215-3.

This companion volume to *Contemporary Gay American Novelists*, contains a series of chapters each dealing with the work of living or recently deceased American lesbian writer. In addition to a bibliography of the author's works and some basic biographical material, each entry contains a rundown of the critical response to the writer and a bibliography of these secondary sources. This work is somewhat specialized and expensive, but will find a place in many academic and public libraries, particularly where resources on women's studies are sought. *Lesbian Writers*

A

1312. Fifty Southern Writers After 1900: A Bio-Bibliographical Sourcebook, by Joseph M. Flora and Robert Bain. Greenwood, 1987. 628p. $95. 0-313-24519-3.

This is a sourcebook on 50 prominent Southern poets, novelists and short story writers. Different literary specialists wrote the articles. Each article is about 10 pages in length and contains a biographical sketch, a discussion of major works, and themes. At the end of each article, there is a list of important critical writing with often as many as 20 citations. By the same editors there is a companion volume, *Fifty Southern Writers Before 1900* (Greenwood, 1987, 601p. $75. 0-313-24518-5). These will be helpful in colleges and large public library or regional collections. *American Literature; Authors, American*

A

1313. Handbook of American Popular Literature, by M. Thomas Inge. Greenwood, 1988. 408p $55. 0-313-25405-2.

Fifteen bibliographic essays covering such topics as comic books, children's literature, young adult literature, detective and mystery stories, gothic novels, science fiction, and popular verse form the body of this work. Each was written by a different specialist and follows the same format: introductory and historical surveys; basic reference sources; an overview of critical and historical sources; and a general bibliography of books, articles, and magazines. This bibliography lists only secondary sources, i.e., materials about these genres. This along with its companion set, *Handbook of American Popular Culture*, will be helpful in large library collections. *Popular Culture; Fiction*

A

1314. Humor in American Literature: A Selected Annotated Bibliography, by Don. L. F. Nilsen. Garland, 1992. 580p. $75. 0-8240-8395-4.

This selective bibliography cites about 1,300 books, chapters in books, and articles that comment critically on humor as found in American literature. The main body of the work deals with secondary sources on specific authors, from seventeenth-century authors through such contemporaries as Irma Bombeck. They are arranged by birth date. For each item cited there is a lengthy, informative annotation. Eleven shorter chapters follow, each devoted to a particular topic related to humor such as ethnic literature, regional humor, parody, and sex-role humor. Title and author indexes are included. For large academic collections. *Humor*

A

1315. Magill's Survey of American Literature, Ed. by Frank N. Magill. Marshall Cavendish, 1991. 6v. $369.95. 1-85435-437-X.

An excellent reference set which presents almost 200 American authors from the "classic" authors such as Emerson, Hawthorne, and Faulkner to current favorites such as Bly, Walker, and Kingston. The selection of authors include novelists, poets, dramatists, etc. Articles are arranged alphabetically, and each entry includes a brief biography, analysis of the author's works (each title analyzed contains full bibliographical data), and a selected bibliography of additional biographical/critical works. This highly selected bio-bibliography is recommended as a standard reference aid and selection guide for secondary, undergraduate academic, and public libraries. *American Literature; Authors, American*

A
1316.   **Modern American Women Writers**, Ed. by Elaine Showalter et al. Scribner, 1991. 583p. $85. CC
0-684-19057-5.   MSU

This volume and *African American Writers* complement the well-known older parent set *American Writers* also published by Scribner. In an attempt to update the parent set, there is some inevitable duplication of women covered, e.g., of the 41 women included in this volume, 22 are also included in *American Writers*. Long biographical and critical essays are followed by detailed references to complete works by and selected works about each writer. This scholarly bio-bibliography is recommended for most academic, public, and many secondary school libraries for general reference, interloans, and collection building.   *Authors, Women; Women Authors; Authors, American*

C; Y; A*
1317.   **The National Book Awards—Forty-one Years of Literary Excellence: Winners and Finalists, 1950-1991**. Baker and Taylor, [1992].

This short booklet lists all of the winners and finalists of the very prestigious National Book Award, since its inception in 1950. The titles listed perhaps represent the finest in American literature. Areas include biography, poetry, general nonfiction, science, history, translations, adult fiction, children's fiction, and picture books. The 76 page booklet also has an author index. A free copy is available by contacting a Baker & Taylor representative or: Baker & Taylor Books, Information Service, P.O. Box 6920, Bridgewater, NJ 08807-0920, or calling, 800-235-4490.   *National Book Awards*

A
1318.   **Vietnam War Literature: An Annotated Bibliography of Imaginative Works about Americans   MSU Fighting in Vietnam**, by John Newman. 2nd ed. Scarecrow, 1988. 285p. $27.50. 0-8108-2155-9.

This greatly expanded second edition contains more than 750 annotated entries. A chapter is devoted to each category of "imaginative" work, such as, novels, short stories, poetry, drama, and miscellaneous. Entries are arranged chronologically under each category by publication date. Each entry includes complete bibliographical information and a descriptive annotation which is generally a plot summary. An author and title index are also provided. This comprehensive bibliography of imaginative literature is recommended for most academic and many public libraries for reference as well as for collection building.
Vietnam War—Fiction

African American

A
1319.   **African American Writers**, Ed. by Valerie Smith et al. Scribner, 1991. 544p. $90. 0-684-19058-3.

A collection of well-written and scholarly essays on well-known African American writers. The presentation of each author includes a brief biographical sketch, a list of major writings with an appraisal, and a bibliography of books and articles for further study. Though limited to only 34 writers, this complement to the basic *American Writers* (Scribner, 8 vols., $499. 0-684-17332-0) is recommended for most secondary school, undergraduate college and public libraries.
Authors, African American; Authors—Biography

Y; A
1320.   **Black American Women in Literature: A Bibliography, 1976 through 1987**, by Ronda Glikin.   CC
McFarland, 1989. 251p. $35. 0-89950-372-1.

This bibliography of 300 black American women writers of essays, poetry, novel, short stories, and plays is arranged alphabetically by author and numbered sequentially. Each entry lists works by the author, followed by criticism. Both scholarly and popular sources were consulted, including 80 periodicals and about 200 books. The two appendixes add strength to this useful work: Appendix A is a bibliography of 112 general works about black women writers; Appendix B lists the writers by genre of their work, e.g., children's literature, science fiction, etc. As a guide to interlibrary loan or collection development, this bibliography is recommended for most libraries—secondary school, academic, and public.
American Literature; Authors, African American; Authors; Women

A

1321.   **Harlem in Review: Critical Reactions to Black American Writers, 1917-1939,** by John E. Bassett. Susquehanna University, 1992. 232p. $36.50 0-945636-28-8.

This chronologically-arranged bibliography covers the critical response to works published during the Harlem Renaissance. There are five main chapters with individual titles being treated in these chapters by date of publication. Most entries are annotated and often contain sizable quotations from the reviews. Each chapter has a section on general criticism. The last chapter extends coverage selectively from 1940 through 1944. Recommended for academic libraries with strong African American programs.

African American Literature; Authors, African American

A

1322.   **Harlem Renaissance and Beyond: Literary Biographies of 100 Black Women Writers, 1900-1945,** by Lorraine Elena Roses and Ruth Elizabeth Randolph. G. K. Hall, 1989. 413p. $45. 0-8161-8926-9.

This valuable bio-bibliography supplies information on 100 famous and not-so-famous black women writers. Each is given an extensive biography with critical commentary, followed by a selective list of primary and secondary sources. Appendixes list the authors by genre, geographic location and dates. There is a title index of the primary sources cited. Valuable in academic and public libraries where there is interest in women's studies and African American literature.

African American Literature; Authors, African American

Y; A*

1323.   **Masterpieces of African-American Literature,** Ed. by Frank N. Magill. HarperCollins, 1992. 593p. $40. 0-06-270066-9.

This guide to about 150 titles represents the works of more than 90 African American writers (37 of whom are women) and includes novels, plays, autobiographies, and poetry. It serves as a companion volume to the many other titles in the *Masterpiece* series edited by Magill. The entries are organized alphabetically by the titles of the works. Each entry includes full bibliographic data, as well as other important information such as principal characters, plot, analysis, and critical comment. Descriptions of standard works covering over 200 years and a number of young adult titles are included. Author and title indexes complete the volume. Although it covers only 150 titles, this convenient collection is highly recommended as a reference tool and selection guide for high school, public and undergraduate college libraries.

American Literature; Authors, African American

A

1324.   **Southern Black Creative Writers, 1829-1953 Bio-Bibliographies,** by M. Marie Booth Foster. Greenwood, 1988. 130p. $35. 0-313-26207-1. (Bibliographies and Indexes in Afro-American and African Studies, 22).

This is an unusual bio-bibliography which identifies known and lesser known black writers from the South who lived and wrote between 1829 and 1953. After a brief biographical sketch that includes place of birth and residence, and occupation, there is a listing of creative writings and the publications in which they appeared. This will be of value in libraries where there is a need for African American materials.

African Americans; Authors, African American

Asian American

C; Y; A

1325.   **Asian American Literature: An Annotated Bibliography,** by King-Kok Cheung and Stan Yogi. Modern Language Association, 1988. 276p. $37 hardcover, 0-87352-960-X; $19.95 paper, 0-87352-961-8.

More than 3,000 briefly annotated entries are included in this, the first major bibliography that includes the works of all Asian-American ethnic groups. Prose, poetry, and drama are identified and full bibliographic citations of anthologies, journals, and monographs are listed. Entries are arranged by ethnic group, e.g., Chinese-American, Japanese-American, etc. Special bonuses are the lists of subject bibliographies, biographical sources, and the section titled "Literature for Children and Young Adults: Selected Books." This seminal work is recommended for most libraries, especially those serving an Asian-American population. *Asian Americans*

Hispanic American

Y; A

1326. **Biographical Dictionary of Hispanic Literature in the United States: The Literature of Puerto Ricans, Cuban Americans, and Other Hispanic Writers**, Ed. by Nicholas Kanellos. Greenwood, 1989. 357p. $49.50. 0-313-24465-0.

This biographical dictionary is a "reference guide to representative figures in Hispanic literature within the geographic, political, and cultural boundaries of the United States." About 50 novelists, poets, and dramatists are included. Mexican Americans who are covered in Greenwood's *Chicano Literature: A Reference Guide* are not included. The importance of this reference tool, for our purposes, are the very fine and extensive bibliographies of works by and about each author that are included at the end of each biographical profile. This basic reference tool is recommended for most secondary school, academic, and public libraries where Hispanic studies are dealt with or in areas where there is an Hispanic population of any size. *Hispanic Americans; Authors, Hispanic American*

A

1327. **Chicano Anthology Index: A Comprehensive Author, Title and Subject Index to Chicano Anthologies, 1965-1987**, by Francisco Garcia-Ayvens. Chicano Studies Library Publication Unit, University of California at Berkley, 1990. 704p. $150.

More than 280 anthologies and other collective works that have been published in the past 25 years are indexed by author, title, and subject in this guide to fiction, plays, poems, and book reviews by Chicano writers. For each of the 500 titles, the main entry gives author, title, source, page numbers, and subjects. The listing of works indexed can help both in collection development and inter-library loan in libraries serving a Chicano population. *Mexican Americans*

A

1328. **Chicano Literature: A Reference Guide**, by Julio A. Martinez and Francisco A. Lomeli. Greenword, 1985. 576p. $55. 0-313-23691-7.

This guide to Chicano literature since 1848 covers the topic in 10 lengthy bibliographic essays like " Chicano Children's Literature" and 29 critical biographies of important authors who are Americans of Mexican descent or Mexicans living in the United States. Each chapter contains a bibliography of primary and secondary sources, and there is, as an appendix, a helpful bibliography of general works on Chicano studies. Libraries that deal with a Chicano population will find this volume useful both for reference and collection development. *Mexican Americans*

A

1329. **Literatura Chicana: Creative and Critical Writings Through 1984**, Comp. by Roberto G. Trujillo and Andres Rodriguez. Floricanto, 1987. 95p. $23. pap. 0-915745-04-6.

The aim of this work is to disseminate knowledge about, and assist in collection building for Chicanos and other Hispanics in the U.S. This is an expansion and updating of Antonia Castaneda Shular's *Literatura Chicana*, 1979 (o.p.). The work is aimed at those who are fluent in English. The bibliography is divided into sections by form, including novels, poetry, theater, literary criticism, oral tradition, literary periodicals, anthologies, dissertations, biographies, and video and sound recordings. Complete author and title indexes are provided. This work is recommended for academic and public libraries, especially those that serve Hispanic patrons. *Hispanic Americans; Mexican Americans*

A

1330. **U.S. Latino Literature: An Essay and Annotated Bibliography**, by Marc Zimmerman. MARCH/Abrazo Press; Dist. by Independent Literary Publishers Association, 1992. 156p. $10.95. pap. 1-877636-01-0.

This work deals with the major U.S. Latino writers and their literature. The major groups considered here are Mexican Americans (Chicanos), Cubans, and Puerto Ricans. The first part of the book consists of an extensive essay describing Latinos and their cultural, especially literary, contributions. The last two thirds of the work comprises the annotated bibliography, which is also divided into the three main groups. The dates of the titles of the items range from the 1970's to the 1990's. Each entry contains full bibliographic data and the descriptive annotations vary in length. This inexpensive work is recommended for all academic and public libraries, especially those supporting a Hispanic studies program or serving a large Hispanic population.

Authors, Hispanic American; American Literature—Hispanic American Authors;
Hispanic Americans; Mexican Americans

Native American

A

cl

MyA

1331.   **American Indian Literatures: An Introduction, Bibliographic Review, and Selected Bibliography**, by LaVonne Brown Ruoff. Modern Language Association, 1990. 200p. $45. 0-878352-187-0. $19.50. pap. 0-87352-192-7.

This unique and scholarly work brings together hundreds of titles of native American literature, heretofore ignored. The time period covered is 1500 to the present. The work is divided into three major sections: an introduction into the literature of the native American, from the 18th century to the present; a bibliographic review; and, important as a selection guide, a selected and rather extensive bibliography of titles. Another special feature is that tribal affiliation is indicated for native American authors. Few, if any, similar works are available and, therefore, this is a highly recommended guide for all libraries building a collection in native American literature.   *Indians of North America—Literature*

Y; A

MyA

1332.   **The Native American in American Literature: A Selectively Annotated Bibliography**, Comp. by Roger O. Rock. Greenwood, 1985. 211p. $42.95. 0-313-24550-9. (Bibliographies and Indexes in American Literature, 3).

Rock states that this volume is "the most eclectic collection available that focuses on literature." The work which includes almost 1,600 references, many of which are annotated, is a good starting point for those doing research on either the American Indian in literature or works by and about native American authors. There is a useful subject index and an author index; a title index would also have been desirable. The division sometimes causes some overlapping, and the subject index not being divided is another disadvantage. Despite these limitations, the bibliography is recommended for most libraries wherever material on native Americans is requested from very basic to more scholarly.

Authors, Indians of North America; Indians of North America;
Indians of North America—Literature

Poetry

Y; A

Ref
PS153
.NSA38
1985

1333.   **Afro-American Poets Since 1955**, Ed. by Trudier Harris and Thadious M. Davis. Gale, 1985. 401p. $112. 0-8103-1719-2. (Dictionary of Literary Biography).

Each of the biographical essays of the 51 Afro-American poets included is preceded by a bibliography of the author's works encompassing books, recordings, television and periodical citations. In some cases, but not all, additional references to other sources about the poet are listed. Like other volumes in this standard series, the book is attractive and well-written and is therefore recommended for all high school and public libraries whose budget can bear the rather high cost.

African Americans—Poets; Poets—African American

Y; A

1334.   **American Poetry Index: An Author, Title and Subject Index to Poetry by Americans in Single-Author Collections**. Roth Pub., 1988. v.4. $52. 0-89609-268-2.

As the title implies, this unique aid indexes works of single authors; unlike the familiar *Granger's Index...* which analyzed primarily anthologies. The rather extensive lists of collections index could serve as buying guides and help round out poetry sections of libraries. However, the index has been published irregularly and the promise of an annual volume has not yet materialized. At present there are two other volumes available, each indexing approximately 200 titles and each costing $52:

V. 2, 1983. 0-89609-241-0. published in 1985.
V. 3, 1984. 0-89609-262-3. published in 1987.

Poetry; American Poetry

A

PS323.5
.M27
1986

1335.   **The Bibliography of Contemporary American Poetry, 1945-1985: An Annotated Checklist**, by William McPheron. Greenwood, 1986. 72p. $35. 0-313-27703-6.

This bibliographic checklist on American poetry is a welcome addition to the study of American Literature. Its intent and format are similar to *The Bibliography of Contemporary American Fiction, 1945-1988*, which serves as a complementary aid. Included are "bibliographically serious accounts" of over

120 contemporary poets, many who are relatively unknown. This volume, along with its companion bibliography is recommended for all libraries that are developing collections for the serious student of American literature. *American Poetry; Poets, American*

A

1336. Guide to American Poetry Explication: Colonial and Nineteenth-Century, by James Ruppert. G. K. Hall, 1989. 239p. $35. 0-8161-8919-6.

This first volume of a projected five volume set is followed by the *Guide to American Poetry Explication: Modern and Contemporary* (1989, $50, 0-8161-8918-9). Future volumes will cover British poetry. Each volume is arranged by poet, followed by the name of the poem then by unannotated critical citations. The lists of the books and periodicals cited may help collection development, although the primary aim of these scholarly volumes is to aid research. For large collections. *American Poetry*

A

1337. Index to Poetry by Black American Women, by Dorothy Hilton Chapman. Greenwood, 1986. 424p. $55. 0-313-25152-5.

This work is an index to 4,000 poems arranged by title and first-line plus a 1,100 entry subject index. It includes poetry written by more than 400 African American women. The list of works indexed will have some use for collection development in large collections where there is a demand for this kind of poetry.

Poetry; African American Women; American Poetry; African Americans—Poets

A

1338. Nineteenth Century American Poetry: An Annotated Bibliography, by Philip K. Jason. Salem, 1990. 257p. $40. 0-89356-651-9. (Magill Bibliographies)

This bibliography has citations to criticism in general and on selected works of 16 well-known nineteenth century American poets, including Bryant, Emerson, Longfellow, Whittier, Poe, Whitman, and Dickinson. After giving biographical information and criticism of each poet's work as a whole, Jason provides us with a 21 page bibliography of "general treatments of the period." Sources are from books, parts of books, and some periodical articles. The annotations are both descriptive and critical. This bibliography is an important purchase for all academic and public libraries maintaining a collection of American poetry. *American Poetry*

A

1339. Poetry by American Women, 1975-1989: A Bibliography, by Joan Reardon. Scarecrow, 1990. 232p. $29.50. 0-8108-2366-7.

This nonselective, comprehensive bibliography lists about 2,900 separately published volumes of poetry by American women that were published from 1975 through 1989. The volume is arranged alphabetically by author's name and for each entry in addition to title, the publisher, pagination, and place and date of publication are given. There are no annotations. This is a companion work to the author's earlier *Poetry by American Women, 1900-1975* (Scarecrow, 1979. $37.50. 0-8108-1173-1). Both will be of value in identifying works prior to consideration for purchase. *Poetry—Women; Women Poets*

Drama

A

1340. American Drama Criticism: Supplement II to the Second Edition, Comp. by Floyd Eugene Eddleman. Shoe String Press, 1989. 269p. $47.50. 0-208-02138-8.

This highly reputable index to American dramatic criticism includes about 350 books (in addition to about 350 journals) that are indexed in a period covering about 1984-1988. One is offered pages of bibliographic citations on a specific playwright. "A library deciding to improve its dramatic literature collection would do well to use the checklist of books provided here as a starting point on recent and worthy additions" (*Recommended Reference Books*, 1990). The basic volume and supplement are still available for this recommended title: *American Drama Criticism: Interpretations, 1890-1977* (Shoe String, 1979. $45. 0-226-16061-0). and *American Drama Criticism: Supplement* (Shoe String, 1984. $39.50. 0-208-01978-2). Certainly the latest supplement, if not all the other volumes, is recommended for most libraries.

American Drama—History and Criticism

A

cc
MSU

1341. **American Playwrights since 1945: A Guide to Scholarship; Criticism, and Performance**, Ed. by Philip C. Kolin. Greenwood, 1989. 595p. $85. 0-313-25543-1.

This in-depth study of 40 American playwrights is not a collection development aid per se. It is a well-written series of essays written by authorities in the field and each includes (in addition to criticism, production history, biographical data, etc.) a primary bibliography and a survey of secondary sources. The dramatists chosen include the most influential in American theater since World War II. The overall usefulness of this identifying tool is reserved perhaps for the serious theatergoer, and therefore is especially recommended for the academic and public library that serves that special breed.

Authors, American; Dramatists, American

A

1342. **American Women Playwrights, 1900-1930: A Checklist.** by Frances Diodato Bzowski. Greenwood, 1992. 420p. $59.50. 0-313-24238-0.

The preface indicates that many writers included are not necessarily American. Entries are arranged by author, with no index by title or subject—a serious limitation. And despite the title, another limitation is that many titles are included that do not fall within the stated scope. Despite this limitation and a number of minor technical errors, this work is recommended for large academic libraries needing a checklist of retrospective titles by women playwrights. *Women Playwrights; Women Studies*

A

cc
MSU

1343. **Contemporary Black American Playwrights and the Their Plays: A Biographical Directory and Dramatic Index,** by Bernard L. Peterson. Greenwood, 1988. 625p. $75 0-313-25190-8.

This source gives biographical information on more than 700 African American writers of plays, and scripts. As well there are bibliographies of each author's play and other writings. Appendixes include a bibliography of general writings on black drama and a listing of libraries with extensive collections in this field. There are title and general indexes. For large libraries or those specializing in African-American material. *African Americans; American Drama; Dramatists, American*

Fiction

Y; A

MSU

1344. **American Best Sellers: A Reader's Guide to Popular Fiction**, by Karen Hinckley and Barbara Hinckley. Indiana University Press, 1989. 270p. $29.95. 0-253-32728-8.

The *World Almanac's* annual lists of best selling books in the U.S. from 1965 to 1985 form the basis of this compilation. The first chapter is the most useful for the purpose of selection development; it lists 468 best sellers under 216 authors. Each title entry gives publisher, date, genre, and a 25- to 100-word descriptive annotation (plot summary). Additional chapters are of added reference value including a great deal of information on best sellers generally. Recommended for most public libraries and other libraries where readers are interested in this genre of literature or in popular culture.

Best Sellers; Adult Books and Reading; Popular Culture

A

1345. **American Novelists**, ed. by James J. Martine. Gale, 1986. 300p. $108. 0-8103-2225-0. (Contemporary Authors Bibliographical Series, v. 1).

This open-ended series is a spin-off of the familiar and highly reputable *Contemporary Authors*. Each volume contains lists of primary and secondary works and extensive bibliographic essays on approximately 10 major novelists. Libraries might purchase all volumes in the series since they do contain additional material not found in the original set of *Contemporary Authors*. Smaller libraries or those with limited budgets may want to purchase specific volumes because of their inclusions of needed authors. For example, volume 1 has bibliographical essays on Baldwin, Barth, Bellow, Cheever, Heller, Mailer, McCullers, Malamud, Updike, and Welty. *Authors, American*

Y; A

1346. **Beacham's Popular Fiction in America**, Ed. by Walton Beacham and Suzanne Niemeyer. Beacham Publishing, 1986. 4v. $249. 0-933833-10-5.

The works of almost 200 best-selling authors are analyzed in the form of critical essays by over 100 contributors. Beacham indicates that: "The criteria for including an author here is that he was a best selling author and that his works reflect social concerns." The only other multivolume works that are similar to the

Beacham series are the Magill/Masterplots series by Salem. The works are arranged alphabetically by author. Each entry includes the following sections: publishing history, critical reception, honors, etc., and an analysis of selected titles by that author. Individual titles are examined in terms of social issues, themes, characters, techniques, literary precedents, related titles, adaptations, and additional sources. A cumulative index of authors and their specific works is included in the 4th volume. This title and others in the Beacham series is recommended for most secondary school, academic and public libraries, and, because there is surprisingly less duplication than might be expected from the Salem Press titles, many libraries might want to consider both series. *American Fiction; Fiction*

Y; A
1347. **Beacham's Popular Fiction, 1991 Update**, Ed. by Walton Beacham. Beacham Publishing, 1991. 2v. $159. 0-933833-26-1.
    This two volume set includes many updated entries for many of the authors from the four volume basic set and entries for newer authors. Criteria and format are similar to those used in *Beacham's Popular Fiction in America* (see above entry). *American Fiction; Fiction*

A
1348. **The Bibliography of Contemporary American Fiction, 1945-1988: An Annotated Checklist**, by William McPheron and Jocelyn Sheppard. Greenwood, 1989. 190p. $42.95. 0-313-27702-8.
    This checklist "records and describes bibliographical accounts of contemporary American fiction writers... and concentrates on writers of adult fiction whose reputations have been established since 1945." It also serves as a companion volume to McPheron's *Bibliography of Contemporary American Poetry.* The work is divided into two sections: " Multiauthor studies" (53 citations) and "Single Author Studies" (550 bibliographies for 125 authors). Arrangement is alphabetical by author and each item is then arranged chronologically. Each entry includes full bibliographic data and an annotation. A subject index of authors who are the subjects of the studies and an index to authors of the studies are included; there is no title index. This checklist is particularly recommended for the larger library needing reference/research materials on individual writers. *American Fiction; Authors, American*

A
1349. **Black American Women Novelists: An Annotated Bibliography**, by Craig Werner. Salem Press, 1989. 286p. $40. 0-89356-651-1.
    Werner presents not only a selected bibliography of the works of 33 black American women novelists, but also a fascinating historical overview in this area. The introduction contains the overview and about 250 annotations to books, scholarly journal articles, mass media reviews, reference sources, etc. The second section, and main part of the book, contains bibliographic entries and annotations to the works of the 33 novelists. An index to authors and reviewers are also provided. This work is a fine complement to Glikin's *Black American Women in Literature: A Bibliography*, and both are recommended for all academic and public libraries that support or have collections in women's studies or African American studies.
American Literature;
Authors, African American; Authors, Women

C; Y; A
1350. **Civil War Novels: An Annotated Bibliography**, by Albert J. Menendez. Garland, 1986. 192p. $32. 0-8240-9933-8. (Garland Reference Library of the Humanities, 700).
    The novels included in this bibliography were published between 1860 and 1985 (with a few exceptions like *Uncle Tom's Cabin*) and cover the American Civil War period and into the Reconstruction period. There are more than 1,000 entries all arranged alphabetically by author. About 120 children's and young adult books are included in this number. These are identified in the index under the heading "Younger Readers." Each citation contains bibliographic information and a descriptive, sometimes-critical annotation. There is a title index and a subject index that lists titles under such headings as battles, locales, military and political figures, and topics like the underground railroad. This will be helpful for reference work and collection development in large public libraries. *United States—History—Civil War—Fiction*

A

1351. Contemporary Gay American Novelists: A Bio-bibliographical Critical Sourcebook, by Emmanuel S. Nelson. Greenwood, 1993. 456p. $69.50. 0-313-28019-3.

This work analyzes the works of 57 male novelists from Christopher Isherwood and James Baldwin to the present. For each, there is a biography, summary of major works, a critical review, plus lists of primary and secondary sources. Preceding this is an introductory essay defining gay literature. A companion volume on lesbian novelists is forthcoming. Both will be important assets in collections, principally in colleges, where there is an interest in gay studies. *Gay Literature; Literature; Homosexuality*

Y; A

PS374
.H52993
1986

1352. Dickinson's American Historical Fiction, by Virginia Brokaw Gerhardstein. 5th ed. Scarecrow, 1986. 352p. $35. 0-8108-1867-1.

This, the fifth edition of a work first published in 1958 under the title *American Historical Fiction*, now contains a listing with annotations of 3.048 novels published between 1917 and 1984 (plus some earlier important ones). The body of the work is divided into 12 chronological divisions, plus subdivisions. The annotations are noncritical. There are author/title and subject indexes. Although some critics find the subject headings confusing and have pointed out omissions in the main entries, this is still considered a valuable guide to in- and out-of-print historical fiction for high school and public libraries. Librarians will find this bibliography useful for identification purposes but will have to check further in critical sources to determine a particular book's suitability for purchase. *United States—History*

Y; A

CC
MSU

1353. Growing Up Female: Adolescent Girlhood in American Fiction, by Barbara White. Greenwood, 1985. 260p. $42.95; $12.95 pap. 0-313-24826-5; 0-313-25065-0, pap. (Contribution in Women's Studies, 59).

Though not intended as a selection aid, this gives a fascinating portrayal of female adolescence in over 200 adult novels, beginning with some published at the turn of the century and extending to such contemporary works as Marge Piercy's *Braided Lives* and Rita Mae Brown's *Rubyfruit Jungle*. However, this study of the adolescent experience can give insights into possible avenues for collection development in both senior high school and public libraries. *Adolescence*

A

MSU

1354. Jewish American Fiction Writers: An Annotated Bibliography, by Gloria L. Cronin and others. Garland, 1991. 1,250p. $167 0-8240-16-19-X.

Sixty-two Jewish American fiction writers from the late nineteenth century for whom no individual bibliography exists are featured in this work. Although authors like Bellow, Malamud, Singer and Wiesel are thus eliminated, others such as Walter Abish, Leon Uris, Herman Wouk and Scholem Asch are included. Only secondary source material is listed, but a wide variety of types, including reviews, articles, chapters from books, interviews, biographical sources and dissertations is drawn on. Each is annotated. This will be used in large academic or public libraries or where there is a keen interest in Jewish-American literature.

Jewish-American Literature

Y; A

cc

1355. Modern American Novel: An Annotated Bibliography, by Steven G. Kellman. Salem Press, 1991. 162p. $40. 0-89356-664-0. (Magill Bibliographies).

This slim volume is designed to be a beginning guide to accessible materials about major modern novelists. Kellman has selected for inclusion 16 novelists of the first half of the 20th century, including Cather, Dreiser, Faulkner, Fitzgerald, Hemingway, Lewis, London, Steinbeck, Wilder, and Wolfe. Entries are arranged alphabetically by author. General studies about each author are followed by entries on the individual works. Full bibliographic information and a brief annotation are included with each entry. This is a part of the "Magill Bibliographic Series" which also includes Taylor's *Restoration Drama...* and Aubrey's *English Romantic Poetry....* This brief, well-focused volume is recommended for many high school and public and all undergraduate academic libraries for general reference and collection development. *Authors, American; Fiction—History and Criticism*

A

1356. The Sports Pages: A Critical Bibliography of Twentieth-Century American Novels and Stories Featuring Baseball, Basketball, Football, and Other Athletic Pursuits, by Grant Burns. Scarecrow, 1987. 274p. $27.50 0-8108-1966-X.

This highly-selective bibliography is a guide to good reading in the area of sports fiction. In it are listed 631 twentieth-century novels and short stories that deal with a wide range of sports including swimming, tennis, hunting, boxing, bullfighting, billiards, horse racing, and wrestling, although the emphasis is understandably on baseball, basketball, football, and golf. Excluded are juvenile titles and mysteries. Each sport has a separate chapter, and for each entry there is full bibliographic information and a lengthy critical annotations. The indexes are by title, author, and themes. Samples from the latter are entries for brothers, cheating, death, and father-daughter relationships. An appendix lists recent critical studies. This excellent bibliography will help in collection development in public and academic libraries and perhaps have value in some secondary schools. *Sport Stories*

A

1357. **War and Peace Through Women's Eyes: A Selective Bibliography of Twentieth-Century American Women's Fiction**, by Susanne Carter. Greenwood, 1992. 293p. $55. 0-313-27771-0.

This compilation of about 350 fiction titles deals with war and peace from World War I to Vietnam (including nuclear war). Since all of the writers are female, it is Carter's intention to reflect a women's attitude toward war through the chosen works. The novels and shorter fiction are organized into separate chapters, each dealing with a major war. Each entry includes a descriptive and critical annotation. Author, title, and subject indexes round out this interesting bibliography which is recommended for all academic and public libraries interested in the peace and/or women's movements. *Peace; War; Women's Studies*

Canadian Literature

A

1358. **The Annotated Bibliography of Canada's Major Authors...**, Vol. 7, Ed. by Robert Lecker and Jack David. ECW Press; distr. by G. K. Hall, 1987. 477p. $50. 0-920763-11-1. (Available in Canada in paperback from ECW Press for $28. 0-920763-12-X).

This volume, which is fully-annotated, is one of a series of bibliographies of 19th and 20th century French-Canadian and English-Canadian major authors. Each bibliography includes only 4 to 6 authors, and each includes a very comprehensive bibliography of works by and about the author in a variety of formats, e.g., periodical articles, books, audiovisual materials, etc. Volume 7 includes the following authors: Marian Engel, Anne Hebert, Robert Kroetsch, and Thomas H. Raddall. Most of the earlier volumes are still available. Most Canadian libraries and many United States libraries will want to consider this major reference resource. *Authors, Canadian*

A

1359. **A Comprehensive Collection of English-Canadian Short Stories, 1950-1983**, by Allan Weiss. ECW Press (University of Toronto), 1989. 973p. $70. 0-92076306707.

In an alphabetical arrangement by author name, over 14,000 English-Canadian short stories by almost 5,000 writers that were published between 1950 and 1983 are listed. There is also an index by titles. This massive bibliography may be of value in acquisition work in large Canadian libraries because of its listings of the books and periodicals analyzed. *Short Stories; Canadian Literature*

A

1360. **French-Canadian Authors: A Bibliography of Their Works and of English-Language Criticism**, by Mary Kandiuk. Scarecrow, 1990. 222p. $27.50 0-8108-2362-4.

For each of the 36 major French-Canadian writers highlighted in this work, there are two bibliographies given. The first is of the works of the author translated into English, and the second is a listing of English-language secondary sources. These include books and part of books, periodical articles, and dissertations. There is also a separate listing of book reviews and a directory of Canadian publishers. This will be of value in Canadian libraries and in developing collections in large libraries in the United States. *French Canadian Literature*

Classical Literature

Y; A

CC

1361. The Classical Epic: An Annotated Bibliography, by Thomas J. Sienkewitz. Salem Press, 1991. 265p. $40. 0-89356-663-2. (Magill Bibliographies)

This bibliography is intended for the nonscholar and the high school or college student who is approaching the reading and study of the *Iliad*, *Odyssey* or *Aeniad* for the first time. It includes books, chapters in books, periodical articles, plot summaries, literary studies, and related material on each of these epics, plus listings of material on their authors. The reference should be easily available in public and small college libraries. This work will be useful in public, college and some large high school libraries.

Latin Literature; Greek Literature; Classical Literature

Y; A

CC MSU

1362. Classical Greek and Roman Drama: An Annotated Bibliography, by Robert J. Forman. Salem Press, 1989. 239p. $40. 0-89356-659-4. (Magill Bibliographies).

Following an overview of Greek and Roman drama that lists general works, there are individual chapters on nine playwrights, including Aeschylus, Aristophanes, Euripides, Seneca, Sophocles, and Terence. There are three sections in each chapter: the first lists various editions of the writer's work, and the second and third cover recommended criticism and general criticism. All the titles listed are recommended and annotated. As well as a tool to identify critical studies, this work can be used as a collection building source in public libraries and high school libraries where material on classical drama is needed. Also in the same series is Thomas J. Sienkewicz's *The Classical Epic* (1991, $40 0-89356-663-2).

Latin Literature; Greek Literature; Classical Literature

East Asian Literature

A

MSU

1363. Chinese Drama: An Annotated Bibliography of Commentary, Criticism and Plays in English Translation, by Manuel D. Lopez. Scarecrow, 1991. 525p. $57.50 0-8108-2347-0.

This extensive bibliography of 3,300 items is divided into two parts: the first lists reference to Chinese drama in a variety of formats from its beginnings to 1985; the second gives the titles of all plays translated into English. About one quarter of the entries are annotated briefly. Though noncritical, this work will by useful in theater collections in college libraries, particularly where there is a department for Asian or Chinese studies. *Drama—Chinese; China*

A

1364. Modern Japanese Novelists: A Biographical Dictionary, by John Lowell. Kodansha Anerica, 1993. 497p. $50. 4-7700-1849-2.

Fifty-seven Japanese writers (all writing in this century) are included in this needed bio-bibliography. Each profile, ranging in length from 3 to 20 pages, contains a biographical sketch, a list and an evaluation of the writers works, and a bibliography of additional critical studies. All works cited are translated into English. There is also a section that explores Japanese writing in general and includes additional references. The work should prove useful to academic libraries with Japanese studies programs as well as all libraries with an interest in Japanese literature. *Japanese Literature*

Y; A

CC

1365. A Reader's Guide to Japanese Literature, by J. Thomas Rimer. Kodansha International, 1988. 208p. $14.95. pap. 0-87011-896-X.

At long last, a guide to Japanese literature in English, and representative of the Japanese tradition, for readers new to the subject. Rimer, an expert in Japanese literature, has compiled a list of 50 titles: 20 written before the opening of Japan to the West, and 30 modern works. A variety of literature is included—poetry, fiction, essays, and dramatic works. Each detailed description is about three pages in length and becomes a bio-bibliography of the author. An index and a bibliography of further reading are also provided. This inexpensive guide is recommended to all secondary school, academic, and public libraries.

Japanese Literature

West European and East European Literature

A

1366. **Bibliography of Ukrainian Literature in English and French: Translations and Critical Works (1950-1986)**, by Oksana Piaseckyj. University of Ottawa Press, 1989. 386p. $19.95. pap. 0-7766-0264-0.

Piaseckyj's work is very broad in scope, covering almost 40 years. Unfortunately, many of the works are not annotated, unlike the Taranawsky, *Ukrainian Literature in English: Books and Pamphlets, 1890-1965*, (o.p.) which this work complements and updates. The material is arranged in five major chapters covering major periods of Ukrainian literature: Kievan, Ukrainian literature from the 13th to the 18th centuries, modern literature, Soviet Ukrainian literature, and literature of the Diaspora. Special features include lists of bibliographies and reference books consulted, journals surveyed, an index to authors, and an index to critics. Most academic libraries and many public libraries (particularly those serving a Ukrainian-American population) will want to consider this bibliography which is intended to serve the student and scholar alike. *Ukrainian Literature*

A

1367. **Dictionary of Scandinavian Literature**, by Virpi Zuck. Greenwood, 1990. 792p. $99.50. 0-313-21450-6.

Using a dictionary format, this book consists of a series of bibliographical essays on various topics related to Scandinavian literature, including important authors, Norse poetry, children's literature, and the literature of various language groups like the Inuit. Works mentioned in the entries are supplemented by short bibliographies after each entry. There is a section on bibliographic sources in an appendix, plus a chronology. This work will serve as a basic guide to the literature of Scandinavia and will be useful in libraries serving a large population from this part of the world. *Scandinavian Literature*

Spanish and Latin American Literature

A

1368. **A Bibliographical Guide to Spanish American Literature: Twentieth-Century Sources**, by Walter Rela. Greenwood, 1988. 400p. $55. 0-313-25861-9. (Bibliographies and Indexes in World Literature).

Rela, an internationally-recognized scholar and bibliographer of Spanish American literature has compiled a bibliography of almost 1,900 entries which, as stated in his Foreword, is a "selective inventory of sources that must necessarily serve as an initial point of departure for serious scholarship." Emphasis is on works published in Spanish and English. Brazilian literature is excluded. The volume is divided by type of publication: bibliographies, dictionaries, history and criticism, and anthologies. Annotations are included when the title is not self-explanatory. The author index is an index of both critics of the works and the authors mentioned in the annotations. This scholarly and well-researched work is recommended for all academic or public libraries with patrons interested in Spanish American literature.

Spanish American Literature

A

1369. **Caribbean Women Novelists: An Annotated Critical Bibliography**, by Lizabeth Paravisini-Gebert and Olga Torres-Seda. Greenwood, 1993. 428p. $38. 0-313-28342-7. (Bibliographies and Indexes in World Literature Series).

A total of 149 women writers who were born or spent a considerable time in the Caribbean and who have had at least one novel published since 1950 are included in this interesting work dealing with an often neglected part of the literary world. The entries, arranged alphabetically by the author's last name, contain a critical bibliographic review of the author's work. They vary in length from less than a page to many pages. The longest, on Jean Rhys, is about 50 pages and the shortest, less that a page. The lists are comprehensive and include, as well as novels, books of short stories, essays, and other literary forms.

This will be primarily of interest in academic libraries or libraries that have many patrons from Caribbean lands. *Women Authors—Caribbean; Caribbean Islands Literature*

A

CC

1370. **Contemporary Latin American Fiction: An Annotated Bibliography**, by Keith H. Brower. Salem Press, 1989. 218p. $40 0-89356-660-8. (Magill Bibliographies).

The author has chosen 23 prominent authors (six Brazilian and 17 Spanish American) for extensive coverage. Preceding this part of the book is a 600 entry annotated general bibliography on Latin American literature. Most of the material appeared between 1965 and 1989 and is in English. The entries for each writer contains three section: a biography, a survey of his or her works and bibliography of criticism. It will be useful in libraries where there is an interest in Latin American and comparative literature.

Latin American Literature

A

1371. **Contemporary Spanish American Poets: A Bibliography of Primary and Secondary Sources**, by Jacobo Sefami. Greenwood, 1992. 245p. $45. 0-313-27880-6. (Bibliographies and Indexes in World Literature, 33).

Poets born between 1910 and 1952 are included in this work that lists both primary and secondary sources for each entry. Although the coverage is somewhat erratic, this is a valuable addition for Spanish language collections in academic libraries. *Spanish American Literature*

A

1372. **Dictionary of Brazilian Literature**, by Irwin Stern. Greenwood, 1988. 402p. $75. 0-313-24932-6.

This 300 entry dictionary gives material on Brazilian authors and literary movements and themes from colonial times to the contemporary scene. Forty-six specialists on this subject worked on this volume which contains both primary and secondary bibliographies scattered throughout the text. There is also a special bibliography on Brazilian studies. This will be of value in large or specialized collections.

Brazil; Brazilian Literature

A

CC
MЧЛ

1373. **Dictionary of Mexican Literature**, by Eladio Cortes. Greenwood, 1992. 768p. $85. 0-313-26271-3.

With emphasis on the twentieth-century, this work gives coverage on 534 Mexican authors. After biographical information, there are extensive bibliographies, the first of which is a complete list of the works of the author and the second an extensive run down on works about the author. There are also a few topical entries and an interesting overview introduction that describes the history and present status of Mexican literature. The bibliographies, however, are the outstanding feature of this work. They will be very useful in building library collections on this topic. *Mexican Literature*

A

1374. **Dictionary of Twentieth-Century Cuban Literature**, by Julio A. Martinez. Greenwood, 1990. $75. 0-313-25185-1.

In a series of signed articles on literary genres and movements and on 120 Cuban authors active from 1900 on, this dictionary reviews Cuban literature of the twentieth century. Each author entry contains biographical and critical information and concludes with a selected bibliography of both the author's work as well as critical assessments. Spanish-language works predominate. There are also other general bibliographies found within the text plus a general index by name, title and subject. This is intended for academic libraries or large public libraries which serve a Cuban-American population. *Cuban Literature*

A

MЧЛ

1375. **Fifty Caribbean Writers: A Bio-Bibliographical Critical Sourcebook**, by Daryl Cumber Dance. Greenwood, 1986. 530p. $75. 0-313-23939-8.

Caribbean literature has recently received increased prominence. This work focuses on 50 authors both of the past and present from the area. For each author, there is a short biography, a critical analysis of the writer's work, and a bibliography of both primary and secondary works. The latter could be of help in collection development in public libraries. *Caribbean Islands Literature; Authors, Caribbean*

A

МЧЛ

1376. **Guide to Reference Works for the Study of the Spanish Language and Literature and Spanish American Literature**, by Hensley C. Woodbridge. Modern Language Association of America, 1987. 183p. $37.50 0-87352-958-8; pap. $17.50. 0-87352-959-6.

This annotated bibliography of 908 titles lists and evaluates important reference materials published from 1950 through 1985. It includes many types of materials, including bibliographies, indexes, encyclopedias, and dictionaries. The arrangement is by subjects like "The Spanish of Spain" and "American Spanish." The thorough table of contents acts as a guide to the subjects included. There is also an author index. For large collections. *Spanish Language; Spanish Literature; Spanish American Literature*

A

1377. **Handbook of Latin American Literature**, by David W. Foster. Garland, 1987. 608p. $60. *CC*
0-8240-8559-0. *MSU*

This work provides a country-by-country (21 including Puerto Rico) bibliographic overview of Latin American literature. Each section is written by a specialist. There is an introductory chapter that outlines general references, and each of the country chapters list more specific secondary works. All entries are annotated. This book can serve as a general introduction to critical works for the nonspecialist and therefore can be of value in academic and public libraries where there is an interest in Hispanic literature.

Latin American Literature

A

1378. **Hispanic Writers: A Selection of Sketches from Contemporary Authors**, by Bryan Ryan. Gale, *CC*
1990. 514p. $75. 0-8103-7688-1.

This spin-off from *Contemporary Authors* contains sketches of Spanish and Spanish-American writers that have already appeared in it (40%) or will appear in future volumes (60%). There are over 400 writers profiled, and in addition to biographical and critical information on the authors, there are bibliographies of both primary and secondary sources. For large collections that have patrons interested in Hispanic studies.

Authors, Hispanic

A

1379. **The Latin American Short Story: An Annotated Guide to Anthologies and Criticism**, by Daniel *MSU*
Balderston. Greenwood, 1992. 525p. $65. 0-313-27360-X.

This extensive and well-indexed work is divided into two major parts: Part 1 includes over 1300 anthologies of Latin American short stories (Latin American, as defined by the author includes Spanish America and relevant areas of the Caribbean, and Brazil).The works are in the original languages or Spanish or Portuguese or English translations. Part 2 lists about 400 works of criticism dealing with Latin American short stories. The entries are arranged in alphabetical order by region and then country. The introduction to each section is a general overview in the form of a bibliographic essay and also very useful. There are detailed indexes of authors of the short stories, critics and titles. This work is recommended for all libraries with a strong need for materials on Latin American or world literature.

Latin American Literature; Short Story

A

1380. **Latin American Writers**, Ed. by Carlos A. Sole and Maria Isabel Abreu. Scribner, 1989. 3v. *CC*
1,497p. $250. 0-684-18463-X. *MSU*

This major bio-bibliography is similar in purpose to other distinguished Scribner works, e.g., *American Writers*, *British Writers*, and *European Writers*. This work includes biographical information, criticism, and bibliographies of 176 major Latin American writers. it is highly recommended, but the cost may limit its purchase to the very large academic or public libraries or those that support a Latin American studies program. *Authors, Latin American*

A

1381. **Mexican Literature: A Bibliography of Secondary Sources**, by David William Foster. 2nd ed. Scarecrow, 1992. 698p. $67.50. 0-8108-2548-1.

There are two major parts to this rather comprehensive work. Part 1 contains general references list from broad to more specific topics. Part 2 cites the secondary sources of 83 authors, chosen because there exists significant literary scholarship about them. The entries cited under each author range from only a few to hundreds, and most of the works listed in this recommended volume are in Spanish. This work would be useful for academic and larger public libraries with research needs or developing collections in this area.

Mexican Literature

A

1382.   **Modern Spanish and Portuguese Literatures**, Ed. by Marshall J. Schneider and Irwin Stern. Ungar, 1988. 640p. $85. 0-8044-3280-5. (Library of Literary Criticism).

This work explores in 800 excerpts a selection of critical opinions on "80 twentieth-century authors of the Iberian Peninsula, writing in Spanish, Catalan, Galician, and Portuguese." Among the writers included are: Garcia Lorca, Ortega y Gasset, and Ramon J. Sender. Each writer is entered alphabetically, with criticism appearing chronologically. In addition, each entry includes bibliographic information for the excerpts as well as additional sources. An author and title index are provided. This biographical/bibliographical reference work is recommended for all academic and many public libraries.

Authors, Portuguese; Literature—History and Criticism;
Spanish Literature; Portuguese—Literature

A

1383.   **Writers of the Caribbean and Central America: A Bibliography**, by M. J. Fenwick. 2 vols. Garland, 1992. 1, 606p. $200. 0-8240-4010-4.

Fenwick has compiled an amazing multilingual bibliography of over 11.000 writers (some well-known, some very obscure). This very comprehensive bibliography, which is divided into 42 countries, lists writers by country of birth. Arrangement is by country. Writers are listed under country of birth and are cross-listed by country of residence. Bibliographic data is provided, but unfortunately, full citations are not always given. Individual works, as well as titles in magazines, are listed. An index of authors is provided to round out this bibliography. Recommended for all libraries serving advanced students, as well as others serving individuals interested in modern Hispanic, English, or world history, or the Caribbean area.

Hispanic Literature; Caribbean Islands Literature

Performing Arts

Theater

Y; A

1384.   **American Theater and Drama Research: An Annotated Guide to Information Sources, 1945-1990**, by Irene Shaland. McFarland, 1991. 157p. $29.95. 0-89950-626-7.

More than 500 sources are listed in this well-developed guide to American theater and drama since World War II. The emphasis is on the "history" of the American theater and drama. All of the entries listed were published since 1965. Entries are listed under five major sections which include most aspects of the subject. The first two sections list general and specialized reference sources. Each entry includes author, title, publication information and date, and pagination. Annotations range from one line to a paragraph and are both descriptive and critical. An author index is provided. The strength of this work is the currency of most of the entries; the limitations are the lack of a subject index and the lack of indication of in-print status. Despite these minor flaws, this work is recommended for most high school, academic, and public libraries.

Theater—United States; American Drama

A

1385.   **American Theater History: An Annotated Bibliography**, by Thomas J. Taylor. Salem Press, 1992. 162p. $40. 0-89356-672-1.

This bibliography, which traces the history of the American theater, is arranged into three important periods: The beginnings until 1914; 1914 to 1945; and New York: 1945-to the Present. The fourth section deals with specific types of American theater such as regional, children's, experimental, and ethnic theater. There is also a section on periodicals dealing with American theater. Entries are arranged alphabetically by author within each section. Complete indexing includes authors, subjects, and periodical titles. The annotations are well-developed, often referring to additional works. Another strong feature is the inclusion of dissertations which are not usually listed elsewhere. This bibliography is recommended for most libraries which have strong theater collections, and especially most academic libraries   *Theater—United States*

Y; A

1386.   **The Book of a Thousand Plays**, Comp. by Steve Fletcher and Norman Jopling. Facts on File, 1989. 352p. $24.95. 0-8160-2122-8.

This guide, according to the authors, lists the most popular plays of the last century in Great Britain and the United States. The titles are arranged alphabetically, and each entry provides full title, author, type of play (tragedy, comedy, musical, etc.), date and place of first production, a plot summary, and a list of characters. An index of authors is also provided. This directory is intended for a wide audience, from the theater buff to the researcher, and the price is right to recommend it to all libraries as a reference guide and an aid for collection development. *Drama*

A
1387. **Broadway on Record: A Directory of New York Cast Recordings of Musical Shows, 1931-1986,** Comp. by Richard Chigley Lynch. Greenwood, 1987. 347p. $45. 0-313-25523-7.

*ML156.4
.O46 L9
1987*

Over 450 original cast albums are indexed in this discography of New York musicals from 1931 to 1986. Entries are arranged alphabetically by show titles. A "Performer Index" and "Technical Index" are also provided. Unfortunately, with the gradual demise of the LP phonorecording, the titles listed in this very comprehensive discography will be increasingly more difficult to acquire in that format. However, this work is recommended as a reference tool and as an identification guide and it is recommended for academic and public libraries serving patrons interested in the Broadway musical.

Musical Revues, Comedies, etc.; Phonorecordings

A
1388. **Theatrical Movement: A Bibliographical Anthology,** Ed. by Bob Fleshman. Scarecrow, 1986. 756p. $69.50. 0-8108-1789-6.

*PN2071
.G4 T46
1986*

This bibliographic guide deals with theatrical movement and performance for both amateurs and professionals in theater, dance, and related forms. The book is divided into two major parts: Part 1, "Preliminary Studies" which includes such topics as movement training, body language, mime and pantomime, and commedia dell'arte; and Part 2, "Sources of information on movement performance in Asia, Africa, Oceania, and the Americas." Each topic includes an essay averaging about 10-12 pages and an annotated bibliography. The book can serve the needs of some experts, although it intended more for the nonexpert. It is recommended for all academic and public libraries having special collections on dance, theater, and related areas. *Theater; Dance and Dancers*

Film, Video, and Television

General Sources and Miscellaneous

C; Y; A
1389. **Bowker's Complete Video Directory, 1993**. Bowker, 1993. 2v. $205. 0-8352-34225-5.

Video sales, rentals, and public library loans have been increasing dramatically. This revised edition of a very comprehensive directory can be called the "Books in Print" of the video world. Over 75,000 videos are included in this 2 volume set: v. 1, "Entertainment" and v. 2, "Education/Special Interest." The publisher claims that this directory provides "ordering information on more foreign films, Spanish-language films, children's films, silent films, and feature films ... than anyone else." The set also has many indexes, for title, genre, subject, etc. A similar work is Gale's *Video Sourcebook* which claims to list more titles, but is more expensive. Libraries developing and maintaining video collections will want one or the other of these sources, but probably not both. *Videocassettes*

A
1390. **The Film Catalog,** by Jon Gartenberg. G. K. Hall, 1985. 443p. $65 0-8161-0443-3.

This catalog lists the holdings of the film library of the Museum of Modern Art in New York. There are now about 5,500 films dating as far back as the 1890s. The catalog is arranged alphabetically by title, and for each title basic information is given but there are no cast listings. This filmography has historical importance but it should not be confused with the *Circulating Film Catalog* (1984) which lists the films that are available from MOMA for rentals. *Motion Pictures*

A
1391. **Film Study: An Analytical Bibliography,** by Frank Manchel. Four volumes. Fairleigh Dickinson University, 1990. $55 per volume. V.1 0-8386-3186-X; V.2 0-8386-3412-5; V. 3 0-8386-3413-3; V. 4 0-8386-3414-1.

The first three volumes of this lengthy bibliography of materials relevant to the study and teaching of film are divided into seven lengthy chapters, each subdivided into small subjects. Each section contains lists of recommended books, articles, and films each thoroughly annotated. There are a total of about 2,000 books cited in this bibliography. Volume four contains glossaries and appendixes, plus seven indexes by authors, titles of various media, film personalities and subjects. A massive work that is of value in film libraries or large public libraries. *Motion Pictures*

A

1392. Film, Television and Video Periodicals: A Comprehensive Annotated List, by Katherine Loughney. Garland, 1991. 431p $50. 0-8240-0647-X.

There are about 900 popular and scholarly journals included in this bibliography. Some are in foreign languages, but most are in English. They are arranged by title, and for each, full bibliographic information is given, including ISSN and OCLC numbers. The annotations are evaluative, and there are cross references to variant titles. The eight indexes are by country, different media, and suitability levels. A thorough work that can be used for collection development in large collections.

Periodicals; Motion Pictures—Periodicals; Video Recordings—Periodicals; Television—Periodicals

A

1393. The Films of the Eighties: A Complete, Qualitative Filmography to Over 3400 Feature-Length English Language Films, Theatrical and Video-Only Released between January 1, 1980 and December 31, 1989, by Robert A. Nowlan and Gwendolyn Wright Nowlan. McFarland, 1991. 852p. $68.50 0-89950-560-0.

The subtitle of this work accurately describes its contents. For each of the titles listed there is given the year of release, production company, country of origin, leading performers and the characters they portrayed, and comprehensive credits. A brief description, review, and evaluation are also given. There is a name index. The distinguishing element of this filmography is that is lists all the films released in the 1980s and is not selective as are many of the general film guides available (e.g., *Halliwell's Film and Video Guide*). However, its price will perhaps restrict its purchase to large libraries. There is a companion volume by Mark Sigoloff, *The Films of the Seventies: A Filmography of the American, British and Canadian Films, 1970-1979* (1984, $29.95, 0-89950-095-1). *Motion Pictures*

A*

PN1994
.Z99F535
1986

1394. On the Screen: A Film, Television, and Video Research Guide, by Kim N. Fisher. Libraries Unlimited, 1986. 209p. $35. 0-87287-448-6. (Reference Sources in the Humanities).

This guide serves as a general reference tool as well as a bibliographic aid to research-oriented, English-language materials in the areas of motion pictures, television, and video. It identifies and offers critical evaluations of more than 700 resources. All works are published between 1966-1985. The entries are arranged by type of reference, such as bibliographical guides, indexes, dictionaries and encyclopedias, abstracts, and databases; they are then further subdivided by motion pictures or television. Each entry has full bibliographic information and a succinct annotation. An author/title and subject index are also provided. This outstanding book is recommended for research/reference and as a guide to collection development in the fields for all public libraries and academic libraries supporting programs in film and television studies.

Motion Pictures; Television; Videocassettes

A

1395. The Video Annual, 1991, Ed. by Jean Thibodeaux. ABC-Clio, 1992. 260p. $49.50. 0-87436-597-X.

With the assistance of experts in the field, Thibodeaux has done an excellent job of editing the first of ABC-Clio's annual in the video field and it "presents to the librarian and video aficionado information most often sought but frequently difficult to locate." This volume includes several major sections of interest to all librarians involved in video collections, for example: "Reports from the Field;" "Statistical Survey of Video Collections;" and "Resource Materials." The last mentioned is very important for collection development. While much of what is included here is also available in other sources such as *AV Market Place*, the big advantages of this annual is the convenience of having all video-related information in one handy volume and at a reasonable price. For these reasons and others stated, it is recommended for all libraries that have developed video collections. *Videocassettes*

A

1396. The Video Sourcebook, 1991, Ed. by David J. Weiner. 12th ed. Gale, 1991. 2,745 p. in 2 v. $220. 0-8103-6978-8.

With the rapid growth of the video industry has come the need for comprehensive listing of what is available. *The Video Sourcebook*, with 64,000 entries which describe 125,000 currently available titles, is the most comprehensive of several lists available. All areas of entertainment, education, culture, medicine, and business are included. It is designed to aid in both evaluation and in acquisition. Entries contain full information needed for acquisition as well as other valuable information, such as running time, date of release, subject category, age suitability, etc. A listing of names, addresses, and phone numbers of almost 1,500 distributors is provided in a separate section. As well, there are extensive indexes by titles, subjects, close caption, casts, etc. A similar work is *Bowker's Complete Video Directory*, which is less expensive but not as comprehensive, and does not include thousands of technical, scientific, and medical titles. Libraries developing and maintaining video collections will want one or the other of these comprehensive sources but probably not both. *Videocassettes*

Guides and Selection Aids

A
1397. **AFVA Evaluations, 1991**, by the American Film & Video Association. Highsmith Press, 1992. 340p. $40. 0-917846-07-9.
The American Film & Video Association which has been sponsoring an annual festival for over a quarter of a century has compiled this excellent annotated guide to the more than 1200 titles submitted for competition in the 1991 Festival. Each entry contains a descriptive annotation and an evaluative rating. About 100 subject areas are represented. There is some overlap with *Video Sourcebook* and *Media Review Digest*; however, the inclusion of both evaluations and its overall diversity make this relatively inexpensive work recommended for academic, public, and school libraries at all levels.

Videocassettes; Motion Pictures

Y; A
1398. **The Book of Video Lists**, by Tom Wiener. 3rd ed. Madison Books, 1991. 608p. $12.95. 0-8191-7825-X.
Unlike *Video Sourcebook* and *Leonard Maltin's TV Movies & Video Guide*, this list is limited to home video. The first part lists titles under a large number of categories, e.g., action and adventure, classics, comedy, cult films, foreign films science fiction, mystery, westerns, etc. There are also checklists by star and by director; this new edition added a list of Academy Award winners. The second part of this guide is a single alphabetical list of all films listed; each entry contains year of release, running time, MMPA rating, a brief plot synopsis, cast members, and a code number referring to the subject lists where it can be found. This inexpensive and useful guide is recommended for all libraries maintaining video collections for home use. *Videocassettes*

A
1399. **Building a Video Media Arts Collection**. Facets Video, 1991. 100p.
Intended for video stores, this guide of 500 video titles of foreign, classic American, independent, documentary, silent, fine arts, and children videos should prove valuable to librarians building high quality video collections. For more information write to: Facets Video, 1517 W. Fullerton Ave., Chicago, IL 60614, or call 800-331-6197 *Videocassettes*

C; Y; A
1400. **The Family Guide to Movies on Video: The Moral and Entertainment Values of 5,000 Movies on TV and Videocassette**, by Henry Herx and Tony Zaza. Crossroad, 1988 331p. $12.95 pap. 0-8245-0817-3 pap.
The key word in the title is "family," because, in addition to listing and annotating 5,000 motion pictures released in the U.S. from 1966 to 1987, this guide identifies their value and appropriateness for various age groups. The annotations include specific information on what is violent, obscene, etc. Two ratings are also included: the United States Catholic Conference Department of Communication and the Motion Picture Association of America. In an appendix on films for family viewing, they are listed by such subjects as adventure, fantasy and comedy. There are also lists by type of audience (e.g., teen, adult). Both librarians and parents can use this guide. *Motion Pictures; Videocassettes*

C; Y; A
1401. **Family Video Guide**, by Terry Catchpole and Catherine Catchpole. Williamson Publishing, 1992. 188p. $12.95. 0-913589-64-0.

The Catchpoles have compiled a list of more than 300 films available on video that, in their judgment, are suitable for parents to share with their children. Most of the films were considered nonobjectionable; however, 10 R-rated films are also included for the purposes of family discussion of the "real world." Each film entry contains adequate identifying information for purchase as well as descriptive information. Films are categorized under 15 popular themes, for example, race relations. The initial list of 100 titles are deemed suitable for the entire family, regardless of age, and a list of films selected for older children is appended. This inexpensive list is recommended as a selection guide for all public libraries, along with a similar but earlier list: *The Family Guide to Movies on Video*. *Motion Pictures; Videocassettes*

A

1402. 500 Best British and Foreign Films to Buy, Rent or Videotape, by Jerry Vermilye. Morrow, 1988. 510p. pap. $15.95 0-688-06897-9.

These 500 films were selected by The National Board of Review of Motion Pictures and the editors of their publication *Films in Review*. The films are arranged alphabetically by title, and for each there is information covering cast, director, release date, and running time, plus a one page review. This can be used for patrons as well as a buying guide of quality motion picture cassettes in public libraries.

Motion Pictures; Videocassettes

Y; A*

1403. Halliwell's Film and Video Guide, by Leslie Halliwell. 8th ed. Harper, 1991. 1264p. $50 0-06-270037-5.

Most of this volume is taken up with brief reports on over 13,000 motion pictures (with an indication if they are available on videocassette). As in previous editions, the films are arranged in alphabetical order by titles. Entries include title, country of origin, running time, color or black and white, director, principal cast members, and awards. Films are given one to four stars. The annotations are brief but pithy and critical. There are list of alternate titles, English language titles of foreign films, and original titles of foreign films. This is now considered the standard film guide in print although libraries will probably want quite a number of different titles. A companion paperback edition is *Halliwell's Filmgoer's and Video Viewer's Companion* (1990, pap. $19.95 0-06-096392-1). *Motion Pictures; Videocassettes*

Y; A

1404. HBO's Guide to Movies on Videocassette and Cable TV, 1991. 2nd ed. Harper, Collins, 1990. 857p. $14.95 pap. 0-06-273074-6.

From the early silents to the latest Hollywood smashes, this is a guide to over 7,000 feature-length movies available on videocassette. The arrangement is alphabetical by title. In addition to standard background information like running time, genre classification, director, cast and a plot summary, there is a rating for each film (one to five stars), a cautionary note if the film might be offensive to some, plus an indication of the film's Motion Picture Association rating (e.g., G, PG, etc.). Although there are many other more extensive film listings like *Halliwell's Film Guide*, this one is unique in the amount of viewer advisory material cited. There are no indexes. This is an inexpensive tool to help libraries build their video collections. *Videocassettes*

A

1405. Home Video in Libraries: How Libraries Buy and Circulate Home Videos, by Martha Dewing. G. K. Hall, 1988. 209p. $35. pap. 0-8161-1914-7.

The body of this work is a tabulated summary of a 1987 survey of 3,000 public libraries on how they acquire, organize, and circulate their collections of videocassettes. Of value in collection development are the appendixes, one of which lists 150 recommended videos for small and medium-sized libraries and another on basic reviewing and information sources. *Videocassettes*

A

1406. The Laserdisc Film Guide: Complete Ratings for the Best and Worst Movies Available on Disc, 1993-1994, by Jeff Rovin. St. Martin's, 1993. 350p. $15.95. 0-312-08703-9.

This relatively inexpensive guide evaluates more than 300 films on laserdisc of the more than 6,000 now available. This newer format using the latest technology may soon be commonplace in libraries. The entries are arranged alphabetically by title; each receives a rating and a brief critical and descriptive annotation including a synopsis. Audio and video quality as well as other technical qualities are discussed. A guide of this type may well-serve as a starting point in collection development. This guide is especially recommended for public libraries developing collections in this exciting area that is bound to grow as the hardware becomes more readily available. *Laser Film Recordings; Compact Discs*

Y; A

1407. **Rating the Movies**, Ed. by the Editors of *Consumer Guide* and Jay A. Brown. Rev. ed. Outlet Book Co., 1990. 600p. $7.99. pap. 0-517-05654-2.

This guide lists thousands of films released from about 1930 to 1989. It is arranged in alphabetical order by title. Each entry contains release date, availability on videocassette, rating from 0 to 4 stars, and a brief descriptive/critical annotation. This review gives performers, director, awards, etc. This guide which is priced for the homeviewer can serve as an excellent reference and selection guide for public (and school) libraries developing video collections. Perhaps, libraries should buy several copies for reference and circulating. *Motion Pictures; Videocassettes*

A

1408. **Roger Ebert's Movie Home Companion, 1992**, by Roger Ebert. Andrews, McMeel & Parker, 1992. 750p. $13.95. pap. 0-8362-6242-8.

Reviewing hundreds of films, each edition grows about 50% larger as the popularity of videocassettes soared since Ebert compiled his first "Companion" in 1986. Ebert lists each film's title, rating, running time, year of release, and his personal rating from one to four stars. The index highlights the years "Ten Best." Another useful title is Lynn Minton's *Movie Guide for Puzzled Parents* (Delacorte, 1984, $12.95, 0-385-29284-8). The big difference, however, is that Minton evaluates films for suitability for children, whereas, Ebert highlights films suitable for parents. Obviously, most libraries will want to have both guides side by side. This annual guide is recommended for all public libraries having or contemplating video-cassette collections for home viewing. *Motion Pictures; Videocassettes*

A

1409. **Variety Movie Guide**, Ed. by Derek Elley et al. Prentice-Hall, 1992. 704p. $20. pap. 0-13-928342-0.

This volume contains about 5,000 film views from 1914 to the present (1992); however, the emphasis is on vintage films. As well, this guide, which is a spin-off from the 21-volume *Variety Film Reviews,* contains excerpts from the opinion of contemporary critics rather than retrospective reviews. Rating symbols are not used, nor are criteria for choosing the titles stated. However, this listing would be useful as a starting point for building a collection of videos, especially if the reviews of the firsthand critics are sought. This inexpensive guide is recommended as an additional title for all libraries as a reference tool and as a selection aid, especially for those libraries that do not have the 21-volume set or those libraries that feel they need several guides to movies/videos. *Motion Pictures; Videocassettes*

A

1410. **Video and Other Non-Print Resources in the Small Library**, by Alan L. Kaye. ALA, 1991. 15p. $5. 0-8389-5734-X.

This very brief pamphlet is a useful guide to getting started with developing a collection of nonprint resources in the *very small* library. Many practical tips are offered. As well, there are several lists of helpful resources, books, AV materials, reference books, databases, periodicals and contacts. Amazingly, a great deal is included in only 15 pages. So despite the rather steep price of almost 35 cents a page, this handy guide is recommended for most libraries with a felt need. *Audiovisual Materials; Videocassettes*

A*

1411. **Video for Libraries: Special Interest Video for Small and Medium-Sized Public Libraries**, Ed. by Sally Mason and James Scholtz, American Library Association, 1988. 163p. $20. 0-8389-0498-X.

This authoritative list of 1,000 titles is intended to serve as a basic or core collection for small and medium-sized public libraries. Selections were chosen on the basis of superior content, quality, currency, and patron popularity. Titles are arranged by subject under broad Dewey Decimal headings, then by title; each entry includes producer, date, distributor, running time, price, subject headings, and availability of public performance rights. As well, a brief descriptive note is included. The first section includes a short chapter on feature films on video in public libraries (with a list of almost 500 which are recommended) and a list of major video reviewing sources. Appendixes include a list of videos for a professional library, producers/distributors, and video wholesalers and retailers. A comprehensive title index is also provided. Despite the date, this guide is highly recommended for all public libraries, especially those just starting video collections. *Videocassettes*

Y; A

1412.   **Video Movie Guide 1993**, by Mick Martin and Marsha Porter. Ballantine, 1992. $7.99 pap. 0-345-37944-6.

This work contains ratings for over 10,000 movies that are available on videocassettes. There are many helpful indexes including those by title, director and stars, a rating system and by categories. Another popular annual guide is Leonard Maltin's *TV Movies and Video Guide* (Signet, 1992, $14,95, 0-452-26522-3).

Motion Pictures; Videocassettes

C; Y; A*

1413.   **Video Movies: A Core Collection for Libraries**, by Randy Pitman and Elliott Swanson. ABC-Clio, 1990. 266p. $39.50. 0-87436-577-5.

Pitman and Swanson, experienced video librarians, have undertaken the difficult task of creating a "core list" of thousands of feature films available on video. They note that the 500 selected titles "include most of the staples of cinema." The introduction discusses purchasing guidelines and gives criteria for inclusion of titles in this recommended collection. The list is arranged alphabetically by title and covers the time span from 1915 (Birth of A Nation) through 1988. Each entry includes date, running time, color or black and white, MPAA rating, distributor, price, director, cast, and a critical synopsis and review. A bibliography of reference and review sources is also provided. This work complements Mason and Scholtz's *Video for Libraries...* which lists 1,000 recommended videos and includes a chapter on feature films. Both guides are highly recommended for public libraries beginning or developing video collections.

Videocassettes

A

1414.   **Viewer's Choice Guide to Movies on Video**, by Joe Blades and the editors of *Consumer Reports Books*. Consumer Report Books, 1991. 351p. $16.95 pap. 0-89043-476-X.

This list of about 3,500 recommended movies on video was selected from the Consumer Reports Movie Poll which started in 1947. All movie titles that are rated excellent or very good and are also available in videocassette format are included. The entries are arranged alphabetically by title under 10 main interest categories such as biographies, comedies, dramas, family viewing/children, suspense and mystery, etc. Each entry indicates title, rating, release date, distributor, running time, black and white or color, director and cast. A brief synopsis of the film is also included. A list of lower rated films are appended. The only drawback to this valuable reference and selection aid for library collection development is the lack of a schedule for updating. Recommended for all libraries with video collections. *Videocassettes*

Special Interests and Genres

A

1415.   **Baseball in the Movies: A Comprehensive Reference, 1915-1991**, by Hal Erickson. McFarland, 1992. 402p. $39.95. 0-89950-657-7.

In the form of lengthy essays Erickson has provided us with perhaps the most complete list of baseball films released through 1991. Each entry is a well-written synopsis and critique. Entries also contain a cast list, production credits, production company, year of release, and other bibliographical data. The work also contains a list of baseball short films, as well as baseball in nonbaseball films. This definitive work is recommended as a reference guide as well as an aid to collection development for all libraries with baseball buffs or strong film collections. *Baseball*

A*

1416.   **Blacks in Film and Television: A Pan-African Bibliography of Films, Filmmakers, and Performers**, Comp. by John Gray. Greenwood, 1990. 496p. $55. 0-313-27486-X.

This international bibliography consists of over 6,000 entries to books, dissertations, articles, films, videotapes, and audiotapes. Though English and French predominate, most major languages are included. The work is divided into chapters which represent the scope of this undertaking, e.g., general materials, blacks by geography (including a separate chapter on blacks in American television and video), and a chapter on individual performers arranged by name. Artist, title, subject, and author indexes facilitate the use of this extensive bibliography which is especially recommended for interlibrary-loans and collection development for all academic and public libraries supporting television, filmmaking, and acting curricula or serving a large African American population. *African Americans; Mass Media; Television; Films*

A

1417.   **Celluloid Wars: A Guide to Film and the American Experience of War**, by Frank J. Wetta and Stephen J. Curley. Greenwood, 1992. 296p. $45. 0-313-26099-0 (Research Guides in Military Studies, 5).

This chronological listing of films involving America at war begins with Colonial wars and ends with the cold war. Each chapter has a historical chronology followed by a listing of films containing such information as release date, title, running times, director, cast, and an interest rating. The final chapter contains a bibliography of books about war films and a resource guide. There is a title index. This interesting guide is recommended for large collections. *Motion Pictures; War*

A

1418.   **The Complete Guide to Special Interest Videos: More Than 7,500 Videos You've Never Seen Before**, by James R. Spencer. James-Robert Publishing (Ontario, CA), 1991. 602p. $14.95 pap. 0-9627836-0-9.

This reasonably-priced paperback is designed to help individuals locate chiefly nonfiction titles of videos on special subjects. The book is divided into 40 main subject areas with many subdivisions. Some of these main subjects are sports, health, travel, cooking, and biography. Samples of subdivisions are baseball, acupuncture, Bermuda, Cajun cooking, and Charles Dickens. Information such as title, running time and price is given plus an annotation. There is a title and series index. This will be particularly valuable in libraries for determining the existence of selected videos on subjects. More extensive listings can be found in *Video Sourcebook* and *Bowker's Complete Video Directory*. *Videocassettes*

A

1419.   **Ethnic and Racial Images in American Film and Television: Historical Essays and Bibliography**, by Allen L. Woll and Randall M. Miller. Garland, 1987. 408p. $48. 0-8240-8733-X.

In each of 12 chapters, the authors trace the history of the images in TV and film of a particular race or ethnic group such as African American, Arabs, Asians, Germans, Irish, etc. This fascinating study has an extensive bibliography of books, dissertations, government documents, and journal, magazine and newspaper articles. Recommended for large academic and public libraries.

Motion Pictures; Television; Ethnic Groups

A

1420.   **Fantastic Cinema Subject Guide: A Topical Index to 2,500 Horror, Science Fiction, and Fantasy Films**, by Bryan Senn and John Johnson. McFarland, 1992. 682p. $45. 0-89950-681-X.

This guide covers movies available in English that were released before May, 1991. Fantasy films without some elements of horror or science fiction are excluded. The book is organized into 100 sections each dealing with a specific subject such as mad scientists or time travel. Each section contains an introductory note and an alphabetical listing by title of the films. For each film, there is a suitable information given including production facts, cast, and a summary. Some films are listed several times under different subject headings. There are reproductions of stills from some of the films, and in one of the many indexes the films are lists by title and given a quality rating from 1 to 10. This is a fascinating book but will be useful mainly in specialized or very large collections. *Fantasy; Motion Pictures*

A

1421.   **Filmed Books and Plays: A List of Books and Plays from Which Films Have Been Made, 1928-90**, by Mandy Hicken. 5th ed. Gower, 1991. $59.95 0-566-03655-X.

This fascinating bibliography lists films made from the beginning of talkies that are based on published novels or plays. The first section lists films by title and gives their film company and date of release plus the name of the original author and the work. The second section lists each author and the books that have been filmed. There is also an index to titles that were changed for the screen. This will be used more to identify films than as a film buying guide. *Motion Pictures*

Y; A

1422.   **Films and Video for Africana Studies**. Pennsylvania State University, 1992. free.

This catalog lists over 400 films and videos that focus on the culture, religion, and history of Africa and gives a summary of each, plus format and price information. This list, compiled by Penn State's Audio Visual Services department, is free from: Audio-Visual Services, Pennsylvania State University, Special Services Building, 1127 Fox Hill Road, University Park, PA 16803-1827.

Africa; Motion Pictures; Videocassettes

A

1423. **The Great Gangster Pictures II**, by James Robert Parish and Michael R. Pitts. Scarecrow, 1987. 398p. $37.50 0-8108-1961-9.

This is a sequel to the authors' first volume which covered releases through 1975 (*The Great Gangster Pictures* 1976, $37.50, 0-8108-0881-1). This book contains information on over 400 films. In addition to technical and cast information, there is a lengthy plot summary and critical evaluation. Some photographic stills are included. Though useful primarily for circulation, this can also serve as a guide for selecting films and videocassettes for large libraries. Others in this series are *The Great Detective Pictures* (1990, $59.50, 0-8108-2286-5), *The Great Spy Pictures* (1974, $39.50, 0-8108-0655-X), *The Great Spy Pictures II* (1986, $39.50, 0-8108-1913-9), *The Great Western Pictures* (1976, $35, 0-8108-0980-X) and *The Great Western Pictures II* (1988, $45, 0-8108-2106-0). *Motion Pictures*

A

1424. **The Great Hollywood Musical Pictures**, by James Robert Parish and Michael R. Pitts. Scarecrow, 1992. 806p. $79.50. 0-8108-2529-5.

This is an entertaining evaluation of the important Hollywood musicals released through 1988. Each entry is about three pages in length and contains such information as the songs with performers names, release and production information, and cast lists. With many of these movies now available on videos, this book can help guide collection development in this area. For public libraries. *Motion Pictures*

A

CC

MSU

1425. **Handbook of American Film Genres**, by Wes D. Gehring. Greenwood, 1988. 405p. $59.95 0-313-24715-3.

This books contains information on 18 major film genres that cover such areas as comedy, adventure, science fiction, fantasy, and musicals. Each chapter contains an overview essay plus several bibliographies: one on a review of the literature of the genre, a second of recommended readings, and the last a highly selective listing of important films in the genre. Some genres such as disaster films, sports movies, or detective and mystery films are not included. The index contains entries for individuals, and film and publication titles. This handbook will be useful in large collections. *Motion Pictures*

A

CC

MSU

1426. **Haven't I Seen You Somewhere Before? Remakes, Sequels, and Series in Motion Pictures, Videos and Television, 1896-1990**, by James L. Limbacher. Pierian Press, 1991. 438p. $65. 0-87650-244-3.

This revision and updating of a book that originally appeared in 1979, deals with interrelated foreign and domestic films released between 1896 and 1990. It is divided into three sections: remakes (about ¾ of the book), sequels, and series. The first two sections are arranged by title and give production information for each entry. The last section is on series and is arranged by the series title. Each film in the series is listed with background material. There is no index. Public and academic libraries that have strong film collections or film programs will find this useful for both reference and acquisitions work.

Motion Pictures; Videocassettes; Television

A

1427. **Jewish Film Directory: A Guide to More than 1,200 Films of Jewish Interest from 32 Countries over 85 Years**, Ed. by Matthew Stevens. Greenwood, 1992. 298p. $65. 0-313-28279-X.

The 1,200 films in this listing are arranged in the main body of the work by title. For each, various kinds of screen credits are given including cast, director, and producer. Country of origin, category (e.g., documentary, feature), format, and brief summaries are also given. There are indexes by director, country, subject, and source material. This work will be used principally in college libraries that support programs in Jewish or film studies. *Motion Pictures; Jews*

A

MSU

1428. **Keep Watching the Skies! American Science Fiction Movies of the Fifties**, by Bill Warren. McFarland, volume 1, 1982; volume 2, 1986. 1344p. $65. 0-89950-19-5.

This exhaustive bibliography lists all of the science-fiction movies released over a 12 year period. Volume one covers 1950 through 1957 and volume two, 1958 through 1962. Movies announced but not produced are also included. Each receives a thorough synopsis and analysis plus quotes from reviews, and full cast and production credits. Fun to browse through but of limited value in collection development at any level. *Science Fiction; Motion Pictures*

A

1429.   **Movie Musicals on Record: A Directory of Recordings of Motion Picture Musicals, 1927-1987**, Comp. by Richard Chigley Lynch. Greenwood, 1989. 445p. $45.95. 0-313-26540-2.

Phonorecordings for 60 years of motion picture musicals are included in this discography of over 650 albums. The recordings are listed in alphabetical order by title entry which includes film company and release date. Each entry also includes such information such as record company, record number, credits, cast members, and a list of songs. Unfortunately, with the gradual demise of the LP phonorecording, titles listed in this discography will be increasingly more difficult to acquire in that format. However, this work is recommended as a reference tool and as an identification guide to a title that may be available in another format such as audiotape cassette or compact disk. It is recommended for public, and performing arts libraries, and academic libraries supporting programs in film or music.

Motion Picture Music; Musical Revues, Comedies, etc.

A

1430.   **Native Americans on Film and Video. v. 2**, by Elizabeth Weatherford and Emelia Seubert. National Museum of the American Indian, 1988 112p. $6. 0-934490-44-9.

This volume supplements v. 1 which was published in 1981 and lists about 200 films and videos produced since 1980 about Inuit and Indians of the Americas. Included are documentaries, animations, and short features. Selection for inclusion was "on the basis of the quality of the productions research, filming and editing, and on the uniqueness of their approach or subject matter..." Many of the films were either produced or aided by native Americans. The detailed annotations both describe and analyze the content of the film or video. Entries include release date, running time, credits, formats available, languages, and distributors for either rental or sale. Most of the films are intended for adult audiences which would eliminate serious purchase by school media centers; however, this important filmography is recommended for most academic and public libraries supporting native American studies, film studies, or anthropology programs.

Videocassettes; Indians of North America; Films

Y; A

1431.   **On Being Black: A Selected List of Books, Films, Filmstrips, Recordings for Young Adults, 1985**. New York Public Library, 1985. 19p. $3. 0-87104-675-X. *MSU*

The title and subtitle say it all. This title is still timely and still available for $3 plus $1 for shipping and handling from: The New York Public Library, Office of Branch Libraries, 455 Fifth Avenue, New York, NY 10016.

African Americans; Authors, African American; Films; Filmstrips; Phonorecordings; Young Adult Literature

A

1432.   **Picture This!: A Guide to Over 300 Environmentally, Socially, and Politically Relevant Films** *CC* **and Videos**, by Sky Hiatt. Noble Press, 1992. 389p. $12.95. 1-879360-05-5.

Hiatt has compiled a rather extensive list of activist films on such topics as poverty, race, war, gay rights, etc. Many, though not all, are readily available in video format. This timely list can serve as a companion to Kevin Brownlow's *Behind the Mask of Innocence...* (Univ. of Calif. Pr., 1992. $25. pap. 0-520-07626-5). Recommended for those libraries having a large film/video collection or special collections in the topics cited in the subtitle. *Motion Pictures; Videocassettes*

Y; A

1433.   **Revenge of the Creature Features Movie Guide: An A to Z Encyclopedia to the Cinema of the** *CC* **Fantastic; or, Is There a Mad Doctor in the House?** by John Stanley. 3rd ed. Creatures at Large Press, 1988. 420p. $40. hardcover 0-940064-05-7; $11.95 pap. 0-940064-04-9.

This 3rd edition of this "fantastic" guide includes almost 4,000 annotated film entries on science fiction, horror, suspense, mystery, and offbeat movies. Following a long introduction on the genres is an alphabetized list of the films indicating year of release, main actors, director, producer, and a note on whether the film is available on video. Annotations are succinct and generally positive. Two important drawbacks are lack of indexes and no indication as to running time (limitations for selection by subject or aid in programming). Still, with the relatively inexpensive paperback price and the popularity of the subject, this guide is recommended for its reference value and possible selection aid for most public libraries and academic libraries supporting film studies programs. *Motion Pictures; Videocassettes*

Y; A

1434.   **Rock Films: A Viewer's Guide to Three Decades of Musicals, Concerts, Documentaries and Soundtracks, 1955-1986**, by Linda J. Sandahl. Facts on File, 1987. 240p. $27.95. 0-8160-1281-4.

"This helpful book covers directors, performers, songs and subjective descriptions of over 400 rock films. All entries are indexed by movie title, proper name, and song titles." (*Reference Quarterly*, Summer 1987). Those with videos or soundtracks available are so noted. *Rock Films* is the first truly comprehensive guide to rock and pop music in these movies. This relatively up-to-date guide is recommended as a reference aid and selection tool for music, academic, and public libraries developing collections on the genre.

Rock Music; Videocassettes; Motion Pictures

A

1435.   **Safe Planet: The Guide to Environmental Film and Video**. Alternative Media Information Center, 1991. 40p. $13.50; $9.50. (pap.).

This booklet lists and provides descriptive annotations on over 80 new films and videos dealing with the environment. Information on how to rent or purchase is given with appropriate addresses. Copies are available for $13.50 including postage and handling ($9.50 for individuals) from Alternative Media Information Center, 121 Fulton St., Fifth Floor, New York, NY 10038.

Environment; Motion Pictures; Videocassettes

A

1436.   **Shakespeare on Screen: An International Filmography and Videography**, by Kenneth S. Rothwell and Annabelle Henkin Melzer. Neal-Schuman, 1990. 400p. $59.95 1-55570-049-7.

Arranged alphabetically by play title, this work lists over 750 films and video productions that have used Shakespeare's works as bases including abridgments, ballets, excerpts and documentaries on Shakespeare and his times. In each listing extensive credits are given and critical annotations. There are six indexes to provide multiple access to the information in the main body of this work. This will be valuable in specialized collections.   *Shakespeare, William*

A

1437.   **Short Stories on Film and Video**, by Carol A. Emmens. Libraries Unlimited, 1985. 337p. $25. 0-87287-424-9.

This is a listing of 1,375 short stories arranged by author that have been the bases of films. For each entry, information is given such as the title, date of the film (from 1920 to 1984), cast, director, distributor and a brief descriptive annotation. Availability of video versions is noted. Information on the print version includes where it first appeared and the date. There are two indexes, one by the titles of the films and the other by print titles. This is still valuable particularly for educators who are trying to locate filmed versions of stories, but it now needs an updating.   *Motion Pictures; Short Stories; Videocassettes*

A

1438.   **Sound Films, 1927-1939: A United States Filmography**, by Alan G. Fetrow. McFarland, 1992. 954p. $75. 0-89950-546-5.

This filmography lists 5,418 United States feature films that were released in the first eleven years of sound. For each film, title, studio, cast, director, running time, and awards are given. For large public library collections or where there is a particular interest in film studies.   *Motion Pictures*

A

1439.   **Sports Films: A Complete Reference**, by Harvey Marc Zucker and Lawrence J. Babich. McFarland, 1987. 612p. $49.95 0-89950-227-X.

This guide supplies information on over 2,000 sports related films released between 1896 and 1984. Both full length and important short films are included though films for television and educational films are excluded. The book is divided into 12 categories, one for each major sport like baseball and others that combine topics like "Horses and Other Animals," and "Soccer, Rugby, Cricket and Hurling." Within these categories, films are arranged by title. For each, information is given on release date, producers, casts, a plot summary and critical comments. There are comprehensive indexes, plus 63 photographs of stills from major films. For public library and academic collections.   *Sports; Motion Pictures*

Y; A

1440.   **The Third World in Film and Video, 1984-1990,** by Helen W. Cyr. Scarecrow, 1991. 256p. $29.50. 0-8108-2380-2.

This is Cyr's third edition in a series of filmographies on the Third World (the earlier two, titled: *Filmography of the Third World* were published in 1976 (o.p.) and 1985 (1985, $25. 8-8108-1783-3). The latest edition, renamed to reflect the fact that videocassettes have been added, lists over 1100 titles, not included in the earlier editions, relating to Third World countries and what Cyr calls "the third world in our midst," the major ethnic minorities in North America. Entries are arranged geographically by region and country. Annotations and full bibliographic information are provided, including distributors' names and addresses. This guide will be well-used in most secondary school and public libraries for reference, library programming, and collection development.   *Developing Countries; Motion Pictures; Videocassettes*

Y; A

1441.   **Video Classics: A Guide to Video Art and Documentary Tapes,** by Deirdre Boyle. Oryx, 1986. 184p. $23.50. 0-89774-102-1.

Boyle has compiled a list of award winning art and documentary videos that is intended to form a core collection of those independently produced. Entries are arranged alphabetically by title, and each includes a lengthy review ranging from about 250 to 750 words. Also provided are film maker, date, length, distributor, and credits. These videos document contemporary American social issues and art and would be useful in history or social studies classes, to members of the general public interested in noncommercial film. Recommended for secondary school, academic, and public libraries developing video collections.

Videocassettes

A

1442.   **Western Movies: A TV and Video Guide to 4,200 Genre Films,** by Michael R. Pitts. McFarland, 1986. 623p. $45. 0-89950-195-8.

This very inclusive list of 4,200 feature films (over 40 minutes in length) is "intended to provide the Western film viewer with a comprehensive handbook of films available plus a fair amount of information about them." The alphabetically arranged entries include the releasing company and year; running time; black & white or color; director; screenwriter; cast, a one-sentence plot summary; and a one-sentence review. For several hundred entries, a video source is also listed. One of the bonuses of this work is the long, selected bibliography dealing with films generally and the western genre specifically. This work is recommended for academic and public libraries as a reference guide to the western film buff, and as a selection aid for video collections and reference sources on the enduring western.

West (U.S.); Videocassettes; Motion Pictures

Television

A

1443.   **Animated TV Specials: The Complete Directory to the First Twenty-five Years, 1962-1987.** by George W. Woolery. Scarecrow, 1989. 570p. $59.50. 0-8108-2198-2.

This rather specialized filmography identifies and annotates 434 animated films which were shown as TV Specials from 1962 through the 1986-87 season. The entries are arranged alphabetically by title, and each entry includes a broadcast listing, credits, characters, songs, a plot summary. Also given is adequate information for acquiring the film (videocassette). Appendixes and an index provide additional information, e.g., Specials arranged by holiday and subject; series; distributors, etc. This unique guide is recommended for the general library interested in popular culture as well as the specialist in the film/television field.

Animation; Television

A

1444.   **Blacks on Television: A Selectively Annotated Bibliography,** by George H. Hill and Sylvia Saverson Hill. Scarecrow, 1985. 223p. $25.00. 0-8108-1774-8.

The Hills have compiled an annotated bibliography of over 2,800 magazine, newspaper, books, dissertations, and theses tracing the role of blacks on television since its inception over 50 years ago. There are entries suitable for the beginning student as well as the serious researcher. A list of "Emmy Winners" is appended. Useful indexes for programs, subjects, and authors are also provided. Gray's *Blacks in Film and Television* covers a more international role and only overlaps in part. This bibliography is still valuable from a historical perspective, especially since a special emphasis has been made in tracing the inequities that have existed. Therefore, it is recommended as a complement to the Gray's bibliography for the same general audience in academic and public libraries. *African Americans; Television*

C; Y; A

1445. The Great Plains National Instructional Television Library (GPN) Catalog. Great Plains National Instructional Television Library, annual, free.

This annual catalog describes educational products such as video tapes, slides, and videodiscs available to schools (K-12) and colleges. This agency also prepares new and original materials for educational media users. The materials in the catalog are arranged by subject and given lengthy annotations that include running time, price, teacher's guides, and suitability. This listing is updated quarterly with the free GPN Newsletter. Copies of these publications are available from: Great Plains National Instructional Television Library, P.O. Box 80669, Lincoln, NE 68501. *Videocassettes; Slides; Videodiscs*

A

1446. Role Portrayal and Stereotyping on Television: An Annotated Bibliography of Studies Relating to Women, Minorities, Aging, Sexual Behavior, Health, and Handicaps, Comp. and ed. by Nancy Signorielli. Greenwood, 1985. 214p. $45. 0-313-24855-9. (Bibliographies and Indexes in Sociology, no. 5).

The subtitle aptly gives the full scope of this interesting bibliography of 423 citations of research on stereotypical portrayals published in both popular and scholarly books, journals, and government publications. The work is divided into five sections: Women and Sex-Roles; Racial and Ethnic Minorities; Aging and Age Roles; Sexual Behavior and Orientations; and Health and Handicaps. Entries under each section are arranged in alphabetical order by author. Full bibliographic information and an abstract of the findings are included. Author and very broad subject indexes are provided. This work which includes both popular and scholarly sources is recommended as a bibliographic reference tool for special, educational, and academic libraries concerned with the problem. It may also be of value for libraries with patrons interested in the topic. *Television; Stereotypes*

Y; A

1447. Television: A Guide to the Literature, by Mary Cassata and Thomas Skill. Oryx, 1985. 160p. $12.50. 0-89774-140-4.

This series of bibliographic essays covers many aspects of television from about 1965 through 1985. The chapters deal with such topics as the historical development of television, television's effects on children, television news, the television industry, television and politics, and other related topics. The first part of each chapter is a brief bibliographic essay; the second part is a bibliography of the items discussed. Over 450 popular and scholarly books and reports are included. One of the essays is a discussion of other reference books dealing with television. Thorough author, title, and subject indexes conclude this well-written work which is recommended for academic, high school, and public libraries. *Television*

A

1448. Television & Ethics: A Bibliography, by Thomas W. Cooper et al. G. K. Hall, 1988. 203p. $50. 0-8161-8966-8.

Many aspects of television *and* ethics are included in this unique bibliography. Cooper indicates that there are more appropriate bibliographies that deal with either television or ethics, he further states that "in this bibliography we have selected books, articles, speeches, and theses that treat the ethical dimensions of television programs and practices." The work is divided into two major sections: Part 1, "Ethical Contexts" includes citations related to classical ethics, professional ethics, communication and mass media ethics, etc.; and Part 2, Television and Ethics" includes chapters on topics such as advertising, children and television, politics and television, law and courtroom coverage, and public television. This work was created by a thorough online searching of a number of databases such as ERIC. More than 1,000 sources are included, with about half of them with an abstract or brief note. Author and subject indexes are provided. This comprehensive work is recommended for those academic or special libraries supporting communication studies courses or programs. *Television Broadcasting; Ethics*

Music and Dance

General and Miscellaneous

A

1449. All-Music Guide: The Best CDs, Albums & Tapes, Ed. by Michael Erlewine. Miller Freeman, 1992. (Dist. by Publishers Group West). 1,176p. $19.95. pap. 0-87930-264-X.

As the title implies, this extensive selection aid covers all types of music, including country, rock, rap, and classical. Actually, more than 23,000 recordings of more than 6,000 artists are included under 27 music subject categories, with a chapter devoted to each music category. Entries within each chapter are arranged alphabetically by artist or composer; each entry includes title, recording company, year of distribution, and a brief annotation. A symbol designates those considered by the editor to be "landmarks, the best an artist has to offer." Indexing is minimal; however, an artist index is included for most popular works and a composer index is included for most classical titles. Despite the editor's subjectivity, this comprehensive and inexpensive guide is recommended for most libraries developing a collection in this area.

Audiocassettes; Compact Discs; Phonorecordings

Y; A

1450. Bibliographical Handbook of American Music, by D. W. Krummel. Univ. of Illinois Press, 1988. 288p. $29.95. 0-252-01450-2. (Music in American Life).

This handbook serves as a bibliographic sourcebook in all areas of American music, geared primarily for the researcher but also useful to the beginning student. Approximately 700 items, including books, articles, dissertations, and databases that offer guidance in locating music, writings, recordings, etc., from sources dealing specifically with music as well as more general sources. There are four major sections to the work. They deal with major national resources, regional and ethnic groups, various types of music, and bibliographic forms such as collections about music and discographies. Most of the entries are annotated and include bibliographic data for retrieval or ordering. Recommended for all academic and public libraries with strong music collections. *Music—United States*

A

1451. Computer Applications in Music: A Bibliography, by Deta S. Davis. A-R Editions, 1988. 537p. $49.95 0-89579-225-7 (The Computer Music and Digital Audio Series).

The entire range of subjects involving computer music up to mid-1986 is covered in this 4,585 item unannotated bibliography. There are chapters on such areas as aesthetics, composition, electronic and pipe organs, and computers in music education, plus an author and title index. Large libraries with a demand for material on this subject will find this extensive work of value. *Music; Computer Music*

C; Y; A

1452. Computer Software in Music and Music Education: A Guide, by Barton K. Bartle. Scarecrow, 1987. 252p. $29.50 0-8108-2056-0.

This is an evaluative listing of 105 software products in music, mostly in the areas of composition and performance with a heavy emphasis on drill and practice exercises. Entries are arranged by title. Information given includes author, publisher, hardware and memory needed, date, cost, documentation, and intended audience (elementary school through adult). Following this is a lengthy section describing and evaluating the contents of each package based on author's own use. There are indexes by intended audience, hardware, and subject, as well as a brief bibliography. This is an thorough treatment of a very specialized area.

Computer Music; Music; Computer Software

A

1453. Guide to Opera and Dance on Videocassette, by Robert Levine and the Editors of *Consumer Reports Books*. Consumers Union, 1989. 213p. $16.95 pap. 0-89043-261-9.

This very selective bibliography lists about 175 recommended performances of opera and dance, both live and studio produced, plus a few documentaries, concerts, and educational features. The choices are well made, making this a useful acquisition guide for medium and large public libraries.

Opera; Dance and Dancers; Videocassettes

A

1454. Index to Biographies of Contemporary Composers, Volume Three, by Storm Bull. Scarecrow, 1987. 854p. $65 0-8108-1930-9.

This is the third volume (the two previous ones are out of print) of a series that analyzes reference sources for biographical material about contemporary composers. Most of the 98 works indexed in this volume were published between 1975 and 1985. The body of the work is an alphabetical listing of over 13,500 composers, with a listing for each of the reference books in which biographical material can be found. Almost half of the works cited are in foreign languages. The reference books analyzed are listed with annotations at the front of the book. This index will be valuable in libraries with large music collections.

Music; Composers; Classical Music

A

1455. Instrumental Virtuosi: A Bibliography of Biographical Materials, by Robert H. Cowden. Greenwood, 1989. 349p. $55. 0-313-26075-3 (Music Reference Collection, 18).

This companion volume to the author's *Concert and Opera Singers* (separate entry) and *Concert and Opera Conductors* (1987, $37.95, 0-313-25620-9) indexes biographical information on 1,215 instrumentalists in both classical and popular music. A total of almost 200 publications are analyzed. These are listed at the beginning of the book. The body of the work is an alphabetical list of the musicians with reference to appropriate biographical sources. For large collections. *Musicians*

A

1456. Keyboard Music of Black Composers: A Bibliography, Ed. by Aaron Horne. Greenwood, 1992. 331p. $55. 0-313-27939-X.

This bibliography is in two main sections, the first with references cited for biographical material on black composers for the piano, and the second an index to their keyboard music. The first is subdivided by categorizing the composer as African, African American, Euro-African, or Afro-Latino. Others in this series include *String Music of Black Composers* (Greenwood, 1991, 327p., $55. 0-313-27938-1) and *Woodwind Music For Black Composers* (Greenwood, 1990,168p., $35. 0313-27265-4) These volumes will have value in large public libraries and colleges with extensive music programs. *Piano; Music; African Americans*

A

1457. Music: A Guide to the Reference Literature, by William S. Brockman. Libraries Unlimited, 1987. 254p. $38.50. 0-87287-526-1 (References Sources in the Humanities).

This highly-praised bibliography is a selective list of important works on various aspects of music and its many forms, including jazz. With a concentration on English language materials, the book is arranged under such categories as key references works like encyclopedias and guides to the literature, musical instruments, theory, recordings, performers and performances, and written music. There are special sections on resource guides, current periodicals, organizations, and research centers. In addition to full bibliographic information, each book receives an annotation and a concise critical comment. This basic bibliography in music will be useful in both public and academic libraries. *Music*

A

1458. Music Analyses: An Annotated Guide to the Literature, by Harold J. Diamond. Schirmer Books, 1991. 716p. $39.95. 0-02-870110-0.

This work is really a updated edition of Diamond's *Music Criticism: An Annotated Guide to the Literature* (1980). The focus of this volume is to direct "students, concertgoers, and nonprofessionals" to materials analyzing the work of the world's most famous composers. The more than 4,600 entries are arranged alphabetically by composer. General references are followed by citations for individual works. The annotations are merely notes indicating technical level and say little to indicate content of article, book, or dissertation. However, this is recommended for most larger academic and music libraries, and for smaller academic and public libraries that have many music lovers and do not subscribe to *Music Index*.

Composers; Music

A

1459. Music and Dance Periodicals: An International Directory and Guidebook, by Doris Robinson. Peri Press, 1989. 395p. $65. 0-96178444-X.

This basic directory lists U.S. and foreign periodicals and annuals on music and dance and related subjects. *Choice*, in its review, stated that "no comparable publication is available. Here is a wealth of information concisely and clearly presented." Arrangement is by subject, e.g., reference works, composers, songwriters, etc, Each entry includes bibliographic identification, language summaries or abstracts, type of music covered, reviews, indexing, etc. The annotations are descriptive, pointing out scope, purpose, and special features. This guide is appropriate for students and researchers alike, and is therefore recommended for all music libraries and academic and public libraries with strong music collections.

Music; Periodicals—Music; Dance and Dancers; Periodicals—Dance

A

1460. **Music and the Personal Computer: An Annotated Bibliography**, by William J. Waters. 175p. $35. Greenwood, 1989. 0-313-26790-1.

Music vis-à-vis microcomputers is not a new concept, but it is increasing in interest as more individuals acquire computers, etc. Reflecting this interest, a number of useful bibliographies have been published in recent years: Davis's *Computer Applications in Music*, for example, is an excellent bibliography, but the emphasis is more on theory and research. Waters, on the other hand, has given us a very practical bibliography designed for the practicing musician as well as the music educator. More than 1,300 succinctly annotated books and periodical sources are included, most published between 1983 and 1989. Most are selected to relate to specific computers, e.g., Commodore, IBM, and Macintosh. Although a bit pricey for its size, this bibliography is recommended for academic and public libraries.

Music; Composition (Music); Microcomputers; Computer Music

A

1461. **Music Reference and Research Materials**, by Vincent Duckles and Michael A. Keller. Schirmer, 1992. 715p. $45. 0-02-870821-0.

Since its first edition in 1964, Duckles has become a standard and basic reference source in the field of music reference and research (Keller has carried out the revisions since his death in 1985). This edition has well over 3,000 entries and is undoubtedly the most comprehensive of any bibliographies in the field. Entries include books, articles, and nonprint sources in European languages published from about the 18th century to 1986.

The succinct annotations are mainly descriptive; however, scholarly reviews are cited. This ambitious work includes three indexes—authors, editors and reviewers; subjects; and titles. This extensive reference work is recommended for students and musicologists alike and should be available in every academic and public library serving such clientele. The revised 5th edition is expected to be published soon.

Music; Reference Books—Music

A

1462. **Piano Information Guide: An Aid to Research**, by Robert Palmieri. Garland, 1989. 329p. $51. 0-8240-7778-4. (Music Research and Information Guides, 10); (Garland Reference Library of the Humani- ties, 806).

This very comprehensive and well-documented bibliography about the piano deals with the instrument and the literature that describes music for the piano, but it does not include biographies and performances. The volume is divided into many sections including encyclopedias and dictionaries, historical works, construction of the piano, pianos of specific composers, electronic piano, buying and caring for a piano, etc. Books and periodical literature in many languages are included. Each entry gives bibliographic data as well as an annotation which is both critical and descriptive, e.g., assessing its value for the scholar or novice and pointing out strengths and weaknesses of the content. This unique and interesting bibliography is recommended for most academic and public libraries and all libraries that have special music collections.

Music; Piano

A

1463. **Schwann Artist Issue**. Schwann, 1992. $15.

This annual publication is the artist index to the Fall, 1991-92 *Schwann Opus Guide* (described below). It lists Compact Discs and cassettes only in six different sections. The first section is an alphabetical listing of orchestras and ensembles with further subdivisions by conductors, composers and title of work. Lastly there is a listing of the record release which identifies it by label, number, analog or digital recording, and format (CD or cassette). There is a separate section on conductors which gives only the name of their orchestras. The last four sections give full record listings under instrumental soloists (arranged by instrument them by artist), choral groups, opera groups, and vocalists. There are two other discographies from Schwann that are also essential collection developing tools in this medium: *Schwann Spectrum* which lists pop music including rock, jazz and soundtracks. An average issue contains information on about 65,000 CDs, LPs, cassettes and laserdiscs (quarterly, $24.95 per year; Canada $34.95). The other is *Schwann Opus*, which lists recorded classical music by composers names. There are about 45,000 CDs, Cassette tapes and laserdiscs in each issue (quarterly, $29.95; Canada $39.95). Schwann editorial offices are at 535 Boyston St., Boston, MA 02116. These are very valuable reference and collection building tools in both public and academic libraries. *Compact Discs; Audiocassettes*

Y; A

MyU

1464. Twentieth-Century Choral Music: An Annotated Bibliography of Music Suitable for Use by High School Choirs, by J. Perry White. 2nd ed. Scarecrow, 1990. 226p. $ 25. 0-8108-2394-2.

This is a critical, selective bibliography of twentieth-century choral compositions accessible to the high school choir. It represents major composers and stylistic trends during this century. Each of the 360 entries (120 new in this edition) include composer, title, voicing, accompaniment, text, range, difficulty, style, comments, publisher, usage, date, and level (junior high school through college). Appended is a list of major music publishers. A composer index and a title index are also provided. This valuable bibliographic guide is recommended for all music, high school, academic libraries and public libraries with strong music interests. *Choirs (Music); Choral Music*

Classical Music and Opera

A

1465. A Basic Classical and Operatic Recordings Collection for Libraries, by Kenyon C. Rosenberg. Scarecrow, 1987. 255p. $29.50. 0-8108-2041-2.

Rosenberg, an experienced librarian, music critic/reviewer, and unchallenged authority, has compiled a core collection of recordings. This up-to-date evaluative guide rates more than 1,200 recordings. He ranks each recording as A (required in every library), B (useful in medium-sized and large libraries,) and C (recommended only for large public and academic libraries). Each entry is arranged alphabetically by composer, with a lively and rather detailed account of the composer's life and works and recommended and available recordings. While this list is still useful, the movement of libraries toward collections of audio-cassettes and compact disks (see following entry) may make this list obsolete very shortly.

Classical Music; Opera; Phonorecordings

A*

CC

1466. A Basic Classical and Operatic Recordings Collection on Compact Discs for Libraries: A Buying Guide, by Kenyon C. Rosenberg. Scarecrow, 1990. 375p. $39.50. 0-8108-2322-5.

Like the author's *Basic Classical and Operatic Recordings Collection for Libraries* (see entry above), this up-to-date guide of compact discs is intended to aid the librarian in developing and/or evaluating a collection of classical music and operatic recordings. Over 1,200 works are arranged by composer and recommended for various size libraries. This timely guide will be a welcome asset to the busy librarian and will also prove useful to patrons building up collections of CD's. Recommended for most libraries.

Classical Music; Opera; Compact Discs

ML128
.B45G7
1988

A*

1467. Blacks in Classical Music: A Bibliographical Guide to Composers, Performers, and Ensembles, Comp. by John Gray. Greenwood, 1988. 280p. $45. 0-313-26056-7. (Music Reference Collection, 15).

Gray culled newspaper and periodical indexes, biographical dictionaries, bibliographies, dissertations, music collections, and discographies to compile this extraordinary list of over 300 black composers, performers, conductors, symphony orchestras, and ensembles. The scope of the work is also extensive, spanning the time period from the mid-1700's to the late 1980's, and geographically covering Europe, Africa, Latin America and the Carribean in addition to United States. In addition to a comprehensive listing of bibliographical citations relating to the artists and ensembles, a detailed bibliography of important reference sources, such as indexes, biographical dictionaries, and bibliographies of books and recordings is provided. Indexes of artists and authors complete this excellent work. Other bibliographies covering blacks in classical music exist; however, they all pre-date the 1985 cutoff date of this guide. This relatively inexpensive work is highly recommended for all academic and music libraries and public libraries developing collections in music.

African Americans; Musicians, African Americans;
Composers, African American; Classical Music

A

1468. CD Review Digest: Classical Peri Press (Voorheesville, NY) quarterly with annual cumulations. $15 per issue, $75 per year. ISSN 1045-0114.

A

1468a. CD Review Digest: Jazz, Popular, Etc. Peri Press (Voorheesville, NY) quarterly with annual cumulations. $15 per issue, $75 per year. ISSN 1045-0122.

These compilations of reviews of CD recordings that began in 1983 attempt to do what *Book Review Digest* does for the print medium. The classical part tabulates reviews that have appeared in over twenty publications. Some are specialized reviewing sources like *Gramaphone* and *American Record Guide*, and others are more general in nature like *Opera News*. Reviews are listed alphabetically by composer and then by composition, and there is a selection on collections. Full information is given on each recording, followed by complete bibliographic information on the review, including its length. About 80% of the citations contain a critical excerpt from one of the reviews. Music videodiscs are also included. These are indexed by label, performers, and reviewers, plus by a listing of mail order houses where CD's can be purchased. The jazz, popular, etc. publication does essentially the same, except that its primary arrangement is by performer with a separate section for collections and movie and show albums. In this publication there is an excerpt from a review for every album discussed. Indexes are by title of selection, label, and reviewer. Prior to 1989, these publications were issued jointly and the cumulations of these reviews are still available. There is a cumulation covering 1893 through 1987 for $175 and an annual volume for 1988. From 1989 on, there are separate annual cumulations (one for classical, one for popular) available at $75 each. This guide will be valuable for collection building and reference in large public libraries. *Compact Discs*

A

1469. Chamber Music: An International Guide to Works and Their Instrumentation, by Victor Rangel-Ribeiro and Robert Markel. Facts on File, 1993. 271p. $45. 0-8160-2296-8.

The compilers have created a very comprehensive list of about 8,000 entries of musical works suitable for 3 to 24 performers in an innumerable number of combinations. Works can be retrieved by composer as well as by specific combinations of instruments. This easy-to-use guide is recommended for all music libraries and other libraries serving musicians and other interested professionals as the best current source available in this area. *Chamber Music; Music; Classical Music*

A

1470. Concert and Opera Singers: A Bibliography of Biographical Materials, by Robert H. Cowden. Greenwood, 1985. 278p. $42.95 0-313-24828-1. (Music Reference Collection, 5).

The principal section of this work lists alphabetically more than 700 opera and concert singers, gives a little biographical information for identification purposes, and then gives sources where biographical information can be found. For collection-building purposes, there is an annotated list of more than 100 collective biographies of singers and a listing of 150 related works. Reference materials are listed in a separate appendix, and there is an index to authors of works listed. These bibliographies total over 1,000 titles. Another work of similar scope and purpose is Andrew Farkas' *Opera and Concert Singers: An Annotated International Bibliography of Books and Pamphlets* (Garland, 1984, $65. 0-8240-9001-2). These works will be useful in large collections. *Music; Singers; Opera*

A

1471. How Quaint the Ways of Paradox! An Annotated Gilbert and Sullivan Bibliography. Scarecrow, 1991. 208p. $25. 0-8108-2445-0.

There are 968 entries in this bibliography, including books, articles, conferences papers, librettos, chapters in books, and scores all written by or about Gilbert and Sullivan. There are short descriptive annotations and author, title and subject indexes. Of value in specialized collections. *Gilbert and Sullivan*

A

1472. Music Theory from Zarlino to Schenker: A Bibliography and Guide, by David Damschroder and David Russell Williams. Pendragon Press, 1990. 522p. $54. 0-918728-99-1.

The works of over 200 musical theorists are included in this detailed bibliography. The works are arranged chronologically from the 16th century to the 1960's. The focus is on the theorists rather than the topics or the periods. Each entry follows a similar pattern: beginning with a brief essay on the theoretical writings, listing citations of extant primary sources, and concluding with a bibliography of related literature. Also included is a special 51 page Literature Supplement that lists more general literature. This work makes an important contribution to music scholarship and is highly recommended for all academic, public, and special libraries with specialized music collections. *Music—Theory*

Y; A

1473. **The New Penguin Guide to Compact Discs and Cassettes Yearbook, 1990**, by Edward Greenfield, Viking/Penguin, 1990. 512p. $13.95. 0-14-012377-6.

Penguin guides to classical music have been appearing under various titles for about 10 years. With the explosive emergence of the compact disc (CD) there was a gap; the Penguin guides soon filled that gap, certainly since the 1990 edition, and with the issuance of annual supplements. The CD has replaced the LP and is on the way to replacing the audiocassette. This yearbook (even with its slight British accent) is a welcome addition to the bibliographic control of this rapidly growing medium. Entries are arranged by composer; some are further sub-divided by type, e.g., orchestral, chamber music, vocal music, etc. There is a need, perhaps, for a performer index; nevertheless, this guide is recommended as a purchasing guide for every academic, public, and even school library that has developing collections of classical music on compact discs. *Music; Compact Discs*

A

1474. **Opera Performers in Video Format**. Music Library Association, P.O. Box 487, Canton, MA 02021, 1991. $15. 0-914954-43-1.

About 300 commercially-produced and still available videos are included in this handy and inexpensive guide. The videos are arranged by composer and opera titles. Each entry indicates running time, cast members, language of opera, VHS or Beta, and distributor. Indexes of titles, performers, ensembles and performance location complete this volume which has the endorsement of the Music Library Association and is recommended for most academic and public libraries, and all libraries that have a special interest in music or clientele who are opera buffs. *Opera; Videocassettes*

A

1475. **Opera Plot Index: A Guide to Locating Plots and Descriptions of Operas, Operettas, and Other Works of the Musical Theater, and Associated Material**, by William E. Studwell and David A. Hamilton. Garland, 1990. 466p. $54. 0-8240-4621-8. (Garland Reference Library of the Humanities, 1099).

Studwell and Hamilton have compiled an index, arranged by title of composition, of interesting information found in about 160 sources, on operas, operettas, and musicals. Entries include codes which point to additional description, critical analyses, bibliographies, and most important resources. The list of the books indexed becomes a useful bibliography for collection development. This index is presently the most complete opera index available and is recommended for public and academic libraries serving patrons who are students of opera or merely opera lovers. *Opera*

Y; A

1476. **Penguin Guide to Compact Discs**, by Edward Greenfield. Penguin, 1990. 1392p. $19.95. 0-14-046887-0.

This edition updates the earlier (1986) edition of the *Penguin Guide...*. This latest edition, not surprisingly, drops cassettes and LPs. This edition is primarily new titles or titles that have been transferred to CD's. Preceding the listing there is an excellent essay discussing the advantages and disadvantages of CD's. Entries are arranged by composer, followed by type of composition; they contain evaluations of performances, as well as recording quality. This guide has a strong British bias, however, an attempt was made to include most important U.S. discs. This inexpensive guide is recommended for all libraries building or maintaining collections of classical music. *Compact Discs; Music*

Ethnic and Folk Music

A

MSU

1477. **African Music: A Bibliographical Guide to the Traditional, Popular, Art, and Liturgical Musics of Sub-Saharan Africa**, By John Gray. Greenwood, 1991. 544p. $59.95. 0-313-27769-9. (African Special Bibliographic Series, 14).

This volume of more than 5800 entries from books, articles, theses, and dissertations to newspaper columns. A fair number of audiovisual materials and a short discography are also included. Many items listed are unpublished and difficult to retrieve; however, despite these limitations, this is a valuable source for all academic, music, and other libraries serving students and scholars of African music.

Africa—Music; Music—Africa

A

1478. Ethnomusicology Research: A Select Annotated Bibliography, by Ann Briegleg Schuursma. Garland, 1992. 173p. $24. 0-8240-5735-X. (Garland Library of Music Ethnology, 1). *MSU*

This bibliography covers about thirty years (roughly 1960 through 1990) of publications related to music in culture. Dance and popular music have been excluded because separate volumes on these topics will be published later. The 468 publications cited are annotated and arranged in five separate sections dealing with history, theory, fieldwork studies, musical analysis, and publications from related fields. All publications are in English. This will be useful primarily in academic institutions with active music or anthropology departments *Music*

A

1479. Folk Music in America: A Reference Guide, by Terry E. Miller. Garland, 1986. 424p. $48. *ML128 .F74M5 1986* 0-8240-8935-9. (Garland Reference Library of the Humanities, 496).

This annotated bibliography includes books, articles from scholarly publications, sections from encyclopedias, and dissertations on folk music in America. Most of the citations date from the 1950s to the mid 1980s. There are descriptive annotations for each. The almost 2,000 entries are arranged in nine subject-oriented chapters like, "General Resources," "Music of the American Indians and Eskimos," and "Afro-American Music." Short essays introduce each section, and there are author and subject indexes. Because many of the citations are to popular books, this can be useful in colleges and large public libraries.

Folk Music

Y; A

1480. Literature of American Music in Books and Folk Music Collections: A Fully Annotated Bibliography: Supplement I, by David Horn and Richard Jackson. Scarecrow, 1988. 570p. $49.50. 0-8108-1997-X. *MSU — We have 1977 ed) @ML120 .U5H7*

Two noted authorities, Horn, music librarian at the University of Exeter in England, and Jackson, music specialist at the New York Public Library, have corroborated to produce an invaluable reference source. The number of entries from the basic volume has doubled and, with the assistance of Jackson, the Horn work has added a needed American accent. The main volume, with its almost 1900 annotated and 800 unannotated titles, was published in 1977 (1977 $35. 0-8108-0996-6). Supplement I adds about 2,100 additional titles published prior to 1980. More than half are described with very lengthy evaluative annotations. The entries are arranged by a broad classified subject arrangement. The work has three separate indexes: author, title and specific subject. This work (along with the basic volume) is recommended for all libraries which serve a clientele interested in music. *Music—United States; Folk Music*

Cinematic Music

A

1481. Cinema Sheet Music: A Comprehensive Listing of Published Film Music from Squaw Man (1914) to Batman (1989), by Donald Stubblebine. McFarland, 1991. 628p. $65. 0-89950-569-4. *MSU*

From over 6,000 films from various countries, this directory lists about 15,000 pieces of published sheets music of the past 75 years. The works are arranged alphabetically by title of the movie, and for each there is given such information as the studio, release date, stars, song title, composer and lyricist, publisher, and cover art. No orchestral scores are included, but there is a 52 item bibliography, a song index and an index by composer. This extensive bibliography is unique and extensive in scope and therefore should find a place in libraries where material on the performing arts is stressed. *Motion Pictures; Music*

A

1482. Film and Television Composers: An International Discography, 1920-1989, by Steve Harris. McFarland, 1992. 302p. $55. 0-89950-553-8.

This is a listing of about 750 international composers of film and television music with emphasis on American, British, French, and Italian composers. Only significant phonograph records (no CD's) are listed alphabetically under the composers' names. For each of the 7,980 entries, disc information such as record label, number, format, and country of pressing is given. There is an index by production title. This volume essentially updates the author's earlier (1988) *Film, Television and Stage Music on Phonograph Records*, although stage music is not included in the newer book. This will be a useful bibliographic source in large or specialized libraries involved in music or the performing arts.

Phonorecordings; Music; Motion Pictures; Television

A

1483.   Film, Television and Stage Music on Phonographic Records: A Discography, by Steve Harris. McFarland, 1988. 445p. $49.95. 0-89950-251-2.

There are over 12,000 entries in this discography divided into three sections: films (8,000 entries), television productions (2,000 entries), and stage musicals (2,000 entries). These cover discs released in both the United States and Great Britain. Shows are arranged by title, and under each, basic information is given (i.e., composer, record label, number, date) but no list of cast members. There is a composer index. This is of value in medium and large-sized collections more for reference than collection building.

Phonorecordings; Motion Picture Music; Television Music;

Musical Revues, Comedies, Etc.; Music

A

MSU

1484.   Keeping Score: Film and Television Music 1980-1988 (with Additional Coverage of 1921-1979), by James L. Limbacher and H. Stephen Wright. Scarecrow, 1991. 916p. $92.50 0-8108-2453-1.

This combined update and revision of two of Limbacher's earlier books is divided into three parts. The first lists films and television programs chronologically, with fullest coverage for the years 1980 through 1988. For each the name of the composer is given. The second section lists these films again, but alphabetically by composer's name. The last is a discography which includes phonograph records, CD's, and tapes. There is a title index of the films and the television programs. In large academic and large public libraries, this could be valuable for research and collection building.

Films; Music; Phonorecordings; Compact Discs

Popular, Rock, Jazz, and Blues

Y; A

1485.   The Beatles: A Bio-bibliography, by William McKeen. Greenwood, 1989. 181p. $39.95. 0-313-25993-3.

In the first half of this relatively brief work, McKeen summarizes more than 30 sources in a biographical essay; this is followed by a series of short essays which discuss the work and influence of the Beatles. The second half of the book contains a discography, bibliography, and a list of performances. The discography provides brief identifying information: title, record number, release date, and song titles and writers from the album. The bibliography is divided by format and includes about 150 books and over 300 periodical articles (most of the citations are drawn from Terry's *Here, There, and Everywhere* (Popular Culture, 1985. $34.50 0-7650-163-3), perhaps the most comprehensive bibliography on the Beatles. The concluding section lists in chronological order the Beatles' performances and films with brief notes on each. This bio-bibliography is recommended as a reference aid and collection development guide for all libraries that serve Beatles fans.   *Beatles*

A

1486.   Best Rated CDs: Jazz, Popular, Etc. Peri Press, 1992. 678p. $19.95. 1-879796-06-6.

This guide of the "best" in popular music is based on selections culled from the first five volumes of *CD Review Digest,* which cover the years 1983-1991 inclusive. This compilation of almost 2,100 titles includes blues, jazz, pop-rock, and show music. Selection is based on at least two favorable reviews from the many reviewing periodicals included in the *CD Review Digest*. The guide is arranged alphabetically by the surname of the artist or group's name and is divided into four sections by type of music. Each entry contains complete discographic information, excerpts from the reviews, and bibliographic data of original reviewing sources. The publishers also issue a companion guide which is similar in purpose and format: (*Best Rated CDs: Classical*. Peri Press, 1992. 1-879796-06-6). Both of these guides are important evaluative aids and selection tools for most academic and public libraries.   *Compact Discs; Music*

A

1487.   The Blackwell Guide to Blues Records. Basil Blackwell, 1989. 347p. $19.95 0-631-16516-9.

This book combines a historical overview of blues music with a discography of key recordings. Each of the twelve chapters is written by a specialist and deals with a particular aspect of blues music such as "Rhythm and Blues" and "Piano Blues and Boogie-Woogie." Within each chapter, is a listing of 10 "essential" recordings, plus a supplementary list of 30 highly recommended titles. Unfortunately, many of these recordings have not been transferred to CDs and are now out-of-print or otherwise not readily available; therefore, the lists will have only limited value as acquisition tools in public libraries.

Blues Music; Phonorecordings; Music

Y; A

1488.   **The Blackwell Guide to Recorded Jazz**, Ed. by Barry Kernfeld. Basil Blackwell, 1991. 474p. *CC* $24.95. 0-631-17164-9.

This work identifies about 125 jazz artists and highlights the single most important work of each. Jazz music from all genres and time periods is represented, from the birth of jazz through the 1980's. The work is chronologically arranged in 11 chapters representing the major styles of jazz and spotlighting the most important artists within each category. Bibliographic data is provided for each format currently available— LP, cassette, or compact disk. All songs on the recording and all artists are listed. All names mentioned are included in the very comprehensive index. This work will be of more than passing interest to all jazz fans and to all libraries building collections to satisfy these buffs.   *Jazz; Phonorecordings*

A

1489.   **The Blues: A Bibliographic Guide**, by Mary L. Hart et al. Garland, 1989. 636p. $66. 0-8240-8506- X. (Garland Reference Library of the Humanities, 565); (Music Research and Information Guides, 7).

This compilation of bibliographic citations of one of America's original musical forms include books, journals, newspapers, reports, book reviews, films, and notes from record albums. It is comprehensive in scope and intended for the general listener as well as the blues scholar. It is inclusive in sources used and time span covered (the twentieth century up to 1985). The work is divided into 12 broad chapters, each compiled by a subject specialist. Major topics include "Blues Biographies," with reference to hundreds of performers; "Blues on Film," which lists 177 titles; and "Blues Research," which lists basic blues reference works including dictionaries, discographies, and other bibliographies. Indexes of authors and titles complete this unique and one-of-a-kind guide, which is recommended for interlibrary loan and as a collection development tool for all academic and public libraries that can afford it.   *Blues Music*

Y; A

1490.   **The CD Rock and Roll Library: 30 Years of Rock and Roll on Compact Disc**, by Bill Shapiro. Andrews and McMeel, 1988. 188p. $8.95 pap. 0-8362-7947-6.

The author comments on 467 works by 200 different artists in this selective discography arranged by decade (i.e., the 50s, the 60s, the 70s and the 80s). Each decade has a written introduction, and there is a 90 item supporting bibliography. The annotations for each recording include biographical, as well as critical information. A somewhat similar listing is found in David Prakel's *Rock 'n' Roll on Compact Disc*. Both lists are valuable for collection development.   *Compact Discs; Rock Music*

A

1491.   **Down Home Guide to the Blues**, by Frank Scott et al. A Cappella Books, 1991. 250p. $14.95 pap. 1-55652-130-8.

This discography is a compilation of 3,500 record reviews that have appeared in 12 years of the newsletter on blues recordings published by Down Home Music. The entries are arranged alphabetically by performer with a separate section on anthology records. The reviews include label name, identification numbers, comments on the style and quality of the records and a partial list of song titles. A core collection of 100 records is also identified. There are no indexes but there are a few black and white photographs. This current, comprehensive list will be helpful in academic and public libraries for public use and collection development.   *Blues Music; Phonorecordings; Music*

A

1492.   **Find That Tune: An Index to Rock, Folk-Rock, Disco and Soul in Collections**, volume 2, by *MSU* Sue Sharma and William Gargan. Neal/Schuman, 1989. 387p. $49.95. 1-55570-019-5.   *NDSU has*

The first volume of *Find That Tune* appeared in 1984 ($47.50 0-918212-70-7). This second volume updates and adds to the first volume by listing 4,000 popular rock songs (about 50% of them were also in *1st ed)e* the first edition) as they appear in 202 new sheet music collections. The book is indexed by collection, title, *Ref* first line, composer, lyricist and performer. For libraries that contain collections of sheet music, this can be *ML128* used both for reference and collection building.   *Rock Music; Music*   *.R6F56*   *1984*

A

1493.   **Fire Music: A Bibliography of the New Jazz, 1959-1990**, by John Gray. Greenwood, 1991. 515p. *CC* $75. 0-313-27892-X. (Music Reference Collection).

There are about 7,100 unannotated citations in this book that include books, articles, newspapers, dissertations, films, videos, and audiotapes on the subject of jazz published between 1959 and 1990. These works are international in scope and are organized in six major sections including a chronology and chapters on topics like country and regional studies, and jazz collectives. Over two thirds of the book is devoted to listing material on more that 400 individual artists and groups. There are artist, subject, and author indexes and appendixes that cover such material as sources consulted and locations of resource centers for jazz. This is an important resource for libraries needing material on the contemporary jazz scene.   *Jazz; Music*

A

CC

1494.   The Grove Press Guide to the Blues on CD, by Frank John Hadley. Grove Press, 1993. 256p. $14.95. pap. 0-8021-3328-2.

Hadley, a frequent contributor to *Down Beat*, defines the blues as a "common language of virtually all American musics." Rhythm and blues, jazz, rock, and even country and western are included along with what we traditionally consider as pure blues. The more than 700 recent or reissued compact discs included are arranged by performer. Each entry includes very specific detailed information such as: album name, recording company, running time, a star rating (one to five stars), year of issue, and a brief critical annotation. A list of CD anthology entries arranged by title, as well as an album title index, are also included. This very inexpensive guide is recommended for all libraries that support music studies programs as well as those who simply cater to music lovers.   *Blues Music; Compact Discs*

A

MSU

1495.   The History of Rock and Roll: A Chronological Discography, by Mirik Kocandrie. G. K. Hall, 1988. 297p. $45. 0-8161-8956-0.

This discography of about 12,000 recordings defines rock and roll very broadly so that the chronologically-arranged chapters cover such styles as boogie-woogie, gospel and country music, as well as soul music, doo-wop, heavy metal, and new age music. Asterisks identify very important discs. Very basic background information is given for each record, but unfortunately record numbers are not given. The work is also marred by lack of annotations and sometimes inaccurate classification of performers and general misinformation. For large libraries with extensive popular music collections.

Rock Music; Music; Phonorecordings

Y; A

1496.   Jazz on Compact Disc: A Critical Guide to the Best Recordings, by Steve Harris. Harmony, 1987. 176p. $13.95 (pap.). 0-517-56688-5.

The author, a British jazz critic, has chosen 79 important performers to highlight in this highly selective discography of CD's that represent the best in the past and present of jazz recordings. For each performer, there is a short biographical sketch followed by a listing of his or her most important discs. For each disc appropriate background information is given, including contents of the disc, timings, recording dates, labels, numbers, and author's comments. The work is also attractively illustrated with photographs of the artists and album dust jackets. For small libraries only able to purchase a basic collection, there is an introductory selection of the 100 best recordings. This is a fine acquisition tool for both public and academic libraries as well as school libraries where there is an interest in jazz.   *Jazz; Compact Discs*

A

1497.   Jazz Performers: An Annotated Bibliography of Biographical Materials, by Gary Carner. Greenwood, 1990. 364p. $45. 0-313-26250-0.

The main section of this work is an alphabetical listing of jazz performers. For each, there is brief information for identification of the performers (e.g., instrument, place and date of birth) and a bibliography materials (chiefly magazine articles) about them. There is also a section on supplementary bibliographies and author and subject indexes. For large collections where there is a great interest in jazz.   *Jazz*

Y; A

MSU

1498.   The Literature of Rock II, 1979-1983, by Frank Hoffmann and B. Lee Cooper. Scarecrow, 1986. 2v. $85. 0-8108-1821-3.

This very extensive bibliography updates and expands the earlier volume which covered the years 1954-1978 (1981. $29.50. 0-8108-1371-8). Nearly 10,000 entries, from more than 500 book and 130 periodicals, are arranged under 21 broad subject areas and then further subdivided into more specific areas. Most citations are not annotated. There is a performers index, which list identifying citation numbers, and two useful appendixes, one which lists books and periodicals indexed and the other, a core collection of rock records. This very comprehensive work will be useful to rock fans as well as to scholars of popular culture, and is therefore recommended for most libraries building a collection in this area.

Rock Music; Rock Musicians

① MSU

A

1499.   **The Penguin Guide to Jazz on CD, LP, and Cassette**, by Richard Cook and Brian Morton. *MSU* Penguin, 1992. 1,287. $22.50. pap. 0-14-015364-0.

Cook and Morton have provided us with a comprehensive discography to recorded jazz from about 1917 to the present. They state that "this is the first attempt to bring the whole spectrum of jazz recording within a single volume." The work consists of more than 1,300 jazz musicians and groups organized alphabetically by name. Each entry includes background and critical information on individual musicians or groups, as well as a list of recording titles preceded by a rating of 1 to 5 stars. The extensive index lists the musicians and every performer on every record. This guide to jazz serves as a companion volume to the latest edition of *Penguin Guide to Compact Discs...* (which focuses on classical music) and is recommended for all academic, public, and music libraries developing collections in the area of jazz music.

Phonorecordings; Compact Discs; Jazz; Music

A*

1500.   **Popular Music: A Reference Guide**, by Roman Iwaschkin. 2nd ed. Garland, 1992. 672p. $94. 0-8240-4449-5. (Garland Reference Library of the Humanities, 642).

This comprehensive bibliography of over 5,000 entries is an attempt by the author to include every English-language book and periodical on American and British popular music published through 1984. The guide is divided into seven parts, of which the first two parts make up more than half of the volume. Part 1 deals with the various genres of popular music and Part 2 concentrates on collective and individual biographies. The remaining parts constitute a miscellany on aspects of popular music, including technical questions, collecting, discographies, literary works, and periodicals all dealing with popular music. The annotations are basically descriptive. The index is in dictionary form including authors, titles, and subjects in one alphabet. This bibliography is recommended for public and academic libraries as a beginning reference source and as a guide for collection development. *Music, Popular*

Y; A

1501.   **Rap Music in the 1980's: A Reference Guide**, by Judy McCoy. Scarecrow, 1992. 261p. $32.50. 0-8108-2649-6.

McCoy has compiled a bibliography/discography on one of the newest forms of music which is very much related to Black oral-tradition improvisation and the everyday experiences of Black youth. More than 1,000 entries on the literature of the field are included, as well as entries for about 75 recordings. All of the entries contain bibliographic information and brief annotations. Indexes by artist, album titles, and subject are also included. This work may be considered for academic and public libraries that have collections or are building collect-ions on popular culture, black studies as well as music.

Rap Music; African Americans; Compact Discs

Y; A

1502.   **Rock & Roll Review: A Guide to Good Rock on CD**, by Bill Shapiro. Andrews & McMeel, 1991. 299p. $9.95. pap. 0-8362-6217-4.

This is the 2nd edition, under a new title, of Shapiro's *The CD Rock and Roll Library: 30 Years of Rock and Roll on Compact Disc*. More than 1,000 short reviews are cited in this edition. Each entry includes title, year of publication, label, catalog number, a rating (A-F) with notes on the technical and aesthetic quality indicating the basis for the rating. There is some question on the subjectivity of Shapiro in selecting both the artists and the reviews; however, the work does serve a useful reference purpose, and it is helpful in identifying many rock and roll selections that are currently on CD for collection building in this area. This very inexpensive guide is recommended for most secondary school and public libraries.

Rock Music; Compact Discs

Y; A

1503.   **Rock 'n' Roll on Compact Disc: A Critical Guide to the Best Recordings**, by David Prakel. Harmony Books/Crown, 1987. 176p. $13.95. pap. 0-517-56687-7.

Prakel has compiled an interesting guide on a popular topic on a very popular format. Even the introduction is a bonus: "Introducing Compact Disc" is a fascinating discussion of CD technology, including the processes of recording and manufacturing compact discs. The CD reviews are arranged alphabetically by artist; each entry contains a brief history of the performer or group. This is followed by specific album entries with complete ordering information, including American and English release numbers and labels, and total playing time. Prakel also rates each album 1-3 both for desirability and for quality of the recording. Following this main section is a list of "Other performers" which adds another 100 albums for consideration.

A final bonus is the list of 100 albums recommended for purchase for a basic collection (a big help to busy or not rock-inclined librarians). This guide is highly recommended for both high school and public libraries as a reference tool for their rock fans or as a guide for development of CD collections.

Rock Music; Compact Discs

Y; A

1504.   **Rockabilly: A Bibliographic Resource Guide**, by B. Lee Cooper and Wayne S. Haney. Scarecrow, 1990. 372p. $39.50. 0-8108-2386-1.

More than 35 years of rockabilly music are included in extensive lists of printed resources. Most of the well-known performers such as Charlie Feathers, Carl Perkins, Jerry Lee Lewis, Elvis Presley, Shakin' Stevens, The Cramps, and The Stray Cats are represented among the more than 220 rockabilly singers and instrumentalists. The bibliographic survey includes biographies, historical studies, concert and record reviews, discographies, and articles from magazines. Author and name index are provided. This bibliography is recommended as a reference aid and collection building guide for secondary school, academic, and public libraries supporting collections or programs in rock and country music, popular culture, and American studies.   *Rock Music; Country Music; Popular Culture; Music*

Y; A

1505.   **The Trouser Press Record Guide**. Ed. by Ira A. Robbins. 4th ed. Macmillan/Collier, 1991. 800p. $18.95. pap. 0-02-036361-3.

Following the pattern established by *Trouser Press* magazine, which was published from 1974 to 1984, the type of music included in this revised edition of a popular guide includes new wave, punk, roots music, rap, heavy metal, speed metal, electronic, and esoteric folk music. The works of 2,500 artists are reviewed in this guide. Guides to LP records are generally only useful for purposes of identification rather than for collection development; however, this guide includes extended play, compact discs, and cassette availability as part of its entries. The 1,600 alphabetically-arranged, signed reviews range from several hundred to several thousands of words in length. This guide to alternative music is recommended for high school, academic, and public libraries as a reference tool and as a aid in collection development.

Music, Popular; Phonorecordings

Dance

A

1506.   **Black Dance: An Annotated Bibliography**, by Alice J. Adamczyk. Garland, 1989. 213p. $33.50. 0-8240-8808-5.

The 1,400 entries to books, articles, reviews, and dissertations come from sources ranging from the very popular such as *Village Voice* and *Ebony* to the very scholarly such as the *Journal of American Folklore* and the *University of Pennsylvania Museum Journal*. Entries are in alphabetical order by author and include a brief annotation as well as bibliographic data. The subject index includes names of individuals, groups, types of dance, and other topics. This specialized bibliography is recommended for academic libraries supporting programs in dance or black culture as well as public libraries supporting collections in the per-forming arts.   *African Americans; Dance and Dancers*

A

1507.   **Dance: An Annotated Bibliography, 1965-1982**, by Fred R. Forbes, Jr. Garland, 1986. 261p. $39. 0-8240-8676-7.

This 1,166 item bibliography was culled from a number of different existing databases and represents writing in books, parts of books, articles, and dissertations that appeared between 1965 and 1982. The scope of subjects is wide—from dance history and dance therapy to disco and belly dancing. The entries are arranged alphabetically by author in eight chapters. There is a subject and author index. This will be useful in academic and many public library collections.   *Dance and Dancers*

A

1508.   **Dance Film and Video Guide**, by Deirdre Towers. Princeton Book Co./Dance Horizons, 1991. 233p. $24.95 pap. 0-87127-171-0.

There are over 2,000 films and videos listed by title in this filmography which covers all types of dancing around the world. For example, not only are there listing for ballet and modern dance, but also entries for the films of Fred Astaire and Gene Kelly. Each entry gives credits (e.g., choreographer, director, dancers, etc.) and a brief descriptive annotation. There are indexes by choreographer, dancer, dance company, composer, and director, and a subject index by type of dance and geographical location. This work will be of value in libraries with large dance and/or video collections.

Motion Pictures; Videocassettes; Dance and Dancers

Religion and Philosophy

Philosophy and Ethics

A

1509. **A Bibliographic Guide to the Comparative Study of Ethics**, Ed. by John Carman and Mark Juergensmeyer. Cambridge, 1991. 811p. $100. 0-521-34448-4.

This guide includes ethical writings within a variety of religious and ethical traditions. It is intended for both the beginning student and the scholar, and it deals with 24 related topics such as wealth, evil, equality, etc. The volume consists of 15 bibliographic essays; each one of which reviews the ethical writings of a basic tradition, e.g., Islam, Judaism, Western philosophical ethics, etc. The bibliography is classified and annotated and contains both primary and secondary sources. Though expensive this volume is recommended for most academic and large public libraries. *Ethics; Religion*

A

1510. **Ethics: An Annotated Bibliography**, by John K. Roth et al. Salem Press, 1991. 169p. $40. 0-89356-662-4. (Magill Bibliographies).

This is a beginner's guide to the literature of both the abstract and practical aspects of moral philosophy. This annotated bibliography of books is arranged into four parts. The first two cite works of a general nature and those on ethical theory. The third is a chronologically arranged list of the masterpieces of ethical literature from Plato to the present, and the fourth, "Applying Ethics," contains material on current issues such as ethics in relation to business and medicine. Generally the works cited are current and available. Because of the breath of its coverage and the quality of its selections, this bibliography is recommended for both public and college libraries. *Ethics*

A*

1511. **Philosophy: A Guide to the Reference Literature**, by Hans E. Bynagle. Libraries Unlimited, 1986. 170p. $35. 0-87287-464-8. (Reference Sources in the Humanities).

This work encompasses "the entire realm of philosophy: works dealing with any period, movement, school, branch, major figure, or geographical-cultural subdivision, non-Western as well as Western." More than 200 works are described and evaluated. Its strongest feature is its annotations which are well-written and are useful for reference work with patrons. The author also includes a list of core journals in the field. Author/title and subject indexes are provided. While there are many bibliographies in the field of philosophy, Bynagle's work tends to update two similar ones: De George's *Philosopher's Guide* (Univ. of Kansas, 1980, $25, 0-7006-0200-3) which is older and has few annotations; and Tice and Slavin's *Research Guide to Philosophy* (o.p.) which is really a long essay with a bibliography included. Both works predate the scope of this guide. Byngagle's is highly recommended for all academic and public libraries as a reference tool and as an aid to collection development. *Philosophy*

A

1512. **Resources in Ancient Philosophy: An Annotated Bibliography of Scholarship in English, 1965-1989**, by Albert A. Bell and James B. Allis. Scarecrow, 1991. 799p. $79.50. 0-8108-2520-1.

Bell and Allis have produced a very thorough bibliography of over 7,000 items in the field of Ancient Philosophy. Actually, several delimitations were established: Only Western philosophy was considered and, except for a number of surveys and bibliographies, all of works included were published after 1965. The work was intended to meet the needs of both the beginning student as well as the specialist. The entries are arranged in 21 chapters that encompass Western philosophy, from Thales to Augustine. The chapters are subdivided into many subheadings. Each entry includes full bibliographic data and a brief descriptive annotation. There are no author indexes, and the subject index may list very large blocks of item numbers, necessitating a lengthy browsing time. Despite this flaw, the volume should be very useful and is therefore recommended for most academic libraries and other libraries that need a basic bibliography in this field.

Philosophy, Ancient

A

MSU

1513. **Women Philosophers: A Bibliography of Books Through 1920,** by Else M. Barth. Philosophy Documentation Center, 1992. 236p. $39. 0-912632-91-7.

Barth has compiled an extensive bibliography of about 2,000 works about and/or by women "philosophers" from Western Europe and English speaking countries throughout the world. Authors selected include women holding a position in the philosophy department of a university, or those who are recognized philosophers by one of the current definitions. A number of lists and indexes facilitate the work: a list of major philosophers; an index of names; a detailed table of contents. The major limitation is the lack of evaluative or even descriptive annotations. However, this work will fill a gap in any academic library with a women's studies program or public library serving those with an interest in this area and is therefore recommended. *Philosophers; Women's Studies*

Religion

A

1514. **A Basic Book List for Church Libraries,** by Bernard E. Deitrick. 4th Rev. ed. Church and Synagogue Library Association, 1992. 16p. $5.95. 0-915324-10-5.

This "core collection," representing some 190 annotated titles of basic books for church libraries of all denominations, was selected and annotated by CSLA's former book review editor. It is available for $5.95 from: Church and Synagogue Library Association, P.O. Box 19357, Portland, OR 97219.

Church Libraries

A

BS659
.ZZM35
1988

1515. **Anti-Evolution: An Annotated Bibliography,** by Tom McIver. McFarland, 1988. 385p. $39.95. 0-89950-313-5.

Most of the more than 1,800 books and pamphlets included in this bibliography espouse the Christian creationist theory, but other anti-evolution beliefs are also represented, namely, theosophy, Hinduism, and some material with no religious leaning. Most of the annotations are quite brief, and each entry includes full bibliographic information. The works are arranged by author, and there are name and title indexes and a limited subject index, which makes it is very difficult to retrieve by specific subject. Despite this limitation, this bibliography is highly recommended for most academic libraries and for all libraries with a special religious focus. *Anti-Evolution; Creationism; Evolution*

A

1516. **The Bible and Modern Literary Criticism: A Critical Assessment and Annotated Bibliography,** by Mark Allan Powell. Greenwood, 1992. 469p. $65. 0-313-27546-7.

This interesting bibliography cites works published through 1990 that study biblical texts by using current literary techniques. Following a brief bibliographic essay which serves as an overview to the topic, are several sections dealing with the current theories of literary criticism. The fourth section is the body of the volume and lists the literary studies on the Bible. Indexes by author, title, and subjects are included. The work is of interest, but is not as useful, nor as expensive, as Mark Minor's *Literary-Critical Approaches to the Bible: An Annotated Bibliography*, 1992, which has a stronger emphasis on literary studies of biblical works, and is therefore recommended for libraries needing a bibliography in this area.

Bible—Criticism; Bible as Literature

A

CL

1517. **Black Theology: A Critical Assessment and Annotated Bibliography,** Comp. by James H. Evans. Greenwood, 1987. 205p. $42.95. 0-313-24822-2.

Evans, an African American professor of theology and black church studies, has compiled a selective bibliography of publications based on a survey of black theology spanning about two decades—the mid-1960's to the mid-1980's. Journal monographs, journal articles, anthologies, and essays within collections are included among the more than 450 items. Entries are arranged in alphabetical order by author under three large categories: Origin and Development of Black Theology; Liberation, Feminism, and Marxism; and Cultural and Global Discourse. Each entry includes full bibliographic data and an annotation ranging in length from one sentence to a paragraph or more. Indexes for names, subjects, and titles complete this generally scholarly and useful bibliography, which is recommended for most academic libraries and special theological libraries. *African Americans; Theology*

A

1518. **Books for Believers: 35 Books That Every Catholic Ought to Read**, by Raymond A. Schroth. Paulist, 1987. 135p. $6.95. 0-8091-2911-6.

The 35 titles that Schroth has selected in this brief bibliography would be of interest to anyone concerned with morality, social action, threat of nuclear war, and other serious issues of modern society. This would be a worthwhile list for members of other religions denominations, as well. *Catholics*

A

1519. **Church and State in America: A Bibliographic Guide: The Civil War to the Present Day**, by John F. Wilson. Greenwood, 1987, 452p. $55. 0-313-256914-3.

This is a companion volume to the author's previously published *Church and State in America: A Bibliographic Guide: The Colonial and Early National Periods* (Greenwood, 1986, $69.95. 0-313-25236-X). Like the earlier book, this work is divided into eleven critically annotated bibliographic essays that deal with religion as it relates to such topics as law, education, women and specific historical periods. After each essay, is a selected list, averaging about 250 titles, of books, periodical articles, and other sources on the topic. Most are recent, some as late as 1986. There are author and title indexes. This bibliography will be a good starting place for researchers as well as librarians who wish to increase holdings in this area.
Church and State Relations; Religion

A

1520. **Cities and Churches: An International Bibliography**, by Loyde H. Hartley. 3 vols. American Theological Library Association/Scarecrow, 1992. 2,764 p. $195. 0-8108-2583-X. (ATLA Bibliography Series).

This mammoth, three-volume work traces the history of church-city relations for a period of almost 200 years as it has appeared in books, articles, pamphlets, doctoral dissertations, motion pictures and other media. It emphasizes the United States and England. Works are arranged chronologically by year of publication with an author index and detailed subject index. Though unannotated, there is no other bibliography as comprehensive on this often unexplored topic. Recommended for large religious collections. *Religion; Church and State Relations*

A

1521. **The Contemporary Islamic Revival: A Critical Survey and Bibliography**, by Yvonne Yazbeck Haddadd and others. Greenwood, 1991. 230p. $45. 0-313-24719-6.

The emergence of a strong Islamic fundamentalist movement is being felt around the world. This bibliography covers this revival in 1,225 entries to books, articles, and dissertations published in English between 1970 and 1988. The bibliography is divided into a section that covers general works and such topics as economics and women, and one which is arranged by geographical areas. Specific countries in the Middle East are listed, as are Africa, Asia, Europe and the Americas. About one third of the entries are annotated and there are author, title, and subject indexes. This bibliography will be of value in academic libraries and public libraries that serve a large Islamic population or support collections on programs dealing with Islamic studies. *Islam*

A

1522. **A Critical Bibliography of Writings in Judaism: Parts 1 and 2**, by David B. Griffiths. E. Mellen, 1989. 2 volumes. 804p. $99.95. 0-88946-254-2.

This extensive bibliography on all aspects of Jews and Judaism includes books, articles, and entries from major encyclopedias arranged in two volumes under topics that are arranged in rough chronological order. Volume one lists general resources (e.g., reference works) and covers the ancient and medieval periods. Volume two deals with modern times. Most items are annotated, and there are frequent cross-references and an extensive table of contents but no general index. For large collections. *Jews; Judaism*

A

1523. **Critical Guide to Catholic Reference Books**, by James P. McCabe. 3rd ed. Libraries Unlimited, 1989, 323p. $47. 0-87287-621-7.

Now in its third edition, this has become the standard bibliography in its field. Its lists and annotates critically, 1,500 books in five main sections: general works, theology, the humanities, the social sciences, and history. The annotations are comprehensive and often contain quotes from reviews. The majority of entries are for English language publications, but there are several in other European languages. There are also extensive indexes in the work. It will have use in specialized collections and large public libraries.
Catholics; Reference Books

A

1524. The Divine Guide: A Comprehensive Guide to the Sacred Texts and Spiritual Literature of the World, by Rufus C. Camphausen. Inner Traditions, 1992. 182p. $10.95 pap. 0-89281-351-2.

This international bibliography lists over 120 important works on world religion from both the past and present. Available editions are listed, and annotations explain the importance of the work. There is also a glossary and index. This work will be of use in building collections needing a strong component of books in religion and philosophy. *Religious Literature*

A

1525. Goddesses and Wise Women: The Literature of Feminist Spirituality, 1980-1991; An Annotated Bibliography, by Anne Carson. Crossing Press, 1992. 200p. $39.95 0-89594-536-3.

The annotations in this listing of books and articles are summaries of the contents. The material garnered from nineteen year of publishing is arranged by such topics as "The Goddess through Space and Time," "Witchcraft," "Christianity and Judaism," "Audio Visual Materials," and "Bibliographies." Useful in large collection for both reference and selecting materials. *Women; Feminism*

A

1526. Index Islamicus, 1981-1985: A Bibliography of Books and Articles on the Muslim World, Ed. by G. J. Roper. Mansell, 1991. 2v. 1,347p. $295. 0-7201-2009-8.

This, the sixth supplement to the established bibliography in European languages of published materials on Islam, contains over 34,000 entries arranged by a classified subject system. There is an extensive name index that includes authors, translators, and persons who are subjects. This is an important research tool for academic libraries and those public libraries who have a special need. *Islam*

A

1527. International Meditation Bibliography, 1950-1982, by Howard R. Jarrell. Scarecrow, 1985. 444p. $35. 0-8108-1759-4. (American Theological Library Association Bibliography Series, 12).

This annotated bibliography includes 2,200 entries for books, theses. periodical articles, motion pictures and recordings all dealing with various aspects of meditation. The body of the work is by form and then by author; therefore, the use of the subject index will be necessary to locate material on a particular aspect of the topic. This will be a useful reference work where there is an interest in such types as Christian, Zen, Yoga and transcendental meditation. *Meditation*

A

1528. Jewish-Christian Relations: An Annotated Bibliography and Resources Guide, by Michael Shermis. Indiana University Press, 1988. 291p. 0-253-33153-6.

This extensive bibliography on relations between Christians and Jews is divided into several different sections. The major one, which is further subdivided into various historical and topical subjects such as intermarriage and the Vatican Council II, contains an annotated listing of about 600 important books and pamphlets on these subjects. There follows a similarly annotated list of 25 key periodical articles on Jewish-Christian relations, followed by a larger unannotated supplementary list also of articles. In the concluding sections, there is a great deal of supplementary material: one section lists important journals and others cover conferences, nonprint media, college syllabi, organizations, and speakers. This bibliography will have a place in academic libraries and in public libraries where the community has an interest in this subject. *Jewish-Christian Relations*

A

1529. Judaism and Christianity: A Guide to the Reference Literature, by Edward D. Starkey. Libraries Unlimited, 1991. 256p. $42. 0-87287-533-4.

This is an annotated bibliography of approximately 800 English language titles published between 1970 and 1989 (and a few older important works) that deal with Judaism and Christianity. The first of two parts treats the reference literature and includes encyclopedias, dictionaries, handbooks, statistical sources, directories, biographical sources, and atlases. The second covers biblical studies and lists reference works and concordances. There are also special chapters on journals, organizations, research institutes and electronic databases. The annotations are descriptive and critical. This scholarly work will be useful in large public libraries. *Judaism; Christianity; Bible*

A

1530. **Literary-Critical Approaches to the Bible: An Annotated Bibliography**, by Mark Minor. Locust Hill Pr., 1992. 520p. $50. 0-933951-48-5.

The purpose of this work is to "help critics of all persuasions understand how the relationship between biblical and literary studies has developed. Non-English language works, book reviews, and dissertations are excluded. The entries contain helpful critical and descriptive annotations arranged according to the books of the Bible. There are also special sections on biblical narratives, poetry, and parables. A complete author index is included, but the lack of a subject index (although there are many cross-references) is an important shortcoming. Still, the work is recommended for academic and public libraries interested in either literary criticism especially as it relates to biblical texts.

Bible—Criticism; Bible as Literature; Religious Literature

A

1531. **Religion and American Life: Resources**, Ed. by Anne T. Fraker. Univ. of Illinois Press, 1989. *MSU* 236p. $24.95. 0-252-01588-6.

The focus of this reference book is the interaction between American culture and religion. The annotated bibliography of 116 books and 121 journal articles grew out of a two-year series of symposia held on the topic. The work is divided by format, and entries are arranged in alphabetical order by author. The titles chosen for inclusion were selected and evaluated by authorities including several clerics and academicians in the fields of history, literature, and religious studies. Full bibliographic citations are provided as well as author and title indexes. The main drawback is the lack of a subject index which would have made this much more useful as a reference tool and as an aid in collection development. Still, this well-done resource guide is recommended for all academic, religious, and public libraries.

Religion; United States—Religion

A

1532. **Religious Colleges and Universities in America: A Selected Bibliography**, by Thomas C. Hunt *eC* and James C. Carper. Garland, 1988. 374p. $62. 0-8240-6648-0. (Garland Reference Library of Social Science, 422).

About 2,300 entries make up this extensive bibliography on "private colleges and universities that are, or have been, religiously affiliated." After the opening chapters on general works and background information on religious colleges, the major part of this work is the 25 chapters organized by denomination. There are some inconsistencies in format due, perhaps, to the fact that 35 contributors combined their effort in the project. For example, some chapters have introductory essays and annotated entries, others have neither; some are arranged alphabetically by school name, others by authors of entries. Nevertheless, these problems are minor, especially since author and subject indexes tie it all together. This bibliography will be an important asset to public libraries, academic libraries generally, and more specifically to all religious colleges. *Colleges and Universities; Religion; United States—Religion*

A

1533. **Religious Information Sources: A Worldwide Guide**, by J. Gordon Melton and Michael A. *CC* Koszegi. Garland, 1992. 569p. $75. 0-8153-0859-0.

The stated purpose of this rather extensive guide is "to provide in one volume broad coverage of the major sources of information in religion." Further, it is intended to serve anyone interested in religion, from the beginning student of the discipline to the scholar. Over 2,5400 entries are included in this guide which is organized into four main sections geographically. Though worldwide in scope, North American and Christianity receive the greatest emphasis, and most of the items are in English. Microform and electronic materials, in addition to print materials, are included. Unfortunately, most of the entries are not annotated. Author, title, subject, and organization indexes complete the volume and do aid in accessing materials. The scope and size of the work make it a useful addition to most academic, public and other libraries having special collections in religion. *Religious Literature*

A

1534. **Women in American Religious History: An Annotated Bibliography and Guide to Sources**, by *CC* Dorothy C. Bass and Sandra Hughes Boyd. G. K. Hall, 1986. 205p. $35. 0-8161-8151-9. (Reference Publication in Women's Studies).

Bass and Boyd, two scholars on the topics of church history and women's studies, have used their research skills to connect the two areas and produce this much-needed work. It is of interest to a wide audience as "it embraces social, economic, political, and regional issues as well as denominational, doctrinal, and devotional themes." The first chapter identifies general works in American religious history and American women's history. The succeeding chapters include more specific sources on the history of women in particular religious traditions: Protestantism; Roman-Catholicism; Judaism, etc. Two-thirds of the book deals with the various denominations of Protestantism and Roman Catholicism—newer religious movements or cults are not covered. Over 550 annotated secondary sources are included (many primary sources are mentioned at the end of each chapter). The table of contents serves as a detailed outline, as well; there is also an index of proper names including authors, editors, and historical figures mentioned in the text. This work is recommended as a scholarly addition to any library with collections in American history, religious history, or women's studies. *Religion; United States—Religion; Women in Religion*

15 Science and Technology

General and Miscellaneous

Y; A

1535.   **AAAS Science Book List 1978-1986: A Selected and Annotated List of Science and Mathematics Books**, Ed. by Kathryn Wolff et al. American Association for the Advancement of Science, 1986, 568p. $25. 0-87168-315-6.

Though somewhat dated (it includes titles published in all fields of science from 1978 through 1986), this list is still useful for building an in-depth, retrospective collection particularly one focusing on historical and background information in the sciences. Intended for junior and senior high school, under-graduate college, and public libraries. Librarians must proceed with caution if this aid is used for selection purposes, especially in such fields as computer science and life sciences, e.g., genetics, etc. It should be used in conjunction with the science sections of such aids as *Senior High School* and *Junior High School Catalog*, as well as those in current reviewing journals. While there is a need to have this important list updated, it remains the most comprehensive guide in the field and is therefore recommended. *Science; Mathematics*

A

1536.   **Abstracts and Indexes in Science and Technology: A Descriptive Guide**, By Dolores B. Owen. 2nd ed. Scarecrow, 1985. 235p. $22.50. 0-8108-1712-8.

Owen indicates in the introduction that "the purpose ... is to provide a description of the materials one would encounter in conducting a literature search in science and technology." This is not a definitive bibliography, about 250 titles are indexed. Each entry includes arrangement, coverage, abstract, type of index, and other important user information. Titles are arranged by broad topics, e.g., General Science, Chemistry, Mathematics, etc. Although, this work is quite old for the field of science, it may still be useful for retrieving background data. *Abstracts; Science; Technology*

A

1537.   **Bibliography of Bioethics**. v. 16, Ed. by LeRoy Walters and Tamar Joy Kahn. Kennedy Institute of Ethics, 1990. 600p. $45. 0-9614448-6-X.

Bioethics, a field of study concerned with the ethics and philosophical implications of certain biological and medical procedures, treatments, etc., is currently a high interest topic at all levels in our society. This annual bibliography has been issued since 1975 by the Kennedy Institute of Ethics of Georgetown University. The current volume has over 2,500 English-language books, articles, legal and government reports, and AV items. Among the many topics included are such bioethical questions as abortion, AIDS, euthanasia, in vitro fertilization, organ transplantation, and surrogate motherhood. Access is through an author/title index and a thesaurus of specific subjects. Many back volumes from v. 10 are still available. This bibliography is recommended for all health, academic, and many public libraries providing literature on ethical, legal, and public policy questions to bioethical concerns. *Bioethics; Ethics; Medical Ethics*

A

1538.   **Core List of Books and Journals in Science and Technology**, by Russell H. Powell and James R. Powell. Oryx, 1987. 134p. $38.50. 0-89774-275-3.

This core list consists of annotated entries for 760 books, published from 1980 through 1986, and 780 unannotated entries for periodicals in all the fields of science and technology. The arrangement is by 10 subject areas like agriculture, astronomy, mathematics, and engineering. There is also a reference section listing 43 basic reference books. This judiciously chosen bibliography of scholarly materials is not for the layman. Unfortunately, it is beginning to show its age. There are author, title, and subject indexes. Recommended for large public and academic libraries. *Science; Technology*

A

1539. **Directory of Technical and Scientific Directories**, by A. P. Harvey. 6th ed. Oryx, 1990. 410p. $125. 0-89774-637-6.

This is an international listing of nearly 1,500 directories involving the disciplines of science and technology. Edited in England, this work will be of value in large academic collections and special libraries dealing with these subjects. *Science; Technology*

Y; A

1540. **History of Science**, by Gordon L. Miller. Salem Press, 1992. 193p. $40. 0-89356-675-6.

Miller has compiled a bibliography of about 500 works dealing with the history of science. The focus is on Western science; however, important works from other cultures are included. All branches of science are represented. Each entry contains a descriptive annotation, and though the author indicates that the works range in level from high school to the scholarly, the annotations do not indicate level. An author index completes the work. Although the works are arranged under broad subject area, a specific subject area would foster an ease in use. The work is recommended for all libraries. *Science—History*

A*

1541. **Information Sources in Science and Technology**, by C. D. Hurt. 3rd ed. Libraries Unlimited, 1994. 412p. $55 (cloth); $32 (pap.). 1-56308-034-6 (cloth); 1-56308-180-6 (pap.). (Library Science Text Series).

This text, formerly edited by Malinowsky, begins with a chapter that defines science and technology and their areas of study. The body of the work is a series of chapters on such areas as astronomy, general biology, botany and agriculture, chemistry, geosciences, physics, mathematics, zoology, energy and environment, biomedical sciences, and various types of engineering. In each chapter there is a subdivision by specialized areas, plus a listing of informational sources by type. Each is critically annotated, and there is an emphasis on in-print titles and online and software sources. A total of over 2,000 reference sources are included. There are author/title and subject indexes. This valuable literature guide should be found in all academic as well as medium and large public libraries. *Science; Technology*

C; Y; A

1542. **Integrating Aerospace Science into the Curriculum: K-12**, by Robert D. Ray and Joan Klingel Ray. Teacher Ideas Press, 1992. 191p. $15.95. 0-87287-924-0.

This is a book of ideas, activities, and projects that teachers could use to teach aerospace science to students in all public school grades. Of particular value to librarians are the many bibliographies and resource listings that follow groups of activities. The materials are current, recommended for inclusion in school and library collections, and therefore of value in collection development.

Children's Literature; Young Adult Literature; Science; Aerospace Science

Y; A

1543. **Prominent Scientists: An Index to Collective Biographies**, Ed. by Paul A. Pelletier. 3rd ed. Neal-Schuman, 1992. 400p. $49.95. 1-55570-140-0.

More than 12,000 leaders in the field of science are included in this index to 262 collective biographies and other works that include biographical information. All of the works are published in English from 1960-1983. Current men and women, as well as historical figures, are included. The work is divided into two major parts: an alphabetical list of scientists by surname, and a second section which lists the scientists by more than 100 scientific fields. The list of sources in the front of the volume includes complete bibliographic information. This excellent index is recommended for most secondary school and public libraries. *Scientists*

A*

1544. **Science and Technology (year): A Purchase Guide for Branch and Public Libraries**. Carnegie Library of Pittsburgh (annual), 70p. $7. (pap.).

This annual annotated listing of outstanding new books in science and technology first appeared in 1960. At present, it consists of approximately 1,000 titles chosen both for their content and their suitability for the adult general reader. A few reference books and textbooks are included. Books are arranged by subjects according to the Library of Congress classification. Annotations are brief but informative. Of particular interest to smaller libraries is a coding system that indicates books for libraries only purchasing 50 books and for those purchasing 100. Author and series indexes are included. This is a practical list that emphasizes topics of current interest and importance. *Library Journal* also has an annual list of the 101 "Best Sci-Tech Books" of the year in the March 1 issue. *Science; Technology*

A

1545. **Science and Technology Annual Reference Review, 1991,** by H. Robert Malinowsky. Oryx, 1991. 376p. $74.50 0-89774-608-2.

This annual collection-development tool, which began with the 1989 volume, is a survey of the year's reference literature in the fields of science and technology. It includes handbooks, texts, manuals, dictionaries, encyclopedias, abstracts, and other reference materials. There are also 800 titles in the current edition arranged by disciplines like agriculture, astronomy, chemistry, computer science, and mathematics. Each is given a lengthy review written by a subject expert. There are four indexes, by title, author, subject, and type of library. The latter indicates suitability for academic, public, high school, and special libraries. The price of this useful bibliography, however, might limit its purchase to larger libraries. Both the 1990 and 1989 editions are also currently available. *Science; Technology*

C; Y; A

1546. **Science Education,** by Eileen E. Schroder. Oryx, 1986. 103p. pap. $18.75. 0-89774-227-3. (Oryx Science Bibliographies, 6).

This annotated bibliography of references about science education in elementary and secondary schools consists of some books but chiefly periodical articles published from 1980 through 1985. There are separate chapters on various educational levels, teacher education, special populations, different subject disciplines, and other related topics. The annotations are not critical, but key articles are indicated. There is an author index. An updating would be welcome. *Science—Study and Teaching*

C; Y; A

1547. **Science for Children: Resources for Teachers,** by the National Science Resources Center, Smithsonian Institution. National Academy Press, 1988. 176p. $9.95 pap. 0-309-03934-7.

This is a guide to educational resources in the teaching of science to children in kindergarten through eighth grade. The first of the three sections in this helpful work contains a list of 300 published lesson plans, activity guides, and instructional materials. The second section is an annotated bibliography of activity books, books on science teaching, and science magazines for teachers and students, and the third gives directory information on museums, associations, and publishers. The work does not list textbooks, audiovisual materials, software or trade books but it is an excellent tool for building collections of curriculum materials for science teaching. *Science—Study and Teaching*

A

1548. **Science Tracer Bullets: A Reference Guide to Scientific, Technological, Health, and Environmental Information Sources,** 4 vols. ed. by Helene Henderson. Omnigraphics, 1990. 1,687p. $192. 1-55888-925-6.

In these four volumes, there are reprints of 173 bibliographies prepared by the Library of Congress Science and Technology Division between 1973 and 1989. Each of the four volumes deals with large subjects. They are "Earth and Natural Sciences," "High Technology," "Medical and Biological Sciences," and "Socio-Political Aspects of Science and Technology." There is a short subject index. The lists contain government documents as well as trade books, journal articles, and foreign government documents. Most of these individual bibliographies are available from the Library of Congress free of charge.
Science; Technology; Health; Environment

A

1549. **Scientific and Technical Information Sources,** by Ching-chih Chen. 2nd ed. MIT Press, 1987. 824p. $55. 0-262-03120-5.

This excellent guide to the literature of science and technology now contains brief annotations for 5,300 works most of which were published between 1980 and February 1986, although a few date back to 1976. The work is divided by type, that is, there are separate chapters under such formats as encyclopedias, dictionaries, indexes, reviews of the literature, government documents, proceedings, patents and standards, trade literature, nonprint materials, society publications and databases. Within these chapters there are subdivisions by scientific disciplines. This arrangement is helpful for acquisition purposes but somewhat difficult for researchers interested in a particular discipline. A detailed table of contents and author and title indexes, however, help in accessing material. For many of the materials, reviews are cited in a wide variety of science and nonscience sources. This is recommended for academic plus medium and large public libraries. *Science; Technology; Engineering*

C; A

1550. **Teaching Science to Children**, by Mary D. Iatridis. 2nd ed. Garland, 1993. 199p. $30. 0-8153-0090-5. (Garland Reference Library of Social Science, 747).

The purpose of this bibliography is to provide all those involved with the teaching of science to children from preschool through grade three with the awareness and access of current theories, strategies, and instructional materials. Each chapter of this annotated bibliography has an introductory essay, followed by a list of materials or a bibliography of resources. The areas covered by the various chapters include: Chapter 1, a review of science textbooks; Chapter 2, a rundown on science activities with books which help children learn scientific principles; Chapter 3, a bibliography of titles included in a section "Science Books for Children;" and Chapter 4, a brief discussion of science education for the special child with a list of recommended titles. Because of the importance of the topic and the dearth of similar guides, this work is recommended for all libraries that serve those involved with the teaching of science for children.

Science; Science—Study and Teaching

A

1551. **Women in Science: Antiquity Through the Nineteenth Century: A Biographical Dictionary with Annotated Bibliography**, by Marilyn Bailey Ogilvie. MIT Press, 1990. 272p. $13.50 Pap. 0-262-65038-X.

This bio-bibliography includes 186 women scientists born before 1885; it is international in scope, but more Americans than European are included. Ogilvie provides both biographical information and bibliographic sources for further study. An extensive historical overview which includes an annotated bibliography precedes the biographical sketches. Each biographical entry contains detailed information relating to birth, nationality, branch of science, education, professional positions, etc. At the end of each sketch is a list of works by the subject as well as a list of items in the bibliography that will provide further information on the biography. This bio-bibliographic reference source is recommended for academic and public libraries that support science and women's studies collections. *Scientists; Women in Science*

Astronomy, Aeronautics, and Space Exploration

Y; A

1552. **Air and Space Catalog: The Complete Sourcebook to Everything in the Universe**, by Joel Makower. Vintage/Random, 1990. 336p. $16.95. pap. 0-679-72038-3.

As the subtitle indicates, this unique publication deals with astronomy, aviation, weather, space flight, planetariums, etc. It lists many sources for purchasing telescopes, weather equipment, model airplanes, and more directly related to the purposes of this guide, many books and AV materials on the subject. This interesting and inexpensive catalog is recommended for most public and high school libraries.

Astronomy; Space Exploration; Aeronautics

A

1553. **Air and Space History: An Annotated Bibliography**, by Dominick A. Pisano and Cathleen S. Lewis. Garland, 1988. 571p. $75. 0-8240-8543-4. (Garland Reference Library of the Humanities, Vol. 834).

With the cooperation of the National Air and Space Museum, the compilers of this bibliography have produced this annotated bibliography of about 2,000 important books that deal with the historic aspects of aeronautics and space science. The book is divided into three parts. The first lists general sources on air and space involving bibliographies, general works, research sources, issues, and biographies. The second covers such areas related to aircraft as engineering, military aircraft, meteorology, navigation, balloons and helicopters; and the third deals with topics related to space such as early rockets, missiles, launch sites, applications of space explorations, and manned programs. The annotations are full and there is an author index. This impressive work will be used in science collections in public and academic libraries.

Aeronautics; Space Exploration

A

1554. **The Airline Bibliography: The Salem College Guide: The Salem College Guide to Sources on Commercial Aviation. v. 1: The United States**, by Myron J. Smith. Locust Hill Press, 1986. 238p. $45. 0-933951-00-0.

A comprehensive bibliography on commercial aviation in the United States from its inception through 1985. Its intended audience is for the scholar as well as the aviation buff. There are four sections to the bibliography which contains over 6,000 entries: reference sources, historical, economic and operational aspects, and information on specific airlines; each section is further subdivided. Author and title indexes are included. This unique and specialized bibliography is recommended for all public libraries having a need for such a specialized collection. *Aeronautics, Commercial; Airlines*

A

1555. America in Space: An Annotated Bibliography, by Russell R. Tobias. Salem Press, 1991. 327p. $40. pap. 0-89356-69-1.

More than 30 years of America's space program are covered in this well-developed bibliography. The entries are arranged under very broad topics, such as Propulsion, Manned Spacecraft, etc. Each entry includes a well-written annotation and adequate bibliographic data for retrieval and ordering. The titles included will be of interest to both the specialist and general reader. Recommended for most academic and public libraries. *Space Exploration*

A

1556. Astronomer's Sourcebook: The Complete Guide to Astronomical Equipment, Publications, Planets, Planetarium, Organizations, Events, and More, by Bob Gibson. Woodbine House, 1992. 302p. $19.95. 0-933149-43-3.

The author, an amateur astronomer and writer, has compiled a comprehensive guide to all sorts of information on astronomy suitable for the beginning stargazer as well as the more sophisticated. The 19 chapters lists organizations, written guides, planetariums, etc. Of particular usefulness to library collection development are the lists of publications. The indexing is very complete. This inexpensive and popularly-oriented directory should prove useful as a reference tool and selection aid for most public and undergraduate academic libraries. *Astronomy*

Y; A

1557. Astronomy and Astronautics: An Enthusiast's Guide to Books and Periodicals, by Andy Lusis. Facts on File, 1986. 292p. $35. 0-8160-1469-8.

Lusis has compiled for us an exciting list of almost 1,000 titles of books (some periodical titles but not articles) on astronomy and related areas. All works were published between 1976 and 1986 and "are intended for a wide-ranging level of readership, from complete beginners to professionals...." The bibliography is organized under broad categories, e.g., general astronomy, history, solar system, astronautics, etc. Entries are arranged by author under each subdivision and include full bibliographic data and well-written evaluative annotations which give references to similar titles, published reviews, intended reader-ship, and a brief summaries of the books. Also provided are rather complete author, title and subject indexes. The price is right; therefore, this book is highly recommended for all libraries—academic, public, and secondary school. *Astronomy; Astronautics*

Y; A

1558. A Basic Astronomy Library. Astronomical Society of the Pacific, [1990]. $3.

A brief pamphlet listing, with descriptive notes, the best astronomy books published during the last decade (1980's) is available from: Astronomical Society of the Pacific, Book List Department, 390 Ashton Avenue, San Francisco, CA 94112. *Astronomy*

Y; A

1559. Black Holes: An Annotated Bibliography, 1975-1983, by Steven I. Danko. Scarecrow, 1985. 282p. $27.50. 0-8108-1836-1.

There is perhaps no more fascinating a subject than Black Holes. Danko has identified almost 1,900 English-language citations published between 1975-1983, ranging from the very popular to the technical. The work is divided into eight sections including books, popular journal articles, technical journal articles, government documents, nonprint media, etc. Each entry has complete bibliographic data and a brief annotation. Author and title indexes are provided. This bibliography, which pulls together many sources including online databases, is recommended for high school, public and academic libraries. *Black Holes*

Y; A

1560. **Space Exploration: A Reference Handbook**, by Mrinal Bali. ABC-Clio, 1990. 240p. $39.50. 0-87436-578-3. (Contemporary World Issues Series).

This is similar in content and arrangement to other reference books in this fine series. After an introductory essay by former astronaut Harrison H. Schmitt, there is a historic overview of space exploration with a chronology of events followed by brief biographies of key contributors to space exploration and tables on various kinds of space activities. The annotated bibliography lists key books, periodicals, films, videos, and sources of electronic information related to this topic. There is also an international directory of organizations and agencies engaged in various space exploration activities that are also potential sources of information. This source of quick information and basic bibliographies can be useful in high schools and undergraduate collections plus public libraries. *Space Exploration*

A

1561. **UFOs and the Extraterrestrial Contact Movement: A Bibliography**, by George M. Eberhart. Scarecrow, 1986. 2v. 1298p. $97.50. 0-8108-1919-8.

This exhaustive guide contains over 15,000 citations on all aspects of the fascinating subject of unidentified flying objects and related topics of extraterrestrial intelligence. Eberhart attempts to be very comprehensive by citing references that deal with the subject from ancient times to the present, in foreign languages, as well as in English, in nonfiction and fiction, motion pictures, television, government documents, etc. Each of these sections has a brief introduction, followed by an unannotated listing of books, articles, etc. Name, periodical, and organization indexes keyed to the numbered items are provided. Also included are recommendations for a core collection. The strength of this work, however, is the large number of citations. Larger libraries and those serving students and other ufology buffs may want to consider this definitive bibliography in the field. *Extraterrestrial Beings; Unidentified Flying Objects*

Biological Sciences

A

1562. **Birds: A Guide to the Literature**, by Melanie Ann Miller. Garland, 1986. 887p. $86. 0-8240-8710-0.

Miller, an ornithologist and librarian, has compiled a very comprehensive annotated bibliography of almost 2,000 books on birds published from 1800-1984. Her stated criterion for inclusion was simply that the book be "readily accessible in libraries...and appear with regularity in bird bibliographies."

All of the titles are in English, though many are international in scope. Entries are divided into eight broad headings and then further divided into almost 20 subdividions. Subjects include reference, artists and illustrators, bird classification, migration, field guides, children's literature, and biography and fiction. Annotations range from one sentence to almost a quarter of a page. An author, illustrator, and title index complete this ambitious project. This work is recommended for all academic and public libraries that have special collections in this area or budgets large enough to afford it. *Birds*

A

1563. **The Gardener's Book of Sources**, by William Bryant Logan. Viking Penguin, 1988. 271p. $12.95 (pap.). 0-14-046761-0.

This source book on gardening lists, in addition to key books, catalogs and magazines, the names of companies, nurseries, clubs, and individuals that can supply resources and services to help even the most specialized of gardeners. Entries are organized under suppliers' names with addresses and detailed information on services and products given under each entry. Prices are also given, but, in many cases, these will now be out of date. This work will be useful for reference and collection building in public libraries where gardening is a hot topic. *Gardening*

A

1564. **The Gardener's Reading Guide**, by Jan Dean. Facts on File, 1993. $23.95. 0-8160-2754-4.

Most of the 2,300 books on gardening included in this volume were published from the late 1970s on (with the exception of a few "classics" in the field). They are arranged in six chapters by subjects: "The Personal Side of Gardening" (narratives and books of essays), "How-to Gardening," "Specific Gardening Methods" (e.g., oriental, topiary), "Special Types of Gardens," "Regional Gardening," and "Miscellaneous Gardening Topics" (e.g., gardening for children or the elderly). For each entry, there is bibliographic information and a brief annotation. Author and subject indexes conclude the work. This is a fine reference and selection guide for public libraries. *Gardening*

A

1565. Guide to Information Sources in the Botanical Sciences, by Elizabeth B. Davis. Libraries Unlimited, 1987. 175p. $35. 0-87287-439-7. (Reference Sources in Science and Technology).

Excluding agriculture, horticulture, and gardening, this is an excellent guide to botanical literature. The approximately 600 publications are well organized into three major sections with appropriate subdivisions. The main headings "Bibliographic Control," "Ready Reference Sources," and "Additional Sources of Information," cover such materials as guides to the literature, indexes, abstracts, databases, dictionaries, encyclopedias, handbooks, histories, major textbooks, and important monographs. All entries are annotated. A list of key publishers and a title index are appended. This guide can serve as both a guide for students interested in the field, as well as a selection aid for collection building. *Botany*

A

1566. The History of Biology: A Selected Annotated Bibliography, by Judith A. Overmier. Garland, 1989. 157p. $20. 0-8240-9118-3. (Garland Reference Library of the Humanities, 419; Bibliographies of the History of Science and Technology, 15).

This highly selective bibliography of 619 entries covers publications on the history of biology from the 1800s through the 1950s. Books, chapters from books, and journal articles are included and arranged in 36 subject areas such as anatomy, evolution, and taxonomy. Each entry is annotated, and there are subject and author indexes. For large collections. *Biology*

A

1567. Index to Illustrations of Animals and Plants, by Beth Clewis. Neal-Schuman, 1991. 217p. $49.50. 1-55570-072-1.

This volume indexes the pictures found in 142 works (some multivolumed) that contain extensive pictures of plants and animals and have been published recently. An introduction explains how to use the volume. This is followed by the body of the work, an alphabetical listing of plants and animals (common names are used with scientific names in parenthesis) with citations to works where pictures can be found. There are many indexes, but acquisition librarians will be most interested in the nine page appendix which lists the books that have been indexed. A more comprehensive work is the multivolume, *Illustration Index*, which is available from Scarecrow Press (e.g., *Vol. VI, 1982-1986*, Scarecrow, 1988, $42.50, 0-8108-2146-X), but the present volume is still recommended for use in both public and academic libraries.

Illustrations; Plants; Animals

A

1568. Information Sources in the Life Sciences, by H. V. Wyatt. 4th ed. Saur, 1992. 250p. $65.

Using subject subdivisions such as biochemistry, microbiology, biotechnology, genetics, zoology, ecology, and botany, this is a guide to important resources, organized under types of material such as handbooks, dictionaries, and basic periodicals. There are also chapters on online searching, databanks, and the history of biology. In spite of its British bias and steep price, this is useful in large collections for collection development purposes. *Biology; Life Sciences*

A

1569. Keyguide to Information Sources in Animal Rights, by Charles Magel. McFarland, 1989. 267p. $39.95 (pap.) 0-89950-405-1.

This extensive, highly regarded bibliography on animal rights consists of several parts. The first is a collection of six bibliographic essays on animals rights issues like philosophy and animals, science and animals, education and animals, and religion and animals. Books, articles, databases, works for children, some fiction, and organizations are cited. Citations for the approximately 1,000 items listed in these essays, are given in a separate "Literature Cited" section. Section two is a chronological list of 355 major works on the subject from Ovid to the 1980s. It includes prose, poetry, films, position papers, and juveniles. Each is extensively annotated. Almost 200 U.S. and foreign rights groups are listed in another separate section. The book ends with appendixes that include material on audiovisual sources and periodicals, plus a detailed index by author, title, and subject. This work will be of value in medium and larger public libraries plus selected secondary schools. *Animal Abuse*

A

1570.   **Keyguide to Information Sources in Aquaculture**, by Deborah A. Turnbull. Mansell, 1989. 137p. $55. 0-7201-1853-0. (Keyguide to Information Series).

This bibliography on a variety of informational sources on aquaculture follows the standard pattern of organization used in other volumes of the Keyguide series. It consists of three parts. The first surveys the topic and gives an historical overview plus a general introduction to the types of information available on aquaculture. Part two is the actual bibliography divided by types of sources, such as encyclopedias, periodicals, and visuals. Databases, annuals, and newsletters are also included. Both British and American sources are included. The third part is a listing of important national, regional, and international organizations. The index is by author, title and subject. For large libraries. *Aquaculture*

A

1571.   **The Literature of the Life Sciences: Reading, Writing, Research**, by David A. Kronick. ISI Press, 1985. 219p. $29.95. 0-89495-045-2. (Library and Information Science, 1).

This interesting work is both a bibliography and a useful library guide. It provides a basic outline of the history and development of scientific literature in the life sciences. Many aspects of the literature are dealt with—primary sources, indexes, online searching, etc. Despite the fact that there is a need for an update, this guide is still useful and recommended for most academic and public libraries. *Life Sciences*

A

1572.   **The Origin and Evolution of Life on Earth: An Annotated Bibliography**, by David W. Hollar. Salem Press, 1992. 235p. $40. 0-89356-683-7.

Hollar has provided us with a comprehensive bibliography of over 800 books on evolution, from the 1800's to the present time. All of the entries contain full bibliographic data, as well as rather lengthy descriptive annotations. A detailed table of contents facilitates subject access, and an author index is also provided. The work is intended for the general reader, as well as students of the subject and is therefore recommended for academic, public, and secondary school libraries. *Evolution*

Computer Sciences

General and Miscellaneous

A

1573.   **Computer Catalogs**, by Barry Klein. Todd, 1992. 114p. $12.95 pap. 0-915344-27-0.

This work lists alphabetically 300 mail-order computer companies that sell hardware, software, furniture, accessories, and supplies. Information in each entry includes company name, address, credit cards accepted, telephone and fax numbers, and products available. Most of the companies are in the United States, though some Canadian companies are also included. There is an index by company name and one divided into such subjects as software, furniture, and programming. This useful guide will be consulted both by patrons and librarians in reference collections in public libraries. *Computers; Computer Software*

A

1574.   **Computer Publishers and Publications 1991-92**, Ed. by Efrem Sigel and Frederica Evan. 4th ed. Gale, 1992. $205 (including supplements). 0-8103-8407-8.

The two largest sections of this directory list publishers of materials on computers and the periodicals in the field. For each of the publisher entries, information includes full name, address, phone number, contact person and key personnel, year founded, brief description of the company, and details concerning the books and periodical published. Standard directory information is given for each of the periodicals plus advertising rates. Coverage includes the U.S., U.K., Canada, Australia, and other English speaking countries. There are numerous indexes, for example, the publishers section is indexed by type of market (consumer, professional, etc.), type of machines covered, and geographic location of the firm. There is also a title and author index to books cited. Similarly, the periodical section has indexes by type of market, machines covered, geographic location, and frequency of publication. The final master index lists all periodicals, publishers, and parent companies. This exhaustive directory will be of value in large public and academic libraries. *Computers; Periodicals; Publishers and Publishing*

A

1575.   **The Computer Resource Guide**, by Charles E. LaGasse. Computer Insights (Concord, MA), 1991. diskette, $9.95.

This is a highly selective 100-item guide from over 90 companies including books, organizations, magazines, newsletters, and important events involving computers listed under 40 subject headings. Under these, there are subdivisions by such formats as bibliographies, books, buyer's guides, newsletters, and magazines. Each resource has a descriptive annotation. This electronic book is available in a diskette version for use in IBM PCs and compatibles. The price is $9.95 plus $1.55 postage and is available from: Computer Insights, 2090 Main Street, Concord, MA 01742-3805. Some high schools and public libraries might find this list and its companion, *The Directory of Free Computer Publications*, of value.   *Computers*

A

1576.   **Computers and Computing Information Resources Directory**, by Martin Connors. 2nd ed. Gale, 1993. 1,300p. $195 0-8103-2743-0.

This is a conglomerate of information about computers. There is a massive amount of information on trade and professional associations, user groups, trade shows, consultants and consulting organizations, research organizations, university computer facilities, special libraries and information centers, online services, and association conventions. For collection building, there are also about 1,500 print sources listed in these journals, newsletters, abstracting and indexing services and directories. There are many indexes, including those by title and keyword. For use in large collections.   *Computers*

A

1577.   **Computing Information Directory**, Ed. by Darlene Myers Hildebrandt. Hildebrandt, 1992. $229.95. pap. 0-933113-13-7.

This directory lists vast amounts of material about computers, the industry, and users. For collection development there are chapters on journals, dictionaries, glossaries, indexing and abstracting services, software resources, hardware resources, directories, encyclopedias and handbooks, and computer languages. There is a "Master Subject Index" and a "Master Title Index." This work is comparable in coverage to *Computers and Computing Information Resources Directory* from Gale.   *Computers*

Y; A

1578.   **Directory of Free Computer Publications**, by Charles LaGasse. Computer Insights, 1991. diskette, $9.95.

This diskette, usable on IBM PC and compatible computers, contains listings of 200 publications from over 150 companies, including books, catalogs, magazines, newsletters, and publication types covering over 60 subject areas related to computers. It is available for $9.95, plus $1.55 for postage and handling, from Computer Insights, 2090 Main Street, Concord, MA 01742. The companion diskette *The Computer Resource Guide* is available from the same publisher.   *Computers; Free Material*

A

1579.   **A Guide to the Literature of Electronic Publishing: CD-ROM, Desktop Publishing, and Electronic Mail, Books and Journals**, by Michael R. Gabriel. JAI Press, 1989. 187p. $58.50. 1-55938-044-6. (Foundations in Library and Information Science, Vol. 24).

This bibliography, though now somewhat out of date, gives an overview on the three types of electronic publishing: paper-based printing like desktop publishing and computerized typesetting, optical disk technology, and machine readable formats. The books, articles, and reports cited are arranged by author in various subject-oriented chapters, the largest of which is the one on electronic books and journals and their place in libraries. The items included were published between the 1940s through 1988. This bibliography is recommended where there is demand for material on electronic publishing.

Electronic Publishing; CD-ROM; Electronic Mail; Desktop Publishing

C; Y; A

1580.   **Interactive Fiction and Adventure Games for Microcomputers 1988: An Annotated Directory**, by Patrick R. Dewey. Meckler, 1988. 189p. $39.50 (pap.) 0-88736-170-6.

This is a detailed guide to the adventure and fiction games available for the home computer as of 1988. In addition to a listing for each game which includes grade or difficulty level, producer, cost, and hardware necessary, there is a detailed description of the contents of the game, plus an evaluation, when the author is familiar with the game. This will be useful in libraries serving players anxious to find out about various games on the market, as well as parents, educators, and librarians who might wish to choose the best and most appropriate games for patrons.   *Video Games*

A
1581. **Microsource: Where to Find Answers to Questions About Microcomputers,** by Sayre Van Young. Libraries Unlimited, 1986. 220p. $23.50. 0-87287-527-X.

Van Young provides us with a handy little guide to information about microcomputers, telecommunications, and electronic information retrieval. About 500 books, periodicals, online sources, and ephemera are described. As well, an extensive list of nonannotated references are also included. Also provided is a detailed index by author, title, and subject. Despite the date of the volume, it is still useful, but one would hope for an update in the near future. Recommended for both public and school libraries.

Microcomputers; Telecommunication

A
1582. **Modem USA: Low Cost and Free Online Services for Information, Databases, and the Electronic Bulletin Boards via Computer and Modem in 50 States,** by Lynne Motley. Allium Pr., 1992. 190p. $16.95. 0-9631233-4-3.

The cost of modems has decreased drastically and many libraries (as well as private individuals) are attaching them to their personal computers. Motley has provided us with a guide to low-cost and free online services throughout the United States. About 1,000 electronic bulletin boards and databases are listed in this book. The volume is arranged by subject and then further subdivided by state. Entries include name of database, organizations responsible for development and maintenance, connect numbers, and a brief descriptive annotation of the information included in the database. Useful for interlibrary loan purposes is are the listing of college and university library catalogs that are available through a modem. This work has a table of contents, but no index, and there is some duplication of sources. An introductory section which deals with connecting and using databases and a brief bibliography on Bulletin Boards and databases are special bonuses. This inexpensive guide is recommended for all academic and public libraries with or without modems. *Computer Bulletin Boards; Databases; Modems*

Software Programs

Y*; A*
1583. **Alfred Glossbrenner's Master Guide to Free Software for IBM and Compatible Computers,** by Alfred Glossbrenner. St. Martin's Press, 1989. 530p. $18.95. pap. 0-312-02157-7.

Glossbrenner provides us with a great deal of valuable information about public domain and low-cost shareware, down-loading software from online bulletin boards, modem software concerns, and commercial vendors. But even more exciting, he provides us with a goldmine of ideas and ways of obtaining free software for IBMs and compatibles. The author also gives us a "Core Collection for All PC Users." This inexpensive handbook/guide is a must purchase for all public and school libraries.

Computer Software; Computers; IBM Personal Computers

C, Y, A
1584. **Free (and Almost Free) Software for the Macintosh: An Illustrated and Rated Guide to over 1,000 of the Best Programs.** dilithium, 1987. 413p. $19.95 (pap.). 0-517-56585-4.

For users of Apple Macintosh computers, this is an excellent albeit somewhat dated guide, to recommended public domain and shareware programs for users at various age and interest levels (although the emphasis is on materials for adults). The items are arranged in chapters under broad subjects. For each entry, there is a lengthy description, sometimes an illustration, and an objective evaluation. Unfortunately, there are no indexes, so the reader will often have to browse to find programs on specific topics. In spite of this inconvenience, this work will be of interest and value where Macintosh computers are in use.

Computer Software; Computers

Y; A
1585. **Free and User Supported Software for the IBM PC: A Resource Guide for Libraries and Individuals,** by Victor D. Lopez and Kenneth J. Ansley. McFarland, 1990. 216p. $20.95 pap. 0-89950-499-X.

Of the thousands of public domain or shareware programs now available, the authors have chosen 61 to highlight. They are arranged by categories such as word processing, spreadsheet, database management, and games. Descriptions of each program range from one to seven pages each and include important features, illustrations of sample screens, information where they can be obtained, and a rating from poor to excellent. Recommended for libraries where there is an interest in shareware.

Computer Software; IBM Personal Computer; Free Material

A

1586. **ICP Software Directory.** 68th ed. 9 vols. ICP (Indianapolis, IN) . 1991. 2,400p $432 0-88094-218-5.

International Computer Programs is a large corporation that publishes many directories of software products mainly for the business community. The biggest, the *ICP Software Directory*, lists about 13,000 programs for mainframes, minicomputers, and microcomputers. The nine-volume set is arranged by large topics like banking and manufacturing and is updated three time per year. Recently (1990), the material relating to microcomputers has been repackaged into 15 different volumes, some organized around the type of hardware used, other by kinds of applications (e.g., office management, construction, and engineering). Again the focus is on the business community. These smaller volumes average $20 to $25 each. The large directory is also available in a CD-ROM version call *ICP's Software Information Database (SID) on CD-ROM* ($585) again updated three times a year. For very large libraries, although others may want to consult this publisher's catalog for individual titles in the 15 volume spin-off. *Computer Software*

Y; A

1587. **Macintosh Word Processing: A Guide to Software,** by William Saffady. Meckler, 1989. 155p. $29.95. 0-88736-343-1.

This handy little volume evaluates and compares the word processing programs that are commonly used with the Apple Macintosh. Among those examined are Macwrite, Microsoft Word, and WordPerfect. This guide will be useful for a number of years in the future and is recommended for all libraries that have or serve patrons that have Macintosh personal computers. *Computer Software*

C; Y; A

1588. **Micro: Educational Software Evaluations.** Florida Center for Instructional Computing (Tampa, Fla.), 1989. $25.

Most of the 200 software programs described and evaluated in this directory have been field tested in Florida schools and given written evaluations by practitioners. The programs are either administrative or instructional in nature and are useful in preschool through adult settings. Sources are disk, online, or paper in format. The programs are arranged under broad subject areas like writing or algebra, and for each, there is a one-page critique which gives information on hardware needs, length of program, contents, audience, instructional value, reliability, and minimum students performance standards. Two other sources of educational software reviews are *Only the Best* (see entry 286) and *T.E.S.S: The Educational Software Selector* (Teachers College Press, 1986, $59.95, 0-916087-00-X). The latter is edited by the EPIE (Educational Products Information Exchange) Institute and, though the main volume is now seriously dated, there is a supplement which appeared in 1988. All of these have various strengths and weaknesses, but lack of currency is a problem with all three. They are, however, still important in locating and evaluating software programs designed for schools. *Computer Software*

Y*; A*

1589. **Microcomputer Software Sources: A Guide for Buyers, Librarians, Programmers, Businesspeople and Educators,** by Carol Truett. Libraries Unlimited, 1990. 176p. $28.50. 0-87287-560-1.

Truett, an Assistant Professor of Library and Information Science, has produced a much-needed guide which lists and evaluates published aids such as "bibliographies, directories, catalogs, review services, journals with regular software review sections, etc.." Also included are sources of "shareware" and online sources of software and electronic bulletin boards. Entries include full bibliographic information and detailed descriptive and evaluative annotations. Because of the nature of the topic, it is hoped that this excellent source is updated often. This inexpensive guide is highly recommended for contemplating or developing personal computer software collections for library use or for their users. *Computer Software*

Y; A

1590. **Public Domain Software and Shareware: Untapped Resources for the PC User,** by George R. Fontine and Rusel DeMaria. 2nd. ed. M and T Publishing, 1988. 498p. $19.95 (pap.). 1-55851-011-7.

This extremely valuable, though unfortunately somewhat out of date, volume lists and reviews hundreds of electronic products including databases, graphics, utilities, and tutorials that are either in the public domain or available at a modest cost. Specific sources are identified, as well as many shareware computer bulletin boards. Although it is impossible to produce a definitive list of these often ephemeral products, this work does describe and evaluate the major ones that were available at print time. Additional sections cover such topics as basic telecommunications, and tell ways to locate and use commercial and private bulletin board services. This book will be popular with computer buffs in high school, academic, and public libraries, and, in some cases, may serve as an acquisition tool for librarians. *Computer Software*

A

1591.   **The Software Catalog: Science and Engineering**. 4th ed. Elsevier, 1987. 706p. $ 73.75. pap. 0-444-012700-2.

This bibliography describes around 4,000 science and engineering programs for micro- and minicomputers as taken from MENU, the international software database. After an introduction on how to evaluate software products, the body of the work is arranged by vendor. There are detailed descriptions of each of the software packages that include scope and content, price, and date of release. There are several indexes including one each for computer and operating systems, program languages, titles and keywords in titles, subjects, and applications. A useful tool in large academic libraries. Others in this series from Elsevier include *The Software Catalog: Business Software* (1985, $62.25 pap. 0-440-85023-6), *The Software Catalog: Systems Software* (1986, $114.25 pap. 0-440-01013-0) and *The Software Catalog: Microcomputers* (1990, 2 vols, $250 pap. 0-44001554-X).

Computer Software; Computers; Science; Engineering; Business

A*

1592.   **The Software Encyclopedia, 1992**. Bowker, 1992. 2 vols. 2191p. $209.95 0-8352-3180-1.

This annual compilation has become the software counterpart of *Books in Print*. The present volume lists and describes approximately 22,000 software programs from about 3,000 publishers and producers. Each of the two volumes contains a usage guide. The first volume on titles and publishers is in two parts. The first is an alphabetical listing of the programs. Information given under title includes scope, coverage, versions, compatible hardware, requirements, disc size, and price. The second section is a list of publishers. The second volume titled, System Compatibility/Applications, lists the programs by subjects and contains a Guide to Applications, Guide to Systems, and a System Compatibility/Applications Index. The current guide includes desktop publishing and word processing programs. Though somewhat expensive, this guide will be of importance in academic and public libraries.   *Computer Software; Computers*

C; Y; A

1593.   **Software Information! for Apple II Computers**. Black Box, 1990. 829p. $19.95 pap. 0-942821-18-1.

This is a guide to 12,000 programs that are available for the Apple II personal computer. The software is divided into eight categories: productivity, education, industries, personal, entertainment, sciences, professions, and systems (e.g., operating systems, programming languages, utilities). Within each category there are further subdivisions. Under these headings, software packages are listed alphabetically by title. For each entry information is given on such topics as publisher, system information, disk medium, RAM requirements, scope and coverage, and retail price. There are indexes by product name and software title. Fuller information on each package is given in the separately published two-volume work that is part of this publisher's professional series. It costs $59.95. This directory in available online through DIALOG and a CD-ROM version is also being prepared. There is also a companion volume available from the same publisher that lists the software programs available for IBM-PCs and compatible computers.

Computer Software; Apple Computers; Computers; IBM Personal Computers

A

1594.   **Software Reviews on File**. Facts on File, 1985- . $221. annual, loose-leaf 0-685-54353-6.

This is the software counterpart to *Book Review Digest*. Each month a loose-leaf supplement of 64 pages is supplied as part of an annual subscription. In it are summaries and condensations of reviews of approximately 45 programs. For each entry there is a factbox that gives bibliographic material, a contents note, system requirements, and price. Following this is a description supplied by the producers and excerpts from reviews with full bibliographic citations. About 300 publications are consulted for their reviews. The arrangement of programs is by type (e.g., education, business, programming languages, games). The monthly index which is cumulative for an entire year includes entries for software producers, titles, hardware, and subjects. This is an excellent access point to reviews and a particular boon to libraries that cannot afford a great number of the journals that review software. Recommended for medium and large public and academic libraries.   *Computer Software; Computers*

Y; A

1595.   **Video Game Quest: The Complete Guide to Home Video Game Systems**. Video Games and Accessories. DMS CA, 1990. 256p. $14.95 pap. 0-9625057-2-2.

This guide identifies and describes more than 700 games available from the major systems. Games are arranged by title in alphabetical order under eight major categories, e.g., Arcade Action, Educational, Sports, etc. Each entry includes software manufacturer, system, number of players, and a brief descriptive note. Prices, age levels, or ratings unfortunately are not provided. However, with the growing popularity of video games, this inexpensive guide is recommended for all libraries both for patron use and for building library collections. *Video Games*

Earth Sciences— Geology and Paleontology

Y : A

1596. **Death of the Dinosaurs and Other Mass Extinctions**, by Gary Fouty. Oryx, 1987. 96p. $18.95 pap. 0-89774-432-2. (Oryx Science Bibliographies, 10).

This work includes 275 annotated entries that provide background information on the mass extinctions of animal life on earth. Entries explore the current debate involving conflicting theories under such subjects as "Impact Theory," and "Man as a Cause of Extinction." Current material only is included, and the scholarship is roughly at the undergraduate level of detail. This is a good overview that will be of value in public and academic libraries and some secondary schools.

Dinosaurs; Extinct Animals; Prehistoric Animals

A

1597. **Dinosaurs: A Guide to Research**, by Bruce Edward Fleury. Garland, 1992. 468p. $73. 0-8240-5344-3.

This guide to the literature pertaining to dinosaurs is aimed at students in undergraduate and advanced high school courses. Each of the entries is annotated. The book begins with a chapter on 78 general and introductory works followed by chapters on specific topics like extinction. The number of citations totals almost 1,200. This bibliography will be of use particularly in college collections. *Dinosaurs*

C; Y; A

1598. **Earth Science Resources for Teachers, 1992**. American Geological Institute. free.

This leaflet lists reports, activity sheets, magazines, and other aids for teaching earth science that are available from 53 nonprofit sources. It is available free from: National Center for Earth Science Education, American Geological Institute, 4220 King St., Alexandria, VA 22302-1507.

Earth Sciences—Study and Teaching

A

1599. **Gemology: An Annotated Bibliography**, By John Sinkankas. Scarecrow, 1993. 2v. 1,216p. $179.50. 0-8108-2652-6.

Since Sinkankas is perhaps the world's leading authority on gems, this bibliography is undoubtedly the definitive work in the field. This monumental work contains about 7,500 entries, each fully annotated. Included are books, journal articles, catalogs, pamphlets, government publications, and ephemera. The entries are arranged alphabetically by author and then chronologically by title. Every aspect of gemology is represented, for example, cultural aspects, ornamental and decorative use, mining, extracting, processing, cutting, marketing, and evaluation. While most of the titles are in English, many other languages are included. A subject index is included. Though somewhat expensive, this work is recommended for most academic and public libraries and other libraries serving patrons with an interest in gems.

Gems; Precious Stones

A

1600. **Information Sources in the Earth Sciences**, by David N. Wood et al. 2nd ed. Bowker-Saur, 1989. 518p. $85. 0-408-01406-7.

In the introductory chapters of this work, the earth sciences and subdisciplines are introduced, plus a rundown on the kinds of literature available, how they can be searched by various classification systems used in libraries, and the use of computers in resources seeking. There follows fourteen chapters, each written by an expert and consisting of a bibliographic essay on a particular specialized area in the earth sciences. Both primary and secondary sources are listed and evaluated. Many are international in scope. Though somewhat specialized, this work will certainly be used in academic libraries, as well as public libraries where there is a particular interest in the earth sciences. *Earth Sciences; Geology*

Environmental Sciences and Energy Studies

Y; A

1601. **Acid Rain: A Bibliography of Research Annotated for Easy Access**, By G. Harry Stopp, Jr. Scarecrow, 1985. 174p. $20.00. 0-8108-1822-1.

This is a bibliography of 886 books, articles, conference proceedings, technical reports, and government documents published through 1984. Stopp, an authority in the field, is Director of Research and Sponsored Programs at the University of North Carolina at Greensboro. The compilation is intended for scientists, policymakers, and all others interested in the scientific, political, and social implications of the growing problem of acid rain. The subject index is essential since the entries (which include complete bibliographic data) are arranged by author. Because of the date of this publication, most of the data is most useful for background and historical information in all types of libraries. *Acid Rain*

A

1602. **Changing Wilderness Values, 1930-1990: An Annotated Bibliography**, by Joan S. Elbers. Greenwood, 1991. 138p. $39.95. 0-313-27377-4.

This is a listing of 300 scholarly essays and articles dealing with the wilderness that appeared from 1930 through 1990. Excluded are those that appeared in popular magazines or newspapers. Articles are summarized and are arranged by specific subjects such as special issues, environmental ethics, and reflective essays. For large collections that specialize in environmental issues. *Wilderness; Environment; Ecology*

A

1603. **Ecophilosophy: A Field Guide to the Literature**, by Donald Edward Davis. R and E Miles, 1989. 137p. $8.95 pap. 0-936810-18-1.

Ecophilosphy is a branch of philosophy that deals with human relations with nature. There are 334 items in this bibliography. The main section is a list of 280 books arranged under author's name. In addition to giving bibliographic information, each entry is fully annotated and includes critical comments. Most of the titles were published during the 1980s. There are two appendixes which list periodicals and organizations. There are several indexes. This interdisciplinary bibliography, though intriguing, will probably be of value only in large collections. *Philosophy; Ecology*

A

1604. **Endangered Vertebrates: A Selected, Annotated Bibliography, 1981-1988**, by Sylva Baker. Garland, 1990. 197p. $30. 0-8240-4796-6. (Garland Reference Library of Social Science, Vol. 480).

This bibliography of about 900 books and periodical references covers eight important years (1981 through 1988) of publishing on currently endangered or recently extinct species. After an introductory chapter introducing the topic, important terms, and key organizations, there is a section on general sources followed by separate chapters that deal with mammals, birds, amphibians and reptiles, and fishes with sub-divisions on such topics as habitats, conservation, and laws and legislation. The annotations are concise and informative, and there is an appendix which lists conservation organizations with addresses and lists of publications. Indexes are by the animals' common names, scientific names, authors' names, and geographical areas. This is an extremely useful tool for collection building on endangered species.

Endangered Species; Biology; Animals

A

1605. **Energy Update: A Guide to Current Reference Literature**, by R. David Wever, Energy Information Press (San Carlos, CA), 1991. 455p $42.50. 0-9628518-5-X.

This bibliography is arranged by subject and updates the author's *Energy Information Guide* (o.p.) that appeared early in the 1980s. This deals selectively with materials on the production, distribution, storage, and consumption of energy that appeared from the 1980s through 1990. There are critical annotations for many specialized books, articles, and documents, plus standard reference tools like encyclopedias and bibliographies and material on 75 online databases. It also contains author, title and subject indexes. For use in large public and academic libraries. *Energy Resources; Energy Conservation*

A

1606. Environmental Hazards: Air Pollution: A Reference Handbook, by Willard E. Miller and Ruby M. Miller. ABC-Clio, 1989. 250p. $39.50. 0-87436-528-7. (Contemporary World Issues).

As in other volumes in this series, there is an introductory essay on the issue in question; an historical overview; short biographies of prominent people in the area; annotated surveys of important books, magazines and documents; information on databases, electronic bulletin boards, and audiovisual materials; plus a directory of private, governmental and international organizations. A companion volume by the Millers is *Environmental Hazards: Toxic Waste and Hazardous Materials* (ABC-Clio, 1991, $39.50, 0-87436-596-1. *Air-Pollution; Environmental Health*

A

1607. The Environmental Sourcebook, by Edith Carol Stein. Lyons and Burford, 1992. 264p. $16.95 pap. 1-55821-164-0.

This guidebook gives sources of information on eleven different major issues related to the environment and ecology: population, agriculture, energy, climate and atmosphere, biodiversity, water, oceans, solid wastes, hazardous substances and waste, endangered lands, and development. For each there is a general introduction to the problem, a bibliography of selected recent books and reports, an annotated list of periodicals, and directories of important organizations a grant-giving foundations. A comprehensive index is included. Two somewhat similar sources in content are the *Gale Environmental Sourcebook* (Gale, 1992, $75, 0-08103-8403-5) and *Your Resources Guide to Environmental Organizations* (Smiling Dolphin Press, 1991, pap. $15.95, 1-879072-00-8), but this work is outstanding in its ease of use and the details it supplies on foundations, periodicals and organizations. Recommended for public and academic libraries and high schools where there is need for this kind of information. *Environment; Ecology*

Y; A*

1608. Environmentalist's Bookshelf: A Guide to the Best Books, by Robert Meredith. G. K. Hall, 1993. 272p. $40. 0-8161-7359-1.

This excellent "guide to the best books ... on nature and the environment" is based on the recommendations of 200 leaders in the field who were sent a questionnaire. The final list of about 500 books "selected" is divided into three major sections: a core list of 100 most recommended; a second list of 250 titles that were recommended several times; and a third list those mentioned only once, but still deemed important. These lists could be interpreted as priority lists for building a collection of environmental materials. Most of the annotations are in the form of selected quotes from the respondents. All entries contain full bibliographic data, and author, title, and subject indexes are provided. As well, a list of sources for further reference is appended. This bibliography is an excellent aid to collection development for all academic and public libraries and would also be useful for larger secondary school libraries. *Environment; Ecology*

Y; A

1609. Green Earth Resources Guide: A Comprehensive Guide about Environmentally-Friendly Services and Products, by Cheryl Gorder. Blue Bird, 1991. $12.95 (pap.) 0-9333025-23-8.

In the tradition of the *Whole Earth Catalog* of many years ago, this work is a guide to many environmentally sound products, services, organizations, and publications. The first part is a series of short essays on people and companies who deserve commendation for their environmentally conscious policies and products. The second is more valuable for collection building. It lists resources including bibliographies, books, pamphlets, periodicals, and specific products under a variety of subjects, such as baby and children's products, "eco-tourism," and educational materials. Although this is chiefly useful for patron browsing, acquisition personnel in public, high school and college libraries should find this a storehouse of ideas for out-of-the-way materials. *Ecology; Environment*

A

1610. The Greenhouse Effect: A Bibliography, by Joan Nordquist. Reference and Research Services, 1990. 60p. $15. pap. 0-937855-34-0. (Contemporary Social Issues, 18).

This bibliography of about 500 entries lists references by topics such as causes, solutions, forests, and ozone depletion. Under each heading, books and pamphlets are listed separately from periodical articles. The titles are well chosen but unannotated. Organizations are also listed. For information on other bibliographies in this series see *Contemporary Social Issues: A Bibliographic Series*. *Greenhouse Effect*

A

1611. Island Press Bibliography of Environmental Literature, by Joseph A. Miller et al. Island Press, 1993. 320p. $48. 1-55963-189-9.

More than 3,000 books, monographs, journals, government publications, and report abstracts are listed in this timely bibliography on the environment, a subject of global concern. The annotated citations are listed under 156 environmental topics, arranged alphabetically by title, and numbered consecutively under two main parts: Part I deals with the natural environment and includes such topics as air, water, land, plants, trees, and animals. Part II, the human environment, includes such areas as ethics and philosophy, the arts, education, economics, health, and science and technology. The reference index in the beginning of the book is subject oriented. As well an author and title index are provided. This bibliography is recommended for all libraries serving patrons studying the environment or involved in saving our planet.

Environment; Ecology

Y; A

1612. Reading About the Environment: An Introductory Guide, by Pamela Jansma. Libraries Unlimited, 1993. 252p. $27.50. 0-87287-985-2.

This bibliographic guide includes about 800 entries from books and popular magazine articles on important environmental issues as they relate to business, government, and personal decision-making policies of today. Each citation lists full bibliographic data as well a brief annotation which discusses the scope, organization, and particular slant of the work. This up-to-date and easy-to-use bibliography is intended for the layperson, student, and professional in the field of environmental studies, and therefore is recommended for all libraries. *Environment; Ecology*

A

1613. Resource-Efficient Housing: An Annotated Bibliography and Directory of Helpful Organizations, Rev. ed. by Robert Sardinsky and the Rocky Mountain Institute. 161p. $15. spiral-bound.

Produced by the staff of the Rocky Mountain Institute, this guide to publications and organizations dedicated to energy saving housing includes books, periodicals, and names of national and state organizations that provide information. In addition to a listing and description of periodicals (and some specific articles) focusing on energy/environment, there is extensive list of annotated books arranged by subjects such as landscaping, energy-efficient applicances, household environmental quality, and efficient water use. Most of the titles are quite recent, having been published since 1985. Perhaps the biggest limitation to this otherwise invaluable guide is the lack of an index, though there is a very detailed table of contents. This book should prove useful to homeowners throughout the country and is highly recommended for all public libraries for reference and collection development. It is available for $15. from: Rocky Mountain Institute, 1739 Snowmass Creek Rd., Snowmass, CO 81654-9199.

Energy Conservation; Environment; Housing

A

1614. Solar Home Planning: A Bibliography and Guide, by Stevan D. Atkinson. Scarecrow, 1988. 343p. $29.50 0-8108-2098-6.

This nonselective, comprehensive bibliography contains 2,036 entries of English language materials published between 1975 and 1986 on the subject of solar energy and the home. The book is organized by type of material such as bibliographies, directories, data bases, software, periodicals, articles, monographs, indexes, and libraries. The monograph and article sections comprises about half of the book. Within each of these categories there are subdivisions by subject. Print items are unannotated, but non print materials recieve brief descriptive annotations. There are author and title indexes. This book is suitable for public and academic libraries. *Solar Energy*

A

1615. Synerjy: A Directory of Renewable Energy. Synerjy, semiannual issues. $45. per year.

This combination bibliography and directory is over 15 years old and has as its purpose to give "information about practical, nonpolluting alternatives to fossil fuels and nuclear energy." Each issue has nine separate subject areas like solar energy, wind power, water power, and geothermal energy. In each are listed appropriate reference books, journal articles, government documents, and news about conferences and associations. Most of the publications cited are technical in nature, although a few are popular. There is neither an index nor annotations. The summer/fall issue cumulates the citations from the winter/spring issue and can be ordered separately for $30. This will be of value in large libraries where there is a demand for material on alternative or renewable energy sources. *Energy Resources*

A
1616. **Toxic and Hazardous Materials: A Sourcebook and Guide to Information Sources**, Ed. by James K. Webster. Greenwood, 1987. 431p. $55. 0-313-24575-4. (Bibliographies and Indexes in Science and Technology, 2).

More than 1,600 information sources on toxic and hazardous materials are identified and described in this sourcebook compiled by Webster and 10 librarians. Included are monographs, periodicals, newsletters, indexes, audiovisual materials, and databases. Most of the entries refer to publications and other sources written since 1980. Though international in scope, most of the citations come from U.S. sources. The introductory chapter presents information from general sources. Some of the topics covered in the various chapters include acid rain; health; disposal of wastes; radioactive materials; laws and regulations; and accidents, spills, and cleanups. The pattern followed in most of the chapters is a brief essay on the topic, followed by lists of materials under special headings such as books, periodicals, abstracts, reviews, etc. Each list is in alphabetical order by author or title. Bibliographic information and an annotation are also provided. A detailed title index is provided. The index for subject headings is spotty. This important and timely guide is recommended for all academic and public libraries. *Hazardous Wastes*

A
1617. **Wetland Economics and Assessment: An Annotated Bibliography**, by Jay A. Leitch and Brenda L. Ekstrom. Garland, 1989. 194p. $27. 0-8240-3648-4.

This bibliography of about 500 annotated citations mainly from North American sources published between 1975 and 1988, covers one of the world's formerly scorned but now considered productive geographical areas, the wetlands. The sources, that include books, periodical articles, reports, proceedings, and documents, are divided into six sections that include economic valuation, regulations and policies, social values, and management. The annotations are full, and there are author and subject indexes. This is a valuable guide particularly for libraries situated in areas where the future of wetlands is a vital topic.

Wetlands; Geography

Health Sciences

General and Miscellaneous

A
1618. **Alternative Therapies, Unproven Methods, and Health Fraud: A Selected Annotated Bibliography**, By Micaela Sullivan-Fowler et al. American Medical Association, 1988. 47p. $20. 0-89970-319-4.

This slim volume of only 117 books and journal articles has the authority, and understandable bias, of the American Medical Association's Division of Library and Information Management behind it. Though highly selective, the works are evenly divided between those for the specialist as well as the layperson. The entries are annotated and include complete bibliographic citations; they are arranged alphabetically under 18 categories. Only works against alternative therapy are included. Librarians may also want to consider West and Trevelyan's *Alternative Medicine* (o.p.) which advocates alternative therapeutics.

Alternative Medicine; Quacks and Quackery; Therapeutics

Y; A
1619. **Alzheimer's Disease**, Comp. by Margaret Eide and Twyla Mueller Racz. Oryz, 1987. 72p. $18.75. pap. 0-89774-324-5. (Oryx Science Bibliographies).

This important and timely work presents a review of the basic facts—history, causes, treatment, and psychosocial aspects—about Alzheimer's disease and includes a bibliography of almost 300 current references on the topic. The annotated entries are arranged by broad topic such as symptoms and causes, treatment and care, research, etc. There is also an author index which refers to entry numbers. Despite the lack of a subject index, this is still a useful source and is recommended for most libraries.

Alzheimer's Disease

A

1620. The Best of Health: The 101 Best Books, by Sheldon Zerden. Four Walls Eight Windows, 1989. 306p. $28.95. 0-941423-22-0; $14.95. pap. 0-941423-23-9.

This listing of "best health books" intended for the layperson is perhaps the only bibliography of its kind at the present time. The 101 titles concern nutrition, weight control, exercise, minerals, psycho-logical fitness, etc. Authors include doctors, psychologists, nutritionists, laypersons, etc. The books are arranged under broad subjects. Each entry presents a detailed summary of the book. A subject index is lacking, but would be useful. Despite this minor limitation, the book is recommended for most public libraries. *Health*

A

1621. Black American Health: An Annotated Bibliography, Comp. by Mitchell F. Rice and Woodrow Jones. Greenwood, 1987. 140p. $45. 0-313-24887-7. (Bibliographies and Indexes in Afro-American Studies, 17).

This annotated, timely and comprehensive bibliography of 370 entries deals with the health of black Americans during the 1970's and 80's. The entries are arranged sequentially and are grouped into seven major headings including: the cardiovascular system, health care problems, mental health, and sickle cell anemia. While there are some bibliographies dealing with specific health concerns of blacks, this is the only book-length bibliography dealing with the overall problems of black American health care and, therefore, it is recommended for most academic and public libraries, especially those serving a health care or a black community. *African Americans; Health*

Y; A

1622. Cancer: A Bibliography of Resources; Mental Health: A Bibliography; Nutrition Bibliography; Women's Health, by the Connecticut Consumer Health Information Network [1988]. $1 each.

These four brief bibliographies contain books, periodical articles, and audiovisuals on the subject of cancer, mental health, nutrition and women's health. For each item, bibliographic material and an annotation are supplied. They are available for $1 each or $3.50 for all four from HEALTHNET, Lyman Maynard Stowe Library, University of Connecticut Health Center, Farmington, CT 06032.

Cancer; Mental Health; Nutrition; Women's Health

A*

1623. The Consumer Health Information Source Book, by Alan M. Rees and Catherine Hoffman. 3rd ed. Oryx, 1990. 210p. $39.50 pap. 0-89774-4-8-X.

This is an evaluative guide to approximately 1,000 popular health publications. The chapters are arranged topically and collectively contain evaluative annotations on 750 books, 79 magazines and newsletters, 30 information clearinghouses, 175 health-related organizations, and 103 toll-free hot lines. There is also a list of 49 professional publications for reference purposes. Many of the book annotations are designated 'recommended' or 'highly recommended.' This is an excellent collection building tool on this subject. Another title in this area is *Core Collection in Nursing and the Allied Health Science*. *Health*

A

1624. Core Collection in Nursing and the Allied Health Sciences: Books, Journals, Media, by Annette Peretz and others. Oryx, 1990. 236p $42.50 pap. 0-89774-464-0.

This bibliography contains about 1,000 entries for materials published between 1980 and 1988. The material indexed is arranged by broad subject headings like AIDS, Computers, and Nutrition. Each of these sections begins with a listing of books giving bibliographic information and a brief descriptive annotation followed by a similar listing of nonprint items such as tapes, recordings, and computer software. There is a separate section on periodicals which lists indexes, magazines, and yearbooks and annuals. There are also author, title, and subject indexes. Large public libraries will find this valuable but should also check *Consumer Health Information Source Book*. *Health; Nursing; Medicine*

A

1625. Current Bibliographies in Medicine, by the National Library of Medicine.

This series of bibliographic pamphlets of 15 to 50 pages each is edited at the National Library of Medicine and contains listing of books, journal articles, and audiovisual materials on currently popular medical topics. Recent titles with SuDoc numbers are *Nutrition and AIDS* (817-007-00003-1), *Medical Waste Disposal* (817-007-00001-5), *Laboratory Animal Welfare* (817-007-00001-5), *Therapy-Related Second Cancers* (817-007-00002-3), and *Human-Pet Relationships* (817-007-00001-5). Each cost $3 but a subscription to the 20 issue series is $52. Order from Superintendent of Documents, Government Printing Office, Washington, DC 20402-9322. *Health; Medicine; United States—Government Publications*

A

1626. **Drug Information: A Guide to Current Resources**, by Bonnie Snow. Medical Library Association, 1988. $32. 0-912176-24-5.

This is a guide to current and important information in many types of print materials (e.g., books, articles) as well as on-line sources that deal with drugs and their use. The book's arrangement and practice exercises make it also useful as a self-study text. For academic and public libraries. *Drugs*

A

1627. **Encyclopedia of Health Information Sources**, by Paul Wasserman. 1st ed. Gale, 1987. 483p. $155 0-8103-2135-1.

Using a total of 450 alphabetically arranged medical subjects (many on specific diseases), this bibliography lists thousands of resources published from 1980 through 1986. Sources listed include abstracting services, indexes, yearbooks, associations, online databases, periodicals, popular works, research centers, statistical sources, and textbooks. Specialized sources are listed, as are general ones if part of their coverage pertains to the subject. Although there are no annotations or indexes, the bibliographic information is complete. This volume has value in collection development in academic and large public libraries. *Health*

C; A

1628. **Environmental Hazards to Young Children**, by Dorothy N. Kane. Oryx, 1985. 256p. $39.95. 0-89774-221-4.

This bibliography contains citations and annotations for about 3,000 books and articles on various environmental hazards as they relate to young children. The book is arranged by the nine most significant threats to the safety of children, such as traffic, fire and burns, falls, toxins and gases, and noise. There are extensive indexes. Useful in collections where adults need material on child safety.

Health; Children; Environmental Health

A

1629. **Federal Information Sources in Health and Medicine: A Selected Annotated Bibliography**, by Mary Glen Chitty and Natalie Schatz. Greenwood, 1988. 306p. $55 0-313-25530-X. (Bibliographies and Indexes in Medical Studies, 1).

This is a thorough, annotated bibliography that lists a total of 1,200 government publications and 90 databases on health related topics from almost 90 federal agencies. Practically all the items are dated 1980 or later. After several introductory chapters on the structure of federal publishing and how to gain access and use federal publications, databases and allied information sources, there are 37 chapters outlining resources on such subjects as 'accidents and injuries' and 'women's health.' Entries include author, title, document availability, publication date, and SuDoc and NTIS numbers (but no GPO stock numbers). There is a 28-page index of individual titles. This will be a useful selection aid for large libraries with need for material in this area. *Health*

A

1630. **Finding the Source of Medical Information: A Thesaurus-Index to the Reference Collection**, by Barbara Smith Shearer. Greenwood, 1985. 225p. $49.95. 0-313-24094-9. (Finding the Source).

Using the same arrangement as others in this series, a thesaurus orientation, this volume gives access to a listing of 450 of the most used and useful reference medical references and texts. The annotations are clear and the choices excellent. There are two sections. The first lists the books, and the second refers to them under terms in the thesaurus. There are also indexes to facilitate identifying individual resources. Recommended as a reference work and selection guide for large libraries. *Medicine*

A

1631. **Guide to Library Resources for Nursing**, by Katina Strauch. 2nd ed. Oryx, 1992. 224p. $45. 0-89774-491-8.

This is a guide to information sources in the field of nursing arranged by important subjects on the topic. As well as full bibliographic information, each citation is well annotated. There are also special sections on how to use the library and methods of accessing information. *Nursing*

Y; A

1632. **Health Resource Builder: Free and Inexpensive Materials for Librarians and Teachers**, by Carol Smallwood. McFarland, 1988. 251p. $18.95 pap. 0-89950-359-4.

Under a listing of over 200 topics involving physical and mental health and safety, there are enumerated pertinent health organizations, information clearinghouses and resource institutions, and the kinds of free and inexpensive information available from each. A sample of the subjects are aging, AIDS, drug abuse, smoking, child safety seats, and medical ethics. The types of materials listed include pamphlets, magazines, audiovisual materials, kits, and health care databases. There is an index which classifies the organizations by the type of material available. This is an excellent help in developing both general collections and the vertical files in high school, college and public libraries. *Health; Vertical File Materials; Free Material*

A

1633. **Home Health Care: An Annotated Bibliography**, by Ada Romaine-Davis, et al. Greenwood, 1992. 145p. $42.95 0-313-28334-6.

There are 370 citations to books and articles in this timely bibliography. The works are organized under eight main subjects including, "Care in the Home," "Care of the Terminally Ill," "Administration," and "Education of the Caregivers." Each of the listings is annotated, and there is a subject index. Recommended particularly for academic and large public libraries. *Home Care: Health*

A

1634. **Medical and Health Information Directory, v. 2: Publications, Libraries, and Other Information Services**, Ed. by Karen Backus. 6th ed. Gale, 1992. 721p $185. 0-8103-7522-2.

Volume 2 of a three volume set (v.1 lists organizations and agencies; v. 3 lists health services) identifies and describes more than 9,700 libraries, audiovisual producers and services, publications, and databases related to the medical and health fields. This specialized directory is intended for "medical and health professionals, government officials, medical librarians, and consumers..." and, despite its cost, it is recommended for all special, academic, and public libraries that serve such clientele.

Medicine; Health; Medical Care

A

1635. **Minority Health Resources Directory**. ANROW Publishing, 1991. 355p. $50. pap.

This directory describes the special resources offered by 360 organizations representing selected minority groups. Some of the organizations are quite well-known, such as Alcoholics Anonymous and the American Red Cross, while others are little known, such as the People of Color against AIDS Network and the Organizacion de la Salud de la Mujer Latina. Each organizational profile gives procedures for contacting the organization, an overview of their purpose, and an outline of services offered, including publications available. This may be helpful to build an information file of resources (local as well as national) in public libraries serving patrons represented by organizations included in the directory. If this publication is not available from a library's regular jobber, it may be purchased direct from: ANROW Publishing, 5515 Security Lane, Ste 510, Rockville, MD 20852. *Health Care; Minorities; Multiculturalism*

A

1636. **The Native Peoples of Canada: An Annotated Bibliography of Population Biology, Health, and Illness**, Comp. by C. Meiklejohn and D. A. Rokala. Canadian Museum of Civilization; distributed by Univ. of Chicago, 1988. 564p. $29.95. pap. 0-660-10774-0. (Archaeological Survey of Canada, 134).

This bibliography is an expansion of a previously published work and a portion of a large database of biological and health-related materials about native Americans, *Manitoba Masterfile*. The vast majority of the 2,100 citations are annotated. A few entries are in French or German; however, most are in English. Author and subject indexes are provided. This rather specialized bibliography is recommended for most academic, health sciences, and public libraries (but especially Canadian) supporting programs relating to health care of native Americans. *Health Care; Indians of North America—Canada*

A

1637. **PMS: The Premenstrual Syndrome**, Comp. by Lorna Peterson. Oryx, 1985. 76p. $18.95. 0-89774-205-2. (Oryx Science Bibliographies, 3).

This work on a current science topic lists journal articles discussing the symptoms and etiology of PMS (premenstrual syndrome). As well, this bibliography lists items on related topics such as pharmacological, hormonal, nutritional, and exercise treatments; its psychological and sociological aspects; and its legal implications and feminist perspectives. The 237 articles were chosen on the basis of their availability and their comprehensibility to the nonspecialist. This brief work is recommended for all academic and public libraries, especially those that do not have specialized medical indexes.

Premenstrual Syndrome

A
1638. **Post-Traumatic Stress, Disorder, Rape, Trauma, Delayed Stress and Related Conditions: A Bibliography; With a Directory of Veterans Outreach Programs**, Comp. by D. Cheryn Picquet and Reba A. Best. McFarland, 1986. 204p. $29.95. pap. 0-089950-213-X.

This bibliography pulled together books and articles concerned with post-traumatic stress disorder (PTSD) in "war veterans, disaster victims, concentration camp survivors, victims of incest, rape, child and spouse abuse, prisoners of war, refugees, and evacuees, and civilian victims and survivors of war." Despite this lofty aim of the compiler, the vast majority of the entries of this bibliography deal with PTSD in Vietnam veterans. Entries are arranged alphabetically by author. There is an author index, but still the volume is not easy to use without a subject arrangement. The title is somewhat of a misnomer as indicated; however, this is an excellent bibliography of PTSD and is therefor recommended for most academic and public libraries where this is a concern of researchers as well as the interested general reader.

Post-Traumatic Stress Disorder; Vietnam War Veterans

A
1639. **A Research Guide to the Health Sciences: Medical, Nutritional, and Environmental**, by Kathleen J. Haselbauer. Greenwood, 1987. 655p. $65. 09-313-25530-9. (Reference Sources for the Social Sciences and Humanities, 4).

Haselbauer, a science librarian at Western Washington University, has compiled this extensive, annotated guide to reference sources in selected health sciences which includes over 2,000 entries to English-language items. There are four major parts to the guide: General Works arranged by type; Basic Sciences Supporting Clinical Medicine; Social Aspects of the Health Sciences; and Medical Specialties. The first part identifies and describes general works such as research guides, indexes, biographical sources, dictionaries, handbooks, and data-bases. The remaining sections are arranged by broad subject and subdivided by format. The annotations are critical and compare the title with similar works where appropriate. Full bibliographic information is included. As well, a combined author, title, and subject index is provided. This guide is recommended as a reference guide and collection development aid for all libraries serving health science students and professionals. *Health; Medicine; Nutrition; Environment*

A
1640. **Sickness and Wellness Publications, Volume 1**, by Janet R. Utts. John Gordon Burke Publisher, 1989. 288p. $50 0-934272-21-2.

This bibliography consists of coverage of about 400 newsletters and publications on health and various diseases and ailments. There are many cross references and a title index. Volume 2 has also been published (1990, $19.95 pap. 0-934272-26-3). Updates are planned and a diskette version is also available in a combined print/electronic version for $89.50. For large libraries.

Health; Illness; Diseases

AIDS

A
1641. **AIDS: Abstracts of the Psychological and Behavioral Literature, 1983-1989**. Ed. by James M. Jones et al. 2nd ed. American Psychological Association, 1989. 113p. $20.00 pap. 1-55798-062-4. (Bibliographies in Psychology, 6).

This highly selected bibliography of works on the psychological and behavioral aspects of AIDS was taken from about 1,300 journals reviewed for *Psychological Abstracts*. This second edition published only one year after the first includes a section of selected books. Annotated entries are listed under broad subject categories such as treatment, risks, education, and societal concerns and arranged alphabetically by author. A detailed subject and author index is included. This is recommended as a selection guide for most libraries needing more information on this specialized aspect of AIDS. *AIDS*

A

1642. AIDS and Women: A Sourcebook, By Sarah Barbara Watstein and Robert Laurich. Oryx, 1990. 159p. $36.50. 0-89774-577-9.

This bibliography is primarily a listing of journal articles on the specific subject of women and AIDS. However, it is recommended for most libraries, if for no other reason than that it includes an excellent list of audiovisual resources and a basic list of reference sources (helpful for background information) in its special appendix of resources. *AIDS*

A

1643. AIDS Crisis in America, by Mary Ellen Hombs. ABC-CLIO, 1992. 280p. $39.95. 0-87436-648-8. (Contemporary World Issues).

There are many recent titles on the subject of this devastating disease. Like most of the currently available titles, this work also presents a good overview of the history, events, personalities, and public policy. However, the real strength of this work is the excellent annotated bibliographies. Another bonus is the directory of organizations concerned with aids which also includes their major publications. This source is recommended for all libraries building collections on this dreaded illness. *AIDS*

Y; A

1644. AIDS Information Sourcebook, Fourth Edition 1993-94, Ed. by H. Robert Malinowsky and Gerald J. Perry. Oryx, 1993. 312p. $39.95 pap. 0-89774-740-2.

This handbook, now in its fourth edition in about 5 years, deals with many aspects of the AIDS epidemic, and therefore belongs in most libraries. However, the final section is the most directly related to our purposes; it consists of a detailed and annotated bibliography of articles, bibliographies, books, films, periodicals, audio and video tapes, and databases on the subject of AIDs. A separate subject index to these items is provided. As with all lists of materials on a rapidly changing subject, one must be alerted to revised editions and newer bibliographies. *AIDS*

Y; A

1645. AIDS Research and Resource Guide. The Free Library of Philadelphia, [1992]. $.75.

A useful and up-to-date guide for building up a collection of information on this dreaded disease. Included in the guide are "recommended reading list, a survey of films and videos dealing with AIDS-related issues." This professionally prepared publication is recommended for both school and public libraries. To obtain a copy, send 75 cents in postage to: The Free Library of Philadelphia, Office of Work With Adults/Young Adults, Logan Square, Philadelphia, PA 19103. *AIDS*

A

1646. How to Find Information about AIDS, by Jeffrey T. Huber. 2nd ed. Haworth, 1991. 130p $29.95; $14.95 pap. 1-56024-140-3; 0-918393-99-X.

This is basically a directory of sources of information about AIDS with chapters devoted to different resources. The organizational section lists local, state, and national agencies and describes briefly their services. There are also sections on state health departments, government sources of information and research agencies. For collection development there is coverage on pertinent databases, print sources, and audiovisual material. The chapter on print sources covers indexing and abstracting services, journals, newsletters, reference works, and monographs. There is an index by place and subject. This is an excellent complementary volume to H. Robert Malinowsky's *AIDS Information Sourcebook* which contains somewhat similar information. *AIDS*

Y; A

1647. Learning AIDS: An Information Resources Directory, Ed. By Trish Halleron et al. 2nd ed. American Foundation for AIDS Research (AmFAR), dist. by R. R. Bowker, 1989. 270p. $26. 0-9620363-1-5.

This is a very comprehensive and informative bibliography of more than 1700 items of print and nonprint titles (an increase of 600 over the first edition). More than half of the items were carefully evaluated by a panel of 30 experts in the medical or educational fields; these titles are fully annotated and listed in the first chapter under target audiences such as adolescents, blacks, health care workers, the gay community, and the general public. The second chapter lists other items that were not evaluated. Chapter three, the final chapter, lists producers and distributors. There are also three useful indexes by title, product type, and non-English language materials (mainly Spanish). This relatively inexpensive, comprehensive, and current guide is recommended for all libraries needing additional material on this subject. *AIDS*

A
1648.   **The National Directory of AIDS Care**. 2nd ed. [1992].

Over 14,000 entries of sources which offer a variety of resources are included in this second edition of an important and timely location tool. Each entry includes such information as names and addresses, phone numbers, and contact persons of national, state, county, and city agencies and organizations (both governmental and private) concerned with HIV/AIDS. A copy is available for $75 plus $5. for shipping from: National Directory of AIDS Care, 11927 Menaul Boulevard NE, Suite 105, Albuquerque, NM 87112-2457, or call, 800 584-7972 or 505 271-1277. *AIDS*

A
1649.   **The Psychological Aspects of AIDS: An Annotated Bibliography**, by Paula L. Levine et al. Garland, 1990. 540p. $70. 0-8140-5835-6. (Garland Reference Library of Social Science, 547).

The publishing output on the topic of AIDS is extensive and increasing. One of the problems, of course, is keeping current with a subject that is changing almost daily. Under these circumstances, can one justify a huge expenditure for a hardbound bibliography? Levine has chosen, perhaps, the one aspect of this dreadful disease that has not changed and will not change in the foreseeable future—the psychological impact on every individual in our society touched by this plague as well as the unfortunate victims. More than 1,200 books, chapters of books, articles, bibliographies, and dissertations are listed by type under broad aspects of the subject. Critical annotations and perhaps greater selectivity would make this more useful to the users. Still, this volume will be helpful for reference, interlibrary loan, and collection development for academic and many public libraries. *AIDS*

Nutrition and Cookery

A
1650.   **The American Regional Cookery Index**, Comp. by Rhonda H. Kleiman. Neal-Schuman, 1989. 221p. $55. 1-55570-029-2.

In addition to serving as a locational aid to hard-to-find regional recipes, the 25 regional cookbooks indexed serve as an excellent selection and buying guide for a core collection of this genre. As well, there is added bibliography of additional related cookbooks, which would help public libraries expand their collection of "All-America" cookery, if so desired. *Cookbooks*

A
1651.   **Cook's Index: An Index to Cookbooks and Periodicals from 1975-1987. volume 1**, by John Gordon Burke and others. John Gordon Burke Publisher (Evanston, IL), 1989. 536p. $55 0-934272-09-3.

This guide to published works on cookery is in two sections. The first lists, without annotations, thousands of cookbooks arranged by subject. Full bibliographic information is given. The second section is an index to magazine articles that contain one or more recipes from such periodicals as *Gourmet*, *Family Circle* and *House Beautiful*. Again a subject approach is used. An update is planned every three years. This printed volume is supplemented by the *Cook's Index Information Service* on diskette. A unique source for large public and specialized collections. *Cookbooks*

A
1652.   **Current Cookbooks**, by Christine Bulson. Choice, 1990. $12.

This booklet lists and annotates 250 recent cookbooks arranged by cuisine (e.g., Armenian), cooking techniques (e.g., microwave), courses (e.g., appetizers), foods (e.g., candy), and audience (e.g., Kosher). Most of the books listed were published after 1970. This bibliography can be ordered directly from Choice, 100 Riverview Center, Middletown, CT 06457. *Cookbooks*

A
1653.   **Ethnic Cookbooks and Food Marketplace: A Complete Bibliographic Guide and Directory to Armenian, Iranian, Afghan, Middle Eastern, North African and Greek Foods in the U.S.A. and Canada**, by Hamo B. Vassilian. 2nd ed. Armenian Reference Books, 1991. 128p. $29.50. 0-931539-00-5.

This unique source includes a guide to printed materials on Middle Eastern, North African, and Greek food, as well as information on where foods and ingredients can be purchased. The first part is an alphabetical listing by author, title and subject of 239 cookbooks in English. Other parts give a guide to the food marketplace with listings of caterers, bakeries, grocers, restaurants, and manufacturers under various categories. There are indexes by business names and geographic locations. Large public and academic libraries where there is a demand for material on ethnic foods may find this valuable. *Cookbooks*

A

1654.   **Food Additives and Their Impact on Health**, by Mary Ellen Huls. Oryx, 1988. 76p. $18.95 pap. 0-89774-433-0. (Oryx Science Bibliographies, 12).

This bibliography contains 251 fully annotated English language citations culled from a wide spectrum of both popular and scientific journals. After a seven page introduction that gives an overview of the topic, the sources are listed by such subjects as adverse affects, nitrites and nitrates, monosodium glutamate, and artificial sweeteners. There are author and title indexes. This will be of interest in public and undergraduate college libraries.   *Food Additives; Health*

A

1655.   **Food and Nutrition Information Guide**, by Paula Szilard. Libraries Unlimited, 1987. 358p. $37.50. 0-87287-457-5.

This guide to reference materials on nutrition and food science begins with an overview of the field, its literature, types of resources, and a beginner's guide to doing research in this area. The bibliographies which follow are arranged under topics like nutrition and dietetics. They include important reference sources, diet manuals, nutrition, and food consumption surveys, government publications, handbooks, indexes, and periodical articles. Most of the entries were published from 1976 to 1986. There are sections that cover food standards, food service, and social and cultural factors related to food. This will be useful in large collections.   *Food; Nutrition*

A

1656.   **Food Safety, 1990: An Annotated Bibliography of the Literature**, by the Food Research Institute, University of Wisconsin. Butterworth/Heinemann, 1991. 511p. $95. 0-7506-9210-3.

This comprehensive publication, now updated annually, contains hundreds of listings on food safety arranged under three main headings, "Diet and Health," "Safety and Food Components," and "Foodborne Microbial Illness," with a number of subdivisions. After an alphabetical listing of the citations, each of these sections contains a brief bibliographic essay which comments on the contents of each item. This will be of use primarily in academic and large institutions.   *Food*

A

1657.   **Health-Related Cookbooks: A Bibliography**, by Tian-Chu Shih. Scarecrow, 1991. 427p. $42.50 0-8108-2513-9.

This bibliography of health-related cookbooks contains over 1,000 titles published commercially or by vanity, government, or university presses. Most appeared in the 1980s, although in the case of some subjects, coverage begins in the 1970s. The books are arranged under such subjects as weight reduction, heart disease, cancer, diabetes, and food intolerance. Each chapter begins with a short description of the subject or disease and ends with a list of pertinent organizations and agencies. Unfortunately, most of the entries are not annotated and the list is unselective, so that there is no way of determining the quality of the book listed. There are indexes by author, keyword, and title. In spite of shortcomings, this will be useful in collection development, particularly in public libraries.   *Cookbooks*

A

1658.   **Melting Pot: An Annotated Bibliography and Guide to Food and Nutrition Information for Ethnic Groups in America**, by Jacqueline M. Newman. Garland, 1993. 240p. $38. 0-8240-7756-3. (Garland Reference Library of Social Science, v. 708).

This greatly revised and expanded edition of Newman's 1987 work continues to explore the nutrition and food, cuisine and dietary habits of America's diversified ethnic groups. Hundreds of new entries have been added to this update. The references were culled from many scholarly as well as popular books and journals and bibliographies of cookbooks. While African

Americans and Native Americans are included in-depth, there are many entries from Asian-Americans, including Asian Indians. European American groups are deleted. There are no indexes; however, retrieval of data about specific groups is not difficult because of the overall arrangement. Public libraries and academic libraries with patrons and/or programs in nutrition, food and health, and culinary arts will want to consider this relatively inexpensive work which is useful as a reference and selection aid.

Food; Nutrition; Cookery, Ethnic

A

1659. **Specialty Cookbooks: A Subject Guide, Vol. 1,** by Harriet Ostroff and Tom Nichols. Garland, 1992. 659p. $90. 0-8240-6947-1.

There are 4,500 specialized cookbooks listed without annotations in this bibliography that concentrates on the decade 1980 through 1990. General, ethnic, and health-related cookbooks are going to appear in volume 2. This work is divided into four parts. The first and largest is on "Specific Ingredients," i.e., cookbooks that specialize in an ingredient like rice or chocolate. The other three are on specific courses, specific meals, and special techniques (e.g., microwaving). The general index in by author and title. For large collections   *Cookbooks*

Physical Sciences and Mathematics

Y; A

1660. **The Atomic Bomb: An Annotated Bibliography,** By Hans G. Graetzer and Larry M. Browning. Salem Press, 1992. 168p. $40. 0-89356-677-2.

The authors have produced a rather comprehensive bibliography in this short bibliography of less than 200 pages. The 10 chapters include fully-annotated titles on the background of radioactivity, fission, and fusion; biographies of atomic scientists; the atomic bombs of Hiroshima and Nagasaki; and the arms race to the early 1990's. The hundreds of titles should prove useful for high school and college students as well as adult peace groups and general readers. Therefore, despite the rather steep price, this work is recommended for most libraries.   *Atomic Bomb*

A

1661. **Chemical Industries: An Information Sourcebook,** by Phae H. Dorman. Oryx, 1988. 158p. $32.50. 0-89774-257-5. (Oryx Sourcebook Series in Business and Management).

This annotated bibliography contains citations for over 500 sources on chemical industries in books, journals, databases, reference works, and associations and research centers. In addition, there is a section which lists 158 core collection titles. Another important title in this series on business and management from Oryx is *Mining and Mineral Industries* by Marilyn McAnally Stark (19988, $38.50 0-89774-295-8) which list a total of 549 sources of information in these areas.

Chemical Industries; Mines and Mineral Resources

A

1662. **Encyclopedia of Physical Sciences and Engineering Information Sources,** by Steven Wasserman et al. 2nd ed. Gale, 1993. 800p. $155. 0-8103-6911-7.

This bibliography, arranged by subject, with author and title indexes, is a guide to hundreds of human, print, and electronic sources of information in the physical sciences and engineering. This is an expensive specialized item but will be of value in collections where these topics are given particular attention.

Science; Engineering

A

1663. **How to Find Chemical Information: A Guide for Practicing Chemists, Educators and Students,** by Robert E. Maizell. 2nd ed. John Wiley, 1987. 402p. $59.95 0-471-86767-5.

This excellent guide to the literature of chemistry is divided by type of material. In addition to coverage for standard works like dictionaries and handbooks, there are chapters on *Chemical Abstracts*, online searching, U.S. Government document information centers and sources, and analytical chemistry sources. Each piece of material is well-annotated with tips on usage. Chemistry is emphasized with some coverage for chemical engineering. A good reference work for larger collections and all college libraries.   *Chemistry*

A

1664. **Information Sources in Physics,** by Dennis F. Shaw. 2nd ed. Butterworths, 1985. 456p. $80. 0-408-01474-1.

In spite of a somewhat British emphasis, this is an excellent overall guide to the literature of physics. Twenty-two specialists have contributed chapters that deal with the types of phenomenon studied in physics or with types of sources like abstracts, online sources, science libraries, and the history of physics. The latest date of the material listed was 1983, which would indicate that the work needs updating. The readable, clear text and the nature of the materials included, however, make this volume still of value in public and academic library collections. *Physics*

A

1665. **Mathematical Book Review Index,** by Louise S. Grinstein. Garland, 1992. 448p. $72. 0-8240-4114-3.

The stated purpose of this excellent reference work is to provide a handy source for reviews of books on pure and applied mathematics from the elementary school to the graduate school level and beyond. Coverage ranges from English language reviews from Canada and the United States, published from about 1800 to 1940. Entries are arranged alphabetically by author and include standard bibliographic data and review information. A list of the journals and other reference sources consulted and a subject index are also included. This is perhaps the only index to book reviews in mathematics, and despite the limitation of not going beyond 1940, the work is recommended for academic libraries where the retrospective study of mathematics is important. *Mathematics*

A

1666. **Mathematical Journals: An Annotated Guide,** Comp. by Diana F. Liang. Scarecrow, 1992. 235p. $29.50. 0-8108-2585-6.

This much-needed reference work lists and describes 350 mainly English language journals in mathematics and related disciplines (such as statistics and mathematical applications in computer science). The entries are arranged alphabetically by title and include standard bibliographic information such as price, ISSN, publication history, editor, manuscript requirements for authors, frequency, and sources that index or abstract the journal. As well, a short descriptive annotation is included which indicates the scope, purpose, and target audience. Despite the limitation of not including a subject index of the various branches and subdivisions of mathematics, this inexpensive guide is recommended for all academic and larger public libraries. *Mathematics; Periodicals*

A

1667. **Time: A Bibliographic Guide,** by Samuel L. Macey. Garland, 1991. 426p. $62. 0-8153-0646-6.

Macey has compiled a selected and yet an almost unbelievable number of about 6,000 items on the subject of time. The items were drawn worldwide (though most of the items are in the English language). The work is divided into 25 sections based on typical academic disciplines. The work is intended to help advanced researchers as well as beginning students. This bibliography is a welcome addition to research-oriented academic and public libraries for reference, research, and collection development. *Time*

Technology and Applied Sciences

A

1668. **Biotechnology and the Research Enterprise: A Guide to the Literature,** by William F. Woodman et al. Iowa State University Press, 1989. 358p. $49.95. 0-8138-0164-8.

This comprehensive, annotated bibliography describes recent publications dealing with agricultural biotechnology. The detailed entries are arranged into seven major sections which include: federal research policy, university-industry relationships, conflicts of interest, university research, biotechnology industry, international biotechnology research, and related issues. A list of additional recommended sources is appended. This bibliography would be helpful for collection development in special libraries and academic libraries supporting agricultural biotechnology programs. *Agricultural Research; Biotechnology*

A

1669. **From the Titanic to the Challenger: An Annotated Bibliography on the Technological Failures of the Twentieth Century,** by Susan Davis Herring. Garland, 1989. 459p $62. 0-8240-3043-5.

This collections of accounts in books, journals, and government publications, chronicles in bibliographic form the technological disasters of the twentieth century, from the Quebec Bridge failure in 1907 through Chernobyl. The 1,354 entries are arranged by type of industry or structure such as aircraft, automobiles, dams, and railroads. Each entry is annotated in approximately 10 lines. There is an introductory chronology of events and indexes by type of failure, author, and title. A fascinating bibliography for large libraries where technical information is needed. *Disasters; Technology*

A

1670. **The History of Engineering Science: An Annotated Bibliography,** by David F. Channell. Garland, 1989. 311p. $48. 0-8240-6636-7. (Garland Reference Library of the Humanities, 1150; Bibliographies of the History of Science and Technology, 16).

This bibliography covers the historical, philosophical and social aspects of the history of engineering and the relationship between science and technology. Most of the works cited are from the 1960s through the 1980s and are in English. The entries are arranged under broad subjects and are briefly annotated. There is no subject index. For large collections. *Engineering; Science*

A

1671. **Women and Technology: An Annotated Bibliography,** by Cynthia Gay Bindocci. Garland, 1993. 243p. $39. 0-8240-5789-9.

This is possibly the only current full-length bibliography on a timely and important issue. Bindocci introduces the topic with a lengthy overview which includes general resources such as dissertations, monographs, and journal articles. The main body of the work is organized under 16 categories including such areas as Agriculture and Food, Architecture, Communication, Industrial Work, Military, and Transportation. Bibliographic data is provided, and most of the annotated entries were published between 1979 and 1991. A useful index completes the work. Recommended for most public libraries and academic libraries which have women's studies or technology programs. *Technology; Women's Studies*

Author-Title Index

Note: Reference is to entry number. The letter "n" following entry numbers refers to titles mentioned in annotations.

Subject Index

Note: Reference is to entry number.

African Americans—Poets
Afro-American Poets Since 1955, 1333
Index to Poetry by Black American Women, 1337

African Literature
Bibliography of African Women Writers and Journalists: Ancient Egypt-1984, 660

Africans
Negritude: An Annotated Bibliography, 633

Aged. *See* **Senior Citizens**

Agent Orange
Agent Orange and Vietnam: An Annotated Bibliography, 835

Aging
Aging with Style and Savvy: Books and Films on Challenges Facing Adults of All Ages, 968a
Anthropology of Aging: A Partially Annotated Bibliography, 612
Building Library Collections on Aging: A Selection Guide and Core Collection, 969
Crime and the Elderly: An Annotated Bibliography, 887
The Encyclopedia of Aging, 971
Families and Aging: A Selected Annotated Bibliography, 973
Federal Public Policy on Aging Since 1960: An Annotated Bibliography, 974
Of a Certain Age: A Guide to Contemporary Fiction Featuring Older Adults, 1227
Where Do We Come From? What Are We? Where Are We Going? An Annotated Bibliography of Aging and the Humanities, 1097
Women and Aging: A Selected, Annotated Bibliography, 979

Agricultural Laborers
Mexican and Mexican-American Agricultural Labor in the United States: An International Bibliography, 714

Agricultural Research
Biotechnology and the Research Enterprise: A Guide to the Literature, 1668

AIDS
AIDS: Abstracts of the Psychological and Behavioral Literature, 1983-1989, 1641
AIDS and Women: A Sourcebook, 1642
AIDS Crisis in America, 1643
AIDS Information Sourcebook, Fourth Edition 1993-94, 1644
AIDS Research and Resource Guide, 1645
How to Find Information about AIDS, 1646
Learning AIDS: An Information Resources Directory, 1647
The National Directory of AIDS Care, 1648
The Psychological Aspects of AIDS: An Annotated Bibliography, 1649

Air—Pollution
Environmental Hazards: Air Pollution: A Reference Handbook, 1606

Airlines
The Airline Bibliography: The Salem College Guide: The Salem College Guide to Sources on Commercial Aviation. v. 1: The United States, 1554

Alcoholism
Biomedical and Social Aspects of Alcohol Use: A Review of the Literature, 1028
Prevention Education: A Guide to Research, 1029
Substance Abuse: A Resource Guide for Secondary Schools, 459
Work and Alcohol Abuse: An Annotated Bibliography, 1031

Aliens, Illegal
The New American Immigration: Evolving Patterns of Legal and Illegal Immigration: A Bibliography of Selected References, 883

Alphabet Books
Alphabet Books as a Key to Language Patterns: An Annotated Action Bibliography, 186

Alternative Medicine
Alternative Therapies, Unproven Methods, and Health Fraud: A Selected Annotated Bibliography, 1618

Alzheimer's Disease
Alzheimer's Disease, 1619

American Civil Liberties Union
American Civil Liberties Union: An Annotated Bibliography, 893

American Drama
American Theater and Drama Research: An Annotated Guide to Information Sources, 1945-1990, 1384
Contemporary Black American Playwrights and the Their Plays: A Biographical Directory and Dramatic Index, 1343

American Drama—History and Criticism
American Drama Criticism: Supplement II to the Second Edition, 1340

American Fiction
Beacham's Popular Fiction in America, 1346
Beacham's Popular Fiction, 1991 Update, 1347
The Bibliography of Contemporary American Fiction, 1945-1988: An Annotated Checklist, 1348

American Literature
Black American Women in Literature: A Bibliography, 1976 through 1987, 1320
Black American Women Novelists: An Annotated Bibliography, 1349
Chelsea House Library of Literary Criticism, 1196
Concise Dictionary of American Literary Biography, 1310
Critical Surveys, 1173
Dictionary of Literary Biography, 1188
Facts on File Bibliography Series, 476
Fiction Catalog, 1223
Fifty Southern Writers After 1900: A Bio-Bibliographical Sourcebook, 1312
Gale Literary Criticism Series, 1200
Good Reading: A Guide for Serious Readers, 1175
Magill's Survey of American Literature, 1315
Masterpieces of African-American Literature, 1323
Masterplots II, 1176
The New Moulton's Library of Literary Criticism: British and American Literature to 1904, 1285
Reference Works in British and American Literature, 1288
A Research Guide for Undergraduate Students: English and American Literature, 1289

Art, Chicano
Arte Chicano: A Comprehensive Annotated Bibliography of Chicano Art, 1965-1981, 1143

Art, Modern
Twentieth-Century Artists on Art: An Index to Artists' Writings, Statements, and Interviews, 1152

Art Films
Art on Screen: A Directory of Films and Videos on the Visual Arts, 1142
artsAmerica Fine Art Film and Video Source Book, 1144

Artificial Intelligence
Artificial Intelligence and Instruction: A Selected Bibliography, 773

Artists
Contemporary Artists, 1145
Old Master Print References: A Selected Bibliography, 1149
Twentieth-Century Artists on Art: An Index to Artists' Writings, Statements, and Interviews, 1152
Women Artists in the United States: A Selective Bibliography and Resource Guide on the Fine and Decorative Arts, 1750-1986, 1155
Women in the Fine Arts: A Bibliography and Illustration Guide, 1156

Arts and Crafts. *See* **Handicraft**

Asia
Good Books for the Curious Traveler: Asia and the South Pacific, 825
Literature for Children about Asians and Asian Americans: Analysis and Annotated Bibliography, with Additional Readings for Adults, 303
Selection of Library Materials for Area Studies, Part I: Asia, Iberia, the Caribbean and Latin America, and the Soviet Union and the South Pacific, 654

Asian Americans
American Ethnic Literature: Native American, African American, Chicano/Latino, and Asian American Writers and Their Backgrounds, 1306
Asian American Literature: An Annotated Bibliography, 1325
The Asian American Media Reference Guide: A Catalog of More Than 500 Asian American Audio-visual Programs for Rent or Sale in the United States, 634
Asian American Studies: An Annotated Bibliography and Research Guide, 635
Asian Americans Information Directory: A Guide to Organizations, Agencies, Institutions, Programs, Publications, and Services Concerned with Asian American Nationalities and Ethnic Groups in the United States, 636
Cultural Diversity Videos, 299
Literature for Children about Asians and Asian Americans: Analysis and Annotated Bibliography, with Additional Readings for Adults, 303
Substance Abuse among Ethnic Minorities in America: A Critical Annotated Bibliography, 1030
Understanding Asian Americans: A Curriculum Resource Guide, 637

Astronautics
Astronomy and Astronautics: An Enthusiast's Guide to Books and Periodicals, 1557

Astronomy
Air and Space Catalog: The Complete Sourcebook to Everything in the Universe, 1552
Astronomer's Sourcebook: The Complete Guide to Astronomical Equipment, Publications, Planets, Planetarium, Organizations, Events, and More, 1556
Astronomy and Astronautics: An Enthusiast's Guide to Books and Periodicals, 1557
A Basic Astronomy Library, 1558

Athletes
The Neal-Schuman Index to Sports Figures in Collective Biographies, 1052

Atlases
General Reference Books for Adults: Authoritative Evaluations of Encyclopedias, Atlases, and Dictionaries, 503

Atomic Bomb
The Atomic Bomb: An Annotated Bibliography, 1660

Audiocassettes
All-Music Guide: The Best CDs, Albums & Tapes, 1449
Audiocassette Finder: A Subject Guide to Educational and Literary Materials on Audiocassettes, 767
British Words on Cassette, 1992, 1135
Growing Up with Music: A Guide to the Best Recorded Music for Children, 280
The Integrated Library: Encouraging Access to Multimedia Materials, 913
National Information Center for Educational Media (NICEM), 772
Phonolog, 97
Radio Soundtracks: A Reference Guide, 1132
Schwann Artist Issue, 1463
The Spoken Audio Source Guide, 1138
Words on Cassette, 1139

Audiorecordings
Media Review Digest, 1991..., 1136

Audiovisual Materials. *See also* **Instructional Materials**
American Library Association's Best of the Best for Children..., 264
The Asian American Media Reference Guide: A Catalog of More Than 500 Asian American Audio-visual Programs for Rent or Sale in the United States, 634
AudioVideo Review Digest, 1133
AV Market Place, 1992: The Complete Business Directory..., 1134
Best Science Books & A-V Materials for Children: An Annotated List of Science and Mathematics Books, Films, Filmstrips, and Videocassettes, 326
Creating Connections: Books, Kits and Games for Children: A Sourcebook, 271
The Elementary School Library Collection: A Guide to Books and Other Media, 121
Film Library Quarterly, 91
The Integrated Library: Encouraging Access to Multimedia Materials, 913
Introducing Children to the Arts: A Practical Guide for Librarians and Educators, 297
Kits, Games and Manipulatives for the Elementary School Class-room: A Sourcebook, 284
Media and Methods: Educational Products, Technologies and Programs for Schools and Universities, 59

Business—Information Services
Through a Glass Clearly: Finding, Evaluating and Using Business Information from the Soviet Region, 743

Business Communication
Better Said and Clearly Written: An Annotated Guide to Business Communication Sources, Skills, and Samples, 693

Business Education
Videos for Business and Training, 1989: Professional and Vocational Videos and How to Get Them, 715

Business Ethics
Business Ethics and Responsibility: An Information Sourcebook, 696
Public Relations and Ethics: A Bibliography, 605

Cable Television
Cable Television: A Reference Guide to Information, 1100

Caldecott Medal Books
The Newbery and Caldecott Awards: A Guide to the Medal and Honor Books, 1993 Edition, 158
Newbery and Caldecott Medal and Honor Books in Other Media, 159
Newbery and Caldecott Medalists and Honor Book Winners: Bibliographies and Resource Material Through 1991, 160

California
The California Handbook: A Comprehensive Guide to Sources of Current Information and Action, with Selected Background Material, 678

Canada
Canada: A Reader's Guide. Introduction Bibliographique, 679
Canadian Books for Children: Guide to Authors and Illustrations, 111
Canadian Books for Young People. Livres Canadiens pour la Jeunesse, 112
Canadian Picture Books. Livres d'Images Canadiens, 195
Canadian Selection: Books and Periodical for Libraries, 472
Guide to Reference Materials for Canadian Libraries, 520
Read! A Guide to Quality Children's and Young Adult Books, 133

Canadian Literature
Books in Canada, 64
Canadian Selection: Books and Periodical for Libraries, 472
A Comprehensive Collection of English-Canadian Short Stories, 1950-1983, 1359
Dictionary of Literary Biography, 1188
Notable Canadian Children's Books: 1975-1979 Cumulative Edition, 129
Subject Index to Canadian Poetry for Children and Young People, 361

Canadian Literature—History and Criticism
Research Guide to Biography and Criticism: 1990 Update, 1291
Research Guide to Biography and Criticism: Poetry and Fiction, 1292

Research Guide to Biography and Criticism: Volumes 5 and 6, 1290

Canadian Periodicals
Canadian Serials Directory. Repertoire des Publications Seriees Canadiennes, 543

Cancer
Cancer: A Bibliography of Resources; Mental Health: A Bibliography; Nutrition Bibliography; Women's Health, 1622

Capital Punishment
Capital Punishment in America: An Annotated Bibliography, 885

Careers. *See* **Occupations; Vocational Guidance**

Caribbean Islands
Latin America and Caribbean: A Directory of Resources, 689
Latin America and the Caribbean: A Critical Guide to Resources, 690
Selection of Library Materials for Area Studies 654

Caribbean Islands Literature
Caribbean Women Novelists: An Annotated Critical Bibliography, 1369
Fifty Caribbean Writers: A Bio-Bibliographical Critical Sourcebook, 1375
Writers of the Caribbean and Central America: A Bibliography, 1383

Catalogs—Commercial
The Kids' Catalog Collection: A Selective Guide to More Than 500 Catalogs, 283

Catholic Literature
Biographical Dictionary of Contemporary Catholic American Writing, 1309

Catholics
Books for Believers: 35 Books That Every Catholic Ought to Read, 1518
Books for Catholic Elementary Schools, 109
Books for Religious Education in Catholic Secondary Schools, 386
Critical Guide to Catholic Reference Books, 1523

Cats
Dogs, Cats and Horses: A Resource Guide to the Literature for Young People, 293

CD-ROM
The CD-ROM Directory, 1992, 560
CD-ROM for Librarians and Educators: A Resource Guide to Over 300 Instructional Programs, 561
CD-ROM Information Products: An Evaluation Guide and Directory, 562
CD-ROM Librarian: The Optical Review Media Review for Information Professionals, 87
CD-ROM Market Place: An International Guide: 1992 ed., 563
CD-ROM Periodical Index: A Guide to Abstracted, Indexed, and Fulltext Periodicals on CD-ROM, 564
CD-ROM Professional, 88
CD-ROM Research Collections: An Evaluative Guide to Bibliographic and Full-Text CD-ROM Databases, 565

Children's Literature, British

Children's Literature, Canadian

Children's Literature, Spanish

Children's Periodicals

Children's Plays

Genocide
First-Person Accounts of Genocidal Acts in the Twentieth Century: An Annotated Bibliography, 853
Genocide: A Critical Bibliographic Review, 854
Genocide in Our Time: An Annotated Bibliography with Analytical Introductions, 855

Geography
A Bibliography of Geographic Thought, 813
Encyclopedia of Geographic Information Sources: United States Volume, 814
Geographical Bibliography for American Libraries, 815
Geography: A Resource Book for Secondary Schools, 816
Wetland Economics and Assessment: An Annotated Bibliography, 1617
World Bibliographical Series, 822

Geology
Information Sources in the Earth Sciences, 1600

Gerontology
Anthropology of Aging: A Partially Annotated Bibliography, 612
Families and Aging: A Selected Annotated Bibliography, 973
A Guide to Research in Gerontology: Strategies and Resources, 975
The Image of Older Adults in the Media: An Annotated Bibliography, 976
Retirement: An Annotated Bibliography, 977

Gifted Children
Books and Real Life, 366
Books for the Gifted Child. v. 2, 367
Educating the Gifted: A Sourcebook, 787
Gifted, Talented and Creative Young People: A Guide to Theory, Teaching, and Research, 788
Resources for Educating Artistically Talented Students, 790

Gilbert and Sullivan
How Quaint the Ways of Paradox! An Annotated Gilbert and Sullivan Bibliography, 1471

Gothic Fiction
Through the Pale Door: A Guide to and through the American Gothic, 1271

Great Britain
British Sources of Information: A Subject Guide and Bibliography, 672

Great Britain—Description and Travel
Before You Go to Great Britain: A Resource Directory and Planning Guide, 823

Greek Art
Guide to Research in Classical Art and Mythology, 1147

Greek Literature
The Classical Epic: An Annotated Bibliography, 1361
Classical Greek and Roman Drama: An Annotated Bibliography, 1362

Greenhouse Effect
The Greenhouse Effect: A Bibliography, 1610

Guidance
Educators Guide to Free Social Studies Materials, 343

Haiti
Haiti: A Research Handbook, 686
Haiti: Guide to the Periodical Literature in English, 1800-1990, 687

Handicapped. *See* **Disabilities; Physical Handicaps**

Handicraft
Crafts Index for Young People, 292
The Crafts Supply Sourcebook: A Comprehensive Shop-by-Mail Guide, 1163
Fun for Kids II: An Index to Children's Craft Books, 294
Handweaving: An Annotated Bibliography, 1165
Index to Handicraft Books, 1974-1984, 1167
Make It—II: An Index to Projects and Materials, 1974-1987, 1168

Hazardous Wastes
Toxic and Hazardous Materials: A Sourcebook and Guide to Information Sources, 1616

Health. *See also* **Medicine**
The Best of Health: The 101 Best Books, 1620
Black American Health: An Annotated Bibliography, 1621
Consumer Health and Nutrition Index, 68
The Consumer Health Information Source Book, 1623
Core Collection in Nursing and the Allied Health Sciences: Books, Journals, Media, 1624
Current Bibliographies in Medicine, 1625
Educators Guide to Free Social Studies Materials, 343
Encyclopedia of Health Information Sources, 1627
Environmental Hazards to Young Children, 1628
Federal Information Sources in Health and Medicine: A Selected Annotated Bibliography, 1629
Food Additives and Their Impact on Health, 1654
Health Resource Builder: Free and Inexpensive Materials for Librarians and Teachers, 1632
Medical and Health Information Directory, v. 2: Publications, Libraries, and Other Information Services, 1634
A Research Guide to the Health Sciences: Medical, Nutritional, and Environmental, 1639
Science Tracer Bullets: A Reference Guide to Scientific, Technological, Health, and Environmental Information Sources, 1548
Sickness and Wellness Publications, Volume 1, 1640

Health Care
Choices and Challenges: An Older Adult Reference Series, 970
Minority Health Resources Directory, 1635
The Native Peoples of Canada: An Annotated Bibliography of Population Biology, Health, and Illness, 1636

High Interest-Low Vocabulary Books
The Best: High/Low Books for Reluctant Readers, 443
Books for Adult New Readers: A Bibliography Developed by Project: LEARN, 466
Choices: A Core Collection for Young Reluctant Readers, Volume 2, 371
Easy Reading: Book Series and Periodicals for Less Able Readers, 446
High-Interest Books for Teens: A Guide to Book Reviews and Biographical Sources, 449
High Interest-Easy Reading: A Booklist for Junior and Senior High School Students, 450
High/Low Handbook: Encouraging Literacy in the 1990s, 451

Videodiscs

Videodiscs—Education

Vietnam War, 1961-1977

Vietnam War—Fiction

Vietnam War Veterans

Violence

Visual Literacy

Vocational Guidance